Management

JAMES A. F. STONER
Fordham University

Management

Prentice-Hall, Inc., Englewood Cliffs, New Jersey

To my parents

Library of Congress Cataloging in Publication Data
Stoner, James A. F.
    Management.
    Includes bibliographical references and indexes.
    1. Management.   I. Title.
HD31.S6963   658.4   77-21259
ISBN 0-13-549303-X

© 1978 by Prentice-Hall, Inc., Englewood Cliffs, N.J. 07632

All rights reserved. No part of this book
may be reproduced in any form or
by any means without permission in writing
from the publisher.

Printed in the United States of America

10 9 8 7 6

Prentice-Hall International, Inc., *London*
Prentice-Hall of Australia Pty. Limited, *Sydney*
Prentice-Hall of Canada, Ltd., *Toronto*
Prentice-Hall of India Private Limited, *New Delhi*
Prentice-Hall of Japan, Inc., *Tokyo*
Prentice-Hall of Southeast Asia Pte. Ltd., *Singapore*
Whitehall Books Limited, *Wellington, New Zealand*

Cover Photo: Mitchel Funk/The Image Bank

Contents

Chapter 3 Managers and the External Environment of Organizations 58

PART II Planning and Decision Making 85

Chapter 4 Planning and Plans 90

Chapter 5   Strategic Planning   112

Chapter 6   Making Planning Effective   140

Contents

Contents

Chapter 10   Coordination and Span of Management 241

Chapter 11   Authority, Delegation, and Decentralization 264

Chapter 12   Groups and Committees 289

Chapter 13   Organizational Design for Changing Environments   314

Chapter 14   Managing Organizational Conflict and Creativity   342

Chapter 15 Managing Organizational Change and Development 371

PART IV Leading 397

Chapter 16 Motivation, Performance, and Satisfaction 404

Chapter 17 Leadership 436

Chapter 18   Interpersonal and Organizational Communication   464

Chapter 19   Staffing and the Personnel Function   494

Contents

Chapter 20   Organizational Careers and Individual Development   526

PART V   Controlling   557

Chapter 21   The Control Process   564

Preface

This book is about the job of the manager. It describes how men and women go about managing the people and activities of their organization so that the goals of the organization, as well as their personal goals, will be achieved.

I have attempted in this book to convey the very positive view I have of the manager's job. I believe the job of a manager is among the most exciting, challenging, and rewarding careers a person can have. Individuals can, of course, make great contributions to society on their own. But it is much more likely that major achievements will occur in *managed* organizations—not only businesses, but also universities, hospitals, research centers, governmental agencies, and other organizations. Such organizations bring together the talent and resources that great achievements require. The individual manager, therefore, has a much greater chance to be involved in a significant and far-reaching activity than the individual working alone.

I also believe that in addition to being fun and rewarding, a managerial career is critically important. The problems our society faces today—and, most likely, the problems it will face in the foreseeable future—require the type of large-scale solutions only governments and other organizations can provide. How well we learn to manage such problems as pollution, the energy crisis, overpopulation, and poverty may help determine whether we survive as nations, cultures, or even as a species. The skill of organizational managers will be a vital factor in our ability to meet our society's tasks and challenges. The information in this text is designed to help you, the reader, develop these vital managerial skills.

In this text I have chosen to address the reader as a potential manager. At times, in fact, I even adopt a tone that suggests the reader already is a manager. This decision was a deliberate one: I want to encourage the reader to start thinking like a manager as soon as possible. Obviously, the earlier one learns to think like a manager, the quicker one can develop managerial effectiveness. But there is another, more basic reason I approach the reader as if he or she already were a manager. All managers, but especially young managers just beginning their careers, are evaluated in large part on how effective they are as *subordinates*. The more successful an individual is as a subordinate, the more successful his or her career is likely to be. And one of the best ways of learning how to be an excellent subordinate is to learn how to think like a manager. Thus, addressing the reader as a manager (or at least as a prospective manager) is meant to be a helpful way of improving the reader's chances for future managerial *and* career success.

The material in this text has been selected with two objectives in mind: to provide the reader with information that is useful and relevant and to give the reader an understanding of the management field. Thus, most chapters have a practical orientation — how organizational realities affect the ethical behavior of managers (Chapter 3); how managers carry out the strategic planning process in their organizations (Chapter 5); when managers and subordinates should make decisions together (Chapter 7); how many subordinates should report directly to each type of manager (Chapter 10); how managers can be effective participants and leaders of groups and committees (Chapter 12); how organizational conflict can be managed (Chapter 14); what leadership styles are most effective in different types of situations (Chapter 17); what organizational realities and career strategies young managers should be aware of in order to manage their careers effectively (Chapter 20); and how managers can devise control systems that will be accepted by their subordinates (Chapters 21 and 24). Every attempt has been made to eliminate the use of management jargon, which so often hampers the readability of books on management. Instead, clear and familiar language is used so that the material will be easily accessible to the reader. Where a new term is introduced, it is set off in italics and clearly defined. The text has also been made more useful to students by covering different types of organizations — nonprofit, governmental, *and* business — in the belief that students will be assuming a wide variety of management positions.

The field of management has grown so rich that it is impossible to describe the work of all management writers and theorists in an introductory text. Instead, this text describes the major schools of management thought in one introductory chapter (Chapter 2); the remainder of the text includes material from a wide variety of sources that seemed most useful to the reader. The text does not, however, neglect the classical works in the field of management and in addition often includes the first pieces of research in a new area of inquiry.

This book attempts to integrate the major approaches to the basic introductory management course — the classical, behavioral, and quantitative approaches — and the emerging systems and contingency perspectives. The structure of the book is based, in large part, on the classical approach because (1) managers themselves still seem to find it quite useful; (2) students find it to be a good "handle" and lead-in to the management field; and (3) it provides an excellent organizing framework for all the management approaches. I believe that the various schools and perspectives in management have been growing closer for a number of years and that the reader's best interests are served by a text that takes an integrative point of view. Of course, wherever appropriate, I have specifically noted some of the important differences in the underlying values, assumptions, and action implications of the various approaches.

I have tried to present the material in such a way as to be most helpful to students and teachers alike. The chapters in the text are designed to stand on their own, so instructors can deal with the various topics in whatever order they choose. However, in order to show how integrated the management field is, I have included a large number of chapter cross-references. The book as a whole is organized in a way that has proven successful in many introductory management courses.

Objectives. Each chapter begins with a list of learning objectives. These tell the reader specifically what he or she should know after reading the chapter. The reader can use these objectives as a study aid.

Illustrations and Tables. A large number of colorful and informative charts, tables, cartoons, and other illustrations have been included in this text. They have been designed to convey information in an attractive and readily comprehensible form. The boxed inserts in the text provide the reader with interesting supplementary information or summarize important material in the text.

Summary. A summary at the end of each chapter helps the student review the material presented in that chapter. The summary contains key information, concepts, and terms.

Review Questions. An additional study aid is the list of review questions that follows each chapter. These questions help students pull together and integrate the basic contents of the chapter. In addition, the questions give students an opportunity to see how their own values will affect the way they apply management principles.

Case Studies. The case study method has long been recognized as an effective means for helping students acquire and learn to apply management concepts. This text contains a total of twenty-nine cases, most of which have been classroom-tested for effectiveness. The cases describe situations in business as well as nonbusiness organizations. Each of the five units in the text opens with a major case that is designed to cover the key concepts of the entire unit. Each chapter closes with a shorter case study or incident that is designed to highlight key concepts of the chapter. Both types of cases are followed by case questions that are designed to help students focus on the important aspects of the case.

Supplements. A Study Guide and Workbook is available to help the student review, understand, and integrate the material in the text. Each chapter in the workbook includes a review outline, a list of key terms and concepts, and a series of self-test questions. A separate Instructor's Manual, Test Item File, and set of Transparency Masters are also available.

Acknowledgments One of the more pleasant parts of writing a book is the opportunity to thank those who have contributed to it. Unfortunately, the list of expressions of thanks — no matter how extensive — is always incomplete and inadequate. These acknowledgments are no exception.

First thanks must go to my editor, Sheldon Czapnik, whose unflagging patience, constant good humor, and astounding capacity for creative work and long hours made the book possible. Without Sheldon, there would have been no book. I am deeply indebted to Charles Wankel, Peter Pfister, Dr. Samuel Dekay, and Della Dekay for performing much useful research, completing many detailed tasks, and frequently suggesting alternative approaches. On this text I had professional writing assistance, and I would like especially to thank Arthur Mitchell and Jim McDonald for their contributions. Earl Kivett and Paul Atkinson, at that time Prentice-Hall acquisitions editor and area sales representative, respectively, first interested me in this project. Paul was particularly helpful in encouraging me to go ahead. I would also like to give special thanks to the production editor, Eleanor Perz, for her good spirits, professionalism, and dedication to the project.

Many of my colleagues in academia contributed directly and indirectly to this text. My advisor on two theses and early academic mentor, the late Donald G. Marquis, placed his own imprint indelibly and permanently upon me. I have frequently drawn heavily on the research and the recalled classes and conversations of Professors George Farris, Thomas Ference, Edgar Schein, and Kirby Warren, and my own interpretation of how they might have thought through problems. Tom was helpful on numerous occasions, and I am very grateful to him and to our colleague Jerome Schnee for allowing me to use their teaching notes and other materials at critical times. Deans Senkier, Jordan, and McDermott at Fordham provided consistent encouragement for my involvement in this project. They were always understanding during my various stages of work overload. From the time I was considering embarking on the project until its completion, they each had only one question: "What can I do to help?" I couldn't have asked for better management. James Gatza, Curtis R. Clarke, David E. Risch, Mahmoud A. Moursi, David A. Tansik, and F. Glenn Boseman provided needed reviews and guidance at critical stages.

Because this book is about management and about managers, I am indebted to the many outstanding managers and consultants with whom I have worked. These are far too many to list, but a few simply must be credited: Joseph Voci, David Gleicher, Malcolm MacGruer, and the late Victor Milton have all influenced me profoundly. As consultants, Joe and David can conceptualize and guide the practice of management as well as anyone I have ever met. As practicing managers, Joe, Malcolm, and Victor have always been a joy to watch in action.

Finally, in a strictly personal vein, my thanks for multiple types of encouragement go to Bill, Diane, Lynn, and Sandy.

J.A.F.S.

Management

Part

Introduction to Management

Case on Introduction to Management

LEIS ELECTRONICS COMPANY

"I really enjoyed Bill Grant's lecture and handling of the discussion," Tom Griffin said, "but I wish we had gotten to the Grossinger Corporation case as the schedule indicated. Now I'm afraid we won't get to it this afternoon and I'll never know how good my solution is."

"Come on, Tom," Phyllis Selden said as she scanned the menu. "You know these things never have right answers. They're just supposed to get us into the habit of developing and analyzing alternatives so we'll take a problem-solving approach to our jobs." Then she smiled and added with a chuckle: "Of course, we would have gotten to it on schedule if you and Sloane hadn't asked so many questions."

As Sloane Evans and Tom Griffin started to protest their innocence, the fourth member of the group—Richard Niles—laughed and added: "Yeah, Phyl's right. For a moment there, I thought Tom and I were back in "Pappy" Voelker's solid-state physics class and that Tom was trying to stretch out the lecture long enough until it was too late to give tomorrow's assignment. But then I realized you two were really turned on."

The four people kidding each other over lunch at the Harrington Inn dining room are employees of Leis Electronics, a multidivisional company that produces electrical and electronic products for consumer, industrial, and military uses. Tom Griffin, 31, was a math and physics major in college. He joined the company three years ago after a stretch in the army and two years as a salesman with a computer company. Tom was a divisional sales manager until nine months ago when he was promoted to senior product manager for small electrical appliances. Phyllis Selden, 29, has been with Leis for five years. She came straight from graduate school, where she received an M.S. in industrial engineering. After two and a half years in the design department, she was promoted to a first-line supervisory position in quality control and last year assumed her new job of department head in product engineering. Richard Niles went to the same college as Tom. Tom and Richard had a couple of mathematics and physics classes together, but they did not get to know each other well until Tom joined the company. Richard had been with Leis since graduation and was quick to show Tom the ropes when he first arrived. Richard's first position was a brief training assignment in sales, and then he moved to R&D. Following two promotions, he is currently a department head in R&D with four technical supervisors reporting to him. All three have advanced rapidly with Leis Electronics—in part because of the combination of their technical abilities and their active efforts to develop their management skills, and in part because the rapid growth of Leis in the last ten years has

Case copyright © 1977 by James A.F. Stoner. Used by permission.

pulled many individuals into management positions faster than would have happened in slower growing companies.

The remaining member of the foursome, Sloane Evans, has been with the company for fifteen of his 45 years. He is currently the chief financial officer of the consumer electronics division. Normally he joins more actively in the repartee of the younger managers, but today his thoughts are distracted. Within a few days of the end of this semiannual three-day seminar for managers of the consumer electronics division, the president of the company will announce Sloane's promotion to general manager of the industrial electronics division.

Sloane is thinking about his conversation with his wife two days ago. When she was joking with him about the president's enjoyment in making dramatic announcements, such as the acquisitions of new companies, major new products, or the promotions of key executives, Sloane said: "Well, I couldn't care less *when* Sam makes the announcement, what's bugging me is who I should choose to be my assistant. I've narrowed it to Phyl, Tom, and Rich, but beyond that I'm having trouble." Sloane's thoughts were interrupted by Phyl's response to Richard: "Hey, I can't wait till this evening to listen to you two guys fight about Grossinger's problems—let's start right now."

"Fine," Tom replied, "But you start Phyl, so Rich will have a chance to collect his *thought*. But I'll give you only three minutes so your Reuben sandwich won't get cold."

"Fair enough, Tom. Now you get serious while I explain the problem. It's really quite simple. Grossinger's major difficulties occur in meeting production schedules, maintaining quality, and dealing with special, rush orders from customers. The problem lies in the ambiguities and confusion in the chain of command and in the way the whole operation is organized. Or, maybe I should say disorganized. The manufacturing VP's authority and responsibilities are unclear. He is second-guessed by the president half the time, and the other half of the time he is bypassed by the two plant managers who think they have a direct line to the president. Besides, the manufacturing VP's span of management is too wide—he simply can't train, supervise, and help all those different managers reporting to him. And he doesn't have the authority to carry out his responsibility. In addition, there's no mechanism for coordinating production, sales, and R&D. They'll never be able to get special orders out on schedule and within budget until they resolve those interdepartmental conflicts and start working together."

Pausing for a breath, Phyllis reached under her chair for her copy of the case. "Now, if you all will compare the new organization chart I've sketched out on the back page with the one they show in Figure II, I'll explain how Grossinger should be reorganized to get around these problems."

"Hold it," Tom pleaded, "take that organization chart out of my mushroom soup. You're going to move all those people around and create a whole bunch of new settling-in difficulties, without solving the problems. You're right that things are a bit messy organizationally, but the problems really come from the lack of proper capital equipment and a misdesigned production system.

I left my case back in the seminar room, but if Rich will let me use the front of his turtleneck as a scratch pad, I can show you pretty quickly what new equipment they need and how a simple rearrangement of the manufacturing operation will increase their output by 20 to 30 percent. To see the problem you have to push a few numbers, but once you do, it's crystal clear. I worked out the numbers last night, and for about $200,000—which is peanuts for them to spend—they can meet their regular production schedules *and* handle the special orders without disrupting their operations. I've outlined the operations research program to confirm my rough analysis. Since most of the quality control problems almost certainly come from the schedule interruptions, the unnecessarily short production runs, the rush to fill late orders, and the whole crisis atmosphere, quality will pick up dramatically once they conduct the study and make the changes I've tentatively outlined."

"Cease and desist, my number-happy friend," Richard interjected. "No need to unbutton your calculator nor to incur a dry cleaning bill for my high-fashion turtleneck. Actually, I had more than one thought to collect, so I appreciated the extra time. My first thought *was* about the capital equipment situation, but I think those numbers they give you in the case are just a red herring to lead the unwary astray. You could spend a million bucks on new equipment and on revamping the production process without solving the basic problems. And reorganization is tempting, but look at the way people interact in that company. There's no cooperation anywhere in that organization. The place is rife with competition, hostility, and distrust. Everybody spends his time blaming someone else for the difficulties, going over his boss's head, or trying to develop liaisons and coalitions with other managers. And the problem starts at the top. The president got so uptight the first couple of times they were late with important orders that he turned a moderate training and re-staffing problem into a major organizational crisis. Rather than trying to find out where to place the blame for specific foul-ups, he should have focused on developing the capacities of the people below him and supported their efforts to deal with the problems. He undercut his key managers when they were in a problem-solving mode, and now we see the result. It's clearly a team-building problem: he needs help in developing his key executives into an effective working team. Until he tackles *that* problem, anything else will just be window dressing! Right, Sloane?

Although Sloane Evans thought he had been listening intently to the conversation, Richard's quick question caught him off balance as he realized he had been listening with only half of his attention. While they were talking, he had also been recalling the rest of that conversation with his wife. Sloane had continued: "They're all excellent and I think equally deserving of what will clearly be a significant promotion and a great learning opportunity. But their strengths and approaches are quite different. I'm sure they would each tackle the job from a different angle. Each will be exciting and fun to work with, but each would give me somewhat different results. I wish I had a clear decision rule for making this choice. It's important for them and it's important for me."

Breaking off his second reverie, Sloane set down his coffee cup and tried to recall what had struck him about the case when he had read it hurriedly that morning. Smiling, he said: "Well, I'm not sure I can add much to what you have already said. I think each of you has a handle on significant parts of the problem. And since I would bet Rich has sketched out a top management team-building program that is just as solid as Phyl's reorganization and Tom's operations research and investment programs, each of you appears to have a logical action plan. I wouldn't be too surprised if one or even all of them improved things. But what kept occurring to me this morning when I read the case and thought about it—between questions to Professor Grant—was that I couldn't figure out what Grossinger's strategy is. Maybe that is in there implicitly somewhere, but it seemed to me that the confused decisions and inconsistent actions were partially the result of not having a clear idea of what business they're in and what they're *not* going to try to do. For example, those conflicts between their major product lines and the special orders. There are a lot of ways to resolve them, but it all depends on what their major strengths and opportunities are and how they are going to leverage those strengths. Personally, I think they should turn down all special orders that do not contribute to the development phase of their major R&D activities. Then the special orders would make sense in furthering the development of new product lines. Otherwise, they're just frittering away key resources on Mickey Mouse activities. As another example, take the situation—oops, it looks like everybody is heading back to the seminar room. Maybe we'll get a chance to find out how the others look at Grossinger's problem."

As the four managers left the dining room, Sloane Evans's attention once again drifted away from the Grossinger Corporation case and back to the decision he would have to make in a few days.

1. What factors should Sloane Evans take into account when deciding which of the three young managers should be his assistant?
2. What are likely to be the major strengths and weaknesses of each individual as a subordinate?
3. What additional training should be arranged for the individual whom he selects to be his assistant? What additional training should the others receive?
4. How should Sloane decide what his major priorities in his new job should be? How should those priorities influence his choice among Phyllis, Tom, and Richard?
5. What additional information about Sloane Evans would you like to have to help you decide whom he should choose as his assistant?
6. Which of the three young managers would *you* be most comfortable working with? Why?
7. From which of the three would you *learn* the most? Why?
8. Which of the three young managers do you think was the best individual contributor when he/she first started work? Which was the best first-line supervisor after the first promotion? All three managers are just getting into the middle management level. Who do you think will be the best middle manager? Who has the most potential for top management?

Chapter 1

Managing and Managers

Upon completing this chapter you should be able to:

1. Define the concept of management and discuss why managers and organizations are needed.

2. List and describe the four basic functions of managers.

3. Describe several additional roles and responsibilities of managers.

4. Identify what is meant by top, middle, and first-line managers, and functional and general managers, and describe how their work activities differ.

5. Describe what management education can and cannot do for you, and explain why you must be actively involved in learning to become an effective manager.

At various times in our lives, each of us will be a member of some kind of organization—a college, a fraternity or sorority, a sports team, a musical group, a branch of the armed forces, or a business. The organizations we belong to will obviously differ from one another in many ways. Some, like the army or a large corporation, may be organized very formally. Others, like a neighborhood basketball team, may be less formally organized. But regardless of how they differ, all the organizations we belong to will have a few basic things in common.

Perhaps the most obvious common element our organizations will have is a goal or purpose. The goals will vary—to win a league championship, to entertain an audience, to sell a product—but without a goal no organization would have any reason to exist. Our organizations will also have some program or method for achieving their goals—to win a certain number of games, to rehearse a certain number of times before each performance, to manufacture and advertise a product. Without some idea of what it must do, no organization is likely to be very effective. Finally, our organizations will all have leaders or managers responsible for helping the organizations achieve their goals. Who the leaders actually are probably will be more obvious in some organizations than in others. But without some manager — a coach, a conductor, a sales executive—the organization is likely to flounder like a ship without a helm.

This book is about how organizations are managed or, more specifically, how managers can best help their organizations set and achieve their goals. Our emphasis will be on the so-called formal organizations—such as businesses, religious or philanthropic organizations, or hospitals—that provide goods or services to their customers or clients and offer career opportunities to their members. It is easier to discuss the management of these organizations, because in such organizations people will usually have various well-defined responsibilities, and the role of the manager will be clear-cut and visible. But regardless of just how formal their role is, all managers in all organizations have the same basic responsibility: to help other members of the organization set and reach a series of goals and objectives. Helping you to understand how managers accomplish this task is the purpose of this book.

DEFINING MANAGEMENT

Like many areas of study that involve people, management is difficult to define. In fact, no definition of management has been universally accepted. One popular definition is by Mary Parker Follett: Management, she says, is "the art of getting things done through people." This definition calls attention to the fact that managers achieve their goals by arranging for *others* to perform whatever tasks may be necessary—not by performing the tasks themselves.

We will use a somewhat more elaborate definition to begin our discussion in this chapter, because we will want to call attention to other important aspects of managing:

Management is the process of *planning, organizing, leading, and controlling* the efforts of organizational members and the use of other organizational resources in order to achieve *stated organizational goals*.

7

The reader will notice that we have used the word "process" rather than "art" in defining management. To say that management is an art implies that it is a personal aptitude or skill. A process, on the other hand, is nothing more than a systematic way of doing things. All managers, regardless of their particular aptitudes or skills, engage in certain interrelated activities in order to achieve their desired goals.

We have called these management activities planning, organizing, leading, and controlling. (Others have expanded this list, but for the sake of convenience we will use just these four activities.) *Planning* means that managers think their actions through in advance. Their actions are usually based on some method, plan, or logic, rather than on a hunch. *Organizing* means that managers coordinate the human and material resources of the organization. The strength of an organization lies in its ability to marshal many resources to attain a goal. Obviously, the more integrated and coordinated the work of an organization, the more effective it will be. Achieving this coordination is part of the manager's job. *Leading* means that managers direct and influence subordinates. They do not act alone, but get others to perform essential tasks. Nor do they simply give orders. By establishing the proper atmosphere they help their subordinates do their best. *Controlling* means that managers attempt to assure that the organization is moving toward its goals. If some part of their organization is on the wrong track, managers try to find out about it and set things right. (We will expand our discussion of these activities later in this chapter.)

Our definition also indicates that managers use *all* the resources of the organization—its finances, equipment, and information as well as its people—in attaining their goals. While people are any organization's most important resource, managers would be limiting themselves if they did not also rely on the other organizational resources available to them. For example, a manager who wishes to increase sales might try not only to motivate the sales force but also to increase the advertising budget.

Finally, our definition says that management involves achieving the organization's "stated goals." This means that managers of any organization—a hospital, a university, the Internal Revenue Service, or the Washington Redskins—try to attain specific ends. These ends will, of course, vary with each organization. The stated goal of a hospital might be to provide comprehensive medical care to a community. The stated goal of a university might be to give students a well-rounded education in a congenial environment. Whatever the stated goals of a particular organization, management is the process by which the goals are achieved.

WHY ORGANIZATIONS ARE NEEDED

Almost every day, it seems, headlines like these greet us from the front pages of our daily newspapers:

—"City Charged with Wasting Millions in Medicare Funds"
—"Detroit Recalls 20,000 New Cars, Found Defective"
—"Study Asserts Many College Students Have Serious Reading Problems"

Even as members of a society in which the certainty of change seems to be the only thing that never changes, we cannot help but be affected by the stories behind such headlines. Some Americans are afraid that organizations designed to serve them are letting them down. There is a feeling that the organizations of government, business, and organized labor have become too large, that they may have lost touch with people's needs, and that their leaders lack high ethical standards.

Criticizing our organizations is, of course, a time-honored American custom and helps to keep them on their toes. However, it is not enough simply to criticize organizations. We must at the same time constantly seek new ways to improve our organizations and make them more effective tools for serving human needs. The reason for this is that organizations, in one form or another, will always be with us. They are a necessary element of civilized life because they perform a number of vital functions:

1 They enable us to accomplish things that we could not do as well—or at all—as individuals.

2 They help provide a continuity of knowledge.

3 They serve as an important source of careers.

The Effectiveness of Organizations

Let us consider for a moment how many organizations were needed just to bring us the tuna in that sandwich we had for lunch: a fishing fleet, a cannery, manufacturers of various types of equipment and supplies, distributors, truckers, telephone and electric power companies, fuel producers, a supermarket chain, and so forth. (And this list would get even larger if we included the organizations that were needed to produce the bread in that sandwich.) Even if an individual acting alone could do all the things those organizations did to produce a can of tuna, which is doubtful, it is clear that he or she could never do them as well or as quickly.

We can also look at a less mundane example: the Apollo moon-landing mission. This mission required the combined knowledge and coordinated efforts of scores of physicists, mathematicians, biologists, chemists, geologists, computer technicians, engineers, and astronauts, and years of dedicated work. It took a huge government agency, NASA, to plan the mission and to coordinate and control the enormous quantities of people and resources required. Possibly, some large corporation might have succeeded in carrying out a project of this magnitude, but certainly no single individual could have done it.

It is clear, then, that organizations perform this essential function: *By overcoming our limitations as individuals, they enable us to reach goals that would otherwise be much more difficult or even impossible to reach.*

Continuity of Knowledge Provided by Organizations

We know from history that when recorded knowledge is destroyed on a large scale (as in the barbarian invasions of Rome, for example) much of it is never regained. We depend on records of past accomplishments, because they provide a foundation of knowledge on which we can build to acquire more learning and achieve greater results. Without such records, science and other fields of knowledge would stand still.

Organizations (such as libraries, museums, and corporations) are essential because they store and protect most of the important knowledge that our civilization has gathered and recorded. In this way, they help to make that knowledge a continuous bridge between past, present, and future generations. In addition, organizations themselves add to our knowledge by developing new and more efficient ways of doing things.

Organizations as a Source of Careers

Organizations are important for still another reason: they provide their employees with a source of livelihood and perhaps even personal satisfaction and self-fulfillment. Many of us tend to associate career opportunities with corporations and other businesses, but in fact a variety of other organizations, such as churches, government agencies, schools, hospitals, and so on, also offer rewarding careers.

Thus, we can see that organizations are vital elements of our society and that they do serve useful functions. The question we should be concerned with is not, Do we need so many large organizations? but, How can we make these organizations more effective in meeting our needs?

The Purpose of This Book

Most of the readers of this book will spend a good part of their lives working in organizations, either as subordinates or managers or both. The chief purpose of this book is to prepare them for both of these roles. To accomplish this, it will help the reader to understand how organizations are managed; that is, what tasks managers must perform to keep their organizations running smoothly and effectively. The reader will also learn how managers accomplish those tasks, what managers need to know in order to manage effectively, and how they apply their skills and knowledge in order to meet organizational goals (as well as their own).

Usually, when people become employees, their first task is learning to be successful subordinates. The importance of being a good subordinate should not be underestimated. In order to become managers, most people first have to prove themselves as subordinates. Besides, virtually every member of an organization is someone's subordinate. Even an organization's president is subordinate to the board of directors, and the board members in turn are, in principle, responsible to the shareholders.

The person who acquires a good basic understanding of how organizations are managed will be able to use it to learn effectively when he or she becomes a member of an organization. For example, by watching various managers in action, an alert, knowledgeable employee can identify the kinds of managerial behavior that seem to be successful (or unsuccessful) in moving the organization toward its goals. The employee can use this learning experience to improve his or her chances of becoming not only a manager but an *effective* manager.

Last but not least, an understanding of management, as implied earlier, should prove helpful to the reader in many situations and activities outside the formal organization.

WHAT MANAGERS DO

Our working definition describes the manager as an organizational planner, organizer, leader, and controller. Actually, every manager—from the program director of a college club to the chief executive of a major steel corporation—takes on a much wider range of roles to move the organization toward its stated objectives. This section, by discussing some of the more important aspects of what the manager *does,* will add more detail to our concept of what a manager *is.*

The manager assumes responsibility. A manager is in charge of specific tasks and must see to it that they are done successfully. The manager is usually evaluated on how well he or she arranges for these tasks to be accomplished. In addition, since the manager works through subordinates, he or she is responsible for the actions of subordinates. Their success or failure is the manager's success or failure.

The manager must balance competing goals. At any given time, a manager faces a number of organizational goals, problems, and needs—all of which compete for the manager's precious time and resources (both human and material). Because such resources are always limited, each manager must strike a balance between the various goals and needs. Many managers, for example, arrange each day's tasks in order of priority—those things that need to be done right away are attended to first, while those things that can be postponed are looked at later. In this way managerial time is used more efficiently.

Competing
Goals

The manager must also decide who is to perform a particular task, assigning each task to the person most able to perform it. While ideally each person should be given the task he or she would most like to do, the limited resources of the organization often make this impossible. The manager must decide when the wishes of a subordinate should be secondary to the need to have a task performed efficiently and effectively.

The manager is a conceptual thinker. Every manager must be an *analytical thinker;* that is, he or she must be able to think a specific, concrete problem through and come up with a feasible solution for it. But even more importantly, the manager must be a *conceptual thinker,* a person able to think about the entire task in the abstract. For the manager, this job is no simple matter, for it means working to achieve the larger organizational goals as well as the goals of the manager's own unit.

The manager works with and through other people. The word "people" here refers not only to subordinates and supervisors but also to the manager's peers. In fact, the manager works with anyone at any level in the organization who can help him or her achieve unit or organizational goals.

In addition, managers work together in the organization to provide one another with accurate information needed to perform tasks. In other words, a manager acts as a *channel of communication* within the organization. Managers also must work together to establish the organization's long-range goals and to plan how to achieve them.

The manager is a mediator. Organizations are made up of people, and sometimes people disagree or quarrel. Disputes within a unit or organization can affect morale and productivity and may even cause some competent employees to leave the organization. No manager wants any of these things to happen, so he or she must take on the role of mediator and try to iron out all disputes before they get out of hand. Of course, settling a dispute requires skill and tact, and a manager who is careless in handling such a problem may find that he or she has only made it worse.

The manager is a politician. This does not mean, of course, that the manager actually runs for political office. It simply means that a manager, like a politician, must use the arts of persuasion and compromise in order to promote organizational goals.

Every effective manager "plays politics" by developing networks of mutual obligations with other managers in the organization, and he or she may also have to build or join alliances or coalitions. Managers draw upon the relationships established in those ways to win support for critical proposals, decisions, or activities.

The manager is a diplomat. The manager is an official representative of his or her work unit at organizational meetings. When dealing with clients, customers, contractors, government officials, and personnel of other organizations, the manager is usually considered a representative of the entire organization as well as of a particular unit.

The manager makes difficult decisions. No organization runs smoothly all the time. There is almost no limit to the number and types of problems that may occur: financial difficulties, problems with employees, or differences of opinion concerning organization policy, to name just a few. Managers are the people who are expected to come up with solutions to difficult problems, and to follow through on their decisions even when doing so may be unpopular with some person or persons. One of the most unpleasant measures a manager has to take is to terminate an employee, and managers—even good ones—often put off dismissing someone, even though they know that the morale of their whole unit may suffer until action is taken.

A manager *is* what a manager *does,* and a manager obviously does many different things—so many, in fact, that the roles described above do not begin to exhaust the list of possibilities. However, the roles we have examined here should help the reader to be aware that managers need to "change hats" frequently and must be alert to the particular role needed at a given time. The ability to recognize the appropriate role to be played and to change roles readily is the mark of an effective manager.

Some Gaps in Our Working Definition We have just seen a part of the wide range of roles—often conflicting ones—that managers play in their organizations. Obviously, there are important aspects of the manager's activities that were not mentioned in the brief working definition above. This section will discuss several other important aspects of the manager's role.

Accountability. As we have seen, managers are people who assume responsibility—but this alone does not make them different, because those members of an organization who are not managers are also responsible for their particular tasks. The difference is that managers are held responsible, or accountable, not only for their own work but also for the work of others.

Because managers have subordinates and other resources to use in getting a job done, they are able to accomplish more than nonmanagers, who have only their own efforts to rely on. This, of course, means that managers are also *expected* to accomplish more than other members of the organization; that is, they are also held accountable for greater achievement. Obviously, there is an element of risk involved here, because the manager's need to get more work done is coupled with the need to rely on others to do that work. Managers, in fact, sometimes feel anxiety because of this responsibility for achieving things beyond their immediate control.

Effectiveness and Efficiency. Our working definition says, in effect, that managers are doers, but it mentions nothing about their responsibility to perform well. A manager's performance can be measured in terms of two concepts: *efficiency* and *effectiveness*. As Peter Drucker, one of the most respected writers on management, puts it, efficiency means "doing things right," and effectiveness means "doing the right thing."

Efficiency—that is, the ability to get things done correctly—is an "input-output" concept. An efficient manager is one who achieves outputs, or results, that measure up to the inputs (labor, materials, and time) used to achieve them. In other words, if the manager is able to minimize the cost of the resources he or she uses to attain a given goal, that manager is acting efficiently.

People provide a major input of an organization, its labor and talent. It may not be enough, then, to measure the efficiency of a manager's use of labor inputs only in terms of keeping their cost down. Efficiency here might also mean developing or upgrading the people who do the work.

Effectiveness, on the other hand, is the ability to choose appropriate objectives or the appropriate means for achieving a given objective. In other words, an effective manager selects the right things to get done or the right method for getting a particular thing done. For example, a manager who insists on producing only large cars when the demand for small cars is soaring is an ineffective manager, even if those large cars are produced with maximum efficiency.

A manager's responsibilities require performance that is both efficient and effective, but although efficiency is important, effectiveness is critical. For Drucker, effectiveness is the key to the success of an organization. The manager's need to make the most of opportunities, says Drucker,

implies that effectiveness rather than efficiency is essential to business. The pertinent question is not how to do things right, but how to find the right things to do, and to concentrate resources and efforts on them.[1]

[1] Peter F. Drucker, *Managing for Results* (New York: Harper & Row, 1964), p. 5.

Is Management
an Art, a Science,
or a Profession?

Follett defined management as an art, but there is no universal agreement with her point of view. In fact, there has been considerable debate for many years over just how management can be classified. Most writers agree that management does involve some degree of skill, but beyond that attitudes vary. In this section we will look at two interesting, though opposing, classifications of management.

Is Management a Science? In a speech he delivered at an international management conference, Luther Gulick defined management as a "field of knowledge" that "seeks to systematically understand why and how men work together systematically to accomplish objectives and to make these co-operative systems more useful to mankind."[2] According to Gulick, management already meets the requirements for a field of knowledge, because it has been studied for some time and has been organized into a series of theories. (See Chapter 2.) These theories, he admits, are still too general and subjective. But he is optimistic that management is on its way to becoming a science, because it is being studied systematically and because the management theories that exist are being tested against experience. Once it is a science, the field of management will reliably inform managers what to do in a particular situation and enable them to predict the consequences of their actions.

Gulick would probably be the first to admit that for the foreseeable future, and perhaps even beyond, the practice of management will remain in many ways an art. It is true that we are learning more about management every day, and in many situations we can safely recommend a specific course of action. Furthermore, the use of the computer has vastly improved the manager's ability to judge the outcome of an individual decision (such as the decision to manufacture a certain product mix). But our knowledge is far from complete in any science, and certainly in a field like management, which involves working with people, we still have a great deal to learn. Perhaps someday our understanding of human behavior will be complete; until then managers will have to rely on their fallible judgment and on insufficient information a great deal of the time. In short, while aspects of management are becoming more scientific, much of management will remain an art.

Is Management a Profession? We have seen that management is part art and part science. Is it a profession? Edgar H. Schein has defined the characteristics of professionals and has evaluated managers against those characteristics.[3] We will discuss three of Schein's criteria here.

According to Schein, professionals make decisions based on general principles. The existence of management courses and training programs indicates that there are certain dependable management principles. Professionals also

[2] Luther Gulick, "Management Is a Science," *Academy of Management Journal,* Vol. 8, No. 1 (March 1965), pp. 7–13.

[3] Edgar H. Schein, "Organizational Socialization and the Profession of Management," *Industrial Management Review,* Vol. 9, No. 2 (Winter 1968), pp. 1–16.

"Stop complaining. You knew what you were getting into when your father left you the business."

Reproduced by special permission of *Playboy* Magazine; copyright © 1974 by *Playboy*.

attain their status by meeting certain objective standards of performance, not because of favoritism or because of their race or religion. By this criterion managers still have a way to go before they achieve professionalism. Unfortunately, in practice, managers are not always judged by their accomplishments alone.

Finally, because professionals have superior knowledge in a particular field, their clients are dependent on them. Thus, professionals must be governed by a strong code of ethics so that their clients, who are in a vulnerable position, will be protected. Schein believes that no management code of ethics has yet been developed.

Schein concluded that according to some criteria management is a profession, but by other criteria is not yet a profession. We should note, however, that there are signs that management is working toward increased professionalism. Current social pressures may be succeeding in bringing about improvement in the ethical standards of business, government, and other organizations. (See Chapter 3.) Also, management is becoming more professional through the accelerated growth of formal management training in graduate schools and through executive development programs.

TYPES OF MANAGERS

We have been using the term "manager" in a very broad sense to mean anyone who is responsible for subordinates and other organizational resources. There are, however, many different types of managers, with diverse tasks and responsibilities. In this section we will discuss the various types of managers that exist and the different things that they do.

Managers can be broadly classified in two ways: by their level in the organization — so-called first-line, middle, and top managers — and by the range of organizational activities for which they are responsible — so-called functional and general managers.

Management
Levels

First-Line Managers. The lowest level in an organization at which individuals are responsible for the work of others is called *first-line* or *first-level* management. (See Figure 1-1.) First-line managers direct operating employees only; they do not supervise other managers. Examples of first-line managers are the foreman in a manufacturing plant, the technical supervisor in a research department, and the clerical supervisor in a large office.

Middle Managers. The term *middle management* can encompass many levels in an organization. Middle managers direct the activities of other managers and sometimes also those of operating employees. One of the principal responsibilities of middle managers is to direct the activities that will actually implement the broad operating policies of the organization. The head of a subdivision in an electronics firm is an example of a middle manager.

Top Managers. This comparatively small group of executives makes up the highest classification of managers. *Top management* is responsible for the overall management of the organization. It establishes operating policies and guides the organization's interactions with its environment. Typical titles of top managers are "chief executive officer," "president," and "senior vice president." However, titles vary from one organization to another and are not always a reliable indication of membership in this group.

FIGURE 1-1
Levels of
Management in
an Organization

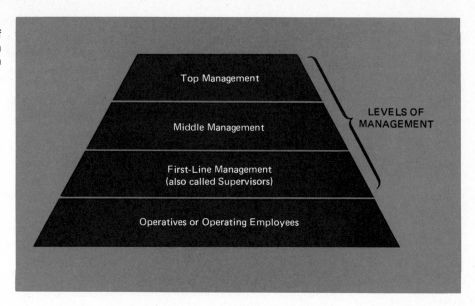

Functional and
General
Managers

Apart from their rank in the organization, managers can also be classified as functional or general managers, depending on the scope of the activities they manage. The *functional manager* is responsible for only one organizational activity, such as production, marketing, sales, *or* finance. The people and activities headed by a functional manager will have an underlying common purpose. The *general manager,* on the other hand, oversees a complex unit, such as a company, a subsidiary, or an independent operating division. He or she will be responsible for all the activities of that unit—its production, marketing, sales, *and* finance, for example.

A small company may have only one general manager—its president or executive vice president—but a large organization may have several, each one heading a relatively independent division. In a large food company, for example, there might be a grocery products division, a refrigerated products division, and a frozen food products division, with a different general manager responsible for each. And, like the chief executive of a small company, each of these divisional heads would be responsible for all the activities of his or her respective unit.

THE PROCESS OF MANAGEMENT

It is easier to understand something as complex as management when it is described as a series of separate parts, or *functions,* that make up a whole process. Descriptions of this kind, known as *models,* have been used by students and practitioners of management for decades. We, in fact, used a

17

model—without identifying it as such—when we said earlier in this chapter that the major management activities were planning, organizing, leading, and controlling. This model of management was developed at the end of the nineteenth century and, as a glance at our table of contents will indicate, is still in use today.

We have already described briefly these four main management activities. Now that we have acquired some new insights into the manager's many roles and responsibilities, we will examine these activities or functions in greater detail. This will increase our general understanding of the management process.

Planning   Plans are needed to give the organization its goals and to set up the best procedure for reaching them. In addition, plans permit (1) the organization to set aside the resources it will need for required activities, (2) members of the organization to carry on activities consistent with the chosen procedures, and (3) the progress toward the objectives to be monitored and measured, so that corrective action can be taken if the rate of progress is unsatisfactory.

The first steps in planning involve the selection of goals for the organization. Then goals are established for the subunits of the organization—its divisions, departments, and so on. Once the goals are decided upon, programs are established for achieving them in a systematic manner. Of course, in selecting the goals and developing the programs, the manager considers their feasibility and whether they will be acceptable to the organization's managers and employees.

Plans made by top management for the organization as a whole may cover periods as long as five or ten years. In a large organization, such as a multinational energy corporation, those plans may involve commitments of billions of dollars. Planning at the lower levels, by middle or first-line managers, covers much shorter periods. Such plans may be for the next day's work, for example, or for a two-hour meeting to take place in a week.

Organizing   Once managers have established objectives and developed plans or programs to reach them, they must design and develop an organization that will be able to carry out those programs successfully. Different objectives will require different kinds of organizations to achieve them. For example, an organization that aims to write a new encyclopedia will have to be far different from one that wants to manufacture automobiles. Producing cars requires assembly-line techniques, while producing an encyclopedia requires teams of professionals— writers, editors, and experts in various subjects. Such people cannot be organized on an assembly-line basis. It is clear, then, that managers must have the ability to determine what type of organization will be needed to accomplish a given set of objectives. And they must have the ability to develop (and later to lead) that type of organization.

Many students of management consider *staffing* an organization to be part of the organizing function. Staffing is the recruitment and placement of the qualified personnel needed to do the organization's work. Others list staffing as a separate management function or consider it to be a part of the leadership function, which is discussed next.

Leading
After plans have been made and the organization has been established and staffed, the next step is to arrange for movement toward its defined objectives. This function can be called by various names: "leading," "directing," "motivating," "actuating," or others. But whatever the name used to identify it, this function involves getting the members of the organization to perform in ways that will help it achieve the established objectives.

While the planning and organizing functions will focus, at least in part, on more abstract aspects of the management process, the activity of leading focuses directly on the people in the organization.

Controlling
Finally, the manager must ensure that the actions of the organization's members do in fact move the organization toward the stated goals. This is the controlling function of management, and it involves three elements:

1 Establishing standards of performance.
2 Measuring current performance and comparing it against the established standards.
3 Taking action to correct any performance that does not meet those standards.

Through the controlling function, the manager can keep the organization on the right track before it strays too far from its goals.

What we have presented here is a model of the management process. A model is a simplification of the real world used to convey complex relationships in more understandable terms. The relationships described above are by no means as straightforward as our model implies.

For example, we saw that standards and benchmarks are used as a means of controlling employees' actions, but, obviously, establishing such standards is also an inherent part of the planning process. And taking corrective action, which we also introduced as a control activity, often involves an adjustment in plans. In other words, the management process does not involve four separate or loosely related sets of activities but a group of closely interrelated functions.

We should also point out that the four functions do not necessarily occur in the sequence presented in our model (except perhaps when a new organization is being formed). In fact, various combinations of these activities usually go on simultaneously in an organization.

In addition, the existence of these management functions should not be taken to mean that any manager has complete freedom to perform them when he or she wishes. Managers generally are faced with various limitations on their activities, depending on their rank, their role in the organization, and the kind of organization they work for. Some managers, for example, may find that limits are set on their handling of subordinates — on what they can do to direct, guide, or motivate them — because they have a leadership style that conflicts with the style that prevails in their organization. And a manager may not be able to hire a new staff to pursue a new set of objectives, because the organization cannot carry the added expense of their salaries.

Nevertheless, a model can be a very useful approach to learning, provided that we remember its shortcomings and that it is not meant to be an exact description of the real world. By analyzing the management process—that is, by separating it into distinct pieces we call "management functions"—a model can improve our understanding of what managers do. And that, after all, is the purpose of this book.

HOW MANAGERS SPEND THEIR TIME

Managers at all levels of the organization need to plan, organize, lead, and control. There are, however, differences between managers in the amount of time they devote to each of these activities. Some of these differences will depend on the kind of organization the manager works for and on the type of job the manager has.

For example, we would expect the manager of a small private clinic to spend his or her time quite differently than the head of a large teaching and research hospital. The clinic manager will probably spend comparatively more time practicing medicine and less time managing the organization than the administrator of a large hospital. Similarly, the technical supervisor of a group of research physicists at Bell Laboratories will perform activities that are different from those of a foreman on the General Motors assembly line—yet both the supervisor and foreman are first-line managers. (Of course, there will also be some similarities in how they spend their time.)

Other differences in how managers spend their time will depend on the level of the individual manager in the organizational hierarchy. In the sections below we discuss how management skills and activities will differ at the various levels of the organization.

Management Levels and Managerial Skills

Robert L. Katz, an educator and businessman, has identified three basic types of skills—*technical, human,* and *conceptual*—which he says are needed by all managers.[4]

Technical skill is the ability to use the tools, procedures, or techniques of a specialized field. A surgeon, an engineer, a musician, or an accountant all have technical skill in their respective areas. The manager needs enough technical skill "to accomplish the mechanics of the particular job" he or she is responsible for.

Human skill is the ability to work with, understand, and motivate other people, either as individuals or as groups. The manager needs enough of this human relations skill to be able to participate effectively in and lead his or her group.

---

[4] Robert L. Katz, "Skills of an Effective Administrator," *Harvard Business Review,* September-October 1974, pp. 90–102.

Conceptual skill is the mental ability to coordinate and integrate all of the organization's interests and activities. It involves the manager's ability to see the organization as a whole and to understand how its parts depend on each other, and how a change in any given part can affect the whole organization. A manager needs enough conceptual skill to recognize how the various factors in a given situation are interrelated, so that the actions he or she takes will be in the best interests of the organization.

Katz suggests that although all three of these skills are essential to effective management, their relative importance to a specific manager depends on his or her rank in the organization. Technical skill is most important at the lower levels of management; it becomes less important as we move up the chain of command. The foreman in a manufacturing plant, for example, is likely to need more technical skill than the company president, because he or she will have to deal with the day-to-day manufacturing problems that arise. Similarly, while human skill is important at every level of the organization, it is probably most important at the lowest level, where the greatest number of manager-subordinate interactions are likely to take place. (See Figure 1-2.)

On the other hand, the importance of conceptual skill increases as we rise in the ranks of management. The higher the manager is in the hierarchy, the more he or she will be involved in the broad, long-term decisions that affect large parts of the organization. For top management, which is responsible for the entire organization, conceptual skill is probably the most important skill of all.

FIGURE 1-2

Relative Skills Needed for Effective Performance at Different Levels of Management

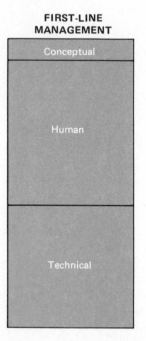

FIRST-LINE MANAGEMENT

Conceptual

Human

Technical

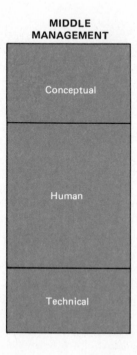

MIDDLE MANAGEMENT

Conceptual

Human

Technical

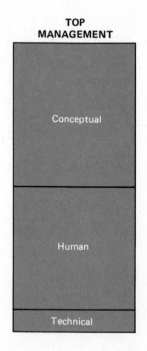

TOP MANAGEMENT

Conceptual

Human

Technical

Katz was concerned with the skills that managers need, not with the amount of time spent on various activities. However, it is obvious that managers at different levels of the organization need different skills because they spend their time differently. First-line managers need greater technical skill because a greater portion of their work time is likely to involve technical activities. Conversely, middle and top managers spend more of their time making conceptual decisions.

How Managers Allocate Their Time

Katz developed his concepts from firsthand experience in working with and studying managers. On the other hand, the work of Mahoney, Jerdee, and Carroll was the product of detailed research and thus rests on a broader base of empirical data.[5]

Mahoney and his colleagues concentrated on measuring management performance itself in terms of the amount of time that managers set aside for accomplishing various activities. Their study involved 452 managers representing all levels of management, from first-line supervisor to president. The managers were employed in 13 companies that varied in size from 100 to more than 4,000 employees and represented a typical cross section of business and industry.

The managers in the study received questionnaires instructing them to estimate how much time they usually spent on each of eight management functions: *planning, investigating, coordinating, evaluating, supervising,*

TABLE 1-1
Percentage of Workday Spent by Managers on Various Functions

Function	Percentage of Workday	Function	Percentage of Workday
Supervising	28.4	Investigating	12.6
Planning	19.5	Negotiating	6.0
Coordinating	15.0	Staffing	4.1
Evaluating	12.7	Representing	1.8

Source: T. A. Mahoney, T. H. Jerdee, and S. J. Carroll, "The Job(s) of Management," *Industrial Relations,* Vol. 4 (February 1965), p. 103. Used by permission.

staffing, negotiating, and *representing.* (These categories are essentially a more detailed breakdown of our own four management functions.) As a group the managers reported that they spend more of their workday performing supervising activities (28.4 percent) than any other single function. The planning function came next, taking up 19.5 percent of their average workday. (See Table 1-1.)

This information was based on the performance of the surveyed group of managers as a whole. Thus, it was a useful indicator of how the "average" manager spends his or her time. But Mahoney and his colleagues were also

[5] T. A. Mahoney, T. H. Jerdee, and S. J. Carroll, "The Job(s) of Management," *Industrial Relations,* Vol. 4 (February 1965), pp. 97–110.

interested in finding out if the time spent on a given activity varied with the level of the manager. They therefore grouped the managers in their survey into the appropriate three management levels to see if any differences in management activities would appear.

As the accompanying illustration indicates, Mahoney and his associates did find evidence for Katz's contention that specific skills are more important at some levels of management than at others. Supervising, which involves mostly

FIGURE 1-3
Distribution of
Assignments
among Job Types
at Each
Organizational
Level

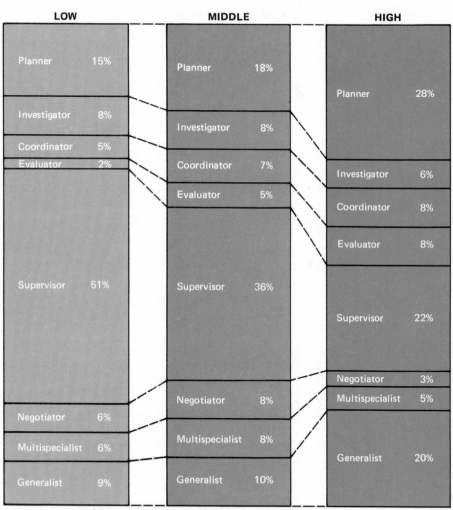

Note that generalists were those managers who did not concentrate an unusually large proportion of time on any one function. Multispecialists spent a good deal of time on two functions. The staffing and representing functions made too small a showing in the sample to qualify as job types.

Source: T. A. Mahoney, T. H. Jerdee, and S. J. Carroll, "The Job(s) of Management," *Industrial Relations*, Vol. 4 (February 1965), p. 103. Used by permission.

human and technical skills, is the dominant activity for lower and middle levels of management. The proportion of time that managers spend as supervisors decreases with each rise in organizational level. Planning, on the other hand, largely involves conceptual skill. It is the dominant activity of top managers, while middle and lower-level managers engage in correspondingly less planning.

How Managers Spend Their Time: An Alternate View

Henry Mintzberg offers an alternative view of the job of managing that throws some new light on how managers spend their time and perform their work.[6] Mintzberg made an extensive survey of existing research on this subject and integrated those findings with the results of his own study of the activities of five chief executive officers. The combined survey covered all kinds and levels of managers: factory foremen, sales managers, administrators, presidents, and even some street gang leaders.

Mintzberg concluded that there is considerable similarity in the behavior of managers at all levels. All managers, he argued, have formal authority over their own organizational units, and they derive status from that authority. This status causes all managers to be involved in interpersonal relations with subordinates, peers, and superiors, who in turn provide managers with the information they need to make decisions. These different aspects of a manager's job cause managers at all levels to be involved in a series of interpersonal, informational, and decisional *roles,* which Mintzberg defined as "organized sets of behaviors." (See Figure 1-4.)

The Manager's Interpersonal Roles. Three interpersonal roles help the manager keep the organization running smoothly. Thus, although the duties associated with these roles are often routine, the manager cannot ignore them.

The first interpersonal role is that of *figurehead.* As head of his or her unit, the manager sometimes acts as a figurehead by performing certain ceremonial duties—greeting visitors, attending a subordinate's wedding, taking a customer to lunch, and so on. Second, the manager adopts the *leader* role—hiring, training, motivating, and encouraging employees. Finally, the manager must play the interpersonal role of *liaison,* by dealing with people other than subordinates or superiors (such as suppliers or clients). Managers develop such contacts mainly to build up personal sources of information.

The Manager's Informational Roles. Mintzberg suggests that receiving and communicating information are perhaps the most important aspects of a manager's job. A manager needs information in order to make the right decisions,

---

[6] Henry Mintzberg, "The Manager's Job: Folklore and Fact," *Harvard Business Review,* July-August 1975, pp. 49–61. Important precursors of Mintzberg's work were Sune Carlson, *Executive Behavior: A Study of the Work Load and Working Methods of Managing Directors* (Stockholm, Sweden: Stromberg Aktiebolag, 1951); Rosemary Stewart, *Managers and Their Jobs: A Study of the Similarities and Differences in the Ways Managers Spend Their Time* (London: Macmillan, 1967); L. R. Sayles, *Managerial Behavior* (New York: McGraw-Hill, 1964); and Peter F. Drucker, *The Practice of Management* (New York: Harper & Row, 1954).

FIGURE 1-4
The Manager's
Roles

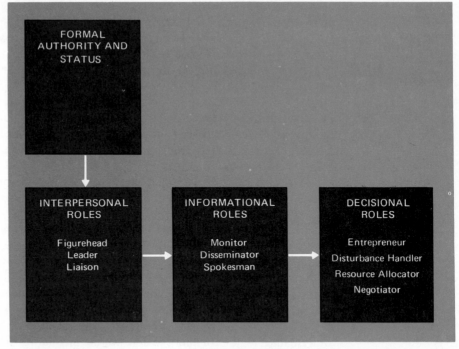

FORMAL
AUTHORITY AND
STATUS

INTERPERSONAL
ROLES

Figurehead
Leader
Liaison

INFORMATIONAL
ROLES

Monitor
Disseminator
Spokesman

DECISIONAL
ROLES

Entrepreneur
Disturbance Handler
Resource Allocator
Negotiator

Source: Henry Mintzberg, "The Manager's Job: Folklore and Fact," *Harvard Business Review,*
July-August 1975, p. 55. Copyright © 1975 by the President and Fellows of Harvard College; all
rights reserved.

and others in the manager's unit or organization depend on the information
they receive.

There are three informational roles in which managers gather and disseminate information. The first is the *monitor* role. As monitor, the manager constantly looks for information that can be used to advantage. Subordinates are
questioned, and unsolicited information is also collected, usually through the
manager's system of personal contacts. The monitor role usually enables the
manager to be the best-informed member of his or her group. Second, in the
disseminator role, the manager distributes to subordinates important information that would otherwise be inaccessible to them. Finally, as *company representative,* the manager transmits some of the information he or she has
collected to individuals outside the unit — or even outside the organization.
Keeping superiors in the organization satisfied by keeping them well informed
is one important aspect of the role of company representative. Another aspect
is communicating outside the organization — when a company president makes
a speech before a group of consumer advocates, for example, or when a foreman suggests how a supplier should modify a product.

The Manager's Decisional Roles. So far, we have seen the manager distributing
to other people information he or she has taken pains to collect. But, of course,
information is also "the basic input to decision making" for managers.

25

According to Mintzberg, there are four decisional roles the manager adopts. In the role of *entrepreneur,* the manager tries to improve the unit. For example, when the manager receives a good idea, he or she launches a development project to make that idea a reality. As an entrepreneur, the manager initiates change voluntarily. In the role of *disturbance handler,* on the other hand, the manager responds to situations that are beyond his or her control, such as strikes, bankrupt customers, breach of contract, and the like. As a *resource allocator,* the manager is responsible for deciding how and to whom the resources of the organization and the manager's own time will be allocated. In addition, the manager screens all important decisions made by others in the unit before they are put into effect.

The fourth and last decisional role is that of *negotiator:* A company president works out a deal with a consulting firm, a production head draws up a contract with a supplier, an office manager irons out a problem with a clerk. Managers spend a great deal of their time as negotiators, because only they have the information and authority that negotiators require.

Mintzberg's work is particularly interesting because it calls attention to the uncertain, turbulent environment in which the manager operates. Real-life events and situations, he stresses, are only partially predictable and controllable, and the manager often must deal with them as they come. In his view, managers have neither the time nor the inclination to be reflective thinkers —they are, above all, *doers* coping with a dynamic parade of challenges and surprises.

Thus, Mintzberg's concept of the manager's job offers a useful reminder that our definition of management as a series of functions — planning, organizing, leading, and controlling — is a somewhat idealized but useful overview of what managers try to do. In fact, managers operate in a constantly changing environment. Although they attempt to follow systematic and rational procedures, they are often interrupted in their work.

THE TRAINING OF MANAGERS

We will discuss the training of managers at some length in our chapters on "Staffing and the Personnel Function" and "Organizational Careers and Individual Development." However, a few words on the subject are appropriate here.

Most people would agree that the technical, human, and conceptual skills Katz described are important to managers. How effectively can these skills be taught? Katz believes that technical skill is the easiest for a manager to acquire. It is generally well covered in courses at the undergraduate and graduate levels and in company-sponsored training programs.

As we might expect, however, human skill is far more difficult to teach or learn than technical skill. Human relations involve many complex emotional elements, and it is difficult to demonstrate that a particular interpersonal approach is more effective than another. Also, while it may be easy for us to admit that we are ignorant about some technical matter, it is much harder for us to admit that we need to be taught new ways of dealing with people. It is harder still to change our habitual and well-rationalized ways of relating to others. Nevertheless, serious attempts are being made in business schools and company programs to help present and future managers improve their methods of dealing with people. These programs are based on the social sciences of anthropology, sociology, and, most importantly, psychology.

Katz believes that conceptual skill has been difficult to teach, mainly because it involves intellectual ability that has to be developed early in life. Courses in strategic planning are one method designed to help future managers increase their conceptual skill. The need to improve this skill is a principal reason why managers who are likely to be promoted to general management are frequently sent to executive development programs.

A Critique of Management Education

J. Sterling Livingstone, in an article entitled "The Myth of the Well-Educated Manager," argues that most management training programs neglect to teach people what they must do in order to become fully effective managers.[7] These programs, Livingstone maintains, only emphasize problem solving and decision making. Thus, they help to develop analytical ability, but do little to improve other, more important capacities a manager will need.

What managers really should be taught, Livingstone says, is problem finding and opportunity finding. Analytical skills are important, but a manager's success will ultimately depend on his or her ability to anticipate problems long before they arise.[8] Even more important to the manager is the ability to find and take advantage of opportunities. After all, it is not problem solving but making the most of opportunities that helps organizations succeed.

While Livingstone suggests that these abilities can and should be taught, he also maintains that certain characteristics of effective managers are almost impossible to teach. These characteristics are personal qualities, which people develop long before they enter management training programs. (See our discussion of managerial traits in Chapter 17.) According to Livingstone, there are three such qualities associated with successful managers:

1   *The need to manage.* Only those people who want to affect the performance of others and who derive satisfaction when they do so are likely to become effective managers.

2   *The need for power.* Good managers have a need to influence others. To do this they do not rely on the authority of their positions but on their superior knowledge and skill.

3   *The capacity for empathy.* The effective manager also needs the ability to understand and cope with the often unexpressed emotional reactions of others in the organization in order to win their cooperation.

[7] See *Harvard Business Review,* January-February 1971, pp. 79–89.
[8] For a good discussion of problem finding, see W. F. Pounds, "The Process of Problem Finding," in David A. Kolb, Irwin M. Rubin, and James M. McIntyre, eds., *Organizational Psychology: A Book of Readings,* 2nd ed. (Englewood Cliffs, N.J.: Prentice-Hall, 1974).

With his discussion of the limitations of management education, Livingstone has joined Katz and Mintzberg in arguing that there are a wide variety of skills and abilities successful managers must have. Many of these skills can be and are being taught. It seems fair to say, however, that prospective managers will have to take the initiative in developing the personal qualities and abilities they will eventually need.

Books and the Classroom

It is obvious by now that no textbook can by itself teach you how to become a manager. Learning how to be an effective manager requires not only knowledge and personal ability but also considerable practice in the various management skills.

However, a major advantage of a textbook is its ability to present relevant information in an orderly, systematic way. We say "relevant," because the knowledge in this textbook is based on the experience of managers and on accepted studies by management researchers. You will not be ready to assume all the responsibilities of a manager when you finish this book, but you will know many of the tools you will be using as a manager, and you will be more aware of the kinds of problems and opportunities you will be facing.

In order to help you develop your managerial abilities, this book includes case studies that require you to describe and anticipate problems and decide what to do about them. These case studies will provide you with an opportunity to develop your judgment and skill. To the extent that you will work with others in analyzing the cases, you will also be able to practice the human skills Katz described.

Wider experiences in school and life can, by broadening your perspectives, supplement what you learn in the classroom and be of great help in planning and developing a managerial career. You might, for example, work in and lead group projects that many schools offer in connection with formal course work. In addition, you can take advantage of whatever skills-oriented courses are available. These courses help develop specific abilities through the use of experiential exercises, unstructured groups, role playing, and other techniques. The individual who is successful in learning how to be a manager integrates the knowledge that is available both inside and outside the classroom and consciously tries to develop management skills.

Summary

Organizations are needed in our society, because they accomplish things that individuals could not do, help provide continuity of knowledge, and are a source of careers. The management of organizations involves planning, organizing, leading, and controlling organizational members in order to achieve stated goals.

In moving organizations toward their goals, managers adopt a wide range of interpersonal, informational, and decisional roles. For example, they act as leaders, work with and through other people, and balance competing goals. The fact that managers need to rely on their fallible judgment in dealing with people and in making decisions suggests that management is still in many ways an art.

There are two ways that managers can be classified: by level and by organizational activity. Management levels include *first-line, middle,* and *top* managers. *Functional managers* are responsible for only one organizational activity, such as sales. *General managers* are responsible for all the varied activities in a complex organizational unit.

Managers at different levels of the organization require and use different types of skills. Lower-level managers require and use a greater degree of technical skill than higher-level managers, while higher-level managers require and use a greater degree of conceptual skill. Human skills are important at all managerial levels.

Review Questions

1. In light of what you have read in this chapter, are the organizations you belong to managed effectively? What do you think can be done to improve them?
2. What are the four functions of managers, and how do they help organizations achieve their goals?
3. Do you agree with our assessment that organizations are needed? Why or why not?
4. What is the difference between an efficient manager and an effective manager?
5. What are the major differences in how the various types of managers spend their time?
6. What are the three types of management skills identified by Katz?
7. What is Mintzberg's view of the job of managing? Do you think it is important for you to be aware of his view? Why?

CASE STUDY: TALKING WITH GEORGE

The scene: The controller's office in a large corporation on a Monday morning. George, director of economic planning, has just submitted a report to his immediate superior, the controller.

Controller: Sit down, George, while I look this over.

George: (virtually collapsing into a chair before the desk) This is the first chance I've had to sit down for a week.

Controller: (after examining major aspects of the report carefully but briefly) This is fine, George, just what we need. But why couldn't it have been ready for the treasurer on Friday, as we had agreed?

George: Frank became ill on Monday, that new girl's husband decided to accept a job in Des Moines—that makes three good girls I've lost in as many weeks—and by the time I had a look at the first draft, it was already late and the draft was absolutely incomprehensible. Irving could have worked on it with me, but he has been scheduled for months to go on vacation to California as of last Wednesday, and all his plans were made and I couldn't ask him to delay leaving. So, hard as we tried, and God knows we slaved over this report, it was just impossible to finish it by Friday. As it was, I finished it up on Saturday and Sunday. I've worked like a dog on this project, and all I get are questions about why it wasn't ready sooner. There is very little appreciation around here for what goes into a report like that. The treasurer wants something, probably minor to him, and the word filters down to us until it is a major project. We go all out on it, then no one gives a damn what we put into it. You can ask Phil, I was here until six o'clock Saturday working on that damn thing.

Controller: I know you work hard, George. I have never suggested that you don't. This report is an excellent job, just what I wanted—but *you* shouldn't have done it. We have had this assignment for two weeks. We discussed it again ten days ago at my initiative. You

Case copyright © 1968 by the President and Fellows of Harvard College. Reproduced by permission.

	never at any time during that period said it wouldn't be ready — until you came in here Friday morning asking me to phone the treasurer for an extension.
George:	He didn't really need it until tomorrow, anyhow. The board meeting isn't until then.
Controller:	But he asked us to have it ready by Friday and we had plenty of time to do it. Why can't we schedule jobs and be sure they come out on time?
George:	(Repeats his previous explanation for the delay, putting added emphasis on his own hard work and on the amount of overtime he had devoted to the report [for which he received no extra compensation].)
Controller:	George, I don't want you to work harder. I don't want you to work overtime. I want you to organize your department so that jobs come out when they are scheduled.
George:	I don't know *what* you want. I work harder than anyone around here. (Again repeats explanation for the report's delay, with some elaborations and additions.)
Controller:	Let's go to lunch and talk some more about this.
George:	I can't go out for lunch. I don't have time. My desk is piled high with papers. I'll probably be here until eight o'clock tonight. You don't have any idea how much work goes through my office. I've got to get back to work. (Gets up and moves toward the door, muttering that he works harder than anyone else in the company and no one gives a damn. "Those people in investment go home right on the dot of five o'clock............")

Case Questions

1. Why is George having so much trouble meeting deadlines?
2. How does George define his responsibilities as a manager?
3. How do you think George got into the habit of managing the way he does? Do you think the controller contributed to George's development of these habits?
4. What should the controller do to help George perceive his job differently and to change his ways of managing his job?
5. What do you think it would be like to have George as your supervisor? as a co-worker? as a subordinate?

Chapter 2

The Evolution of Management Theory

Upon completing this chapter you should be able to:

1. Describe the three major schools of management thought and how they evolved.
2. Discuss how each of these schools can help you perform your job as a manager.
3. Identify the models of human nature that underlie each of these schools.
4. Discuss the contributions and limitations of each school.
5. Describe two recently developed approaches to management that attempt to integrate the various schools.
6. Form your own working synthesis of the various management schools.

The theory of relativity helps physicists control the atom. Through the laws of aerodynamics, engineers can predict the effects of a proposed change in airplane design. Similarly, the theories and principles of management make it easier for us to decide what we must do to function most effectively as managers. Without theories, all we can have are intuition, hunches, and hope, which are of limited use in today's increasingly complex organizations.

Unfortunately, there is as yet no verified general theory of management that we can apply to all situations.[1] As managers, we will have at our disposal many ways of looking at organizations and at the activities, responsibilities, and satisfaction of people in organizations. Each of these ways may be more useful for some problems we will face than for others. For example, a management theory that emphasizes the importance of a good work environment may be more useful in helping us deal with a high employee turnover rate than with production delays. Because there is no general management theory, we must be familiar with the major theories that exist. We will then be able to match the insights and guidance available in each theory to the appropriate situation.

Like all useful theories, management theory is not an end in itself. Rather, it serves as a tool to increase our effectiveness as managers. The manager who is up-to-date on existing management theories will be more likely to remain up-to-date on management practices. A sad and frustrating sight is the mid-career or senior executive who has had an impressive past career, but who has remained attached to a theory of management that has become progressively out of step with current organizational and managerial realities. Those of us who are informed about management theories will be able to form our own "working synthesis" of the various approaches. In this way we will be able to guide our own actions as managers with greater flexibility.

In this chapter we will review the major management theories and describe each theory in some detail.[2] We will focus on three well-established schools of management thought—the *classical school* (which has two branches, *scientific management* and *classical organization theory*), the *behavioral school*, and the *quantitative school*. We will also discuss two recent approaches to management that attempt to integrate the various theories—the *systems approach* and the *contingency approach*. All these schools and approaches differ in their assumptions about how individuals in an organization behave, in what they see as the key goals of the manager, in the problems they emphasize, and in the solutions they suggest to these problems.

---

[1] In 1963, William C. Frederick (in "The Next Development in Management Science: A General Theory," *Journal of the Academy of Management,* Vol. 6, No. 3 [September 1963]) was optimistic about the emergence of a general theory within ten years. We are well past that time period, but the development of a general theory has turned out to be a more difficult task than he anticipated.

[2] Much of the discussion in this chapter on the evolution of management theory is based on Claude S. George, Jr., *The History of Management Thought* (Englewood Cliffs, N.J.: Prentice-Hall, 1968), and Daniel A. Wren, *The Evolution of Management Thought* (New York: Ronald Press, 1972).

THE CLASSICAL MANAGEMENT THEORISTS

People have been managed in groups and organizations since the beginning of history. Even the most primitive villages generally had a recognized leader or a council responsible for the welfare of the group and empowered to make decisions that others were obliged to obey. As societies grew larger and more complex, the need for organizations and managers became even more apparent. Governments, for example, could no longer be run by a few individuals. Administrators and bureaucrats became necessary to direct the operations of the state. Similarly, the military and the Roman Catholic church had to develop complex organizational structures in order to manage growing numbers of people effectively.

Attempts to develop *theories and principles* of management, however, occurred relatively recently. In particular, it was the industrial revolution of the nineteenth century that gave rise to the need for a sophisticated approach to management. The development of new technologies at that time concentrated great quantities of raw materials and large numbers of workers in factories. And it was difficult to coordinate all these elements into a smooth, productive flow. For this reason, people began to pay increasing attention to the problems of management.

The Forerunners of Scientific Management

Imagine for a moment that you are a resident of England in the early 1800s. Because of the industrial revolution, the factory system has started to spread. The need to discover new ways to manage the work force and to improve productivity is becoming increasingly evident. You find yourself in charge of one of the emerging factories. What do you think would be foremost in your mind — profits, efficiency, craftsmanship? What would you look for in your employees? To what extent would you feel responsible for their welfare? The forerunners of scientific management confronted questions very much like these, only they had no previous experience to guide them.

Robert Owen (1771–1858). Robert Owen was a manager of several cotton mills at New Lanark, Scotland, during the early 1800s. At that period in history, working and living conditions for employees were very poor. Child workers of 5 or 6 years of age were commonplace, and the standard working day was 13 hours long.

Owen conceived of the manager's role as one of *reform*. He built better housing for his workers and operated a company store where goods could be purchased cheaply. He reduced the standard working day to 10 1/2 hours, and refused to hire children under the age of 10.

Owen never claimed that he fought for reform on humanitarian grounds alone. Instead, he argued that improving the condition of employees would inevitably lead to increased production and profits. Where his fellow managers put their money into technical improvements, Owen stressed the fact that a manager's best investment was in the workers, or "vital machines," as he called them.

MANAGER

↓

Reform

↓

Improved Employee Morale

↓

Increased Productivity

Aside from making general improvements in working conditions at his mills, Owen instituted a number of specific work procedures that also served to increase productivity. For example, an employee's work was rated openly on a daily basis. Owen believed that these open ratings not only let the manager know what the problem areas were but also served to instill pride and spur competition. In our organizations today, the public posting of sales and production figures follow the same basic psychological principles.

Charles Babbage (1792–1871). A British professor of mathematics, Babbage spent much of his time studying ways to make factory operations more efficient. He became convinced that the application of scientific principles to the work process would both increase productivity and lower expenses.

Babbage was an early advocate of the division of labor principle. He believed that each factory operation had to be closely analyzed so that the different skills involved in the operation could be isolated. Each worker would then be trained in one particular skill and would be responsible for only one part of the total operation (rather than for the whole task). Babbage believed that in this way expensive training time could be cut. And the constant repetition of each operation would improve the skills of workers and enhance their efficiency. Our modern assembly line, in which each worker is responsible for a different repetitive task, is based on many of Babbage's ideas.

Frederick W. Taylor (1856–1915) and Scientific Management

Scientific management arose in part from the need to increase productivity. In the United States especially, labor was in short supply at the beginning of the twentieth century. To expand productivity, ways had to be found to increase the efficiency of workers.

Could some element of the work be eliminated or some parts of the operation combined? Could the sequence of these tasks be improved? Was there "one best way" of doing a job? In his pursuit of answers to such questions, Taylor slowly built the body of principles that constitute the essence of scientific management.

Taylor's ideas grew primarily out of years of experience and experiment in three companies: Midvale Steel, Simonds Rolling Machine, and Bethlehem Steel.

The Midvale Years. Taylor based his managerial system on his own production-line *time studies*. This approach marked the true beginning of scientific management. Instead of relying on the traditional work methods, Taylor analyzed and timed steel workers' movements on a series of jobs. He thereby established how much workers *should* be able to do with the equipment and materials at hand. With time study as his base, Taylor could now break each job down into its components and design the quickest and best methods of operation for each part of the job.

At Midvale, Taylor had to contend with the fact that workers were afraid to work fast, because they believed they would be laid off if they completed their tasks too quickly. To counter these fears, Taylor took the first step toward developing his *differential rate system*, which tied a worker's earnings to scientifically set performance standards for his or her job. If the worker met the standard, he or she earned the base rate. If the worker surpassed the standard, his or her pay would go up. The increased wage rate was carefully calculated so that companies would be making greater profits from the increase in production, even though they would be paying more in wages. Thus, workers were encouraged to surpass previous performance standards and earn more pay. They did not have to fear layoffs, Taylor argued, because their companies benefited from the increased productivity.

The Consulting Years: Simonds. By 1893, Taylor decided he could best put his ideas into effect as a private consulting management engineer. He was soon able to report impressive improvements in productivity, quality, worker morale, and wages while working with one client, Simonds Rolling Machine Company. Simonds employed 120 women to inspect bicycle ball bearings. The work was tedious and the hours were long, and there seemed little reason to believe improvements could be made. Taylor proved otherwise. First, he studied and timed the movements of the best workers. Then he trained the rest in the methods of their more highly skilled co-workers and transferred or laid off the poorest performers. He also introduced rest periods during the workday, along with his differential pay rate system and other improvements. The results were impressive: expenses went down, while productivity, quality, earnings, and worker morale went up. (See box.)

Improvements in Productivity at the Simonds Rolling Machine Company	
Task:	Inspection of the balls used in bicycle ball bearings. An established operation employing 120 workers who were "old hands" and skilled at their jobs.
Major Changes Made:	Additional training based on study of higher-performing workers. Selection on the basis of appropriate skills, laying off or transferring lower performers. Workday shortened from 10½ to 8½ hours. Rest periods introduced. Efficiency of control system increased (but with no change in inspection standards).
Results Reported:	Thirty-five inspectors did work formerly done by 120. Accuracy improved by two-thirds. Wages received rose by 80 to 100 percent. Apparent improvements in worker morale.

The Consulting Years: Bethlehem Steel. In 1898, Bethlehem Steel Company engaged Taylor as a consultant. Taylor set out to make the work of the company yard gang more efficient. The members of the yard gang unloaded raw materials from incoming railcars and loaded the finished product on outgoing cars. Each man earned $1.15 a day for loading an average of 12 1/2 tons. Taylor was told that the workers were habitually slow and that they were not willing to work faster.

After he and a co-worker studied and timed the operations involved in unloading and loading the cars, Taylor concluded that with frequent rest periods, each man could handle about 48 tons a day. Setting 47 1/2 tons as the standard, Taylor worked out a piece rate that would net $1.85 a day to those who met that standard. The workers were thus encouraged to adopt Taylor's work methods, because they could then earn more pay.

Although Taylor's methods led to dramatic increases in productivity and to higher pay in a number of instances, workers and unions eventually became uncomfortable with Taylor's approach. Like the workers at Midvale, they feared that working harder or faster would exhaust whatever work was available and bring about more layoffs. The fact that workers had been laid off at Simonds and in other organizations using Taylor's methods encouraged this fear. As Taylor's ideas spread, opposition to them continued to grow. Increasing numbers of workers became convinced that they would lose their jobs if Taylor's methods were adopted.

The Philosophy behind the Technique. By 1912, resistance to Taylorism had caused a strike at the Watertown Arsenal in Massachusetts, and hostile members of Congress called on Taylor to explain his ideas and techniques. Both in his testimony and in his two books *Shop Management* and *The Principles of Scientific Management*, Taylor outlined his philosophy.[3] It rested, he said, on four basic principles:

1 *The development of a true science of management,* so that, for example, the best method for performing each task could be determined.
2 *The scientific selection of the worker,* so that each worker would be given responsibility for the task for which he or she was best suited.
3 *The scientific education and development of the worker.*
4 *Intimate, friendly cooperation between management and labor.*

Taylor testified, however, that in order for these principles to succeed "a complete mental revolution" on the part of management and labor was required. Rather than quarrel over whatever profits there were, they should both try to increase production. By so doing, profits would be increased to such an extent that labor and management would no longer have to compete for them. In short, Taylor believed that management and labor had a common interest in increasing productivity.

Other Contributors to Scientific Management

Henry L. Gantt (1861–1919). Gantt collaborated with Taylor at Midvale, Simonds, and Bethlehem Steel. But after he began to work on his own as a consulting industrial engineer, Gantt reconsidered Taylor's incentive system.

Abandoning the differential piece rate as having too little motivational impact, Gantt came up with a new idea. Every worker who finished a day's assigned work load would win a 50¢ bonus for that day. Then he added a second

[3] Both books, in addition to Taylor's testimony before the Special House Committee, appear in Frederick W. Taylor, *Scientific Management* (New York: Harper & Brothers, 1947).

new twist. The *foreman* would earn a bonus for each man or woman who made the daily standard, plus an extra bonus if *all* the workers made it. This, Gantt reasoned, would spur a foreman to train his or her workers to do a better job.

Gantt also built upon Owen's idea of rating an employee's work publicly. Every worker's progress was recorded on individual bar charts — inked in black on days he or she made the standard, in red on days he or she fell below. Going beyond this, Gantt originated a charting system for production scheduling. This system, called the "Gantt chart," is still in use today.

The Gilbreths. Frank B. and Lillian M. Gilbreth (1868–1924 and 1878–1972) made their contribution to the scientific management movement as a husband and wife team. Lillian's doctoral thesis, which later appeared in book form as *The Psychology of Management,* was first published in *Industrial Engineering Magazine* in 1912, under the publisher's condition that the author be listed as L. M. Gilbreth with no indication she was a woman. Although she and Frank collaborated on fatigue and motion studies, Lillian also focused her attention on ways of promoting the welfare of the individual worker. To her, scientific management had one ultimate aim: to help workers reach their full potential as human beings.

Frank Gilbreth began work as an apprentice bricklayer and worked his way up the managerial ladder. Bricklayers, he noticed, used three different sets of motions: one for teaching apprentices, another for working fast, and a third for deliberately holding down the pace. After careful study of the different motions involved, Frank was able to develop a technique that tripled the amount of work a bricklayer could do in a day. His success led him to make motion and fatigue study his lifework.

In Gilbreth's conception, motion and fatigue were intertwined — every motion that was eliminated also reduced fatigue. Using motion picture cameras, Gilbreth tried to find the most economical motions for each task, thus upgrading performance and reducing fatigue. According to both Gilbreths, motion study raised worker morale not only because of its obvious physical benefits but because it demonstrated management's concern for the worker.

The *three-position* plan of promotion the Gilbreths developed was meant to serve as an employee development program as well as a morale booster. According to the plan, a worker was training his or her successor, doing his or her present job, and preparing for the next highest one all at the same time. Thus, a worker could constantly look forward to promotion and avoid dead-end jobs.

THE THREE-POSITION PLAN

prepares for promotion

Worker does job

trains successor

Contributions and Limitations of Scientific Management

Contributions. A team of men or women working together, each person tending expertly to one task, can outproduce by far the same number of people each performing a variety of tasks. The prime example of this is the vastly increased productivity of the modern assembly line, in which conveyor belts bring to each employee the parts he or she needs to do one specific job. Today's assembly lines pour out their finished products faster than Taylor himself could have conceived. This American production "miracle" is the legacy of scientific management.

The methods of scientific management can be applied to a variety of organizational activities, besides those of industrial organizations. The *efficiency techniques* of scientific management, such as time and motion studies, have made us aware that the tools and physical movements involved in a task could be made more efficient and rational. The stress it placed on *scientific selection* of workers has made us recognize that without ability and training a person cannot be expected to do his or her job properly. Finally, the importance that scientific management gave to *work design* encouraged managers to seek

© 1976 Bruce Ackerman

the "one best way" of doing a job. Thus, scientific management not only developed a rational approach to solving organization problems but also contributed a great deal to the professionalization of management.[4]

Limitations. Unfortunately, only part of the "mental revolution" called for by Taylor came about in practice. Labor and management have remained at odds. The higher wages and better working conditions enjoyed by today's workers did not result solely from the voluntary redistribution of increased profits by management. Instead, the tremendous growth of unionism after the depression and the labor shortage in the years following World War II produced many of labor's gains.

Proponents of scientific management were also hampered by the notions of human behavior that were prevalent at the time. In brief, the then popular model of human behavior was that people were completely rational — that they were motivated primarily by a desire for gain and would act in a manner best suited to satisfy their *economic* and *physical* needs.[5] Thus, Taylor and his followers overlooked the *social* needs of workers as members of a group and never considered the tensions created when these needs were frustrated. They assumed one had only to tell people exactly what to do to increase their earnings and they would go right ahead and do it, as "rational" people would. In fact, as many managers have since discovered, people need to feel important and want a say in the things that matter to them.

Finally, the proponents of scientific management overlooked the desire for job satisfaction. Paradoxically, as the principles of scientific management were successfully applied and affluence spread, there was a growing willingness on the part of workers to question traditional management practices. Thus, for example, workers became more willing to go out on strike over job conditions rather than salary and to leave a job if they were unhappy in it.[6] The result was that the scientific management model of a purely "rational man," interested *only* in higher wages, became increasingly inappropriate for modern managers.

Henri Fayol (1841–1925) and Classical Organization Theory

Scientific management was concerned with increasing the productivity of the shop and the individual worker. The other branch of classical management — classical organization theory — grew out of the need to find guidelines for managing complex organizations, such as factories. We acknowledge Fayol as founder of the classical management school, not because he was the first to

---

[4] Another important contributor to scientific management was Harrington Emerson. See his book *The Twelve Principles of Efficiency,* published in 1913.

[5] For a rich discussion of rational, economic, social, self-actualizing, and complex man, see Edgar H. Schein, *Organizational Psychology,* 2nd ed. (Englewood Cliffs, N.J.: Prentice-Hall, 1970), pp. 55–76.

[6] One observer, reporting on an automobile plant, wrote: "Some assembly line workers are so turned off, managers report in astonishment, that they just walk away in midshift and don't even come back to get their pay for the time they have worked." See Judson Gooding, "Blue Collar Blues on the Assembly Line," *Fortune,* July 1970, pp. 69–70.

investigate managerial behavior, but because he was the first to systematize it. Fayol believed that sound managerial practice falls into certain patterns that can be identified and analyzed. From this basic insight, he drew up the blueprint for a cohesive doctrine of management—one which retains much of its force to this day.

Trained as a mining engineer, Fayol made his mark as an industrialist with the firm of Commentry-Fourchambault, the French coal and iron combine where he spent his entire working career. He joined the firm as a junior executive in 1860, and rose quickly through the ranks until his retirement as a director of the company in 1918. Fayol always insisted that his success was due not to his personal abilities as a manager but to the methods he used. In fact, he believed that "with scientific forecasting and proper methods of management, satisfactory results were inevitable."

Fayol's insistence that management was not a personal talent but a skill like any other was a major contribution to management thought. It had generally been believed that "managers were born, not made," that practice and experience would be helpful only to those who already had the innate qualities of a manager. Fayol, however, believed that management could be taught, once its underlying principles were understood and a general theory of management was formulated.

Fayol spent much of the later years of his life trying to prove that, when properly applied, his methods and principles would ensure a manager's success. However, widespread recognition of his work came very slowly, partly because his writings were not translated into English until several years after his death. For example, few, if any, American managers were aware of his work even as late as the 1930s. Yet many of the managerial concepts we take for granted today were first articulated by Fayol.

The Activities of a Business and the Functions of a Manager. In setting out to develop a science of management, Fayol began by dividing business operations into six activities, all of which were closely dependent on one another. These activities were (1) *technical*—producing and manufacturing products; (2) *commercial*—buying raw materials and selling products; (3) *financial*—acquiring and using capital; (4) *security*—protecting employees and property; (5) *accounting*—recording and taking stock of costs, profits, and liabilities, keeping balance sheets, and compiling statistics; and (6) *managerial*.

Fayol's primary focus, of course, was on this last managerial activity, because he felt managerial skills had been the most neglected aspect of business operations. He defined managing in terms of five functions: planning, organizing, commanding, coordinating, and controlling. In this definition, *planning* means devising a course of action that will enable the organization to meet its goals. *Organizing* means mobilizing the material and human resources of the organization to put the plans into effect. *Commanding* means motivating employees and getting them to do their work. *Coordinating* means making sure that the resources and activities of the organization are working harmoniously to achieve the desired goals. (For example, a manager in a new automobile assembly plant would make sure car parts are delivered *before* the production line is ready for operation, so that the production line would not remain idle waiting for parts to arrive.) *Controlling* means monitoring the plan to ensure that it is being carried out properly. (See Figure 2-1.)

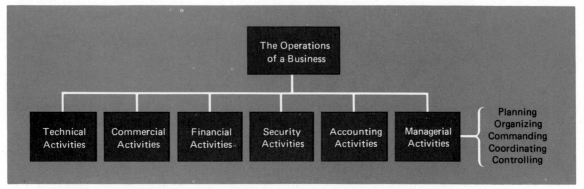

FIGURE 2-1   The Operations of a Business and the Functions of a Manager (Fayol)

Readers will recognize that Fayol's five management functions are similar to the four functions of planning, organizing, leading, and controlling we are using in this book and which are described in Chapter 1. The model of management as a series of functions originated with Fayol, and is one reason why we owe him an enormous debt today.

The Abilities of Managers. Fayol observed that the types of abilities needed by managers in a given organization depend on the managers' position in its hierarchy. For example, if we are in a lower-level job, we may need specific technical skills but very little managerial ability. As we move up the hierarchy, however, we find that managerial abilities become more important as compared to technical skills. Thus, if we are a general manager of a firm, we need a good deal more managerial ability and much less technical ability than a lower-level manager. Fayol noted, too, that the need for managerial abilities is also related to the size of the organization. As chief executives in a large business, for example, we need a relatively greater measure of managerial skill than chief executives in a small one. (See our discussion of management levels and skills in Chapter 1.)

This last point had a strong influence on the development of Fayol's idea that management should be taught. He noted that as the number of large businesses grew, the need for more and better managers increased. Fayol therefore called for the introduction of formal managerial training in schools rather than reliance on the sink-or-swim approach then in use. An added benefit of

41

such managerial training, he suggested, would be that people could function better in all areas of life. Fayol always believed managerial ability could be applied to the home, the church, the military, and politics as well as industry.

The Principles of Management. Fayol carefully chose the term "principles of management" rather than "rules" or "laws":

I prefer the word principles in order to avoid any idea of rigidity, as there is nothing rigid or absolute in administrative matters; everything is a question of degree. The same principle is hardly ever applied twice in exactly the same way, because we have to allow for different and changing circumstances, for human beings who are equally different and changeable, and for many other variable elements. The principles, too, are flexible, and can be adapted to meet every need; it is just a question of knowing how to use them.[7]

Fayol's 14 Principles of Management	
1. Division of Labor	7. Remuneration
2. Authority	8. Centralization
3. Discipline	9. The Hierarchy
4. Unity of Command	10. Order
5. Unity of Direction	11. Equity
6. Subordination of Individual Interest to the Common Good	12. Stability of Staff
	13. Initiative
	14. Esprit de Corps

The fourteen principles Fayol chose were the ones he "most frequently had to apply":

1 *Division of Labor.* The more people specialize, the more efficiently they can perform their work. As we have already suggested, this principle is epitomized by the modern assembly line.

2 *Authority.* Managers need to be able to give orders so that they can get things done. While their *formal* authority gives them the right to command, managers will not always compel obedience unless they have *personal* authority (such as intelligence) as well.

3 *Discipline.* Members in an organization need to respect the rules and agreements that govern the organization. To Fayol, discipline will result from good leadership at all levels of the organization, fair agreements (such as reasonable provisions for salary increases), and judiciously enforced penalties for infractions.

[7] Henri Fayol, *Industrial and General Administration*, trans. J. A. Coubrough (Geneva: International Management Institute, 1930). Fayol used the word "administration" for what we call "management."

42

4   *Unity of Command.* Each employee must receive his or her instructions about a particular operation from only one person. Fayol believed that if an employee was responsible to more than one superior, conflict in instructions and confusion of authority would result.

5   *Unity of Direction.* Those operations within the organization that have the same objective should be directed by only one manager using one plan. For example, the personnel department in a company should not have two directors, each with a different hiring policy.

6   *Subordination of Individual Interest to the Common Good.* In any undertaking, the interests of employees should not take precedence over the interests of the organization as a whole.

7   *Remuneration.* Compensation for work done should be fair to both employees and employers.

8   *Centralization.* Decreasing the role of subordinates in decision making is centralization; increasing their role is decentralization. Fayol believed that managers should retain final responsibility but also need to give their subordinates enough authority to do their jobs properly. The problem is to find the best amount of centralization in each case.

9   *The Hierarchy.* The line of authority in an organization—often represented today by the neat boxes and lines of the organization chart—runs in order of rank from top management to the lowest level of the enterprise.

10 *Order.* Materials and people should be in the right place at the right time. People in particular should be in the jobs or positions most suited for them.

11 *Equity.* Managers should be both friendly and fair to their subordinates.

12 *Stability of Staff.* A high employee turnover rate is not good for the efficient functioning of an organization.

13 *Initiative.* Subordinates should be given the freedom to conceive and carry out their plans, even when some mistakes result.

14 *Esprit de Corps.* Promoting team spirit will give the organization a sense of unity. To Fayol, one way to achieve this spirit is to use verbal communications instead of formal written communications whenever possible.

It is likely that at least some of these principles had been practiced by astute managers long before Fayol appeared. But it was Fayol who first codified these principles, making it possible for all managers to learn them. He thus helped lay the foundation for management as a profession.

Contributions and Limitations of Classical Organization Theory

Contributions. Like all theorists, the classical organization theorists were limited by the knowledge that was available to them and the conditions that existed in their time.[8] Nevertheless, much in classical organization theory has endured. For example, the concepts that management skills apply to all types of group activity have, if anything, increased in importance today—in our

[8] Other important classical theorists were James D. Mooney and Alan C. Reiley, who wrote *Onward Industry* (New York: Harper & Brothers, 1931), and Lyndall F. Urwick, who wrote *The Elements of Administration* (New York: Harper & Brothers, 1943).

schools, government, and other institutions. The concept that certain identifiable principles underlie effective managerial behavior and that these principles can be taught also continues to have validity. (For one thing, it is the justification for this book.)

Although classical organizational theory has been criticized by members of other schools of management thought, its assumptions have been better received by practicing managers than any other. This may be because classical organization theory helped to isolate major areas of practical concern to the working manager.

Take, for example, the classical concept of initiative — that subordinates need to be given a certain amount of freedom. This principle is accepted by almost all managers today. There is considerable disagreement on how much freedom subordinates should have, but nevertheless the need for initiative is recognized and accepted. More than anything else, then, the classical organization school raised issues that are important to managers. It made them aware of certain basic kinds of problems that they would face in any organization.

Limitations. Classical organization theory has been criticized on the ground that it was more appropriate for the past than for the present. When organizations were in a relatively stable and predictable environment, the classical principles seemed valid. Today, with organizational environments becoming more turbulent, the classical organization guidelines seem less appropriate. For example, it was important to classical theorists that managers maintain their authority. Today's more knowledgeable and affluent employees, however, are likely to resent authority, especially when it is applied arbitrarily. They are also more likely than workers of the past to leave an organization if they are dissatisfied in it.

The principles of classical organization theorists have also been criticized by many modern writers as being too general for today's complex organizations. For example, in modern companies specialization has increased to the point where the lines of authority are sometimes blurred. The maintenance engineer, for instance, may take orders from the plant manager *and* the chief engineer. Here we have a conflict between the classical principles of division of labor and unity of command. Yet there is little or no guidance in classical theory on how such problems might be resolved.

Bridging the Classical, Behavioral, and Systems Schools

Mary Parker Follett and Chester Barnard built on the basic framework of the classical school. However, they introduced so many new elements which were closer to the emerging behavioral and systems approaches that they cannot be easily classified in any one management school. Thus, we can say that their contributions extended one line of management thought and anticipated others that followed.

Mary Parker Follett (1868–1933). Follett was convinced that no one could become a whole person except as a member of a group. Thus, she took for granted Taylor's assertion that labor and management shared a common purpose as members of the same organization. She believed, however, that the artificial distinction between managers and subordinates — order givers and order takers — obscured this natural partnership.[9]

Follett argued that in order for management and labor truly to become part of one group, traditional views would have to be abandoned. For example, she believed leadership should no longer come from the power of formal authority, as was traditional, but from the manager's greater *knowledge* and expertise. The manager should simply be the person best equipped by know-how, talent, and experience to head the group. Follett felt that because such a manager would be more acceptable to the group, the group would operate in a more unified way.

Individual

Needs

of

Employees

ORGANIZATIONAL
SUCCESS

Organization

Goals

Chester I. Barnard (1886–1961). Barnard became president of New Jersey Bell in 1927. He used his work experiences and his extensive readings in sociology and philosophy to formulate his theories on organizational life.

According to Barnard, people come together in formal organizations to achieve things they could not achieve working alone. But as they pursue the organization's goals, they must also satisfy their individual needs. And so Barnard arrived at his central thesis: An enterprise can operate efficiently and survive only when both the organization's goals and the aims and needs of the individuals working for it are kept in balance.[10]

For example, to meet their personal goals within the confines of the formal organization, people come together in informal groups, such as cliques or clubs. To ensure its survival, the firm must have consideration for these informal organizations, even if its immediate goals sometimes suffer. This was a major contribution to management thought and anticipated the human relations theorists, who would later make the same point. (We discuss Barnard's work in more detail in Chapter 11.)

THE BEHAVIORAL SCHOOL: THE ORGANIZATION IS PEOPLE

The behavioral school emerged in part because managers found that the classical approach did not quite achieve complete production efficiency and workplace harmony. Managers still encountered difficulties and frustrations because people did not always follow predicted or rational patterns of behavior. Thus, there was an increased interest in helping managers deal more effectively with the "people side" of their organizations. Several individuals tried to strengthen scientific management and organization theory with the insights of sociology and psychology.

[9] See Mary P. Follett, *The New State* (Gloucester, Mass.: Peter Smith, 1918) and H. C. Metcalf and L. Urwick, eds., *Dynamic Administration* (New York: Harper & Brothers, 1941).

[10] See Chester I. Barnard, *The Functions of the Executive* (Cambridge, Mass.: Harvard University Press, 1938).

"Our incentive plan is quite simple. Make one mistake and you're through!"

Cartoon by George Dole

Hugo Münsterberg (1863–1916) and the Birth of Industrial Psychology

Münsterberg's major contribution was to apply the tools of psychology to help meet the demand of scientific management for increased productivity. In his major work, *Psychology and Industrial Efficiency,* he suggested that productivity could be increased in three ways: (1) through finding the *best possible man*—the worker whose mental qualities single him or her out as best suited for the job; (2) through creating the *best possible work*—the ideal psychological conditions for maximizing productivity; and (3) through the use of psychological influence, which Münsterberg calls the *best possible effect,* to motivate employees.

In each area Münsterberg suggested the use of techniques taken from experimental psychology. For example, psychological testing could be used to help select qualified personnel. Learning research could lead to improved training methods. And the study of human behavior could help formulate psychological techniques for motivating workers to greater effort. The use of vocational guidance techniques to identify the skills needed on a job and to measure the skills of candidates for the job were offshoots of Münsterberg's studies.[11]

[11] See Hugo Münsterberg, *Psychology and Industrial Efficiency* (reprint of 1913 edition, New York: Arno Press). An interesting discussion of Münsterberg's work appears in "Measuring Minds for the Job," *Business Week,* January 29, 1966, pp. 60–63.

46

Elton Mayo and
the Human
Relations
Movement

"Human relations" is frequently used as a general term to describe the ways in which managers interact with their subordinates. When "people management" stimulates more and better work, we have "good" human relations in the organization. When morale and efficiency deteriorate, human relations in the organization are "bad." To create good human relations, managers must know why employees act as they do and what social and psychological factors motivate them.

The Hawthorne Experiments. Elton Mayo (1880–1949) and his Harvard associates conducted a famous study of human behavior in work situations at the Hawthorne plant of Western Electric from 1927 to 1932. Mayo was called in by Western Electric when other researchers, who had been experimenting with work-area lighting, reported some rather peculiar results. They had divided the employees into a "test group" that was subject to deliberate changes in illumination, and a "control group" whose illumination remained constant throughout the experiment. When the test group's lighting conditions improved, productivity increased, just as expected. But what mystified the researchers was a similar jump in productivity when illumination was *worsened.* To compound the mystery, the control group's output kept rising with each alteration in the test group's lighting conditions, even though the control group experienced no such changes. In his attempt to solve this puzzle, Mayo ushered in the new era of human relations.

In a new experiment, Mayo and his Harvard co-workers placed two groups of six women each in separate rooms. In one room the conditions were varied and in the other they were not. A number of variables were tried: salaries were increased; coffee breaks of varying lengths were introduced; the workday and workweek were shortened; the researchers, who now acted as supervisors, allowed the groups to choose their own rest periods and to have a say in other suggested changes.

Once again, output went up in both the test and control rooms. The researchers felt they could rule out financial incentives as a cause, since the control group was kept to the same payment schedule. Mayo concluded that a complex emotional chain reaction had touched off the productivity increases. Because the test and control groups had been singled out for special attention, they developed a group pride that motivated them to improve their work performance. The sympathetic supervision they received had further reinforced their increased motivation.

The result of this experiment gave Mayo his first important discovery: when special attention is given to workers by management, productivity is likely to increase regardless of actual changes in working conditions. This phenomenon became known as the *Hawthorne effect.*

One question, however, remained unanswered. *Why* should special attention plus the formation of group bonds elicit such strong reactions? To find the answer, Mayo launched a massive interview program, which led to his most significant finding: that informal work groups—the social environment of employees—have a great influence on productivity. Many of the employees found

47

their lives inside and outside the factory dull and meaningless. But their workplace associations, based in part on mutual antagonism toward the "bosses," imparted some meaning to their working lives. For this reason, group pressure, rather than management demands, had the strongest influence on how productive they would be.

To maximize output, Mayo and his associates concluded, management must recognize the employees' needs for recognition and social satisfaction. It had to turn the informal group into a positive, productive force by providing employees with a new sense of dignity and a sense of being appreciated. To Mayo, then, the concept of *social man* — motivated by social needs, wanting on-the-job relationships, and more responsive to work-group pressures than to management control — had to replace the old concept of rational man motivated by personal economic needs.[12]

Contributions
and Limitations
of the Human
Relations School

Contributions. By stressing social needs, the human relations movement improved on the classical approach, which treated productivity merely as an engineering problem. In a sense, Mayo had rediscovered Robert Owen's century-old dictum that a true concern for workers, those "vital machines," paid dividends.

His studies revealed a fact that seems commonplace today: that an office, factory, or shop is not merely a workplace but also a social environment, with employees interacting with each other. And this social environment is very influential in determining the quality and quantity of work produced.

In addition, Mayo spotlighted the importance of a manager's style and thereby revolutionized management training. More and more attention was focused on teaching people-management skills, as opposed to technical skills. Finally, his work led to a new interest in the dynamics of groups. Managers began thinking in terms of *group* incentives to supplement their former concentration on the individual worker.

Limitations. The concept of "social man" was an important counterweight to the one-sided "rational-economic man" model. But it, too, did not completely describe individuals in the workplace. Many managers and management writers assumed that satisfied workers would be more productive workers. However, attempts to increase output during the 1950s by improving working conditions and the human relations skills of managers did not result in the dramatic productivity increases that had been expected.

---

[12] For extensive discussion of Mayo's work, see Elton Mayo, *The Human Problems of an Industrial Civilization* (New York: Macmillan, 1953), and F. J. Roethlisberger and W. J. Dickson, *Management and the Worker* (Cambridge, Mass.: Harvard University Press, 1939). Analysis, criticism, and defense of the Hawthorne studies can be found in G. C. Homans, *The Human Group* (New York: Harcourt, Brace, and Co., 1950), pp. 48–155; A. Carey, "The Hawthorne Studies: A Radical Criticism," *American Sociological Review,* Vol. 32, No. 3 (June 1967); H. A. Landsberger, *Hawthorne Revisited* (Ithaca, N.Y.: Cornell University Press, 1958); and J. M. Shepard, "On Carey's Radical Criticism of the Hawthorne Studies," *Academy of Management Journal,* Vol. 14, No. 1 (March 1971), pp. 23–32.

Apparently, economic aspects of work *do* play an important role in worker motivation and productivity. Employees may enjoy their co-workers, but if salary levels are too low, turnover rates are still likely to be high. In addition, it is not reasonable to expect that tensions between labor and management, which can affect productivity, will cease to exist simply because supervisors are skilled in human relations. Finally, the emphasis on the social aspects of work neglects the effects that the work task itself and the structure of the organization can have on productivity. If employees see the work task as extremely boring, for example, they are not likely to be motivated to do their best, regardless of the social environment at the workplace. Thus, the entire matter of productivity and worker satisfaction has turned out to be more complex than it originally appeared to be.

From Human Relations to the Behavioral Science Approach

Mayo and his colleagues pioneered the use of the scientific method in their studies of people in the work environment. Later researchers were more rigorously trained in the various social sciences (such as psychology, sociology, and anthropology). They also tended to use more sophisticated research methods. Thus, these later researchers became regarded as "behavioral scientists" rather than members of the "human relations" school.[13]

Mayo and the theorists of the human relations school introduced "social man," motivated by a desire to form relationships with others. Some behavioral scientists, such as Argyris, Maslow, and McGregor, believed that the concept of "self-actualizing man" would more accurately explain the motivations of people.[14]

According to this concept, the needs that people are motivated to satisfy fall into a hierarchy. At the bottom of the hierarchy are the lower-level needs, such as physical and safety needs. At the top are the higher-level needs, such as ego needs (the need for respect, for example) and self-actualizing needs (such as the need for meaning and personal growth). In general, the lower-level needs must be satisfied before the higher-level needs make themselves felt. Since many of our lower-level needs have been satisfied in our society, most of us are motivated, at least in part, by the higher-level ego and self-actualizing needs. Being aware of these different needs enables a manager to use different ways to motivate subordinates.

Some later behavioral scientists feel that even this model is inadequate to explain fully what motivates people in the workplace. They argue, for example, that not everyone goes predictably from one need level to another. Some

---

[13] See B. Berelson and G. A. Steiner, *Human Behavior: An Inventory of Scientific Findings* (New York: Harcourt, Brace, and World, 1964). Berelson and Steiner define science as a form of inquiry in which procedures are public, definitions are precise, data collection is objective, findings are replicable, the approach is systematic and cumulative, and the purposes are explanation, understanding, and prediction. This is the ideal toward which behavioral science (or any science) strives.

[14] See C. Argyris, *Integrating the Individual and the Organization* (New York: Wiley, 1964); A. Maslow, *Motivation and Personality* (New York: Harper & Row, 1964); and D. M. McGregor, *The Human Side of Enterprise* (New York: McGraw-Hill, 1960).

people see working only as a way to meet their lower-level needs. Others are satisfied with nothing less than the fulfillment of their highest-level needs, and may even work in jobs that threaten their safety. To these behavioral scientists, the more realistic model of human motivation is *complex man*. This model suggests that different people will react differently to the same situation or will react the same way to different situations. The effective manager is aware that no two people are exactly alike, and tailors his or her attempts to influence people according to their individual needs. (In later chapters we will be discussing in much greater detail how managers can use the insights of behavioral science.)

Contributions and Limitations of the Behavioral Science School. Behavioral scientists have made enormous contributions to our understanding of individual motivation, group behavior, interpersonal relationships at work, and the importance of work to human beings. Their findings have caused managers to become much more sensitive and sophisticated in dealing with subordinates. They continue to offer new insights in such important areas as leadership, conflict resolution, organizational change, and communication.

However, many management writers—including behavioral scientists—believe that the potential contribution of behavioral science to managers has not been fully realized. Many managers resist the behavioral scientists' suggestions, because they do not like to admit they are unable to handle people without help. The tendency of behavioral scientists to use their own technical terms rather than everyday language in communicating their findings has also inhibited acceptance of their ideas. Finally, because human behavior is such a complex area, behavioral scientists often differ in their recommendations for a particular problem, making it difficult for managers to decide whose advice to follow.[15]

THE QUANTITATIVE SCHOOL: OPERATIONS RESEARCH AND MANAGEMENT SCIENCE

During the first years of World War II, Great Britain was faced with a number of new, complex problems in warfare that it needed desperately to solve. (For example, new tactics in antisubmarine warfare had to be developed.) With their survival at stake, the British formed the first *operational research (OR)* teams—groups of mathematicians, physicists, and other scientists who were brought together to solve such problems. Because they pooled the expertise of various specialists in these OR teams, the British were able to achieve significant technological and tactical breakthroughs. And because OR

[15] See Edgar H. Schein, "Behavioral Sciences for Management," and E. W. Flippo, "The Underutilization of Behavioral Science by Management," in J. W. McGuire, ed., *Contemporary Management: Issues and Viewpoints* (Englewood Cliffs, N.J.: Prentice-Hall, 1974), pp. 15–32 and pp. 36–41. See also J. A. Lee, "Behavioral Theory vs. Reality," *Harvard Business Review*, March-April 1971, pp. 20–28, passim.

teams were so successful, the Americans formed what they called *operations research* teams to solve similar problems when they entered the war.

When the war was over, the applicability of OR to problems in industry gradually became apparent. New industrial technologies were being put into use. Transportation and communication had become more complicated. These developments brought with them a host of complex problems that could not be easily solved by conventional means. OR specialists began to be called on with increasing frequency to help managers come up with new answers to these new problems. With the development of the electronic computer, OR procedures eventually became formalized into what is now called the "management science school."[16]

Today the OR–management science approach to solving a problem works in approximately the following manner. A mixed team of specialists from relevant disciplines is called in to analyze the problem and propose a course of action to management. The team constructs a mathematical model to simulate the problem. The model shows, in symbolic terms, all the relevant factors that bear on the problem and how they are interrelated. By changing the values of the variables in the model (such as increasing the cost of raw materials) and analyzing the different equations of the model with a computer, the team can determine what the effects of each change would be. Eventually, the OR team presents management with a rational base for making a decision.[17] (See Chapter 8 for a further discussion of OR.)

Contributions and Limitations of the Management Science Approach

The techniques of management science are a well-established part of the problem-solving armory of most large organizations, including the civilian as well as the military branches of government. Management science techniques, which we will describe later in this book, are used in such activities as capital budgeting and cash flow management, production scheduling, development of product strategies, planning for manpower development programs, maintenance of optimal inventory levels, and aircraft scheduling.[18]

In spite of its widespread use in many problem areas, however, management science has not yet reached the stage where it can effectively deal with the

[16] See R. J. Thierauf and R. C. Klekamp, *Decision-Making through Operations Research,* 2nd ed. (New York: Wiley, 1975), and H. M. Wagner, *Principles of Management Science* (Englewood Cliffs, N.J.: Prentice-Hall, 1970).

[17] The management science approach has been applied to other uses besides industrial problem solving. Jay Forrester and his colleagues, for example, have pioneered attempts to simulate the operations of whole enterprises. He and others have also simulated economic activities of Third World nations and even of the world system as a whole. See J. W. Forrester, *Industrial Dynamics* (Cambridge, Mass.: MIT Press, 1961); E. P. Holland and R. W. Gillespie, *Experiments on a Simulated Underdeveloped Economy* (Cambridge, Mass.: MIT Press, 1963); D. H. Meadows et al., *The Limits to Growth* (New York: Universe Books, 1972); and Mihajlo Mesarovic and Eduard Pestel, *Mankind at the Turning Point* (New York: Dutton, 1975).

[18] For a rich discussion of the directions in which management science may evolve in the future and an indication of its increasingly close connections with systems analysis, see M. K. Starr, "Management Science and Management," and D. B. Hertz, "The Changing Field of Management Science," in McGuire, *Contemporary Management,* pp. 72–92 and pp. 95–98.

people side of an enterprise. Its contributions to management have been greatest in planning and control activities. But they are still very modest in the areas of organizing, staffing, and leading the organization. Some management scientists also feel that they have not achieved their full potential for solving management problems because of their remoteness from and lack of awareness of the problems and constraints actually faced by managers.[19]

ATTEMPTS TO INTEGRATE THE SCHOOLS

The classical, behavioral, and quantitative schools offer different perspectives on the management of organizations. Each of these perspectives is useful in the appropriate setting. However, it is difficult to know which perspective is most useful and appropriate in a given situation.

As an example, let us look at a city administration faced with the declining use of mass transit and the accompanying problems of traffic tie-ups and revenue loss. From the classical viewpoint, the mass transit system might require a strengthening of the organizational structure, with areas of responsibility more clearly defined in order to break through repair backlogs and parts shortages. A behavioral scientist might suggest that people dislike using the system because of crowding, noise, dirt, and the unpredictability of schedules. A management scientist might suggest determining the most efficient routes through OR. All three approaches might apply, or two, or one, depending on the specific system involved. Yet members of the city administration would have no easy way of knowing which one to use.

What is needed is one broad, detailed, conceptual framework that can help a manager diagnose a problem and decide which tool or combination of tools will best do the job. Many theorists point to the new *systems* and *contingency* approaches as the most likely candidates to provide this integrated approach to management problems.

The Systems Approach

When we look at a painting, we see neither lines nor points nor individual splotches of color. What we see are patterns—the intertwining of lines, points, and colors that makes the painting *more* than the sum of its parts. Similarly, we experience a melody only because we tune out the sound of each individual note; we take in only the pattern of notes that makes the melody. In this sense, a painting or a piece of music can be seen as a *system*—an interdependent group of items that form a unified whole.

The systems approach to management attempts to view the organization as a unified, purposeful system composed of interrelated parts. Rather than dealing separately with the various parts of an organization, the systems

[19]Suggestions on how to bridge the gap between manager and management scientist are offered by C. Jackson Grayson, Jr., "Management Science and Business Practice," *Harvard Business Review,* July-August 1973, pp. 41–48, and by J. L. McKenney and P. G. W. Keen, "How Managers' Minds Work," *Harvard Business Review,* May-June 1974, pp. 79–90.

approach tries to give managers a way of looking at organizations as a whole. In so doing, systems theory tells us that the activity of any part of an organization affects the activity of every other part.[20]

As production managers in a manufacturing plant, for example, we would ideally like to have long uninterrupted production runs in order to maintain maximum efficiency and low costs. Marketing departments, on the other hand, would like to offer quick delivery of a wide range of products and therefore may want a flexible manufacturing schedule that can fill special orders on short notice. As systems-oriented production managers, we would make our scheduling decisions only after we have identified their impact on other departments and the entire organization. This means that systems managers cannot function wholly within the confines of the traditional organization chart. To mesh their department with the whole enterprise, managers must be in frequent contact with other employees and departments.[21]

Some Key Concepts. Many of the concepts of general systems theory are finding their way into the language of management. As managers, we should be familiar with the systems vocabulary, so that we can keep pace with current developments.

Subsystems. The parts that make up the whole of a system are called "subsystems." And each system in turn may be a subsystem of a still larger whole. Thus, a department is a subsystem of a plant, which may be a subsystem of a company, which may be a subsystem of a conglomerate or industry, which is a subsystem of the economy as a whole, which is a subsystem of the world system. From such a perspective, the manager is able to see the needs and operations of various departments as a part of a larger whole.

Synergy. Synergy means that the whole is greater than the sum of its parts. In organizational terms, synergy means that as separate departments within an organization cooperate and interact, they become more productive than if they had acted in isolation. For example, it is obviously more efficient for each department in a small firm to deal with one financing department than for each department to have a separate financing department of its own.

Open and Closed Systems. A system is considered open if it interacts with its environment; it is considered closed if it does not. All organizations interact with their environment, but the extent to which they do so varies. An automobile plant, for example, is a far more open system than a monastery or a prison.

System Boundary. Each system has a boundary that separates it from its environment. In a closed system this boundary is rigid; in an open system, the boundary is more flexible. The system boundary of many organizations has become increasingly flexible in recent years. Oil companies that wished to

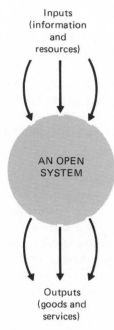

Inputs (information and resources)

AN OPEN SYSTEM

Outputs (goods and services)

---

[20] See Ludwig von Bertalanffy, C. G. Hempel, R. E. Bass, and H. Jonas, "General System Theory: A New Approach to Unity of Science," I–VI, *Human Biology 23* (1951), pp. 302–361, and Kenneth E. Boulding, "General Systems Theory – The Skeleton of Science," *Management Science,* April 1956, pp. 197–208.

[21] See S. Tilles, "The Manager's Job—A Systems Approach," *Harvard Business Review,* January-February 1963, pp. 73–81.

engage in offshore drilling, to cite one example, have increasingly had to consider public reaction to the potential environmental harm.

Flow. A system has flows of information, material, and energy (including human). These enter the system from the environment as *inputs* (raw materials, for example) and exit the system as *outputs* (goods and services).

Feedback. Feedback is the key to system controls. As operations of the system proceed, information is fed back to the appropriate people or perhaps to a computer so that the work can be assessed and, if necessary, corrected.[22]

Our discussion implies that managers at any level can use systems theory to keep their separate functions more closely in line with the overall goals of the organization, and integrate their activities with those of other departments. But systems theory may be especially useful to the general manager. With a systems perspective, general managers can more easily maintain a balance between the needs of the various parts of the enterprise and the needs and goals of the firm as a whole. A common pitfall of managers is to stress one aspect of the organization at the expense of others — to concentrate on building a strong sales organization, for example, and ignore product quality. The systems approach helps managers avoid this pitfall.

The Contingency Approach

The contingency approach is the second approach that attempts to integrate the various schools of management thought.[23] Its development was stimulated by managers, consultants, and researchers who tried to apply the concepts of the major schools to real-life situations. They often found that methods that were highly effective in one situation would not work in other situations. They then sought an explanation for these experiences. Why, for example, did a behavioral scientist's concept work brilliantly in one situation and fail miserably in another? The contingency approach that was developed attempted to answer such questions simply and logically: Results differ because situations differ. A technique that works in one case does not necessarily work in all cases.

According to the contingency approach, then, *the task of managers is to try to identify which technique will, in a particular situation, under particular circumstances, and at a particular time, best contribute to the attainment of management goals.* Where workers need to be encouraged to increase productivity, for example, the classical theorist may prescribe a new incentive scheme. The behavioral scientist may create a psychologically motivating climate. The manager trained in the contingency approach will ask, Which method will work best here? If the workers are unskilled, struggling to meet car or mortgage payments, then financial incentives might work well. With

[22] F. E. Kast and J. E. Rosenzweig, "General Systems Theory: Applications for Organization and Management," *Academy of Management Journal,* December 1972, pp. 447–465.

[23] See F. Luthans, "The Contingency Theory of Management: A Path Out of the Jungle." *Business Horizons,* June 1973, pp. 62–72, and F. E. Kast and J. E. Rosenzweig, eds., *Contingency Views of Organization and Management* (Chicago: Science Research Associates, 1973).

skilled workers, driven by pride in their abilities, a job enrichment program might be more effective.

As managers in the contingency school, we would not be satisfied with just analyzing the particular problem, however. We would be equally concerned with how well a particular solution would fit in with the structure, resources, and goals of our entire organization. If top management is opposed to incentive plans for policy reasons, then clearly such plans could not be applied as solutions. Similarly, we would take environmental factors into consideration when deciding what to do. In a depressed economy, for example, job enrichment programs might be too expensive or too uncertain in their outcome to be considered. The contingency approach means that we must be aware of the complexity in every situation and that we must take an active role in trying to determine what would work best in each case.

The insights available from both the systems approach and the contingency approach look very promising for managers and the future of management thought. However, both approaches are still sufficiently new to make it difficult to predict just how they will eventually develop. We will have to wait and see whether either one or both together achieve the goal of integrating the various schools of management thought.

Summary Three well-established schools of management thought—classical, behavioral, and quantitative—have contributed to managers' understanding of organizations and to their ability to manage them. Each offers a different perspective for defining management problems and opportunities and for developing ways to deal with them. In their current state of evolution, however, each approach also overlooks or deals inadequately with important aspects of organizational life. The newer systems approach, based on general systems theory, and the contingency approach have already been developed to the point where they offer valuable insights for the practicing manager. Eventually they may lead to the integration of the classical, behavioral, and quantitative schools; or, some new approach not yet perceived on the horizon may accomplish this end.

It is also possible that the theoretical breakthrough may never occur.[24] Managers will then have to continue on their own to select the appropriate perspective or perspectives for each situation. They may, of course, become lost in what one writer has called "the management theory jungle."[25] But it is at least as likely that managers will find such a multiplicity of theories useful. It may be that no one theory could encompass a field like management, in which the complexities of human behavior play such a central role.

[24] For an excellent treatment of the process of change in theories, see T. S. Kuhn, *The Structure of Scientific Revolutions,* 2nd ed., enlarged (Chicago: University of Chicago Press, 1970).

[25] See Harold Koontz, "The Management Theory Jungle," *Journal of the Academy of Management,* Vol. 4, No. 3 (December 1961), pp. 174–188. When Koontz wrote his now classic article, the systems and contingency approaches had not yet developed sufficiently for Koontz to deal with them. See also Lyndall F. Urwick, "The Tactics of Jungle Warfare," *Journal of the Academy of Management,* Vol. 6, No. 4 (December 1963), pp. 316–329, and Richard G. Brandenberg, "The Usefulness of Management Thought for Management," in McGuire, *Contemporary Management,* pp. 99–112.

Review Questions

1. Why is it important for you to understand the various management theories that have developed?
2. What problems and developments caused each of the three major schools to arise?
3. What methods did Taylor use to increase productivity? How would you have proceeded in his place?
4. Was Taylor naive to believe that management and labor had a common interest? Why or why not?
5. What are the major contributions and limitations of each of the three schools?
6. Which of Fayol's principles and functions of management do you believe still apply today?
7. What was Mayo's principal contribution to management knowledge? What is the Hawthorne effect?
8. Which "model of man" characterized each major school?
9. What is OR and how does it work?
10. Does the systems approach seem more valid for our time than for Fayol's? Why?
11. What is the major task of the manager according to the contingency approach?
12. With what elements of each approach we have described are you most comfortable? least comfortable?

CASE STUDY: GRANDVIEW MORNING PRESS

The *Grandview Morning Press* is published seven days a week in the city of Grandview, an area that undergoes a large increase in population every summer due to its fine scenery and excellent climate. Normally the paper consists of a single section with occasional advertising supplements. However, in the summer, a second, "Summer Living," section is added, and the number and frequency of advertising inserts increases drastically in an effort to profit as much as possible from the summer trade.

The insertion of the advertising supplements and the collating of the two sections is done by hand. The publishers of the *Morning Press* feel it would be too costly to purchase the necessary machinery when most of the time it would be used only during the summer months. Besides, they feel that hiring a number of vacationing students is a step toward better community relations. Each summer they hire approximately a dozen college students to work in the printing press building each night, usually for between 7 and 14 hours. Because some editions have more advertising "stuffers" than others, the students do not know until they report for work whether that evening's work will be long or short. All time over 8 hours is considered overtime and is paid at time and a half. The normal hourly rate is $2.10.

The summer workers have a code among themselves that no matter what the work load, they will decide exactly how long to work each night. For example, if there seems to be an 8-hour load, the stuffing crew will purposely slow down in order to take 9 hours and thereby get paid overtime. On those occasions when the crew wants to finish early and get to the local disco before the 4 a.m. closing time, an estimated 7- or 8-hour job will be completed in about 6 hours. Newcomers to the crew are made to conform to the group's production norms through verbal abuse for noncompliance.

A member of the stuffing crew for the past two summers, Barbara Warren has supported this code. This summer, however, Barbara was asked by the pressroom chief to supervise the work of the stuffing crew. She welcomed the extra 20¢ an hour she would be making and viewed with pride the thought of being able to apply her business school theories to her new "management level" position.

After the first few nights, she noticed the code was working as it had for untold summers past. But this year she viewed its effects from the "other side." She realized that the slowdown lowered the profits of the paper by raising the labor costs. The drivers were delayed in making their deliveries. On occasion even the janitors had to sit about idle, waiting for the stuffing crew to finish their work.

At first Barbara was puzzled as to what her proper course of action should be. Should she lower the boom and stop the wasteful practice, or should she let it continue? Neither alternative would be satisfactory to everyone concerned.

Case Questions

1. Does Barbara have more than the two choices she is considering? If so, what choices?
2. What will be the consequences of her actions, both for herself and the paper?
3. How would the situation differ if these were full-time employees on a regular job?
4. Why does the *Morning Press* management permit the code to operate?
5. How would you handle the code?

Chapter 3

Managers and the External Environment of Organizations

Upon completing this chapter you should be able to:

1. Describe the *direct-action* and *indirect* environments of organizations and explain why it is important for managers to be concerned about them.

2. Describe the ways you as a manager can keep abreast of changes in the environment.

3. Describe how concepts of managerial and organizational responsibility have been changing.

4. Discuss the role of ethics in organizational life.

5. Discuss how the values of managers have changed and how your own values are likely to affect your actions as a manager.

6. Describe the barriers to increased social responsibility by organizations.

7. Define and explain the *corporate social audit*.

The classical, behavioral, and quantitative schools of management thought tended to focus on those aspects of the organization that managers could *control.* They told managers how many subordinates they should have, why it was important to improve the work environment, and how the computer could be used to help them make decisions. But they tended to underplay the importance of the external environment for managers. The political climate of society and how people outside the organization felt about the organization were never the main concerns of the three management schools.

This was not necessarily bad. If the external environment of organizations is fairly stable and predictable, there is less need for managers to be directly concerned with it. In our time, however, the external environment has been undergoing rapid and even accelerating changes. These changes are having significant and sometimes unpredictable effects on organizations and their management.

Once, for example, it seemed to be enough for organizations to maximize profits; now they must consider how they will affect the quality of life. Once, increased productivity appeared to be sufficient in itself; now the ecological balance must be maintained. The ups and downs of the economy; the changing attitudes and requirements of customers; the actions of government agencies; the inflated costs of money, materials, and manpower; all these and more affect and are affected by the organization and its management. As Murray D. Lincoln, long-time head of Nationwide Insurance, once put it, in a world in which change is the only constant, "every firm needs one vice president in charge of revolution" to cope with change and prevent organizational hardening of the arteries.[1]

With or without a "vice president in charge of revolution," managers today must establish some method or approach that will enable them to maintain and improve their performance in a changing environment. Take, for example, some of the problems hospital managers have had to contend with in the past decade, as their social and technological environments changed:

— pressures on space and costs because of the rising demand for in-patient treatment occasioned by Medicare and Medicaid programs
— increased wages and better working conditions as nurses, orderlies, custodians, and other staff members escalated their demands
— similar demands from and changes for interns
— new pressures from government agencies to meet local and national performance standards
— escalating costs from the rapid development of expensive and sophisticated equipment and treatment procedures
— pressures from insurance companies because of a new wave of malpractice suits

It is obvious that only an approach to management that takes the external environment into account will enable organizations to function effectively.

[1] Quoted in Arthur Mitchell, "Human Relations." Unpublished work.

Here is where the "systems" and "contingency" approaches come into their own. Both take explicit account of the total environment within which an organization operates. And both focus specifically on the adjustments that must be made as the manager attempts to dominate, control, neutralize, or adapt to that environment.

With the systems and contingency approaches as our guides in this chapter, we will focus first on the *direct-action* environments of organizations—that is, on those elements of the total environment that directly affect and are affected by the organization's major operations. Then we will consider the *indirect* environments—those which do not directly touch on the work of the organization but which can, nonetheless, influence its decisions.[2]

An example may make clear the distinction between direct-action and indirect environments. A steady flow of raw materials from its steel suppliers is essential to the day-to-day work of General Motors. Thus, these steel suppliers are part of GM's direct-action environment. GM's daily operations do not depend directly upon the activities of consumer advocate Ralph Nader. Yet Nader's activities may well influence indirectly any number of decisions the GM management might make. To make effective decisions, a manager must first identify those elements of the environment involved in a given situation.

THE "DIRECT-ACTION" ENVIRONMENTS

For most organizations, the major direct-action environments are suppliers, customers, competitors, and government agencies. These will be specific to a given organization (U.S. Steel will interact often with the Occupational Safety and Health Administration but rarely with the Food and Drug Administration), and they will change in composition over time (some customers will be lost, new ones picked up). The accompanying chart illustrates the importance of the direct-action environments. It shows how these environments interact not only with the manager but also with the subunits (departments, divisions, and so on) of the organization.

Suppliers
Each organization takes in raw materials, parts, energy, equipment, and labor from the environment and uses them to produce its output. Thus, no organization can be independent of its suppliers of materials and labor.

As purchasing manager or agent, we would usually deal with several competing suppliers, sometimes paying a higher unit price in the process. But this is acceptable if it keeps our firm from becoming overly dependent on a single supplier. A company tied to one supplier has no other place to turn. Besides, by dividing our purchases among various vendors, we will be able

[2] See Alvar O. Elbing, "On the Applicability of Environmental Models," in Joseph W. McGuire, ed., *Contemporary Management: Issues and Viewpoints* (Englewood Cliffs, N.J.: Prentice-Hall, 1974), pp. 283–289.

FIGURE 3-1
The Direct-Action
Environments

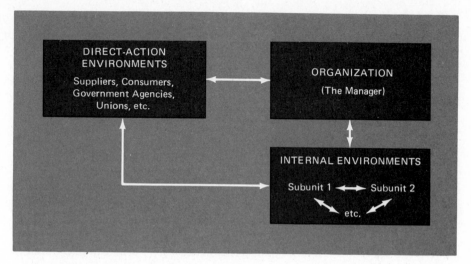

Source: Alvar O. Elbing, "On the Applicability of Environmental Models," in J. W. McGuire, ed., *Contemporary Management: Issues and Viewpoints* (Englewood Cliffs, N.J.: Prentice-Hall, 1974), p. 284. Used by permission.

to take advantage of price cuts initiated by one or another competing supplier. We will also be able to use the competitors to keep suppliers in line on quality and delivery-time requirements.

The interaction between management and employees will depend on the specific labor market conditions that prevail. In a "tight" market, with few qualified people available to meet the firm's needs, managers may have to better the going wages, working conditions, and fringe benefits. In a "loose" market, with many qualified individuals competing for each job, wages may be average. Similarly, a department (such as a research and development department) that requires many highly skilled technicians and where a high personnel turnover may disrupt ongoing projects will be generous in its offerings. An organization like a hamburger chain, on the other hand, which employs large numbers of unskilled employees who come and go at frequent intervals, will try to keep wages and benefits to a minimum. However, regardless of labor conditions, all managers must deal with such factors as employee turnover, absenteeism, time lost through work stoppages, and training budgets.

Customers   In selling our firm's goods and services, our tactics will vary with the kind of customer and the type of market involved. Our customer may be an institution, such as a school, hospital, or government agency; another firm, such as a contractor, distributor, or retailer; or an individual consumer.

Our market may be fairly competitive, with large numbers of buyers and sellers seeking the best deal. There we will have to be especially concerned with price, quality, service, and product style if we want to keep old customers and attract new ones. Our market may be oligopolistic, with a handful of sellers confronting large numbers of buyers, as in the steel industry. In such cases,

61

price and market share may be determined by tacit or informal industry agreement, while firms compete on quality, advertising claims, corporate image, and the like. Or there may be a monopoly, with every customer having to buy from just one available source, as with an electric utility. In that case, relations with government regulators will be one of our major concerns. Sometimes our firm may enjoy a temporary monopoly until competitors enter the field, as was the case with Xerox when it introduced the electrostatic copier.

Competitors

Closely linked to the customer environment are the type, number, and norms of behavior of the organization's competitors. To increase its share of the market, the firm must take business away from somebody else. This means it must provide superior customer satisfaction. Where products and prices are the same, the firm must create differences in packaging, service, or corporate image.

Firms like General Motors, Ford, Chrysler, American Motors, and their foreign counterparts are clearly competitors in the American automobile market. But competition can also come from organizations that provide substitute products or services. In New York City, for example, the rapid transit network competes to some extent with the automobile manufacturers. The world petroleum crisis in the 1970s has drawn attention to the complex competitive interrelationships in the energy industry. Thus, while Texaco, Mobil, and Exxon compete with each other in the sale of fuel, all of them together face the competition of energy-producing substitutes from the coal, nuclear, solar, and geothermal industries.

Government Agencies

Organizations have become increasingly involved with government agencies. Of course, when the federal government appears in the role of consumer (sometimes the sole domestic consumer, as with the defense industry), such involvement is welcomed. More controversial is an organization's relation to the growing number of regulatory agencies. These agencies establish ground rules under which an industry may operate, and they police the industry to ensure that those rules are obeyed.

Some agencies focus on selected industries. For example, the Federal Communications Commission (FCC) focuses on telecommunications, the Securities and Exchange Commission (SEC) focuses on the securities industry, and the Food and Drug Administration (FDA) focuses on the food and drug industries. Other agencies like the Occupational Safety and Health Administration (OSHA) and the Environmental Protection Agency (EPA) leave their mark on a broad spectrum of industries. In addition to these federal agencies, management must also cope with a plethora of state and local agencies. And given the pressures on government from public interest groups which insist that social needs must take precedence over the drive for maximized profits, the likelihood is that such agencies will continue to proliferate.

Because many of these agencies must explore new ground, their activities inject a new degree of uncertainty into the environments of the organizations they regulate and thereby limit a manager's freedom of action. Unlike the accepted roles of customers, suppliers, and competitors, the role of government has been a subject of heated debate. As some see it, government "encroachment" impairs the efficiency of both profit and nonprofit organizations. Others insist that government must protect the community from the "antisocial" side effects of unregulated industrial activity and must also maintain a fair competitive system.

There can be little question that the organizational *cost* of government regulation has climbed very high. Vulcan, Inc., a medium-sized manufacturer, pays out $88,000 a year in salaries just to process the 480 forms required by a variety of federal and state agencies. Eli Lilly & Co., a billion-dollar pharmaceutical company, fills out a staggering 27,000 forms a year at a cost of $15 *million*.[3] In addition, there are "opportunity costs" an organization must bear — for example, the losses borne because of work that does not get done while government forms are being filled out. One of Vulcan's divisions suffered losses from underpricing a product because its chief auditor was so tied down by Department of Labor paperwork that he could give no time at all to the pricing calculations.

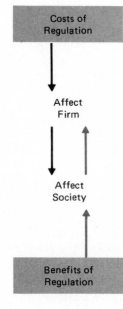

Costs of
Regulation

Affect
Firm

Affect
Society

Benefits of
Regulation

Certainly, government agencies too often do tend toward rigidity, entangling themselves and the organizations that must deal with them in reams of red tape. On the other hand, an increasing number of managers have come to recognize that costs to the organization must be balanced against the gains to the community achieved by government regulation. After all, the FDA tries to keep noxious foods and drugs off the market, the EPA tries to keep our air and waterways from being polluted, and so on.

There are also costs that would be incurred by the organization if there were no government regulation. A quality-control technician in the Vulcan firm admitted that before strict emission-control standards went into effect, the air surrounding the company's plant was always smog-ridden — cinders "would float out across the parking lot, land on your car, and burn right into the paint." Besides, one top executive added, the safer, cleaner plants required by OSHA now attract those good workers who had previously shunned foundry work.

Government regulatory agencies and nongovernmental organizations are engaged in a continuing process of defining areas of responsibility. Under these circumstances, mistakes, inefficiencies, and frustrations are bound to occur. It is likely that as both the agencies and the organizations they regulate gain experience, a more efficient way will be found to balance the needs of the community and the needs of the firm.

[3]"Paper Weight: Companies Often Find They Must Put Forms Ahead of Substance," *Wall Street Journal,* July 16, 1976, p. 1 ff. See also "Red Tape Blues," *Newsweek,* August 30, 1976, p. 77, and "Why Nobody Wants to Listen to OSHA," *Business Week,* July 14, 1976, pp. 64–69.

THE "INDIRECT" AND GENERAL ENVIRONMENTS

While the various elements of the indirect environment may not have a direct impact on our organization's operations, they cannot be safely ignored. A "Friends of the Earth" antipollution campaign, for example, may knock a proposed new smelting plant completely off the planning boards. Thus, the ecologist's likely reactions must be factored into the decision-making process beforehand, even though that ecologist may have nothing directly to do with the firm or its products. In today's world, relations with the indirect environment must be actively "managed" if the organization is to grow and prosper.

The accompanying chart illustrates the groups that make up the indirect environment, which the manager must actively deal with. However, the chart leaves out of the picture other important general factors in the environment that also influence the organization and that must be considered by managers. These are the environment's technological, economic, sociocultural, political-legal, and international variables.

Technological Variables

In any society or industry, the level of technology plays a significant role in determining what products and services will be produced, what equipment will be used, and how various operations will be managed. For example, some see in our continuing technological advance the imminent death of middle managers. Many companies now use computers for operations forecasts and production scheduling, which had been middle management functions.

Certainly, changes in technology affect the competitive position of companies — even those in the same industry — on an almost daily basis. A company like Polaroid, for example, could compete against a giant like Eastman Kodak, because it focused new production know-how around a single product protected by a network of patents. When Kodak developed an alternative technology, it threatened Polaroid's unique market position and led to an extensive series of lawsuits.

Between industries, the transfer of technology can also affect the competitive standing of companies. With the development of the integrated circuit, Texas Instruments and other electronics firms burst into the wristwatch market with high-volume, low-cost electronic digital watches. This brought a new competitive dimension to the field, catching the well-established mechanical watch manufacturers like Timex, Seiko, and the Swiss firms badly off guard. Managers need to monitor new technological developments, both inside and outside their industry, in order to help their organizations retain a competitive edge.

Economic Variables

Managers will always have to take into account the major costs — such as labor and raw materials — that their organizations require. Since such costs vary over time, they must also assess the prospects for price stability or inflation in the foreseeable future. In much of the post–World War II period, it seemed

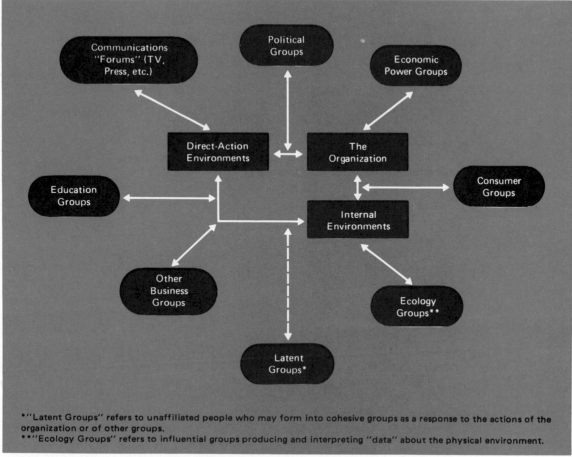

FIGURE 3-2   The Indirect Environments

Note that members of the indirect environment affect the direct-action environments as well as the organization itself and its subunits.

Source: Alvar O. Elbing, "On the Applicability of Environmental Models," in J. W. McGuire, ed., *Contemporary Management: Issues and Viewpoints* (Englewood Cliffs, N.J.: Prentice-Hall, 1974), p. 288. Used by permission.

possible for most developed and some underdeveloped countries to achieve fairly steady rates of economic growth while holding the line on price inflation. But experience in the 1970s has shown that controlling inflation is a more difficult task than economists had realized.

The prices set by competitors and suppliers, and the government's fiscal and monetary policies, will significantly influence the costs of producing a firm's products or services and the market conditions under which it sells those products or services. Given the importance of such economic factors, business managers must devote considerable time and resources to forecasting the future state of the economy and to anticipating changes in prices.

Sociocultural Variables

The values, mores, and customs of a society establish guidelines that determine how most organizations and managers will operate. Sometimes the guidelines will be relatively narrow—like the restrictions on black workers in South Africa who are denied both by law and by custom the right to managerial positions where they might have to supervise whites. Or, as in most countries, social barriers are raised against women who seek managerial careers, although a few do make it to the top against all the odds and at the cost of considerable personal sacrifice.[4]

In other areas the guidelines may be quite broad—like the wide latitude of acceptable boss-subordinate relationships that can be found in a single city or even within the same organization. In some cases, the normal relationship may be very formal, with a great show of outward respect by the subordinate for those above him or her in the hierarchy. In other organizations, an egalitarian atmosphere may prevail, with little outward evidence of differences in rank.

The values and customs of society will also be reflected in a firm's organizational structure. American companies are structured and managed somewhat differently from the Japanese, and both differ somewhat from the French. In Japan, where an employee has a vested interest in his or her job for life, lower-level workers participate in policy and decision making more freely than American workers do. French companies, operating in a society where relationships are somewhat stiff, tend to be more formally structured than their American and Japanese counterparts.

Perhaps most importantly, the values and customs of a society will influence how individuals feel about the organization they are in and how they feel about work. The changes in attitudes toward authority and toward work itself that have occurred in our own society have complicated the task of managers enormously. As managers, we will need to recognize and anticipate changes in the social climate and develop ways to deal with them.

Political-Legal Variables

Will a government agency adopt a hard or soft stance in its relations with management? Will antitrust laws be rigidly enforced or ignored? Will government policy curb or enhance management's freedom to act? The answers to such questions depend in large part on the political and legal climate in a given period of time.

In the United States, the political climate has ranged from strong support of

---

[4] See Michael Fogarty et al., *Women in Top Jobs* (London: George Allen and Unwin, Ltd., 1967); Eli Ginzberg and Alice M. Yohalem, eds., *Corporate Lib: Women's Challenge to Management* (Baltimore: Johns Hopkins University Press, 1973); and Francine E. Gordon and Myra Stroeber, eds., *Bringing Women into Management* (New York: McGraw-Hill, 1975).

corporate autonomy—epitomized in President Coolidge's dictum that "the business of America is business"—to the deep suspicion and distrust of business and government that marked the 1970s. By and large, government has steadily escalated its involvement in the affairs of business and nonprofit organizations. As increasing numbers of people call upon government to protect the consumer, preserve the environment, and put an end to discrimination in employment, education, and housing, pressures are generated that neither political party can withstand. And these pressures have been reinforced by those—many managers among them—who call for adherence to high ethical principles in the conduct of business and the professions.

While many people have deplored the constraints placed upon organizations by our laws and regulatory agencies, the opportunities they create have too often been overlooked. Our antipollution laws, for example, stimulated companies in the pollution-control industry to the point where at one time their securities were counted among the Wall Street "glamour stocks." And as the Office of Economic Opportunity (OEO) enforced its antidiscrimination regulations, it created a demand for training and consulting services—which in turn led to the formation of some profitable new companies.

Government also opened up new opportunities in the past by channeling resources into priority areas like defense and highway construction, and more recently in energy development and rapid transit. On the negative side, shifts in priorities have transformed attractive opportunity areas into problems for companies that suddenly found themselves struggling with reduced budgets, as was the case with the aerospace industry when space exploration was cut back.

As managers we obviously will not be able to insulate ourselves from the outside world. The effective manager keeps a wary eye on the political and social milieu, anticipates changes and the problems or opportunities arising from them, then decides the best way these might be met or exploited.

The International Dimension

Firms that engage in foreign production and sales quickly learn that success or failure may turn on a detailed knowledge of the laws, customs, mores, ethics, economic systems, and methods of management in the countries where they do business. The multinational giants, which establish production facilities in 10 or 20 different countries and sell in 50 or more, have had to accumulate a vast store of knowledge of these variables in the countries in which they operate.

Even companies that restrict themselves to domestic operations may have to become aware of how people in other countries operate. They may, for example, find themselves facing foreign competitors. Companies with no foreign customers or competitors may depend on foreign suppliers for raw materials or production equipment. Just the "simple" act of arranging payment for imported goods requires some knowledge of foreign exchange markets and of trends in foreign exchange rates over time.

RELATING THE ORGANIZATION TO THE ENVIRONMENT

It seems evident that managers today must learn to live with complex, highly unstable environments that can change with bewildering speed. One writer, in fact, has suggested that the ability of organizations to survive has increasingly become a function of their ability to learn about changes in the external environment and to adjust to them.[5] How, then, can we control or adapt to those critical elements in the environment that can shape our organization's future for better or for worse?

In trying to control the environment, managers resort to a number of expedients. They advertise in order to influence consumer preferences. They establish cooperative relations with suppliers in order to ensure an adequate flow of materials at acceptable prices. They enter into agreements with unions in order to stabilize labor market conditions. And they lobby in their state capitals and in Washington to try to forestall unfavorable legislation and regulation.

One major way in which managers attempt to adapt to environmental change and uncertainty is by developing effective systems for *forecasting* trends and changes and translating these forecasts into concrete *plans* for future action. If, for example, forecasts suggest that emissions standards for cars will be tightened, managers in an automobile company must plan to invest funds in antipollution devices. We will be discussing forecasting and planning in Chapters 4, 5, and 8.

Some managers also monitor environmental trends on a continuous basis, hoping to develop a usable understanding of the external environment. A manufacturer of luxury items, for example, may plan to cut back production if consumer spending figures begin to go down.

Most managers involved in producing consumer goods will try to adapt to the needs and expectations of consumers. They usually do this by engaging in some form of *market research,* to determine consumer wants and to enable them to tailor their products accordingly.

A special type of managerial adjustment is sometimes needed. It involves changes in the organization's formal structure—its work flows, authority patterns, reporting relationships among managers, and the like. This form of adjustment to the environment is so important for managers to understand that it is often called "organizational design"—implying a conscious structuring of the organization so it will best meet the demands of the environment at a given time. While few organizations will be "designed" in quite so rational a manner, many are regularly "reorganized" and restructured in accord with environmental dictates. We will describe this process in considerable detail in Part III.

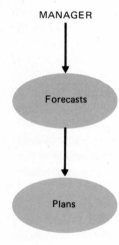

MANAGER

Forecasts

Plans

[5] Shirley Terreberry, "The Evolution of Organizational Environments," *Administrative Science Quarterly,* Vol. 12, No. 4 (March 1968), pp. 590–613. See also Alvin Toffler, *Future Shock* (New York: Bantam, 1970).

CHANGING CONCEPTS OF MANAGERIAL AND ORGANIZATIONAL RESPONSIBILITY

Like technology or the legal system, the moral environment of organizations also changes with time. In this century, the depression of the 1930s and the activist 1960s stimulated in their different ways a mounting criticism of business behavior. This criticism directed itself against the traditional view that business should pursue profit single-mindedly, with little or no consideration of social needs. Today there can be little question that there have been significant changes in what our society expects of its institutions and in what managers believe is their proper role in organizations. Many people, including many managers, believe that managers have a larger responsibility to society as well as a responsibility toward the organizations they serve. They believe that managers should act in accordance with society's laws and mores; that they should take into account the effects of their decisions on the rest of society; and that they should, through their organizations, take an active role in solving some of society's problems.

But where does such responsibility begin and where does it end? What rules of conduct should govern the exercise of executive authority? Should business continue to be governed by the traditional ethic of *caveat emptor* (let the buyer beware), or should business be governed by a new rationale— let the seller beware? Should managers be bound by restrictive laws, regulations, and red tape, or should they be free to act as their judgment and conscience dictate? Should a firm be held responsible for the social consequences of its profitable operations, or should it be commended for placing the stockholders' interests first?

Difficult questions such as these have become a matter of continuing debate, anxiety, and confusion. Although much of the discussion and writing on this subject bears the label "corporate responsibility" or "corporate social responsibility," the underlying issues and problems apply to all institutions in society. The social performance of hospitals and the entire health-care industry, of universities and the total educational system, of the legal and accounting professions, of the defense establishment and all government agencies, has been challenged and scrutinized as never before as both the public and the institutions themselves reassessed priorities, contributions, and performance. A better phrase for this new concern might well be "organizational (or institutional) social responsibility."

In the rest of this chapter we will focus on (1) how managers view their roles today as compared with the past, (2) the values and ethics that guide their actions, and (3) the changing views of organizational responsibility.

Changing Views of the Manager's Role

We would expect that our present view of the manager's role would differ from the views held in the 1870s or 1920s. But just how that role has changed and how deep the change goes are open to question. One interesting way of describing how our concepts of proper managerial behavior have evolved is the one presented by Robert Hay and Ed Gray.[6] They suggest that three distinct phases of management responsibility can be identified:

Phase I—Profit Maximizing Management
Phase II—Trusteeship Management
Phase III—"Quality of Life" Management

The Phase I concept derives from Adam Smith's *Wealth of Nations*. Writing in 1776, when poverty was the common lot of humanity, Smith opened on a paradoxical note. Do we want to promote the welfare of *all?* Then we must cater to the selfish desires of a *few*.

Entrepreneurs produce what people want only when they can earn a profit by doing so. If society allows entrepreneurs to give full rein to their desire to maximize income, then their own self-interest will cause them to increase production. This will make more goods available to all. Of course, in a competitive market, entrepreneurs would not be able to increase prices at will, because people will only pay the prices they can afford. But within the limitations of the market, Smith believed that entrepreneurs should be allowed to pursue their own self-interest for the benefit of all.

For many years the adoption of Smith's philosophy was associated with the reduction of scarcity in America and in most Western countries. The attitude "What's good for me is good for my country" became much more common and perhaps even somewhat justifiable. But there was another, more negative side to the way Smith's ideas were being put into effect. As nineteenth-century railroad tycoon William Henry Vanderbilt once said, "The public? The public be damned!" The depression of the 1930s convinced many that unregulated free enterprise could also cause great harm.

Phase II began with the diffusion of corporate ownership as thousands of shareholders became "partners" in one jointly held enterprise. And where once the owners of a business personally supervised its operations, operating control came to rest in the hands of hired professional managers. It was presumed that managers no longer only sought to maximize profits but also served as "trustees" who mediated the opposing claims of stockholders, suppliers, customers, and the public.

This trusteeship concept was a product of the depression-ridden 1930s when business was under severe attack because of prolonged unemployment. For those who then managed our corporations, the trusteeship notion was an attractive one. It imparted an aura of above-the-battle selflessness to their judgments. For as trustees they were dedicated not to their own enrichment but to the welfare of the many diverse groups in the organization's environment.

The values associated with this phase are somewhat more altruistic. Trusteeship management implies a concern for the interests of others as well as one's

⁶Robert Hay and Ed Gray, "Social Responsibilities of Business Managers," *Academy of Management Journal*, Vol. 18, No. 1 (March 1974), pp. 135–143.

own. "What's good for me..." changes subtly into "What's good for General Motors is good for the country."

Phase III came upon the scene in the 1960s, just about the time when the silent generation was giving way to the committed one. The free speech movement activist whose sign proclaimed—"I am a U.C. student. Please don't bend, fold, spindle, or mutilate!"—articulated a disillusionment and discontent with what was seen as a remote and faceless corporate world. Why should pockets of poverty, deteriorating cities, polluted waterways, and racial discrimination disfigure our affluent society? And as this new mood permeated the ranks of managers, pressures were generated for active corporate involvement in social progress.

The values of the "quality of life" managers contrast sharply with both the profit maximizer and the trustee manager. For the former, the essential equation becomes "What's good for society is good for our company." While accepting profit as essential, the quality of life manager would neither produce nor sell unsafe or shoddy goods. And where the other management types inveigh against government in business, the Phase III manager welcomes government as a partner in a joint effort to solve society's problems.

The Personal Values of Managers

In a given culture at a given time, most people share pretty much the same major values. That is, they agree on what is "good" (for example, the right to vote) and what is "bad" (for example, corruption in government). Not all will hold the same set of values; but the social values of the majority will affect the beliefs and behaviors of most members of society, including its managers.

The values of managers are of interest to us because of their influence on the actions managers take. William Guth and Renato Tagiuri found that the personal values of top managers have a strong effect on the strategies their corporations adopt.[7] For example, managers who are motivated by economic values will tend to stress the importance of growth for their companies. Managers who are motivated more by social values, on the other hand, might be willing to sacrifice some company growth to improve conditions for their employees. Of course, values are not the only factors that will influence a manager's decisions; the specific situation a manager faces will have great influence on (or even dominate) how a manager behaves.[8] But the personal values of managers, which are shaped in large part by the values of society as a whole, will have some effect on management decisions.

What, then, are the values of managers in each of the three phases of management attitudes discussed earlier? The table on the next page lists the values Hay and Gray associate with their three-phase model. Even a quick glance will suggest how the different values in each phase would lead to different decisions

---

[7] William D. Guth and Renato Tagiuri, "Personal Values and Corporate Strategy," *Harvard Business Review,* September-October 1965, pp. 123–132.

[8] See George W. England, "Personal Value Systems of American Managers," *Academy of Management Journal,* Vol. 10, No. 1 (March 1967), pp. 53–68.

TABLE 3-1 Comparison of Managerial Values

Phase I Profit Maximizing Management	Phase II Trusteeship Management	Phase III Quality of Life Management
Economic Values		
1) Raw self-interest	1) Self-interest 2) Contributors' interests	1) Enlightened self-interest 2) Contributors' interests 3) Society's interests
What's good for me is good for my country.	What's good for GM is good for our country.	What is good for society is good for our company.
Profit maximizer	Profit satisficer	Profit is necessary, but....
Money and wealth are most important.	Money is important, but so are people.	People are more important than money.
Let the buyer beware. *(caveat emptor)*	Let us not cheat the customer.	Let the seller beware. *(caveat venditor)*
Labor is a commodity to be bought and sold.	Labor has certain rights which must be recognized.	Employee dignity has to be satisfied.
Accountability of management is to the owners.	Accountability of management is to the owners, customers, employees, suppliers, and other contributors.	Accountability of management is to the owners, contributors, and society.
Technology Values		
Technology is very important.	Technology is important but so are people.	People are more important than technology.
Social Values		
Employee personal problems must be left at home.	We recognize that employees have needs beyond their economic needs.	We hire the whole person.
I am a rugged individualist, and I will manage my business as I please.	I am an individualist, but I recognize the value of group participation.	Group participation is fundamental to our success.
Minority groups are inferior to whites. They must be treated accordingly.	Minority groups have their place in society, and their place is inferior to mine.	Minority group members are people as you and I are.
Political Values		
That government is best which governs least.	Government is a necessary evil.	Business and government must help solve society's problems.
Environmental Values		
The natural environment controls people's destiny.	Man can control and manipulate the environment.	We must preserve the environment if we want a quality life.
Aesthetic Values		
Aesthetic values? What are they?	Aesthetic values are okay, but not for us.	We must preserve our aesthetic values, and we will do our part.

Source: Quoted and adapted from Robert Hay and Ed Gray, "Social Responsibilities of Business Managers," *Academy of Management Journal,* Vol. 18, No. 1 (March 1974), p. 142. Used by permission.

by managers. A Phase I manager, for example, would likely feel far less personal conflict in producing products that pollute than a Phase III manager.

There are those who dispute the Hay-Gray model and argue that managerial behavior has changed more in style than in substance. These critics suggest that innovations in organizations, such as today's greater emphasis on human relations, aim at the traditional goals of improved efficiency and profit maximization. However, a study by Rama Krishnan finds that today's younger managers hold views more consistent with phases II and III than do older managers — thus indicating a shift in managerial values and actions in keeping with the Hay-Gray model.[9]

The Ethics of Managers

Where values define a person's beliefs, ethics concern themselves with moral rights and wrongs or, more specifically, with a person's moral obligations to society. Determining ethical rights and wrongs is complicated by the fact that moral concepts, like all others, change with time. Besides, different groups in the same society may have conflicting ideas of right and wrong. Allowing for all the difficulties of pinpointing anyone's personal ethical code, we may still agree that a manager's ethics may influence a wide range of organizational decisions and actions.

Key Factors in Making Ethical Decisions. There are five factors that affect the manager involved in making decisions on ethical problems.[10] Some of these key factors may simplify the manager's problems, others may complicate them. The factors are: the law, government regulations, firm or industry ethical codes, social pressures, and the tension between the manager's personal standards and the needs of the firm.

The law is a simplifying factor since it defines minimum ethical standards in a given area of practice. For example, deceptive advertising is defined as illegal. One either obeys the law or breaks it; but the standards are clear and the violator risks the stipulated punishment as well as the loss of goodwill.

Government regulations also simplify the issue by mandating what is acceptable and what is not. Rulings on such matters as unfair competition, price discrimination, and unsafe products set guidelines for the manager. Sometimes the government may enforce the standards with a cease and desist order or even a criminal charge. Sometimes a firm or industry will comply with an agency finding voluntarily. But a positive response *at home* to a government ruling does not always resolve the ethical issue. In 1969, the FDA banned the use of cyclamates in food on the grounds that these artificial sweeteners were carcinogenic (cancer-causing). Over the next sixteen months,

---

[9] Rama Krishnan, "Business Philosophy and Executive Responsibility," *Academy of Management Journal,* Vol. 16, No. 4 (December 1973), pp. 658–669. An alternate explanation of Krishnan's findings is that the Phase III values of younger managers tend to change to more traditional values as the managers grow older.

[10] Robert J. Mockler, *Business and Society* (New York: Harper & Row, 1975).

a major food packer sold some 300,000 cases of cyclamate-sweetened food to *overseas* customers.[11]

Firm and industry ethical codes can be seen as simplifying factors, because they expressly spell out the ethical standards a manager should follow. The only question will be whether a given code serves merely as window dressing or is strictly enforced. Even in the former case, codes do clarify the ethical issues and thus leave the resolution to the individual's conscience.

Social pressures complicate the matter because the ethical code of one group is imposed upon another. Boycotts, picket lines, newspaper and television publicity, and political lobbying have all been employed by pressure groups trying to make business management more responsive to the public. Such pressures may alter managerial behavior in some cases, provoke stubborn resistance in others. For example, boycotts during the civil rights drive in the 1960s forced many organizations to open their doors to members of minority groups. On the other hand, community pressures on utilities to halt the installation of atomic reactor generating plants have often resulted in bitter, long-drawn-out battles.

Tension between personal standards and the needs of the organization complicate a manager's task enormously. As a member of management, the manager has a clear-cut mission: produce more, sell more, make more profit. As a citizen, the manager has a commitment to ethical conduct: to avoid harming the welfare of the community. But the two aims may clash. For example, doctors and dentists agree that too much sugar is bad for all of us, and even more so for growing children. Reducing sugar intake might therefore be considered a desirable social aim. But sugar-saturated baby foods and breakfast cereals sell faster than unsweetened foods. How can the dilemma be resolved? It is evident that where ethical problems are concerned, there are no easy answers.

The Ethical Situation Reported by Managers. What ethical codes do business leaders generally subscribe to? And to what extent do their ethics determine their behavior as executives? To get the answers to these questions, Raymond Baumhart posed a number of ethical problems to 1,700 managers and probed their views.[12] (See Table 3-2.) Seven basic findings emerged:

1 Executives recognize the social responsibilities of business in general terms. The corporation, they agree, is but one small part of the total society.

2 When it comes to specific business practices, there is a distinct parting of the ways, with different executives taking different positions.

3 While managers generally paint a flattering picture of their own high ethical standards, they hold a low opinion of the ethical practices of the average manager.

---

[11] *Wall Street Journal,* February 11, 1971.

[12] Raymond C. Baumhart, "How Ethical Are Businessmen?" *Harvard Business Review,* July-August 1961, p. 7 ff. See also "The Pressure to Compromise Personal Ethics," *Business Week,* January 31, 1977, p. 107.

4 The manager most likely to tailor actions to ethics, the respondents agree, is the one with a clearly defined personal code. But even such managers may find it hard to withstand pressures for unethical conduct unless their bosses share the same high standards.

5 Many unethical practices are common to their own industries, executives say, because ethics and economics do not mix.

6 Top management must lead the way if unethical practices are to be minimized.

7 Most executives would welcome a written code of ethics for their firm or industry — if it has teeth and is rigidly enforced.

TABLE 3-2 Influences on Executive Behavior

A. What influences an executive to make ethical decisions?		B. What influences an executive to make unethical decisions?	
Possible Influence	Importance as an Ethical Influence (Average Rank*)	Possible Influence	Importance as an Unethical Influence (Average Rank*)
A man's personal code of behavior	1.5	The behavior of a man's superiors in the company	1.9
The behavior of a man's superiors in the company	2.8	Ethical climate of the industry	2.6
Formal company policy	2.8	The behavior of a man's equals in the company	3.1
Ethical climate of the industry	3.8	Lack of company policy	3.3
The behavior of a man's equals in the company	4.0	Personal financial needs	4.1

*Most influential = 1, least influential = 5. Chart is based on response of 1,700 executives to *Harvard Business Review* questionnaire.

Source: Raymond C. Baumhart, S. J., "How Ethical Are Businessmen?" *Harvard Business Review,* July-August 1961, p. 156. Copyright © 1961 by the President and Fellows of Harvard College; all rights reserved.

Changes in Expected Adherence to Ethical Standards. The public indignation and outcry that resulted from the scandals of the 1970s (such as overseas bribes by scores of American corporations) do not herald the emergence of a whole new set of ethical standards. Rather, they represent intensified pressures for adherence *in practice* to those commonly accepted moral standards that had long been proclaimed *in words* by executives and politicians — including many of the individuals involved in the scandals.

Some guilty individuals maintained that what they had done was no worse than what their peers had done before. Such conduct, they implied, was merely the normal way of doing business and playing politics. As self-serving as such assertions are, they do contain an element of truth, for the unethical and illegal practices that were suddenly being publicly exposed, and in some cases being judicially punished, had been almost a way of life for some politicians and business leaders. All that had changed was that some had been caught, publicly exposed, and even punished.

However, as the disclosures continued, new demands were raised for codifying undesirable business and political conduct and for procedures to prevent or punish such acts. In this sense, pressures were generated for raising adherence to ethical and legal standards. Only time will tell whether these pressures have been translated into a generally heightened level of ethical and legal behavior.

CONCEPTS OF ORGANIZATIONAL OR CORPORATE RESPONSIBILITY

Given the very size of our corporate organizations and the extent to which the economy depends on their continued prosperity, we can understand why the view has grown that as managers we must consider our organization's responsibility to the community as well as to its own interests. This view, of course, reflects the values underlying the notion of "quality of life" management. The discussion of corporate responsibility breaks down into two broad areas: (1) Should the corporation acknowledge its social responsibilities and act on that acknowledgement? And (2) do our corporations generally act in a socially responsible manner?

Two Views of the Proper Role of Business

Responding to the first question positively, one leading business group, the Committee for Economic Development (CED), published a pamphlet on *Social Responsibilities of Business Corporations* that urged management to involve itself actively in such social causes as aid to education, urban renewal, opening up better job opportunities to blacks and women, training the disadvantaged, environmental pollution, and much more.

The most prestigious exponent of the opposing view is Milton Friedman, the internationally known economist who won a Nobel Prize in 1976. "There is one and only one social responsibility of business," says Friedman: "to use its resources and energy in activities designed to increase its profits so long as it stays within the rules of the game...engages in open and free competition, without deception and fraud....Few trends could so thoroughly undermine the very foundations of our free society as the acceptance by corporate officials of a social responsibility other than to make as much money for their stockholders as possible.... Can self-selected individuals decide what the social interest is? Can they decide how great a burden they are justified in placing on themselves and their stockholders to serve that interest?"[13] Managers who devote corporate resources to pursue their own, perhaps misguided notions of social good, Friedman goes on to say, are unfairly taxing their own

---

[13] Milton Friedman, *Capitalism and Freedom* (Chicago: University of Chicago Press, 1963), p. 133. See also "The Social Responsibility of Business Is to Increase Its Profits," *New York Times Magazine*, September 13, 1970, p. 33 ff.

"Warrington Trently, this court has found you guilty of price-fixing, bribing a government official, and conspiring to act in restraint of trade. I sentence you to six months in jail, suspended. You will now step forward for the ceremonial tapping of the wrist."

Drawing by Lorenz; © 1976 The New Yorker Magazine, Inc.

shareholders, employees, and customers. In short, businesses should go on with the business of producing goods and services efficiently, and leave the solution of social problems to government agencies and concerned individuals.

Friedman's views have been faulted on a number of counts.[14] First, he implies that "free competition," which defines the "rules of the game," still exists, when as an economist he knows we have long since mourned its demise. Second, corporations cannot evade their social responsibilities, because their own actions have caused or exacerbated many of the problems with which society is now grappling. Problems of pollution, product safety, job discrimination, and the bribing of public officials are very much a product of past corporate practices. And, as Keith Davis has phrased it, there is "an iron law of responsibility which states that in the long run those who do not use power in a manner that society considers responsible will tend to lose it."[15] Business

[14] See R. Joseph Monsen, Jr., "The Social Attitudes of Management," in McGuire, *Contemporary Management*, p. 616.

[15] Keith Davis, "The Meaning and Scope of Social Responsibility," in McGuire, *Contemporary Management*, p. 631.

must amend its public image voluntarily, or it will almost inevitably be subject to increased government regulation.

Finally, it can be argued that it is in the best interest of corporations to act in a socially responsible way. Corporations have an obvious investment in the society of which they are a part, and for them to ignore social problems might in the long run be self-destructive.

The Levels of Business Activism in Social Areas

To what extent do our major corporations actually discharge their social responsibilities today? Some companies, like Kaiser Aluminum, have contributed to the health care of their employees by developing advanced group health programs. Others have invited their local communities to participate in corporate decisions that affect community welfare. The Long Island Lighting Company, for example, let the community vote on the choice of building a nuclear or conventional generating plant and abided by the majority decision. Other firms have also contributed to urban renewal, minority hiring, and antipollution programs.

There are also many examples on the negative side. For instance, some mining companies routinely submit figures to the government showing that safety standards are too tough and too costly. Yet the dangers of cave-ins and explosions have largely been eliminated in some foreign countries, thanks to the same safety technology available to American mining companies.[16]

R. Joseph Monsen has suggested a four-level hierarchy of business activism. At the first or bottom level is the management which feels that society is well enough served so long as the firm *obeys the law*. The second-level manager goes beyond the legal minimum, accepting the need to cater also to *public expectations,* moving as the winds of public opinion blow. On the third level, management beats the public to the punch, acting so as to *anticipate* public expectations. At the fourth and highest level, we find the manager who *creates* new public expectations by voluntarily setting and following the loftiest standards of moral and social responsibility.[17]

A survey conducted in 1970 found that few organizations went much beyond levels one or two. But a number of more recent studies indicate a growing trend toward greater business activism at the two higher levels.[18]

Create Public Expectations
Anticipate Public Expectations
Cater to Public Expectations
Obey the Law

HIERARCHY OF BUSINESS ACTIVISM

The Role of Profits

Before an organization can devote resources to socially desired objectives, it must make enough profit to maintain the confidence and support of its shareholders and bankers. To the extent that socially oriented actions strengthen

---

[16] *Wall Street Journal,* February 11, 1971.

[17] In McGuire, *Contemporary Management,* pp. 615–629.

[18] See, for example, David C. Aaker and George S. Day, "Corporate Responses to Consumerism Pressures," *Harvard Business Review,* November-December 1972, pp. 114–124; Henry Eilbert and Robert Parket, "The Current Status of Social Responsibility," *Business Horizons,* Vol. 16, No. 4 (1973), pp. 5–14; and Vernon M. Buehler and Y. K. Shetty, "Managerial Response to Social Responsibility Challenge," *Academy of Management Journal,* Vol. 19, No. 1 (March 1976), pp. 66–78.

the organization by preventing conflict with environmentalists, government agencies, and consumer groups, and enhance the organization's public image as a supplier, customer, and employer, the resources allocated to social action also serve the organization's self-interest. But when corporations go too far beyond their self-interest, or when the financial costs of social activism run too high, then the tension between the desire for public acceptance and the need for profits is heightened.

The costs of socially responsible actions can be borne by organizations in four major ways: increased efficiency, higher prices, lowered wages, or reduced profits. The first and most fortunate one occurs when the socially responsible action is actually more profitable for the firm than doing "business as usual." Situations like this do not arise as often as advocates of social responsibility would have us believe, but they do exist. In one such case, a consulting firm offered better than market salaries and career opportunities to women and minority group members at a time when other organizations were not yet feeling OEO pressures and were still following discriminatory procedures. By not discriminating, this firm gained access to more skilled and better motivated individuals than its competitors, at no greater cost.[19]

But in most situations, behaving in a socially responsible manner will boost the firm's costs with no equivalent gain in efficiency. In these cases the company may try to pass the costs along to the consumer in higher prices, to workers by holding the line on wage increases, or to shareholders by accepting the reduced profits and lowering the dividends at the risk of causing a fall in share prices. Should profits fall too drastically, then the continued survival of the organization may be in doubt. Recognition that someone must eventually bear the costs of social responsibility is the crux of Friedman's argument that managers should focus on what they know best: how to make a profit. The same consideration also influences many of the business managers who criticize the growing constraints and pressures placed on business by government agencies and consumer and environmental advocates. Business managers can never forget that every resource allocated to a given activity costs something and that those costs must be recaptured in some way.

Most people outside business believe that corporate profits are higher and corporate taxes lower than they are in reality. For example, a Gallup poll of college students found that they estimated corporate profits at 45 percent of sales, when in reality profits average about 5 percent.[20] To the extent that people grossly overestimate corporate profits and underestimate tax outlays, some of the hostility expressed toward business ("they can afford to behave responsibly and still make plenty of profit") may be misplaced.

---

[19] For baseball fans the classic example might be the benefits the Brooklyn Dodgers derived from Jackie Robinson and Roy Campanella when Branch Rickey, the manager, first broke the color line in professional team sports.

[20] Reported in James J. Kilpatrick, "Why Students Are Hostile to Free Enterprise," *Nation's Business,* July 1975, pp. 11–12.

However, although critics may exaggerate the ability of corporations to pay the cost of social programs, they may not be off-base in arguing that managers too often opt for short-run profits at the expense of much higher long-term social and business costs. For example, the management of one company failed to install pollution-control equipment in a new plant because it was not legally required to do so. When pollution-control standards were tightened, as most observers had predicted they would be, the costs of modifying the original equipment were far greater than the initial installation would have been. By ignoring the health needs of the community, the company made both a bad business and a bad social decision.

Measuring Social Performance

Attempts to develop a systematic measure of an organization's social impact on its environment can be traced as far back as 1940. But the thrust toward conducting *corporate social audits* is largely a post-1970 phenomenon. Thus, methods for conducting such audits are still in a state of evolution.

As Archie B. Carroll and George W. Beiler describe it, the social audit "represents a managerial effort to develop a calculus for gauging the firm's socially oriented contributions. That is, it is an attempt to measure, monitor and evaluate the organization's performance with respect to its social programs and social objectives."[21] One approach to the social audit analyzes the costs and benefits of the organization's major interactions with its environment. Obviously, only the major effects can be evaluated and the values attached to the transactions can only be approximations. The best-known example of this approach is the one used by Abt Associates, a Massachusetts consulting firm. This firm's social audit, which looks somewhat like a profit and loss statement, has been included in the company's annual report since 1972.

A second and more common approach is based on the major social programs engaged in by the organization. The steps in this approach are not uniform for all programs. However, the audits will likely include an inventory of the programs, a determination of their original purpose, an evaluation of the resources devoted to them, and an attempt to measure how well they met their original objectives or new ones that may have evolved since their initiation. This approach has the advantage of focusing on specific programs that can be directly altered in response to the findings of the audit.

At present, many problems and ambiguities plague the social audit movement. For example, what such audits should accomplish, how a manager's resistance to being "audited" can be overcome, and how and to whom the results should be reported are questions that get different answers from each of the various organizations, scholars, and consultants working in this area. Still, it does seem that the use of social audits will increase rather than decrease, and that improved concepts and methods will continue to be developed.

[21] Archie B. Carroll and George W. Beiler, "Landmarks in the Evolution of the Social Audit," *Academy of Management Journal*, Vol. 18, No. 3 (September 1975), pp. 589–599.

**Barriers to
Improved Social
Performance**

In the future, we may expect that pressures for greater social responsibility by managers and their organizations will continue to increase. In order to meet such pressures, we must be aware that barriers to improved social performance exist at every level of the organization—the individual manager, the division, the top management of the organization, or even the industry of which the organization is a part. By becoming aware of these barriers, we can work to overcome them.

The Individual Manager. Most business managers are employees. If something they do meets with their supervisor's disapproval, they may jeopardize their careers. For this reason, most managers are cautious about proposing significant changes in their organization's behavior. Changes that would benefit both society and the firm may never be proposed for fear of "rocking the boat."

Public criticism of an organization's shortcomings—known as "whistle blowing"—is not calculated to win the approval of one's superiors. One widely publicized example of what can happen to whistle blowers occurred in 1968, when A. E. Fitzgerald, a civilian cost analyst working for the Air Force, told a congressional committee about massive cost overruns in cargo jets the Air Force had ordered. First Fitzgerald was reassigned to minor jobs and then he was fired. He was still fighting in court in 1977 for full reinstatement to his original post. Managers who want to "blow the whistle" must make hard choices between socially responsible behavior and their own careers. The fact that most situations are not as clear-cut as the cargo jet cost overruns makes such choices all the more difficult.

To the extent that middle-level and top managers encourage ethical and socially responsible behavior in their subordinates, the need for "whistle blowing" is reduced. By avoiding a psychological investment in the status quo, managers can remain open to socially responsible suggestions that will not threaten the organization's survival or profitability.

The Division. Like the organization of which it is a part, a division must try to maintain itself as a profit center. Any socially responsible decision that reduces the level of profits—say, the expansion of a job-training program—might threaten the division's viability. Thus, most divisions are slow to initiate socially responsible programs until they receive clear instructions to do so from top management.

The head of a division may obtain approval for certain socially responsible programs if he or she can demonstrate that such programs will not be too costly or that they will benefit the organization in other ways—for example, by improving the organization's public relations. Sometimes top management will try such programs on an experimental basis, and then publicize them if they succeed.

The Organization. Even when profits are high, top management must balance social programs against such considerations as plowing the profits back into

81

expanded production or distributing them in the form of dividends. Besides, a company's social actions can affect its competitive position. For example, refusing to buy materials produced in an unpopular, authoritarian country may prove disadvantageous economically if competitors do not follow suit.

In such situations top management is faced with a truly difficult choice. It must weigh the demands of stockholders and the short-term needs of the organization against the unpredictable long-term needs of the organization and often ambiguous standards of right and wrong.

The Industry. Obviously, the danger of a competitor taking advantage of one's socially responsible actions is lessened if an entire industry adopts a similar policy. But there are barriers that can prevent industries from acting in a unified way. Companies that regard each other as competitors may be reluctant to enter into an industry-wide agreement. In an environment where business is already suspect, any industry-wide action would be viewed with skepticism and might even create antitrust problems. Finally, a decision taken by an American industry would not be binding on foreign companies. Thus, the domestic industry might lose its competitive position internationally. For example, a major justification for American arms sales abroad is that "if we don't do it, others will." In this case, it is argued that to forgo revenues (and political influence) from foreign arms sales would achieve little, since the purchasing countries could obtain similar weapons elsewhere.

Individual managers, company divisions, organizations, and industries are still in the process of sorting out the new social values and expectations that are evolving. It is safe to say, however, that some concrete changes have already occurred. For example, the courts are increasingly upholding the right of employees to criticize their employers openly without losing their jobs.[22] Individual employees have also become more willing to articulate their grievances, even at some personal cost. For instance, some atomic physicists with successful careers in a California nuclear power company recently resigned their positions in order to combat the expansion of the nuclear power industry.

Well-entrenched organizations have also experienced changes in attitudes. The problem of increasing the gas mileage of automobiles, for example, was a very difficult one for individual automobile companies to resolve, because of the added costs involved in car design and manufacture. However, applying mileage standards on an industry-wide basis reduced the resistance of the automobile industry. Today, individual companies *compete* to increase the gas mileage of their cars. It seems likely, then, that many of the changes in values we have described will become an accepted part of the environment of organizations, one which we as managers will have to take into account.

---

[22] Kenneth D. Walters, "Your Employee's Right to Blow the Whistle," *Harvard Business Review,* July-August 1975, p. 26 ff.

Summary   Organizations are being increasingly influenced by changes in their external environment. These changes can affect organizations in a number of ways: directly, through members of the "direct-action" environment (such as customers or suppliers); and indirectly, through special interest and pressure groups and general environmental variables (like levels of technology and changes in values).

The changes in the environment of organizations require managers to try to anticipate future changes and to monitor them on a continuing basis. By so doing, they will enable their organizations to adapt to or influence environmental trends so that their survival or profitability will not be threatened.

In one major change, managers as well as the public have been taking a new look at the question of managerial responsibility and organizational social responsibility. In this area, according to one view, three phases of management have evolved: profit maximization, trusteeship, and quality of life. While some doubts have been raised about the commitment to Phase III, or "quality of life" management, some studies indicate a trend in that direction among younger managers.

In the 1970s, managers found themselves increasingly pressed to adhere to society's legal and ethical standards. At the same time, unprecedented attention began to be focused on the organization's response to social issues. This has led to two major consequences. First, many organizations now find it wise to go beyond their primary mission and take into account the needs of the community. Second, better measures of social performance are now being devised to help organizations determine how well they are doing in this regard and also to make them more accountable for the effects of their behavior. How managers choose to deal with the issues raised in this chapter will, of course, reflect their personal ethics, their organization's policies, and the social values that prevail at the time.

Review Questions
1. Why has it become more important now than in the past for managers to take the environment of their organizations into account when making plans and decisions?
2. What are the major elements in the direct-action environment of organizations? In the indirect environment?
3. What are the three phases of management responsibility as described by Hay and Gray? With what phase do your own values seem most compatible?
4. What do you think are the major factors that affect the ethics of a manager's decision?
5. What are the two major views of the proper role of business? With which view are you most sympathetic? How might this affect your performance as a manager?
6. What is the corporate social audit?
7. What are the barriers to improved social performance by organizations? How do you think these barriers can be overcome?

CASE STUDY: TULSA MOTOR INN

Jim Baggett had heard about Oklahoma's penal reform plans. One phase of the plan involved the establishment of prisoner prerelease centers in both Tulsa and Oklahoma City. This idea seemed to make sense in some ways; the cost of rehabilitating a man

Case copyright © 1972 by James C. Johnson and Howard A. Thompson of the University of Tulsa. Used by permission.

might be lowered, and the percentage of parolees who made the transition from tax-using, regimented prisoner to useful, tax-paying citizen might be increased. The basic idea was to provide a halfway house, a boarding house for parolees who had no family anxiously awaiting their release, which would give them an opportunity to readjust to a new job and make new friends—in short, fit into the society that had previously labeled them as misfits.

But as Jim scanned the newspaper that morning his acquiescence toward one particular prisoner prerelease center (PRC) began to change. The headline catching his eye read, "Tulsa Motel to Become Prisoner Prerelease Center." The article went on to explain that the state had entered into a long-term lease with the owners of an existing mismanaged and floundering motel to use that facility as the Tulsa PRC. Another PRC was to be located in Oklahoma City. The most important information in the article to Jim, however, was the location of the PRC motel. It was *next door,* not 50 yards away from his own motel, the Tulsa Motor Inn.

The Baggetts had acquired the Tulsa Motor Inn eighteen months prior to the PRC announcement. After successfully managing a motel in the Oklahoma City area, they had purchased this one in Tulsa, which at the time was also mismanaged and losing money. Jim carefully planned and financed its remodeling and renaming under a nationally franchised motel chain. After investing $1,250,000 and one and a half years of hard work, the operation was beginning to show promise of success. "And now the state wants to locate twenty to thirty parolees within 50 yards of my guests, dozens of new cars, vacation-enlarged billfolds, and dressed-for-the-pool swimmers!" The thought brought with it a vision of empty rooms, forced room-rate reductions, and higher overhead stemming from new security precautions.

During the last twelve months, the Tulsa Motor Inn had grossed $197,000, permitting a net profit before taxes of $41,000. Although he considered this to be less than half of its potential profitability, assuming occupancy percentages continued to improve, Jim Baggett believed the Motor Inn to be "on target" according to his forecast nearly two years earlier. The PRC, however, was definitely not part of the "game plan." He had little doubt but that the excellent repeat business with commercial travelers (sales representatives), now believed to constitute about one-half of total revenue, would shift to a "safer" location once the prisoners were known to be 50 yards away. An earlier advantage of being located near an expressway within 15 minutes of downtown Tulsa while still out of the congested part of the city now seemed almost a disadvantage.

Jim Baggett's business associates counseled him to seek an injunction to prevent the state from locating an "undesirable" facility next door. He, with his son, a management major at the University of Tulsa, had been wrestling with questions of social responsibility, environmental pollution, and the like only a few weeks ago. He was very much in favor of business committing itself to the pursuit of these goals and ideals. But if he failed to act quickly against the state's announced plan for the new PRC, Jim Baggett was certain this could mean a severe financial reversal for the Motor Inn.

Case Question   1. What counsel would you give Jim Baggett?

Planning and Decision Making

Case on Planning and Decision Making

SYSTEM-WIDE SOLUTIONS NEEDED

"Well, if you can't solve the problems in your department, what makes you think you can tell me how to run the entire company?" the president of Mid-State Machinery Company exploded to Craig Anderson, manager of the data processing department, at the end of a difficult hour-long meeting between the two. Anderson had joined the firm only one week earlier after five years of successful experience as a data processing programmer, senior systems analyst, and associate manager of data processing in a firm that was larger and more complex than Mid-State. After coming to Mid-State he immediately began to assess the role, function, and performance of the data processing department. Anderson first talked with Bill Klein, a systems analyst and a long-time employee of the company who was nearing retirement age. Anderson expected Klein to speak freely. He did!

Klein told Anderson, "With the emergence of the computer for business applications, Mid-State created a data processing department as a staff department but located it in the organizational structure at the same level as the operating departments that used its services. Since the data processing department was budgeted as an administrative overhead department, its services were available to the operating departments without direct charge. It was established with little guidance for the general purpose of developing computerized systems for the other departments in the company." (See Exhibit 1.)

"With such a wide mission, we set out to 'computerize' the company. The heads of other departments readily accepted this concept, because electronic data processing looked like the answer to many of their management problems. Our data processing department ballooned in size—almost overnight, it seemed. Many systems had been designed, installed, and were running before we began to realize that company-wide objectives had never been formally established. Each department worked hard to achieve departmental objectives, but quite often the objectives of one department conflicted with the objectives of other departments.

"By this time, several operating departments were heavily dependent upon the data processing department to generate data and reports and to improve their systems as needed. Other departments had not contributed much to the development of the computer system. The computer could do the clerical procedures faster and more accurately than clerks had done them. While fewer clerks were needed in the company after 'computerization,' a larger number of persons with higher skills were required to keep up with what the computer was doing and to correct errors in the input data. In short, our electronic data processing department had grown and developed by doing

Case reprinted with permission from *Critical Incidents in Management,* 3rd ed., by John M. Champion and John H. James (Homewood, Ill.: Richard D. Irwin, Inc., 1975), pp. 185–188.

EXHIBIT 1

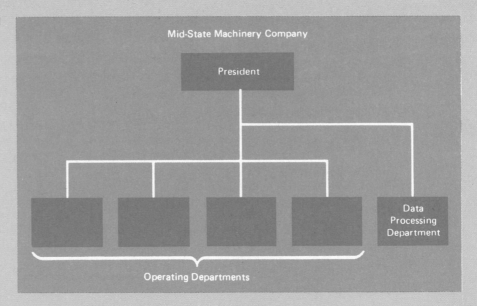

exactly what it thought *its* goal was. Of lesser concern to us was what the user departments actually needed or wanted."

Next, Anderson developed a list of characteristics of the data processing department as follows (see Exhibit 2):

1   Employees of the data processing department are largely college graduates in mathematics and computer science. About half of the supervisors have been with the company a long time, while the other half are relative newcomers. This mixture has its advantages, but conflicting ideas are frequently produced.

2   Most of the personnel joined the data processing department directly from college and with little previous work experience.

3   More than 50 percent of the personnel in the department are female. Data processing is an area that many women are interested in and do well in.

4   The previous manager of the department was an experienced line manager who had not kept up to date with the data processing field.

5   The majority of the women employees are at the lower levels of the department. This is not a policy but is a circumstance that should be adjusted with the passing of time.

6   The data processing environment is a very disciplined one in which to work. There must be standards, rules, and guidelines in order to assure that the problems of the user departments are addressed and solved. Work must be accomplished on schedule. Due to continuing and rapid changes in technology, languages, systems, and procedures, the personnel in data processing are required continually to update their preparation in the field.

Anderson completed his analysis of the data processing department by identifying four crucial problems:

1   Requests from the user departments for data processing services seldom were completed within a reasonable time and almost always *after* established due dates had passed. Some user departments had urgent needs for systems analysis and programming that were not being met. Much of the delay in starting and completing work seemed to be caused by a continuing scheduling battle between the Project Development Section and the Programming Section of the department.

2   The pressure of unmet schedules made most of the employees tense, reduced their morale, and increased their errors. Much poor work was being turned out. Turnover was excessively high and required that a large proportion of new employees be hired and trained. The time spent in training the new employees further reduced the output of the data from the data processing personnel, which in turn caused delays in completing regularly scheduled work.

3   The discouraging climate in the department had caused some otherwise dependable, productive employees to say that they would no longer try to use initiative to solve the problems of the department but would only do what they were told to do.

4   Objectives for the company as a whole had been neither formally established nor communicated to managers within the company. A hierarchy of integrated objectives for units at various levels in the organizational structure was lacking. Apparently planning was done at the department level only—and done there only for the short run. No evidence could be found to suggest the existence of a long-range strategic plan for the company as a whole.

EXHIBIT 2

Characteristics of the Data Processing Department
1. Well-educated but inexperienced personnel
2. Mix of experienced and new supervisors
3. Mostly female personnel
4. Majority of women occupy lower-level positions
5. Highly disciplined work
6. Excessive turnover rate

Anderson had attempted to convince the president that the lack of an integrated, clearly established structure of objectives and performance standards at Mid-State was a problem that should be dealt with by the top management of the company. Moreover, he had explained in detail why he felt that early attention to this problem would greatly facilitate, and should precede or at least be done concurrently with, the efforts by the data processing department in developing effective interface linkages among the computerized systems in the various departments of the company. At present, he had pointed out to the president, system-wide solutions were not being generated. Only local, i.e., departmental, solutions were being produced.

As Craig Anderson sought to formulate a satisfactory course of action for his department and for his next meeting with the president, the challenging words of the president rang repeatedly in his ears: "Well, if you can't solve the problems in your department, what makes you think you can tell me how to run the entire company?"

1. What is the answer to the president's question?
2. To whom is the data processing department accountable?
3. How does the data processing department measure its success? What are the criteria for excellence in a specific job?
4. If two departments submit tasks to the data processing department and these jobs are at cross-purposes to one another, what do you think would be the proper course of action to follow?
5. What is the long-range goal of the data processing department?
6. What is the *stated* long-range goal of the data processing department? How effective is the stated goal in guiding the department's activities?
7. Why do you think the data processing department was budgeted as administrative overhead rather than having the operating departments charged directly for the services they received? What were the consequences of this budgeting decision?
8. How did computerization affect Mid-State's personnel needs?
9. What do you think relations might be like between employees in the data processing department and employees in the other departments?
10. What problem or problems do you think Anderson is overlooking?
11. How would you proceed to generate "system-wide solutions"?

Chapter 4

Planning and Plans

Upon completing this chapter you should be able to:

1. Explain why planning is needed in organizations.
2. Distinguish between planning, plans, and decision making.
3. Identify and describe the different types of plans that exist, and discuss where in the organizational hierarchy they are most likely to be used.
4. Describe the basic steps in the planning process.
5. Explain how the functions of planning and controlling are linked.

Planning occurs in all types of activities. Whether we are planning a party, a vacation, a next step in our career, or a new sales program for our organization, *planning* is the basic process by which we decide what our goals are and how we are going to achieve them.

While planning is useful in our daily lives, planning in organizations is essential. In fact, organizational planning has primacy over the other management functions of organizing, leading, and controlling, because these management functions operate only to carry out the decisions of planning. It is by planning that managers of organizations decide, in the words of one writer, "what is to be done, when it is to be done, how it is to be done, and who is to do it."[1]

Planning is also a pervasive element in any organization. As we shall see, managers at different levels of the organization tend to do different types of planning. For example, the administrator of a hospital might plan to increase staff efficiency so that more patients can be taken care of by existing personnel. In turn, the head nurse might have to plan a more efficient route for making rounds. Regardless of their level in the organization, however, all managers plan.

In this first chapter of Part II (Chapters 4–8), we will focus primarily on the planning that managers do in the course of their daily work. We will also discuss the various types of plans that exist and how planning differs at each level of an organization. In Chapter 5, our main emphasis will be on longer-term strategic planning, as it has become an organizational activity of major importance. Chapter 6 will discuss the barriers that hinder proper planning and the ways that planning can be made more effective. Chapter 7 will focus on decision making, a major managerial activity that is an important part of all planning activities. Finally, Chapter 8 will describe qualitative and quantitative tools that managers can use to improve their plans and decisions.

THE NEED FOR PLANNING

In today's increasingly complex organizations, intuition alone can no longer be relied upon as a means for making decisions. This is one reason why planning has become so important. By providing a more rational, fact-based procedure for making decisions, planning allows managers and organizations to minimize risk and uncertainty. In a dynamic society such as ours, in which social and economic conditions alter rapidly, planning helps us prepare for and deal with change.

Planning also helps us focus the attention of our organization on its goals. This makes it easier to apply and coordinate the resources of the organization

---

[1]George A. Steiner, *Top Management Planning* (New York: Macmillan, 1969), p. 7. Steiner's book has been an important influence in communicating and guiding the evolution of organizational planning. Much of the discussion of planning in these chapters draws upon that book and related articles by Steiner.

more efficiently. For example, if an oil producer plans to search for new wells, a portion of the oil company's finances and personnel will then be directed toward that end. Planning is thus one way of helping the organization define its purposes and activities. Ideally, planning provides the score from which the orchestra of the organization plays in harmony.

Planning also provides us with benchmarks, or points of reference, against which accomplishments can be measured. These help eliminate the chance that we and our organization will proceed erratically or incorrectly. The setting of performance standards, which is a part of planning, allows managers to monitor how well their organization is proceeding toward its goals.

The Need for Flexibility in Planning

It would be convenient if plans did not have to be changed once they have been set. In fact, because conditions both within and outside the organization may change, planning must be a continuous process. Managers must constantly monitor the circumstances of the organization to determine if changes are required in the goals of the organization and the procedures for reaching them.

For this reason, *flexibility* is an important part of the planning process and helps determine whether or not the organization will succeed. Airline executives who plan an expansion program without taking into account the possibility that fuel prices will increase may find that their plans are too costly when the time comes for carrying them out. Similarly, if certain plans depend on key personnel (such as those in a research team), the plans may fail if the key people leave the organization—unless provisions for personnel replacement are part of the manager's plan. Because circumstances change, because devising new plans when old ones fail is costly and time-consuming, and because it is simple common sense to allow for as many contingencies as possible, plans need to have a built-in flexibility.

Planning and the Management Process

Planning is the beginning of the process of management. Before managers can organize, lead, or control, they must make plans that give purpose and direction to those activities. Because planning sets the other functions into action, it can be seen as the most fundamental of the responsibilities and tasks of the manager.

Successful planning is the key to the manager's (and the organization's) effectiveness and success. Even managers who do a good job in carrying out the other managing functions may not achieve the best possible results if they are not good planners. Such managers may be *efficient* but not *effective;* that is, they may be "doing things right" but not "doing the right things."[2] (See Chapter 1.) Since planning is the stage at which managers set objectives that determine the organization's activities in the near and distant future, it is also the stage at which they must set the *right* objectives.

In Chapter 1, we noted that although the need for planning exists at all levels

[2] Peter F. Drucker, *Managing for Results* (New York: Harper & Row, 1964). See also Melville C. Branch, *The Corporate Planning Process* (New York: American Management Associations, 1962).

of management, that need increases as we go higher in the organizational hierarchy. In other words, planning is important to all managers, but in the sense of the time spent on planning, and the potential impact of planning on the organization's success, it becomes more critical at the higher levels of the organization. It is top management that sets the overall strategies and goals of the organization. The further down the organizational hierarchy that managers are, the more likely that their plans will involve only their particular subunits. For this reason, upper-level managers generally devote most of their planning time to the distant future, while lower-level managers plan mainly for the achievement of near-term goals. Figure 4-1 below suggests how

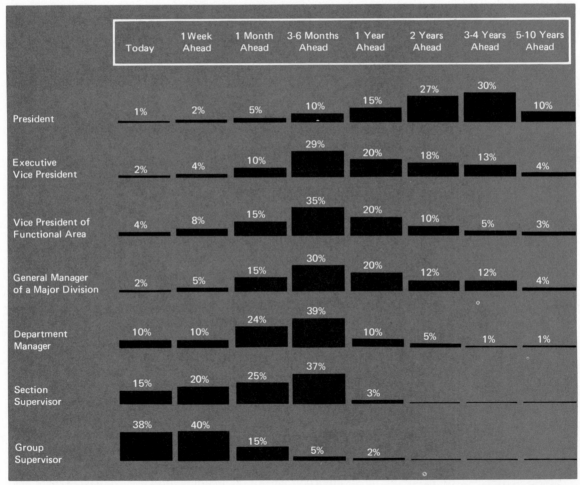

	Today	1 Week Ahead	1 Month Ahead	3-6 Months Ahead	1 Year Ahead	2 Years Ahead	3-4 Years Ahead	5-10 Years Ahead
President	1%	2%	5%	10%	15%	27%	30%	10%
Executive Vice President	2%	4%	10%	29%	20%	18%	13%	4%
Vice President of Functional Area	4%	8%	15%	35%	20%	10%	5%	3%
General Manager of a Major Division	2%	5%	15%	30%	20%	12%	12%	4%
Department Manager	10%	10%	24%	39%	10%	5%	1%	1%
Section Supervisor	15%	20%	25%	37%	3%			
Group Supervisor	38%	40%	15%	5%	2%			

FIGURE 4-1 "Ideal" Allocations of Time for Planning in the "Average" Company

Source: George A. Steiner, *Top Management Planning* (New York: Macmillan, 1969), p. 26. Copyright © 1969 by The Trustees of Columbia University in The City of New York.

© 1976 by United Feature Syndicate, Inc.

planning time might be spent at various levels of an average company under ideal conditions.

Variations in the planning responsibilities of managers also depend on the size and type of organization. A large company, for example, would be more concerned with planning for the distant future than a small or medium-sized company, and this difference would be reflected in the planning responsibilities of its top-level management. Some types of organizations, because of their particular purposes, must make long-range commitments. These might include an oil or mining company, an airline, or the defense department. On the other hand, some organizations require comparatively less long-term planning. Dress manufacturers, for example, can do little to plan styles for the distant future because they cannot safely predict how fashions will change.

Planning, Plans, and Decision Making

It is important to make a distinction between planning and plans. Managers who go through the process of planning but do not come up with a definite *plan* — that is, a specific commitment to present and future actions — are wasting both their and their organization's time. This is because without plans the process of planning has no practical effect.

On the other hand, once a plan has been developed and put into effect, it may require modification if conditions change. The process of *planning,* with its constant monitoring of the organization's circumstances, must remain uppermost in managers' minds, or else they may stay with a plan long after it has ceased to be useful.

Another important aspect of planning is *decision making,* which can be defined as the process of choosing among alternatives. Obviously, decision making will occur at many points in the planning process. For example, in planning for their organizations, managers must first decide which goal to pursue: "Shall our department teach Latin, modern languages, Latin and modern languages, or no languages at all?" In fact, deciding which goal to pursue is probably the most important part of the planning process. Managers must also decide which assumptions about the future and about the environment they will use in making their plans: "Will taxes on our foreign earnings increase, and thus strain our company's cash flow, or can we expect taxes to remain at the

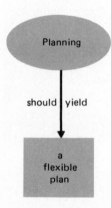

same level?" In addition, managers must decide how they will allocate their resources to attain their goals: "Will we promote one of our sales representatives to head the new sales campaign, or will we hire someone from outside the organization?" Because decision making is such an integral part of planning, we will be discussing it more extensively in Chapter 7.

WAYS OF CLASSIFYING PLANS AND PLANNING

Although the basic process of planning is the same for every manager, planning can take many forms in practice. There are several reasons for this. First, different types of organizations have different purposes; a planning approach that works in one organization will not necessarily work in another. Second, even within the same organization there will be a need for different types of planning at different times. Finally, different managers will have different planning styles. In this section, we will discuss some ways the different types of plans and planning can be conveniently classified.

The Perspectives of Organizational Planning

As Figure 4-2 on the next page illustrates, plans and planning can be viewed from five perspectives:[3]

1. *The time horizon.* In planning, we try to forecast future conditions so that we can decide what problems and opportunities our organization will face. Obviously, the greater the time span between a prediction and the actual event, the more likely it is that the prediction will be wrong. (Compare, for example, the accuracy of short-term and long-term weather forecasts.) For this reason, long-range plans — such as a plan to construct a new manufacturing facility in ten years — are usually less certain than short-range plans — such as a plan to move into a new office within two weeks. Regardless of the type of plan being drawn up, it should cover a time period that is long enough for the desired objectives to be attained. (This rule is called the "commitment principle" by some management writers.) For example, a plan to double profits in three years should cover all the actions during the three-year period that the manager believes will be necessary to achieve that goal.

2. *The subject matter.* Planning for product marketing, for example, will differ in many ways from planning to reorganize the personnel department. A greater financial investment may be required for the marketing of a product, while in reorganizing the personnel department a manager may have to be especially sensitive to the feelings of subordinates. In any case, the different subject matter involved is likely to affect how managers will proceed with the planning process.

3. *The organizational unit.* Planning for a total organization, such as a large hospital, is much more complex than planning for a subunit of that

[3] Steiner focuses on business planning, and the content of his chart reflects that focus. However, the concepts he presents are also applicable to other types of organizations, such as hospitals, schools, and government agencies.

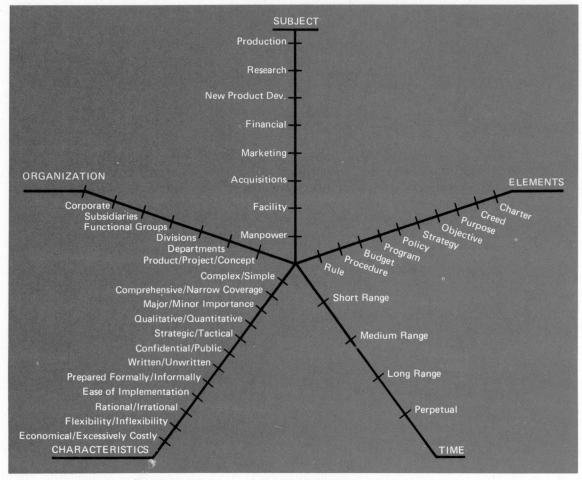

FIGURE 4-2   Five Key Dimensions of Business Planning

Source: George A. Steiner, *Top Management Planning* (New York: Macmillan, 1969), p. 12. Copyright © 1969 by The Trustees of Columbia University in The City of New York.

organization, such as the radiology department. Similarly, different subunits within the organization will have different purposes requiring different types of plans.

4. *The plan's characteristics.* Here the policies of the organization and the different styles of managers will affect the type of planning that takes place. Some managers, for example, will tolerate greater uncertainty in their plans than others. Similarly, an organization such as a consumer goods company planning to develop a new product may prefer to keep its plan confidential, while another company such as a public utility planning to build a nuclear power plant may prefer that its plan be made public.

5. *The elements of the plan.* The major types of plans routinely encountered in organizations bear such names as budgets, programs, rules, procedures,

and policies. Each of these items is part of the larger planning process of the organization; they help guide the execution of its daily activities. Less frequently encountered directly by middle or first-level managers are strategic plans or plans for the attainment of the organization's long-term objectives. However, these inclusive, general plans provide the starting points from which the more familiar types of plans are derived. Each type mentioned here will be described later in this chapter.

Strategic and Tactical Plans

Another useful way of classifying plans is to distinguish between strategic and tactical planning. *Strategic planning* involves deciding what the major goals of the entire organization will be and what policies will guide the organization in its pursuit of these goals. *Tactical planning* involves deciding specifically how the resources of the organization will be used to help the organization achieve its strategic goals.

Compared to tactical planning, strategic planning occurs at higher levels of management. It usually involves a longer period of time than tactical planning because the overall goals of the organization are involved. For this reason, strategic planning is more uncertain than tactical planning. Stragegic planners have to rely heavily on long-term forecasts of such matters as future developments in technology and changes in the political environment. Tactical planners, on the other hand, can rely more heavily on the past performance of the organization in allocating its resources. Because strategic planning is not involved with the day-to-day operations of the organization, it can be considerably less detailed than tactical planning.

We should note that in practice the distinction between strategic and tactical plans is not always as clear-cut as presented here. For example, as part of an organization-wide strategic plan, a divisional plan may be considered a tactical plan. At the same time, it may serve as a strategic plan for the development of more-detailed tactical plans for subunits in the division.

TYPES OF PLANS

The plans discussed above are arranged in a hierarchy within the organization. Each plan at a given organizational level serves two functions: it provides a means for achieving the objectives outlined in the plans at the next higher level; it also provides the ends or objectives for the plans at the next lower level in the organization. A general plan at the top level of management will give rise to a series of increasingly detailed plans, each contributing its part to the success of the general plan. For example, a general decision by the top management of an automobile company to produce compact cars would generate a whole series of plans in the engineering, production, and marketing departments. These in turn would generate more detailed plans, until the lowest level of management was reached.

The hierarchy of plans can be divided into three broad groups, as shown in the accompanying illustration: goals, single-use plans, and standing plans. *Goals* are the broad ends of the organization toward which the more detailed single-use and standing plans are directed. *Single-use plans,* as their name suggests, are developed to achieve a specific end; when that end is reached, the plan is dissolved. *Standing plans,* on the other hand, are designed for situations that recur often enough to justify a standardized approach. For example, it would be inefficient for an accounting firm to develop a single-use plan for processing the tax return of each new client. Accounting procedures have become sufficiently uniform to justify a broader standing plan.[4]

Goals   Goals provide the basic sense of direction for the organization's activities. They consist of the purpose, mission, objectives, and strategies of the organization. (See Figure 4-3.) Using the purpose of the organization as a framework, managers define the unique mission of the organization and then its narrower objectives, which are aimed at achieving that mission. They next translate the objectives of the organization into strategies, and perhaps even into formal strategic plans.

Those concepts will be defined and discussed below, but we must caution that the words used here to identify the various aims of an organization are not universally accepted. Many authors and managers, for example, use the words "goal" and "objective" interchangeably. Also, in their attempt to achieve the goals of their organizations, managers may follow different procedures from those described here.[5]

Purpose. The *purpose* of an organization is its primary role as defined by the society in which it operates. It is therefore a broad aim that applies not only to that organization but to all organizations of its type in that society. In free enterprise economies, for example, the purpose, or primary role, of business organizations is to earn a profit by producing goods and services within a set of guidelines and restrictions determined by society. The purpose of universities is to develop knowledge through research and to transmit knowledge to students through formal teaching programs. Hospitals are expected to provide health care, and the armed forces are expected to provide protection against attack by other nations.

Mission. The *mission* of an organization is the broad, unique aim that sets the organization apart from others of its type. It is the broadest aim that the organization chooses for itself. This definition implies a distinction between

[4] See William H. Newman, *Administrative Action: The Techniques of Organization and Management,* 2nd ed. (Englewood Cliffs, N.J.: Prentice-Hall, 1963). Our discussion draws upon the classification and description of plans by Newman, but the types of plans we include in the classification and our specific interpretation of their use differ somewhat from Newman's version.

[5] For example, a more extensive and detailed description of the hierarchy of goals is given in Charles H. Granger, "The Hierarchy of Objectives," *Harvard Business Review,* May-June 1964, pp. 63–74. Granger obviously uses the word "objectives" for what we call "goals."

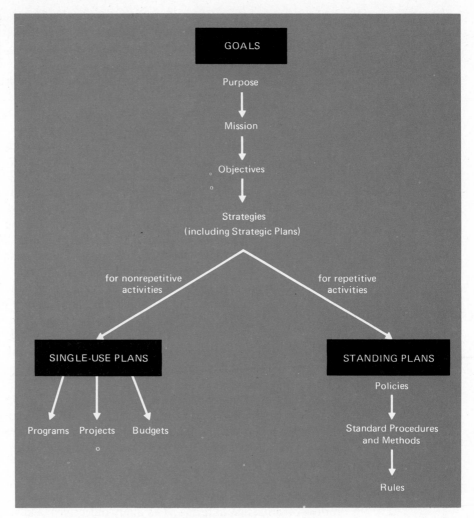

FIGURE 4-3
The Hierarchy of
Organizational
Plans

"purpose" and "mission" that is overlooked by many writers, who use those terms interchangeably. However, our awareness of the difference can help increase our understanding of organizational goals. As we have seen, a particular purpose is defined by society and applies to all organizations of a particular type. That purpose sets broad limits within which all those organizations must operate. But within those limits, each organization chooses its own unique mission—a narrower, more specific version of its societal purpose. Where the purpose of business organizations is to produce goods and services in general, the mission of a particular business would be to produce certain types of goods or services. For example, the Rival Manufacturing Company produces only small kitchen appliances, and the Katharine Gibbs School specializes in secretarial training.

The way in which a given organization defines its mission is seen by many management writers as crucial to its prosperity and even to its survival.[6] The dramatic decline in this century of the competitiveness and profitability of the U.S. railroads is often blamed on the failure of their managements to adapt their mission to changes in technology and economic conditions. If they had redefined their mission from "building rail lines and running trains" to "providing transportation services," they might have benefited rather than suffered from the development of the automobile, truck, and airplane.

Objectives. An organization's *objectives* are those ends that it must achieve in order to carry out its mission. Objectives are by nature more specific than the mission statement. Objectives can be considered as the translation of the mission into specific, concrete terms against which actual results can be measured more easily. Suppose the mission of a hospital is "to establish a capacity for outstanding care of patients with heart ailments." It would then translate that broad goal into specific objectives, which might include "performing at least six heart transplants each year" and "publishing annually five papers by resident doctors on diseases of the heart."

To take another example, an airline defines its mission as "providing transportation for passengers and high-value freight within a six-state area in the Middle West." The objectives it selects to implement this mission might include "achieving 15 percent rate of return on equity capital," "establishing a reputation for on-time service," and "being able to transfer air freight between any two cities in our operating areas in less than 24 hours." Note that not only can there be objectives for entire organizations but there can also be objectives for subunits within the organization. For example, an objective of the air freight department of the same airline might be "being able to put on any given flight any acceptable item of freight received as late as 15 minutes before scheduled time of departure."

Strategies. *Strategies* are broad programs for achieving the organization's objectives and thus implementing its mission. They create a unified direction for the organization in terms of its many objectives, and they guide the deployment of the resources that will be used to move the organization toward those objectives. Strategic plans and strategies are carried out by means of the two other major groups of plans — single-use plans and standing plans.

Single-Use Plans   *Single-use plans* are used to carry out courses of action that probably will not be repeated in the same form in the future. For example, a firm planning to set up a new warehouse because it is expanding rapidly will need a specific single-use plan for that project, even though it has established a number of other warehouses in the past. It will not be able to use an existing warehouse plan, because the projected warehouse presents unique requirements and

---

[6] See Peter F. Drucker, *Management: Tasks, Responsibilities, Practices* (New York: Harper & Row, 1974).

100

problems: location, construction costs, labor availability, zoning restrictions, and so forth. The major types of single-use plans are programs, projects, and budgets.

Programs. A *program* is a single-use plan covering a relatively large set of activities. The program shows (1) the major steps required to reach an objective, (2) the individual or organization responsible for each step, and (3) the order and timing in which the steps will be completed. The program may be accompanied by a budget or a set of budgets for the activities required.

Some programs are quite large and costly, like the one initiated by President Kennedy to place a man on the moon before 1970. Others are much more modest in their objectives and in the human and other resources used. These might include, for example, a program set up by an R&D firm to develop the managerial skills of its technical supervisors, or a program of a local school board to improve the reading level of fourth-grade children in its district.

Projects. A *project* is a single-use plan that consists of the same steps as a program but does not cover as large a set of activities. A project can be formulated and executed as an independent plan or as a relatively separate and clear-cut part of a program. The previously mentioned plan to build a warehouse, for example, might be an independent project to meet a limited need for more storage space, or it might be part of a company program "to double the capacity of our warehouse facilities by 1982."

The moon-landing program provides another example of the possible relationship between programs and projects. At the outset that program was divided into a large number of subprograms, and these in turn were broken down into numerous projects for assignment to different organizations. One such project covered the development of the moon buggy, which the astronauts used to travel on the moon's surface. In fact, the buggy project itself was broken down into a series of subprojects.

Budgets. *Budgets* are statements of the financial resources set aside for carrying out specific activities. As such, they are primarily devices used to *control* all kinds of organizational activities. For example, sales budgets show sales targets for a given area in which the sales force operates, and profit budgets are sometimes established for each division and department of an organization. As financial control devices, budgets are of course important components of programs and projects.

However, budgets can also be considered single-use plans in their own right, because managers often use the budget-developing process *as a guide to making decisions on how to allocate resources among various alternative activities.* If the allocation of resources during the budgeting process does not take strategic objectives into account, the organization's strategy can, at best, have only a limited effect on its actual activities. For this reason, the budgeting process is often the key planning process around which other activities are planned and coordinated.

Standing Plans   Because a bank regularly decides whether to grant requests for car loans, it does not need a different plan to handle each specific request. Instead, it uses one *standing plan* that anticipates in advance whether to approve or turn down any request based on the information furnished, credit ratings, and the like. Standing plans are used wherever an organizational activity occurs repeatedly, because they enable a single decision or set of decisions to guide those repeated actions. Thus, once established, standing plans allow managers to conserve planning time and decision-making time and to handle similar situations in a consistent manner. Of course, standing plans can sometimes be disadvantageous, because they commit the organization's managers to decisions made in the past and thus may limit their ability to handle new situations and problems flexibly.

The major types of standing plans are policies, procedures, and rules.

Policies. A *policy* is a general guideline for decision making. It sets up boundaries around decisions, including those that can be made and shutting out those that cannot. In so doing, it channels the thinking of organization members so that it is consistent with organizational objectives. Some policies deal with very important matters, like those requiring strict sanitary conditions where food or drugs are produced or packaged. Others are concerned with relatively less important issues, such as the dress and general appearance of employees.

Policies are usually established formally and deliberately by top managers of the organization. These managers may set a policy because (1) they feel it will improve the effectiveness of the organization; (2) they want some aspect of the organization to reflect their personal values (for example, dress codes); or (3) they need to clear up some conflict or confusion that has occurred at a lower level in the organization. Often, however, policies emerge informally and at lower levels in the organization from a seemingly consistent set of decisions on the same subject made over a period of time. For example, if office space is repeatedly assigned on the basis of seniority, that may become organization policy. In recent years policy has also been set by factors outside the organization, such as government agencies, which set limits and guidelines for the organization's activities (such as requiring certain safety procedures).

Standard Procedures. Policies are carried out by means of more detailed guidelines called "standard procedures" or "standard methods." A *procedure* provides a detailed set of instructions for performing a sequence of actions that occurs often or regularly. For example, suppose a refund department of a large discount store has a policy of "Refunds made, with a smile, on all merchandise returned within seven days of purchase." The procedure for all clerks who handle merchandise returned under that policy might then be a series of steps like this: (1) Smile at customer. (2) Check receipt for purchase date. (3) Check condition of merchandise... and so on. By providing such detailed instructions for various actions, the organization insures that there will be a high level of consistency in the way in which different members carry out a frequently occurring activity.

Rules. *Rules* are statements that a specific action must or must not be taken in a given situation. As the most explicit of the standing plans, they do not serve as guides to thinking and decision making but rather as substitutes for them. The only element of choice a rule leaves to the individual is whether or not to apply the rule to a specific situation. For example, in an office that has a rule requiring all employees to work until five o'clock, the office manager may suspend the rule and let everyone go home early on a hot day when the air-conditioning system breaks down.

THE FOUR BASIC STEPS IN PLANNING

Since planning is such an important activity at all levels of the organization, it is extremely desirable to understand what managers actually do when they engage in the general planning process. In this chapter, we will describe in abbreviated form the basic steps all managers engage in when they plan. Knowledge of these steps will help you understand the planning process, particularly the planning that occurs in the day-to-day operations of the organization. In the next chapter we will discuss in greater detail some of the techniques and perspectives that are especially appropriate and useful for strategic planning, which is a more comprehensive and longer-term type of planning.

In a simplified form, the basic process of planning (see Figure 4-4) involves four major steps:

1 *Establishing a goal or set of goals to be achieved;* that is, deciding what the organization or subunit wants or needs.

2 *Determining where the organization or subunit is relative to the goal.* This means deciding how far the unit is from the goal, what resources it has for reaching the goal, and what its limitations are.

3 *Determining which factors in the environment will help the organization or subunit reach its goal and which factors will act as barriers.* This step includes predicting, or *forecasting,* which factors will appear in the future or how present factors will change.

4 *Developing a plan, that is, a set of actions for reaching the goal.* This is done by generating a set of alternative courses of action, evaluating them, and then choosing among them.

Step 1: Establishing a Goal

From our own experience, we know that it is often difficult to decide on the goals we want to pursue, especially when (as is sometimes the case) we can choose only one goal among two or more attractive alternatives. For example, suppose a recent business school graduate who wants to find a job in international finance also would like to live and work in a small midwestern town. These are potentially conflicting goals, because most jobs in that particular field are located in New York and other major cities. Therefore, unless this

103

FIGURE 4-4
The Four Basic
Steps in Planning

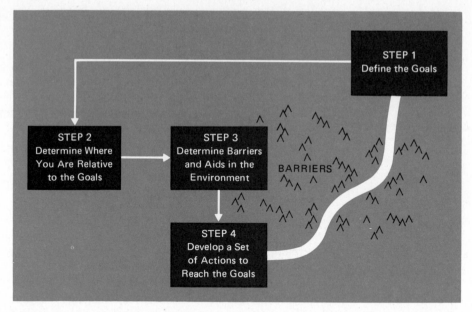

FIGURE 4-4
The Four Basic
Steps in Planning

graduate is unusually persistent or lucky, he or she will probably have to decide between the two competing goals.

Sometimes one goal must be chosen over another because the individual or organization does not have enough resources to achieve both at the same time. A hospital, for example, may simultaneously need a new radiation device for treatment of cancer patients and several new ambulances that are specially equipped to save the lives of victims of heart attacks. Both these objectives are consistent with the hospital's mission, which in this case happens to be "providing excellent health care for the people of our community." But if the hospital's budget does not allow for both expenditures, it will have to make a choice between the two alternatives.

The task of translating broad goals—such as the organization's mission or its broad objectives—into more concrete, measurable objectives varies in difficulty, depending on the specific situation. One of the trickier problems in this process is to avoid losing sight of the true meaning and intention of the organization's broad goals while concentrating on the selection of more specific aims. For example, many philanthropic organizations find that an ever-increasing proportion of charitable contributions is used to pay the costs of solicitation and staff salaries. The original broad commitment to the needy has been somewhat diluted by the specific need for advertising and personnel.

Step 2:
Determining the
Present
Situation

No goals exist in a vacuum. A person who wants to become a corporate treasurer, for example, does not decide on that goal without evaluating it in terms of his or her actual and potential abilities. In other words, the future must have a realistic basis in the present.

The same is true for organizational goals. That is, once the desired future situation (the goal) has been established (usually on a tentative basis), the manager must evaluate it in the light of the organization's or subunit's present situation. Suppose the marketing manager of a company sets an objective of achieving a 5 percent profit margin for a given product line within the next three years. The manager then evaluates the current situation: The present profit margin for that line is 3 percent, and it is estimated that the company's chief competitor is marketing a similar line at a 5 percent margin. In the light of this information, the manager would then probably decide that the 5 percent objective is a reasonable one.

Note that in practice it is difficult to distinguish steps 1 and 2 as separate activities. In the previous example the marketing manager might have first evaluated the current situation and then established the goal on that basis instead of working the other way around. And even after the goal has been firmly established, it can be influenced by changes in the current situation. Suppose that after establishing the 5 percent goal, the marketing manager later discovers that the competitor's product line is actually achieving a 12 percent profit margin. He or she would then probably go through the whole planning process again to try to determine the reasons for such a large difference in the performance of the two companies. As a result of this replanning, the manager may come up with a much higher expected rate of return (that is, a new goal), or he may decide it would be best to eliminate the lagging product line altogether.

Managers need to gather data to understand the present situation, for without such data informed planning cannot take place. This is why managers need to keep all lines of communication open. If necessary, they may have to develop a formal *information system* for collecting relevant data. (We will be discussing management information systems and the importance of communication for managers in future chapters.)

Step 3: Determining Aids and Barriers to Goals	Once managers have selected their goals, they must determine what factors will aid or hinder them in pursuit of these goals. Often, the resources of the organization—its finances, equipment, and personnel—will be the main aids available to the manager. For example, if a goal of an automobile manufacturer is to reduce the size of all its cars over a period of time, the equipment on hand and the capital available for retooling this equipment will help it reach its goal. If the goal of an advertising agency is to attract ten new clients a year, the creativity of its copywriters will be an aid. Conversely, insufficient organizational resources may be a barrier to the attainment of goals. In our example, if the caliber of the copywriters in the advertising agency is insufficient to attract new clients, the head of the agency will probably have to provide for hiring new copywriters in order to achieve his or her goal.

Sometimes barriers to goals exist as part of the structure of the organization. For example, the goal of a manager may be to increase a sense of unity in the organization. If communication in the organization tends to be overly formal, however, or if the physical layout of the workplace inhibits communication, these barriers may have to be removed before the goal can be achieved. More frequently, however, barriers to goals will exist outside the organization. These may be market conditions that inhibit the introduction of a new product, competitors who are known for their low-pricing policies, legal restrictions that prevent a merger, or any factor in the external environment. (See Chapter 3.)

The Role of Forecasting. It will be a comparatively easy task for us to determine those aids and barriers to goals that already exist. A much harder and more uncertain task is to predict what aids and barriers (or opportunities and problems) *will* exist. Planning, by definition, involves the future. We plan now to achieve something later. No usable plan can therefore be developed unless possible future events are taken into account. For this reason, forecasting is a critical element in the planning process.

Forecasting is often involved with the environment in a special way because it includes predictions of how other individuals, groups, or organizations will respond to the actions that are planned. If a company plans to continue its present sales program, its management must predict how the company's customers, sales force, and competitors will react. The company may also wish to reduce the price of a product to increase sales volume. However, if management predicts that competing companies would follow suit, then it is probable that another method of increasing sales volume will have to be found.

Other types of forecasting will not involve the interaction of the organization with the environment. For example, a manager may wish to predict the gross national product or the national employment rate. Such variables are unlikely to be appreciably affected by the actions of the organization, though they may well influence how successful the organization will be.

Well-established tools of economic and statistical analysis are widely used in forecasting. These are sometimes supplemented by less-established approaches, such as game theory. We will be discussing the techniques and tools of forecasting in Chapter 8.

Step 4: Developing a Plan for Reaching the Goal

The final step in the planning process involves developing various alternative courses of action for reaching the desired goal or goals, evaluating these alternatives, and choosing from among them the most suitable (or, at least, a satisfactory) alternative for reaching the goal.

This fourth step in planning will not be necessary if the manager, after examining current trends, predicts that the plan already in effect will carry the organization or subunit to its desired goal. In such a case, the manager usually watches (that is, *controls*) progress under the old plan very closely and is ready to react quickly if it deviates from expectations. Most of the time, however, we will engage in planning because present conditions are not meeting goals and expectations. In such cases a new plan has to be developed.

FIRST QUARTER   PROJECTED 2ND QUARTER   FANTASIZED 2ND QUARTER

Cartoon by Henry Martin

Planning
involves

developing
alternatives

A   B   C

and

choosing
the most
satisfactory
alternative

Developing Alternative Courses of Action. If the existing plan is no longer usable, the manager must develop alternatives from which to choose a new plan. These alternatives must be realistic—that is, they must be based on organizational resources that exist or can be obtained without unusual difficulty.

Let us assume, for example, that as part of its plan to increase its reputation as a center for heart disease a hospital offers a $500 bonus to each resident who publishes a paper on heart disorders. If over a six-month period only one acceptable paper has resulted, the administrator will have to develop alternative courses of action in order to achieve the objective. The administrator might: (1) increase the bonus to $750 for a publishable paper; (2) give doctors interested in participating in the project additional time off to conduct research; (3) combine the $750 bonus with the additional time off; (4) free doctors who produce satisfactory papers from unpleasant responsibilities, such as emergency room duty, for a six-month period. Because the first plan did not succeed, the administrator would probably consult with the residents before developing this new set of alternatives.

Evaluating the Alternatives. After the manager draws up a set of feasible alternatives, he or she then evaluates and compares them. In this process the

107

manager estimates the cost of carrying out each alternative and balances it against the probable benefits that will be derived from it. The costs to be considered include not only the financial expense of the control system that will be used to implement the plan but also the costs in social and psychological terms—that is, the effects of the planned activities on members of the organization, customers, suppliers, and the like. (We will discuss the evaluation of plans in greater detail in Chapter 6.)

Making a Selection among Alternatives. As might be expected, most managers try to choose the best, or "optimal," alternative—that is, the one which best balances the costs, benefits, and uncertainties and is therefore most likely to achieve the most satisfactory results. *Optimizing* a decision means making the best one available to the organization at a given time.

In practice, however, there are often great limitations placed on the planning/decision-making process:

1 The manager may lack important information when making the decision.
2 There is always pressure on the manager to act quickly and with apparent decisiveness.
3 The manager may have overlooked more attractive alternatives in the early stages of the process.

James G. March and Herbert A. Simon have argued so persuasively about the limits on rational decision making that their word *satisficing* has become an accepted part of the management vocabulary.[7] Satisficing means finding and selecting a satisfactory (as opposed to the best) alternative—one which achieves a minimally acceptable outcome.

Although March and Simon have a valid point, it perhaps can be over-emphasized by managers so that it discourages them from trying to make the best possible decision when it is possible to do so. In fact, one of the advantages of following the formal procedures of the planning process is that this activity increases our chances of developing more of the good alternatives and minimizes the possibility that we will simply select the first satisfactory alternative developed.

THE LINKAGE OF PLANNING AND CONTROLLING

We have chosen to describe planning as an analytical and decision-making process that ends with the development of a specific plan for action. But every plan must, of course, be translated from intention into action. For this reason, there is a direct relationship between planning and the other management functions, particularly the function of controlling.

On a fairly simple level, control can be defined as "the process of making

[7] See James G. March and Herbert A. Simon, *Organizations* (New York: Wiley, 1958).

sure that performance takes place in conformance with plans."[8] While this definition distinguishes controlling from planning, it also points out that the two functions are very interrelated. No controlling can take place unless a plan exists, and the success of a plan would be uncertain at best unless some effort were made to monitor its progress.

Thus, not only does planning lead to controlling, but the reverse is also often true. A manager who is controlling an activity often sees the need to alter the original plan to meet changing or unforeseen conditions.

The most common link between planning and controlling in organizations is through a budget. As we suggested earlier, budgets are often a key part of the planning process, because they help determine what resources will be directed toward the attainment of the desired goal. If the implementation of a part of the plan threatens to exceed the budget, it is a sign that an unforeseen problem has arisen. The manager may have to revise the plan to take new problems into account.

In some organizations, planning and controlling are also linked together by the process of employee participation in planning. It is assumed that when employees participate in establishing goals, they will be more likely to control their own activities to make sure the goals are met. For example, if employees agree to submit sales reports by a certain date, they might voluntarily work longer hours to make sure the reports are completed on time.

We should note that despite the linkage of planning and controlling, it is important for managers to keep the two functions formally separated. A formal commitment to controlling is usually necessary to ensure that employees will take the concept of control seriously and that the controlling activities themselves will not be haphazard. We will be discussing controlling in greater detail in Part V.

Summary

Planning has primacy over the other management functions and is a pervasive element in organizations. By planning, managers minimize uncertainty and help focus their organization on its goals.

The types of planning that managers engage in will depend on their level in the organization and on the size and type of their organization. *Strategic planning,* for example, which involves deciding the major goals of the organization, usually occurs at the top management level. *Tactical planning,* which is usually concerned with the implementation of strategic plans, involves middle and lower-level management. In general, plans parallel the organizational hierarchy, with broader, longer-range plans at the top level generating increasingly narrower, shorter-term plans at lower levels of the organization.

Plans can be conveniently divided into three broad groups. *Goals* are the broad ends of the organization. They include the organization's purpose, mission, objectives, and strategies. *Single-use plans* are developed for a specific activity that will probably not be repeated. They include programs, projects, and budgets. Conversely, *standing plans* are used for methods of operation that have become standardized. They include policies, procedures, and rules.

[8] Steiner, *Top Management Planning,* p. 41.

The basic process of planning includes four major steps: (1) deciding what goals are to be achieved, (2) establishing where the organization is relative to those goals, (3) determining what aids and barriers to these goals exist, and (4) developing a plan for reaching the goals. Once plans have been made, they must be implemented and monitored in order to have practical effects. For this reason, the other management functions, particularly controlling, are closely related to the planning function.

Review Questions

1. Why do you think planning is important in organizations?
2. How does planning fit into the management process?
3. How will your awareness of the distinction between planning and plans affect your performance as a manager?
4. According to this chapter, what are the five perspectives from which planning and plans can be viewed?
5. What is the difference between strategic and tactical plans? How are these types of plans related to the organizational hierarchy?
6. What are goals, single-use plans, and standing plans? What is the difference between an organization's purpose and its mission?
7. What is the importance of forecasting in the planning process?
8. Describe the basic steps in the planning process. Why do you think each step is important?
9. Do you think "satisficing" is a more acceptable term for managerial decision making than "optimizing"? Why?
10. How are planning and controlling linked? Why will it be important for you as a manager to keep these two management functions formally separated?

CASE STUDY: A PROBLEM OF TIRES

Because of the strike in the rubber industry in the summer of 1976, about 2.5 million cars and trucks were produced without spare tires. Automakers had to make do with existing supplies, and by producing motor vehicles without spare tires, they were able to stretch their inventories by 20 percent and produce more cars. It was important for automakers to continue to produce as many cars as they could, since the auto industry was just beginning to recover from a prolonged sales slump.

When the strike was over, the automakers presented the tire manufacturers with a list of vehicles that had been produced without a spare. The tire manufacturers were supposed to ship extra tires to the appropriate auto and truck dealers, who would in turn get the spares to those customers who did not have them. Automakers were unable to handle the tire distribution themselves. As one spokesman for an auto manufacturer was quoted as saying, "We didn't have a distribution system. We aren't in the business of shipping spares."

Unfortunately, the tire manufacturers were not in position to ship spare tires immediately. They were under pressure to fill a backlog of orders as well as new tire orders for cars that were now being produced. Making additional spares did not have top priority. In addition, the tire companies were not properly prepared to ship tires directly to car and truck dealers.

By late March 1977, when the strike had been over for six months, it was estimated that about 200,000 people had still not received spare tires. Moreover, many people who received spares found that the tires were of the wrong size or type. Customer resentment was high—not only were customers bothered by the long and highly inconvenient wait for the spares, but they also deeply resented paying full price for their vehicles when they were sold to them with one tire missing. In addition, the Federal Trade Commission was investigating reports that some buyers were not told their vehicles were without a spare. (Reported in the *Wall Street Journal*, March 21, 1977.)

Case Questions

1. What was wrong with the automakers' plan?
2. How did the divided responsibility for getting spare tires to customers dilute the effectiveness of the plan?
3. How could dealers have offset some of the problems created by the automakers' plan?
4. How would you have coordinated the activities of automakers, tire manufacturers, and dealers in getting spare tires to consumers?
5. Why do you think the automakers did not try harder to get spare tires to their customers?
6. Construct an alternative plan for marketing "spare-less" vehicles.

Chapter 5

Strategic Planning

Upon completing this chapter you should be able to:

1. Explain why it is important for you to understand strategic planning.

2. Describe how managers can devise a correct strategy for their organizations.

3. Identify and describe the three modes of strategy making, and discuss which mode is most effective for a particular organization.

4. Identify and describe the nine steps in the formal strategic planning approach.

5. Describe how strategic planning takes place in large organizations.

6. State the disadvantages and advantages of strategic planning.

In the previous chapter we discussed why planning in general is important to managers and how managers plan. In this chapter, we will focus on a specific type of planning called *strategic planning*. It is through strategic planning that managers define the basic mission of their organization and decide what resources will be devoted to its accomplishment.

For a number of reasons it has become desirable for managers and prospective managers to understand strategic planning. First, strategic planning is the most important type of planning we may do. Managers direct the detailed operations of their organization only after they have determined what their basic goals are and how they will achieve them. In short, the activities of an organization — and thus its survival and growth — will ultimately depend on its strategic plan. Second, as we shall see, strategic planning has increasingly become a fact of organizational life. More and more organizations are using this type of planning to help them develop and succeed. It is therefore likely that prospective managers will be playing some role in their organization's strategic planning process. Finally, an understanding of the process will give prospective managers a useful insight into the operations of an organization and the concerns of managers at different levels of the organization.

WHY STRATEGIC PLANNING?

The importance of strategic planning for managers and organizations has grown in recent years. Managers found that by defining the mission of their organization in specific terms, they were better able to give their organization direction and purpose. For example, the international car rental firm of Avis operated at a loss for many years. Management initiated several action programs, including a number of acquisitions, but still the firm did not prosper. Then Robert Townsend stepped in as president, gave Avis a sorely needed sense of direction, and in three short years made it number two in its field.

The first thing Townsend did was to define Avis's mission as "the renting and leasing of vehicles without drivers." Overnight, this clear concept put an end to the less purposeful activity that had gone on before. In Townsend's words, defining the firm's purpose, "Let us . . . stop considering the acquisition of related businesses like motels, hotels, airlines and travel agencies. It also showed us we had to get rid of some limousine and sightseeing companies we already had."

Townsend then went on to formulate long-range objectives. "It took us six months," he wrote, "to define one objective: 'We want to become the fastest-growing company with the highest profit margins in the business of renting and leasing vehicles without drivers.' . . . I used to keep a sign where I couldn't miss it: 'Is what I'm doing or about to be doing getting us closer to our objective?'" That sign, he concluded, kept him from getting caught in a lot of useless activity.[1]

[1] Robert Townsend, *Up the Organization* (Greenwich, Conn.: Fawcett, 1971), pp. 111–112.

Strategic planning, then, will help us develop a clear-cut concept of our organization. This, in turn, will make it easier for us to formulate the plans and objectives that will bring our organization closer to its goals. In short, by defining the mission of the organization in specific terms we will be able to focus the organization's resources more efficiently and effectively.

The Changing Environment of Organizations

Another reason strategic planning has become important for managers is that it enables them to prepare for and deal with the rapidly changing environment of their organizations. When the pace of life was slower, managers operated on the assumption that the future would be substantially like the past. They could establish goals and plans simply by extrapolating from past experience. Today, events are moving too rapidly for experience always to be a reliable guide. Managers must develop new strategic plans that will be suited for unique problems and opportunities in the future. (See Table 5-1 for some differences between an emphasis on strategy and one on the day-to-day operations of an organization.)

TABLE 5-1
Operating Management vs. Strategic Management

	Operating Management	Strategic Management
Focus	Operating Problems	Longer-Term Survival and Development
Objective	Present Profits	Future Profits
Constraints	Present Resources Environment	Future Resources Environment
Rewards	Efficiency, Stability	Development of Future Potential
Information	Present Business	Future Opportunities
Organization	Bureaucratic/Stable	Entrepreneurial/Flexible
Leadership	Conservative	Inspires Radical Change
Problem Solving	Reacts, Relies on Past Experience	Anticipates, Finds New Approaches
	Low Risk	Higher Risk

Source: Bernard Taylor, "Strategies for Planning," *Long-Range Planning,* Vol. 8, No. 4 (August 1975), p. 38. Used by permission.

Since World War II there have been several major developments that have increased the importance of strategic planning:

1. *The tempo of technological change.* In the wake of the postwar technological explosion, whole new industries have sprung into being — from photocopiers to pocket calculators. This new tempo has made it necessary for a firm actively to seek new opportunities, instead of reacting defensively to competition.

2. *The mounting complexity of the managerial job.* Management today must deal with such matters as the growing size and diversity of organizations, increasing overhead costs, the shift of people — and markets — from cities to

suburbs, and the relationship between social responsibility and managerial practice. It is only through long-range planning that managers can anticipate such problems and opportunities.

3. *The mounting complexity of the external environment.* As we have seen in Chapter 3, management can no longer enjoy the luxury of focusing exclusively on the firm's internal affairs. Changes in social values, government regulations, union activities, and so on must enter into managerial calculations today. Several years ago, for example, a realtor committed himself to building a new shopping center without anticipating that the local planning board would require him to provide an environmental impact statement. The result was a considerable financial loss for the realtor.

4. *The longer lead time between current decisions and their future results.* A growing number of management decisions rest more upon long-term profit expectations than upon immediate sales prospects. This means that planners must look farther ahead than ever before. The prospects for the economy as a whole, the development of new materials, the growth and decline of whole industries—all these and more must be projected many years into the future. For example, airlines must plan ahead for planes and landing facilities that will not be operational for ten to twenty years.[2]

Through strategic planning, then, better preparation can be made for the future. Managers can avoid costly investments in goods or services for which there will be no demand and, in addition, plan now to produce those goods or services for which there will be a demand.

THE CONCEPT OF STRATEGY

In the 1920s, General Robert E. Wood was president of Sears, Roebuck & Co., a giant mail-order house. Wood realized the growing popularity of the automobile would allow increasing numbers of people to move to the cities. And a population no longer confined to the countryside, he reasoned, would abandon the mail-order catalog in favor of the retail store. So Sears embarked on a long-range strategy of converting to a retail chain. According to Wood, the company "made every mistake in the book" at first, but its carefully laid plans spelled success in the end. "Business is like war in one respect," the general wrote. "If its grand strategy is correct, any number of tactical errors can be made and yet the enterprise proves successful."[3]

How will we go about devising an effective strategy? The first thing we will do is find a "common thread" or theme for the activities of our organization. For example, the top management of Hertz, the well-known car rental

[2] See George A. Steiner, *Top Management Planning* (New York: Macmillan, 1969), and Ernest Dale and Michael J. Kami, "Long-Range Planning," in Dale, ed., *Readings in Management* (New York: McGraw-Hill, 1965), pp. 252–259.

[3] Quoted in Alfred D. Chandler, Jr., *Strategy and Structure* (Cambridge, Mass.: MIT Press, 1962), p. 325.

agency, could conceivably have defined the common thread of the company as "the renting of cars." This, however, would not have distinguished the firm from its competitors. Hertz management would have had a difficult time devising a marketing strategy for the company. But when management defined the firm as "the number one car rental agency," an effective marketing strategy quickly became apparent: the company could use its top position in the car rental industry to convince the public of its superiority. Hertz began to stress "we're number one" in its print advertising, and it used football's top running back, O. J. Simpson, in its television commercials.

Finding the common thread allows managers to determine the true capabilities of their organization. This, in turn, enables them to plan strategically how they will best apply these capabilities.

Finding the Common Thread

In certain organizations, or in certain circumstances, the theme of the organization will suggest itself fairly quickly. (For example, it is likely that Hertz management found the firm's common thread with little effort.) More often we will have to explore several possibilities and make many false starts before we can find a useful theme. Many managers find the common thread of their organizations by asking themselves some of the questions listed below.[4]

1. *What is our business and what should it be?* This seems like a minor question, but in reality the answer to it can determine the success or failure of the organization. If an organization's business or purpose is defined too broadly, the organization may lack a sense of direction. Conversely, if its business or purpose is defined too narrowly, the organization may overlook attractive opportunities.

For example, at the end of World War II International Rayon was the sole manufacturer of rayon filament yarn. Aware that competition would soon press into this lucrative field, top management initially decided to invest in new and improved machinery. But the director of research and development, who had been conducting an informal survey of customer needs, found a growing demand for completely new fibers. He therefore persuaded management to redefine its concept of the business from providing the best in rayon yarn to providing the best and largest variety of fibers for industrial uses.

Three years later the firm's chief competitor entered the market with a better and cheaper rayon yarn. But by that time International Rayon had perfected a process for tire and industrial fibers which enabled it to maintain its leading position in the field. Identifying the common thread—fibers for industrial uses—helped redefine the corporation's basic mission and redirected management into a lucrative new market.

2. *Who are our customers and who should they be?* In the case cited above, management's first plan was inwardly oriented—that is, management aimed to improve an existing manufacturing capability. It was the R&D director's survey of *customer needs* that put the firm on the right track.

Identifying customer needs is important for all organizations, not just busi-

---

[4] See H. Igor Ansoff, *Corporate Strategy* (New York: McGraw-Hill, 1965), and Peter F. Drucker, *Management: Tasks, Responsibilities, Practices* (New York: Harper & Row, 1974).

nesses. Barry Commoner, the world-famous biologist and ecologist, serves as director of Washington University's Center for the Biology of Natural Systems. When asked to describe how the Center planned its projects, Commoner replied, *"It's really a question of whom you're working for.* [Emphasis added.] If you're working for your peers, you do discipline-oriented work. If you're doing it for the public... you do task-oriented work."[5] Here we see how even in a nonprofit organization, defining the nature of the "business" and pinpointing the "customer" is the basic starting point for planning future work projects.

3. *Where are we heading?* Even when an organization produces generally unrelated goods or services, managers can find its common thread by determining in which direction the organization is moving. Is the organization's share of the market growing or declining? Is it developing new products or services? Does it need to diversify? By asking such questions, managers can determine where new growth opportunities might be sought in the years ahead.

4. *What major competitive advantages do we enjoy?* Managers can identify and isolate those factors that give the firm a strong competitive position, such as patent-protected processes or unique products. By so doing, managers can focus on missions that hold the greatest promise for the future development of the organization.

5. *In what areas of competence do we excel?* Sometimes industry boundaries are ill-defined or changing. In such cases, special capabilities of the organization, such as an outstanding information processing capability or a comprehensive distribution network, could suggest the common thread.

6. *Shall we acquire new resources or develop them internally?* Managers must decide whether their organization will emphasize internal growth or growth through acquisition. Growing through acquisition may be preferred if the organization wants the resources it is purchasing fairly quickly. For example, if a television network wishes to expand into radio broadcasting, it may prefer to purchase a radio station, with its existing facilities and experienced personnel, rather than go through the laborious and time-consuming process of obtaining a license and building its own station from the ground up. On the other hand, if the organization has enough time and resources of its own, managers may decide to expand internally—particularly if acquisition of another organization would be too expensive. (This is a larger-scale, strategic version of the common *make-or-buy* decision—that is, whether to produce a part or product internally or purchase it from another firm.) Whatever decision the manager makes will help define the organization's purpose and mission.

APPROACHES TO STRATEGIC PLANNING

Once the common thread of their organization has been found, managers can begin the strategic planning process. However, the form of strategic planning that managers will engage in varies according to the personal style of the manager and the type of organization involved. Before focusing on the formal

[5] *New York Times Magazine,* November 17, 1976.

steps in strategic planning, we will consider the different ways strategic plans and decisions can be made.

The Three Modes
of Strategy
Making

According to Henry Mintzberg, there are three modes of managerial strategy making: the entrepreneurial, the adaptive, and the planning mode.[6]

In the *entrepreneurial* mode, one strong leader, usually the founder of the business or a descendant, makes bold, risk-taking decisions more or less intuitively. That is, he or she relies on personal judgment formed by experience. With power centralized in the chief executive's hands, the entrepreneurial organization is motivated essentially by one overriding goal: constant growth. Strategy making is dominated by an active search for new opportunities with choices guided not by charted rule but by the chief's personalized plan of attack. (See Figure 5-1.)

FIGURE 5-1
Paths of the
Three Modes

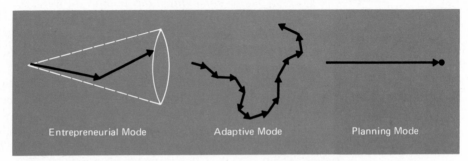

Entrepreneurial Mode   Adaptive Mode   Planning Mode

Source: Reprinted from *California Management Review*, Vol. 16, No. 2 (Winter 1973), p. 49, by permission. © 1973 by the Regents of the University of California.

The *adaptive* mode has been called "the science of muddling through."[7] Where the entrepreneur confronts the environment as a force to be controlled, the adaptive manager reacts to each situation as it arises. Where strategy in the entrepreneurial organization consists typically of dramatic leaps forward in the face of uncertainty, the adaptive organization moves ahead timidly in a series of small, disjointed steps. And where the entrepreneur constantly seeks to beat competition to the punch, the adaptive manager tends to react defensively to the actions of competitors.

The difference stems from the lack of a central source of power. Caught in a web of conflicting forces—owners, unions, government, and so on—management cannot always negotiate a clear statement of objectives. Hence the reactive, fragmented, disjointed strategy making that, oddly enough, adds an element of flexibility—one that accounts largely for the organization's ability to muddle through.

[6] Henry Mintzberg, "Strategy-Making in Three Modes," *California Management Review*, Vol. 16, No. 2 (Winter 1973), pp. 44–53.

[7] Charles E. Lindblom, "The Science of 'Muddling Through,'" *Public Administration Review*, Vol. 19, No. 2 (1959).

The *planning* mode provides the guiding framework and strong sense of direction the other modes lack. Where the entrepreneur trusts to judgment and the adaptive manager waits to see the shape of the future, the planner turns to the professional practitioners of management science: the analysts, game theorists, model simulators, and computer programmers. While planners must also make risk-taking decisions, their choices are systematic and structured; that is, they are based on a rational estimate of costs and benefits and are tailored to fit the overall strategy of the organization.

Selecting the Approach

No one approach to strategy making will work best for all organizations and in all situations. Indeed, the same organization may benefit from using different approaches at different stages in its evolution or when it faces different types of strategic issues. We shall discuss first the conditions under which each mode may most effectively guide the organization and then how the modes might be mixed for optimum effectiveness.

A small, relatively young organization with a strong chief executive addicted to the quick, bold stroke is made to order for the entrepreneurial mode. Too young for policies and procedures to be frozen by precedent, with few irreversible investments to hold it back, the organization can plunge ahead boldly with little to lose and a lot to gain from every risk-taking action. This entrepreneurial behavior may also suit an organization in trouble, when the bold stroke may be the only hope of salvation.

The adaptive mode would be the choice for the large organization in a complex, unstable environment, committed to irreversible investments and overhead, and with a management composed of competing groups holding each other in check. Most universities, many large hospitals, government agencies, and some of our larger corporations fit this description.

To make effective use of the planning mode, an organization must be able to afford the costs in manpower and finance of formal analysis. In addition it must be able to formulate objectives and, according to some authors, must be operating in a reasonably stable environment. A good-sized firm in a basically noncompetitive industry would best fit this description.

Mixing the Modes. In practice, most firms combine these three modes in various ways to meet their particular needs. In one case, the management of a leading city hotel decided to build a luxury motel in an outlying suburb. This in itself was an adaptive reaction to motel competition. But in choosing a location, management adopted the planning mode. A task force weighed such factors as the possibility of traffic being diverted from proposed sites by new thruways and the possibility that a proposed site might divert guests from the parent hotel.

An organization may also operate with different modes of strategy making in different functional areas. Plant managers, who usually have to concern themselves with precise production goals and schedules, may lean toward the planning mode. In marketing, where imagination and boldness are often needed, managers might act in a more entrepreneurial fashion. The adaptive approach

119

might be found in personnel departments, which must cope with a complicated labor market.

Two Types of Strategic Planning

Mintzberg's attempt to describe when each type of strategy making will be effective may be the beginning of a contingency approach to strategic planning. (See Chapter 2.) That is, managers can now attempt to tailor their planning approach to each situation. An additional step was taken in this direction by Michael B. McCaskey, who distinguishes between two types of strategic planning: planning with specific goals and "directional planning."[8]

Planning with specific goals is the type of planning described in Chapter 4 and discussed further in this chapter. This kind of planning tends to be formal and structured. Managers decide what the organization is going to do and how it is going to do it. Through goal-oriented plans, managers provide the organization with a strong sense of focus and efficiently channel the organization's resources.

In *directional planning,* managers first decide what they would *like* to do, rather than what they *should* do. What accomplishments in the past have satisfied them most deeply? In what direction do they personally want to see their organization move? Only after managers have selected a desired direction or activity for their organization do they decide how best to go about making their desire a reality.

Directional planning may involve greater expenditures than planning with goals, because managers may have to spend more before finalizing their plans. For example, it may be necessary to do more extensive market research to determine if there is a demand for the goods or services the managers would like to produce. In addition, directional planning is less likely than goal-oriented planning to give the organization a strong sense of purpose, because it may not involve commonly accepted goals. On the other hand, directional planning may be more flexible than planning with goals, because the manager and the organization are not tied down to a firmly defined set of goals and methods for reaching them. (See Table 5-2.)

For these reasons, directional planning may be more suited to the early stage of an organization's life, before managers have decided precisely what the organization should do. Directional planning may also be useful when the environment of the organization is very fluid and unpredictable. The mayor of a large city, for example, might find that planning for specific goals is sometimes unrealistic, considering the shifts in population, employment, and revenue that typically occur in a city. Instead, the mayor may establish a set of desirable guidelines and try to win broad-based political support for his or her aims.

[8] Michael B. McCaskey, "A Contingency Approach to Planning: Planning with Goals and Planning without Goals," *Academy of Management Journal,* Vol. 17, No. 2 (June 1974), pp. 281–291.

TABLE 5-2
Contrast between
Planning with
Goals and
Directional
Planning

Planning with Goals	Directional Planning
Characteristics	
Teleological, directed toward external goals	Directional, moving from internal preferences
Goals are specific and measurable	Domain is sometimes hard to define
Rational, analytic	Intuitive, use unquantifiable elements
Focused, narrowed perception of task	Broad perception of task
Lower requirements to process novel information	Greater need to process novel information
More efficient use of energy	Possible redundancy, false leads
Separate planning and acting phases	Planning and acting not separate phases
Contingent upon	
People who prefer well-defined tasks	People who prefer variety, change, and complexity
Tasks and industries that are quantifiable and relatively stable	Tasks and industries not amenable to quantification and that are rapidly changing
Mechanistic organization forms, "closed" systems	Organic organization forms, "open" systems
"Tightening up the ship" phase of a project	"Unfreezing" phase of a project

Source: Michael B. McCaskey, "A Contingency Approach to Planning: Planning with Goals and Planning without Goals," *Academy of Management Journal,* Vol. 17, No. 2 (June 1974), p. 290. Used by permission.

The Need for the Formal Approach to Planning

Regardless of the type of planning actually used by managers, there is evidence that a formal, step-by-step, long-range approach to the planning process is more effective than a short-term informal approach. Using a sample of 36 firms drawn from six industries, Stanley S. Thune and Robert J. House found that companies that adopted formal, long-range planning procedures consistently outperformed companies that confined themselves to informal planning. The advantage of formal strategic planning was most evident in industries where the environment was rapidly changing (such as the drug and the machinery industries). Managers in such industries had to chart their course carefully to help their organizations survive and grow.[9] (See Figure 5-2 on the next page.)

In a follow-up study, David M. Herold collected additional information on

[9] Stanley S. Thune and Robert J. House, "Where Long-Range Planning Pays Off, *Business Horizons,* Vol. 13, No. 4 (August 1970), pp. 81–87. See also H. Igor Ansoff et al., "Does Planning Pay?" *Long-Range Planning,* Vol. 3, No. 2 (December 1970), pp. 2–7.

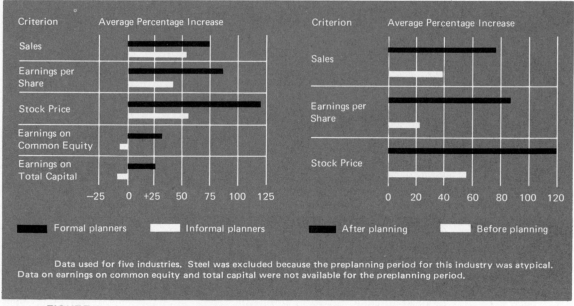

FIGURE 5-2 Performance of Formal and Informal Planners during Planning Period (left) Performance of Companies before and after Formal Planning (right)

Source: Stanley S. Thune and Robert J. House, "Where Long-Range Planning Pays Off," *Business Horizons*, Vol. 13, No. 4 (August 1970), p. 83. Copyright 1970 by the Foundation for the School of Business at Indiana University. Reprinted by permission.

the same firms. His findings supported the original study by Thune and House: formal planners had higher sales and profits than informal planners.[10]

The experience of these organizations suggests that the formal planning approach has become more important to managers. The environment of today's organizations has become less predictable. In an atmosphere of uncertainty, managers are more likely to make a wrong decision. And the costs of wrong decisions have risen: overhead costs have gone up; raw materials, machinery, and personnel have become more expensive; and competition has become more intense. It appears that managers who take the time and effort to plan carefully and logically are more likely to be successful. And organizations whose managers engage in formal planning are likely to be better prepared for the future.

THE FORMAL PLANNING APPROACH

In this section we will describe the formal approach to strategic planning. We will use an approach suggested by many management writers and try to explain how managers should execute the planning process so that their plans will

[10]David M. Herold, "Long-Range Planning and Organizational Performance," *Academy of Management Journal,* Vol. 15, No. 1 (March 1972), pp. 91–102.

be effective.[11] Readers should keep in mind that the process we describe applies mainly to large or complex organizations. Smaller organizations can simplify considerably their strategic planning approach.

Step 1: Select the Goals

Setting the goals of the organization is the most critical step in the strategic planning process. The goals selected will take up a large amount of the organization's resources and will govern many of its activities for a considerable length of time. For this reason, strategic goals are most often set by upper-level or top managers, usually after a number of possible goals have been carefully considered.

There are many types of goals managers can select: a desired sales volume or growth rate, the development of a new product or service, or even a more abstract goal such as becoming more active in the community. The type of goal selected will depend on a number of factors: the basic mission of the organization, the values its managers hold, and the strengths and weaknesses of the organization.

The mission of the organization, as we have already suggested, can take managers a long way toward deciding what goals they will pursue. For example, AT&T's visionary mission some seventy years ago was described by a recent former chairman in this way: "The dream of good, cheap, fast, worldwide telephone service . . . is not a speculation. It is a perfectly clear statement that you're going to do something."[12] Before deciding what their goals are going to be, managers must know the purpose and mission of their organization.

The values held by managers will also affect the kind of goals they select.[13] These values may involve social or ethical issues, or they may involve neutral areas, such as the size they would like their organization to be, the kind of product or service they would like to produce, or simply the way they prefer to operate as managers. They may be greatly influenced by aesthetic values, and so may seek improvements in the design of their corporation's products— even if this entails a lower rate of profit. Conversely, if they are motivated by a desire for economic growth, they may wish to maximize profit at the expense of design. Managers who consciously seek a better understanding of their own

---

[11] See, for example, Steiner, *Top Management Planning,* pp. 31–37, and especially J. Kalman Cohen and Richard M. Cyert, "Strategy: Formulation, Implementation, and Monitoring," *Journal of Business,* Vol. 46, No. 3 (1973), pp. 349–367, for the step-by-step approach used here. For other approaches to strategic planning, see F. T. Haner, *Business Policy, Planning, and Strategy* (Cambridge, Mass.: Winthrop, 1976), and Frank T. Paine and William Naumes, *Strategy and Policy Formation: An Integrative Approach* (Philadelphia: W. B. Saunders, 1974).

[12] Quoted in Charles H. Granger, "The Hierarchy of Objectives," *Harvard Business Review,* May-June 1964, p. 70.

[13] See William D. Guth and Renato Tagiuri, "Personal Values and Corporate Strategy," *Harvard Business Review,* September-October 1965, pp. 123–132. See also Bernard Taylor, "Conflict of Values—the Central Strategy Problem," *Long-Range Planning,* Vol. 8, No. 6 (December 1975), pp. 20–24. Taylor suggests that a clash between the goals and values of business and those of society is changing planning from an internal process concerning managers to an "open debate involving public servants, employees, and self-appointed representatives of community interests."

123

"Dear Shareholder: The planetary vibrations this quarter were directed toward partnership association. As a result we are happy to announce the acquisition of Croghan Industries as a wholly owned subsidiary. Mars was adverse in the fourth house from the twenty-third to the thirtieth so we have avoided legal matters and thus have nothing to report on the pending Briggs suit this quarter. Certain days were favorable for following hunches so your management is pleased to announce the following new members to the board."

Copyright © 1976. Reprinted by permission of *Saturday Review* and Henry Martin.

and their associates' values will find themselves setting goals that provide more effective guidance for their organizations.

The setting of goals is a major step in the strategic planning process. For this reason, it is important to assess correctly the strengths and weaknesses of the organization before selecting its goals.[14] In making this assessment, the obvious question to ask is, Can we realistically expect to achieve our goals, considering the talent, resources, *and* limitations of our organization?

This kind of self-examination becomes especially important when com-

---

[14] See William D. Guth, "Formulating Organizational Objectives and Strategy: A Systematic Approach," *Journal of Business Policy,* Vol. 2, No. 1 (Autumn 1971), pp. 24–31.

petitors are trying to achieve the same goals we are. In such a case, the organization that is most suited for the particular goal will be more likely to succeed. Some years ago, for example, Union Carbide decided to develop a synthetic leather similar to Du Pont's Corfam. Market research established that there was a demand for such a product; Union Carbide had enough capital to invest; and the firm had access to the shoe and leather industries, which would most need the new synthetic. Nevertheless, Union Carbide sustained a large loss in developing the product, because it had overlooked an internal weakness: it did not have the technical capability to find a profitable way of producing the synthetic. Had the company examined its strengths and weaknesses more carefully *before* trying to develop the synthetic, the loss might have been avoided.

Step 2:
Analyze the
Environment

In selecting goals, managers must also consider the problems and opportunities presented by the environment.[15] This is a crucial step, because, whatever the goals may be, they will in some way be affected by factors outside the organization. (See Chapter 3 for an extensive discussion of this topic.) It would normally be unrealistic, for example, to plan for rapid expansion of a company in a period of economic stagnation. Similarly, it would obviously be unwise to plan to introduce a new product—even if the organization is ideally suited to produce the product—if there is no demand for it. For this reason, managers try to analyze or forecast the environment (through market research, for example) so that they will be able to judge how feasible or attainable their goals are.[16] (See Figure 5-3.)

FIGURE 5-3
Basic Foundations
for the Strategic
Planning Process

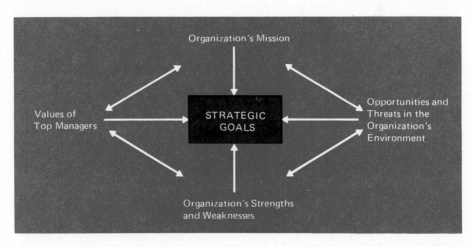

---

[15] See Carl R. Anderson and Frank T. Paine, "Managerial Perceptions and Strategic Behavior," *Academy of Management Journal,* Vol. 18, No. 4 (1975), pp. 811–823.

[16] See, for example, Ian H. Wilson, "Futures Forecasting for Strategic Planning at General Electric," *Long-Range Planning,* Vol. 6, No. 2 (June 1973), pp. 39–42.

Step 3:
Establish
Measurable
Goals

We have stated that goals can be as specific as a desired rate of growth or as general as a commitment to be more active in the community. Regardless of the type of goal selected, however, it will be most effectively met if it is spelled out in precise, measurable terms.

There are several reasons for this:

1   The more precise the goal, the easier it is to decide how to achieve it. For example, the goal of "becoming more active in the community" leaves managers in doubt as to how to proceed. If, instead, managers select as their goal "the creation of four hiring offices in the community over the next three years," they have described their goal in much more meaningful terms.

2   Specific goals are better motivators of people than general goals. Members of the organization will be much more willing to work to achieve goals when they understand exactly what they are.

3   Precise, measurable goals make it easier for lower-level managers to develop their own plans for actually achieving those goals. For example, if a general manager is aiming for a 15 percent growth rate over the next four years, the sales manager can determine how sales must increase in order to meet this goal.

4   It is easier for managers to establish whether they are succeeding or failing if their goals are precise and measurable. For example, if they are aiming for a profit of $1.5 million over the next two years, they can check their progress as profit and loss figures come in. They would then be in a better position to take whatever corrective action may be necessary to help them meet their goal.

Step 4:
Subunits Develop
Their Own Plans

Once upper-level management tentatively selects and states its basic, long-term goals, lower-level managers in turn must decide what their own subunits will do to help meet these goals. Planning by lower-level managers is necessary, because only in the simplest organizations will top management be able to produce detailed plans for all subunits. In addition, lower-level managers will do a better job of implementing the strategic plan if they have contributed to it.

In developing their own plans, lower-level managers take steps similar to those taken by upper-level managers: selecting realistic goals, assessing their subunit's particular strengths and weaknesses, and analyzing those parts of the environment that can affect them. For example, to meet top management's desire to expand the facilities of a university, the chairman of the economics department must decide how many new instructors can be hired, what these instructors' specialties should be, and whether or not there will be federal funding for new programs.

Step 5:
Compare Lower-
Level Plans with
the Strategic Plan

When lower-level managers have formulated their plans, they send these plans up the organizational hierarchy to middle and upper-level managers for review and approval. Usually, the plans for subunits in a particular division are integrated and made part of an overall plan for the division. Whether at the division level or the top management level, the plans are examined to see how close to or far from the original strategic goals they are. For example, if the strategic plan calls for $1.5 million profit in three years, the profit goals for each subunit are added together to see if they reach that figure. If they do not reach the $1.5 million figure, then a gap exists between the organization's goals and what it actually expects to achieve.

Step 6:
Close the Gap

If there is a gap between the goals of the overall strategic plan and those of the organization's subunits, new changes in the strategic plan must be made. A properly drawn-up plan — that is, a plan with sufficient flexibility (see Chapter 4) — rarely has to be completely scrapped. Instead, managers usually have to develop several new alternatives to make the original plan workable.

The most logical area to develop these alternatives is inside the organization. For example, if a desired profit level is part of the strategic plan, lower-level managers could be asked to suggest ways for cutting costs. A price cut for the organization's products can be considered in the hopes of increasing sales and revenues. Perhaps some aspect of the original plan's timetable could be speeded up, in order to reduce overhead costs or introduce a new product to the market earlier. Managers can usually establish a variety of alternatives from within the organization to help it achieve its long-term goals.

To help make the strategic plan feasible, managers can also look outside the organization. For example, if more money than originally anticipated is needed for expansion, managers might try to find new sources of financing. If managers want the organization to enter a new market area, but the expected development costs are too high, an established company in the new market could be acquired. If the organization has insufficient technical ability in a key area, people with the desired technical knowledge can be hired. Again, managers develop a variety of alternatives to close the gap between the goals they desire and the present capabilities of their organization.

Step 7:
Select the Best
Alternatives

While managers will develop any number of alternatives to help make their strategy feasible, not all these alternatives will become part of the strategic plan. There are several reasons for this. First, not all the alternatives will be necessary. If the original strategic plan called for profits of $1.5 million, and the lower-level plans of the organization indicate that just a $1.2 million profit is possible, managers need select only as many alternatives as it takes to close the $.3 million gap. Second, some of the alternatives might be inappropriate for the organization. For example, a company that already has a large debt but that needs to raise additional revenues may be unable to obtain a loan. It will have to consider other ways of increasing revenues (or reducing costs). Finally, managers may find some alternatives preferable to others. For example, let us assume a company needs to obtain additional technical ability before it can carry out its plan to computerize its operations. It may prefer to hire a team of technical consultants for a short period of time, rather than hire a permanent full-time staff of computer specialists.

Managers will have to select the best alternatives from among all those they have developed — deciding which alternatives will help "close the gap" most efficiently and effectively and which alternatives will be best suited for them and their organization. The alternatives they finally select then become part of the revised strategic plan.

Step 8: Implement the Strategic Plan

Once the final strategic plan has been formulated, its broad goals must be translated into the detailed day-to-day operations of the organization. Middle and lower-level managers must draw up the appropriate plans, programs, and budgets for their subunits. (See Figure 5-4.)

Let us assume, for example, that we have developed a strategic plan that calls for our organization to introduce a new line of products in ten years. The personnel department might have to develop a short-term hiring program. The marketing department might have to make up a short-term budget for the first year of the plan—perhaps to begin preliminary market testing for new product concepts. The research and development department might develop a preliminary set of plans to cover the entire period of the strategic plan—for example, setting-up and basic research to take place the first two years, additional research to occur the next three years, testing and evaluation to take place the next three years, ending with final testing and modification of the new product line. The production department may plan preliminary cost estimates during the early stage of the strategic plan, and become more actively involved as the new products achieve final form in the R&D department.

In short, our total strategic plan will be translated into a series of closely meshed "subplans" by the appropriate divisions and subunits of our organization. Each subplan will reflect the particular subunit producing it—the personnel department's plan may be a simple, short-term one, while the plan by

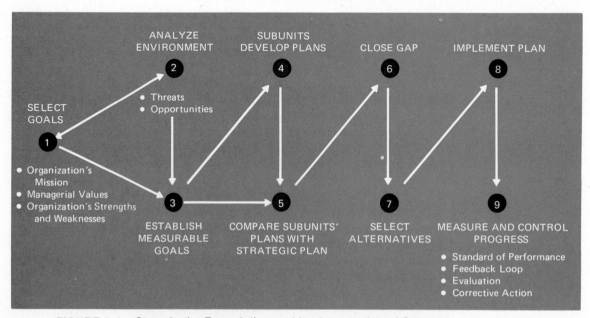

FIGURE 5-4   Steps in the Formulation and Implementation of Strategy

the R&D department may be complex and long-term, involving a considerable amount of our organization's resources. Nevertheless, each plan and each subunit will play its assigned role in achieving our organization's overall strategic goals.

Step 9:
Measure and
Control the
Progress of
the Plan

As we have already indicated in previous chapters, the process of *controlling* is a critical part of any plan. Managers need to check the progress of their plans so that they can (1) take whatever remedial action is necessary to make the plan work or (2) change the original plan if it is unrealistic. Obviously, it is foolish to let a plan run its course without monitoring its progress, since a bad plan or a plan that has gone off course can prove extremely costly and even threaten the survival of an organization.

There are four basic elements to a sound control system: the standard of performance, the feedback loop, evaluation, and corrective action.

The Standard of Performance. These are the benchmarks against which the progress of a plan can be measured. In a three-year plan to increase profits to $2 million annually, the standard of performance might be $800 thousand profit the first year and $1.4 million the second year. If profits for any of these years are lower than planned, managers would review their operations to see why revenues are too low or expenses too high. They would then revise their methods or goals accordingly.

Most strategic plans, at least in their preliminary stages, use budgets as standards of performance rather than profit and loss statements. This is because strategic plans usually involve considerable start-up costs or investment at the beginning, and do not show a profit until fairly late in the time period covered by the plan. Thus, if the budget for a certain subunit or period is exceeded, the manager tries to discover what the cause of the cost overrun might be.

Sometimes even the budget does not provide an adequate standard of performance. This is because a plan can be on budget and still be off course or misguided—for example, the development of a new product may be proceeding smoothly, but the demand for it may have declined. In such cases managers try to use a variety of benchmarks to measure the progress of the plan. For example, they may insist that market surveys be updated to determine if the demand for the new product is still strong.

The Feedback Loop. In order for the control process to be meaningful and effective, there must be a free flow of information between managers and their operating units. Managers must receive feedback from subordinates whenever a significant deviation from the plan occurs. (We say "significant," because if every minor deviation is reported to managers they will soon get bogged down in trivia.) In turn, managers must help subordinates find ways to get the plan back on track.

People often find it difficult to admit that something they are working on is not proceeding according to plan. For this reason, managers need to maintain an open, uncritical atmosphere so that subordinates will be willing to come to them if something goes wrong. In addition, managers can formalize the feedback process (and so make it less threatening) by requiring periodic schedule updates or written reports.

Evaluation. As information is received, managers must evaluate it to see if some corrective action should be taken. No plan is perfect, so some deviation from the plan is bound to occur. Managers must decide how great a deviation can be tolerated for what length of time.

Corrective Action. If deviation from the plan is significant enough, managers must decide what action is necessary to bring the plan back on course. Often, a manager's course of action will be suggested by contingency plans that have been drawn up along with the basic strategic plan. For example, if sales of a new product are less than expected, contingency plans will usually exist for cutting prices to increase sales, increasing the advertising budget, or simply revising the original sales estimate.

Perhaps the greatest danger a manager must face when presented with a severe problem in the plan is the temptation to scrap the plan completely. This is sometimes the correct action to take, but more often than not it is simply the easiest action to take. It takes confidence in one's original plan, persistence, and perhaps some courage to try to iron out the problems that a plan has run into and make it work.

One word of caution: We have simplified our description of the formal strategic planning process in order to make it easier to understand. In practice, the neat and orderly step-by-step approach we have indicated here is a rarity. Planning is a continuous process, and the outside world changes constantly. Most managers and organizations are engaged in any number of planning steps at the same time.

THE PLACE OF STRATEGIC PLANNING IN ORGANIZATIONS

Organizations differ in their approach to strategic planning.[17] For example, smaller companies are likely to use a less formal approach. Managers might communicate their strategic plans verbally, instead of writing them down. Top and lower-level managers might meet informally to select goals and methods of operation without elaborate, systematic review. In larger organizations, on the other hand, the strategic process is likely to be much more formalized. In fact, the larger the organization, the more likely it is to have a specialized staff responsible for the planning process.

[17] Much of the discussion in this section is based on Steiner, *Top Management Planning,* pp. 108–121.

There are several factors that will affect the way an organization structures its planning activities:

1 *The size of the organization.* As we have already suggested, larger organizations will tend to have a carefully structured and professionally staffed planning department.

2 *Centralized or decentralized management.* In a centrally controlled organization, such as a chain of supermarkets directed from office headquarters, strategic goals will be set by top management. Planning directives will flow down the organizational hierarchy to middle and lower-level managers. In a decentralized organization, such as a company with separate divisions producing different products, planning authority may be more diffuse. Divisional managers or their planning staffs may set the strategic goals for their division. They may then work together with the central planning authority of the organization to help set its overall strategic goals.

3 *The nature of the product.* The planning structure of an organization will also vary with the goods or services it produces. For example, in the meat-packing industry a formal, long-term forecasting capability may not be crucial. Consumer habits and distribution channels in the industry are fairly predictable from year to year. In an oil company, on the other hand, all aspects of the formal planning process are probably essential. The oil industry is involved with huge investments, rapidly changing market conditions, and long-term technological development; a planning error could have severe financial implications.

4 *The personality of top executives.* Executives who like to work independently may want to avoid hiring a separate planning staff. Instead, they may do their own planning with the aid of assistants and specialists. Other executives may prefer to use a separate planning division or to have division managers assume planning responsibility.

The Role of the Planning Staff

As organizations grow, they often find that a formally staffed planning department becomes a necessity. Large organizations are usually too complex for their managers to be able to plan without the help of a planning staff. In addition, large organizations tend to be involved in long-term projects that require a considerable investment of time and resources. The careful and complete planning a special planning staff can provide gives such projects a greater likelihood of success. Finally, large organizations usually have the stability and resources needed to set up a planning staff. An effective planning group cannot be established quickly or easily. For example, it may take from five to eight years to develop fully a formal planning staff in a corporation. (See Table 5-3 on next page.) Only an organization with enough time and money can afford to make the commitment a formal planning staff requires.[18]

The Responsibilities of the Planning Staff. The primary responsibility of the planning staff is to help top managers formulate their strategies and goals.

[18] See Erwin von Allman, "Setting Up Corporate Planning," in Bernard Taylor and Kevin Hawkins, eds., *A Handbook of Strategic Planning* (London: Longman, 1972), pp. 34–47. See also R. Hal Mason, "Developing a Planning Organization," *Business Horizons,* Vol. 12, No. 4 (August 1969), pp. 61–69; E. Kirby Warren, *Long-Range Planning: The Executive Viewpoint* (Englewood Cliffs, N.J.: Prentice-Hall, 1966); and Rudolph W. Knoeppel, "The Politics of Planning," *Long-Range Planning,* Vol. 6, No. 1 (March 1973), pp. 17–21.

TABLE 5-3
The Time
Sequence of
Planning
Organization

Phase	Action	Time Span	Total Elapsed Time
I	Establish executive planning committee	6–12 months	6–12 months
II	Select director of planning and provide *ad hoc* staff committee	About 12 months	18–24 months
III	Director develops permanent planning staff at corporate level; division planning committees added	12–36 months	30–60 months
IV	Appoint vice president of planning and corporate development reporting to president and executive planning committee; select division planning coordinator	12–24 months	42–72 months
V	Specialize corporate development, planning, and evaluation functions; provide division planning staffs reporting to division heads but with relationship to corporate development and planning department	12–36 months and beyond	60–108 months

Source: R. Hal Mason, "Developing a Planning Organization," *Business Horizons,* Vol. 12, No. 4 (August 1969), p. 62. Copyright 1969 by the Foundation for the School of Business at Indiana University. Reprinted by permission.

Usually the planning staff does this by constantly monitoring, through surveys and research, those factors that are likely to affect the organization. For example, the planning staff will try to monitor and forecast the changing needs of the organization's customers, the shifts in the organization's economic environment, advances in technology that can affect the organization, and the development of new market opportunities for the organization. In light of the information it gathers, the planning staff will recommend appropriate strategies and goals to top managers. The planning staff may also evaluate the strategies and goals that top managers propose.[19]

The second major responsibility of the planning staff is to coordinate the planning efforts of the organization. As we described earlier, once top-level strategic plans have been made, lower-level managers are asked to make up plans for their own subunits to help top managers achieve their goals. It is the

[19] See Seymour Tilles, "How to Evaluate Corporate Strategy," *Harvard Business Review,* July-August 1963, pp. 111–121. Tilles suggests six criteria for the evaluation of strategy: internal consistency, consistency with the environment, appropriateness in the light of available resources, satisfactory degree of risk, appropriate time horizon, and workability.

planning staff that provides lower-level managers with the background information they will need to make up their plans, such as the organizational resources each lower-level manager can count on.

Once lower-level managers complete their plans, they send them to higher-level managers for review. The planning staff then goes over these plans and compares them with the strategic plan. If gaps exist, the planning staff works with top and lower-level managers to find ways the gaps can be closed.

The final major responsibility of the planning staff is to help divisional managers who are inexperienced with formal, long-term planning develop such plans for their divisions. This usually occurs when a new division has been created or acquired by the organization.

Strategic Planning in Large, Diversified Companies

Richard J. Vancil and Peter Lorange have described how strategic planning takes place in a large, diversified, multinational corporation.[20] Their analysis broadens our understanding and provides a useful review of the strategic planning process.

The Three Levels of Strategy Making. The strategy of an organization emerges from the interaction of managers at three levels of the organization: top-level corporate managers (including the planning staff), division-level general managers, and functional managers within each division.

Top-level managers establish, with the aid of the planning staff, overall strategies and goals for the entire corporation. They decide what resources the organization will need to make their strategies feasible and how these resources will be allocated among the various divisions. For example, the head of a transportation firm may aim for a rapid increase in sales and profits over a three-year period. The head may decide that the company should concentrate its major efforts in its automobile division.

Within the framework of the overall strategic plan, middle-level managers formulate the strategies and goals for their divisions. They decide how the resources of the division will be used to help the organization achieve its goals. The head of the automobile division, for example, may decide that a major effort to increase the production and sale of compact cars would result in the largest profits for the division.

The lower-level functional managers of the division (frequently called department heads) develop action programs to meet the goals of their division. Each department head decides what the objectives of the department will be, what actions will be taken to reach these objectives, and what the timing and sequence of the actions will be. For example, the production head for the compact car line may establish tentative cost estimates for the raw materials needed, set up a series of meetings with potential suppliers, and make up a preliminary production schedule for a one-year period.

[20] Richard F. Vancil and Peter Lorange, "Strategic Planning in Diversified Companies," *Harvard Business Review,* January-February 1975, pp. 81–90.

FIGURE 5-5   Steps in the Planning Process in a Large, Diversified Company

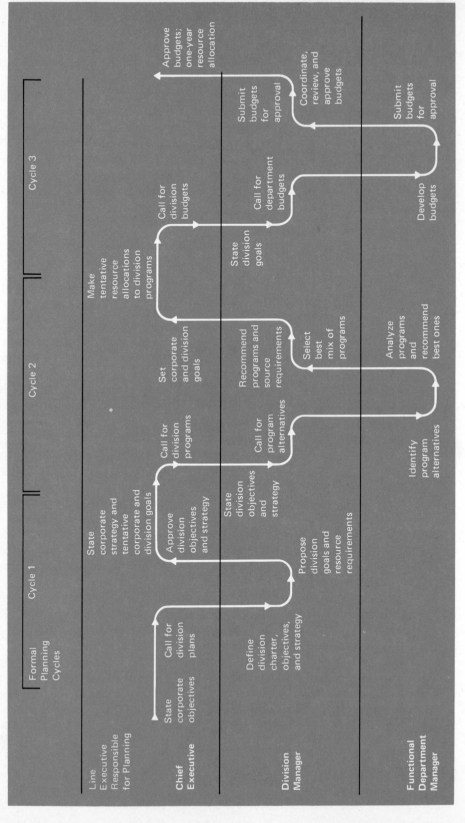

Source: Richard F. Vancil and Peter Lorange, "Strategic Planning in Diversified Companies," *Harvard Business Review*, January–February 1975, pp. 84–85. Copyright © 1974 by the President and Fellows of Harvard College; all rights reserved.

The Three Cycles of Corporate Strategic Planning. As managers in an organization, we would not develop our strategies and plans in isolation. We would constantly interact with our colleagues above and below us in the hierarchy — asking that plans be drawn up, offering plans for review, and approving the strategies and goals that have been established.

The activities of managers involved in the planning process can be divided into three cycles. During the *first cycle,* corporate executives and division managers meet to select tentatively the strategic goals of the organization. In addition, the responsibilities of each division for meeting these goals are broadly outlined. Functional managers will play a minor role during this cycle. They may, however, be called in on an informal basis — if, for example, the division manager wants to make sure that a certain goal is practical.

Functional managers play a much more important role during the *second cycle.* First, they meet with their division managers to develop preliminary strategies and objectives for their departments. During this process, they will be working under the constraints imposed by the divisional plan. For example, they will know approximately how much money will be available to them, and so their own plans will not be able to exceed this amount. Within these limits, however, they will still suggest a variety of ways their departments can help the division meet its goals. The production head of the compact car line, for instance, might suggest increasing overtime or hiring new workers as ways production can be stepped up. Offering division managers a number of alternatives is one of the most important contributions that functional managers can make to the planning process.

Once several possible strategies have been selected, functional managers must draw up *formal* action programs for carrying them out. It would be impossible to review and evaluate informal programs in a large company, with its many departments. Formalizing action programs also makes it easier to decide whether or not they can actually be carried out.

In the *third cycle,* the resources of the organization are finally allocated. Division managers are asked to draw up budgets for their divisions; functional managers are asked to draw up budgets for their departments. Usually the budget-approval process is not as structured as the process of selecting strategies and goals. The amount of money received will depend not only on the managers' actual needs but also on their persuasiveness and political influence within the company. (See Figure 5-5.)

Budgets usually cover a one-year period. Normally, a shorter budget span would be inconvenient, while a longer span would not allow for a timely review of the organization's progress.

THE DISADVANTAGES AND ADVANTAGES OF STRATEGIC PLANNING

Now that we have discussed the strategic planning process, we can better analyze its drawbacks and advantages.[21] It is important for us to be aware of the problems and opportunities strategic planning can create, since we may

[21] See Ansoff, *Corporate Strategy,* pp. 113–115.

eventually have to decide whether or not to use strategic planning in our organizations.

<table>
<tr><td>

The
Disadvantages

</td><td>

As might already be evident, the major disadvantage of strategic planning is that it requires a considerable investment in time, money, and people. It may take years before the planning process in an organization begins to function smoothly. Sometimes planning decisions are deferred until review and evaluation have been completed. This can result in lost opportunities for the organization. There are also many expenses involved in strategic planning. For example, there are start-up costs, such as the expense of hiring new people and renting new office space, the costs of market research, surveys, and model building that often involves expensive data processing activities. In addition, there are the training and salary costs of planners. For these reasons, smaller organizations are usually unable to afford a formal strategic planning program.

</td></tr>
</table>

Another disadvantage of strategic planning is that it sometimes tends to restrict the organization to the most rational and risk-free opportunities. Managers might wish to develop only those strategies and goals that could survive the detailed analysis of strategic planning. Attractive opportunities that involve high degrees of uncertainty or are difficult to analyze might be avoided or overlooked.

The Advantages The major advantage of strategic planning is that it provides consistent guidelines for the organization's activities. By using strategic planning, managers give their organizations clearly defined goals and methods for achieving these goals. Thus, their organizations have purpose and direction. In addition, managers do not have to let problems and opportunities overtake them. Instead, they can try to anticipate problems before they arise and can actively seek ways to help their organizations develop and grow.

Another important advantage of strategic planning is that it helps managers make decisions. Sometimes opportunities that seem too risky might in fact be quite feasible. At other times, opportunities that seem quite safe might in fact prove disastrous to the organization. Without strategic planning, managers would have a difficult time discovering the pertinent facts in each case. The careful analysis provided by strategic planning gives managers more of the information they need to make good decisions.

Strategic planning also minimizes the chance of mistakes and bad surprises, because strategies and goals are analyzed several times. They are therefore less likely to be faulty or unworkable. In addition, strategic planning helps managers anticipate future events (through environmental analysis and forecasting, for example). Managers who use strategic planning are, therefore, more likely than others to adapt successfully to change.

The advantages provided by strategic planning are particularly important in organizations where there is a long time period between a manager's decision and its results. For example, in a manufacturing company, there is often a considerable delay between the decision to manufacture a product and the moment the first product rolls off the assembly line. Research, development, and the process of setting up production facilities may take years. Many events can occur during this intervening period to nullify the effectiveness of the manager's original decision. Through strategic planning, managers can increase their chances of making decisions that will stand the test of time.

Summary   Strategic planning has become more important to managers in recent years. Defining the mission of their organizations in specific terms has made it easier for managers to give their organizations a sense of purpose. In addition, the changing environment of organizations has pointed up the importance of preparing more carefully for the future.

To devise a correct strategy, managers must first find the "common thread" of their organizations. What should the business of the organization be? What are the needs of its customers? In what direction is the organization heading? By asking such questions, managers can determine the true capabilities of their organizations and devise the most effective strategies.

There are several modes and types of strategic planning managers can use. Each is best suited to a particular organization or situation. However, studies have suggested that the formal approach is more effective than the informal approach.

In the formal strategic planning approach, managers (1) select their goals, (2) analyze the environment of their organizations, (3) establish measurable goals so that their goals will be easy to work with, (4) ask subunits to develop their own plans to help meet the strategic goals, (5) compare subunits' plans with the strategic plan to see if a gap exists, (6) close the gap by developing alternatives inside and outside the organization, (7) select the best alternatives, (8) implement the strategic plan, and (9) evaluate the progress of the plan to see if any action is needed to make it work.

These basic steps in the formal planning approach are likely to be structured differently in various types of organizations. Large organizations, for example, are likely to use a specialized planning staff to formulate strategies and goals and to coordinate the other planning activities of the organization. Smaller organizations are unlikely to have a formal planning staff.

In large organizations the formal planning process usually moves through three cycles. In the first cycle, top managers meet with division managers to select tentative strategies and goals. During the second cycle, functional managers meet with division managers to develop goals and formal action programs for their departments. In the third cycle, budgets are drawn up and approved and the resources of the organization are finally allocated.

Review Questions   1. Why do you think it is important for you to understand strategic planning?

2. Why has strategic planning become important to managers and their organizations?

3. How can managers find the "common thread" of their organizations? Why do you think finding the common thread will help them devise correct strategies?

4. What are the entrepreneurial, adaptive, and planning modes of strategy making? Under what conditions might each mode be used? Which mode is most appealing to you?

5. What is the difference between planning with specific goals and directional planning?

6. What are the nine steps in the formal planning approach?

7. How might your own values affect the kinds of goals you select for your organization?

8. Why do you think it is important that managers establish measurable goals for their organizations?

9. What are the four basic elements in a manager's control system?
10. What factors might affect the way an organization structures its planning activities?
11. Describe the responsibilities of a planning staff.
12. What are the three cycles of strategic planning in a large corporation? Describe the role of managers at each level of the organization during each cycle.
13. What do you think are the advantages and disadvantages of strategic planning?

CASE STUDY: TAPPAN ZEE TIN CONTAINER COMPANY

The Tappan Zee Tin Container Company is a small, family owned manufacturer of decorative tin boxes used by specialty tea packing companies. The Tappan Zee tins are made in five basic shapes and are printed in bright designs according to the tea companies' needs. The same size and shape container, then, can be printed to order and will serve for any number of customers.

The operation employs few people. The draftsmen make the design according to customer specifications and prepare it for the printers. The operators of the printing presses print large tin sheets with the design. These sheets are then cut and bent into shape by other machines, and the finished tins are packed into cardboard boxes for shipment to the tea companies.

Most of Tappan Zee's customers are small, regional herbal tea packers whose varying output prohibits them from ordering tins from large container companies. The normal order ranges in size from 1,000 to 5,000 tins.

A few months ago one of the tea companies asked Tappan Zee if they could print a decorative box and attach a removable label so that the buyers of the herbal teas could reuse the boxes when the tea was used up.

The suggestion made Voss Winkler, president of Tappan Zee Tin Container, look into the possibility of selling empty, unlabeled, decorative tin boxes to the general public. He reasoned that if his bright boxes helped sell tea, the boxes themselves might be salable items. Tappan Zee could save money by printing much larger quantities of a single design than they had for the tea companies. They should be able to sell more boxes by making them available to the general public, rather than to just a few small tea packers. They could probably also get more money per container, Voss imagined. He didn't think the extra costs would be too high, and even so, they would be covered by the extra profits.

The problem did not seem insurmountable to him, either. He foresaw only two at the moment. First, Tappan Zee Tin had never sold on a retail or wholesale level to a general market. Their business was always to the tea companies, and the tea companies had sought out Tappan Zee Tin. As a result, Tappan Zee Tin had not advertised or used salesmen for the past thirty or forty years. The second problem was what sort of design to use. All previous work had been dictated by the customer. Tappan Zee Tin had no idea of the kind of design to put on an empty tin box.

Hubert Van Kant, the bookkeeper, pointed out to Mr. Winkler that although the cost of manufacture could probably be made up in the profits, he was not so sure about the extra costs of salespeople. If Mr. Winkler wanted to stay mostly in the local area, Mr. Van Kant thought that maybe one salesperson could cover the stores that might sell the box, even though Mr. Van Kant admitted he was not certain what type of store would sell them.

Mr. Winkler's niece had joined the firm eight months ago after graduating from business school. She felt that it was silly to stay small, local, and unknown. She said that the way to make real profits was through mass distribution. The costs would be much, much higher, but the returns, she felt sure, would be astronomical and would spread the name of Tappan Zee Tin Container Company. She assured her uncle that a simple market survey would help them decide what type of design to print.

Case Questions

1. In what area does Tappan Zee's expertise lie?
2. What information should Voss Winkler try to obtain to find out if his idea is feasible? How can this information be located?
3. What are the extra costs involved in marketing the empty containers?
4. What problems are possible if Tappan Zee goes nationwide?
5. What sort of retail outlets should be chosen?
6. What designs might be selected?
7. How might this proposed change affect Tappan Zee's relationship with the tea packers?
8. How should Voss Winkler react to his niece's assurances?

6

Making Planning Effective

Upon completing this chapter you should be able to:

1. State why some managers are reluctant to plan or resist carrying out planned activities.

2. Describe how the barriers to planning can be reduced or eliminated.

3. Identify the obstacles to the use and implementation of strategic plans.

4. Explain the concept of management by objectives (MBO).

5. Describe the assumptions that underlie management by objectives and how they differ from traditional assumptions about how people are motivated to work.

6. Identify the common elements of effective management by objectives programs.

7. State the strengths and weaknesses of management by objectives, and describe how the weaknesses can be overcome.

After many years of success as a supplier to basic processing industries, Ento International[1] began to see that its future profitability was being threatened. New steel industry processes were slowing the growth of demand for Ento's products, and it was widely believed that present developments in the aluminum industry would soon have a similar effect.

Ento's top managers watched these developments with growing concern and finally concluded that the company could no longer afford the luxury of concentrating only on production improvements. They decided that what Ento needed in order to prepare for a less certain future was a formal strategic planning program.

Ento's management made what it considered a good start on the program. They created a central planning department to develop the planning system and put the executive vice president in charge. The vice president hired a prestigious consulting firm, and with its help the planning department staff was soon hard at work on Ento's first strategic plan. Planning procedures recommended by the consultants were adopted, and guidelines were issued to the company's divisional managers for gathering planning data. The department also developed sophisticated mathematical techniques to help in analyzing and evaluating alternatives and instructed the divisional managers in their use. Each manager was also given a planning manual with step-by-step instructions for producing a long-range plan for his or her division.

All this activity kept a lot of people busy, and top management was at first very impressed. However, after two years it became clear that strategic planning was not succeeding in clearing up some of Ento's major problems. Sales and profits had not improved, and the implementation of the long-range plan had not been effective. Furthermore, people throughout the organization were frustrated about having to complete complex forms and carry out elaborate procedures as part of the planning activities each year.

What went wrong at Ento International? We will find the specific answer later in this chapter, when we discuss how some of the people involved missed some of the basic principles of planning. For the moment let us focus on the broad question that this case suggests: How can organizations make their planning effective (or more effective)? How can managers implement their plans so that they will get the results they want and, at the same time, make that implementation as efficient, easy, and cost-free as possible?

We will begin by recognizing that there are typical problems that arise when managers develop or try to implement plans. Those problems become barriers to effective planning when managers do not recognize them or cannot overcome them. In the first section of this chapter, we will briefly discuss those barriers that apply to all types of planning. In the second part, we will deal in greater detail with the barriers to strategic planning. Of course, most of the statements that refer to planning in general will also apply to strategic planning.

In the last section of this chapter, we will discuss one popular and well-

[1] This case appears in Kjell A. Ringbakk, "Why Planning Fails," *European Business*, Spring 1971, pp. 15–27.

known approach to planning that can be used to overcome some of the barriers to planning and to make plans effective. This approach is known as *management by objectives* (MBO).

BARRIERS TO EFFECTIVE PLANNING

There are two major types of barriers to developing effective plans. The first is the would-be planner's internal resistance to establishing goals and making plans to achieve them. In other words, the individual is unwilling or unable to engage in meaningful goal-oriented activities.

The second barrier, which exists not within but outside the planner, is the general reluctance of organization members to accept planning and plans because of the kinds of changes they bring. It should be understood that this is not a rejection of planning but only of the new activities and goals it imposes on those who must implement the plan. Both types of obstacles to effective planning are discussed below.

Reluctance to Establish Goals

As we know, establishing a goal is the essential first step of the planning process. A manager who is unable to set meaningful goals will also be unable to make meaningful plans. There are at least five main reasons why some managers hesitate — or fail entirely — to set goals for their organizations or subunits:[2]

1. *Unwillingness to give up already established alternative goals.* The decision to establish specific goals and commit resources to their achievement requires that other alternatives be forgone. Each of us will at times find it difficult to accept the fact that we cannot achieve *all* of the goals that are important to us. We may be reluctant to make firm commitments to specific goals in order to avoid the painful task of giving up other desirable goals.

2. *Fear of failure.* Whenever someone sets a definite, clear-cut goal, that person takes the risk that he or she will fail to achieve it. Managers, no less than other people, see failure as a threat to their self-esteem, to the respect that others have for them, and even to their job security. Thus, their fear of failure keeps some managers from taking necessary risks and establishing specific goals.

3. *Lack of organizational knowledge.* In order to set effective goals, a manager needs a good working knowledge of three areas of the organization: (1) the organization as a whole, (2) other subunits of the organization, and (3) his or her own subunit.

No manager can establish meaningful objectives for a subunit without understanding the broad goals, objectives, and strategies of the organization.

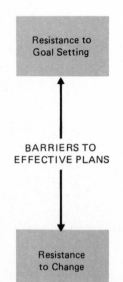

Resistance to Goal Setting

BARRIERS TO EFFECTIVE PLANS

Resistance to Change

[2] See David A. Kolb et al., *Organizational Psychology: An Experiential Approach,* 2nd ed. (Englewood Cliffs, N.J.: Prentice-Hall, 1974), pp. 296–297. The authors discuss why individuals are reluctant to set personal goals regarding their careers, but their reasons are also applicable to the reluctance of managers to commit themselves to setting organizational goals. Similarly, the solutions that the authors offer can be applied to improving a manager's effectiveness in goal setting.

© 1975 by United Feature Syndicate, Inc.

The objectives of the subunit must contribute to the broader goals and plans of the total organization. A manager who is new in the organization or who does not keep informed about its latest plans will be understandably hesitant to set new objectives, because they might conflict with those established by higher-level management.

Similarly, the manager must be aware of the objectives of other subunit managers to avoid establishing objectives that conflict with or duplicate theirs. A manager with an undeveloped or faulty information system may therefore try to avoid goal setting altogether, and, instead, fall back on already established subunit goals.

4. *Lack of knowledge of the environment.* In addition to understanding the organization's internal environment, the manager needs to understand the external environment—the competition, clients or customers, suppliers, government agencies, and the general public. The opportunities that an organization needs to fulfill its major goals, as well as the pitfalls it must avoid in order to survive, are in the external environment. Without knowledge of the external environment, managers are apt to become confused about which direction to take and are reluctant to set definite goals.

5. *Lack of confidence.* To commit themselves to goals, managers must feel that they and the subunit or organization have the ability to achieve those goals. Obviously, if the manager lacks self-confidence or confidence in the organization, he or she will hesitate to establish difficult goals.

What can a manager do to overcome these impediments to effective goal setting? Some of the answers are implied by the problems themselves; for example, a manager who is not adequately informed about the organization or external environment can correct this situation by developing a viable information system. Acquiring this knowledge will in turn help, at least in part, to overcome the fear of failure and the lack of self-confidence.

Another way commitment to a specific goal can be increased is by carefully comparing the value of a chosen goal with that of each rejected alternative. Such comparisons are reassuring, because they help to convince the person that the chosen goal is superior.

Furthermore, once a goal is established, it can be continually reevaluated in the light of new information from the organization and the external environment and of feedback from other members of the organization. Such reassessments of the goal often not only reinforce the manager's commitment to it but also enable him or her to replace it with a more suitable goal if it should turn out to be unrealistic or lose its viability.

Resistance to Change

The obstacle to planning we have just discussed consists of shortcomings in the would-be planners themselves. Resistance to change, on the other hand, occurs among the organization's members—managers as well as operating employees—who must carry out the planned activities.[3] (The subject of acceptance of and resistance to change will be discussed more extensively when we deal with managing organizational change in Chapters 13–15.)

The widely recognized tendency for organization members to resist planning and plans has been identified by one writer as "the most universal" barrier to effective planning.[4] Obviously, if the very people who are meant to carry out planned changes resent them, then it may be difficult to implement these changes. Moreover, the morale of the organization may be affected. People may openly object to the plan, gripe behind the scenes, implement the plan halfheartedly, or even try to sabotage the new system or get the planner out of the organization.

There is no single or simple reason why organization members resist change. (We can gain insight into resistance by others to our plans by observing our own resistance to the plans of others.) Some fear of the unknown probably exists in all of us, and people often prefer the security of familiar activities to potentially threatening new situations and responsibilities. In addition, most people dislike feeling manipulated, and they may get this feeling if plans are developed without their involvement or knowledge.

Frequently the members of an organization resent a new plan because it conflicts with their interests; that is, it may eliminate or reduce benefits or rewards that they enjoy, such as power, career opportunities, or prestige. For example, middle managers might well object to a reorganization plan that reduces the size of their departments.

Planning may also be resented because it restricts people's freedom to engage in a preferred work activity or imposes unwanted tasks on them—or simply because they fail to see the value of the planned changes. Suppose a new school program required that teachers spend more time on clerical activities (such as recordkeeping and entering grades) and less on classroom teaching. Most teachers would probably resist such a plan, because it would limit their teaching time and they would not agree that it is desirable for them to perform activities that could be done equally well by clerks and aides.

---

[3] This discussion is based chiefly on Ronald N. Taylor, "Psychological Aspects of Planning," *Long-Range Planning,* Vol. 9, No. 2 (April 1976), pp. 66–74.

[4] David W. Ewing, *The Human Side of Planning: Tool or Tyrant?* (New York: Macmillan, 1969), p. 44.

Most organization members also object to new policies that increase their work load, especially when they feel that their rewards have not been increased as much as the amount of work. For example, assembly-line workers who are asked to speed up their production by x number of items per day will balk at this new requirement unless their take-home pay reflects the increased work load.

At this point the reader may be wondering whether we are describing the meeting of an irresistible force (planning) and an immovable object (resistance to change). Such a situation would of course destroy any chance that a plan could succeed, because success requires the cooperation of the people who will carry out the planning decisions. Fortunately, there are several ways to reduce or eliminate resistance to planned change:

— By providing organization members with all possible information about the plan so that they can understand why changes are needed and how the changes will benefit the organization.

— By making plans that take into consideration the feelings of those affected by them.

— By rewarding members of the organization when they contribute to planning activities or to the successful implementation of a plan.

— By encouraging the participation of organization members in the planning process.

When used in suitable situations, participation can not only help to bring about the acceptance and implementation of planning decisions but also improve the quality of the plans themselves. In one survey of the management of change in large organizations, all the successful cases studied involved some participation in planning decisions by those who were to implement them.[5] We will be discussing the relative merits of the participative and nonparticipative approaches, as well as the situations in which each type of approach is preferable, in this and later chapters.

BARRIERS TO FORMAL STRATEGIC PLANNING

The barriers we have just discussed apply to all types of planning, including formal strategic or long-range planning. However, long-range planning is also more complex, costly, and time-consuming than the short-range varieties, and its results are much less clear-cut. Therefore, those same characteristics that make formal strategic planning unique in many ways also make the obstacles and difficulties that apply to it equally unique. Such barriers can be divided into two groups:

[5] R. J. Mockler, *Readings in Business Planning and Policy Formulation* (Englewood Cliffs, N.J.: Prentice-Hall, 1972), p. 293.

1   Those characteristics of formal strategic planning that prevent or discourage its use under certain conditions.

2   Those difficulties in developing or implementing a formal planning system that arise because the organization's managers do not fully understand the process or do not use it properly.

Factors That
Discourage
Strategic
Planning

Formal planning is a useful tool when used at the right time and in the right place. It is not—nor is it meant to be—the answer to the problems of all organizations or the answer to all the problems of a given organization. In the section below, we will describe those characteristics of formal strategic planning that discourage or prevent its use by some managers.[6]

Inconsistency between Strategic Planning and Management Style. As we saw in Chapter 5, some approaches to planning may be more useful or acceptable to a given organization than others. When formal planning and control are imposed on managers who are unwilling or unable to accept them, the results can be damaging to the organization. As reported in newspaper accounts, CBS Inc. discovered this fact in the mid-seventies.[7] A dramatic decline in the network's ratings early in the 1976 season was blamed, at least in part, on bureaucratic corporate policies—including formal strategic planning—introduced a few years earlier. Under those bureaucratic policies, CBS had lost more than ten of its most experienced executives in a two-year period, some of them to competing networks. Several of those who resigned from CBS explained that they had done so to escape what they described as "a corporate bureaucracy that imposed meetings, reports and five-year plans upon the program work that had to be performed on a daily basis....According to sources close to CBS management, the systems...designed for business efficiency might have been appropriate for other large corporations, but not for one whose product is entertainment and news."

Even in organizations that recognize a need for "business efficiency," formal planning often meets with the resistance of many key executives, because it conflicts with their personal style of managing. By nature or necessity, most managers prefer action and making decisions quickly and spontaneously as problems come up, rather than the slower, more analytical approach that long-range planning requires.

Possible Inappropriateness of Strategic Planning. Formal strategic planning is usually of little use to a small organization or to an organization struggling hard to survive on a day-to-day basis. A business organization with very limited resources that faces very strong competition, for example, must con-

---

[6] This discussion is adpated from E. Kirby Warren, *Long Range Planning: The Executive Viewpoint* (Englewood Cliffs, N.J.: Prentice-Hall, 1966); George A. Steiner, *Top Management Planning* (New York: Macmillan, 1969); and Bernard Taylor, "Strategies for Planning," *Long-Range Planning,* Vol. 8, No. 4 (August 1975), pp. 27–40.

[7] Les Brown, "CBS Shake-Up Traced to Taylor Policies," *New York Times,* October 16, 1976.

centrate on making profits in the present and near future. Any planning its management does will be short-term; it cannot afford the luxury of diverting limited resources, which are needed to relieve immediate pressures, to making plans for a distant future the company may never live to see. Similarly, small enterprises — many of which are struggling for survival — simply cannot afford the time, money, and human resources needed to install and maintain a formal strategic planning system.

In addition, the development and maintenance of a formal planning system require the continuous heavy use of written communications, such as reports, directives, questionnaires, budgets, and forecasts. Large organizations are comfortable with such devices; they use them continuously and find them indispensable. In small enterprises, on the other hand, more informal communications (either oral or written) are preferred, because they work better within the less complex structure of those organizations.

Expense of Strategic Planning. As was stated in Chapter 5, formal strategic planning is expensive. The time and efforts of many organization members and significant amounts of money are required to set up a viable planning system and to gather the information needed to make it work. Managers who introduce formal planning into their organization must be able to justify those high costs with tangible results.

Overemphasis on Measurable Aspects of Strategic Planning. Formal planning systems have often placed too much emphasis on the quantitative (measurable) and economic aspects of strategic planning and little or none on its social, political, and creative aspects. For managers who find complex quantitative matters difficult, or who believe the other areas of organizational life are more important, strategic planning may seem inappropriate. (See box on next page for one company's approach to dealing with some nonquantitative aspects of planning.)

Vulnerability of Strategic Planning to the Unexpected. The strategic plan can be disrupted by unexpected changes in the environment. Formal strategic planning depends heavily on assumptions about the future environment based on long-range forecasts. However, predictions — especially those of the distant future — are never completely accurate, and unexpected things can happen to upset even the most carefully made plans.

For example, a government body may pass a law or issue a ruling that makes the goals of a formal plan either meaningless or impossible to achieve. Foreign governments can unexpectedly raise the prices of raw materials or of energy sources. Labor unions can disrupt production by strikes or slowdowns. Even natural events can adversely affect the operation of an organization (a drought can destroy crops, for example).

A well-constructed strategic plan will not usually be disrupted by unexpected events. However, some unexpected changes in the environment can make a particular plan impractical. The possibility that all the time, expense, and effort that go into formal planning can be lost because of an unforeseeable

147

General Electric's "Stoplight Strategy" for Planning

General Electric Co. thinks it has found at least a partial solution to an age-old corporate planning problem: how to put a value on those critical elements in planning it is impossible to attach a number to. In a decision on whether a product will live or die, for example, the value of a patent or the impact of social change cannot be quantified. By using its Strategic Business Planning Grid, or "stoplight strategy," GE can at least evaluate such factors with something more than just a gut reaction.

In every annual planning review, each individual business is rated not only on numerical projections of sales, profit, and return on investment but also on such hard-to-quantify factors as volatility of market share, technology needs, employee loyalty in the industry, competitive stance, and social need. The result is a high, medium, or low rating on both attractiveness of an industry and GE's strengths in the field.

How It Works If industry attractiveness is seen as medium and GE's strengths as high (Chart A), an "invest and grow" ...decision would result, because the evaluation bars cross in a "growth" square. Both industry attractiveness and business strength are low in Chart B, indicating a "no-growth" strategy, or a business which will continue to generate earnings but no longer warrants much additional investment by GE. Chart C represents a business with high industry attractiveness but low GE strength—a "borderline" business that might go either way.

A "growth" business is expected to expand. A "no-growth" operation's strategy, on the other hand, may involve consolidation of plants, limited technology infusion, reduced investment, and strong cash flow. A "borderline"... business—say, electronic components—could be diverse enough to have both no-growth and growth units.

After three or four critiques at various levels, the final grids—and decisions—are made by the corporate policy committee—the chairman, three vice-chairmen, five senior vice-presidents, and the vice-president for finance.

The process is not just window dressing. It may prevent costly mistakes. "Interestingly," says one GE planner, "the financial projections are often best on businesses that turn up worst on the grid."

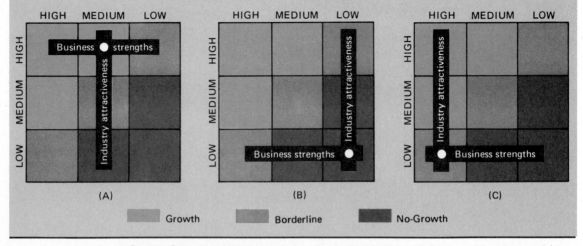

Source: Quoted and adapted from the April 28, 1975 issue of *Business Week* by special permission. © 1975 by McGraw-Hill, Inc.

occurrence is a key factor in the decision by many managers to avoid this form of planning.

Obstacles to the Effectiveness of Strategic Planning

In the previous section, we discussed some of the reasons why managers avoid using strategic planning in their organizations. In this section, we will describe some of the barriers to effective implementation of strategic planning after it has been introduced. By becoming aware of these barriers, managers can increase considerably their chances of carrying out the steps in the formal planning process (described in Chapter 5) as successfully as possible.

The barriers to be discussed here are based on a survey of 286 American and European corporations by means of a detailed, open-ended questionnaire that covered "the most important aspects of planning and decision-making philosophy and practices."[8] An additional 65 companies participated in in-depth interviews on the same topics. The findings of this study suggest that there are ten major reasons why organizations can fail in their formal planning efforts. Usually, when planning failure occurs, two or more of these reasons occur together in the organization:

1. *Formal planning is not accepted into the organization's total system of management.* In many organizations, managers lack a proper understanding of the potential benefits of formal planning, and therefore they fail to cooperate when attempts are made to develop a planning system. Obviously, those executives who reject the need for formal strategic planning or consider it unimportant will not devote the time and effort needed to make it succeed.

2. *The planners do not fully understand certain aspects of formal planning.* For example, an organization's managers may overlook some necessary step or steps in the planning process because of carelessness or lack of knowledge. In addition, they may not be able to evaluate alternative strategies properly or to select the best ones.

3. *Managers at every level of the organization do not participate in planning activities.* Top management must initiate, sponsor, and give direction to an organization's planning efforts, but the real job of planning must be performed by the other managers in the organization. Those who must actually implement the plans should play a major role in producing them.

4. *A planning department is given the primary responsibility for planning.* Here again top management mistakenly delegates the responsibility for planning to a specialized planning staff or department instead of to the appropriate managers. Often a planning staff will work hard to develop a complicated, overrefined plan in order to impress top management. When the completed plan is turned over to the other managers in the organization, they may be unwilling or unable to carry it out. As we indicated in the previous chapter, a planning staff or department can coordinate an organization's planning activities and even help managers develop their plans. It should not be given full responsibility for the entire planning process.

---

[8] Ringbakk, "Why Planning Fails," pp. 16–24.

5. *The organization's managers consider the long-range plans to be unchangeable.* Far too often, managers think of a strategic plan as something that necessarily remains in effect without modification until its goals are achieved. This could not be further from the truth. In fact, effective long-range planning requires managers who do not hesitate to abandon or change plans when they are no longer useful.

During the life of any plan, especially a long-range one, changes are bound to take place in the organization and its environment. For example, competitors may enter the market with new products, affecting the organization's market share and profitability. Managers must be alert to such unexpected major events and quickly modify their plans accordingly.

6. *Managers choose the wrong system.* Sometimes a planning system fails because it just is not the right one for the people using it. Some systems, often those designed by outside consultants, are too complex and elaborate to be useful to any organization. For example, organization members may simply not have the time, personnel, or resources necessary to evaluate and coordinate such a complex plan.

7. *A good plan is disregarded by managers.* There is obviously no chance to win a horse race, even with the fastest thoroughbred, if the jockey refuses to ride. When the plan has been developed carefully and — at that point in time — seems to meet the organization's needs better than any other alternative, then management should use it. Too often managers will develop a plan and then revert to old patterns of behavior.

8. *Managers confuse forecasting and budget projections with planning.* Extrapolation of past events and results into the future is forecasting, not planning. Of course, forecasting is a part of planning but it is certainly not the whole. For a time, management may get away with substituting extrapolation for planning, but when future events do not conform to their expectations, they will find themselves — and their organizations — in trouble.

Some companies similarly confuse extended budgeting with planning. In so doing, they place too much emphasis on financial and other measurable results and not enough on the underlying factors, such as constant monitoring and updating of plans, that make those results a reality.

9. *The available information is inadequate for planning.* Managers often fail in their planning efforts because they do not realize that the information normally available to them — in the form of monthly reports, say — is produced for the purpose of control and is not useful for planning. A broader base of information is needed — that is, information must represent not only the actions of each unit of the organization but also the activities of competitors and other aspects of the external environment.

10. *Managers get bogged down in the details of planning.* Sometimes managers fail to see the forest for the trees; they pay so much attention to small details that they lose sight of what they are trying to accomplish through their planning efforts. For example, division managers may continuously

strive to meet the plan's established objectives, and forget that these objectives must be periodically reevaluated to see if they are still realistic or desirable.[9]

Now that we have examined some of the reasons for planning failure, we can go back to the case history introduced at the beginning of the chapter. We will briefly explore the reasons why the formal strategic planning system developed by Ento International failed to achieve its intended results.

Probably the worst mistake the management of Ento made was to deprive the division heads of the direct responsibility for making the strategic plans. Top management did this by creating a central planning department under the control of the executive vice president. In its legitimate attempt to make certain that strategic planning was seen as having top-level support, Ento's management had inadvertently kept the real planning activities out of the hands of the managers who were most familiar with the problems and abilities of the organization. Thus, management lost any chance that the planning process would develop realistic plans that could be carried out effectively.

Because they were not involved in the formal planning process in any meaningful way, the division chiefs did not take it very seriously. They also were perplexed and annoyed by the elaborate models and sophisticated techniques that the planning department presented to them. These practical executives had little interest in such complex devices and did not really understand them. In fact, they saw them as toys rather than tools for effective planning. Each division, sensing its own chief executive's disenchantment with the formal planning system, came to view strategic planning as a crash program run once a year to produce a plan that nobody really cared about or used.

Fortunately, Ento's story had a happy ending, because its top managers realized and corrected their planning mistakes before strategic planning was completely rejected by operating managers. But these top managers could have spared themselves unnecessary problems if they had foreseen the potential roadblocks *before* they tried to set up their planning system.[10]

MANAGEMENT BY OBJECTIVES

The term "management by objectives" (MBO) was first applied by Peter Drucker in 1954 to an approach to planning that he detailed in his book *The Practice of Management*.[11] Since that time, MBO has attracted a great deal of discussion, evaluation, and research. There is widespread agreement that

---

[9] Another writer, Paul J. Stonich, offers similar explanations of why planning systems fail, in "Formal Planning Pitfalls and How to Avoid Them—Part 1," *Management Review*, Vol. 64, No. 6 (June 1975), pp. 5–6, and "Part 2," *Management Review*, Vol. 64, No. 7 (July 1975), pp. 29–35.

[10] Ringbakk, "Why Planning Fails," pp. 15–16.

[11] Peter F. Drucker, *The Practice of Management* (New York: Harper & Brothers, 1954).

through MBO, managers can avoid some of the barriers to and pitfalls of planning described earlier in this chapter. This section will examine the philosophy of MBO, its weaknesses and strengths, and ways of evaluating it and making it more effective.

What Is Management by Objectives?

In *The Practice of Management,* Drucker contrasted management by *objectives* with management by *drives.*[12] The latter refers to the attempt to control an organization by responding to sudden financial or market pressures with an "economy drive" or a "production drive." In practice, it produces a temporary improvement at best. More often it results in an increase in inefficiency and dissatisfaction.

In MBO, effective planning depends on every manager having clearly defined objectives that apply specifically to his or her individual functions within the company. Each manager's objectives must also contribute to the objectives of higher management and of the company as a whole.

Management by Drives

How these objectives are arrived at is of crucial importance. As Drucker points out, managers must either set their own objectives or, at the very least, be actively involved in the objective-setting process. Imposing predetermined objectives on managers runs the very real risk of either refusal to cooperate or half-hearted attempts to implement "someone else's" objectives.

In addition, Drucker suggests that managers at every level should participate in setting the objectives for levels higher than their own. In this way, they can get an understanding of the broader objectives of the company and how their own specific objectives relate to the overall picture.

Management by Objectives

For Drucker, this relationship of each individual's objectives to the common goal is of primary importance. The main purpose of implementing MBO is to achieve an efficient operation of the total organization through the efficient operation and integration of its parts.

A different emphasis is stressed by another leading exponent of MBO, Douglas McGregor.[13] He favors MBO because of its value as a performance appraisal program. He recommends that individual managers, after agreeing on their basic job responsibilities with their immediate superior, set their own performance objectives for the immediate short-term period, such as six months. They would also be responsible for outlining specific plans for achieving these goals. At the end of the period, each manager would carry out a self-appraisal. This appraisal would then be discussed with his or her superior and new objectives set for the next period. In this way, the ambiguities and tensions that usually accompany most other appraisal programs can be reduced.

More than twenty years have passed since Drucker first introduced his detailed description of MBO. Has it become an established approach with

---

[12] In addition to Drucker's book, see also Stephen J. Carroll, and Henry L. Tosi, *Management by Objectives—Applications and Viewpoints* (New York: Macmillan, 1973).

[13] Douglas McGregor, *The Human Side of Enterprise* (New York: McGraw-Hill, 1960), and "An Uneasy Look at Performance Appraisal" *Harvard Business Review,* May-June, 1957, pp. 89–94.

American companies? A 1974 survey found that although almost half of the large companies surveyed reported some form of MBO,[14] less than 10 percent felt that they had "highly successful applications."[15] The survey found that while there were many companies with highly successful MBO programs, many more companies misunderstood what MBO was supposed to do or how it should be applied.

To increase our understanding of MBO, we will first look at some of the assumptions and theories upon which MBO is based. We will then describe the common elements in effective MBO programs and discuss how MBO can best be implemented.

The Philosophy behind MBO

McGregor has suggested that there are two sets of assumptions about how people are motivated to work.[16] (See box on next page.) *Theory X* assumptions are based on the traditional view that human beings regard work only as something that must be done to survive. Thus, they will avoid work whenever it is possible for them to do so. According to this view, managers have to be strict or authoritarian with subordinates, because otherwise subordinates would accomplish very little work.

Theory Y assumptions represent a much more positive assessment of human behavior. In this view, people do not inherently dislike work but can find it a great source of satisfaction. If some people avoid responsibility, lack ambition, or are only concerned with security, it is because of their particular life experience or work situation.

Obviously, the extent to which managers subscribe to one theory or another will radically affect their attitudes toward subordinates. Only the most cynical of managers might be expected openly to admit holding Theory X assumptions, but McGregor believes that these assumptions govern traditional management policies and practices. For example, the common requirement in many organizations that employees punch time clocks is based on Theory X assumptions. Managers in these organizations believe that if employees do not have to punch clocks they will not report for work on time. Similarly, many managers periodically bemoan the difficulty of maintaining high productivity. This complaint is usually based on the Theory X assumption that workers are stubborn and unambitious.

Theory Y offers no such convenient rationalization for failing to reach an organization's goals. If there is a lack of motivation among employees, a Theory Y manager will assume that there has been a failure on *management's* part to provide a proper environment for realizing the full potential of employ-

---

[14] Carroll and Tosi, in *Management by Objectives* (p. 3), list other names used for MBO-type programs, such as "management by results," "goals management," "work planning and review," "goals and controls," and so on. Despite differences in name, all these programs are similar.

[15] Fred E. Schuster and Alva F. Kindall, "Management by Objectives: Where We Stand — A Survey of the Fortune 500," *Human Resource Management*, Vol. 13, No. 1 (Spring 1974), pp. 8–11.

[16] McGregor, *The Human Side of Enterprise*, pp. 23–57.

Theory X and Theory Y Assumptions	
Theory X	**1.** The average human being has an inherent dislike of work and will avoid it if he can.
	2. Because of this human characteristic of dislike of work, most people must be coerced, controlled, directed, threatened with punishment to get them to put forth adequate effort toward the achievement of organizational objectives.
	3. The average human being prefers to be directed, wishes to avoid responsibility, has relatively little ambition, wants security above all.
Theory Y	**1.** The expenditure of physical and mental effort in work is as natural as play or rest.
	2. External control and the threat of punishment are not the only means for bringing about effort toward organizational objectives. Man will exercise self-direction and self-control in the service of objectives to which he is committed.
	3. Commitment to objectives is a function of the rewards associated with their achievement.
	4. The average human being learns, under proper conditions, not only to accept but to seek responsibility.
	5. The capacity to exercise a relatively high degree of imagination, ingenuity, and creativity in the solution of organizational problems is widely, not narrowly, distributed in the population.
	6. Under the conditions of modern industrial life, the intellectual potentialities of the average human being are only partially utilized.

Source: Douglas McGregor, *The Human Side of Enterprise* (New York: McGraw-Hill, 1960), pp. 33–34, 47–48.

ees. The task of a manager, according to Theory Y assumptions, is not to control subordinates but to help them achieve their fullest capabilities within the organization. These Theory Y assumptions underlie the MBO system.

The MBO System   MBO programs can vary enormously. Some are designed for use in a small subunit of an organization, while others are used for the organization as a whole. The particular methods and approaches that managers use in an MBO program will differ. There also may be wide differences in emphasis. In the United Kingdom, for example, MBO is known chiefly as a system for corporate planning or strategy development. The emphasis is on efficiency in reaching company objectives. In the United States, individual motivation is more often the focus of attention. Managers concentrate on human needs and on increasing subordinate participation in goal setting rather than on strategy. Nevertheless, in most *effective* MBO systems, there are several common elements, which are described next.[17]

[17] See W. J. Reddin, *Effective Management by Objectives: The 3-D Method of MBO* (New York: McGraw-Hill, 1971), pp. 13–19.

Top-Level Goal Setting. Effective planning programs for an organization usually start with top managers setting preliminary goals after consultation with other managers in the organization. (See Chapter 5.) As much as possible, these goals are stated in specific terms — "a 5 percent increase in sales for the year," "a 15 percent expansion in the number of patients processed in our clinic," "no increase in overhead costs for the year," and so on. With specific goals set, people in the organization will have a clearer idea of what top management hopes to accomplish. They will also be better able to plan realistically for achieving these goals.

Individual Goal Setting. One of the basic characteristics of effective MBO programs is that each manager and subordinate will have clearly defined job descriptions and objectives — for example, "The manager of Subunit A will be responsible for increasing sales by 15 percent over a twelve-month period." Again, the purpose of making objectives at every level of the organization as specific as possible is to help managers and subordinates understand clearly what they should accomplish. In this way, their efforts will be purposeful and efficient, instead of being dispersed in too many directions.

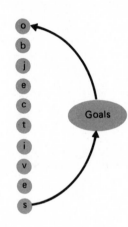

To be most effective, the objectives for each individual are reached by joint manager-subordinate consultation. Subordinates help managers develop realistic objectives, since they know best what they are capable of achieving. Managers help subordinates "raise their sights" toward higher objectives, by indicating confidence in subordinates and a willingness to help subordinates overcome obstacles. Such joint consultation is important, because individuals will be most committed to objectives that they have helped develop and that reflect their own interests and abilities.

Participation. The degree of subordinate participation in the setting of objectives can vary enormously. At one extreme, subordinates might participate only by being present when objectives are laid down by management. At the other extreme, subordinates might be completely free to set their own objectives and methods for achieving them. Neither of these extremes is likely to be effective. Managers might set objectives without full knowledge of the practical constraints under which their subordinates must operate; subordinates might select objectives that are inconsistent with the organization's goals. As a general rule, the greater the mutual participation of managers and subordinates in the setting of goals, the more likely it is the goals will be achieved.

Autonomy in Implementation. Once the objectives have been set and agreed upon, the individual has a wide range of discretion in choosing the means for achieving the objectives. Within the normal constraints of organization policies, managers should have the freedom to develop and implement programs to achieve their goals without being second-guessed by their immediate superiors. This aspect of MBO is one that is most appreciated by managers in an MBO program.

155

Review of Performance. Regular, periodic interviews are held between manager and subordinate to review progress toward the previously set objectives. To be fair and meaningful, the review is based on specific, measurable performance results rather than on subjective criteria, such as attitude or ability. For example, rather than attempting to review how energetic a salesperson has been in the field, emphasis would be placed on actual sales figures and detailed knowledge of specific accounts.

During the review process, manager and subordinate decide what, if any, problems exist and what they can mutually do to help resolve them. If necessary, the objectives will be modified for the next review period.

The MBO Process

Although emphasis and methods vary considerably, most effective MBO programs include the following elements:

1. Effective goal setting and planning by top management.
2. Setting of individual goals by managers and subordinates that are related to the organizational goals.
3. Considerable autonomy in developing and selecting means for achieving objectives.
4. Frequent review of performance as it relates to objectives.
5. Commitment to the approach at all levels of the organization.

Commitment to the Program. It requires a great deal of time and energy to implement a successful MBO program. Managers must meet with each subordinate, not only to set objectives, but to review progress toward these objectives. For this reason, effective MBO programs require the full support of everyone in the organization from top management down. There are no easy shortcuts: setting objectives without periodic review will eventually result in unmet objectives; reviewing the progress of subordinates in an overly judgmental way will result in resentment.

When properly introduced into the organization, MBO can be highly motivating. Managers and subordinates can see their individual position within the organization more clearly and will be motivated to contribute more toward the organization's goals as well as their own.

The Evaluation of MBO
We have implied that MBO programs that include (1) the establishment and acceptance of specific goals, (2) timely and accurate feedback on performance against those goals, and (3) the active involvement of individuals in the goal-setting and review process should improve the individual's and the organization's performance. Stephen J. Carroll and Henry L. Tosi have reviewed the research on these three MBO concepts—goal setting, feedback on performance, and participation—to determine if optimism about MBO is justified.[18]

[18] Carroll and Tosi, *Management by Objectives*.

Goal Setting. One of the main conclusions reached from research into goal setting was that, in effect, nothing succeeds like success. Individuals setting their own goals tend to aim for an improvement on past performance. If they achieve this improvement, they again set themselves a higher goal. If they fail to reach their target, however, they tend to set more conservative levels of aspiration for the next period.

The research also suggests that employees who are given specific goals do reach a significantly higher performance level than those who are merely asked to do their best. However, if employees feel that goals are impossible rather than challenging, their performance is likely to decrease.

Although most of the research Carroll and Tosi reviewed was not performed in organizations with established MBO programs, the research does indicate that MBO should improve performance if the goals are realistic and accepted by the employees involved. The actual degree of improvement, however, will depend on many factors, such as the individual employee's past experience with success or failure in reaching goals and how difficult the actual goals are.[19]

Feedback on Performance. Not surprisingly, providing employees with feedback will generally lead to improvements in their performance. In addition, feedback has been shown to have positive effects on employees' attitudes, creating feelings of friendliness, confidence in management, and a more tolerant acceptance of criticism.

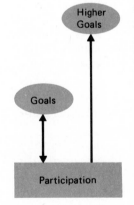

Several studies showed a relationship between the quality of the feedback and the degree of improvement: the more specific and timely the feedback, the more positive the effect. Also, the manner in which the feedback is provided also affects performance. The feedback should be given in a tactful manner, particularly if it conveys a failure to meet objectives. Otherwise, hostility and reduced performance can result.

Participation. Most research studies on participation indicate that subordinates who set or participate in setting their own goals are likely to show higher performance levels than subordinates who have goals set for them. In one well-known study of an MBO program at General Electric,[20] subordinates who had more influence in setting objectives showed more favorable attitudes and higher levels of achievement. On the other hand, subordinates who had

---

[19] A thorough review of the effects of goal setting on performance is provided in Gary P. Latham and Gary A. Yukl, "A Review of Research on the Application of Goal Setting in Organizations," *Academy of Management Journal,* Vol. 18, No. 4 (December 1975), pp. 824–845.

[20] Herbert H. Meyer, Emmanuel Kay, and John R. P. French, Jr., "Split Roles in Performance Appraisal," *Harvard Business Review,* January-February 1965, pp. 123–129. See also John M. Ivancevich, James H. Donnelly, and Herbert L. Lyon, "A Study of the Impact of Management by Objectives on Perceived Need Satisfaction," *Personnel Psychology,* Vol. 23, No. 2 (Summer 1970). pp. 139–151; Anthony P. Raia, "Goal Setting and Self-Control," *Journal of Management Studies,* Vol. 2, No. 1 (February 1965), pp. 34–53; and Anthony P. Raia, "A Second Look at Goals and Controls," *California Management Review,* Vol. 8, No. 4 (Summer 1966), pp. 49–58.

little influence and were dominated by their superiors showed defensive behavior and, in some cases, lower levels of achievement.

Carroll and Tosi concluded from their research that participation will lead to greater employee acceptance of performance goals and management decisions. (See also our discussion of participation in decision making in the next chapter.) The very process of participation, their studies suggest, invariably leads to increased communication and understanding between managers and subordinates.

The Strengths of MBO

A survey[21] of managers about their experience with MBO found that MBO's major advantages were, in the order mentioned, as follows:

1 It lets individuals know what is expected of them.
2 It aids in planning by making managers establish goals and target dates.
3 It improves communication between managers and subordinates.
4 It makes individuals more aware of the organization's goals.
5 It makes the evaluation process more equitable by focusing on specific accomplishments. It also lets subordinates know how well they are doing in relation to the organization's goals.

From this survey and other analyses of MBO,[22] it seems clear that MBO can offer major advantages to the individual as well as to the organization. For individuals, perhaps the main advantage is that MBO allows them to gain an understanding of a superior's expectations. This will allow them to concentrate their efforts where they are most needed and most likely to be rewarded. In addition, individuals will have to worry less about being evaluated on their personal traits or attitudes—which a particular superior may dislike. Rather, they will be evaluated on how well they have accomplished the specific objectives that they have helped to establish. The result is that individuals in the MBO process are more likely than others to perform their responsibilities willingly and well.

All these individual benefits will, at least indirectly, benefit the organization as well. In addition, there are advantages to a successfully implemented MBO program that apply directly to the organization. Since all levels of the organization help in setting objectives, the organization's goals and objectives will be more realistically based. This is particularly important in the planning process, when future goals for the organization are established. In addition, the improved communication that results from MBO can help the organization achieve its goals, since its activities will be better coordinated. Finally, the entire organization has an increased sense of unity: lower-level employees are more aware of

[21] Henry L. Tosi and Stephen J. Carroll, "Managerial Reaction to Management by Objectives," *Academy of Management Journal,* Vol. 11, No. 4 (December 1968), pp. 415–426.

[22] See Robert A. Howell, "A Fresh Look at Management by Objectives," *Business Horizons,* Vol. 10, No. 3 (Fall 1967), pp. 51–58.

top management's expectations and in turn assist in establishing attainable objectives.

MBO does not, of course, solve all the organization's problems. Appraisal of subordinates is a particularly difficult area, because it involves status, salaries, and promotions. The review process might well involve tensions and resentments even in the best MBO program. Not all the accomplishments of a subordinate can be quantified or measured. Even if achievements (or their lack) are measurable—such as the total number of sales in a subordinate's area—the subordinate might not be responsible for them. For example, sales might drop despite the subordinate's best efforts because of some unexpected move by a competitor. The changes MBO requires in a manager's behavior may also cause problems. In the MBO process, the emphasis is shifted from judging subordinates to helping them. This is a difficult shift for many managers to make.

The Weaknesses of MBO

The weaknesses of MBO can be divided into two categories. In the first category are weaknesses *inherent* in the MBO process. These include the considerable time and effort involved in MBO and managers' reluctance to do the considerable paperwork usually required. In the second category are weaknesses that theoretically should not exist but that frequently seem to develop in even properly implemented MBO programs.

This second category includes several key, recurring problems in MBO that must be controlled if the program is to be successful:[23]

1 *Management style and support.* If top managers prefer a strong authoritarian approach with centralized decision making, they will require considerable reeducation before they can implement an MBO program. MBO stands little chance without the full understanding and support of top managers.

2 *Adaptation and change.* MBO may require many changes in organizational structure, authority patterns, and control procedures. They require the full support of the managers involved. Those who participate only because they are forced to go along with the organization may easily doom the program to failure.

3 *Interpersonal skills.* The manager-subordinate appraisal and goal-setting procedure require a high level of skill in interpersonal relations. Many managers have neither previous experience nor natural ability in these areas. Extensive training in counseling and interviewing is usually required.

4 *Job descriptions.* Framing a specific list of individual objectives and responsibilities is difficult and time-consuming, especially when a subordinate's job is complex. In addition, job descriptions must be frequently reviewed and revised as conditions within the organization change. This is particularly critical during the implementation stages, when the impact of the MBO system itself may cause changes in duties and responsibilities at every level. Too often, despite a manager's best efforts, subordinates still fail to understand completely what is expected of them.

[23] Bruce D. Jamieson, "Behavioral Problems with Management by Objectives," *Academy of Management Journal,* Vol. 16, No. 3 (September 1973), pp. 496–505. See also Tosi and Carroll, "Managerial Reaction to Management by Objectives," pp. 415–426.

5 *Setting and coordinating objectives.* Setting challenging, yet realistic, objectives is frequently a source of confusion for managers in an MBO system. Problems may occur in making the objectives measurable, in finding a happy medium between too easily reached and impossible targets, and in describing the objectives in clear and precise terms. In addition, difficulties may be encountered in coordinating objectives not only with the organization's overall aims but also with the personal needs and objectives of the individual.[24]

6 *Control of goal achievement methods.* Considerable frustration can result if one manager's efforts to achieve his or her goals are dependent on the achievement of others within the organization. For example, production-line managers cannot be expected to meet a target of assembling 100 units per day if their department is being supplied with parts for only 90 units. Group goal setting and flexibility are needed to minimize this type of problem.

Making MBO Effective

MBO should not be considered a panacea for an organization's planning, motivation, evaluation, and control needs. And it is certainly not a simple process that can be quickly and easily implemented. Nevertheless, many large organizations are using some form of MBO. There is wide recognition of the advantages of having some mechanism of goal setting and evaluation for managers and of having individual goals integrated within the organization.

Many of us will work in organizations or subunits within an organization that have some form of formal objective-setting program. For this reason, we will list the elements that are needed to make an MBO-type program effective:[25]

Acceptance and use by managers. For MBO to succeed, it must be not only supported by management but also used by management. Subordinates must be aware that the system is company policy in practice as well as in name. For example, if performance levels are set without consultation with subordinates, the system will rapidly fall apart before any appreciable benefit can be achieved.

Clear formulation of objectives. Managers and subordinates must be satisfied that objectives are clearly understood and realistic, and that they will be used to evaluate performance. If managers do not already know how to set useful goals, they may require considerable training to teach them the skill.

Availability of feedback. An MBO system depends on those involved knowing where they stand in relation to their objectives. Setting goals is, in itself, not sufficient as an incentive; regular performance review and feedback of results is necessary to realize the full potential of the program.

Continuing support of program. Initial support and enthusiasm for an MBO program may quickly disappear unless efforts are made to keep the system alive and fully functioning. Managers who find it difficult to set and review objectives may quickly revert to more traditional and authoritarian approaches. Top managers must be aware of these tendencies and make special efforts to keep the program a vital part of the organization's operating procedures.

Encouragement of participation. Managers must realize that participation

[24] See Harry Levinson, "Management by Whose Objectives?" *Harvard Business Review*, July-August, 1970, pp. 125–134.
[25] See Tosi and Carroll, "Managerial Reaction to Management by Objectives," pp. 424–426.

by subordinates in mutual goal setting may mean a reallocation of power. They must be willing to relinquish some control over the work environment and to encourage subordinates to take a more active role in achieving their objectives. Managers may be somewhat uncomfortable with this loss of power, but only if they accept that loss can an MBO program be effective.

Summary

Planning is the first step in managing an organization. To make the planning process effective, two major barriers must be overcome: internal resistance to goal setting and reluctance to accept plans because of the changes they bring.

Resistance to goal setting may result from unwillingness to give up already established goals, fear of failure, lack of knowledge of the organization and its environment, and lack of confidence by managers in their own ability. Resistance to change may simply reflect people's desire for the familiar, or it may result because people feel their interests will be threatened by change.

These barriers apply to planning in general. There are also barriers that apply to strategic planning in particular. These include the fact that strategic planning may be inappropriate for certain managers, in certain types of organizations, or under certain conditions. Even if strategic planning is being used, it may not be properly implemented. For example, managers may not participate sufficiently in planning activities, or the strategic plan may not be revised to reflect changing conditions.

Management by objectives (MBO) is one approach to planning that helps overcome some of these barriers. Essentially, MBO involves managers and subordinates meeting to establish specific objectives and periodically reviewing progress toward those objectives. It is based on a set of assumptions (Theory Y) that under the proper conditions people will find satisfaction in work and will accept responsibility for their results.

The basic elements in effective MBO programs include (1) goal setting by top managers, (2) participation by subordinates in the setting of objectives, (3) autonomy in determining how to achieve objectives, (4) periodic review of performance, and (5) commitment to the program at all levels of the organization. MBO does require a great deal of time and energy to make it work effectively. Properly implemented, however, it results in improved performance and higher morale.

Review Questions

1. Why are some managers personally reluctant to set goals? How can they overcome this reluctance?
2. Why might people in the organization resist plans? How can managers reduce or eliminate this resistance?
3. Identify and describe some of the reasons why managers avoid strategic planning.
4. What are some of the barriers to effective implementation of strategic plans? Why is the participation of all managers in the strategic planning process important?
5. How does management by objectives differ from management by drives?
6. Describe how Drucker and McGregor differ in what they see as the main purpose of MBO.
7. Distinguish between "Theory X" and "Theory Y" assumptions. How might these different assumptions affect a manager's approach to subordinates? Which set of assumptions are you most comfortable with?
8. Identify and discuss the five elements of effective MBO programs.
9. According to available research, how are employee achievement and morale affected by specific goal setting, performance feedback, and subordinate participation in goal setting and review?

10. What are the major strengths of MBO? What are its major weaknesses?
11. Why do you think MBO is particularly useful in planning?
12. What things need to be done to make and keep MBO-type programs effective?

CASE STUDY: DASHMAN COMPANY

The Dashman Company was a large concern making many types of equipment for the armed forces of the United States. It had over 20 plants, located in the central part of the country, whose purchasing procedures had never been completely coordinated. In fact, the head office of the company had encouraged each of the plant managers to operate with their staffs as separate independent units in most matters.... When it began to appear that the company would face increasing difficulty in securing certain essential raw materials, Mr. Manson, the company's president, appointed an experienced purchasing executive, Mr. Post, as vice president in charge of purchasing, a position especially created for him. Mr. Manson gave Mr. Post wide latitude in organizing his job, and he assigned Mr. Larson as Mr. Post's assistant. Mr. Larson had served the company in a variety of capacities for many years, and knew most of the plant executives personally. Mr. Post's appointment was announced through the formal channels usual in the company, including a notice in the house organ published by the company.

One of Mr. Post's first decisions was to begin immediately to centralize the company's purchasing procedures. As a first step he decided that he would require each of the executives who handled purchasing in the individual plants to clear with the head office all purchase contracts that they made in excess of $10,000. He felt that if the head office was to do any coordinating in a way that would be helpful to each plant and to the company as a whole, he must be notified that the contracts were being prepared at least a week before they were to be signed. He talked his proposal over with Mr. Manson, who presented it to his board of directors. They approved the plan.

Although the company made purchases throughout the year, the beginning of its peak buying season was only three weeks away at the time this new plan was adopted. Mr. Post prepared a letter to be sent to the 20 purchasing executives of the company. The letter follows:

Dear _____ :

The board of directors of our company has recently authorized a change in our purchasing procedures. Hereafter, each of the purchasing executives in the several plants of the company will notify the vice president in charge of purchasing of all contracts in excess of $10,000 that they are negotiating at least a week in advance of the date on which they are to be signed.

I am sure that you will understand and that this step is necessary to coordinate the purchasing requirements of the company in these times when we are facing increasing difficulty in securing essential supplies. This procedure should give us in the central office the information we need to see that each plant secures the optimum supply of materials. In this way the interests of each plant and of the company as a whole will be best served.

Yours very truly,

Case copyright © 1942 by the President and Fellows of Harvard College. Reproduced by permission.

Mr. Post showed the letter to Mr. Larson and invited his comments. Mr. Larson thought the letter an excellent one, but suggested that, since Mr. Post had not met more than a few of the purchasing executives, he might like to visit all of them and take the matter up with each of them personally. Mr. Post dismissed the idea at once because, as he said, he had so many things to do at the head office that he could not get away for a trip. Consequently he had the letters sent out over his signature.

During the following two weeks replies came in from all except a few plants. Although a few executives wrote at greater length, the following reply was typical:

Dear Mr. Post:

Your recent communication in regard to notifying the head office a week in advance of our intention to sign contracts has been received. This suggestion seems a most practical one. We want to assure you that you can count on our cooperation.

Yours very truly,

During the next six weeks the head office received no notices from any plant that contracts were being negotiated. Executives in other departments who made frequent trips to the plants reported that the plants were busy, and the usual routines for that time of year were being followed.

Case Questions

1. Why was Mr. Larson assigned as Mr. Post's assistant?
2. To whom was Mr. Post accountable?
3. What is wrong with Mr. Post's plan and the way it was executed?
4. Might the problems (if any) with the purchasing procedures be symptomatic of a larger problem in the company?
5. To whom are the 20 purchasing executives accountable?
6. To whom are the plant managers accountable?
7. What would you have done if you were Mr. Post?
8. What would you have done if you were Mr. Larson?
9. What would you have done if you were a plant executive, either in purchasing or other functions?

Chapter 7

Decision Making

Upon completing this chapter you should be able to:

1. Identify the different types of decisions made by managers.

2. Describe the various conditions under which managers make decisions.

3. Explain why managers often settle for a satisfactory decision, rather than trying to make the ideal decision.

4. Explain why an important part of a manager's job is to find the right problem to work on.

5. Explain why it is important for managers to be aware of their own values and backgrounds when they work on problems.

6. Describe the formal decision-making process and explain why it is preferable to informal methods of decision making.

7. Describe ways in which managers can evaluate the effectiveness of their decisions and make them more acceptable to subordinates.

A manager's life is filled with a constant series of decisions — where to invest profits, what to do about an employee who is always late, where the firm's new warehouse should be built, what subject will have top priority at the department meeting the next morning. Small problem or large, it is the manager who decides what actions need to be taken — or at least arranges for others to decide. The actions are usually carried out by others.

Decision making is thus a key part of a manager's activities. It plays a particularly important role, however, when the manager is engaged in planning. Planning involves the most significant and far-reaching decisions a manager can make. When managers plan, they decide such matters as what goals or opportunities their organization will pursue, what resources they will use, and who will perform each required task. If their plans go off track, they decide what they are going to do about them. The entire planning process involves them constantly in a series of decision-making situations. How good their decisions are will play a large role in determining how effective their plans will be.

In this chapter we will describe how managers can best go about reaching a good decision. For our purposes, we will define a decision as *a choice among alternatives*. This definition implies three things: (1) When managers make decisions they are choosing — they are deciding what to do on the basis of some conscious and deliberate logic or judgment. Even an intuitive decision that they cannot explain is usually based on some judgment they have made in the past. (2) Managers have alternatives available when they are making a decision. It does not take a wise manager to reach a decision when there are no other possible choices. It does require wisdom and experience to evaluate several alternatives and select the best one. (3) Managers have a purpose in mind when they make a decision. There would be no reason for carefully making a choice among alternatives unless the decision had to bring them closer to some goal.[1] Our emphasis in this chapter, then, will be on the formal decision-making process — that is, on how managers systematically go about reaching logical decisions that can best help them reach their goals.

TYPES OF DECISIONS

As managers, we will make different types of decisions under different circumstances. When deciding whether or not to add a new wing to the administration building, or where to build a new plant, we will have to consider our choice carefully and extensively. When deciding what salary to pay a new employee, we will usually be able to be less cautious. Similarly, the amount of information we will have available to us when making a decision will vary. When choosing a supplier, we will usually do so on the basis of price and past performance. We will be reasonably confident that the supplier chosen will

---

[1] See R. W. Morell, *Managerial Decision-Making: A Logical Approach* (Milwaukee: Bruce Publishing Co., 1960).

meet our expectations. When deciding to enter a new market, we will be much less certain about the success of our decision. For this reason, we will have to be particularly careful making decisions when we have little past experience or information to guide us.

In short, the nature and circumstances of a decision can vary enormously. Managers have to vary their approach to decision making, depending on the particular situation involved. For our purposes, it will be useful to distinguish between situations that call for programmed decisions and those that call for nonprogrammed decisions.[2] We will also distinguish between decisions made under conditions of certainty, risk, and uncertainty.

Programmed and Nonprogrammed Decisions

Programmed decisions are those that are made in accordance with some habit, rule, or procedure. Every organization has written or unwritten policies that simplify decision making in a particular situation by limiting or excluding alternatives. (See our discussion of standing plans in Chapter 4.) In many cases, for example, we will not have to worry about what to pay a new employee we have hired. Our organization frequently will have an established starting salary for the position. Similarly, we will not usually have to think about the routine problems we face during the day. Our habits, or those of our peers, will help us decide quickly what to do about them.

To some extent, of course, programmed decisions limit our freedom of action—it is not really us but our organization that decides what to do. However, programmed decisions are really meant to be liberating. The policies, rules, or procedures by which we make our decisions free us of the need to work out new solutions to every problem we encounter. For example, deciding how to handle customer complaints on an individual basis would be time-consuming and costly. Routinized procedures, such as "exchanges will be permitted on all purchases," simplify matters considerably.

Programmed decisions are obviously the easiest for managers to make. It is quicker and simpler to refer to a policy rather than to think some problem through on one's own. We should note, however, that effective managers lean on policy as a time saver but remain alert for any exceptional cases. For example, company policy may put a ceiling on the advertising budget for each product. A particular product, however, may need an extensive advertising campaign to counter a competitor's aggressive marketing strategy. A programmed decision—that is, a decision to advertise the product in accordance with budget guidelines—might be the wrong decision in this case. Ultimately, managers must use their own judgment when a situation calls for a programmed decision.

Nonprogrammed decisions are those that are out of the ordinary or unique. If a problem is complex or exceptional, or if it has not come up often enough to be covered by a policy, it must be handled by a nonprogrammed decision.

---

[2] These terms are from the computer field. A program provides the computer with a sequence of coded instructions for carrying out tasks. See Herbert A. Simon, _The Shape of Automation_ (New York: Harper & Row, 1965), pp. 58–67.

Such problems as how to allocate an organization's resources, what to do about a failing product line, how community relations should be improved—in fact, most of the significant problems a manager will face—will usually require nonprogrammed decisions. (See Table 7-1.)

TABLE 7-1
Traditional and
Modern
Techniques of
Decision Making

Types of Decisions	Decision-Making Techniques	
	Traditional	*Modern*

Programmed:
Routine, repetitive
  decisions
Organization develops
  specific processes
  for handling them
	1. Habit
	2. Clerical routine:
	   Standard operating
	   procedures
	3. Organization structure:
	   Common expectations
	   A system of subgoals
	   Well-defined informa-
	   tional channels
		1. Operations research:
		   Mathematical
		   analysis
		   Models
		   Computer simulation
		2. Electronic data
		   processing

Nonprogrammed:
One-shot, ill-structured,
  novel policy decisions
Handled by general
  problem-solving
  processes
	1. Judgment, intuition,
	   and creativity
	2. Rules of thumb
	3. Selection and training
	   of executives
		Heuristic problem-
		  solving technique
		  applied to:
		a. Training human
		   decision makers
		b. Constructing
		   heuristic com-
		   puter programs

Source: Reproduced with permission from Herbert A. Simon, *The New Science of Management Decision,* rev. ed. (Englewood Cliffs, N.J.: Prentice-Hall, 1977), p. 48.

The ability to make good nonprogrammed decisions helps to distinguish effective managers from ineffective managers. Managers have to rely heavily on their problem-solving ability, creativity, and judgment when they make nonprogrammed decisions. Established procedures are of little use to them, since the important problems confronting them will usually require new or original solutions. For this reason, most management training programs try to improve a manager's ability to make nonprogrammed decisions—usually by trying to teach managers to make their decisions in a logical manner. The decision-making process we describe in this chapter is used mainly for nonprogrammed decisions.

Decisions under Certainty, Risk, and Uncertainty

We stated earlier that managers have a purpose in mind when they make a decision; that is, they decide to do something because they wish to bring about some desired goal. This means that decisions (like plans) are concerned with the future: managers decide to hire a new employee because they believe the employee is best suited to do the work that will be available; they decide to reinvest a portion of their company's profits in new equipment, because they believe that this is the best way to help their company grow.

Unfortunately, the future is not often safe and predictable. Managers make their decisions on the basis of information they have in the present. This information is usually (but not always) inadequate for them to be able to predict with complete confidence what the future will be like. For example, managers hire a new employee on the basis of the employee's past experience, as recorded on his or her résumé, or by references. But managers cannot be completely certain how well the employee will actually work out in their organization.

In general, managers can make decisions under three possible conditions: certainty, risk, and uncertainty.[3] We will discuss each of these conditions in this section.

Conditions of Certainty. Under conditions of *certainty,* managers have enough information to know exactly what the outcome of their decisions will be. Let us assume, for example, that we have to decide what to do with our organization's profits. We know that if we decide to invest the profits in government bonds, they will earn a predictable rate of return. We also know that most of our stockholders would be happy if we distributed the profits as dividends. We make our decision based on which expected outcome we prefer: happy stockholders or a safe return on investment. (Of course, the future is never completely certain. The government could conceivably collapse, and our bonds would be worthless. But at some point, if we have enough information, it simply becomes convenient for us to act *as if* a condition of certainty exists.)

Conditions of Risk. Conditions of certainty are the exception rather than the rule in today's complex, rapidly changing organizations. Managers must usually try to predict in a less certain way the consequences of their decisions. Sometimes, however, managers can know the probabilities of the various possible outcomes associated with a decision, even though they cannot be completely certain which particular outcome will actually occur. (Technically, we would call this "knowing the probability distribution associated with future events.") In such cases, a condition of *risk* is said to exist. Under conditions of risk, managers can determine exactly (within a small margin of error) the probable result of each of the alternatives available to them. They can then decide what to do on the basis of which probable outcome is most desirable.

For example, let us assume we are managers in a homeowner's insurance company and have to decide what rates to charge. We can refer to statistical tables that will tell us what the probabilities are that people in different locations, in various types of houses, will experience theft, fire, or home accidents. We can then set appropriate rates for each type of homeowner. Of course, we cannot be absolutely certain how many claims there actually will be (the

---

[3] See F. H. Knight, *Risk, Uncertainty, and Profit* (New York: Harper & Brothers, 1920); Stephen A. Archer, "The Structure of Management Decision Theory," *Academy of Management Journal,* Vol. 7, No. 4 (December 1964), pp. 269–287; and Kenneth R. MacCrimmon, "Managerial Decision-Making," in Joseph W. McGuire, ed., *Contemporary Management: Issues and Viewpoints* (Englewood Cliffs, N.J.: Prentice-Hall, 1974), pp. 445–495.

Drawing by Ziegler; © 1976 The New Yorker Magazine, Inc.

events being covered have not yet occurred). For this reason, our rate decision will involve risk. But we can be confident that the probabilities in the tables —which are based on the accumulation of many years of statistics—will apply for the foreseeable future, and that our rate decision is a correct one.

Probabilities are also used extensively to help managers make investment decisions. One step in this process involves calculating the *expected value* of a specific investment opportunity and then comparing that expected value with the cost of making the investment. If the expected value is higher, the investment might be worthwhile. If it is lower, the investment might not be worth the risk. The expected value is calculated by multiplying the probability that a given return will be achieved by the value of that return. For example, if we want to decide whether or not to buy a $1 lottery ticket when the odds are 1 in 5 million that $1 million will be won, we can calculate as follows:

$$\frac{1}{5,000,000} \times \$1,000,000 = 20 \text{ cents}$$

The result is smaller than our $1 investment. In this case, we might feel that the chance of a big payoff is well worth the high probability that our small in-certainty

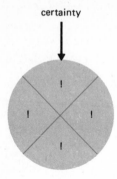

risk

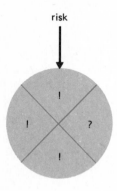

uncertainty

vestment will be lost. When the initial investment is much larger, however, the expected value calculation is a useful tool—together with other tools—in helping managers make their investment decisions. (The values of managers will also play a role here. Cautious managers may insist on a higher probability of success, while other managers may be willing to take greater risks.)

Conditions of Uncertainty. When we do not know the exact probabilities attached to the alternatives available to us, a condition of *uncertainty* exists. Most managerial decisions involve varying degrees of uncertainty. There are usually too many variables or too many unknown facts that can affect a decision for managers to be able to predict precisely its probable outcome. In such cases, managers frequently use their experience, judgment, and intuition to assign approximate probabilities to each of the alternatives available to them. By so doing, they may be able to narrow the range of choices they have and simplify the decision.

For example, let us assume we are managers in a hospital and want to purchase new equipment. There are two suppliers competing for the sale. One supplier has dealt with us before; his equipment is good and his service is reliable. We cannot be certain that this supplier's past performance will continue into the future, but we can be fairly confident that he will meet our expectations. The other supplier has never been used by our hospital. He insists his somewhat more expensive equipment will outproduce and outlast the competition. We have no way of gauging the validity of these claims nor the integrity of the supplier. But having had some experience with similar equipment, we can calculate very loosely the probable life of the equipment and its productivity. We might, for example, see a 50 percent probability that the equipment will do better than the equipment from the old supplier, a 30 percent probability that it will be pretty much the same, and a 20 percent probability that it will do worse. We would then have to decide if the extra cost and uncertainty involved in selecting the new supplier is justified by a 50 percent probability that his equipment will do a better job.

It will not always be possible to assign even approximate probabilities to the available alternatives. However, managers will almost always have at least some vague sense of which future events are more likely than others. If managers increase the price of a product, they may not know what the effect on total revenues will be, but it is almost always safe to assume they will lose some customers. Even in conditions of almost total uncertainty, an educated guess, an intuitive insight, or a hunch will help managers make the right decision.

The Limits of Rational Decision Making

We have said that managers must often make decisions when the information they have is incomplete. One reason for this, as we have already suggested, is that managers cannot always foresee the consequences of their decisions. Of course, if they knew in advance the outcome of a decision, they could easily tell if it was a correct one. But, in reality, they must make decisions without full knowledge of what the future will bring.

Another reason managers have incomplete information when making decisions is that they rarely consider or are even aware of all the alternatives available to them. Most decisions involve too many complex variables for one person to be able to examine them all fully. As a simple example, let us assume we have to decide what name to give a new product. We have available all the words in the dictionary (plus many new words we can invent), but for us to go through the entire dictionary to select a product name would obviously be impractical. What we will probably do is select several possible names, test each in the marketplace, and then choose the one that has the greatest customer approval. Many other—and perhaps better—possible names will never be considered.

The fact that managers often make decisions without knowing all the alternatives available to them and all their possible consequences means that there is a limit to how logical or rational their decisions can be. In organizational life, managers act within what Herbert Simon has called *bounded rationality:* that is, they make the most logical decisions they can, limited by their inadequate information and by their ability to utilize that information.[4] Rather than making the best or ideal decision, managers more realistically settle for a decision that will adequately serve their purposes. In Simon's terms, they *satisfice,* or reach a satisfactory decision, rather than *maximize,* or reach the optimal decision. (See Chapter 1.) In our previous example, it was more practical to select a product name from a few alternatives, rather than examine all possible alternatives. Similarly, it will be more practical to try to decide what we have to do to earn an acceptable level of profits than to try to decide what we have to do to earn the maximum possible profits. As managers, we will rarely have the mental ability, time, or information we need to make perfect decisions.

This does not mean, of course, that managers give up trying to make the best possible decisions. It simply means they recognize that at some point it will become too expensive, time-consuming, or difficult to try to acquire additional information or attempt to analyze it.

There are a variety of techniques and mathematical tools that can be used to help managers make decisions under varying degrees of uncertainty. We will discuss next one main tool, the decision tree. Others will be discussed in the next chapter, "Aids in Planning and Decision Making."

DECISION TREES AND DECISION MAKING

Managers sometimes face complex problems in which the possible outcome of each of the alternative solutions available to them will be hard to foresee. In such cases, they would like to have some way to reduce the element of doubt and uncertainty in the decisions they reach, since each decision or alternative will usually involve some commitment of precious resources.

[4] Herbert A. Simon, *Models of Man: Social and Rational* (New York: Wiley, 1957). See also James G. March and Herbert A. Simon, *Organizations* (New York: Wiley, 1958); Herbert A. Simon, *Administrative Behavior* (New York: Macmillan, 1961); and D. W. Taylor, "Decision Making and Problem Solving," in Richard M. Cyert and Lawrence A. Welsch, eds., *Management Decision Making* (Baltimore: Penguin Books, 1970), pp. 30–63.

Decision trees were developed to help managers make a series of decisions involving uncertain events. A decision tree is a device that displays graphically the various actions that a manager can take and how these actions will relate to the various future events that can occur. Like the other OR (operations research) techniques discussed in Chapter 8, the decision tree will not make the decision for the manager—judgment will still be required. However, in appropriate situations, using a decision tree will help reduce the potential confusion in a complex problem and allow the manager to analyze the problem rationally.

A simple example of a problem analyzed with the help of a decision tree is given below. It will be helpful for the reader to refer to the sample decision tree as the problem is described.

The Problem

The Carter Outboard Motor Company is at present producing only gasoline-powered outboard motors for boats. However, the company's managers believe the market potential for electric motors is growing. They must decide whether to continue producing only gasoline motors or start producing only electric motors. If they continue to produce only gasoline motors, they may subsequently decide to invest in new facilities that will enable them to produce both gasoline and electric motors.

To construct the decision tree that would help their company decide what to do, the appropriate managers would follow a three-step procedure:

1 Identify the decision points (that is, the points at which a decision might be made), the alternative actions available at each point, and the possible events associated with each alternative action. In this case, there are two possible decision points, with two alternatives available at each point: first, "continuing to produce gasoline motors" versus "producing only electric motors," and second, "invest in new facilities to produce both motor types" versus "do not invest in new facilities." The possible outcomes of each alternative action are illustrated in the tree. (See Figure 7-1.)

2 Estimate the probability of each possible event and the payoff associated with each action-event combination. As was stated earlier, under conditions of risk managers will be able to assign precise probabilities for each event; under conditions of uncertainty, approximate probabilities will have to be assigned. In any case, the probability figures give managers a measurable basis for deciding which events are most and least likely to occur. Similarly, the estimated payoffs (or return) will be put in measurable terms—in this case, as profits in dollars.

3 Analyze the decision tree to determine which decision will have the highest expected value in terms of its payoff and the probability that it will occur.

Analyzing the Decision Tree

When the relevant information has been put into graphic form as a decision tree, the managers must analyze the tree to see which action has the highest expected value. The action with the highest expected value would normally be the most attractive, based on the assumptions and expectations underlying the tree.

The managers begin the analysis by working backwards on the tree, from its end branches toward the first decision point. (This process is called "rolling

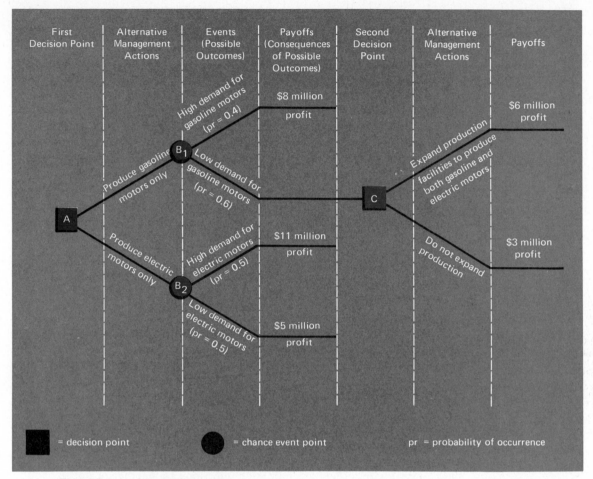

| First Decision Point | Alternative Management Actions | Events (Possible Outcomes) | Payoffs (Consequences of Possible Outcomes) | Second Decision Point | Alternative Management Actions | Payoffs |

High demand for gasoline motors (pr = 0.4)

$8 million profit

Low demand for gasoline motors (pr = 0.6)

Produce gasoline motors only

B₁

Produce electric motors only

B₂

High demand for electric motors (pr = 0.5)

$11 million profit

Low demand for electric motors (pr = 0.5)

$5 million profit

A

C

Expand production facilities to produce both gasoline and electric motors

$6 million profit

Do not expand production

$3 million profit

■ = decision point   ● = chance event point   pr = probability of occurrence

FIGURE 7-1   The Decision Tree

back" the decision tree.) At each stage the expected value is determined by multiplying the probability of each event by the appropriate payoff. The results for all the possible outcomes of each managerial action are then added together. This figure becomes the expected value of the action. It represents the average result the manager can reasonably expect from that action.

The Carter Company managers would start their analysis with the decision at point C. At that point, the outcome is presumed to be known (because sales at that point are predictable). The decision to expand production would be the most logical one to make, since its payoff ($6 million) is greater than the payoff for not expanding production ($3 million). Thus, the expected value of this decision—$6 million—will become the payoff in the event that there is a low demand for gasoline motors at event point B_1.

Moving backwards to event fork B_1, the expected value for the two possible outcomes is calculated. The result is an expected value of $6.8 million for the decision to produce gasoline motors only: $(0.4 \times \$8 \text{ million}) + (0.6 \times \$6 \text{ million})$ $= \$6.8$ million. For event fork B_2, the expected value would be $8 million: $(0.5 \times \$11 \text{ million}) + (0.5 \times \$5 \text{ million}) = \$8$ million.

On the basis of the expected value calculation, the decision to stop producing gasoline motors and start producing electric motors would be most profitable. However, the managers will still have to use their judgment before making the final decision. For example, although the decision to produce only electric motors has the highest expected value, this decision also has the lowest profit if things do not work out well ($5 million versus $6 million). If the managers are reluctant to accept the risk of a profit as low as $5 million, they may not wish to produce electric motors, despite its higher expected value.

Decision trees can become quite detailed and complex if the number of possible alternatives, events, and payoffs increases. Nevertheless, they can help managers think about their decisions in a more logical way and make them more aware of the possible outcomes of their decisions.[5]

THE NATURE OF MANAGERIAL DECISION MAKING

Defining the
Decision-Making
Situation

The idea that managers are decision makers may conjure up an image of managers sitting behind their desks, calmly deciding what to do about every problem that arises. In fact, only mediocre managers try to solve every problem thrust upon them by subordinates, superiors, and peers. Effective managers conserve their time and energy for those problems that really require their decision-making ability. Minor problems are either handled by snap judgment or "feel," or shunted off to a subordinate.

Thus, when managers are presented with a problem, the first thing they should do is ask themselves one or more of the following questions:

1. *Is the problem easy to deal with?* Some problems are difficult and expensive to deal with, others are not. Such questions as whether or not to acquire a subsidiary obviously require extensive consideration. Most problems, however, rarely require more than a small amount of the manager's attention. For example, if a carton supplier finds that the ink on some of the cartons is fading or "bleeding," he or she might quickly decide to order a better grade of ink. Such quick decisions are justified because they resolve insignificant problems. Even if the decision turns out to be wrong, it will be relatively easy and inexpensive to correct. Effective managers reserve the formal decision-making

---

[5] Discussions of decision trees can be found in many operations research textbooks. See, for example, Robert S. Thierauf and Richard A. Grosse, *Decision Making through Operations Research* (New York: Wiley, 1970). Thorough discussions of the technique, with multiple illustrations, are provided in John F. Magee, "Decision Trees for Decision Making," *Harvard Business Review,* July-August 1964, pp. 126–138, and John F. Magee, "How to Use Decision Trees in Capital Investment," *Harvard Business Review,* September-October 1964, pp. 79–96, and in John S. Hammond III, "Better Decisions with Preference Theory," *Harvard Business Review,* November-December 1967, pp. 123–141.

process for those problems that require it. Otherwise, they get bogged down in trivialities.

2. *Might the problem resolve itself?* When presented with a problem, too few managers ever ask themselves, What would happen if I did nothing about this? An amazing number of time wasters can be eliminated if they are left untouched. The classic illustration of this principle concerns Napoleon, who was reputed to let incoming mail pile up on his desk for three weeks. When he analyzed his mail at the end of that time, he would find that most matters had been resolved in the interim.

Effective managers adopt a more active policy, based on the same idea: they place first things first. When they have more problems than they can handle at a given time—and they almost always have—they rank them in order of importance and deal with them one at a time. Those problems at the end of the list that they never get to usually take care of themselves or are dealt with by others. If one of those problems worsens, it simply achieves a higher priority and is then handled by the manager.

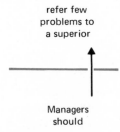

refer few
problems to
a superior

Managers
should

refer many
problems to
subordinates

3. *Is this my decision to make?* Let us assume we are confronted with an important problem requiring a decision. We still must determine if we are responsible for making the decision. Here a general rule can be of help: *the closer to the origin of the problem the decision is made, the better.* This rule has two corollaries: (a) Pass as few decisions as possible to those higher up, and (b) pass as many as possible to those lower down. It is usually those who are closest to the problem who are in the best position to decide what to do about it.

When managers refer an issue to someone higher up for a decision, they have to be sure they are not simply passing the buck instead of being properly cautious. (Referring a matter to a subordinate is not passing the buck, because managers still retain ultimate responsibility.) On the one hand, managers are usually closer to the problem than their superiors; on the other hand, they must pass on all decisions that can be better or more appropriately made by someone else. How can they decide when they should pass a problem on to a superior? If our basic rule and its corollaries do not supply the answer, managers can supplement them with a few basic questions:

—Does the issue affect other departments?
—Will it have a major impact on the superior's area of responsibility?
—Does it require information available only at a higher level?
—Does it involve a serious breach of our departmental budget?
—Will I get into trouble if I do not consult my superior about this?

If managers answer yes to questions like these, it is likely that the issue should be referred to a superior.

If a manager is faced with a problem or issue that is difficult to deal with, if it is an important problem that will not resolve itself, and if the manager must decide what to do about it, then he or she is in a "decision-making situation." It will require the careful, logical, decision-making process described later.

Finding the
Problem to
Work On

Managers do not only wait for problems to come to them. They try to anticipate problems, deciding what to do to prevent them from occurring or what they will do should problems arise. In addition, they actively seek opportunities, deciding first which opportunities to pursue and then what to do to make them a reality. Since there are a great number of problems and opportunities their organization might face, a critically important skill for managers is the ability to select the right problem or opportunity to work on.

As Guth and Tagiuri have noted, the types of problems and opportunities managers choose to work on will be influenced by their values and backgrounds.[6] If managers are motivated primarily by economic values, they will want to make decisions on practical matters, such as those involving marketing, production, or profits. If they have a more theoretical orientation, they might be concerned with the long-term problems and opportunities of their organization. If their orientation is political, they might be more concerned with competing with other organizations, or with their own personal advancement. Clarifying their own values will help them decide what problems and opportunities they would most like to pursue. Remaining sensitive to the values of others will also make it easier for managers to reach decisions that others will accept.

The backgrounds and expertise of managers will also influence what they see as problems and opportunities. A study of executives by De Witt C. Dearborn and Herbert A. Simon found that managers from different departments will define the same problem in different terms.[7] In this study, a group of executives were presented with a complex business case and asked to describe what they saw as the most important problem facing the company. According to Dearborn and Simon, each executive tended to be sensitive to only those parts of the case that were related to his or her department. For example, sales and accounting managers tended to see sales as the company's primary problem, and production managers tended to see as most critical an organizational problem apparently involving the company's factory managers.

Evidently their individual backgrounds and specialties make managers particularly sensitive to certain types of problems and opportunities. This can sometimes be an advantage, as they may be aware of possibilities that others will ignore. But it has a major disadvantage as well, because it may cause them to overlook many other problems and opportunities for their organizations. As managers, we will have to be particularly careful to avoid seeing all problems as being related to our specialties.

Methods of Problem Finding. William Pounds has described four methods managers use to find problems to work on: when there is a deviation from past experience, when there is a deviation from the plan, when other people present

---

[6] See William D. Guth and Renato Tagiuri, "Personal Values and Corporate Strategy," *Harvard Business Review,* September-October 1965, pp. 123–132.

[7] De Witt C. Dearborn and Herbert A. Simon, "Selective Perception: A Note on the Departmental Identification of Executives," *Sociometry,* Vol. 21 (1958), pp. 140–144.

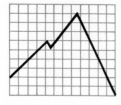

problems to the manager, and when competitors outperform the manager's organization.[8]

When there is a *deviation from past experience,* a previous pattern of performance in the organization is broken. This year's sales are falling behind last year's; expenses have suddenly increased; employee turnover has grown; too many defective products are suddenly coming off the assembly line. Events such as these represent a departure from the past and signal the manager that a problem has developed. The manager will then proceed to figure out what the cause of the problem is and what should be done about it.

When there is a *deviation from the plan,* the manager's projections or expectations are not being met. Profit levels are lower than anticipated; a department is exceeding its budget; a project is off schedule. Such events tell the manager that something must be done to get the plan back on course.

Other people often bring problems to the manager. Customers may complain about late deliveries; higher-level managers may set new performance standards for the manager's department; subordinates may resign. On a day-to-day basis, a large number of the decisions a manager will make often involve problems presented by others.

The *performance of competitors* can also create decision-making situations for the manager. Other companies, for example, might develop new processes or improvements in operating procedures. The manager might have to reevaluate processes or procedures in his or her own organization. "Competitors" within the same organization might also pose problems for the manager. If a company has many plants, for example, top management might compare the performance of each plant. The manager of a plant that is performing below average will have to decide what can be done to bring the plant's performance up to par.

Pounds suggests that management science techniques could also be used to help managers locate problems in addition to solving them. However, such techniques are difficult for many present managers to learn. For this reason, the four methods described above are likely to be the ones most frequently used by managers for the foreseeable future.

THE DECISION-MAKING PROCESS

Many managers who must make a decision rely on informal decision-making methods to give them guidance. They may, for example, rely on *tradition* and make the same decisions that were made for similar problems or opportunities in the past. They may also *appeal to authority;* that is, they will make a decision based on what an expert or a higher-level manager suggests should be done. Finally, they may use what philosophers call *a priori* reasoning: they

---

[8] William F. Pounds, "The Process of Problem Finding," Sloan School Working Paper No. 145-65, Massachusetts Institute of Technology, November 1965. See also Peter F. Drucker, *The Practice of Management* (New York: Harper & Brothers, 1954), pp. 351–354.

will assume that the most reasonable or obvious solution to a problem is the correct one.[9]

Such methods may be useful in some cases. In others, however, they may lead the manager to make the wrong decision. For example, one company was plagued by a serious quality problem: too many of the parts it was making were returned because of defects. The obvious management decision was to tighten up quality control procedures. However, this did not solve the problem. Further investigation revealed that the real culprit was excess worker fatigue caused by a faulty ventilation system. In this case, the correct solution to the problem was not the most obvious one.

The following approach to decision making does not guarantee that a manager will always make the right decision. It is, however, a rational, logical, and systematic approach to decision making. As such, managers who use it are more likely than other managers to come up with more and better solutions to the problems they face.

Rational Decision Making

The basic process of rational decision making involves diagnosing and defining the problem, gathering and analyzing the facts relevant to the problem, developing and evaluating alternative solutions to the problem, selecting the most satisfactory alternative, and converting this alternative into action. There are several stages in this process.[10] (See Figure 7-2.)

Stage 1: Diagnose and Define the Problem. As we have already suggested, the origin of a problem is not always obvious. For example, a newly appointed president of a large chain of retail stores had to reverse his firm's long-term sales decline. He knew it could be due to poor selling procedures, sharp competition, or the saturation of old markets. But when he dug deeper, he found that the cause of the problem was the tight-fisted control of the firm by the previous president. Every expenditure over $2,500 required presidential approval, and no store manager could stock shelves with items of his or her choosing. The result was that no store could move quickly enough to meet changes in customer demand.

If managers are to remedy a situation, they must first find out what the real problem is. One way to do this is to ask, What past action or lack of action might have caused this situation to arise? In this way, managers can focus upon the events or circumstances that most likely led to the problem.

As part of the process of defining the problem, managers should also begin to determine which parts of the problem they *must* solve and which parts they

---

[9] Francis J. Bridges, Kenneth W. Olm, and J. Allison Barnhill, *Management Decisions and Organizational Policy* (Boston: Allyn and Bacon, 1971).

[10] The discussion that follows is based on John Dewey, *How We Think* (Boston: D. C. Heath, 1933), pp. 102–118; Drucker, *The Practice of Management*, pp. 354–365; and Charles H. Kepner and Benjamin B. Tregoe, *The Rational Manager: A Systematic Approach to Problem Solving and Decision Making* (New York: McGraw-Hill, 1965). We have adapted the Kepner-Tregoe approach for our basic model.

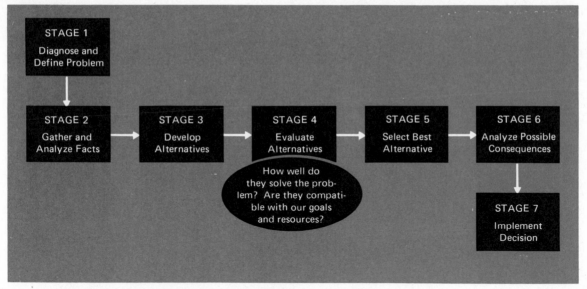

FIGURE 7-2   The Decision-Making Process

should or would like to solve. Most problems involve several elements, and it is unlikely a manager will find a solution that will work for all of them. Managers therefore need to distinguish between their "musts" and their "shoulds" so that they will have a basis for proposing and evaluating alternative solutions. For example, let us assume that we have a staffing problem. We *must* hire someone who can do a good job in a difficult position at a certain salary. We *should* hire someone who has had some experience and who will fit in well with others in the organization. We can eliminate from consideration all candidates who do not meet our "musts" criteria; and we will evaluate all the other candidates by how well they meet our "shoulds."

Stage 2: Gather and Analyze the Relevant Facts. Once managers have determined and defined their problem, they must begin to decide what they are going to do about it. To accomplish this, they must first determine what facts they will need to make a correct decision and then try to obtain as much of this information as possible. They can ask themselves such questions as: Who in our organization is most directly affected by our problem? Can they tell us more about its practical effects? Could they suggest how the problem might be solved? How are our customers or clients affected by our problem, and what do they think should be done about it? Has anyone ever experienced a similar type of problem? Are there certain solutions that people in our organization will oppose? What resources will be available to help us solve the problem? Managers will rarely get all the answers they need to such questions. At some point, however, they should have enough information to be able to formulate possible solutions.

179

Stage 3: Develop Alternatives. No major decisions should be made until several alternative solutions have been developed. Otherwise managers may be tempted to adopt the first solution they find, and the first solution is not always the correct one. Developing alternatives allows managers to resist an understandable inclination to solve their problem quickly and makes it more likely that they will reach effective decisions. (For guidelines on how to avoid prematurely accepting the first feasible solution, see the accompanying box.)

Precepts for Creative Problem Solving

To Prevent Going Off on the Wrong Track:	**Precept 1:** Run over the elements of the problem in rapid succession several times, until a pattern emerges.
	Precept 2: Suspend judgment. Don't jump to conclusions.
	Precept 3: Explore the environment. Vary the temporal and spatial arrangement of the problem's elements.
To Get Back on the Right Track:	**Precept 4:** Produce another solution after the first has been found.
	Precept 5: Critically evaluate your own ideas. Constructively evaluate those of others.
	Precept 6: When stuck, change your representational system. (For example, if you have been thinking about a problem in verbal terms, try using graphs instead.)
	Precept 7: Take a break when you are stuck.
	Precept 8: Talk about your problem with someone.

Source: Ray Hyman and Barry Anderson, "Solving Problems," *Science and Technology*, September 1965, pp. 36–41.

Possible alternatives will often suggest themselves after managers have analyzed a problem and gathered information about it. In addition, managers may use their imagination to come up with other possible solutions to their problem. For example, if we would be faced with a high employee turnover rate, we could obviously (1) raise salaries, (2) increase benefits, and (3) reduce the work load.

Any one of these solutions (or all of them) might apply. But if we investigated further, we might find that other alternatives available to us include (4) do nothing—the expense of raising salaries might wipe out the gain of a stabilized work force, (5) redesign the work area to make it more pleasant, and (6) dismiss or retrain those supervisors who are disliked by employees.

Stage 4: Evaluate the Alternatives. Once managers have developed a set of alternatives, they must evaluate them to see how effective each would be. Effectiveness can be measured by two criteria: how realistic the alternative is in terms of the goals and resources of the organization, and how well the alternative will help solve the problem.

Evaluating alternatives in light of the goals and resources of the organization is an important part of the decision-making process. The alternatives may seem logical, but if they cannot be implemented in the organization, they will be of little use. For example, if our sales are high but our profits are declining, we may want to reduce overhead costs. But if we find that costs have already been cut sharply, or that further cuts would reduce the quality of our product, this alternative would be less feasible. Similarly, alternatives that would strain our organization's resources would also be less desirable than others.

The alternatives must also be evaluated in terms of how well they would solve the "musts" and "shoulds" of the problem. In some cases managers may be able to "experiment" with possible solutions by trying one or more of the alternatives in different parts of their organization to see which is most effective. Usually they will just use their knowledge, judgment, and experience to decide which alternatives are most attractive. When they complete their evaluation, they rank the alternatives in a hierarchy, that is, from most desirable to least desirable. Their top choice will be the alternative that would best solve all the elements of their problem at the lowest cost to their organization.

Stage 5: Select the Best Alternative. This might seem to be an obvious step; after all, the managers have already determined what their best alternative is. However, this best alternative will be based on the amount of information available to the managers and by their imperfect judgment. More likely than not, it will also represent a *compromise* between all the various factors that have been considered. Thus, it is possible that their best alternative will still not adequately solve their problems, in which case the managers would have to begin the decision-making process again.

For example, let us assume our problem is the low productivity of one of our departments. We might believe that productivity would be most conveniently increased if we dismissed the department supervisor. But our investigation discovers that the supervisor is extremely popular and that low departmental morale would result if the supervisor was dismissed. Our best alternative might then be retraining the supervisor or offering financial incentives to the employees to increase productivity. This would be a longer-term, more expensive alternative for our organization, but it might be the "best" one considering all the relevant factors involved.

Stage 6: Analyze the Possible Consequences of the Decision. Once managers have selected their best alternative, they must try to anticipate what problems will occur when implementing their decision. For example, there is often great resistance in organizations to change (as will be discussed in future chapters). Managers must determine how willing their subordinates will be to carry out their decision and what might happen if their decision is not implemented wholeheartedly. There may be practical problems involved in implementing the decision, such as the need to obtain additional funding. Other departments in the organization that might be affected by the decision have to be consulted. Competitors may be affected by the decision, and their reactions will have to be taken into account. Sometimes detailed analysis of such considerations may cause managers to reject their first choice and substitute another alternative that might be more workable. Usually, however, analyzing the possible consequences of their decision will simply allow managers to take the necessary steps to deal with them.

To some extent, of course, managers will have already considered the possible outcomes of their decision while evaluating all the alternatives available to them. Here, however, they are examining one decision in much greater detail. By so doing, it will be easier for them to implement their decision effectively. In addition, they will prevent "smoothing over" the weaknesses of their decision. There is a human tendency to ignore possible problems and alternatives once a decision is made. (In the *theory of cognitive dissonance,* this process is known as *dissonance reduction.*) By taking the extra time to reexamine their decision at this point, managers can counteract this tendency.

Stage 7: Implement the Decision. After managers have taken whatever steps possible to keep adverse consequences from arising, they can implement their decision. Ultimately, no decision is better than the action taken to make it a reality. If the decision is a good one, but subordinates are not willing or able to carry it out, then it is unlikely the decision will be very effective. A frequent error of managers is to assume that once they make a decision, action on it will automatically follow.

Effective implementation of a decision involves much the same steps as implementation of plans. First, managers set up a budget or a schedule for the action they have decided upon, so they can measure its progress in specific terms. There must also be clearly assigned responsibility for carrying out the action. Next, managers set up a procedure for regular, periodic reports on the progress of the action, and they must be prepared to take appropriate measures should some problem arise. Finally, managers set up an "early warning system" to let them know as soon as possible of some problem with the action. In all likelihood, the quicker managers can go to work on a problem, the less drastic their corrective measures will have to be.[11]

IMPROVING THE EFFECTIVENESS OF DECISIONS

Because decision making is such an important part of their job, managers are often evaluated for their ability in this area. However, such an evaluation is not as easy as it may seem. An apparently excellent decision—that is, one based on information that has been gathered, analyzed, and evaluated effectively—might turn out poorly because of an unforeseeable event. Conversely,

---

[11] A good, realistic application of the Kepner-Tregoe approach is demonstrated in Perrin Stryker, "Can You Analyze This Problem?" *Harvard Business Review,* May-June 1965, pp. 73–78, and Perrin Stryker, "How to Analyze That Problem," *Harvard Business Review,* July-August 1965, pp. 99–110.

an unlikely and unpredictable event might turn a bad or illogical decision into a fortunate choice. Even if a decision works as well as predicted, a manager can never be completely sure another one would not have been equally effective or even better.

For these reasons, many managers agree that decisions should be evaluated on the basis of the situation at the time they were made, rather than second-guessed after the results are in. Norman Maier has isolated two criteria by which a decision's potential effectiveness can be appraised. The first is the *objective quality* of the decision, and the second is the *acceptance* of the decision by those who must execute it.[12]

The objective quality of the decision is determined by how well the manager carries out the formal decision-making process. In other words, if the manager fully diagnoses the problem, scrupulously gathers and evaluates facts, and develops alternatives, the decision that results should have high objective quality. Maier suggests that where the problem is largely a technical one, a quality decision may be enough to solve it.

If people are involved in the problem, however, then a quality decision may not be sufficient, according to Maier. The acceptance of the people involved may also be required to make it effective. A difficulty arises for managers if "quality" considerations conflict with "acceptance" considerations. The decision that would objectively work best might not be acceptable to the people affected. On the other hand, the decision most favored by subordinates might not be the best one to make.

Traditionally, this dilemma has been resolved by leaving the final responsibility for making the decision in the hands of the manager. The manager then has to compel or persuade subordinates to obey the decision. The problem with this approach is that it is not always appropriate. Sometimes subordinates may resist a decision because they are aware of alternatives and approaches that were not considered in the original analysis. In such cases, a decision that a manager makes will fail because he or she will be unable to convince subordinates to carry it out willingly.

Maier suggests that managers should evaluate each type of problem to see how important it will be for the solution to have quality and/or acceptance. Managers can then tailor their decision to the particular problem and thus increase its effectiveness. To Maier, decision-making situations can be classified in three ways:

1 *Those where high quality is important but high acceptance is not.* Such problems can be effectively solved by the manager who properly carries out the formal decision-making process. They may include such technical matters as purchasing, engineering, and finance—problems where the application of specialized knowledge is the major consideration. Acceptance by subordinates cannot be completely ignored, but the manager's major emphasis should be on reaching an objectively good decision.

[12] Norman R. F. Maier, *Problem-Solving Discussions and Conferences: Leadership Methods and Skills* (New York: McGraw-Hill, 1963).

2 *Those where high acceptance is important but high quality is not.* Such problems can best be solved by group decision making, because if subordinates do not accept the solution it is likely to fail. Making up schedules for a department and dividing office space fairly are examples of problems best solved through group discussion. In such situations, the manager's role is to present the problem to subordinates and to act as discussion leader.

3 *Those where both high quality and high acceptance are important.* A possible change in production methods that requires the retraining of employees would be an example of this type of problem. It could be solved either by the traditional method of the manager acting alone or through group decision making. For managers skilled in handling group decisions, the latter method would be preferable. There is strong evidence that motivation is increased when individuals are involved in the decision-making process.

A dramatic demonstration of the effectiveness of participation in decision making was provided by Lester Coch and John French in a classic study they conducted three decades ago.[13] A manufacturing company encountered resistance from production workers when it tried to institute changes in production methods. The researchers decided to divide the workers into three groups: one group did not participate in planning production changes; another group participated through worker representatives; and the third group participated totally in planning the changes. The first group resisted the changes that were instituted and showed a sharp decrease in productivity. The second group showed some improvement in productivity. The last group, however, was the most comfortable with the changes and showed dramatic gains in efficiency and productivity.

Matching the Decision-Making Approach to the Problem

In an extension of Maier's work, Victor Vroom and Philip Yetton have developed a method to help managers decide when and to what extent they should involve subordinates in solving a particular problem.[14] First, Vroom and Yetton isolated five styles of decision making (see also accompanying box):

1 Managers make the decision themselves with the information on hand.

2 Managers make the decision themselves, but first get more information from their subordinates.

3 Managers discuss the problem with appropriate subordinates *individually,* but make the decision themselves.

4 Managers discuss the problem with their subordinates as a *group,* but still make the decision themselves with or without letting the group's ideas influence them.

5 Managers arrange for group discussion, but this time have subordinates add and evaluate alternatives with them and arrive at the decision by *consensus.* Managers accept and implement the decision even if it is not theirs.

[13] Lester Coch and John R. P. French, Jr., "Overcoming Resistance to Change," *Human Relations,* Vol. 1 (1948), pp. 512–532.

[14] Victor H. Vroom and Philip W. Yetton, *Leadership and Decision Making* (Pittsburgh: University of Pittsburgh Press, 1973). See also Victor H. Vroom, "A New Look at Managerial Decision Making," *Organizational Dynamics,* Vol. 1, No. 4 (Spring 1973), pp. 66–80.

Types of Management Decision Styles

1. You solve the problem or make the decision yourself, using information available to you at that time.

2. You obtain the necessary information from your subordinate(s), then decide on the solution to the problem yourself. You may or may not tell your subordinates what the problem is in getting the information from them. The role played by your subordinates in making the decision is clearly one of providing the necessary information to you, rather than generating or evaluating alternative solutions.

3. You share the problem with relevant subordinates individually, getting their ideas and suggestions without bringing them together as a group. Then *you* make the decision that may or may not reflect your subordinates' influence.

4. You share the problem with your subordinates as a group, collectively obtaining their ideas and suggestions. Then *you* make the decision that may or may not reflect your subordinates' influence.

5. You share a problem with your subordinates as a group. Together you generate and evaluate alternatives and attempt to reach agreement (consensus) on a solution. Your role is much like that of chairman. You do not try to influence the group to adopt "your" solution, and you are willing to accept and implement any solution that has the support of the entire group.

Source: Reprinted by permission of the publisher from "A New Look at Managerial Decision Making" by Victor H. Vroom, *Organizational Dynamics*, Spring 1973. © 1973 by AMACOM, a division of American Management Associations.

The authors then suggest several questions that managers can ask themselves to help determine which decision-making style to use for the particular problem they are facing (see Figure 7-3 on next page):

—Do we have enough information or skill to solve the problem on our own? If not, then style 1, where we make the decision ourselves, would be inappropriate.

—Do we need to make a high-quality decision, which our subordinates are likely to disagree with? If so, style 5, where we seek the consensus of the group, would not be appropriate. In this case, giving up our authority to make the final decision would probably mean that the decision would not have the objective quality the problem requires.

—Is the problem structured? That is, do we know what information we need and where to get it? If not, then styles 4 and 5, which allow for the greatest group interaction, would be preferable. The other styles would either keep us from getting the information we need or supply us with information in an inefficient manner.

—Is the acceptance of the group critical for the success of the decision? Then styles 1 and 2, which involve subordinates the least, would not be appropriate.

—If acceptance of the decision is important, are our subordinates likely to disagree among themselves about which is the best solution? Then styles 4 and 5, which involve group decision making, are preferable. Only within the group can differ-

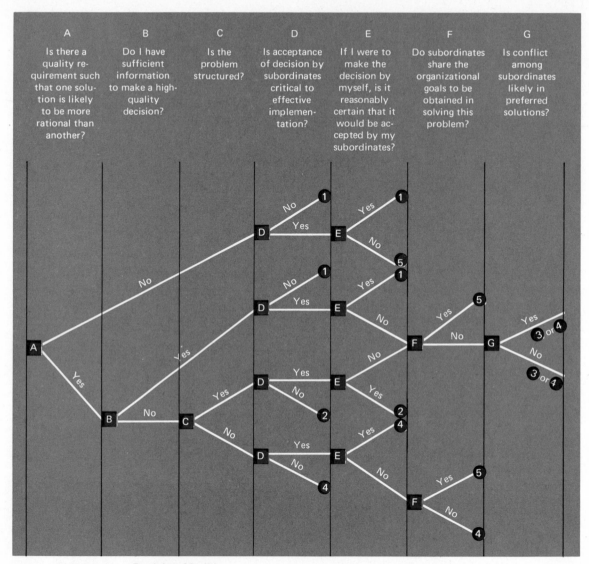

FIGURE 7-3 Decision Model

This model shows the preferred management decision style for each type of problem. The preferred style in each problem situation is indicated by the circled numbers.

Source: Reprinted by permission of the publisher from "A New Look at Managerial Decision Making" by Victor H. Vroom, *Organizational Dynamics*, Spring 1973. © 1973 by AMACOM, a division of American Management Associations.

ences between subordinates be discussed openly and ultimately resolved. The other styles might leave some subordinates dissatisfied with the decision.

—Is acceptance of the decision the most critical factor? Then style 5 would be the most logical choice, since it maximizes the one relevant consideration: acceptance of the decision by the group.

This approach still leaves managers with a great deal of flexibility, since there are many problems where more than one management style will apply. For example, let us assume we are suddenly faced with the problem of high employee turnover. We investigate and find that employee morale is low because of a recent change in company policy regarding overtime pay. Obviously, group ideas and acceptance will be important in devising a solution for this problem. We can either meet with members of the group individually (style 3) or meet with the entire group at once (style 5). Vroom suggests that where several management styles are possible, managers select the one that would cost them least in terms of time or resources. In this case, meeting with the entire group at once would clearly be the least time-consuming way to approach our problem.

Summary   Managers make decisions that must be carried out by others. The types of decisions they make, and the conditions under which they make them, will vary. They must therefore tailor their decision-making approach to their particular problems and circumstances.

Programmed decisions are those that are suggested by habit or policy. *Nonprogrammed decisions* are those that are new or original. Most important decisions will be nonprogrammed; they will require careful and logical consideration.

The conditions under which managers make decisions will vary with the amount of information they have. Under conditions of *certainty,* managers know precisely what the results will be of each of the alternatives available to them. Under conditions of *risk,* they know within a small margin of error the *probable* outcome of each alternative. Under conditions of *uncertainty,* the probabilities are not known precisely. Frequently managers must estimate probable outcomes in order to be able to make a decision. Most management decisions are made under some degree of uncertainty. This is one reason why managers try to reach satisfactory, rather than ideal, decisions.

Managers do not only wait for problems to arise but also actively look for problems and opportunities. Nor do all the problems that managers face require the formal decision-making process. One of the most significant responsibilities of managers is deciding which problems and opportunities should receive their full attention.

When managers face an important problem or opportunity, and it is their responsibility to decide what to do about it, they can best arrive at a good, rational decision by using the formal decision-making approach. This involves seven stages: (1) Diagnose and define the problem; (2) gather and analyze the relevant facts; (3) develop alternatives; (4) evaluate the alternatives; (5) select the best alternative; (6) analyze the possible consequences of the decision; and (7) implement the decision.

In evaluating alternatives, it is often wise to seek insights and reactions from subordinates, especially if their acceptance of the decision is necessary for the decision to succeed. The most effective decisions are those that have the appropriate level of objective quality as well as the appropriate level of subordinate support. The extent to which managers and subordinates should make the decision together will depend on the particular type of problem involved.

Review Questions

1. How are planning and decision making linked?
2. What is the difference between a programmed and a nonprogrammed decision? Which do you think is easier to make? Why?
3. What are the differences between decisions made under conditions of certainty, risk, and uncertainty? Why do managers try to assess probabilities before reaching a decision?
4. Do you agree or disagree with the idea that managers can rarely make the ideal decision? Why?
5. Should managers make decisions on every problem they face? Why? For what decisions should they use the formal decision-making approach?
6. How do our values and backgrounds affect the kinds of problems and opportunities we choose to work on? What are the five methods managers can use to help them find answers?
7. What are the seven steps in the decision-making process, and how are they carried out?
8. Why is it inappropriate or difficult to evaluate decisions after they have been implemented?
9. What are the two criteria by which managers can evaluate their decisions before they are implemented? Why do these criteria sometimes conflict?
10. According to Maier, when should managers involve their subordinates in reaching a decision?
11. What are Vroom and Yetton's five styles of managerial decision making? Which style appeals to you most? How would you match each style to the appropriate decision-making situation? If several styles apply, which should you select?

CASE STUDY: LOCKS VERSUS LIVES

The administrator of the State Mental Hospital learned that keys to security wards for dangerous criminals had been lost or stolen when he received an early morning telephone call the first of May from the night administrator of the hospital. Since duplicate keys were available in the hospital safe, the administrator, Mr. Jackson, knew that loss of the keys would not interfere with the routine functioning of the hospital. But he decided to call a general staff meeting the next morning to consider the problem.

At the meeting, Mr. Jackson explained the problem of the missing keys and asked for suggestions on what to do. The assistant administrator suggested that the matter be kept confidential among the staff since public knowledge could lead to damaging publicity and possibly to an investigation by higher officials in the Department of Health and Rehabilitative Services.

The head of security for the hospital reported that only two keys were missing and that, although he could not yet determine if the keys had been stolen or lost, he

Case reprinted with permission from *Critical Incidents in Management*, 3rd ed., by John M. Champion and John H. James (Homewood, Ill.: Richard D. Irwin, Inc., 1975), pp. 130–131.

thought they probably had been stolen. He emphasized that the missing keys were "master keys" that could open the doors to all the security wards where the most dangerous criminals were housed. In his opinion, immediate replacement of the locks on those doors was required.

The director of accounting estimated the cost of replacing the locks at over $5,000. He reminded the meeting that the operating costs of the hospital already exceeded its operating budget by about 10 percent due to unexpected inflation and other unforeseen expenses, and that an emergency request for a supplemental budget appropriation to cover the deficit had been sent to the Department of Health and Rehabilitative Services the previous week. In sum, he concluded, no funds were available in the budget for replacing the locks, and an additional request for $5,000 might jeopardize the request for supplementary operating funds that had already been submitted. Besides, since it was early May, the hospital would begin operating under the budget for the next fiscal year in approximately sixty days. The locks could then be replaced and the costs charged against the new budget. Another staff member reasoned aloud that if the keys had been lost, any person finding them would not likely know of their purpose, and that if the keys had been stolen they probably would never be used in any unauthorized way.

Mr. Jackson thanked the staff members for their contributions, ended the meeting, and faced the decision. He reflected upon the fact that behind the doors to the security wards were convicted first-degree murderers and sexual psychopaths, among others. He also remembered his impeccable thirteen-year record as an efficient and effective hospital administrator.

As Mr. Jackson continued his deliberations, the thought occurred to him that perhaps the most important action would be to find and place the blame on the person who was responsible for the disappearance of the two keys. Moreover, security procedures might need reviewing, Mr. Jackson could not clearly see how best to proceed.

Case Questions

1. What do you think of Mr. Jackson's idea to find the person responsible?
2. Do you agree with the assistant administrator on the need to keep the matter confidential? What does the administrator's suggestion imply?
3. Why did Mr. Jackson call a staff meeting? Did he call it at the right time?
4. What did the staff meeting accomplish?
5. Why do you think the hospital is having budgetary problems?
6. What should Mr. Jackson do?

Chapter 8

Aids in Planning and Decision Making

Upon completing this chapter you should be able to:

1. Describe the major features of an operations research (OR) program.

2. Identify and describe the five major steps in the management science approach to problem solving.

3. Describe the most popular OR techniques, and discuss the problems to which they are best applied.

4. Discuss the advantages and limitations of OR.

5. Discuss the barriers to effective implementation of OR and how these barriers can be overcome.

6. Discuss why forecasting is an important part of planning and decision making.

7. Identify and describe the various forecasting techniques.

In recent years, the operations of organizations have become more complex and costly. It has therefore become both more difficult and more important for managers to make effective plans and decisions. To help managers improve the quality of their planning and decision making, a variety of techniques and tools have been developed. We will describe these managerial aids in this chapter.

Specifically, we will focus on management science–operations research techniques, which aid in the decision-making process, and on forecasting techniques, which aid in the planning process. We will not be concerned with the technical or mathematical details of these techniques. Instead, we will try to increase the reader's understanding of the underlying assumptions, capabilities, and limitations of the techniques. We will attempt to answer such questions as: How can these techniques improve a manager's judgment? For what types of problems are specific techniques best suited? What are the difficulties associated with using these techniques? We include forecasting—a planning-related activity—in this chapter, because planning and decision making are closely linked and because the techniques of management science and of forecasting require similar skills.

MANAGEMENT SCIENCE APPROACHES TO DECISION MAKING

Management science, or operations research (the terms are used interchangeably in the United States), offers the manager a scientific, quantitative way of analyzing a problem and evaluating the consequences of each possible decision. By using the techniques of science and mathematics, operations research (OR) hopes to increase the logic and reliability of managerial decision making.[1] (See our discussion of management science and OR in Chapter 2.)

There are six major features of an OR program:[2]

1 *A decision-making focus.* The end result of operations research should be information that directly helps managers reach a decision. Moreover, the OR proposal should be capable of implementation. It should not suggest something managers or their organizations would find impossible to do. For this reason, it is important to feed accurate information into the OR process, so the solution offered will be realistically based.

2 *Economic effectiveness.* The financial return on an action suggested by OR should justify the cost of the action in terms of savings or revenues. A suggestion that would solve the problem but that would also result in a net financial loss is not effective. Of course, the solution that results in the greatest return may not be the best one for the organization. (For example, a decision to decentralize distribution facilities may save money but might also result in diminished quality control.) Managers will still have to use their judgment in deciding whether or not to implement the OR solution.

[1] See Frederick S. Hillier and Gerald J. Lieberman, *Operations Research,* 2nd ed. (San Francisco: Holden-Day, 1974).

[2] Harvey M. Wagner, *Principles of Operations Research,* 2nd ed. (Englewood Cliffs, N.J.: Prentice-Hall, 1975). See also David W. Miller and Martin K. Starr, *Executive Decisions and Operations Research* (Englewood Cliffs, N.J.: Prentice-Hall, 1969).

3 *The use of a mathematical model.* A *model,* by definition, is a *representation of reality.* OR reduces the elements of a complex problem to their mathematical equivalents. These are then used to construct a model on which experiments can be made. That is, elements of the model are changed and manipulated, and the results recorded. (We will describe this process in more detail later.) It is assumed that these results would occur in the real situation if it were similarly manipulated.

4 *Reliance on a computer.* A computer is usually necessary to process the model, since the computations involved are often too complex for human beings to handle efficiently. Of course, a computer cannot think for itself; if it is not given the proper data, it will not yield meaningful solutions. (In the computer field, this is known as GIGO—garbage in, garbage out.) For this reason, managers must clarify their assumptions and objectives beforehand, so the information that is given to the computer will accurately describe their problem.

A Team Approach

5 *A team approach.* The problems that OR addresses are frequently too complex for one person to solve alone. The skills and knowledge of a number of specialists—such as statisticians, economists, and psychologists—are often required. The exact composition of an OR team may vary with the problem involved, but in general the team members will represent a number of disciplines. (See box.)

6 *A systems orientation.* OR considers what is best for the organization as a whole, not for a department or division. A special difficulty arises when the OR process must not only mediate differences between the parts and the whole but between the parts as well. A traffic manager, for instance, may seek to minimize freight costs. But the sales manager may insist on fast customer service. These objectives clash: faster deliveries cost more, but if the traffic manager minimizes costs, customers may turn to other sources for faster delivery. The OR analysis will take both cost and service into account, seeking a balance that advances the overall interests of the enterprise even though the special interests of the two managers are not fully satisfied.[3]

Steps in the Management Science Approach

The process we will describe here is quite similar to the decision-making process described in Chapter 7. There are three underlying differences, however. First, the decision-making process relies on logic, while OR usually relies on a mathematical model. Second, managers apply the decision-making process themselves; OR, however, is usually carried out by a team of specialists. Finally, managers automatically implement their decision once they have made it; the OR staff, however, can only propose a solution and try to sell it to managers. As we shall see, this last aspect of OR can lead to some problems.

There are five basic steps in the management science approach to problem solving:[4]

1 Diagnosis of the problem

2 Formulation of the problem

---

[3] Ronald L. Gue and Michael E. Thomas, *Mathematical Models in Operations Research* (New York: Macmillan, 1968). See also Richard I. Levin and Charles A. Kilpatrick, *Quantitative Approaches to Management,* 3rd ed. (New York: McGraw-Hill, 1975).

[4] See Hillier and Lieberman, *Operations Research,* pp. 738–745; Wagner, *Principles of Operations Research,* pp. 9–10; and Levin and Kilpatrick, *Quantitative Approaches to Management,* pp. 15–17.

3 Model building

4 Analysis of the model

5 Implementation of findings

Diagnosis of the Problem. Before problem solving can begin, the major elements of the problem must be identified. The OR staff will try to obtain at least preliminary answers to such questions as: What are the most central parts of the problem situation? What aspects of the problem are outside the manager's control (and are therefore something the manager or the OR team cannot do anything about)? Should an optimum solution be the goal, or will compromise solutions be acceptable or necessary? Seasoned OR personnel will try to approach the problem from the same viewpoint as the manager, who must eventually accept or reject their findings.

Formulation of the Problem. Once the major elements of the problem have been identified, the OR team must begin to formulate the problem in specific terms. In particular, the team must define what elements of the problem can be changed by a decision, and what criteria the proposed solution will have to meet.

For example, as managers we might want to find the most efficient inventory level for a given product. We can contract or expand our storage facilities by

---

OR without the Computer

One possibly apocryphal story, popular among management science writers, is about a New York office building with extremely slow elevator service. Tenants on every floor complained constantly to the management of the building about the long waiting time required for the elevators. Finally, management hired a consulting firm to solve the problem. The firm in turn assigned an interdisciplinary OR team to the job.

The mathematicians and engineers on the team came up with three proposals. However, although the proposals were technically feasible, they were also too expensive to implement. At this point the team psychologist proposed an inexpensive solution. "Install full length mirrors opposite the elevators on each floor," he suggested, "and let human vanity do the rest." Sure enough, complaints about slow service trickled to a halt. People waiting for elevators simply used the extra time to adjust their clothing, fix their makeup, or comb their hair.

This story has two morals. First, it suggests the importance of the interdisciplinary approach to OR. Had the psychologist not been a part of the team, the best solution would have been overlooked. Second, the story shows that an OR team can sometimes do its job without a formal mathematical model or a computer—especially where people problems are concerned.

Source: See Russell L. Ackoff and Patrick Rivett, *A Manager's Guide to Operations Research* (New York: Wiley, 1963), pp. 20–22, and James L. Riggs and Michael S. Inoue, *Introduction to Operations Research and Management Science* (New York: McGraw-Hill, 1975), p. 5.

THE OR PROCESS

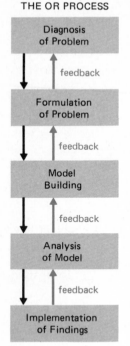

Diagnosis of Problem

↕ feedback

Formulation of Problem

↕ feedback

Model Building

↕ feedback

Analysis of Model

↕ feedback

Implementation of Findings

a simple rearrangement of floor and shelf space. The storage arrangement is a *controllable variable* in the problem; it is something we — and the OR team — can manipulate as part of the solution-finding process. However, our source for the product can supply us with only a certain maximum quantity. The product supply is the *uncontrollable variable;* it defines the limits within which the solution must be confined. An inventory level that calls for larger deliveries than our supplier is capable of handling would not be feasible.

As the major elements of the problem are isolated, the problem variables defined, and the objectives and constraints of the solution identified, the full dimensions of the problem will begin to emerge. The OR team can then proceed to construct a model so the effects of possible solutions can be determined.

Model Building. To determine the best solution to the problem, various solutions must be tested. However, the OR team could hardly experiment in the real world with changes in prices, production rates, and personnel to find a good solution. Obviously, excessive waste and disruption would result. For this reason, the OR team constructs a mathematical model that symbolically incorporates the elements of the problem. Appropriate OR specialists will devise mathematical formulas that describe the interrelationships between elements of the problem (or of a part of the problem). The values of the elements can then be changed at will without interfering with the work of the organization.

Analysis of the Model. Once the basic model has been constructed, a solution to the problem must be derived. Usually the values of the controllable variables will be changed, and with each change the model will be analyzed with the computer. The values that best meet the manager's objectives will represent the solution to the problem.

For example, let us assume we wish to determine the optimum size and cost of our sales force. Controllable variables here might include territory size, commission percentage, salary, and so on. (Uncontrollable variables — the problem limits — might include a minimum and maximum territory size and commission.) The computer will analyze changes in these variables until the best solution is found — that is, the pay scale and sales force size that will lead to the best combination of high sales and low costs.

Implementation of Findings. Of course, the entire OR process will be meaningless to the manager unless the findings are implemented. But the OR staff can only advise; it is the manager who must apply (or file) the findings. And because managers are typically pragmatic individuals, more at home with practice than with theory, they may tend to dismiss OR recommendations as the product of "ivory-tower theorizing." This hurdle can best be surmounted by securing the manager's active cooperation from the very beginning of the project, to make sure the OR team clearly understands what objectives the manager has in mind. (See Figure 8-1 for the results of a study on how management participation in OR affects the implementation of OR solutions.)

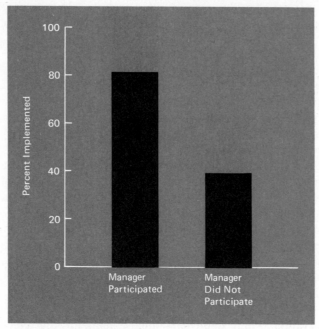

FIGURE 8-1
Relationship between OR Proposals Implemented and Manager's Participation in Problem Definition

Source: Lars Lonnstedt, "Factors Related to the Implementation of Operations Research Solutions," *Interfaces*, Vol. 5, No. 2, Part 1 (February 1975), p. 24. Used by permission.

Types of Models and Management Science Techniques

The models developed in OR must mirror reality as closely as feasible. Otherwise they would be useless. However, there are different types of models and management science techniques that are used for different types of problems.

A useful distinction we can make is between normative and descriptive models. A *normative* model tries to describe what *ought* to be done. It is used to present managers with the best or optimum solution. A normative model (probably linear programming) would be used in our example above, where we wanted to determine the ideal size of our sales force. A *descriptive* model tries to portray things *as they are*. It provides managers with information they need to make decisions—that is, it does not supply solutions to problems but suggests what would happen if problem variables were changed. For example, if a manager wanted to know what the effect of a price increase would be, the OR staff would generate a descriptive model to find the answer—perhaps a simulation model, described below.[5]

Of the many problem-solving management science models and techniques that are available, four that are among the most popular will be described here:

[5] See Miller and Starr, *Executive Decisions and Operations Research*, pp. 147–159. A second major distinction is between deterministic and probabilistic models. Deterministic models deal with exact, precisely identifiable quantities; probabilistic models involve greater uncertainty, because they deal with statistical probabilities. See Robert J. Thierauf and Richard A. Grosse, *Decision Making through Operations Research* (New York: Wiley, 1970).

linear programming models, queuing or waiting-line models, game theory, and simulation models. (Two other models, PERT and CPM, will be described in Chapter 23.)

Linear Programming Models. Linear programming models are widely used to determine the best way to allocate limited resources to achieve some desired end. (Because they seek optimum solutions, linear programming models are considered normative.) The problems for which linear programming might be used are those that can be expressed in terms of linear — that is, directly proportional — relationships.

For example, let us assume company managers want to build a number of warehouses throughout a large area so that their transportation costs will be reduced. There is a linear relationship between shipping distances and costs. (The longer the distance, the higher the cost.) The more warehouses built, the less total shipping distance that will be required. However, there is also a linear relationship between the number of warehouses constructed and building costs. To determine the ideal number of warehouses to be built (that is, the number that results in the lowest total building and transportation costs), a linear programming model would be used.

Linear programming models can be applied to those business and industrial operations where some maximum or minimum value can be derived — establishing maximum machine output, ideal inventory levels, best product mix, and the like.

Queuing or Waiting-Line Models. If trucks arrive at a loading platform at the rate of approximately three per hour, and it takes approximately 20 minutes to load each truck, a queue or waiting line will form when trucks arrive late or when the loading pace slows down. There are costs associated with such a waiting line, and these costs increase as the line grows — gasoline expenses if engines are idling, truck driver wages, and traffic congestion, to name a few. There would also be costs associated with a more efficient loading operation — for example, it may require many extra workers always to load a truck within 10 minutes. Similarly, if customers wait too long at a supermarket checkout counter, they may take their business elsewhere. But it might be too expensive to keep a sufficiently large number of checkout counters operating.

Queuing or waiting-line models are developed to help managers decide how long a waiting line would be most preferable. The models will predict the probable result of various changes in the system involved.

Game Theory. Game theory attempts to predict how rational people will behave in competitive situations. By so doing, it helps people who are competing develop strategies that will combine high gains with low costs. While game theory is most widely used in military strategy, it is also used in industries where individual firms must adjust their actions to the likely actions of their competitors. Game theorists might, for example, attempt to describe how competitors will respond to a price increase, the introduction of a new product, or a new advertising campaign. If, for instance, a price reduction would quickly be matched by competitors, there would be little immediate advantage in lowering prices.

By analyzing what competitors are likely to do in certain situations, game theorists can help managers develop effective strategies. Unfortunately, most competitive situations are extremely complex and involve many possible variables. Game theory has not yet developed to the point where it provides strong guidance for any but the simplest problems in planning and strategy.

Simulation Models. In one sense, all models use the process of simulation in that they imitate reality. Simulation models, however, are specifically designed to be used for problems that are too complex to be described or solved by standard mathematical equations (such as those used in linear programming). They try to replicate a part of an organization's operations in order to see what will happen to that part over time, or to experiment with that part by changing certain variables. (Thus, simulation models are descriptive rather than normative.)

For example, simulation models were used to prepare astronauts for each moon landing. Computers would present the astronaut with a variety of situations to which the astronaut would have to react as if they were really occurring. (The astronaut's controls were a duplicate of the controls in the actual lunar module.) The computer was programmed to react realistically to the astronaut's actions. For instance, a serious mistake by the astronaut resulted in an automatic "abort."

Simulation models have a variety of uses, including the testing of machine systems and large-scale operations such as airports. Like all models, they permit experimentation to take place without interfering with actual operations. Another major advantage of simulation models is that they can be speeded up (through the computer) to indicate within minutes what would occur in the real world over a period of years.

Application of OR Techniques

There are eight types of problems for which OR techniques are most frequently applied:

— Inventory	— Routing
— Allocation	— Replacement
— Queuing	— Competition
— Sequencing	— Search

Before we discuss these problems, we should note that management problems tend to include a variety of overlapping elements — they do not fall neatly into one category or another. Nevertheless, it is convenient to discuss each type of problem separately and see which OR technique is best suited for it.[6]

---

[6] See Russell L. Ackoff and Patrick Rivett. *A Manager's Guide to Operations Research* (New York: Wiley, 1963). See also Gue and Thomas, *Mathematical Models*, pp. 8–12.

versus

Inventory Problems. Inventory problems are among those best approached through OR techniques because they involve the balancing of conflicting objectives. Unit costs of products tend to go down as the quantity ordered (or made in-house) goes up. Large inventories might therefore seem desirable. On the other hand, large inventories tie up capital that could otherwise be invested, and they require greater expenditures on storage and insurance. Similarly, the need for sufficient inventory to meet customer demand conflicts with the need to prevent excessive stockpiling.

As managers, we might have to decide how much inventory to carry and when inventory needs to be replenished. To help us decide, the OR team will try to balance these conflicting cost tendencies so as to find an optimal solution. That is, they will propose an inventory program that will balance the need to satisfy customer demands against the need to maintain low ordering and carrying costs. Linear programming models might well be used for such inventory problems. In more complex cases, simulation models might be required.

Allocation Problems. There are two common types of allocation problems, both of which are best solved through linear programming. In the first type, a given set of resources can be combined in different ways to perform a particular job. For example, in an assembly plant, the same number of products could be produced by many employees and a few machines, or more machines and fewer employees. Assuming managers have the resources to buy the machines or hire new employees, their allocation problem is to find the best mix of machines and employees—that is, the mix that will keep their costs to a minimum.

The other type of allocation problem appears when there are not enough resources available to do all the jobs that managers would like to have done. On an individual and organizational level, managers solve one kind of allocation problem when they make up a budget. A more complex example of this type of problem can be found in organizations that can produce many different kinds of products but only several kinds at the same time (a container manufacturing company, for instance). The allocation problem is to find the most profitable product mix.

Queuing (Waiting-Line) Problems. Queuing problems involve designing facilities to meet a demand for services. Such problems might arise in gas stations, telephone and telegraph switching operations, or, as we mentioned earlier, loading platforms and supermarket checkout counters. Usually, queuing models are used to solve waiting-line problems, but in some complex cases simulation techniques might be required.

Sequencing Problems. Sequencing problems arise when we have to decide in what order the parts of a job are to be performed. For example, in a factory assembly line, a product must pass through several work stations before it is completed. On a poorly planned line, some stations will be idle while others are overburdened. The problem is to sequence the work stations in such a way that idle time is minimized and working time at all stations is roughly equalized. Solutions to sequencing problems are usually found through simulation, which allows the efficiency of different sequences to be tested.

Routing (or Scheduling) Problems. Routing problems arise if we have to decide *when* (rather than in what order) parts of a job are to be done. For example, freight might have to be shipped from point A to point B via a number of intermediate points. Which is the most efficient schedule in terms of time and cost? Similarly, a salesperson might have a certain number of clients or locations to visit. Which route or schedule would allow him or her to make all necessary visits in the shortest possible time (or at the lowest possible cost)? Complex routing problems may be handled by linear programming, queuing models, or some combination of the two.

Replacement Problems. Some expensive items in an organization will deteriorate over time or become obsolete — machinery and trucks are obvious examples. If they are kept for too long a period of time, they become inefficient and increasingly expensive to operate. (They may require increased maintenance, for example.) On the other hand, replacing them may also involve considerable cost. One type of problem, then, is to decide exactly when such items must be replaced.

Another type of replacement problem involves large numbers of inexpensive items, such as light bulbs, which tend to operate fairly consistently until they suddenly stop working altogether. The manager's problem is to decide whether to have each item replaced as it fails or to wait until a set number fails and then have several items replaced simultaneously. Developing a replacement schedule for the bulbs on a bridge or at an airport is a typical example. These types of problems are usually solved through linear programming, which can suggest the least expensive replacement schedule.

Competition Problems. Competition problems develop when two or more organizations are trying to achieve inherently conflicting objectives — such as each trying to increase its market share when an increase for some will obviously mean a decrease for others. Since the decisions made by one competitor can affect and are affected by the decisions of other competitors, the problem becomes to find those strategies and decisions that will maximize one's gains and minimize one's losses. For example, when the managers of store A are considering new price and advertising policies to attract more customers, they have to take into account what store B is doing now and may do in retaliation. Similarly, in competitive bidding for a contract, each bidder must reckon with the actions and reactions of other bidders. Game theory offers guidelines to help managers in competitive situations select the most effective — or least risky — strategies and decisions.

199

Search Problems. As we discussed in Chapter 7, faulty or incomplete information can lead to decision errors. These in turn may require time and expense to correct. Yet, there are also time and monetary costs associated with collecting information. For example, for most production lines, quality inspection of every item would obviously be too expensive, though not inspecting enough items might let a defective batch go by. The problem is to find the right balance between getting enough information to keep decision errors to a minimum and holding down the costs of information gathering. Statistical tools, in combination with linear programming models, are the most widely used techniques for search problems.

Advantages and
Limitations
of OR

Advantages. Management science–OR techniques have but one purpose: to help managers make better decisions. They can fulfill this purpose because they have three major advantages. First, they make it possible to break down a complex, large-scale problem into smaller parts that can be more easily diagnosed and manipulated. Second, in building and analyzing OR models, researchers have to pay close attention to details and to follow logical, systematic procedures. This improves the likelihood of a good decision. Errors creep in more easily when decisions are made on the basis of subjective judgment, past experience, or "rules of thumb," rather than on the basis of a systematic approach. Third, OR is helpful in assessing possible alternatives for the manager. If managers are more aware of the risks and opportunities inherent in the alternatives available to them, they will be more likely to choose the right alternative.

Limitations. As might be expected, OR projects are costly. The expense of the OR specialists' time alone often makes OR too expensive for many organizations or many types of problems. For this reason, each OR study has to be subjected to its own cost-benefit analysis before the decision to do the study is made.

Another disadvantage of OR is that it cannot be effectively applied in many situations. Some problems are simply too complex to be handled by the mathematical tools that are now available. The intuitive judgment of managers will still be required. In crisis situations, there will be no time for the extended analysis of OR; managers will have to respond quickly on their own. Similarly, there are many situations where the available information is inadequate for an OR study. This is particularly true in situations involving human qualities and interpersonal relationships, which cannot yet be quantified.

Perhaps the greatest drawback of OR is that it can easily become a technique divorced from reality—either because of defects in the initial assumptions about a problem or because certain crucial variables are ignored. As we have already mentioned, an OR analysis cannot be more sound than the information it is based upon. Accounting records, for example, are far from exact; they depend heavily on estimates and crude approximations. If an OR analysis relies on such records for figures on manufacturing costs and profits, it may turn out to be faulty. The other great danger in using OR is that researchers may ignore important aspects of a problem because they are not measurable.

© 1970, The Register and Tribune Syndicate

An OR recommendation to increase productivity by changing the work sequence may be logical but irrelevant if the entire plant goes out on strike because of poor working conditions. OR can provide guidance on a problem, but it is not a substitute for managerial judgment.

Problems of
Implementation
Despite the fact that OR has been successfully used to solve many problems in business, nonprofit organizations, and government, OR findings are not always put into effect. For example, in a survey of corporate-level OR groups, Efraim Turban found that only about 60 percent of OR projects were "completely" or "mostly implemented."[7] C. Jackson Grayson, Jr., a manager with a management science background, found OR methods useless when he served as chairman of the Price Commission (which set up and monitored price controls) from 1971 to 1973.[8]

Of course, Grayson had to deal with large-scale problems that had political implications, and the nature of his assignment made fast action particularly important. Still, he was unusually familiar with OR techniques and presumably predisposed toward using them. This fact makes his failure to find OR useful more compelling than if he had been a "stodgy" old manager resisting new technologies.

Grayson offers five reasons many managers do not use OR techniques:

1 *Shortage of time.* Managers bypass OR because it is too time-consuming.

2 *Inaccessibility of data.* It requires too much time, effort, and expense to obtain the information an OR model requires.

3 *Resistance to change.* Everyone encounters resistance in trying to induce people to change well-established ways of doing things. The fact that OR techniques seem so sophisticated and mysterious to many managers makes it even more difficult for the techniques to become accepted.

[7] Efraim Turban, "A Sample Survey of Operations Research at the Corporate Level," *Operations Research,* Vol. 2, No. 3 (May-June 1972), pp. 708–721.

[8] C. Jackson Grayson, Jr., "Management Science and Business Practice," *Harvard Business Review,* July-August 1973, pp. 41–48.

4 *Long response time.* Management scientists approach problems in a highly methodical fashion, rather than begin working on a solution as soon as a problem arises. Managers, however, often need to find solutions quickly. A methodical approach may not seem helpful to them.

5 *Invalidating simplifications.* Because so many of the important areas of management — people problems, organizational politics, power struggles — are hard to quantify, OR simply excludes them from its mathematical equations. The models that result may lead to elegant solutions, but these may be completely useless, because the simplified assumptions they were based on were too far removed from reality.

Grayson does *not* call for the abandonment of OR. Rather, he reaffirms its potential, provided its practitioners rid OR of its defects and limitations. To gain acceptance of their methods, Grayson suggests that management scientists need to become more sensitive to the messy, complicated, time-limited environment of the manager. They also need to try to put all important information in their models, no matter how imprecise and unquantifiable such information may be. Their solutions may then be cruder, but they will also be more workable and useful to the manager.

The Effect of Management Styles. An interesting analysis of why management scientists have problems getting their findings implemented is provided by James McKenney and Peter Keen.[9] These authors suggest that managers differ from management scientists in their information-gathering and problem-solving styles, and that these differences can affect how fully managers will accept OR recommendations.

A person's method of information gathering can either be preceptive or receptive. Those of us who are *preceptive* individuals bring preconceived notions to bear on a situation. We focus on the way various items relate to each other and how they conform to or deviate from our expectations. Those of us who are *receptive* individuals keep our preconceptions under control. We prefer to develop conclusions about the information we have by examining it carefully and in detail.

There are also two problem-solving styles, suggest McKenney and Keen: intuitive and systematic. Those of us who are *intuitive* tend to use trial-and-error methods and readily switch from one problem-solving approach to another. We quickly jump to conclusions based on our past experience. Those of us who are *systematic* tend to approach a problem methodically. We may formally structure a problem in the hope that we will then be more likely to find a solution.

Many types of managerial jobs (such as those in marketing and production) are particularly well suited for those of us with preceptive-intuitive styles. Management scientists, on the other hand, are much more likely to have a systematic style of problem solving and, while their information-gathering styles may vary, they would seem to tend more toward the receptive mode.

[9] James L. McKenney and Peter G. W. Keen, "How Managers' Minds Work," *Harvard Business Review,* May-June 1974, pp. 79–90.

McKenney and Keen hypothesize that managers who are more amenable to systematic approaches and whose own styles are systematic are more likely to be comfortable working with management scientists and to find OR helpful. Intuitive managers who deal in their day-to-day work with more loosely structured problems are less likely to find OR helpful or to feel comfortable working with management scientists. To learn to accept OR, say McKenney and Keen, such managers should interact informally with management science specialists and experiment with using the simpler OR techniques on some of their problems.

The Keys to Implementation. It is obviously to a manager's advantage to increase OR's usefulness and to make it more likely that helpful OR suggestions will be implemented. Wagner has suggested that the most beneficial OR programs contain the following eight elements:[10]

1   *Sponsorship by top management.* Without the support of top management, an OR program will be less likely to have a manager's cooperation. It is also top management's job to make sure an OR program serves the needs of the entire organization, rather than only one part.

2   *Managerial responsibility for the program.* If managers have the ultimate responsibility for the success of an OR project, they are more likely to become actively involved in it. When responsibility for the program is left to the OR staff, it is easier for managers to ignore OR's findings.

3   *Manager participation.* If managers participate in establishing program objectives, the OR models will be much more realistically based. In turn, the solutions suggested by OR studies will be more useful.

4   *Use of managerial judgment.* A manager's advice must be obtained at carefully chosen points in the OR process. Such a procedure will prevent an OR project from going off on a wrong track. It will also make us more open to the solutions offered by OR.

5   *Technical aspects not permitted to dominate.* The mathematical and technical procedures of OR must, of course, be performed competently if the technique is to have any value. However, OR personnel must take into account the less measurable aspects of a problem. They should be particularly aware of how people affect and are affected by the solutions they suggest.

6   *Rapid data collection.* A long, extended process of information gathering will not be helpful to the manager who needs to make decisions as soon as possible. Collecting data quickly and efficiently will shorten the OR process and thus make it more useful.

7   *Preparation for initial difficulties.* When a new OR system is being tested and installed, temporary difficulties are to be expected. If managers anticipate problems and prepare for them, the effectiveness of the system will not be hindered. For example, to prevent resentment when an OR program is begun, managers can work with their subordinates in developing ideas and suggestions to make the program work.

[10] Wagner, *Principles of Operations Research*, pp. 943–951. Lars Lonnstedt (in "Factors Related to the Implementation of Operations Research Solutions," *Interfaces*, Vol. 5, No. 2, Part 1 [February 1975], pp. 23–50) adds one more element: problem scope. He found that OR findings were more likely to be implemented if they were not limited to a small part of the problem.

8 *Accurate recordkeeping.* As an OR program progresses, the assumptions and facts that originally went into the models may become outdated. The organization itself may change over time, or the OR team may have to refine the models as it collects additional information. Instead of building new models each time the situation changes, an effective OR team will periodically bring the original models up to date, saving both time and expense. Keeping OR models current will also make it easier to use the models to solve similar problems in the future.

FORECASTING TECHNIQUES

OR techniques are normally used to solve problems that already exist. Forecasting techniques, on the other hand, are used to anticipate future problems and events. Because they are concerned with the future, forecasts involve a great many uncertainties. Thus, unlike OR, most forecasting techniques tend to be qualitative rather than quantitative.

A popular observation made by many forecasters is that "the only certain thing about a forecast is that it will be wrong." This observation hints at the fact that forecasts do not have to be "right" to be meaningful. They simply have to predict future events closely enough to make our actions in the present valid and purposeful. In essence, the forecaster has the same aim as the OR analyst: to help managers assess alternatives and improve their chances of reaching effective decisions.[11]

The fact that many forecasts by meteorologists, economists, politicians, and managers prove inaccurate may cause us to forget how widespread and important forecasts really are. Most of the actions we will take on a daily basis—as individuals or as managers—will be based on some type of forecast. We may tentatively predict the weather in deciding what to wear before we go out; we may schedule regular meetings in our department, because we foresee that without such meetings the quality of work in our department may decline; we may engage in planning, because we expect that through planning our organization will be better able to meet its goals. Forecasts are necessary, because without them we are at the mercy of future events. By anticipating the future, we make it more likely that our decisions and actions will be sound.

Forecasts as Premises In formulating plans and reaching decisions, managers try to assess the alternatives available to them. In effect, they forecast how events within and outside the organization will affect each alternative and what the outcome of each alternative will be. These forecasts are the *premises,* or basic assumptions, upon which managers' planning and decision making are based.[12] For example, in deciding what fuel to use for heating the new college dormitory under construction, a manager may assume that the natural gas shortage will continue for the foreseeable future and eliminate gas as a possible choice.

---

[11] See James Morrell, ed., *Management Decisions and the Role of Forecasting* (Baltimore: Penguin Books, 1972).

[12] See George A. Steiner, *Top Management Planning* (New York: Macmillan, 1969).

Two broad types of forecasts serve as planning premises: (1) forecasts of events that will not be influenced by the organization, and (2) forecasts of events that will be influenced, at least in part, by the organization's behavior. For the first type, well-established tools of economic analysis are widely employed. For the second type, these tools must be supplemented by less precise qualitative approaches—some of which will be described later in this chapter.

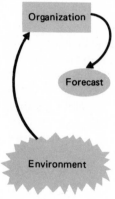

Forecasts Independent of an Organization's Behavior. Certain basic economic and social variables, such as the gross national product, national employment rates, changes in social values, and shifts in immigration patterns, are unaffected by any one organization's behavior. Thus, managers need not take their organization's possible actions into account when making predictions about such variables. Instead, they will look to leading broad-based indicators—such as Department of Health, Education, and Welfare statistics—in finding the information they need. For example, if administrators need to decide whether or not to expand their college's facilities, federal statistics can give them some idea of long-term college enrollment trends.

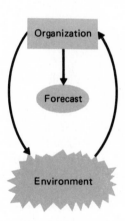

Forecasts Affected by an Organization's Behavior. These types of forecasts are more difficult, because they require some assumptions about the organization's actions as well as assumptions about events outside the organization's control. A sales forecast, for example, starts initially as a company objective. In the planning process, the managers' analyses of anticipated company actions and likely competitor responses—together with their projections of the economic environment—may indicate to them that the sales objective will not be realized if existing programs and policies are left unchanged. In such a case, as described in Chapter 5, a "planning gap" is said to exist. Accordingly, the managers will rework the decisions previously adopted until analysis indicates that the "planning gap" for the sales forecast has been closed—that is, until forecasted sales under the new program and the sales objectives are the same. Once the planning gap has been closed, the sales forecast becomes a *premise* for subsequent parts of the planning process. For instance, the managers might use the sales forecast to help establish production plans and schedules.

Forecasting Techniques for Economic and Sales Information

Because of the importance of predicting future economic and sales information, our discussion of forecasting techniques will focus on these areas. The same techniques can, of course, be used for forecasting other variables (such as the anticipated number of job applicants in a town where the company might open a plant or the number of votes a political candidate will receive). There are essentially three types of forecasting techniques used in these areas: qualitative methods, time series analysis, and causal models.[13]

[13] John C. Chambers, Satinder K. Mullick, and Donald Smith, "How to Choose the Right Forecasting Technique," *Harvard Business Review,* July-August 1971, pp. 45–74. See also Steven C. Wheelwright and Darral G. Clarke, "Corporate Forecasting: Promise and Reality," *Harvard Business Review,* November-December 1976, pp. 40–42 ff.

Qualitative and Judgmental Methods. Qualitative and judgmental methods are appropriate when hard data are scarce or difficult to use. For instance, when a new product or technology is introduced, past experience is not a reliable guide for estimating what the near-term effects will be. These forecasting methods involve the use of subjective judgments and rating schemes to transform qualitative information into quantitative estimates. The purpose of these techniques is to gather information in a logical, unbiased, and orderly manner. Examples of qualitative techniques are the jury of executive opinion, sales force composite, and customer expectations methods.

In a *jury of executive opinion,* the manager may bring together top executives from major functional areas of the organization: sales, finance, production, and purchasing, for example. The manager supplies the group with background information on the item to be forecast, then combines and averages the executives' views. An advantage of this technique is that no elaborate statistics or mathematical calculations are required.

The *sales force composite* is similar to the executive jury, except that it is limited to the sales organization. It includes the opinions of salespeople in the field as well as sales managers, and focuses on forecasting the outlook for specific products or total sales.

The *customer expectations* technique, as its name implies, involves canvassing the organization's customers or clients. The canvass is accomplished either by survey or by the sales force interrogating selected customers. Its purpose is to determine the customers' own estimates of their needs and requirements. Most market research groups use this approach.

Time Series Analysis. Sometimes managers would like to have available a projection of future possibilities, based on some current trend. For example, in long-term planning, they may wish to have an idea of what their product sales for the next five years are likely to be. Or, if they are managers in an automobile insurance company, they might want to know if there is likely to be a seasonal variation in the accident rate. An efficient way to make such a projection is to extrapolate from past experience. If managers can identify a pattern that has appeared in the past, they can predict with some confidence that the pattern will continue in the future.

Time series analysis is a procedure for identifying patterns in information that has been accumulated over time. It is most useful when managers have a great deal of data on hand and when they can discern clear and stable trends. For example, let us assume we want to project what our sales will be for each month over a period of a year, in order to refine our inventory purchases. We would perform a time series analysis on the sales records we have available for, say, the previous six years—first by dividing our sales records into separate twelve-month periods and then by dividing each year's records into months. In all likelihood there will be a pattern of sales from month to month and a pattern of growth from year to year. Projecting these trends into the future will give us roughly the information we need.

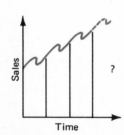

Causal Models. In some situations, there are a number of variables that clearly affect the matter managers would like to forecast. Personal income and consumer confidence, for instance, will obviously affect car sales; fluctuations in weather will directly affect the sale of heating oil. Where the relationships between these variables and the factor to be forecast are known, *causal models* can be constructed. Causal models describe (usually in mathematical terms) the relationship between the elements involved in a situation. If managers have information about the relevant variables, the model allows them to make a prediction about the matter affected by those variables.

For example, John C. Chambers and his colleagues described how the Corning Glass Works Company uses causal models to forecast the demand for its television picture tubes.[14] The company's model takes the form of a flow chart that shows the manufacturing, distribution, and sales network through which the tubes must move to reach the consumer. The critical points on the chart indicate the inventory positions of the various companies in the network. Changes in the inventories allow Corning's managers to forecast sales of the tubes — if inventories pile up, for instance, managers will forecast a slowdown in orders for new tubes.

If the correct causal relationships have been established, causal models are the most accurate of forecasting tools. They are particularly popular and useful in making sales forecasts.

Technological Forecasting

The rapid pace of technological change has led many firms, hospitals, government, and other institutions to recognize the importance of predicting future technological developments. Technological discoveries in such areas as lasers, jet aircraft, nuclear energy, communications devices, desalinization of sea water, and synthetic construction materials have drastically affected many organizations.[15] As managers, we may often have to ascertain what technological developments are likely to occur, so we will be able to prepare our organization for change. (See Figure 8-2 on the next page for an illustration of how technological forecasting is integrated into the management process.)

To make technological forecasts, managers can use any of the techniques described earlier. However, qualitative methods such as the Delphi technique, brainstorming, and scenario construction are especially favored in technological forecasting. These methods allow managers to make predictions when there is comparatively little information available to them.[16]

---

[14] Chambers, "How to Choose the Right Forecasting Technique," p. 47.

[15] See Daniel D. Roman, "Technological Forecasting in the Decision Process," *Academy of Management Journal,* Vol. 13, No. 2 (June 1970), pp. 127–138.

[16] See William F. Butler et al., eds., *Methods and Techniques of Business Forecasting* (Englewood Cliffs, N.J.: Prentice-Hall, 1974); Steven C. Wheelwright and Spyros Makridakis, *Forecasting Methods for Management* (New York: Wiley, 1973); Gordon Willis et al., *Technological Forecasting and Corporate Strategy* (New York: American Elsevier, 1969); and Robert U. Ayres, *Technological Forecasting and Long-Range Planning* (New York: McGraw-Hill, 1969).

FIGURE 8-2
Integrating
Technological
Forecasting into
the Management
Process

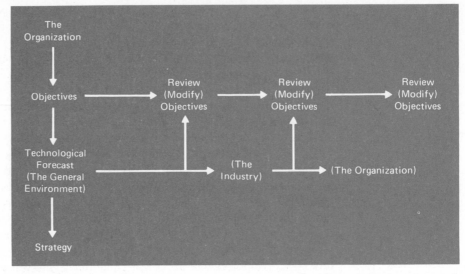

Source: Adapted from Daniel D. Roman, "Technological Forecasting in the Decision Process," *Academy of Management Journal*, Vol. 13, No. 2 (June 1970), p. 133. Used by permission.

The Delphi Method. Developed by the Rand Corporation, the Delphi method is a systematic procedure for arriving at a consensus of opinion among a group of experts.[17] The experts are given a series of detailed questionnaires about a problem. They are also asked to provide their own written opinions. The use of questionnaires avoids direct contact and debate among the experts, which might induce hasty formulation of and commitment to certain ideas. After reading the anonymous answers of the other participants, each expert revises his or her own answers. Eventually, after a series of "rounds" of this type, convergence of opinion usually occurs.

This method can be used to obtain "hard" quantitative data, such as the future sales of refrigerators, or "softer" phenomena, such as projected changes in social and cultural values or the likelihood and time of future technological breakthroughs. Disadvantages of the Delphi method are: insufficient reliability (Would a different panel of experts reach the same conclusions?); oversensitivity to ambiguous questions (Will the particular wording of the questions on each "round" influence the results too much?); and the near impossibility of taking unexpected events into account.

Brainstorming. Brainstorming is often used whenever a large number of new ideas and new alternatives are desired during the decision-making process. It can also be used to forecast possible future events. The brainstorming technique usually involves conducting a group meeting on a specific problem under rules designed to foster freewheeling and creative speculation. One important

[17] See Lesley Albertson and Terrence Cutler, "Delphi," *Futures*, Vol. 8, No. 5 (October 1976), pp. 397–404.

rule is that no participant may criticize any idea that comes up. In a modified version of brainstorming, the participants can role-play the thing or concept central to the forecast. This version is generally used to predict military or political strategy. Group brainstorming can take up a great deal of time, but it is useful for generating ideas that might otherwise never be considered. (See also our discussion of brainstorming in Chapter 14.)

Scenario Construction. Scenario construction is a method that has been used to make very long-range forecasts by "think tanks" (such as that of the Rand Corporation). A *scenario* is a logical, hypothetical description of events. By developing a scenario, the think tank or committee explores the details and dynamics of alternative events, rather than only isolated specific elements of change (as in the OR technique of simulation).

For example, if General Motors aims for a 10 percent increase in its share of the automobile market, management would want to know how competitors, car buyers, and government agencies would be affected by this GM action. Such a forecast is very difficult to obtain with any degree of precision. To achieve that 10 percent increase may call for a complex, multilayered series of market readjustments difficult to predict or simulate with any degree of confidence. But a well-designed scenario might be able to explore each read-justment for a reasonably accurate forecast. It will thus help managers under-stand more fully the possible consequences of pursuing their desired goal.

Morphological Analysis. *Morphological analysis,* the study of structure and form, is not actually a forecasting method. But it has been suggested as a useful technique for systematically structuring a technological forecasting effort and generating ideas. This method consists of identifying the relevant dimensions of the subject, listing all varieties and combinations of those dimensions, and finding practical applications for them. For example, one could explore in this manner all the different ways a new packaging material could be used.[18] How-ever, the ideas that emerge must then be studied through a forecasting tech-nique such as Delphi or scenario construction.

Choosing the Appropriate Forecasting Technique

No single method of forecasting can satisfy the requirements of all types of managers and organizations. The method a manager will select depends on the planning and decision-making context, the amount of information available, the level of accuracy required, the time period to be forecast, the time avail-able to complete the analysis, and the value of the forecast to the organization. (See box on next page.)

A recent survey suggests that organizations generally adopt an "evolu-tionary" approach to forecasting, similar to the way they adopt OR tech-niques.[19] With OR, organizations use the simpler methods first and proceed

---

[18] See Johann G. Wissema, "Morphological Analysis: Its Application to a Company TF Investi-gation," *Futures,* Vol. 8, No. 2 (April 1976), pp. 146–153.

[19] Wheelwright and Clarke, "Corporate Forecasting," p. 60.

Criteria for Selecting a Forecasting Method		
Factor 1: Manager's Technical Ability	—Level of forecasting sophistication	—Understanding of the method —Formal training in forecasting
Factor 2: Cost	—Manager's time —Preparer's time	—Computer time —Data collection
Factor 3: Problem-Specific Characteristics	—Time horizon to be forecast —Length of each time period —Functional area involved	—Degree of top management support —Manager-forecaster relationship
Factor 4: Method Charac- teristics Desired	—Accuracy —Statistics available	

Source: Adapted from Steven C. Wheelwright and Darral G. Clarke, "Corporate Forecasting: Promise and Reality," *Harvard Business Review*, November-December 1976, p. 42. Copyright © 1976 by the President and Fellows of Harvard College; all rights reserved.

to more complex techniques once OR has proved its worth. Similarly, less difficult forecasting methods, such as the executive jury or brainstorming, would first be used in a small part of the organization. Later, as managers gain experience with forecasting, a broader range of techniques will be introduced to other parts of the organization.

Summary   Management science or operations research (OR) techniques help managers improve the effectiveness of their decisions by systematically analyzing a problem and alternative solutions. The basic management science approach is to assemble a group of specialists from a variety of fields and have them diagnose and formulate the problem with the appropriate managers. The specialists will then build a mathematical model that describes the relationship between all the elements of the problem, analyze the model with a computer by changing the values of the problem variables, and then recommend a problem solution. The managers will decide whether or not to implement the OR team's findings.

Some widely used OR tools are *linear programming models, queuing* or *waiting-line models, game theory,* and *simulation models.* Some of these tools, such as linear programming, are *normative* in that they suggest a best solution. Others, such as simulation, are *descriptive* in that they suggest what will happen if a particular solution is adopted. Each OR tool is best suited for certain types of problems.

OR can improve our chances of making good decisions. However, it does have disadvantages. These include its cost, its inapplicability for many problem situations, and its tendency to overlook nonquantifiable aspects of a problem. Defects in OR can be overcome by careful planning and by periodic consultation with the appropriate managers.

Forecasting techniques are used to anticipate future problems and events. Although they are less certain than OR techniques, they can still improve our chances of making effective plans and decisions. Once forecasts have been made, they become the *premises* upon which planning and decision making are based.

Forecasting techniques for economic and sales information include *qualitative methods* (such as a jury of executive opinion), *time series analysis,* and *causal models.* Technological forecasting tools include the *Delphi method, brainstorming,* and *scenario construction.* The best way to introduce OR and forecasting techniques into an organization would seem to be to start with the simpler, qualitative techniques that people can appreciate before turning to the more technical approaches.

Review Questions

1. Why do you think management science and forecasting techniques were developed?
2. What are the six major features of a meaningful OR program? Why do you think each feature is important?
3. What are the steps in the OR approach to problem solving?
4. What are linear programming models, queuing models, simulation models, and game theory? For which of the eight types of problems discussed in the chapter can each OR technique be used?
5. On what bases would you decide whether or not to use OR to help you solve a problem? What role do you think your managerial style would play in your decision?
6. What are the major defects and limitations of OR, and how can they be overcome? Why will your involvement as a manager in the OR process make it more effective?
7. Why do you think forecasts do not have to be completely accurate to be meaningful?
8. Why is forecasting an important part of the planning or decision-making process? What are the two types of forecasts that serve as planning premises?
9. What three types of forecasting techniques are used to generate economic and sales information?
10. Why has technological forecasting become important to managers?
11. What three qualitative methods are used in technological forecasting?

CASE STUDY: CROCKER MACHINING AND FINISHING COMPANY

The Crocker Machining and Finishing Company is a medium-sized manufacturer of component parts in St. Louis. All of its work is done to specifications set by the purchaser. Usually the purchaser contracts out parts to a number of subcontractors and then assembles the unit. Occasionally the purchasers will manufacture some of their own components. Most of the required parts are very similar to previously ordered parts.

When placing an order with Crocker, the purchasing company usually submits a plan of the part or component it wants, Crocker quotes a price, some negotiation follows in which the price may be lowered, and the contract is made. Rarely will bids be solicited because of the well-established working relationships between Crocker, the other machine shops, and the purchasers. The purchasers' stress is on quality components and reliable suppliers rather than on the cheapest price.

The Crocker company's president, Jill Merchant, was attending a management science seminar at the local university when she heard a paper on operations research delivered by Andrew Pittman, a graduating MBA student at the university's School of Business Administration. She was impressed by the paper, and after a series of interviews with Andrew, she offered him a job as Operations Analyst, a position that did not previously exist at Crocker.

211

Andrew accepted the offer and, for the first month, roamed throughout the factory, getting the hang of the floor layout and the various machining operations and asking each worker what he or she did and why he or she did it in that fashion. By the end of that first month, Andrew felt he was a part of the business. The workers, when feeling charitable toward him, felt he was a meddling, troublesome, snoopy busybody.

During his fifth week there, Andrew began looking at the specifications of the orders. He realized many of them were for very similar components but with minor variations. From the engineering and drafting department, Andrew obtained blueprints of components made in the past three years. There were some unique design orders, but most could be put into one of twenty broad types. Andrew suggested to Ms. Merchant that twenty general-type components be designed by engineering, mass-produced, and stocked. The bulk of the orders, he showed her, could be filled, with minor modifications, from stock. The cost of the individual modifications would be more than covered by the savings from mass production, he assured her.

Encouraged by Andrew, Ms. Merchant sent out a policy memo to all department heads announcing the change to mass production and modification for all future contracts. Engineering was the first to complain: "What are you trying to do? Put us out of a job?"

Sales was second: "The clients aren't going to like this. They want what they ask for, not something just as good."

Three days passed before the production department registered its verdict: "The workers won't like handling this stuff twice. They say it's easier to build from scratch than to modify these standard parts."

The next day Quality Control notified everyone that the reject rate for the first batch of standardized parts was triple the normal rate.

One week to the day after sending out the memo, Jill Merchant walked into her office at 8:45 A.M. and found seven very angry department heads waiting for her.

Case Questions

1. Why were the department heads angry?
2. How should Ms. Merchant have gone about hiring Andrew and introducing him into the organization?
3. Can you think of a better way in which Andrew could have obtained the information he wanted?
4. What effect do you think Andrew's suggestion had on the industrial workers' morale?
5. How should Ms. Merchant have handled the policy change?
6. What should she do now?

Part

Organizing for Stability and Change

Case on Organizing for Stability and Change

WILCO, INC.

Shortly after his discharge from the Air Force, Donald Wilson went to work in a small machine shop in Detroit that was run by the father of a former service buddy. Today, eight years later, Donald Wilson owns and operates his own corporation, with sales in excess of $1.6 million.

Donald Wilson had spent six years in the Air Force as a helicopter repairman in Vietnam and Germany. During this time, he became familiar with lathes, grinders, punch presses, and other machinery and equipment. Before going into the military, he had worked one year on an assembly line, but this job had not appealed to him as much as working in machining operations. Upon leaving the Air Force, Wilson decided against going to college. Instead, he chose to enter the machine tool business.

Mr. Wilson proved to be a very fast learner, and after three years he became a foreman supervising a range of casting, molding, metal cutting, and turning operations. While performing his duties, he became acquainted with purchasing agents from General Motors and Ford who liked his work and know-how. Eventually they suggested that it might be feasible for him to start his own business, indicating they would do business with him if he was able to obtain the support necessary to start his own venture.

Mr. Wilson contacted a local Business Development Organization official in Detroit who put him in touch with a branch office of the National Bank of Detroit. The bank's branch manager referred him to a local Minority Enterprise Small Business Investment Company (MESBIC), and the MESBIC officials helped him to prepare a business plan and a loan application. He was subsequently granted a loan by the bank and the MESBIC organization.

With the loan in hand, Mr. Wilson opened up a shop in Livonia, Michigan, and began to produce a line of metal parts, mostly small pins and fittings for the Ford and GM transmission plants in the immediate area. His first orders, he felt, were granted because of his minority status, but the larger, more complex, and more profitable orders that followed were clear indications that he was now seen as just another good and reliable vendor, not a "special case." In consequence, sales expanded from $80,000 in the first year to $1,600,000 in the fifth year. In the fourth year of operation, Mr. Wilson obtained new loans to add a facility in Livonia, and the following year he purchased additional capacity in Wayne, Michigan.

At this point, Wilco, Inc., was over the hump of being a new venture and into the first stages of advanced growth.

Case prepared by John G. Hutchinson. Reprinted by permission.

The primary business of Wilco is the production of standard parts for the General Motors and Ford transmission plants. Some small parts are also sold to the Ford Gear and Axle Division and the Saginaw Steering Gear Division of General Motors. In addition to these parts, other machined and punch press parts are sold to the Burroughs Corporation, Hoover Ball and Bearing, and other companies in the auto parts industry in Cleveland and Toledo as well as Detroit. Big orders and long runs are fairly common in all operations, but some intricate cutting and threading are done in the Livonia shops, particularly on the transmission parts. Both shorter and longer runs are processed in the Wayne operations, and a varied range of customers are serviced by the parts stamped and punched there.

Mr. Wilson has recently looked into the possibility of obtaining government orders, but no government business is now on the books. He has been attending government seminars for minority contractors in the Detroit area, but he has not yet received or even applied for his first order.

In general, selling is done by Mr. Wilson. Some sales contacts come through the shop foremen, but all orders are closed by Mr. Wilson no matter what their origin, since he feels that the bidding and ordering operation is very critical. He is also the only one in the entire organization who knows the details about costs and profits associated with individual orders. Even his accountant, Mr. Dash, does not know all of the details in the final negotiations regarding profits.

The company has no salespeople other than Mr. Wilson. He has indicated that he has thought about the possibility of hiring salespeople to call on purchasing agents in the Big Three auto companies and other Detroit area firms but has not yet done so. Basically, the selling operation is a one-man show with occasional help from specialists in the organization.

The sales growth of Wilco is phenomenal, going from $80,000 in its first year to $1,600,000 in its fifth year of operation. Profits in the first year were 20 percent on sales after taxes, and in the fifth year they had declined to 15 percent on sales after taxes. The downward trend in profits is attributed to higher overhead and smaller margins on bigger orders. In terms of return on owner's equity, Wilco has shown annual figures ranging around 40 percent. The company has good credit lines at two banks, and loan payments have been made on time.

Inventories are very low (less than 5 percent of sales on the average), partially because of the close control demanded by big-company customers who helped Mr. Wilson set up internal inventory control systems. Credit and collections are excellent. In fact, in the five-year history of the company, not a single bad debt has been recorded. Accounts payable averaged less than thirty days, largely due to the quality of the customers, and this means that the cost of credit analysis is near zero.

Donald Wilson knows that added growth would call for additional outside financing since both his facilities are operating very close to capacity. Aside from new demands for plant capacity and equipment, however, Mr. Wilson feels that self-financing could handle any reasonable internal needs.

ORGANIZATION AND MANAGEMENT

The structure of Wilco is not set up in any formal way, but the organization could be charted in the manner shown below:

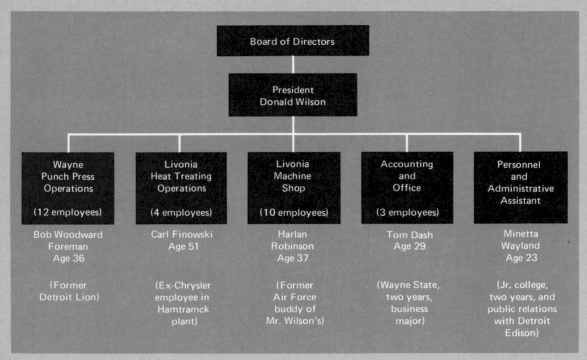

EXHIBIT 1   The Wilco Organization

Exhibit 1 shows that the three main shops (one in Wayne and two in Livonia) report directly to Mr. Wilson, as do the office and accounting functions and a staff assistant who also handles personnel management. The punch press operation in Wayne is headed up by Bob Woodward, 36 years old, who had formerly played football for the Detroit Lions. The Livonia heat treating operation is under the direction of Carl Finowski, 51 years old, who was formerly employed at the main Chrysler plant in Hamtramck. The Livonia machine shop is run by Harlan Robinson, 37, a former service buddy of Mr. Wilson who had worked with him on helicopter maintenance in Vietnam.

Accounting and office functions are under the direction of Tom Dash, who attended Wayne State University for two years, majoring in business. Mr. Dash is 29 and has two bookkeepers and one secretary under his direct control. Minetta Wayland, 23, works in a number of special capacities for Mr. Wilson, as well as being his chief personnel assistant. She attended secretarial school following two years of junior college and formerly worked for two years in public relations with the Detroit Edison Company. It is typical of Mr. Wilson's hiring practices that he had met her at a cocktail party following a Detroit Lions' football game and was impressed with her knowledge and general presence. He believed she would make a good impression on some of his customers and employees and would help by representing the firm to the public as well as large companies. He therefore hired her on the spot.

PRODUCTION

The production operations, located in three separate buildings in the suburban Detroit area, are machining, heat treating, and punching. Machining requires very close tolerances and highly skilled labor. Heat treating calls for some moderate knowledge of metallurgy, but the main characteristic is adherence to the tight specifications drawn up by large customers. Punch press operations require low-skilled labor, and though the tolerances are generally tight, the long runs on most punch press orders make this operation easy to control.

There is some transfer of parts between the two Livonia operations, but the Wayne operation is almost completely independent. Parts that must be heat-treated either before, after, or during a series of machining operations are shuttled back and forth between the plants in Livonia. This has caused some difficulties in scheduling and some loss of parts, and this problem is becoming more pronounced as the company grows in size.

The Livonia machine shop covers 10,000 square feet and is operating close to its capacity. Mr. Wilson believes that if sales rise more than $100,000 in machining operations he will have to build new facilities or go to second- and third-shift operations. He feels that adding shifts is undesirable, since he already has some second-shift operations during the peak months of auto production. The heat treating operation occupies 6,000 square feet. No expansion is needed even for a doubling of capacity, since this facility could easily add a second shift and be utilized more fully. The Wayne shop, like the machine shop, is operating close to capacity. It is now operated on a two-shift basis, and even a small increase in volume would mean that either a third shift would have to be added or new facilities sought.

The crowding in the Livonia machine shop has already caused some difficulty. Harlan Robinson has indicated that overcrowded conditions cause careless work, and that dust and confusion in the shop, as well as the inability to maintain equipment properly, have cost the company an estimated $50,000 in rework in the past six months. Mr. Robinson maintains that it is difficult to tell what specific area caused the rework to be needed since there are no quality controls set up except for personal visits he himself occasionally makes to the shop floor. Both Mr. Robinson and Mr. Wilson recognize this as a deficiency but have taken no action to correct the situation.

PERSONNEL AND LABOR RELATIONS

In general, the company employs no one with formal education beyond two years of college. Ms. Wayland and Mr. Dash attended college for two years. All other employees have only manual training or high school diplomas. There is a great deal of production experience among the group, but little formal knowledge of management systems is evident. Aside from controls over inventory developed by (and demanded by) some of the larger customers, there are few controls over quality, accounting costs, scheduling, and future planning. Mr. Wilson recognizes this deficiency and believes that the company cannot grow unless changes are made. He does not feel that the present staff has the training to make such changes.

Personnel practices are another area in which there is some restiveness. Mr. Wilson has been criticized by several of his immediate subordinates because of the casual way in which he administers hiring procedures. He has often hired people on impulse, relying on first impressions to determine whether or not the individual would be "a good person to work with." Ms. Wayland pointed out that a cocktail party, where Mr. Wilson hired her, was "no place to make such a decision" and that Mr. Wilson needs to formalize hiring policies and procedures. Mr. Wilson, on the other hand, feels that he does not want to be overly structured in running the company and that "too many rules make it difficult for anyone to operate effectively." Mr. Wilson knows everyone in the company and prides himself on being able to greet them all by their first names. He has often made commitments to people off the top of his head that were not consistent with past practice.

In the past year, Mr. Wilson's outside interests have grown rapidly. He has devoted more time to seminars and civic affairs and has become more interested in sports, especially tennis and golf. Ms. Wayland and others have begun pushing very hard to codify rules and regulations before, as she says, "a union comes in and does it for him."

Mr. Wilson is concerned about a union in terms of increasing costs and the kinds of restrictions it might place on moving people across job classifications, but he has decided not to fight one if it comes into the plant. He believes that his main personnel problem is not union relations but in getting the proper people to promote future growth.

PERSONAL ASPIRATIONS AND FUTURE DEVELOPMENTS

In viewing the last five years of his life, Mr. Wilson says, "I've done well but now I want to take a good look ahead. I want to spend more time with my family. I want to improve my golf game and play more tennis. I want to devote more time to civic affairs, and since I spend a lot of time working with kids in the city, I want to be able to let the business run by itself. I haven't told the people in the plant yet, but I'm thinking of moving to Ann Arbor to get out of the city. My wife is pressing me hard to do this because she's worried about my health. In the past year or two, I've had high blood pressure, and the doctor tells me I'm ripe for a heart attack. Besides, I'm getting a little bit tired of running and running and running. It's okay to run when you're a kid, but now I'm 45, and after you're 40, things aren't ever the same again. What's bothering me now is not what I've done so far but what I should be doing. Should I be expanding my present lines? Should I be looking for new work? Should I be more aggressive and concentrate on doing a better internal job with what I've got now? I understand that I've got tough problems in quality, production, personnel, marketing, and so forth, but at this point I don't know how to cope with them. Should I just plunge ahead and keep growing as I have in the past, even though I don't know exactly where I'm going?"

Sitting in his office late one afternoon, Donald Wilson mused, "I know I'm not a big company now, but I'm too big to be small anymore. What should I be doing to cope with the future? How can I find the key problems and solve them? If I can come up with the answers to those questions, Wilco is going to continue to grow rapidly. If not, I don't know where I'll end up."

Questions
1. What do you think are some of the key problems at Wilco?
2. How have Mr. Wilson's values affected the manner in which Wilco has developed and the way it is organized and managed? How are his values likely to affect the future organization and management of the company?
3. What are the advantages and disadvantages of Mr. Wilson's personal style of management?
4. What immediate changes do you think are necessary in the way Wilco is organized?
5. If the company continues to grow, what additional changes in its management and organization will be required?
6. What advice would you give Mr. Wilson?

Chapter 9

Organizational Structure

Upon completing this chapter you should be able to:

1. Describe the organizing process and explain why it is important for organizations.
2. Explain the relationship between strategy and organizational structure.
3. Define the formal structure of the organization, and identify the various ways an organization can be structured.
4. State what is shown on an organization chart.
5. Describe the functional, divisional, and matrix organization, and identify the advantages and disadvantages of each.
6. Describe the relationship between specialization and job satisfaction.
7. Define and describe job enlargement and job enrichment.

The word "organization" has two common meanings. The first meaning signifies an *institution* or functional group—for example, we refer to a business, a hospital, a government agency, or a basketball team as an organization. We discussed the importance of organizations in this sense in Chapter 1. The second meaning refers to the *process of organizing*—the way in which work is arranged and allocated among the members of the organization so that the goals of the organization can be efficiently achieved. We will be dealing with various aspects of the organizational process in this section of the text (Chapters 9–15).

To begin our discussion of organizing, we will focus in this chapter on two major aspects of organizational structure: departmentalization and division of work. *Departmentalization* is the grouping of work activities so that similar and logically related activities occur together. It represents the formal structure of the organization as it might be represented on an organization chart. *Division of work* is the breakdown of a work task so that each individual in the organization is responsible for and performs a limited set of activities rather than the entire task. Both concepts engaged the attention of the earliest management writers and continue to interest present writers and managers. For example, the subject of an individual's work tasks—how specialized and restricted they should be—is still being actively debated and researched today.

In later chapters in this unit, we will discuss other important aspects of the organizing process. Chapter 10 will deal with coordination and span of management; Chapter 11 will discuss authority, delegation, and decentralization; and Chapter 12 will discuss committees and groups. In Chapters 13 through 15 of this unit, we will deal with the different ways organizations can be designed and managed for stability and change.

THE MEANING AND IMPORTANCE OF ORGANIZING

We can describe the organizing process in terms of a three-step procedure:[1]

1. *Detailing all the work that must be done to attain the organization's goals.* Every organization is created with a set of purposes—hospitals are created to care for the sick, basketball teams are created to win games, businesses are created to sell goods and services. Each of these purposes will obviously be accomplished in a different way. For the organization's goals to be achieved, therefore, the tasks of the organization as a whole must first be determined. For example, before the organizers of a hospital can help the sick, they will have to arrange for the purchasing of equipment, the hiring of doctors and other personnel, and the setting up of various medical departments.

2. *Dividing the total work load into activities that can logically and comfortably be performed by one person.* Organizations are created because the work they are meant to accomplish cannot be performed by one person alone. Thus, the work of the organization will have to be appropriately divided among

[1] Ernest Dale, *Organization* (New York: American Management Associations, 1967), p. 9.

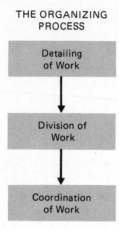

THE ORGANIZING
PROCESS

Detailing
of Work

Division of
Work

Coordination
of Work

its members. By "appropriate" we mean, first, that people will not be assigned tasks for which they are not suited and, second, that people will not be carrying too heavy or too light a work load. Too heavy a work load would mean that the job would not be completed accurately or on time, while too light a work load would result in idle time, inefficiency, and unnecessary cost.

3. *Setting up a mechanism to coordinate the work of organization members into a unified, harmonious whole.* As individuals and departments carry out these specialized activities, the overall goals of the organization may become submerged or conflicts among organization members may develop. For example, production managers in a manufacturing company may press for a standardized product line to hold down costs, when the larger interests of the company may be best served by a diversified product line. In a university, various schools or departments may begin to compete for limited funds. Coordinating mechanisms, as we will describe in the next chapter, enable members of the organization to keep sight of the organization's goals and reduce inefficiency and harmful conflicts.

The need for sound organization is well illustrated in the Old Testament, Exodus 18:13–26. Following the exodus of the Israelites from Egypt, Moses found himself the sole judge of the disputes that arose among the people. Consequently, the people "stood by Moses from the morning unto the evening," waiting for him to make decisions. Jethro, the father-in-law of Moses, saw this spectacle and realized that little could be done with such an unwieldy organization. He offered his advice, thereby becoming the first recorded management consultant. If we translate the language of Exodus into modern management jargon, we find that Jethro's advice to Moses has a decidedly contemporary ring:

> And thou shalt teach them ordinances and laws, and shalt show them the way wherein they must walk, and the work that they must do. [Establish policies and standard practices, conduct job training, and prepare job descriptions.] Moreover thou shalt provide out of all the people able men...and place such over them, to be rulers of thousands, and rulers of hundreds, rulers of fifties, and rulers of tens. [Appoint men with supervisory ability and establish a chain of command.] And let them judge the people at all seasons; and it shall be, that every great matter they shall bring unto thee, but every small matter they shall judge. [Delegate authority and work tasks and follow the *exception principle*—that is, allow routine problems to be handled at lower levels and settle only the big, exceptional problems yourself.]

The obvious effect of this proposed reorganization (which Moses adopted) was to save Moses time and effort. This in itself is no small accomplishment; increased efficiency is one of the desired benefits of the organizing process. However, Jethro's suggestions in fact accomplished a great deal more; they permitted Moses and the Israelites to achieve their goals. Moses' main aim was to lead his people to the Promised Land; yet he was spending all his time settling disputes. The Israelites' main aims were to carry out God's commandments and follow Moses; yet they were spending all their time awaiting Moses' rulings. Through Jethro's reorganization plan, Moses and the Israelites were freed to carry out their major responsibilities. (For example, an Israelite who, after learning the law, still needed a ruling could quickly obtain one from a supervisor and proceed with his or her job.) As a result, the Israelites were able to move more rapidly toward the Promised Land.

The successful accomplishment of the organizing process, then, makes it possible for an organization to achieve its purpose. It lets members of the organization know what their responsibilities are so that they can carry them out. It frees managers and subordinates to concentrate on their major tasks. It coordinates the activities of managers and subordinates so that there is no wasteful duplication of effort or conflict. Finally, the organizing process reduces the chances that doubt and confusion will develop so that the organization can move rapidly and efficiently toward its goals.

STRATEGY AND ORGANIZATIONAL STRUCTURE

We have stated that the purpose of an organization will help determine the way it is organized. A small clinic with the avowed purpose of providing health care to the local community may be run by one physician, who will direct a medical staff and carry out administrative duties in his or her free time. A large hospital, designed to facilitate research and provide long-term patient care, will have several near-autonomous departments and a separate administrative staff. Management writers such as Alfred D. Chandler refer to this phenomenon with the phrase "structure follows strategy":[2] the mission and overall goals of an organization will help shape its design.

We can define organizational *structure* or design as the formal mechanisms through which the organization is managed. In Chandler's words:

> It includes, first, the lines of authority and communication between the different administrative offices and officers, and second, the information and data that flow through these lines of communication and authority. Such lines and such data are essential to assure the effective coordination, appraisal, and planning so necessary in carrying out the basic goals and policies and in uniting together the total resources of the enterprise.

The close relationship between organizational strategy and structure was demonstrated by Chandler in his study of large American industrial enterprises.[3] After analyzing the administrative histories of such companies as Du Pont, General Motors, Standard Oil, and Sears Roebuck, Chandler concluded that changes in corporate strategy precede and lead to changes in organizational design.

[2] See Alfred D. Chandler, Jr., *Strategy and Structure: Chapters in the History of the American Industrial Enterprise* (Cambridge, Mass.: MIT Press, 1962), p. 14.
[3] Ibid., pp. 383–396.

In their initial stages, the companies Chandler studied had a centralized organizational structure that was best suited for the limited products they offered. As population, national income, and rate of technological innovation increased, however, the companies were able to expand their operations. In turn, they had to develop different structures to cope with their expanding markets. For example, to ensure that they would be able to obtain all the raw materials they needed, the companies purchased their own sources of supply. To bring their goods more quickly to market, they created their own distribution network. To produce a greater variety of goods more efficiently, they created separate product groups within their organizations. The greater complexity that inevitably developed made a highly centralized structure inefficient and impractical. The different operations and product units had to have a greater measure of independence in order to be able to respond quickly to the changing demands of their special markets. Some centralized control was (and still is) maintained; but, in general, these companies had to shift to a decentralized structure, with several near-autonomous divisions, in order to remain successful.

We should caution the reader that we do not mean to exaggerate the degree of rationality that goes into organizational design. Many organizations evolve haphazardly, introducing additions and changes from time to time as tactical expedients to meet specific ends. More importantly, strategy is not the only factor that will influence an organization's structure. As we will describe in detail in Chapter 13, there are many other important determinants of structure, including the technology used by the organization, the environment in which it operates, and the values of its members. We simply want the reader to be aware, as we go on to discuss elements of organizational structure, that there is no "one best way" for all organizations to be designed. The most desirable structure will vary from one organization to the next and for the same organization over time.

DEPARTMENTALIZATION

The unity of action, decisiveness, and adaptability typical of the well-run smaller firm are difficult to maintain as organizations grow larger. The number of subunits grows larger; layers of supervision are added; and members of the organization become further removed from the eventual results of their actions. The task of the organization's managers is to allow each individual member and subunit to remain responsive to their particular needs and, at the same time, to coordinate all the organization's disparate elements into an efficient, productive, and unified whole.

One important way managers try to accomplish this task is by establishing a formal structure for the organization. The *formal structure* of the organization is made up of the organization's various departments and individual positions and their relationship to each other. This structure is usually shown on an organization chart.

The Organization Chart

Most organizational structures are too complex to be conveyed verbally. To show the organization's structure, managers customarily draw up an *organization chart,* which is a diagram of the functions, departments, or positions of the organization and how they are related. The separate units of the organization usually appear in boxes, which are connected to each other by solid lines that indicate the chain of command and official channels of communication. (See Figures 9-1 to 9-5 on pages 227–231 for examples of organization charts.)

Not every organization welcomes such charts. For example, Robert Townsend, the former president of Avis, suggests that organization charts are demoralizing, because they reinforce the idea that all authority and ability rest at the top of the organization.[4] Most organizations, however, do develop these charts and find them helpful in defining managerial authority, responsibility, and accountability. The charts illustrate the five major aspects of an organization's structure:

1 *The division of work.* Each box represents an individual or subunit responsible for a given part of the organization's work load.

2 *Managers and subordinates.* The solid lines indicate the chain of command (who reports to whom).

3 *The type of work being performed.* Labels or descriptions for the boxes indicate the organization's different work tasks or areas of responsibility.

4 *The grouping of work segments.* The entire chart indicates on what basis the organization's activities have been divided — on a functional or regional basis, for example.

5 *The levels of management.* A chart indicates not only individual managers and subordinates but also the entire management hierarchy. All persons who report to the same individual are on the same management level, regardless of where they may appear on the chart.[5]

The advantages and disadvantages of organization charts have long been a subject of debate among management writers.[6] Advantages include the fact that the chart permits people to see how the organization is structured. Managers and subordinates and their responsibilities are clearly delineated. In addition, if we need someone to handle a specific problem, the chart indicates where he or she may be found. Finally, the process of making up the chart enables managers to pinpoint organizational defects — such as potential sources of conflict or areas where unnecessary duplication exists.

A major disadvantage of charts is that there are too many things that they obscure or do not show. They do not, for example, indicate who has the greater degree of responsibility and authority at each managerial level. Nor do they indicate the organization's informal relationships and channels of com-

[4] Robert Townsend, *Up the Organization* (New York: Knopf, 1970).

[5] Harold Stieglitz, "What's Not on an Organization Chart," *Conference Board Record,* Vol. 1, No. 11 (November 1964), pp. 7–10.

[6] See Dale, *Organization,* p. 238; Stieglitz, "What's Not on an Organization Chart," pp. 8–10; and Karol K. White, *Understanding the Company Organization Chart* (New York: American Management Associations, 1963), pp. 13–19.

munication, without which the organization could not function efficiently. In addition, people often read into charts things they are not intended to show. For example, employees may infer status and power according to one's distance on the chart from the chief executive's box. These disadvantages can be minimized if we do not expect charts to do more than they were designed to do—reveal the basic framework of the organization.

The Formal Organizational Structure

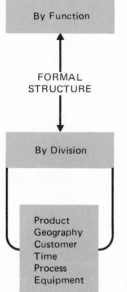

An organization's departments can be formally structured in two major ways: by function or by division.[7]

Organization by *function* brings together in one department all those engaged in one activity or several related activities. For example, the organization divided by function might have separate manufacturing, marketing, and sales departments. A sales manager in such an organization would be responsible for the sale of *all* products manufactured by the firm.

Organization by *division* brings together in one department all those involved in the production and marketing of a product or related group of products, all those in a certain geographic area, or all those dealing with a certain type of customer. For example, divisionalized organization might include separate chemical, detergent, and cosmetic departments. Each division head would be responsible for the manufacturing, marketing, and sales activities of his or her entire unit.

As we shall see, both types of organizational structure have their advantages and disadvantages, and it is unlikely that an organization will use one type exclusively.

The Functional Structure. Functional organization is perhaps the most logical and basic form of departmentalization. It is used mainly (but not only) by smaller firms that offer a limited line of products. A major advantage of a functionalized structure is that it makes supervision easier, since managers have to be expert in only a narrow range of skills. In addition, a functionalized structure makes it easier to mobilize specialized skills and bring them to bear where they are most needed. (See Figure 9-1.)

As an organization grows, either by expanding geographically or by broadening its product line, some of the disadvantages of the functional structure begin to make themselves felt. Obtaining quick decisions or action on a problem can become more difficult, because functional managers have to report to central headquarters. A local plant manager, for example, may have to wait a long time before a request for service is acted on. In addition, it will often be harder to determine accountability and judge performance in a functional

---

[7] See Dale, *Organization,* pp. 105–114; Ernest Dale, *Planning and Developing the Company Organization Structure* (New York: American Management Associations, 1952); Luther Gulick, "Notes on the Theory of Organization," in Luther Gulick and Lyndall Urwick, *Papers on the Science of Administration* (New York: Institute of Public Administration, 1937); and Harold Stieglitz, "Divisionalization and the Work of Top-Level Management," *Conference Board Record,* Vol. 2, No. 3 (March 1965), pp. 7–11.

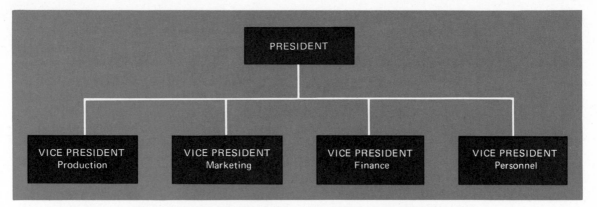

FIGURE 9-1   Functional Organization Chart for a Manufacturing Company

Note that each vice president is in charge of a major organizational function.

organization. If a new product fails, who is to blame—research and development, production, or marketing? Finally, coordination of the entire organization may become a problem for top managers. Members of each department will naturally tend to feel isolated from (or superior to) other departments. It will therefore become more difficult for members of the organization to work in a unified manner to achieve the organization's goals. For example, the manufacturing department may concentrate on meeting cost standards and delivery dates and may neglect quality control. As a result, the service department may become flooded with complaints.

Top managers who wish to use a functional structure or add a functional department to an existing structure must first weigh potential benefits against expected costs. The economic savings brought about by a functional structure (due to its efficient use of specialized resources) may be outweighed by the additional managerial and staff salaries and other overhead costs that will be required. Top managers will also have to consider how often they expect to use the special skills of a functional department. Managers of a small firm, for example, may find it more economical to retain outside legal services whenever necessary rather than set up their own legal department.

The Divisional Structure. Most large, multiproduct companies, such as General Motors, are organized according to a divisional structure. At some point, sheer size and diversity of products make servicing by functional departments too unwieldy. In such a case, top managers will generally create semi-autonomous divisions, each of which designs, produces, and markets its own products.

There are a number of different patterns a divisional organization may follow:

In *division by product,* each department is responsible for a product or related family of products. Product divisionalization is the logical pattern to

227

follow when a product type calls for manufacturing technology and marketing methods that differ markedly from those used in the rest of the organization. For example, General Foods Corporation has a different division for each of its major types of food products. (See Figure 9-2.)

Division by geography brings together in one department all activities performed in the region where the unit conducts its business. This arrangement follows logically when a plant must be located as close as possible to (1) its sources of raw materials, as with mining and oil-producing companies; (2) its major markets, as with a division selling most of its output overseas that must locate abroad; or (3) its major sources of specialized labor, as with diamond-cutting operations in New York, Israel, and Amsterdam. (See Figure 9-3.)

Division by customer occurs when a division sells most or all of its products to a particular class of customer. An electronics firm, for example, might have separate divisions for military, industrial, and consumer customers. As a general rule, manufacturing firms with a highly diversified line of products tend to be organized by customer or by product. (See Figure 9-4 on page 230.) Service, financial, and other nonmanufacturing firms are generally organized on a regional basis.

There are also three minor forms of divisional structure that can be found.

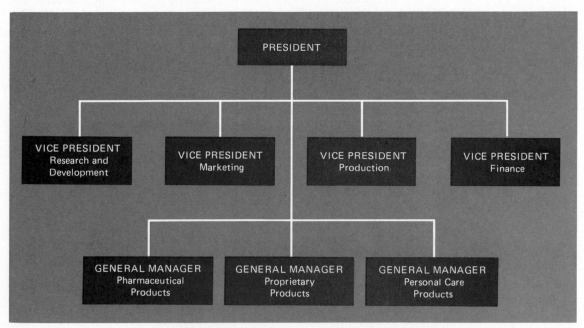

FIGURE 9-2   Product Organization Chart for a Manufacturing Company

Each general manager is in charge of a major category of products, and the vice presidents of the functional areas provide supporting services to the general managers.

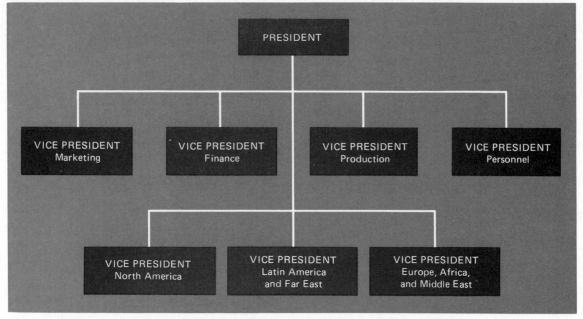

FIGURE 9-3   Geographic Organization Chart for a Manufacturing Company

Each of the area vice presidents is in charge of the company's business in a geographic area. The functional vice presidents provide supporting services and coordination assistance for their areas of responsibility.

In *division by time,* the sequence of the organization's operations determines its structure. Those engaged in initiating activities (such as drawing up goals, forecasts, and plans) may be grouped in one unit; those on the operational side may compose another; and those devoted to control may make up a third.

In *division by process,* the organization is structured according to the specific productive operations in which it is engaged. For example, a textile manufacturer may be departmentalized into spinning, weaving, dyeing, and bleaching subdivisions.

In *division by equipment,* members of the organization are departmentalized according to the different equipment they use. Vocational schools are often divided in this way.

Unlike a functional department, a division resembles a separate business. The division head is accountable for profit or loss, focuses exclusively on the operations of his or her division, and may even compete with other units of the same firm. But a division is completely unlike a separate business in one crucial aspect: it is not an independent entity. The division manager cannot make decisions quite as freely as the owner of a truly separate enterprise, because he or she must still report to central headquarters. As a rule of thumb, a division head's authority is limited to the extent that his or her decisions will affect the workings of other divisions.

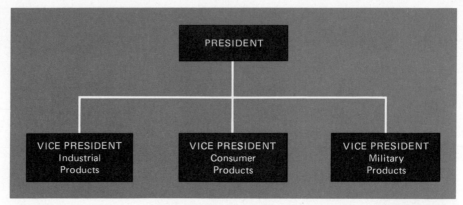

Each vice president is in charge of a set of products grouped according to the type of customer to whom they will be marketed.

Pros and Cons of Organization by Division. Organization by division has several major advantages. Because all the activities, skills, and expertise required to produce and market particular products are grouped in one place under a single head, the whole job can be more easily coordinated and high work performance can be maintained. In addition, both the quality and speed of decision making are enhanced, because decisions made at the divisional level are closer to the scene of action. Conversely, the burden of management at headquarters is eased, because divisional managers are given greater authority. Perhaps most importantly, accountability is clear. The performance of divisional management can easily be measured in terms of that division's profit and loss.

There are, however, some disadvantages to the divisional structure. The interests of the division may be placed ahead of the needs and goals of the total organization. For example, because they are vulnerable to profit-loss performance reviews, division heads may take short-term gains at the expense of long-range profitability. In addition, administrative expenses tend to increase in a divisionalized structure. Each division, for instance, will have its own staff members and specialists, leading to costly duplication of skills.

The Matrix Organization. Neither one of the two types of structures we have discussed will meet all the needs of every organization. In a functional structure, specialized skills may become increasingly sophisticated — but coordinated production of goods may be difficult to achieve. Conversely, in the divisional structure, various products may flourish, while the overall technological expertise of the organization remains undeveloped. The matrix structure attempts to combine the benefits of both types of designs while avoiding their drawbacks.[8]

---

[8] See John F. Mee, "Matrix Organizations," *Business Horizons,* Vol. 7, No. 2 (Summer 1964), pp. 70–72; Jay R. Galbraith, "Matrix Organization Designs," *Business Horizons,* Vol. 14, No. 1 (February 1971), pp. 29–40; and J. Gordon Milliken and Edward J. Morrison, "Management Methods from Aerospace," *Harvard Business Review,* March-April 1973, pp. 6–10 ff.

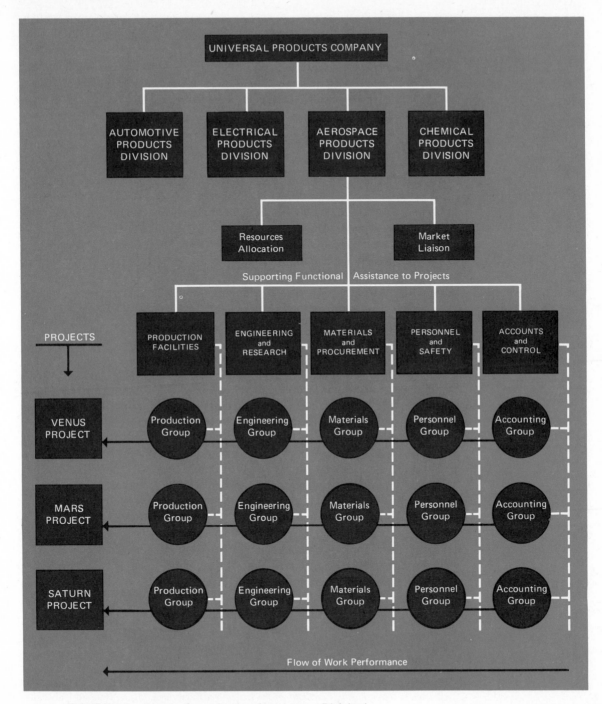

FIGURE 9-5   Matrix Organization (Aerospace Division)

Source: John F. Mee, "Matrix Organizations," *Business Horizons*, Vol. 7, No. 2 (Summer 1964), pp. 70–72. Copyright 1965 by the Foundation for the School of Business at Indiana University. Reprinted by permission.

In a *matrix structure,* two types of organization design exist simultaneously —functional departments and project teams. (On an organization chart, the resulting lines of authority will resemble a grid—hence the term "matrix.") Functional departments are a permanent fixture of the matrix organization; they retain authority for the overall operation of their respective units. Project teams, on the other hand, are created as the need for them arises — that is, when a specific program requires a high degree of technical skill in a concentrated period of time. Members of a project team are assembled from the functional departments and are placed under the direction of a project manager. The manager for each project is responsible and accountable for its success; thus, he or she has authority over the other team members. For the duration of the project, the team can draw on the physical and financial resources of the functional departments. When the project is completed, the members of the team, including the project manager, return to their respective departments until their next assignment. (See Figure 9-5 on previous page.)

The advantage of the matrix structure is that it brings specialized skills to bear on a problem and does it with maximum efficiency. The problem of coordination—which plagues most functional designs—is minimized here, because the most important personnel for the project are working together as a group. In addition, the matrix structure gives the organization a great deal of cost-saving flexibility; each project is assigned only the number of people it needs, thus avoiding unnecessary duplication. One possible disadvantage is that members of the team require some skill in interpersonal relations in dealing intensively with other team members and in getting the help they need from the functional departments. In addition, morale can be adversely affected by the personnel rearrangements as projects are completed and new ones are begun.

The matrix structure was and is widely used in aerospace programs. Such programs involve a large number of separate technological problems and projects that have to be handled on tight schedules. Today, the matrix structure tends to be used in organizations that need a high degree of coordination and technical performance—for example, in some construction companies, consulting firms, and R&D groups.

The Informal Organization

Relationships within an organization are certainly not restricted to those officially described by the formal organization chart. Practical managers have always realized that side by side with the formal organization exists an informal one, growing inevitably out of the personal and group needs of organization members. This informal organization has been defined by Herbert A. Simon as "the interpersonal relationships in the organization that affect decisions within it but either are omitted from the formal scheme or are not consistent with it."[9]

[9] Herbert A. Simon, *Administrative Behavior,* 2nd ed. (New York: Macmillan, 1957). See also Chester I. Barnard, *The Functions of the Executive* (Cambridge, Mass.: Harvard University Press, 1938); Charles Perrow, *Complex Organizations: A Critical Essay* (Glencoe, Ill.: Scott, Foresman, 1972); and F. J. Roethlisberger and William J. Dickson, *Management and the Worker* (Cambridge, Mass.: Harvard University Press, 1947).

Among the first to recognize the constructive aspects of the informal organization was Chester Barnard, whom we discussed in Chapter 2. Barnard suggested that strict adherence to the formal structure—that is, always "going through channels"—could be harmful. In emergencies, for example, an informal communication network makes faster decisions possible. Informal relationships also smooth the flow of personnel and materials across the lines of authority when such a flow is needed and promote interdepartmental cooperation even when the organization chart indicates no point of contact among the departments involved. In short, the informal relationships that develop in an organization not only help organization members satisfy their social needs but also help them get things done.

Barnard, however, overlooked the fact that informal organizations may also arise among employees as a protective device against management. In such cases, the aims of the informal organization may well run counter to the objectives of the enterprise. For instance, the informal group may set work norms well below the standards prescribed by management and enforce a slowdown in various ways, ranging from persuasion to violence. We will be discussing the informal organization in greater detail in future chapters. (See also our discussion of the Hawthorne experiments in Chapter 2.)

DIVISION OF WORK

Up to this point we have discussed specialization from the standpoint of the total organization. Now we shall examine the same subject from the viewpoint of the individual worker and his or her job. We will try to answer such questions as: What are the advantages of job specialization? What effect has such specialization on worker morale? To what extent can job dissatisfaction be eliminated without simultaneously sacrificing the benefits of specialization?

The Advantages of Job Specialization

Only in the last one hundred years or so have most organizations created specialized departments and groups, each confining itself to certain types of work. But at the level of the individual worker, the advantages of specialization were recognized as far back as antiquity. In fact, the rise of civilization can be attributed to the division of labor. The greater productivity resulting from job specialization gave humanity the resources needed for art, science, and education.

Adam Smith's *Wealth of Nations* opens with a famous passage describing the minute specialization of labor in the manufacture of pins. Describing the work in a pin factory, Smith wrote: "One man draws the wire, another straights it, a third cuts it, a fourth points it, a fifth grinds it at the top for receiving the head...." Ten men working in this fashion, he said, made 48,000 pins in one day. "But if they had all wrought separately and independently," each might at best have produced 20 pins a day. As Smith observed, the great gift of the division of labor was that in breaking down the total job into small, simple, and

Cartoon by S. Gross

separate operations in which each worker could specialize, total productivity multiplied geometrically.[10]

Why did division of work arise, and why does it so successfully increase productivity? The answer is that no one person is physically able to perform all the operations in a complex task, and no one person can mentally master the skills different operations require. As a result, it became necessary to parcel out the various parts of a large task among a number of people. Such specialization, in turn, made it easier for people to master their jobs and become more skillful in them. Simplified tasks could be learned in a comparatively short period of time and could be performed more quickly. In addition, with a greater variety of jobs available, people could be matched to the jobs for which they were best suited. The result was greater efficiency and productivity.

The reader should note that, as much as possible, we will be using the more modern phrase "division of work," rather than the classic term "division of labor," because the latter term calls to mind specialization of only routine tasks in the organization. In fact, specialization applies to all types of work activities, including those of the manager and of other professionals.

Specialization and Job Satisfaction

The advantages of specialization in terms of increased productivity received the greatest attention of management writers up to the beginning of the twentieth century. Some writers, however, raised strong questions about the impact of job specialization on the worker. Karl Marx and Friedrich Engels, writing in the middle of the nineteenth century, saw even the most general division of work as a source of alienation and entrapment for the individual:

> ...the division of labor offers us the first example of how...man's own deed becomes an alien power opposed to him which enslaves him instead of being

[10] Adam Smith, *Wealth of Nations* (New York: Modern Library, 1937), pp. 3–4.

controlled by him. For as soon as the distribution of labor comes into being, each man has a particular, exclusive activity...from which he cannot escape. He is a hunter, a fisherman, a shepherd...and must remain so if he does not want to lose his means of livelihood.[11]

And Émile Durkheim, the famous sociological theorist, writing before assembly-line production became the industrial norm, also raised questions about the effects of job specialization. He believed that both the individual and society would be damaged by the widespread demoralizing impact that dull, repetitive jobs would have.[12]

With the development of the assembly line, these apprehensions became more widespread. The extreme division of labor epitomized by the assembly line became the symbol of dehumanizing jobs and the alienation of the individual from the workplace. Perhaps the best-known exposition of this theme occurs in Charlie Chaplin's film *Modern Times,* in which Chaplin as the little tramp is driven to distraction as he mindlessly repeats the same task over and over again while an assembly line moves by at top speed.

Job Definition. We will be going on to discuss more modern views of specialization and job satisfaction. First, we will define two work dimensions that determine the degree to which a job is specialized — depth and scope. By *job depth* we mean the extent to which an individual can control his or her work. When management sets rigid standards, organizes the work down to the last detail, prescribes the methods to be followed, and supervises the work closely, then job depth is low. But if, after objectives and general ground rules are set, employees are free to set their own pace and do the job as they think best, then job depth is high.

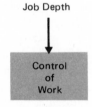

Job Depth

Control of Work

Job Scope

Varied Tasks

By *job scope* we mean the number of different operations a particular job requires and the frequency with which the job cycle must be repeated. The lower the number of operations (and the higher the number of repetitions), the more limited the scope. For example, a hospital nurse who checks temperatures, dispenses medicines, and takes blood samples has more scope than a dishwasher in the hospital kitchen who washes dishes all day.

Of course, different portions of the same job may vary in either depth or scope or both. For example, a university professor who is also a department head may have tasks that run the gamut of possible combinations. He or she chooses and designs a research project (high scope, high depth); teaches three sections of the same course (high depth, low scope); performs a great number of routine administrative tasks (low depth, high scope); and grades a large number of multiple-choice exams (low scope, low depth). Nevertheless, the overall amount of depth and scope will indicate how specialized that job is.

---

[11] Karl Marx and Friedrich Engels, *The German Ideology,* Part I, ed. C.J. Arthur (New York: International Publishers, 1970), p. 53.

[12] Émile Durkheim, *The Division of Labor in Society* (New York: Macmillan, 1933).

235

The Specialization-Satisfaction Trade-Off. Unlike classical theorists, modern management writers like Chris Argyris,[13] Frederick Herzberg,[14] and Douglas McGregor[15] have called attention to the problems that division of work causes for the individual. They argue that when jobs become highly specialized, employees lose their sense of autonomy and challenge and become dissatisfied and dependent. These writers do not claim that all forms of specialization are undesirable — that all employees should engage in all organizational activities during the workday. They do suggest, however, that specialization in some types of work has reached the point where the technical advantages of increased specialization has been overtaken by the human disadvantages.

For example, if we design a group of individuals' jobs in such a way that we are moving from very unspecialized work tasks (high depth and scope) toward very specialized (low depth and scope), we are likely at first to increase productivity greatly as the basic advantages of specialization come into play. In addition, we may well increase satisfaction as individuals have the opportunity to be more effective performers and to develop a few skills in depth. As increasing specialization continues, the big productivity advantages may start to decline, and the increased satisfaction may be replaced by dissatisfaction as the work becomes progressively less challenging. On balance, productivity may still be greater, because the lost motivation, interest, and commitment to the work may not overcome the remaining additional technical efficiencies achieved by the greater specialization.

At some point, however, the work may become so meaningless to the employees that rising dissatisfaction will lead to excessive absences, careless performance, and perhaps even sabotage. These losses will overtake any increased technical advantages from additional specialization. If the employees can insist upon increased financial payment to compensate for their reduced enjoyment, the combination of poorer work performance and higher wages may make increased specialization more costly than less specialization.

These arguments sound persuasive. However, research on the relationship between specialization and job satisfaction has yielded ambiguous results. Some studies have shown decreased satisfaction with increased specialization; others, however, have found no such relationship.[16]

In their review of the research on this subject, Charles L. Hulin and Milton

---

[13] Chris Argyris, *Personality and Organization* (New York: Harper & Brothers, 1957).

[14] F. Herzberg, B. Mausner, and D. Snyderman, *The Motivation to Work,* 2nd ed. (New York: Wiley, 1959).

[15] Douglas McGregor, *The Human Side of Enterprise* (New York: McGraw-Hill, 1960).

[16] See, for example, Nancy Morse, *Satisfaction in the White Collar Job* (Ann Arbor, Mich.: Institute for Social Research, University of Michigan, 1953); E. L. Trist and K. W. Bamforth, "Some Social and Psychological Consequences of the Longwall Method of Coal Getting," *Human Relations,* Vol. 4, No. 1 (February 1951), pp. 3–38; Clayton P. Alderfer, "Job Enlargement and the Organizational Context," *Personnel Psychology,* Vol. 22, No. 4 (Winter 1969), pp. 418–426; and Arthur N. Turner and Paul R. Lawrence, *Industrial Jobs and the Worker* (Boston: Graduate School of Business, Harvard University, 1965). See also *Work in America: Report of a Special Task Force to the Secretary of Health, Education and Welfare* (Cambridge, Mass.: MIT Press, 1973).

R. Blood concluded that whether or not employees with specialized jobs feel dissatisfied depends to a great extent on the backgrounds of the workers being studied.[17] Those employees who believe in the "Protestant work ethic"—that is, who see work as important, meaningful, and leading to success—are likely to become dissatisfied in jobs that are too specialized. Hulin and Blood suggest, however, that those employees who are alienated from work may even prefer narrower, more restricted jobs, because these jobs are easier for them to perform and require little attention or commitment.

Job Enlargement and Job Enrichment

Although Hulin and Blood cast doubts on the relationship between job specialization and worker dissatisfaction, their analysis does suggest that such a connection exists for many workers. And because managers intuitively find this relationship a very logical one, considerable attention has been devoted to ways of making routine jobs more interesting and challenging. These attempts fall into two broad categories: job enlargement and job enrichment. The first category stems from the thinking of industrial engineers (scientific management), the second from motivational theory (human relations and behavioral science).

Job enlargement tackles the problem of dissatisfaction by increasing job scope. Various work functions from a horizontal slice of an organizational unit are combined, thereby giving workers more operations to perform. Perhaps two or three specialized tasks are aggregated into one broader combination; perhaps job rotation is instituted, enabling workers to move from one job to a completely different one. In the first case, some sense of the wholeness of the job is restored. In the second case, the sense of challenge and achievement is awakened as different skills are brought to bear when one task is replaced by another in accordance with the rotation schedule. In both cases, workers are relieved of some of the monotony of a restricted routine and work cycle.

Job enrichment tries to deal with dissatisfaction by increasing job depth. Work activities from a vertical slice of the organizational unit are combined in one job so that employees have greater job autonomy. Individual employees may be given responsibility for setting their own work pace, for correcting their own errors, and/or for deciding on the best way to perform a particular task. Employees may also participate in making decisions that will affect their particular subunits. Such programs are designed to make work more challenging, thereby increasing the employees' motivation and enthusiasm.[18]

There is not yet enough research evidence for us to be able to reach firm conclusions about the effects of job enlargement and job enrichment. Most studies suggest that job enlargement and job enrichment programs will increase

---

[17] Charles L. Hulin and Milton R. Blood, "Job Enlargement, Individual Differences, and Worker Responses," *Psychological Bulletin,* Vol. 69, No. 1 (1968), pp. 41–53.

[18] A paper by Robert N. Ford ("Job Enrichment Lessons from AT&T," *Harvard Business Review,* January-February 1973, pp. 96–106) describes some of the techniques used by AT&T to redesign white- and blue-collar jobs in one of the most extensive job enrichment programs in American industry.

work satisfaction and drive—that is, absenteeism and turnover rates will be lowered considerably and work quality will significantly improve.[19] However, such programs do not seem to increase productivity. This is not a surprising finding, since job enlargement and enrichment programs are meant to counteract the psychic and emotional effects of job specialization; they are not designed to increase productivity, since productivity with job specialization is often already at a high level.

Not all management writers agree that job enlargement and enrichment are desirable or effective in all cases. Some writers, for example, criticize job enlargement on the grounds that "it condenses the monotony and boredom of several jobs into one job."[20] Others, like William Reif and Fred Luthans, suggest that job enrichment will have little effect on employees who "are alienated from the middle class values expressed by the job enrichment concept."[21] Such employees may find their greatest work satisfaction in relating to their co-workers. They may resent any changes in work design that will give them less time or opportunity for social interaction. It seems reasonable to conclude that the effects of job enlargement and enrichment will depend on the backgrounds, personalities, and values of the employees involved.

Summary The organizing process involves determining the work that must be done in order for the organization's goals to be achieved, appropriately dividing this work among organization members, and setting up a mechanism to coordinate the organization's activities. One result of the organizing process will be an organizational *structure,* which represents the formal mechanisms through which the organization is managed. A particular organization's structure will depend to a large extent on its purpose and strategy at a given period of time.

Departmentalization is the grouping together of similar or logically related work activities. Its result is one aspect of the formal structure of the organization. The formal structure is usually shown on an organization chart, which identifies the division of work, managers and subordinates, the type of work being performed, the grouping of work segments, and the levels of management.

The formal structure is usually divided by either *function* or *division.* Organization by function makes supervision easier and allows more efficient use of specialized skills. However, it makes coordination difficult. Organization by division allows greater coordination and accountability, but involves duplication of resources and encourages competition between divisions. The *matrix* structure tries to avoid the disadvantages of these forms by combining functional departments with project teams.

The informal organization coexists with the formal one. It represents the interpersonal relationships that inevitably develop in an organization either to get things done more quickly than the formal structure allows or to protect employees against management.

---

[19] See Hulin and Blood, "Job Enlargement," pp. 41–42, and Frank Friedlander and L. Dave Brown, "Organization Development," in Mark Rosenzweig and Lyman W. Porter, eds., *Annual Review of Psychology,* Vol. 25 (1974), pp. 313–341.

[20] See Friedlander and Brown, "Organization Development," p. 323.

[21] William E. Rief and Fred Luthans, "Does Job Enrichment Really Pay Off?" *California Management Review,* Vol. 15, No. 1 (Fall 1972), pp. 30–37.

Division of work is the breakdown of a work task so that each individual performs a specialized set of activities. Its major advantage is that it greatly increases efficiency and productivity. However, many writers have suggested that overspecialization can lead to employee dehumanization and alienation. In addition, if employee dissatisfaction grows as a result of specialization, there may be increased costs to employers that reduce the benefits of division of work. Job enlargement and job enrichment programs have been developed to improve job scope and depth, respectively, so that the human costs of specialization will be reduced. The evidence suggests, however, that not all workers benefit from such programs.

Review Questions

1. What three steps make up the organizing process? How does the organizing process benefit the organization?
2. What does the phrase "structure follows strategy" mean?
3. What does the organization chart illustrate? What are the major advantages and disadvantages of the organization chart? How do you think you might be affected by seeing your name or position on a chart?
4. What are the advantages and disadvantages of the functional organization structure?
5. How would you decide whether or not the functional structure is appropriate for your organization?
6. What are the different patterns a divisional structure may follow? What are the advantages and disadvantages of a divisional structure?
7. Under what conditions do you think a matrix structure would be most suitable? What are its advantages and disadvantages? What happens to project team members once they have completed their project?
8. What are the positive and sometimes negative aspects of the informal organization?
9. What are the advantages of job specialization? Why do you think specialization developed?
10. How do you feel about assembly-line work? Do you think most people feel the same way you do?
11. What practical consequences of specialization might eventually negate its economic advantages?
12. What do the terms "job scope" and "job depth" mean?
13. What does available research indicate about the relationship between specialization and job satisfaction?
14. What do job enlargement and job enrichment attempt to do?

CASE STUDY: WATERS & CO., INC.

James Waters' hobby of making water skis had gradually grown into a small-scale business before he retired from the U.S. Army. At the time of his retirement, he was selling one hundred pairs a year at a net profit of $10 per pair. His sales were confined to people who had learned of his skis through other customers and who had taken the trouble to contact him for a pair.

After retirement, Mr. Waters placed a few ads in several sports magazines. His sales volume grew rapidly. One year later he had three people working in his garage

Case reprinted by permission of Dr. A. Ranger Curran, Youngstown State University, Youngstown, Ohio.

under the supervision of William Peters, one of the three, who doubled in brass as foreman.

Mr. Waters' son, George, a recent college graduate and a water skiing enthusiast, was now "on the road" throughout the state, selling to sporting goods stores. His wife, Marian, acted as secretary and filing clerk. A bookkeeper, Tobie Black, had just joined the work force.

At this point in time, Mr. White and Mr. James, two neighbors and friends of Mr. Waters, suggested that they contribute some money, incorporate, and buy out the local competition. This was a small ski factory located in an old garage. Its owner, Joseph Blake, was a talented designer but a poor manager. His company was in rather poor straits financially, although business was better than ever and sales had risen every year. (Besides his ski manufacturing, he was also dabbling with custom-made modern furniture, although sales had been small.)

Informal contact with Mr. Blake divulged that he would welcome the opportunity to sell or merge his business with the new combination. He wanted $30,000 in cash and one-eighth of the firm's new stock. This was agreeable to the other parties, and the merger was consummated.

The Blake firm had in its employ at this time the following personnel: ten production people and one production foreman (lumber and materials were bought by the production foreman as needed); three salespeople who covered the Southeast on a territorial basis; and two secretaries who were located in the downtown office of the firm.

In the discussions that followed the merger, Messrs. Waters, White, James, and Blake felt that sales opportunities were virtually unlimited. It was agreed that Mr. Blake would confine himself to design; Mr. James, a retired furniture manufacturer, would look after production; Mr. White, a CPA, would cover financial affairs. The presidency of the company devolved on Mr. Waters, while his son would handle sales.

There was considerable discussion about the possibilities of making snow skis. Mr. Blake was an enthusiastic skier and felt that they should try to crack this market also. Mr. Waters was undecided on this point.

Case Questions

1. What advice would you offer these men to help them make their company a success?
2. What problems and conflicts might develop as a result of the way the company is organized at present? What should be done to prevent these problems and conflicts from arising or to minimize their effects?
3. What will the organization chart for the new company look like?
4. Should the company try to make snow skis as well as water skis? Why or why not?

Chapter 10

Coordination and Span of Management

Upon completing this chapter you should be able to:

1. Explain why coordination of the activities and objectives of an organization is necessary.

2. Define effective coordination, and explain why constructive conflict is an important part of the coordination process.

3. Identify and describe the various coordinating mechanisms that managers can use.

4. Define span of management and explain its relationship to coordination.

5. Distinguish between traditional and modern approaches to selecting a span of management.

6. Describe the effects of too wide or too narrow a span on managerial and organizational effectiveness.

7. Distinguish between "tall" and "flat" organizational structures.

8. Identify and describe the criteria by which managers can decide on an appropriate span of management.

In the preceding chapter we discussed two aspects of the organizing process. The first is division of work: the breakdown of a work task so that each individual is responsible for and performs a limited set of activities rather than the entire task. The second aspect is departmentalization: the grouping of work activities so that similar and logically related activities occur together.

In this chapter we will continue our discussion by examining two more aspects of the organizing process—coordination and span of control. If work activities in an organization are divided and departmentalized, it is necessary for managers to coordinate these activities so that they can efficiently achieve their organizational goals. They will have to communicate their broad goals to each subunit and translate them into appropriate subunit objectives. In addition, they will have to keep each subunit informed about the activities of the other subunits in order to ensure that the separate parts of the organization will be working together harmoniously.

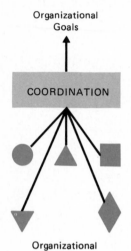

Organizational
Goals

COORDINATION

Organizational
Subunits

How well managers are able to achieve effective coordination will be influenced by the number of subordinates reporting to them and to the other managers in the organization. That number is known as the "span of management" or "span of control." The more subordinates that managers have reporting directly to them (that is, the larger the span of control), the more difficult it may be for them to supervise and coordinate their activities. On the other hand, the more subordinates they and the other managers have, the fewer the number of managers that will be needed by the organization. These fewer managers may have an easier time coordinating work activities with each other. Thus, it is not always a simple task to select the span that will best help managers achieve effective coordination.

In this chapter, then, we will deal with the need for coordination in organizations and how it can be best achieved. We will also discuss how managers can choose the span of management that is most appropriate for their own and their organization's goals.

COORDINATION

The Need for Coordination

When managers divide work into specialized functions or departments, they do so for the purpose of increasing the productivity and efficiency of their organization. At the same time, however, they create a need for the coordination of these divided work activities. *Coordination* is the process of integrating the activities and objectives of the separate units of an organization in order to efficiently achieve organizational goals.[1] Without coordination, individuals and departments would lose sight of their roles within the organization. They would begin to pursue their own specialized interests, often at the expense of the larger organizational goals.

[1] James Mooney defines coordination as "the orderly arrangement of group effort, to provide unity of action in the pursuit of a common purpose." See James Mooney, *The Principles of Organization,* rev. ed. (New York: Harper & Brothers, 1947), p. 5. See also J. A. Litterer, *The Analysis of Organizations* (New York: Wiley, 1965), pp. 28–31.

For example, the purchasing department in a manufacturing company would have no way of knowing the quantity of raw materials the production department required unless the activities of the two departments were co-ordinated. Without such coordination, the organization would become inefficient: too large a quantity of raw materials might be ordered, resulting in increased expenses, or an insufficient quantity, resulting in a failure to meet production goals.

The Difficulty of Coordination

Unfortunately, the more specialized the individuals and subunits within the organization become, the more difficult it is for managers to coordinate their activities. Working on a day-to-day basis on their specialized assignments, surrounded by colleagues who have similar or related tasks, people begin to develop their own ideas about what the organization's goals should be and how they should be pursued. For example, automobile marketing experts might believe strongly in the need to change car models every year in order to increase their marketability, while the production department might want to make only cosmetic changes each year in order to hold down retooling costs. Such a differentiation of attitudes occurs naturally in specialized departments, and it makes coordination of tasks all the more difficult.

Paul R. Lawrence and Jay W. Lorsch have identified four types of differences in attitude and working style that arise among the various individuals and departments in organizations.[2] These differences, they suggest, complicate the task of effectively coordinating an organization's activities:

1. *Differences in orientation toward particular goals.* Members of different departments develop their own views about how best to advance the interests of the organization. To salespeople, product variety may take precedence over product quality. Accountants may see cost control as most important to the organization's success, while marketing managers may regard product design as most essential.

2. *Differences in time orientation.* Some members of an organization, such as production managers, will be more concerned with problems that have to be solved immediately or within a short period of time. Others, like members of a research and development team, may be preoccupied with problems that will take years to solve.

3. *Differences in interpersonal orientation.* In some organizational activities, such as production, there may be relatively abrupt ways of communicating. Decisions may be made in a quick, "let's get on with it" manner in order to keep things moving. In other activities, such as R&D, the style of communication may be much more easygoing. Everyone may be encouraged to have a say and to discuss their ideas with others.

4. *Differences in formality of structure.* Each type of subunit in the organization may have different methods and standards for evaluating progress toward objectives and for rewarding employees. In a production department, for ex-

---

[2] Paul R. Lawrence and Jay W. Lorsch, *Organization and Environment: Managing Differentiation and Integration* (Homewood, Ill.: Richard D. Irwin, 1967).

ample, where quantity and quality are rigidly controlled, the evaluation and reward process might be quite formal. Employees will be judged quickly on how well they meet or exceed well-defined performance criteria. In the personnel department, on the other hand, standards of performance may be much more loosely defined. Employees will be evaluated on the quality of their work over an extended period of time.

Lawrence and Lorsch have called attention to the fact that division of work involves more than a difference in precise activities, such as tightening a bolt or writing advertising copy. It also influences how we perceive the organization, how we perceive our role in it, and how we relate to each other. Of course, these differences are desirable in that they match our individual talents and skills with the tasks best suited for them. Marketing experts, for example, can make effective use of their flair for creativity and communication, while accountants apply their talents to budgets and audits. However, desirable as division of work and specialization are in helping the organization use its resources most efficiently, they do make it more difficult for managers to achieve effective coordination.

Effective and
Ineffective
Coordination

How do we differentiate between effective and ineffective coordination in an organization? Henri Fayol, one of the earliest management writers (see Chapter 2), described in 1916 the following conditions of a well-coordinated organization:

a. Each department works in harmony with the others; the Stores Department knows what it has to supply and when it will be needed; the Production Department knows what it is expected to do; the Maintenance Department keeps the plant and tools in good condition; the Financial Department obtains the necessary capital; the Security Department sees to the protection of goods and persons; every operation is carried out with good order and certainty.
b. Within each department, the various sections and sub-sections are given exact instructions as to the part which they have to play in the common work and how they must combine with one another.
c. The programme of work for each department and section is always kept up to date.[3]

Some modern management writers would add the further condition that there be *constructive conflict* between the different subunits of the organization and that the conflict be effectively resolved on an ongoing basis. By constructive conflict we mean that the various members of the organization present their viewpoints, argue them openly, and in general make certain that they get "heard." Otherwise, managers will make decisions without considering the special needs and knowledge of individual departments. The result may be

[3] Henri Fayol, *Industrial and General Administration*, trans. J. A. Coubrough (Geneva: International Management Institute, 1930), pp. 74–76.

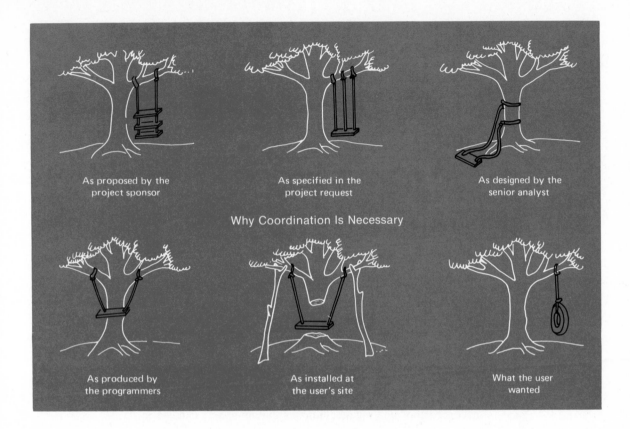

As proposed by the
project sponsor

As specified in the
project request

As designed by the
senior analyst

Why Coordination Is Necessary

As produced by
the programmers

As installed at
the user's site

What the user
wanted

decisions that are unworkable or ineffective or that do not take into account the needs of the organization as a whole.[4]

A typical example of the need for constructive conflict may occur in a manufacturing company. The sales department, in order to meet its objectives, may see the need for multiple product models to give it more flexibility in meeting customer needs. The production department, however, may feel that multiple models will involve it in excessive tooling, inventory, and production costs. Both viewpoints have merit for the departments involved, and both must be expressed and analyzed if a good compromise is to be achieved.

The presence of unresolved conflict in an organization has been recognized as a sign of ineffective coordination. (See Chapter 14 for a full discussion of the management of conflict.) In fact, modern management writers regard the absence of a reasonable level of conflict as a danger sign. Effectively coordinated organizations experience conflict between the different viewpoints and goals of their various departments but resolve these conflicts on an ongoing basis. We will describe in the section that follows some of the coordinating mechanisms available to an organization.

[4] See Lawrence and Lorsch, *Organization and Environment,* p. 12.

Coordinating
Mechanisms

Many managers and organizations seem to operate on the principle that inter-departmental conflicts will sort themselves out through normal day-to-day activities and that coordination will eventually emerge automatically. This approach is generally too haphazard to be effective. There are several recognized mechanisms and procedures that can be used alone or in combination to achieve effective coordination: the managerial hierarchy, interdepartmental communication, committees, and liaison individuals.[5]

Managerial Hierarchy. The traditional method of resolving conflict is to use the organization's chain of command. For example, if two employees have a work-related disagreement, they may ask their manager to make a policy decision. To work efficiently, particularly in larger organizations, this mechanism needs a clearly defined authority structure. Managers at every level must be aware of their responsibilities and have the procedures and authority necessary to carry them out. Formal authority by itself, however, is rarely sufficient to achieve smooth integration. If, as managers, we will answer our subordinates' arguments by issuing directives because "that's the way it has to be," our subordinates will be likely to feel that their objections have been dismissed rather than rationally resolved. The result, at best, will be reluctant submission; at worse, our subordinates may ignore our instructions or even resign.

Considerate and judicious exercise of authority can, however, bring about effective coordination in many cases. The routine control and scheduling procedures (such as policies and rules), discussed in Chapter 4, are commonly accepted coordinating mechanisms that managers can use.

Interdepartmental Communication. Communication between managers in different departments is an integral part of organizational life. When such communication occurs horizontally between managers on the same level (rather than vertically as part of the chain of command), it can be an effective aid to coordination. For example, through interdepartmental communication, the sales department can coordinate sales objectives with the production department. If there is a conflict, it may be resolved by cooperation between the production manager and the sales manager. This type of coordination usually involves the carrying out of policy rather than policy formulation.

Committees. Interdepartmental coordination may also be carried out on a more structured basis through the meetings of formal committees. These meetings may take place as frequently as once a week. They will govern interdepartmental activities until the next meeting is held. Usually committees are formally organized with a designated chairperson and membership and regularly scheduled meetings. This aspect differentiates their function from the often

---

[5] Our discussion of these four topics is based on Ernest Dale, *Organization* (New York: American Management Associations, 1967).

informal and spontaneous interdepartmental meetings in which managers represent the interests of their own departments. (See Chapter 12 for a full discussion of committees.)

The majority of coordinating committees fall into one of three basic types: general management committees, committees dealing with special areas, and multiple-management committees.

General management committees. The basic purpose of this type of committee is to make joint decisions that would otherwise be made by the chief executive. Management committee members — who are all senior managers — operate from the viewpoint of the company as a whole rather than that of their individual departments. Theoretically, each member of the committee has an equal say in its decisions. While this is hard to achieve in practice (some members will in fact be more influential and powerful than others), it is true that no one member will have the power to overrule the committee as a whole. Although its size will vary, a typical committee will have nine or ten members, with the president of the organization acting as chairperson.

The function of general management committees includes both setting policy for the company as a whole and supervising the operations of the various departments. This latter role normally includes approval or disapproval of major proposals from these individual departments.

Committees dealing with special areas. Most large organizations have coordinating committees made up of top managers with special areas of interest. The most common focus of this type of specialization is some aspect of finance, such as salary determination, company investments, and capital expenditures. Other special committees may deal with research and development, planning, or advertising.

Multiple-management committees. This type of committee, less common than those described above, is used to provide a mechanism for lower-level executives to communicate their ideas to top management. A basic format is for individual top managers to hold regular committee meetings at which their immediate subordinates report to them. If the organization is large enough, each of these committee members may meet with lower-level committees composed of their subordinates, and so on down the management hierarchy.

Liaison Individuals. The main function of liaison persons is to help managers achieve more effective coordination of their organization's activities. They provide a means of communication between departments and help clarify the specific roles each must play in meeting the organization's goals. Examples of liaison individuals are product managers, customer coordinators, and project managers.

Product managers are responsible for all activities relating to the sale and marketing of a particular product. Thus, they may coordinate activities in a variety of departments, such as promotion, advertising, and sales. Product managers are usually found in organizations with many product lines, such as consumer packaged goods companies.

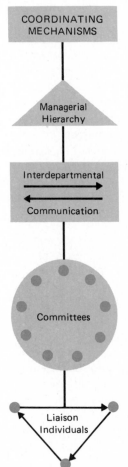

COORDINATING
MECHANISMS

Managerial
Hierarchy

Interdepartmental

Communication

Committees

Liaison
Individuals

Customer coordinators (also called contract managers or company representatives) provide extra service to customers when an organization's business is complex (as in a computer company) or when a customer is particularly important to the organization. For example, a packaging company that is processing a particularly large order of containers might have a customer coordinator to make sure that the production department is meeting the client's specifications and that delivery will take place on time.

Project managers direct a job or a set of related activities until it is completed. For example, a project manager might direct a construction job, a sales campaign, or a research group set up to solve a particular problem. Project managers have to coordinate a wide variety of activities — such as hiring, purchasing, and scheduling — in accomplishing their task.

In many cases, managers can achieve efficient coordination by using only the first two mechanisms — the managerial hierarchy and interdepartmental communication. These methods will usually be sufficient for organizations whose operations follow a relatively predictable and stable form. Also, there are many organizations in which the various departments are not greatly differentiated from each other or which are able to operate somewhat independently of each other. In such cases, the need for coordination may not be great enough to require more than the first two coordinating mechanisms. These may be supplemented by the occasional use of committees or liaison persons.

THE SPAN OF MANAGEMENT

In simple terms, we can define a manager's *span of management* as the number of subordinates who report directly to him or her. We are using the phrase "span of management" instead of the more frequently used "span of control" because we feel that "management" more accurately indicates the breadth and scope of the supervisor's function. As managers, we will do much more than merely control our subordinates' work.

The concept of span of management is certainly not new. At the start of Chapter 9, we described how Moses was initially responsible for all his people, with everyone reporting directly to him. In our terms, his span of management was measured in the thousands. As Jethro, his father-in-law counseled him, "...this thing is too heavy for thee" (Exodus 18:18). One purpose of the reorganization suggested by Jethro was to limit Moses' span of management and thus free him to concentrate on his more important tasks. Managers were established under him, each with their own limited number of subordinates: "...rulers of thousands, and rulers of hundreds, rulers of fifties, and rulers of tens" (Exodus 18:21). As a result, communication, efficiency, and coordination were improved.

Throughout this section we will see a relationship between span of management and coordination. It is often assumed that the greater the number of employees that managers have reporting to them, the more difficult it becomes to achieve effective coordination of the employees' activities. As we have already indicated, however, the relationship is not that simple. The more subordinates there are reporting to each manager, the fewer the number of managers required for a given size of organization. With fewer managerial viewpoints involved, managers may find it easier to coordinate interdepartmental objectives among themselves. This advantage could offset the difficulty of controlling and coordinating a large number of subordinates.

We will be dealing with span of management in considerable detail, because it is one of the aspects of organizational structure to which the reader will be immediately exposed when he or she enters an organization. Overworked or underworked managers are quite common in practice; and it will be helpful for new managers to know how they can seek to establish a span that will enable them to use their time most effectively.

Wide versus Narrow Spans of Management

The search for guidelines by which we can define the ideal span of management has long been a preoccupation of management writers. Fayol referred to the need for different spans at different levels within the organization: each foreman, for example, who is dealing with fairly simple tasks, may supervise twenty or thirty workers, while each superintendent may only supervise three or four foremen.[6] On this basis, Fayol proposed that the number of managers needed in an organization could be determined by a simple geometrical progression—that is, for every three or four supervisors a higher-level manager would be needed, and so on up the chain of command.

Many other attempts at formulating span of management requirements have been made. V. A. Graicunas pointed out that in selecting a span, managers should consider not only the direct one-to-one relationships with the people they supervise but also the relationships with their subordinates in groups of two or more.[7] Thus, with three employees, a manager has a relationship with each one as an individual, with three different groups of two employees each, and with one group of all three. In addition, there are cross relationships between and among the employees to be considered.

The significance of Graicunas's approach is that it suggests how complicated a manager's supervisory task can become. For every single subordinate added to a manager's supervision, the number of possible relationships increases in a mathematically predictable way. Graicunas states this in his formula:

$$R = n(2^{n-1} + n - 1)$$

where R = the number of relationships

and n = the number of subordinates

[6] Henri Fayol, *General and Industrial Management*, trans. Constance Storrs (London: Pitman, 1949), p. 55.

[7] V. A. Graicunas, "Relationship in Organization," *Bulletin of the International Management Institute*, Vol. 7 (March 1933), pp. 39–42; reprinted in Luther H. Gulick and Lyndall F. Urwick, eds., *Papers on the Science of Administration* (New York: Institute of Public Administration, Columbia University, 1937), pp. 182–187.

Even though Graicunas does not include relationships such as those between subordinates and individuals outside their immediate work group, we can see how the number of relationships increases dramatically as the number of subordinates rises. (See Table 10-1.) Another management writer, Lyndall F. Urwick, concluded from Graicunas's work that "no executive should attempt to supervise directly the work of more than five, or at the most six, direct subordinates whose work interlocks."[8]

TABLE 10-1
Graicunas's Calculation of the Number of Possible Relationships between Managers and Subordinates

Number of Subordinates	Number of Relationships	Number of Subordinates	Number of Relationships
1	1	10	5,210
2	6	11	11,374
3	18	12	24,708
4	44	•	•
5	100	•	•
6	222	15	245,970
7	490	•	•
8	1,080	•	•
9	2,376	18	2,359,602

Graicunas and Urwick, of course, were not the only ones to try and define the maximum span of management. General Ian Hamilton, basing his theory on his military experience, reached much the same conclusion as Graicunas:

The average human brain finds its effective scope in handling from three to six other brains.[9]

There are two major reasons why the choice of the appropriate span is important: First, span of management affects the efficient utilization of managers and the effective performance of their subordinates. Too wide a span may mean that managers are overextending themselves and that their subordinates are receiving too little guidance or control. Too narrow a span of management may mean that managers are underutilized and that their subordinates are overcontrolled.

Second, there is a relationship between span of management and organizational structure. A narrow span of management results in a "tall" organization with many levels of supervision between top management and the lowest organizational level. A wide span, for the same number of employees, means fewer management levels between top and bottom. Either structure may influence the manager's effectiveness at any level.

[8] Lyndall F. Urwick, *Scientific Principles and Organization* (New York: American Management Associations, 1938), p. 8. See also Lyndall F. Urwick, "V. A. Graicunas and the Span of Control," *Academy of Management Journal,* Vol. 17, No. 2 (June 1974), pp. 349–354, in which Urwick gives an interesting description of the manner in which Graicunas's original article came to be written.
[9] Ian Hamilton, *The Soul and Body of an Army* (London: Edward Arnold, 1921), pp. 229–230.

Efficient
Utilization of
Managers and
Subordinates

If the situation were as straightforward as that implied by Graicunas, managers could each be assigned five or six subordinates and feel confident that their organization had achieved the correct structure on at least one important aspect of organizational design. Unfortunately it is not that simple. Such formula-based spans may be too broad or too narrow in specific instances, resulting in efficiency.

How can we judge, in particular situations, whether a span is too broad or too narrow? Harold Stieglitz suggests one standard when he states that "harassed supervisors and frustrated subordinates often mean that the supervisor has too broad a span. Conversely, harassed subordinates and frustrated supervisors often indicate too narrow a span."[10] Too broad a span, rather than getting more out of managers by assigning them more responsibilities, is likely to result in an inefficient use of their expensive time. They will have to neglect their own work in order to deal as best they can with all of their subordinates. The time of subordinates may also be underutilized through lack of sufficient control and difficulties getting needed approvals or assistance from an overworked supervisor.

Too narrow a span of management may also prove wasteful of the organization's human resources. Such a situation implies that managers will be constantly peering over their subordinates' shoulders, because they have nothing more pressing to do. The result is likely to be inefficiency and insecurity on both levels.

Span of
Management and
Organizational
Levels

The relationship between span of management and organizational levels is illustrated in Figure 10-1 on the following page. Our theoretical organization, which has 64 operatives, is shown in three span-of-management structures, each requiring a different number of managers. In reality, it would be unusual to have identical spans of management at every level in the way that each of our structures is organized. We have these uniform spans simply for the purpose of illustrating how the span influences both the number of levels between the top and bottom of the organization and the total number of managers needed.

Structure A demonstrates one extreme for our 64-operatives organization. Here we have one manager with direct supervision of the entire staff of 64 subordinates, resulting in an extremely wide span of management and a very flat organizational structure. Structure B shows a narrower span of management and consequently a taller organizational structure. The span of management is 4, which calls for 21 managers and three levels of management. In structure C, we find the opposite extreme of structure A. With a span of management of only 2, there are 63 managers and six levels of management—a very narrow span of management and a very tall organizational structure.

The diagrams also suggest some of the problems that may arise with extreme organizational structures. The opportunities for the 64 subordinates in structure A to have individual communication and direct supervision with one

[10] Harold Stieglitz, "Optimizing the Span of Control," *Management Record,* September 1962, pp. 25–29.

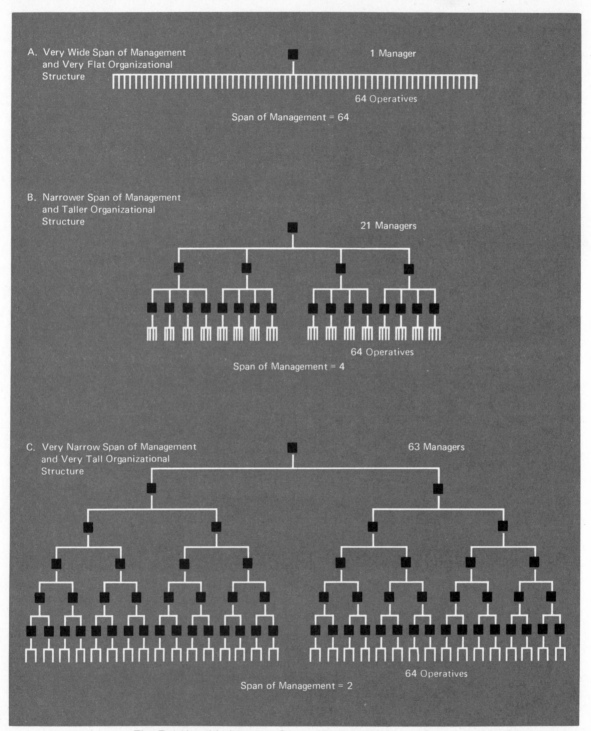

A. Very Wide Span of Management and Very Flat Organizational Structure

1 Manager

64 Operatives

Span of Management = 64

B. Narrower Span of Management and Taller Organizational Structure

21 Managers

64 Operatives

Span of Management = 4

C. Very Narrow Span of Management and Very Tall Organizational Structure

63 Managers

64 Operatives

Span of Management = 2

FIGURE 10-1   The Relationship between Span of Management and Organizational Structure

manager will obviously be limited. In structure C, communication problems may also exist because of the numerous channels that information must go through to get to and from top management and operative employees. In addition, the existence of 63 supervisors, all requiring paychecks, strongly implies that administrative costs are excessive.[11]

While these structures are extreme for the purpose of illustration, the principle applies to all organizational structures: the wider the span of management, the less direct supervision; the narrower the span, the greater the number of managers necessary and, therefore, the higher the cost.

Tall versus Flat Organizational Structures

Not surprisingly, both sides of the tall versus flat organizational structure argument have their supporters and their critics. The two criticisms most often leveled at tall organizations are those mentioned in the previous section: cost and communication.[12] Narrow spans of management require not only more supervisors (and their salaries) but also the added expense of executive offices, secretaries, and fringe benefits. In addition, the more levels of management that communication must pass through, the more diluted and inaccurate it is likely to become. In effect, according to the critics of a tall organizational structure, the decision and communication process takes longer and is of poorer quality. This results not only in inefficiency but also in demoralization among the lower-level subordinates who feel that upper management is out of touch with the realities at their level of operation.

One of the most widely quoted supporters of this viewpoint is James C. Worthy.[13] Based on his 1950 study of Sears, Roebuck and Company, Worthy argued in favor of wide spans of management and flat organizational structures. Worthy observed that small organizations generally have a higher level of employee morale and productivity than large organizations. The way to translate this advantage to a large organization, he reasoned, is to keep the levels of management at a minimum by employing fewer managers with wider spans of management.

Without the easy access to managers and the close supervision that exist with a tall structure, subordinates learn by necessity to take more responsibility and, in effect, learn to manage their own job and to supervise any subordinates they have working under them. Coordination and cooperation are improved, because each individual must learn to manage his or her own function with a minimum of help from superiors. The alternative, Worthy contends, is a tall structure with ever-increasing complexity, depersonalization, and specialization of work, leading to inefficiencies and a deterioration of management-employee relations.

[11] See Herbert A. Simon, *Administrative Behavior,* 2nd ed. (New York: Macmillan, 1961), pp. 26–28.

[12] Rocco Carzo, Jr., and John N. Yanouzas, "Effects of Flat and Tall Organization Structure," *Administrative Science Quarterly,* Vol. 14, No. 2 (June 1969), pp. 178–191.

[13] James C. Worthy, "Organizational Structure and Employee Morale," *American Sociological Review,* Vol. 15, No. 2 (April 1950), pp. 169–179. See also James C. Worthy, "Factors Influencing Employee Morale," *Harvard Business Review,* January 1950, pp. 61–73.

Worthy's arguments against narrow spans of management and tall organizational structures appear to be convincing. However, they are at this point supported mainly by logic and reason. The results of most studies that have been carried out in an attempt to verify relationships between the organizational structure and factors such as employee morale and efficiency have been inconclusive.[14] Some studies have found significantly greater job satisfaction among managers in flat organizations with wide spans of management, provided the size of the organization is about five thousand employees or fewer. Over that number, the reverse is true—the tall structures were associated with the most satisfaction. From these findings, it would seem that organization size could be an important variable in determining the appropriate span.[15]

We cannot, however, select the best span of management for any given organization through a simple formula or set of rules, because there are many variables and contingencies involved in any organization. Perhaps the most we can say is that for some specific tasks a tall structure is likely to yield higher morale and efficiency, while for other specific tasks a flat organizational structure is likely to be more effective. For example, repetitive production operations may be more efficiently carried out in a formalized tall structure than in a flat structure. The management of research and development, on the other hand, may be best handled through a flat structure in which individuals have more freedom and responsibility to work on their own ideas.

Selecting the Appropriate Span

Because of the potential impact too wide or too narrow a span of management may have on organizational productivity and cost, the selection of the appropriate span is important to the efficient operation of the organization.

Early writers on the subject recognized that the appropriate span of management would depend on variables such as the level of the manager in the organization, the nature of the work, and how efficiently the work of each manager's subordinates is coordinated. Most of their creative effort, however, was aimed at establishing broad guidelines for a standard span of, say, six subordinates or a range of spans, such as three to six subordinates. They were generally concerned with defining the best span for the average, nonexceptional organization, and were less interested in viewing the span as something that resulted from a given set of circumstances.

Modern writers have attempted to treat the appropriate span as a dependent variable that is influenced by independent variables in the work environment, such as the similarity of work done by subordinates, the geographic location of subordinates, the degree of training subordinates have, the amount of super-

[14] See, for example, the Carzo and Yanouzas study cited earlier and L. Meltzer and J. Salter, "Organization Structure and the Performance and Job Satisfaction of Physiologists," *American Sociological Review,* Vol. 27 (1962), pp. 351–362.

[15] See Lyman W. Porter and Edward E. Lawler, "The Effects of 'Tall' Versus 'Flat' Organization Structures on Managerial Job Satisfaction," *Personnel Psychology,* Vol. 17, No. 2 (1964), pp. 135–148, and Lyman W. Porter and Jacob Siegel, "Relationships of Tall and Flat Organization Structures to the Satisfaction of Foreign Managers," *Personnel Psychology,* Vol. 18, No. 4 (Winter 1965), pp. 379–392.

vision required, and the nature of the work being performed. In other words, modern writers suggest that the span is likely to be determined by the specifics or characteristics of the manager's particular situation. No one span will apply for all cases.

A Contingency Approach to Span of Management. Graicunas drew our attention to the multiple relationships that exist between managers and subordinates. He then attempted to use this factor as a basis for limiting the span of management to a maximum of six subordinates. His proposal, however, suffered from the following limitations:

1 The list of *possible* relationships does not guarantee that all the relationships actually exist. Furthermore, even if they do exist, it does not necessarily follow that every type of relationship requires supervision by the manager.
2 The relationships may not all be of equal importance to the effective functioning of the organization, and they may not be of equal frequency. In fact, many of the relationships may be quite insignificant.
3 Even relationships that do require supervision by the manager may be far from equal in the amount of time and supervision they need.

Gerald Fisch has urged a less rigid, more analytical approach to the problem of selecting an appropriate management span. Central to his argument is the observation that not all managers at all levels are limited by the same span of management requirements. Fisch divided the management hierarchy into four basic groups — super managers, general managers, middle managers, and supervisors — and analyzed the management span most suitable for each group.[16]

Super managers. Every big company or organization of "super" size has its super managers at the top with duties that are different not only in authority but also in nature from managers at lower levels. Many of the functions of the super manager involve only broad policy control rather than direct, close supervision. Executives under this type of supervision may have limited personal contact with the super manager. They may, in fact, only meet for policy-making sessions, long-term reports, and in times of emergency. This "policy span of supervision," which uses much less of the super manager's time, is quite different from the intensive, day-to-day supervision that the super manager normally has with only a few top executives.[17]

Obviously, then, to limit a super manager's span of management to six, as Graicunas would have us do, is to considerably underutilize a super manager's potential. Fisch feels that a super manager could have as many as one hundred subordinates, with fifty a more workable limit.

General managers. The second of Fisch's managerial types, general managers, includes the top management level in small to medium-sized organiza-

---

[16] Gerald G. Fisch, "Stretching the Span of Management," *Harvard Business Review*, September-October 1963, pp. 74–84.
[17] Keith Davis, *Human Relations at Work* (New York: McGraw-Hill, 1962).

tions. Also included are the managers of subunits in large corporations. At this level, policy supervision may be involved to a certain extent, but there is a more direct, personal contact between managers and subordinates than at the super manager level. General managers are usually involved in some aspects of the instruction and training of subordinates. Their personal leadership becomes an important element in their subunit's success.

Because general managers are more closely involved with their subordinates than super managers, their span of management must be comparatively narrower. However, the span will still not have to be as narrow as Graicunas and Urwick suggested. Technological developments such as the telephone have considerably reduced the amount of time that managers have to spend in a supervisory role. For this reason, a span of management of ten or more subordinates has become common among general managers.

Middle managers. Middle managers may be involved in two kinds of supervision: *executive* supervision and *operative* supervision.[18] Executive supervision refers to the supervision of managers at the next lower levels who have their own executive power and subordinates. Operative supervision is applied to employees such as plant workers or clerical staff who have no managerial status in the organization. Super managers and general managers are involved almost exclusively with executive supervision. Middle managers, however, are usually responsible for executive as well as operative supervision. (See Chapter 1.)

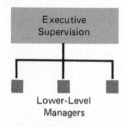

Executive
Supervision

Lower-Level
Managers

The executive span and the operative span of management are likely to be quite different. Operative supervision tends to be of a routine nature. It involves day-to-day decisions (as opposed to longer-term policy decisions) and brief, simple contacts with subordinates. As such, the operative span can be quite large. Executive supervision, on the other hand, involves important leadership functions. Subordinates will require a great deal more individual attention. Thus, the executive span will tend to be limited. For middle managers, then, the appropriate span of management will depend, in part, on the precise mix of executive and operative supervision a specific job requires.

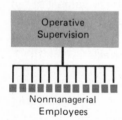

Operative
Supervision

Nonmanagerial
Employees

Supervisors. As managers of operating employees, supervisors are usually well below middle managers in executive authority. They frequently supervise work that is not complex and that rarely requires longer-term policy decisions. Instead, they will usually rely on rules and procedures to help them solve the daily problems that arise. For these reasons, the span of management at the supervisor level will normally be quite wide.

Final Guidelines for Selecting the Appropriate Span. It is already evident that, as managers, we will not be able to select the appropriate span through a single formula or rule of thumb. The span we will find most effective will vary in part according to the management level we occupy.

Economic considerations will also affect our choice of span. As we have

[18] Ralph C. Davis, *The Fundamentals of Top Management* (New York: Harper & Brothers, 1951).

already suggested, smaller spans will mean that our organization will have a larger number of managers, with the added salaries and other costs that they entail. But wide spans will at some point also involve extra costs for our organization — in the inefficiencies that result from diminished managerial leadership. Our job as managers, then, will be to strike an economic balance between cost savings that result from the largest possible span and the added costs that we will begin to incur as the span grows too wide. (See Figure 10-2.)

FIGURE 10-2
Striking an Economic Balance between Span of Management and Cost of Support Activities

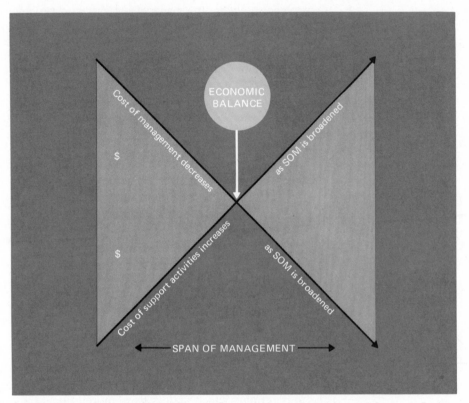

Source: Gerald G. Fisch, "Stretching the Span of Management," *Harvard Business Review,* September-October 1963, p. 79. Copyright © 1963 by the President and Fellows of Harvard College; all rights reserved.

Economic considerations will be most important in selecting a span at the middle management and supervisory levels. Because these levels usually have the greatest number of managers in the organization, keeping the span wide at these levels can result in considerable savings in salaries, office space, and the like. At the general manager level, on the other hand, the organization would usually derive little benefit (and perhaps a great deal of harm) from widening the span. The salaries of a few vice presidents might be saved, but this comparatively small saving might well be offset by a large increase in inefficiency.

What, then, is the widest possible or at least the most reasonable span for middle managers and supervisors? Fisch has suggested three basic criteria by which such managers can decide on an appropriate span:

1 *Business realities.* These include not only the basic economic considerations we have just discussed but also such matters as how diversified the organization's operations are. The more diversified the organization (in terms of function or operation), the more middle and lower-level managers are likely to be required.

2 *Management realities.* The management system of an organization will also affect the kind of span that is required. For example, in an organization where subordinates are permitted a great deal of independence, a wider span is possible. The subordinates will be making more decisions on their own. Similarly, in organizations with effective planning programs, subordinates will be more aware of their responsibilities and will likely require less supervision.

3 *Human realities.* The personalities and abilities of managers and subordinates will also influence the choice of span. Some managers may want to supervise (or are more capable of supervising) their subordinates more closely than others, in which case their span will tend to be narrower. Subordinates who are well trained and very capable will usually require less supervision. Managers with such subordinates can afford a wider span.[19]

As Fisch suggests, the range of possible spans will vary with each level in the organization and with different organizations, managers, and subordinates. Table 10-2 illustrates some methods of determining the maximum span at different management levels.

Span of Management Studies. Harold Stieglitz and C. W. Barkdull[20] have each described how analysts at the Lockheed Missiles and Space Company developed their own contingency approach for selecting the appropriate management span.

The Lockheed analysts first identified seven factors that most affect the choice of span. (These factors are listed in the box on page 260.) Having established what they felt were the most important factors, the analysts then tried to determine which factors were more critical than others. For example, it seems obvious that the more time managers have to spend in planning, the less time they will have for supervision; thus, their span will become narrower. Similarly, the more complex the functions that managers are responsible for, the more difficult their supervisory task becomes; again, the span will narrow. But which factor—planning or complexity—will be *most* likely to affect the width of the span? By using their common sense and experience, and doing some experiments, the analysts were able to answer such questions and arrive at a ranking for the seven factors.

Each factor was then assigned a point value based on its rank; the more

---

[19] Fisch, "Stretching the Span of Management," p. 78.

[20] Stieglitz, "Optimizing the Span of Control," pp. 25–29, and C. W. Barkdull, "Span of Control—A Method of Evaluation," *Michigan Business Review*, Vol. 15, No. 3 (May 1963), pp. 25–32.

TABLE 10-2   The Span of Management and Methods of Determination

Group	Classification	Personnel Involved	Maximum Range of SOM	Analytical Method Recommended
I	Top Management (Large Corporations)	Super Managers	50	*Overall conceptual analysis* of the total enterprise and its needs now and in the future.
II	General Management (Medium to Small Organizational Units)	General Managers	12	*Specific situational analysis* of the overall needs of the unit and personal leadership requirements.
III	Middle Management (All Sizes of Organizations)	Middle Managers	50	*Economic analysis and cost optimization* of the total middle management system, balancing savings of SOM increases against rising support group costs.
IV	First-Line Supervision (All Sizes of Organizations)	Supervisors	100	A. *Specific factor analysis* of each situation or group of situations for separate analysis and simplification; this method is similar in approach to the common industrial engineering sequence of time study, work simplification, restudy, and standard rate setting. B. *Situational evaluation* using analytical techniques similar in kind to those used in job evaluations.

Source: Gerald G. Fisch, "Stretching the Span of Management," *Harvard Business Review*, September-October 1963, p. 84. Copyright © 1963 by the President and Fellows of Harvard College; all rights reserved.

critical the factor in selecting a management span, the higher its point value. The various managerial positions in the company were then analyzed to determine their total point value. For each point total (or position), a "suggested span of management" was established. For example, the positions with the highest point value—that is, the positions with a high proportion of critical factors affecting choice of span—had a suggested narrow span of 4–5 subordinates. Positions with the lowest point values (such as first-line supervisors) had spans as wide as 16–22 subordinates.

Lockheed's managers decided to reorganize several units of their company along these guidelines. The result was an increase in efficiency in these subunits. For example, the number of management levels was reduced from seven to five, resulting in improved coordination and communication. The average span for middle managers was increased from 3.9 to 5.9. Economic savings, though not a primary goal of the program, were significant. The payroll was

Factors Affecting the Choice of Span

Lockheed's analysts selected and defined seven factors that they felt influenced the span of management:

1. *Similarity of functions supervised:* the degree to which the functions or subordinate tasks for which the manager is responsible are alike or different.
2. *Geographic contiguity of functions supervised:* how closely located to the manager the functions or subordinates are.
3. *Complexity of functions supervised:* the nature of the functions or tasks for which the manager is responsible.
4. *Direction and control needed by subordinates:* the degree of supervision that subordinates require.
5. *Coordination required of the supervisor:* the degree to which the manager must try to integrate functions or tasks within the subunit or between the subunit and other parts of the organization.
6. *Planning required of the supervisor:* the degree to which the manager will have to program and review the activities of his or her subunit.
7. *Organizational assistance received by the supervisor:* how much help in terms of assistants and other support personnel the manager can rely on.

Source: Quoted and adapted from C. W. Barkdull, "Span of Control—A Method of Evaluation," *Michigan Business Review*, Vol. 15, No. 3 (May 1963), pp. 27–29. Reprinted by permission of the *Michigan Business Review*, published by the Graduate School of Business Administration, The University of Michigan.

reduced by an estimated $280,000 annually. An additional amount was saved through the elimination of secretarial assistance, office space, and supplies.

Jon G. Udell surveyed the marketing and sales divisions of 67 manufacturing companies to determine if the factors suggested by Lockheed's (and other) analysts actually did affect the management span.[21] He found that some of the factors were related to the span chosen by managers in those firms, particularly the availability of organizational assistance, the similarity of functions supervised, and the length of experience of subordinates. Other factors, however, appeared to have little impact on the choice of span.

Udell's most significant finding was related to the geographic dispersion of subordinates. Most writers have assumed that geographic separation would make supervision more difficult and therefore would narrow the span of management. The Udell study found just the opposite to be true: geographic dispersion appears to encourage a wider rather than a narrower span of management. One possible explanation suggested by Udell is that geographically separated subordinates usually have similar functions, making a less complicated supervision pattern and therefore a wider span possible. It appears that further research is needed before we can say with complete certainty which factors will or should affect our choice of span.

[21] Jon G. Udell, "An Empirical Test of Hypotheses Relating to Span of Control," *Administrative Science Quarterly*, Vol. 12, No. 3 (December 1967), pp. 420–439.

Defining the appropriate span of management has always been a source of concern to managers and management writers. It seems clear that attempting to chart an average span that will be appropriate for all managers or even for managers at a given level in the organization ignores the need to adjust the span to specific situations. (Such an approach may have some usefulness, however, in that it can call attention to spans that are much too large or much too small.) A more dependable procedure is to analyze the specific situation, consider the relevant variables outlined above, and then select the span that seems most appropriate.

Summary   The division of work and departmentalization in organizations make coordination an important managerial activity. Through coordination, the activities and objectives of an organization's subunits are harmoniously integrated so that the organization's goals can be efficiently achieved.

The different working styles and attitudes that develop among specialized personnel and departments complicate the task of coordination. Such differences, however, when effectively resolved and coordinated, serve a useful purpose. They enable the members of the organization to engage in constructive conflict so that the entire organization will benefit from the variety of viewpoints and experiences available to it.

There are several coordinating mechanisms that can be used to achieve effective coordination. The *managerial hierarchy* permits managers to exercise their authority, establish procedures, and resolve disagreements in order to insure efficient operation of the organization. *Interdepartmental communication* permits managers from different subunits to integrate their activities. The various types of organizational *committees* permit the organization's members to meet formally to share information and make joint decisions. The different types of *liaison individuals* provide a means of communication between departments and help clarify the roles each department must play in carrying out the organization's goals.

The number of subordinates reporting to a supervisor is known as that supervisor's *span of management*. Span of management is related to coordination, since in certain cases a wider or a narrower span can make it more difficult for managers to integrate the activities of their subordinates or to integrate their own activities with other managers.

Narrow spans result in "tall" organizational structures, with many levels of supervision. Wide spans result in "flat" structures, with fewer supervisory levels. Too flat a structure might result in a lack of control and inefficient utilization of managers' and subordinates' time. Too tall a structure might lead to oversupervision of subordinates, red tape, and increased expenses for the organization.

Early management writers have attempted to establish a standard span or range of span that would apply for the average organization. Modern writers tend to regard the choice of spans as being contingent on the specifics of a situation. Variables that can affect the span selection include *management level,* with a wider span appropriate at the bottom and top levels of large organizations; *economic costs,* with savings growing as the span widens, until inefficiency costs begin to develop; *business realities,* such as how diverse the organization's functions are; *management realities,* such as the availability of organizational assistance; and *human realities,* including the abilities and personalities of managers and their subordinates.

Review Questions

1. What is effective coordination?
2. What types of differences in attitude and working style can develop among the various departments in an organization? How do such differences make coordination more difficult? How do you think an organization benefits from these differences?
3. What are the four types of coordinating mechanisms that managers can use?
4. What are the functions of the three basic types of committees?
5. What are the responsibilities of the three types of liaison individuals?
6. How are span of management and coordination related?
7. What does Graicunas's formula imply for a manager's choice of span? What are the limitations of Graicunas's approach?
8. What is the relationship between span of management and the number of organizational levels? What are the possible negative effects of too wide or too narrow a span?
9. What are the arguments in favor of a tall organizational structure? a flat organizational structure?
10. What management span is most suitable for each managerial level? Why?
11. What economic considerations affect the choice of span?
12. What are the three basic criteria by which middle and lower-level managers can decide on an appropriate span?
13. What factors did Lockheed's analysts select as significant in selecting a span? Which factors were confirmed by subsequent research? Which factor was found to have an effect the opposite of that suggested by Lockheed's analysts?

CASE STUDY: MAD LUDWIG

The Fullfeder Pen Company was organized about ten years ago by Ludwig Fullfeder, an engineer who simultaneously became its president and general manager of all operations. Initially the firm had about a dozen employees engaged in the manufacturing and assembly of a full line of high quality ball-point and felt-tip pens that Ludwig designed and patented. As sales expanded, Ludwig kept adding both additional plant facilities and employees to handle the increased business that resulted, mainly from customers seeking specialized pens for advertising purposes.

In 1973, Fullfeder Pen was purchased by Macro Pen Industries. Fullfeder was thereupon reorganized and Ludwig elected president of the new company. At the time, Macro Pen also recommended that he develop an organizational structure. Fullfeder never felt one was necessary. "I've always done the thinking here," he once remarked to a friend. Ludwig, a rather stolid individual accustomed to managing his own shop on an informal basis, nevertheless and grudgingly, set up the following organization chart (see Exhibit 1) without consulting the Macro Pen management.

This organizational structure was put into effect and seemed to work satisfactorily for about a year. During this period "Mad Ludwig," as the production workers nicknamed him after a television program on Bavarian King Ludwig II, labored frantically to make the chart work. He worked twelve to fourteen hours each day, much of the time out in the plant supervising the production line. And when not supervising the

Case reprinted with permission from *Contemporary Management Incidents* by Bernard A. Deitzer and Karl A. Shilliff (Columbus, Ohio: Grid, Inc., 1977), pp. 29–31.

EXHIBIT 1

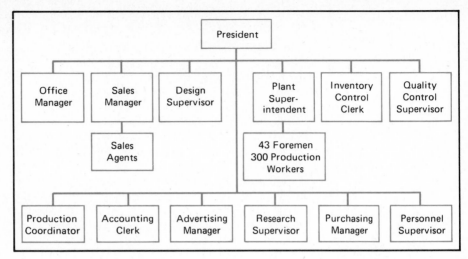

manufacturing process, he would move from department to department solving one problem after another.

On one such typical day, Ludwig:

1   Told purchasing to change suppliers of the basic plastic stock for pen barrels.
2   Hired a new accounts receivable clerk to work in the office.
3   Reviewed and made corrections on advertising copy for a trade journal.
4   Expedited a shipment of pens for a long-time account.

After a year of this kind of managing, Ludwig realized that his structure was not functioning properly. There were continual production breakdowns, sales were down, and profits were off; and to complicate things, his family physician gave him orders to slow down.

The problem, Ludwig felt, was the friction between the department heads. They were just not cooperating. Ludwig felt there was only one solution—dismiss the "troublemakers" in charge of several of the departments and hire new and more cooperative ones.

Case Questions
1. Identify Ludwig's problems. Would dismissing several "troublemakers" remedy the situation?
2. Assume you are a management consultant employed by Macro Pen. How would you handle Ludwig?

Chapter 11

Authority, Delegation, and Decentralization

Upon completing this chapter you should be able to:

1. Define power, influence, and authority and explain their importance in organizational life.
2. Distinguish between the "classical" and the "acceptance" view of formal authority.
3. Identify and describe the bases of managerial power and informal power in organizations.
4. Distinguish between line and staff authority, and describe the various types of personal, specialized, and functional staffs.
5. Explain the importance of delegation in organizations and how delegation can be made effective.
6. Identify and describe the factors that influence the amount of decentralization in organizations.

In the seventeenth century, European traders, soldiers, and missionaries came across an unusual society in the western Great Lakes region. A group of Indian tribes called the Central Algonkians were living harmoniously in the area without a formal leadership system. In fact, the Indians appeared to "carry out their subsistence, religious, administrative, and military activities in the virtual absence of any sort of recognizable authority!"[1]

Not only did the Indians lack an apparent regulatory system, but they also deeply resented any efforts to control their actions. All members of the tribe knew what was required of them by lifelong familiarity with the tasks of the community. These tasks tended to be simple and repetitive, since the rate of social change among the Algonkians was slow. Thus, although groups such as the warriors had their acknowledged leaders, no real authority was required. Rather than issuing direct orders (which were considered insulting), members of the tribe would arouse other members to action by persuasion, flattery, and the setting of examples.

It would be difficult, if not impossible, to implement such a system in our own society. Most of us have grown up in a culture where we have been under the direction of one authority or another for as long as we can remember. Our parents, our teachers, our bosses, our government, all have the acknowledged right under certain conditions to tell us what to do. The concept of authority is so much a part of our culture that it is hard for us to imagine a workable society without it. How, for example, could we hope to manage employees without the authority to direct their activities? We have been culturally pre-disposed to rely on authority to get things done, and would probably be uncomfortable with or incompetent at using the Algonkian method of flattery on a large scale.

There is, of course, another important reason why the Algonkian system would prove inadequate to us: our society has grown far too complex for such a system to work. The wide variety of tasks that members of our society have to perform—often under tight time or budget limitations—makes the Algonkian system impractical. If we attempted to run General Motors or build the Alaskan pipeline without clear lines of authority and accountability, chaos would quickly result. In our modern organizations, the formal authority system is a necessary element in the achievement of organizational objectives.

As we have already suggested in Chapter 9, however, a formal authority system must be supplemented by informal bases of power and influence in order for an organization to function efficiently. For example, managers use more than their official authority in earning the cooperation of their subordinates. They will rely on their intelligence, their experience, and their leadership abilities as well. In fact, effective managers rarely have to resort to their formal authority to influence employees, though that authority is obviously a part of every manager-subordinate interaction. They may, in certain cases, even rely

---

[1] Walter B. Miller, "Two Concepts of Authority," in Harold J. Leavitt and Louis R. Pondy, eds., *Readings in Managerial Psychology* (Chicago: University of Chicago Press, 1964), pp. 557–576.

on the Algonkian method of persuasion, flattery, and the setting of examples to influence employees. In this chapter, we will discuss both the formal and informal bases of influence that managers use to achieve their personal and organizational goals.

INFLUENCE, POWER, AND AUTHORITY

We will start our investigation by looking at the relationship between influence, power, and authority. Writers on management have defined and used these terms in a variety of ways, not all of which are in precise agreement with each other.[2] We will define *influence* as a change in behavior or attitude resulting directly or indirectly from the actions or example of another person or group. For instance, a hard-working person might, by setting an example, influence the other members of his or her department to increase their productivity. Our definition also takes into account those instances of influence in which an actual behavior change does not occur. For example, a manager might use his or her influence to improve morale. The influence here would not necessarily change a behavior; it would simply bring about a change in work attitude.

We will define *power* as the ability to exert influence. In other words, to have power is to be able to bring about a change in the behavior or attitudes of other individuals. In our example above, it is likely that the hard-working person would have more power to influence the work group if he or she were popular than if he or she were disliked. The most powerful managers in an organization are invariably those who can most influence their superiors, peers, and subordinates.

Formal authority is one type of power based on the recognition of the legitimacy or lawfulness of the attempt to exert influence. The individuals or groups attempting to exert influence are seen as having the right to do so within recognized boundaries. This right arises from their formal position in an organization.

The Basis of Formal Authority: Two Views

"What gives you the right to tell me what to do?" This familiar question bluntly suggests that before we comply with an instruction we must be satisfied that the person issuing it has the authority to do so. It is unlikely that we would ask this question of a superior in our organization, since we assume that a superior does have the right to issue instructions to us. Why do we make this assumption? What is the origin of formal authority in organizations? Where do managers get the right to tell other people what to do?

There are two major views on the origin of formal authority in organizations: the classical view and the acceptance view. The *classical view* takes the position that authority originates at some very high level of society and then is lawfully passed down from level to level. At the top of this high level may be

[Figure in left margin: boxes labeled "Power", "Influence", "Change in Behavior or Attitude" connected by downward arrows]

---

[2] See, for example, Herbert A. Simon, "Authority," in Conrad M. Arensberg et al., *Research on Industrial Human Relations* (New York: Harper & Brothers, 1957), p. 103.

God, the bureaucracy (in the form of a king, a dictator, or an elected president), or the collective will of the people.[3]

Figure 11-1 shows a classical view of formal authority in American organizations. Under this view, management has a right to give lawful orders, and subordinates have an obligation to obey. This obligation is, in effect, self-imposed. Members of our society, in agreeing to abide by the Constitution, accept the right of others to own private property and to own and control a business. By entering and remaining in an organization, subordinates in the United States accept the authority of owners or superiors and therefore have a duty to obey lawful directives.

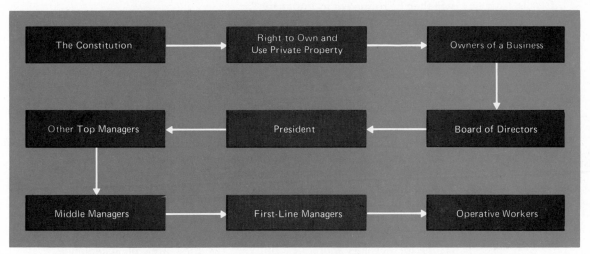

FIGURE 11-1   The Classical View of the Flow of Authority in a Business Organization

This view is normative and idealistic. It describes how individuals should behave and suggests that disobedience of lawful and legitimate orders of managers is wrong and indefensible. That we are all willing to conform to a considerable range of lawful directives is shown by our acceptance of traffic laws, no-smoking signs, and requests to report to the boss right away. The willingness to perceive these various types of formal authority as legitimately based is widespread, even when no explicit reward or punishment is likely to follow compliance or refusal.

The classical view, however, is not fully descriptive. It does not account for the fact that many laws are disregarded and that others are complied with for reasons other than acceptance of authority (such as fear or habit). The classical view also offers only one possible explanation of the process by which authority is obtained.

[3] See Max Weber, "The Three Types of Managerial Rule," *Berkeley Journal of Sociology,* Vol. 4 (1953), pp. 1–11. See also Cyril O'Donnell, "The Source of Managerial Authority," *Political Science Quarterly,* Vol. 67, No. 4 (December 1952), pp. 573–588.

The second theory of the origin of formal authority, the *acceptance view*, finds the basis of authority in the *influencee* rather than in the *influencer*. This perspective starts with the observation that not all legitimate laws or commands are obeyed in all circumstances. Some are accepted by the subordinate or receiver of the order, and some are not. The key point is that it is the *receiver* who decides whether or not to comply. In the acceptance viewpoint, therefore, whether or not authority is present in any particular law or order is a decision of the receiver, not of the person issuing the order. For example, if a supervisor storms along an assembly line shouting at everyone to work harder, the subordinates may not question the supervisor's right to do so but, through anger or indifference, they may choose not to comply with the order. The order will then be robbed of its authority.

Although this approach seems to suggest that insubordination and chaos are the norm in organizations, most formal authority is, in fact, accepted by the members of an organization. Chester I. Barnard, a strong proponent of the acceptance view (see Chapter 2), has defined the conditions under which a person will comply with higher authority:

LEGITIMATE
COMMANDS

Nonmanagerial
Employees

Area of
Acceptance

Possible
Noncompliance

RECEIVER

A person can and will accept a communication as authoritative only when four conditions simultaneously obtain: (a) he can and does understand the communication; (b) *at the time of his decision* he believes that it is not inconsistent with the purpose of the organization; (c) *at the time of his decision,* he believes it to be compatible with his personal interest as a whole; and (d) he is able mentally and physically to comply with it.[4]

In addition to these conditions, cooperation in accepting authority is fostered by what Barnard calls the "zone of indifference" and which Herbert A. Simon refers to, perhaps more descriptively, as the "area of acceptance."[5] Both expressions refer to the inclination of individuals to accept most orders given to them by their superiors, provided the orders fall within a "normal" range. Most of us, for example, will accept the necessity for periodic reports to our superiors, and will not even stop to consider whether or not to comply with a request for such reports.

The Bases of Power

John French and Bertram Raven have suggested that there are five bases or sources of power;[6] these are listed and defined in the accompanying box.

An obvious example of *reward power* is the power of a supervisor to assign work tasks to subordinates. The greater the attractiveness of a particular task in the eyes of the influencee, the greater the reward power is likely to be.

[4] Chester I. Barnard, *The Functions of the Executive,* 30th anniversary ed. (Cambridge, Mass.: Harvard University Press, 1968), pp. 165–166.
[5] Herbert A. Simon, *Administrative Behavior: A Study of Decision-Making Processes in Administrative Organization* (New York: Macmillan, 1961), pp. 133–134.
[6] John R. P. French and Bertram Raven, "The Bases of Social Power," in Dorwin Cartwright, ed., *Studies in Social Power* (Ann Arbor, Mich.: University of Michigan, 1959), pp. 150–167. See also Walter R. Nord, "Developments in the Study of Power," in *Concepts and Controversy in Organizational Behavior,* 2nd ed. (Pacific Palisades, Calif.: Goodyear, 1976), pp. 437–438.

The Five Types of Power

1. *Reward power.* This power is based on one person (the influencer) having the power to reward another person (the influencee) for carrying out orders or meeting the influencer's requirements.
2. *Coercive power.* This power is based on the influencer's ability to punish the influencee for not carrying out the influencer's requirements.
3. *Legitimate power.* This power exists when a subordinate or influencee acknowledges that the influencer has a ''right'' or is lawfully entitled to exert influence. It is also implied that the influencee has an obligation to accept this power.
4. *Referent power.* This power, which may be held by a person or a group, is based on the influencee's desire to identify with or imitate the influencer. The strength of referent power is directly related to factors such as the amount of prestige and admiration the influencee confers upon the influencer.
5. *Expert power.* This power is based on the perception or belief that the influencer has some expertise or special knowledge that the influencee does not.

Coercive power is the opposite of reward power; it represents the threat or possibility of punishment. Coercive power is usually used to maintain a minimum standard of productivity or conformity among employees. Punishment may range from loss of a minor privilege to loss of a job.

Legitimate power is the power we have referred to as formal authority. Subordinates accept that managers have the right — within certain bounds — to make decisions for them and to tell them what to do. The right to increase salaries is an example of legitimate power.

A person in an organization whom others in the organization identify with and wish to imitate has *referent power.* For example, a popular, conscientious manager will have referent power if others are motivated to match his or her work habits. Referent power may apply independently of the organizational structure — the person being influenced may be at the same level as the influencee. A charismatic colleague, for example, may sway us to his or her side in department meetings.

When we do what the doctor tells us, we are acknowledging his *expert power.* Expert power is usually applied to a specific, limited subject area. We may accept the advertising advice of our company's marketing expert but ignore the same person's recommendation on how to lower production costs.

Each of these bases is only a *potential* source of power. They provide the possibility of being able to influence another person. However, simply possessing some or all of these types of potential power does not guarantee the ability to influence particular individuals in a specific way. For example, we may have their respect and admiration as an expert in our field, but we still may be unable to influence them to be more creative on the job or even to get to work on time. Thus, the role of the influencee in accepting or rejecting the attempted influence remains a key one.

269

Normally, each of the five power bases is potentially inherent in a manager's position. A specific degree of legitimate power always accompanies a manager's job. Subordinates are assumed to accept a manager's formal authority and will generally obey him or her within reasonable limits. In addition, managers usually have the power to reward subordinates with money, privileges, or promotions and to punish them by withholding or removing these rewards. Also, managers are assumed to possess some degree of expertise, at least until they prove otherwise. Referent power is perhaps least likely to be an expected part of a manager's position, since it so obviously depends on an individual's style or personality. However, many examples of it exist in most organizations. For instance, there is a tendency among many subordinates to model themselves after senior executives who have had unusually successful careers.

Each of French and Raven's five types of power is important to managers in varying degrees and at varying times. Legitimate power or formal authority, however, is of major importance, because it establishes the ground rules for hiring and firing, for budgeting and allocating resources, and for all the other basic activities necessary for the efficient functioning of the organization.

Power in Organizations

The concept of power is a difficult one for Americans to deal with objectively — perhaps because the United States was founded by waves of immigrants who were seeking to avoid the oppression of authoritarian and despotic regimes in Europe and the Orient. A distrust of excessive power is reflected in the United States Constitution, which, while establishing the powers of government, clearly limits those powers as well. The overall tone of the Constitution is one of concern for the rights of the individual and of minorities; and the Constitution's specific system of "checks and balances" is designed to provide the means for the three branches of government — legislative, executive, and judicial — to prevent each branch from accumulating too much power.

Most Americans, then, tend to have ambivalent feelings about power. They may desire it but are reluctant to admit this openly. They may both admire and resent power in others. This uneasiness about power may explain why it has rarely been examined by management writers, even though power is an obvious part of a manager's position.

David McClelland has suggested that there are "two faces of power" — a negative face and a positive face.[7] The negative face is usually expressed in terms of dominance-submission: "If I win, you lose." To have power implies having power over another person, who is less well off for lack of it. Leadership based on this type of power regards people as little more than pawns to be used or sacrificed as the need arises. Such an approach to power is self-defeating, since people who feel they are pawns tend either to resist leadership or to become overly passive. In either case, their value to the manager is severely limited.

[7] David C. McClelland, "The Two Faces of Power," *Journal of International Affairs,* Vol. 24, No. 1 (1970), pp. 29–47.

The positive face of power is best characterized by a concern for group goals and for helping to find and formulate such goals. It involves exerting influence *on behalf of* rather than *over* others. Managers who exercise their power positively encourage group members to develop the strength and competence they need to succeed as people and as members of the organization.

Whether negative or positive, power is an important fact of organizational life; its existence cannot be ignored. The question is not whether power is an integral part of management but whether it is abused or used constructively.

Norman H. Martin and John H. Sims examined the subject of how power actually is used by managers.[8] They developed a list of "power tactics" that they found to be practiced by most people "whose success rests on ability to control and direct the actions of others":

1 *Taking counsel.* Power-wise managers use caution in taking advice from subordinates, since subordinates may pressure them into making an incorrect decision. (The conditions under which managers and subordinates should reach decisions together are described in Chapter 7.)

2 *Alliances.* Smart managers try to establish relationships with those above and below them in the organization. Forming alliances with people above them can open avenues for advancement; forming alliances with those below them can help build a loyal group of followers.

3 *Maneuverability.* Managers must be ready to adjust smoothly to any major changes in company policy or plans. Therefore, they never commit themselves completely to any one position or program.

4 *Communication.* Giving too much information to subordinates can be a bad idea, since information can arouse unrealistic expectations and conveying it may blur the lines of authority. Many managers therefore use information tactically, by controlling when and with whom they share information.

5 *Compromising.* Managers may give the appearance of accepting compromise at times while actually continuing to press toward their own goals. In this way they attempt to avoid both real concessions and harmful conflict.

6 *Negative action.* Managers may sometimes have to give in to a proposal with which they disagree but which they dare not actively oppose. In such cases they may use the technique of "negative timing." This means that the manager initiates the action desired but postpones actually carrying it out by studying, planning, and indefinitely delaying the program until it quietly dies out on its own.

7 *Self-dramatization.* Managers may consciously shape their speech and their behavior with the skill of an actor in order to accomplish their ends.

8 *Confidence.* After managers make a decision, their inner conviction that the decision is right is less important than an outward appearance of confidence. The manager will behave as if the decision is correct and final.

9 *Always the boss.* Power-wise managers always stay in the role of boss. Emotional ties and friendships with subordinates may erode power and hinder one's ability to view others objectively.

[8] Norman H. Martin and John H. Sims, "Power Tactics," *Harvard Business Review,* November-December 1956, pp. 25–29 ff.

These tactics are presented as "neither immoral nor cynical" by Martin and Sims. They suggest that perhaps in an ideal world managers would not use these tactics, but in the real world these tactics are used daily.

Although the analysis presented by Martin and Sims concentrates on the use of power by managers, the acceptance perspective of Barnard, which was discussed earlier, reminds us that power does not always result from assigned or formal authority. David Mechanic points out that lower-level members of an organization often have a great deal of informal power.[9] This power may be based on their *information* or knowledge about the organization, the *skills* they possess, and the *resources* to which they have access. For example, new doctors in a hospital may have to rely on nurses to "teach them the ropes," and this dependence will give the nurses power to influence the doctors' actions. Similarly, low-level employees with control over special equipment (such as the copying machine) will often have the power to impede or improve a manager's work flow.

LINE AND STAFF AUTHORITY

We have referred to the legitimate power associated with an organizational position as "formal authority." This type of power is based on subordinates' accepting that it is appropriate and desirable to follow orders from certain individuals in the organizational hierarchy.

One of the many other usages of the word *authority* occurs in distinguishing between what is frequently called *line* authority and *staff* authority. Not all authors agree that the line/staff distinction is meaningful.[10] Line and staff authority are, however, such pervasive and often confusing elements in organizations that they need to be recognized and understood.[11]

Line Positions   Every organization exists to achieve specific goals. The line component may be defined as the part of the organization that is directly responsible for achieving these goals. Line authority is represented by the standard chain of command that starts with the board of directors and extends down through the various levels in the hierarchy to the point where the basic activities of the organization are carried out.

Since line activities are identified in terms of the company's goals, the activities classified as line will differ with each organization. For example, a manufacturing company may limit line functions to production and sales, while a department store, in which buying is a key element, will include the purchasing department as well as the sales department in its line activities.

---

[9] David Mechanic, "Sources of Power of Lower Participants in Complex Organizations," *Administrative Science Quarterly,* Vol. 7, No. 3 (December 1962), pp. 349–364.

[10] See, for example, Gerald G. Fisch, "Line-Staff Is Obsolete," *Harvard Business Review,* September-October 1961, pp. 67–79.

[11] Our discussion in this section is based on Louis A. Allen, "The Line-Staff Relationship," *Management Record,* Vol. 17, No. 9 (September 1955), pp. 346–349 ff.

Staff Positions   Staff refers to individuals or groups in an organization whose main function is to provide advice and service to the line. Thus, staff includes all elements of the organization that are not classified as line.

If a staff *department* exists (such as a personnel or accounting department), it may have its own line and staff components. Some parts of the department may exist to carry out the department's objectives; thus, they will be considered that department's line. The other parts of the department will exist to support that line with advice and service. For example, within a personnel department, the personnel manager would be considered part of line; the manager's personal assistants would be considered part of the department's staff.

Theoretically, the distinction between line and staff can be made with reasonable ease and accuracy. In practice, such clarity is often missing. In some complex organizations, for example, the same function may have both line and staff elements. The general manager of a corporate division may use the sales department head as part of his or her staff: the sales department head will also function as a line manager in the division.

Types of Staff   There are two types of staff that provide support services to the line: personal staff and specialized staff. The *personal staff* assists the manager in carrying out some or all of his or her functions. However, the manager will continue to perform and be responsible for those functions, despite the aid of the personal staff. The *specialized staff* performs work requiring skills or objectivity that the line does not possess—a medical staff, for example. Since the work of the specialized staff cannot usually be performed by the line, it may be completely delegated to the staff without involving a line manager. We will discuss both types of staff in greater detail below.

The Personal Staff. A manager's personal staff may involve three kinds of assistants: line assistants, staff assistants, and general assistants.

Line assistants help their managers in *all* their managerial duties rather than in any specific area. Their purpose is to advise, assist, and act on behalf of their chief. As representatives of their managers, line assistants may exercise some authority over other employees or even take over the department in the managers' absence.

Staff assistants will normally have no authority over other employees, because their functions are usually much more restricted than that of line assistants. Their actual duties will depend on the particular company and manager involved and may vary from little more than clerical duties to attending meetings with the power to speak on behalf of the manager.

Staff assistants go under a variety of titles such as "administrative assistant," "special assistant," and "executive assistant," depending on the actual functions they perform.

General assistants are a group of staff assistants functioning at an upper management level. They usually serve as consultants and advisors to top managers in specified areas.

Figure 11-2 shows an example of how personal staff, in the form of an assis-

FIGURE 11-2
Personal Staff

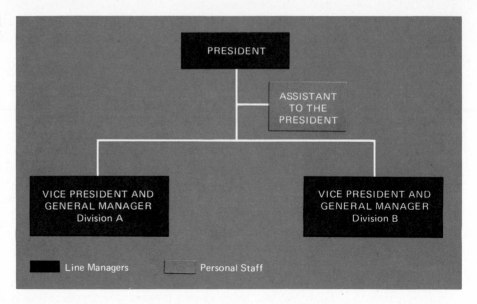

tant to the president, might fit into the organization hierarchy. Depending on the functions he or she performs, this assistant may be considered a line assistant or a staff assistant.

The Specialized Staff. The personal staff, as we have seen, may provide a wide range of services but will concentrate on assisting one department or individual. The members of the specialized staff, on the other hand, concentrate their functions in one specific area of expertise but normally make this service and advice available to a wide range of departments. In fact, specialized staff will usually assist all other departments, line and staff.

Two examples of specialized staff, serving the functions of finance and administration, are shown in a typical company structure in Figure 11-3. The vice presidents of finance and administration are assumed to have full service departments reporting to them and to be responsible for providing staff advice and service to the general managers of all three line divisions.

One identifying characteristic of specialized staff is that it usually has no formal authority over other parts of the organization. Staff members, however, do have access to power. Most of the sources of power defined by French and Raven, which were summarized earlier (see box on page 269), are available to individuals employed in staff functions. They can, for example, develop considerable power through their expertise. Also, by providing needed services quickly and efficiently or by delaying and withholding them, they can exert reward or coercive power.[12] It is even possible for staff individuals to develop referent power if their personal style is particularly appealing. This source of power, however, is less common than other power sources among

[12] See Leonard R. Sayles, *Managerial Behavior* (New York: McGraw-Hill, 1964), p. 79.

staff individuals, since staff positions are generally considered to have lower prestige than line positions.

One example of the successful establishment of referent power by staff specialists is the organizational development specialist who frequently has a professional style that appears to be informal, egalitarian, and antiauthority. This image often appeals to the younger managers in the organization.

In principle, staff carries out specific tasks for the line, with the formal authority for the final decision remaining with the line. For example, the purchasing department may perform the service of ordering raw material, but the final decision as to what type or even what sources are selected may remain with the line. However, even though line managers can legitimately overrule staff recommendations and decisions, in actual practice line managers will often go along with their staff. Only a highly knowledgeable or foolhardy manager would reject the expert decision of staff in such sensitive or high-risk areas as taxation, federal antitrust policies, civil rights legislation, and other matters of law.

Functional Staff Authority

Our description of the role of staff members as that of providing advice and service to line members implies that staff lacks independent, formal authority. In reality, staff departments that have responsibility for carrying out a specific

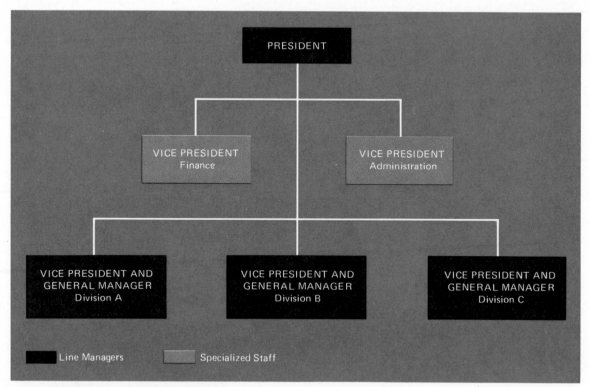

FIGURE 11-3 Specialized Staff

function may have formal authority over line members within the limits of that function. The right to control activities carried out in other departments as they relate to specific staff responsibilities is known as *functional authority*.

In many companies, the personnel manager provides an example of functional staff authority. He or she may have complete control over specific areas such as recruitment procedures, employment testing, and the application of discipline provisions of a labor contract. Specific responsibilities delegated to controllers, such as allocation of overhead and internal auditing procedures, are another typical example of functional authority.[13]

The need for functional authority is very real. It arises from the need to have a degree of uniformity and an unhindered application of expertise in carrying out many organizational activities. For this reason, functional authority is quite common in organizations. Even so, it usually complicates the relationships between line and staff members. The opportunity to confuse the role of given staff individuals in specific situations is high: Are they giving advice, providing a service, or laying down the law on what or how something is to be done by a line member? Such confusion between line and staff authority may hinder the effectiveness of the organization. For example, a staff individual who issues a directive to line members who regard him or her as having only advisory power may well be resented or ignored. The problems arising from staff-line relationships are considerable, and it is important for managers to understand and prepare for them. We will be discussing these problems in greater detail in Chapter 14.

DELEGATION

We may define *delegation* as the assignment of authority and responsibility to another person for the carrying out of specific activities. The delegation of authority by superiors to subordinates is obviously a necessary mechanism for the efficient functioning of any organization, since no superior can accomplish or completely supervise all the organization's tasks. The extent to which managers will delegate authority will be influenced by many factors, such as the style of the organization, the specific situation involved, and the interrelationship, personalities, and capabilities of the people in that situation.[14] However, although there are many "contingency" factors that managers will have to take into account in deciding how much to delegate, there are also

---

[13] See Wendell French and Dale Henning, "The Authority-Influence Role of the Functional Specialist in Management," *Journal of the Academy of Management,* Vol. 9, No. 3 (September 1966), pp. 187–203, and Dale Henning and R. L. Moseley, "Authority Role of the Functional Manager: The Controller," *Administrative Science Quarterly,* Vol. 15, No. 4 (December 1970), pp. 482–489.

[14] See Gerald G. Fisch, "Toward Effective Delegation," *CPA Journal,* Vol. 46, No. 7 (July 1976), pp. 66–67.

"I am perfectly aware, Operator, that I may dial that number directly. I have no wish to do so, however."

Drawing by Richter; © 1976 The New Yorker Magazine, Inc.

some basic guidelines for effective delegation that will apply for most situations.[15] We will discuss these guidelines below.

Guidelines for Effective Delegation

Delegation was a topic treated extensively by the classical management theorists described in Chapter 2. Many of the guidelines to effective delegation are therefore based on classical principles.

Responsibility, Authority, and Accountability. As we have indicated in previous chapters on the organizing process, every position in an organization has, or should have, specified tasks and the responsibility for carrying them out. So that the organization can make efficient use of its resources, *responsibility for*

---

[15] Our discussion in this section is based on S. Avery Raub, *Company Organization Charts* (New York: National Industrial Conference Board, 1954); Bennett E. Kline and Norman H. Martin, "Freedom, Authority and Decentralization," *Harvard Business Review*, May-June 1958, pp. 69–75; and James D. Mooney and Alan C. Reiley, *The Principles of Organization* (New York: Harper & Brothers, 1939), pp. 14–19, 23–24.

specified tasks is assigned to the lowest level of the organization at which there can be found sufficient ability and information to carry them out competently. For example, it would obviously be a waste of a company president's time—most of which should be spent in dealing with the overall goals of the organization—to check personally the time cards of lower-level employees. Such a task can be performed most efficiently by lower-level supervisors.

A corollary of this rule is that *for individuals in the organization to perform their assigned tasks effectively, they must be delegated sufficient authority to carry out those tasks.* For example, as sales managers, we would be responsible for a certain standard of performance in our sales department. But if we did not have the formal authority to assign territories, reward the most effective salespeople, and fire incompetents, we would not be able to fulfill our obligations. Rather than managing and controlling our department, we would be at the mercy of events. Through delegation of authority, then, members of the organization are given the power they need to carry out their assigned responsibilities.

A necessary part of delegation of responsibility and authority is *accountability*—being held answerable for results. By accepting responsibility and authority, individuals in the organization also agree to accept credit or blame for the way in which they carry out their assignments. For managers, the concept of accountability has an added dimension: not only are managers held accountable for their own performance, but they are also held accountable for the performance of their subordinates. In fact, accountability for the actions of subordinates is one of the defining characteristics of a managerial position.

CLASSICAL
DELEGATION
GUIDELINES

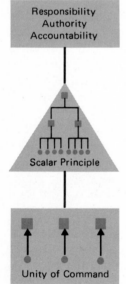

Responsibility
Authority
Accountability

Scalar Principle

Unity of Command

Scalar Principle. For delegation to work effectively, members of the organization should know where they stand in the chain of command. Otherwise, they could neither accept nor assign responsibility with any confidence. The *scalar principle* suggests that there must be a clear line of authority running step by step from the highest to the lowest level of the organization. This clear line of authority will make it easier for organizational members to understand (1) to whom they can delegate, (2) who can delegate to them, and (3) to whom they are accountable.

In the process of establishing the line of authority, *completeness of delegation* is required; that is, all necessary tasks in the organization should be assigned. Unassigned tasks, called *gaps*, have to be avoided, because otherwise it is likely that the tasks will remain unperformed—or the people who voluntarily perform those tasks will resent their extra burden. For example, we will not be able to assume that our purchasing manager will also take care of inventory control. Either we will clearly define the inventory tasks as his or her responsibility or we will delegate the task to someone else. Similarly, there should be no *overlaps* (responsibility for the same task assigned to more than one individual) and no *splits* (responsibility for the same task assigned to more than one organizational unit). Otherwise, confusion of authority and accountability will result.

Unity of Command. The *unity of command* principle states that each person in the organization should report to only one superior. Reporting to more than one superior makes it difficult for an individual to know to whom he or she is accountable and whose instructions he or she must follow. For example, a mail room employee who must report to several managers will frequently receive conflicting orders about whose work has priority. The mail clerk is then likely to feel confused and harassed. Reporting to more than one superior also encourages individuals to avoid responsibility, since they can easily blame poor performance on the fact that with several bosses they have too much to do.

Because of the complexity of many of today's organizations, it has become common for the unity of command principle to be violated. For example, members of a secretarial pool might well have to accept work from a large number of executives. When unity of command cannot be achieved for a person's entire job, it is desirable at least to have the person report to only one superior for each specific task.

Limitations of the Classical Guidelines. The guidelines we have been discussing are representative of the classical "top to bottom" view of authority in organizations. In practice, they suffer from a number of limitations.

One problem with the guidelines is that they overlook the fundamental point we made earlier in this chapter—namely, that members of the organization must accept the legitimacy of higher authority in order for that authority to be able to operate. Managers may have the formal "right" to delegate tasks, but if subordinates do not accept that "right," the delegation process will break down. As we shall see, managers will often have to seek the support of subordinates in order to make delegation effective.

Another problem with the classical guidelines is that there are many situations in which they simply do not apply. For example, it may be fruitless to prepare a precise job description for a project manager in a construction firm, since that manager's responsibilities might differ with each assignment. In a job as complex and changeable as a manager's, some ambiguity in authority is often inevitable. The classical guidelines are useful in many cases, and when overlooked will often lead to predictable types of problems. However, when the situation requires it, managers may intentionally have to violate these guidelines in order to achieve their objectives.

The Advantages of Effective Delegation

When used properly, delegation has several important advantages. The first and most obvious is that the more tasks managers are able to delegate, the more opportunity they have to seek and accept increased responsibilities from higher-level managers. Thus, as managers we will try to delegate not only routine matters but also tasks requiring thought and initiative, so that we can be free to function with maximum effectiveness for our organizations. (See box on next page for a description of the degrees of delegation a manager can use.)

Another advantage of delegation is that it frequently leads to better decisions, since subordinates closest to the "firing line" usually have the best

---

Degrees of Delegation

Harvey Sherman has listed the following as typical degrees of delegation:

1. Take action — no further contact with me is needed.
2. Take action — let me know what you did.
3. Look into this problem — let me know what you intend to do; do it unless I say not to.
4. Look into this problem — let me know what you intend to do; delay action until I give approval.
5. Look into this problem — let me know alternative actions available with pros and cons and recommend one for my approval.
6. Look into this problem — give me all the facts; I will decide what to do.

Source: Quoted from Harvey Sherman, *It All Depends: A Pragmatic Approach to Organizations* (University, Alabama: University of Alabama Press, 1966), pp. 83–84. © 1966 by the University of Alabama Press. Used by permission.

view of the facts. For example, if we are the national sales manager of a company based on the East Coast, our West Coast sales manager will be in the best position to allocate the California sales territories among our salespeople. In addition, effective delegation speeds up decision making. Valuable time is lost when subordinates must check with their superiors (who then may have to check with *their* superiors) before making a decision. This delay is eliminated when subordinates are authorized to make the necessary decision on the spot. Finally, delegation causes subordinates to accept responsibility and exercise judgment. This not only helps train subordinates — an important advantage of delegation — but also improves their self-confidence.

In spite of these advantages, many managers are reluctant to delegate authority and many subordinates are reluctant to accept it. We will discuss the barriers to effective delegation below.

Barriers to Effective Delegation

Barriers to effective delegation generally fall under one of two categories: (1) reluctance to delegate and (2) reluctance to accept delegation.

Reluctance to Delegate. There are a number of reasons that managers commonly offer to explain why they do not delegate: "I can do it better myself"; "My subordinates just aren't capable enough"; "It takes too much time to explain what I want done." These reasons are often excuses that managers use to hide the real reasons why they avoid delegation.

A major cause of reluctance to delegate is often insecurity. Managers are accountable for the actions of subordinates, and this fact makes some managers reluctant to "take chances" and delegate tasks. They would much rather take up their own valuable time and energy to make sure something is done "right," rather than delegate and risk failure. Insecurity of another kind may also

Reluctance
to Delegate

↑

BARRIERS
TO
EFFECTIVE
DELEGATION

↓

Reluctance
to Accept
Delegation

inhibit delegation: the manager may fear a loss of power if the subordinate does too good a job.

Another common cause of reluctance to delegate is a manager's lack of ability. Some managers may simply be too disorganized or inflexible to plan ahead and decide which tasks should be delegated and to whom, or to set up a control system so that subordinates' actions can be monitored.

Lack of confidence in subordinates is a third major reason why managers avoid delegation. In the short run, this lack of confidence may be justified by the fact that subordinates lack knowledge and skill. In the long run, there is no justification for failing to train subordinates. Managers who lack confidence in their subordinates — perhaps because of an inflated sense of their own worth — will either avoid delegation completely or delegate but severely limit their subordinates' freedom to act.

Reluctance to Accept Delegation. Insecurity can also be a barrier to the acceptance of delegation. Many subordinates would like their bosses to make all the decisions so that they can avoid the responsibility and risk of making decisions on their own. The fear of criticism or dismissal for making a mistake, or the personal fear of failure, may also make subordinates reluctant to accept delegation.

Another common cause of such reluctance is that subordinates are often not given sufficient incentives for assuming extra responsibility. Delegating additional responsibility to subordinates means that the subordinates will have to work harder under greater pressure. Without adequate compensation (such as higher salaries or increased promotion opportunities), subordinates may be unwilling to accept a greater work load.

Overcoming the
Barriers

The most basic prerequisite to effective delegation is the willingness by managers to give their subordinates real freedom in accomplishing delegated tasks. Managers have to accept the fact that there are usually several ways of handling a problem and that their own way is not necessarily the one their subordinates will choose. In fact, subordinates may well make errors in carrying out their tasks. The idea that they have to be allowed to develop their own solutions to problems and to learn from their mistakes is very difficult for many managers to face. But unless managers accept this idea, they cannot delegate effectively. They will be so preoccupied with minor tasks or with checking on subordinates that their own important tasks will remain undone. Managers must keep in mind that the great advantages of delegation justify giving subordinates freedom of action, even at the risk of allowing mistakes to occur.

The barriers to effective delegation can also be overcome through improved communication and understanding between managers and subordinates. Managers who make it a point to learn the strengths, weaknesses, and preferences of their subordinates can more realistically decide which tasks can be delegated to whom. They will then have greater confidence in their delegation. Subordinates who are encouraged by their managers to use their abilities and who feel that their managers will "back them up" will in turn become more eager to accept responsibility.[16]

Aside from these general guidelines, there are several specific techniques for helping managers delegate effectively. Louis Allen has listed six useful principles of delegation:[17]

1 *Establish goals.* Subordinates should be told the purpose and importance of the tasks being delegated to them. They should also be told what constitutes effective performance of these tasks so that they will be able to tell how well they are doing.

2 *Define responsibility and authority.* Subordinates should be clearly informed about what they will be held accountable for and what part of the organization's resources will be placed at their disposal.

3 *Motivate subordinates.* The challenge of extra responsibility alone will not always encourage subordinates to accept and perform delegated tasks. Managers can motivate subordinates by remaining sensitive to their needs and goals. (See Chapter 16.)

4 *Require completed work.* The manager's job is to provide guidance, help, and information to subordinates. The subordinates must do the actual delegated work.

5 *Provide training.* Managers need to teach subordinates how to improve their job performance. In addition, managers and subordinates need to work together at bettering their communication skills so that they can help the delegation process run more smoothly.

6 *Establish adequate controls.* Managers should not be spending all their time checking on how well subordinates are doing. A reliable control system (such as weekly reports) should keep time spent in supervising to a minimum.

DECENTRALIZATION

The delegation of authority by individual managers is closely related to an organization's decentralization of authority. Delegation is the process of assigning authority from one level of management down to the next. The concepts of centralization and decentralization refer to the extent to which authority has been retained at the top of the organization (centralization) or has been passed down to the lower levels (decentralization). The greater the amount of delegation of authority throughout the organization, the more decentralized the organization is. For example, to the extent that lower-level managers can expend significant sums for equipment and salary increases without first checking with higher-level managers, the organization is more decentralized.

Considerable confusion often arises between the terms *decentralization* and *divisionalization.* Part of the confusion is due to our tendency to refer to divisionalized firms as decentralized and to functionally structured firms as

---

[16] See Fisch, "Toward Effective Delegation," p. 67, and William Newman, "Overcoming Obstacles to Effective Delegation," *Management Review,* Vol. 45, No. 1 (January 1956), pp. 36–41.

[17] Louis A. Allen, *Management and Organization* (New York: McGraw-Hill, 1958).

centralized. After all, the most obvious example of an increase in decentralization is an organization that moves from a centralized functional structure to a decentralized divisional structure. Furthermore, many of the advantages of divisionalization, as discussed in Chapter 9, also apply to decentralization. The two, however, are not the same and should not be regarded as such. Any divisionalized organization may be relatively centralized or decentralized in its operations.

The advantages of decentralization are similar to the advantages of delegation that were described earlier: unburdening of top managers; improved decision making because decisions are made closer to the scene of action; better training, morale, and initiative at lower levels; and more flexibility and faster decision making in rapidly changing environments. These advantages are so compelling it is tempting to think of decentralization as "good" and centralization as "bad." This temptation is particularly strong for Americans, who, as we described earlier, have a historical distrust of centralized power.

However, total decentralization, with no coordination and leadership from the top, would clearly be undesirable. Without some central authority and power, the various parts of an organization would disintegrate into isolated subunits. The very purpose of organization — efficient integration of various subunits for the good of the whole — would be defeated without some centralized control. For this reason, the question for managers is not *if* an organization should be decentralized but *to what extent* it should be decentralized.

As we shall see, the appropriate amount of decentralization for an organization will vary with time and circumstances. It will also vary for the different subunits of the organization. For example, production and sales departments have gained a high degree of decentralization in many companies, while financial departments have tended to remain comparatively centralized.

| Factors Influencing Decentralization | Decentralization has value only to the degree in which it assists an organization to achieve its objectives efficiently. In determining the amount of decentralization appropriate for an organization, the following factors are usually considered:[18] |

1. Influences from the business environment outside the organization, such as market characteristics, competitive pressures, and availability of materials.
2. Size and growth rate of the organization.
3. Characteristics of the organization, such as costliness of given decisions, top management preferences, history of the organization, and abilities of lower-level managers.

We will be discussing these factors in greater detail below. However, we should note that the first two factors play a large role in determining the logical degree of decentralization — that is, they suggest what top managers *should*

[18] See Ernest Dale, *Organization* (New York: American Management Associations, 1967).

do. The last factor suggests what top managers are *likely* to do. For example, a supermarket chain would logically be better off if each store manager had the freedom to adapt purchasing and pricing policies to local conditions. However, an autocratic top management might be unwilling to delegate this authority. It will either have to change its attitude or accept the fact that the organization will suffer losses in some areas at the hands of competitors.

Strategy and the Organization's Environment. The strategy of an organization will influence the types of markets, technological environment, and competition with which the organization must contend. (We discussed this subject in greater detail in Chapter 9.) These factors will, in turn, influence the degree of decentralization that the firm finds appropriate. Alfred Chandler found, for example, that firms which develop new products through a process of product diversification supported by research (such as Westinghouse and General Electric) chose the decentralized form of organization. Other companies, operating in industries in which markets are less uncertain, production processes less dynamic technologically, and competitive relationships more stable, tend to remain or become more centralized. United States Steel, for example, became more, rather than less, centralized in the first half of this century.[19]

Size and Rate of Growth. It is virtually impossible to run an organization efficiently while retaining all authority to make decisions in one or a few top managers. This factor is almost certainly the strongest single force for delegation and, hence, for decentralization.

As organizations continue to grow in size and complexity, there is a tendency for the process of decentralization to continue. The faster the rate of growth, the more likely that upper management will be forced to accelerate the delegation of authority to the lower levels as they begin to sink beneath the weight of their ever-increasing work loads. When the growth rate slows, however, upper management may attempt to regain the decision-making authority under the guise of "tightening things up" and protecting profits.

Characteristics of the Organization. The extent to which decision-making authority is centralized is also likely to be influenced by the internal characteristics of the company. These might include:

1 *The cost and risk associated with the decision.* Managers may be wary of delegating authority for decisions that could exert a heavy impact on the performance of their own organizational units or of the organization as a whole. This caution is not only out of consideration for the company's welfare but their own as well, since the responsibility for the results remains with the delegator.

2 *Top management's preference for degree of involvement in detail and their confidence in subordinate managers.* Some managers pride themselves in their detailed

[19] Alfred D. Chandler, Jr., *Strategy and Structure: Chapters in the History of the American Industrial Enterprise* (Cambridge, Mass.: MIT Press, 1962).

knowledge of everything that happens within their area of responsibility. (This is known as "the good manager runs a tight ship" approach.) Others take equal pride in confidently delegating everything possible to their subordinates in order "not to get bogged down in petty details" and save their own expertise for the unit's major objectives.

3   *The history of the organization.* Some organizations have a history of tight control and power concentrated at the top. Others have just the opposite. The traditions of the organization can influence not only the choice of managers but also their style once in office. A firm that evolved gradually from a one-person operation may have built up a very centralized structure. In contrast, a firm that has developed through a number of acquisitions probably will have learned to live with the greater independence of the acquired companies.

4   *The abilities of lower-level managers.* This dimension is, in part, circular. If authority is not delegated because of lack of faith in the talent below, the talent will not have as much opportunity to develop. In addition, the lack of internal training will make it more difficult to find and hold talented or ambitious people. This, in turn, will make it more difficult to decentralize.

Trends in Decentralization

Ernest Dale, in his review of trends in the late 1960s, suggested that, following the movement toward divisionalization and decentralization in the 1950s, a movement toward *recentralization* had developed. He noted, however, that recentralization often meant little more than a curtailment of the power of division heads. In addition, he found many examples of companies moving in the opposite direction, toward decentralization.[20]

One reason given for recentralization in the 1960s and 1970s is the pressure of the economy. In times of recession or economic difficulty, company managers are likely to place staff under close scrutiny to avoid costly duplication of functions. Recentralization as a result of recession is often taken as a temporary measure to help ride through an industry slump. It must be viewed, therefore, as a cyclical phenomenon rather than a trend.

Changes in attitude and education in our time may also be exerting an influence on the degree of decentralization. In this country — and, for that matter, in most others — we are seeing higher educational levels among organizational members; an increasing desire for freedom, autonomy, and participation at work; and a growing reluctance to bow to established authority. As a result of these trends, it is reasonable to anticipate pressures on top management from below for more decision-making power at the lower levels. These pressures, in turn, may lead to increased decentralization.

Summary

Power, influence, and authority are necessary elements of organizational life, with formal authority being particularly important. From a classical viewpoint, formal authority is seen as a legitimate managerial right that subordinates are obligated to recognize. From an "acceptance" viewpoint, formal authority is legitimatized by subordinates.

There are five bases of power: reward, coercive, legitimate, referent, and expert.

[20] Dale, *Organization,* pp. 119–122.

Each is a potential source of power for the manager. In exercising their power, managers may use a dominance-submission approach toward subordinates, or they may use a more positive approach based on concern for group goals.

Line positions have been defined as those directly responsible for achieving the organization's goals. *Staff positions,* such as personal staff and specialized staff, provide advice and service to the line. One type of personal staff—line assistants—may sometimes have formal authority over line members. Staff members may also have *functional authority* over line members.

Effective delegation helps an organization use its resources efficiently—it frees managers for important tasks, improves decision making, and encourages initiative. Classical guidelines for effective delegation include the need to give subordinates authority and responsibility and the need to follow the scalar principle and the principle of unity of command. However, these guidelines will not apply to all situations.

Barriers to effective delegation usually involve the reluctance of managers to delegate or the reluctance of subordinates to accept delegation. To overcome these barriers, managers can clearly specify subordinates' responsibilities, motivate and train subordinates, and set up a system of controls.

Delegation is closely related to decentralization in that the greater the amount of delegation, the more decentralized the organization. The appropriate amount of decentralization for a particular organization will depend on environmental forces outside it, its size and growth, and its internal characteristics.

Review Questions

1. What are the two major views on the basis of formal authority in organizations? How do you think each view would affect a manager's attitude and behavior toward subordinates?
2. What is the "zone of indifference"?
3. What are the five bases of power as described by French and Raven? Give one example of the exercise of each type of power by a manager.
4. What are the "two faces" of power? Do you feel the power tactics described by Martin and Sims are cynical or realistic? Why?
5. What are the three bases of informal power in organizations? Do you think lower-level organization members frequently exercise their informal power? Why?
6. What is the difference between line and staff positions? Is the difference always clear in organizations?
7. What are the three types of personal staff assistants? What is the specialized staff? What does the phrase "functional staff authority" mean?
8. What types of staff might have formal authority over line? How might staff develop informal authority?
9. What are the advantages of delegation?
10. What are the classical guidelines to effective delegation? What are the limitations of these guidelines?
11. What are the barriers to effective delegation, and how can they be overcome? Do you anticipate that it will be difficult for you to delegate authority?
12. How are decentralization and delegation related?
13. What factors will influence the extent to which an organization is decentralized? Which of these factors is likely to be most influential?
14. Do you believe there will be a trend toward centralization or decentralization over the next several years? Why?

CASE STUDY: ORGANIZATIONAL REALITIES

Organizing is supposed to be easy. Traditional theory prescribes that an organization be built around the work to be done. For maximum efficiency, work should be divided into simple, logical, routine tasks. These business tasks can be grouped by similar kinds of work characteristics and arranged within an organization under a particularly suited executive. "So," asks Fay Nicely, president of Aerospace Products, Inc., "why are we having so many problems with our executives?"

Fay met with several of her trusted corporate officers in the executive dining room to discuss what was happening to corporate leadership at Aerospace Products, Inc. Fay went on to explain that she was really becoming concerned with the situation. There have been outright conflicts between the vice president of marketing and the controller over merger and acquisition operations. There have been many instances of duplication of work, with corporate officers trying to outmaneuver each other.

"Communications are atrocious," said Fay. "Why, I didn't even get a copy of the export finance report until my secretary made a personal effort to find one for me. My basis for evaluation and appraisal of corporate executive performance is fast becoming obsolete. Everyone has been working up their own job descriptions, and they all include overlapping of responsibilities. Changes and decisions are being made on the basis of expediency and are perpetuating too many mistakes. We must take a good look at these organizational realities and correct the situation immediately."

Jim Robison, vice president of manufacturing, pointed out to Fay that Aerospace Products is not really following the "principles of good organization." "For instance,"

EXHIBIT 1
Aerospace Products, Inc., Corporate Organization Chart

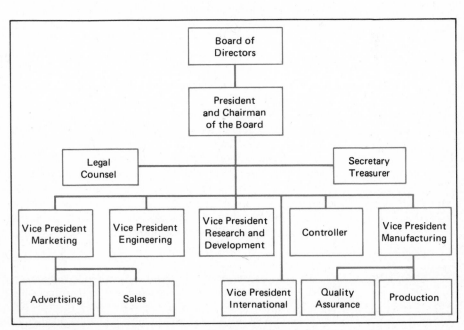

Case reprinted with permission from *Contemporary Management Incidents* by Bernard A. Deitzer and Karl A. Shilliff (Columbus, Ohio: Grid, Inc., 1977), pp. 43–46.

EXHIBIT 2   Corporate Business Tasks

1. Import and export operations	12. Public relations
2. Legal matters	13. Environmental problems
3. Tax matters	14. Administering capital expenditures
4. Coordinating corporate budgets	15. Sales forecasts
5. Coordinating research and development	16. Marketing—pricing policies
6. Engineering design reviews	17. Mergers and acquisitions
7. Operating the research and development center	18. Directing policy and advance planning
8. Operating manufacturing facilities	19. Applying technology
9. Developing advertising and promotion programs	20. Government forms and documents
10. Coordinating safety and training	21. Financing and borrowing
11. Risk and insurance	22. Directing quality assurance operations

explained Jim, "let's review what we should be practicing as administrators. Some of the principles we should be trying are:

1   Determine the objectives, policies, programs, and plans that will best achieve the desired results for our company.

2   Determine the various business tasks to be done.

3   Divide the business tasks into a logical and understandable organizational structure.

4   Determine the suitable personnel to occupy positions within the organizational structure.

5   Define clearly in writing the responsibility and authority of each supervisor.

6   Keep the number of kinds and levels of authority at a minimum."

Jim proposed that the group study the corporate organization chart, shown in Exhibit 1 on the previous page, as well as the various corporate business tasks.

After reviewing the corporate organization chart, Jim, Fay, and the others agreed that the number and kinds of formal corporate authority were logical and not much different from other corporations of like size. The group then listed the various corporate business tasks that went on within Aerospace Products, Inc.

Jim continued, "Exhibit 2 is a typical list of corporate business activities. How did we ever decide who should handle mergers or acquisitions?" Fay answered, "I guess it just occurred over time that the vice president of marketing should have the responsibility." "But," Jim queried, "where is it written down? How would the controller know it?"

"Aha!" Fay exclaimed. "It looks like I'm part of the problem. There isn't anything in writing. Tasks were assigned superficially as they became problems. This has all been rather informal."

Case Questions
1. What are the problems that Fay faces in light of sound organizational principles?
2. Draw a chart showing which executive should be responsible for which tasks. Use the following coding system: A—directly responsible; B—must be included in meetings and final decisions; C—should receive reports and information; and D—may be included—general consulting.

Chapter 12

Groups and Committees

Upon completing this chapter you should be able to:

1. Describe the characteristics of formal and informal groups.

2. State why groups are an important part of organizational life.

3. Explain how group leaders, group norms, and group cohesiveness develop.

4. Identify the factors that can affect group performance.

5. Identify the assets and liabilities of group problem solving, and describe how group performance can be improved.

6. State the roles of task forces and committees in organizations.

7. Describe the advantages and disadvantages of committees and how committees can be made effective.

LOST ON THE MOON: A TEST

Your spaceship has just crash-landed on the moon. You were scheduled to rendezvous with a mother ship 200 miles away on the lighted surface of the moon, but the rough landing has ruined your ship and destroyed all the equipment on board, except for the fifteen items listed below.

Your crew's survival depends on reaching the mother ship, so you must choose the most critical items available for the 200-mile trip. Your task is to rank the fifteen items in terms of their importance for survival. Place number one by the most important item, number two by the second most important, and so on through number fifteen, the least important.

_____ Box of matches

_____ Food concentrate

_____ Fifty feet of nylon rope

_____ Parachute silk

_____ Solar-powered portable heating unit

_____ Two .45-caliber pistols

_____ One case of dehydrated milk

_____ Two 100-pound tanks of oxygen

_____ Stellar map (of the moon's constellation)

_____ Self-inflating life raft

_____ Magnetic compass

_____ Five gallons of water

_____ Signal flares

_____ First-aid kit containing injection needles

_____ Solar-powered FM receiver-transmitter[1]

What do you think? If you were caught in this life-and-death situation, would you have a better chance to survive if you ranked the fifteen items on your own or if you and your crew members ranked the items together? If you and your crew decided to solve this problem as a group, how could you as spaceship captain improve the quality of the solutions offered by your group?

It is likely that most of you who think about these questions will decide that you would be better off making survival decisions on your own, rather than through a group. Working through groups is often a frustrating experience, and the idea that groups actually can be managed to outperform individuals may be difficult for many people to accept. For example, this author has frequently been asked by students how they could chart a management career in which they could avoid the inefficiency and frustration they see as inherent in group work. Such an attempt to escape group work is an unpromising approach for anyone who desires a challenging and mobile managerial career. Groups are an inevitable and useful part of organizational life, and a considerable part of a manager's job will be devoted to group and committee work. As managers, our task will be to manage organizational groups in such a way as to make them more productive and satisfying to their members.[2]

In this chapter we will describe the various types of groups that exist in organizations. We will also describe how group problem solving can be managed and improved. Before we begin our discussion, you might want to take

---

[1] Jay Hall, "Decisions, Decisions, Decisions," _Psychology Today_, November 1971, p. 54.

[2] See Dorwin Cartwright and Ronald Lippitt, "Group Dynamics and the Individual," _International Journal of Group Psychotherapy_, Vol. 7, No. 1 (January 1957), pp. 86–102.

the "Lost on the Moon" test in the following manner: First, get four to seven fellow students to work with you. Each of you should rank the fifteen items on your own, without looking at each other's answers. When you have completed your individual rankings, you and your fellow students should discuss the problem together — sharing your individual solutions — until you reach a consensus. Finally, check both your individual and group answers against the rankings given by NASA experts, which appear in the source article for the test or in your teacher's Instructor's Manual. This procedure may demonstrate in a practical way the relative merits of individual versus group problem solving. It may also give you some insight into the kinds of problems in human relationships that managers of groups can face.

TYPES OF GROUPS

A *group* may be defined as two or more people who interact with and influence each other.[3] There are three types of groups that commonly exist in organizations:

1 *Command groups*, which are composed of managers and their subordinates.
2 *Committees and task forces*, which are formed to carry out specific organizational activities.
3 *Informal groups*, which emerge in the organization whether or not managers desire or encourage them.

The first two types of groups are *formal* groups. Managers determine their membership and direct them in order to achieve specific objectives.

Before we go on to a detailed discussion of these types of groups, we should note that there are other types of groups that managers need to be aware of and understand. For example, *reference groups* are those groups with whom specific individuals identify and compare themselves. A manager's reference group, for instance, might be the other managers on his or her level within the organization or even within the same industry. If the manager strongly desires promotion, his or her reference group is likely to be higher-level managers. In private life, the manager's other reference groups might include members of his or her club or community.

Such groups can affect an individual's attitude and behavior, since people tend to model themselves after the members of their reference group. (If they do not so model themselves, their reference group may punish or reject them. For example, a student who constantly wears a three-piece suit to class when everyone else is wearing jeans may find it difficult to make new friends.) Reference groups therefore can be an important influence in organizational

[3] See Marvin E. Shaw, *Group Dynamics* (New York: McGraw-Hill, 1976).

life, since the members may adopt the performance standards and expectations of their reference group.[4]

Formal Groups

Formal groups exist to carry out tasks that will help the organization achieve its goals.[5] (Informal groups, as we shall see, may sometimes have objectives that run counter to organizational goals.)

The most prevalent type of formal group in organizations is the command group, which includes a manager and his or her subordinates. The formal structure of organizations is built upon a series of overlapping command groups. Managers belong to command groups composed of themselves and their subordinates, and they simultaneously belong to command groups composed of their fellow managers and their mutual higher-level manager. In Rensis Likert's terminology, managers are the "linking pin" between the various formal work groups in their organizations.[6] (See Figure 12-1.)

Permanent formal groups in organizations include command groups and permanent committees. (A planning committee is a common example of a permanent formal group.) Temporary formal groups include committees or task forces that are created to deal with a particular problem and that are disbanded once the problem is solved. We will be discussing committees and task forces later in this chapter.

Informal Groups

Informal groups emerge whenever people come together and interact regularly. Such groups develop within the formal organizational structure. (See Figure 12-2 on page 294.) Members of informal groups tend to subordinate some of their individual needs to the needs of the group as a whole. In return, the group supports and protects them. Informal groups may further the interests of the organization — company bowling clubs, for example, strengthen their members' ties to the organization. They may also oppose organizational objectives, such as high productivity standards, when these are considered harmful to the group. (See Chapter 9 and our discussion of the Hawthorne studies in Chapter 2.)

Functions of Informal Groups. Informal groups serve four major functions:[7]

1. *They perpetuate the social and cultural values the group members hold in common.* Members of the same informal group are already likely to share certain norms and values. In the day-to-day interactions of group members, these norms and values are further reinforced.

---

[4] See Dorwin Cartwright and Alvin Zander, eds., *Group Dynamics: Research and Theory,* 3rd ed. (New York: Harper & Row, 1968), and Harold H. Kelley, "Two Functions of Reference Groups," in Guv E. Swanson, Theodore Newcomb, and Eugene J. Hartley, eds., *Readings in Social Psychology,* rev. ed. (New York: Holt, 1952), pp. 410–414.

[5] See Edgar H. Schein, *Organizational Psychology,* 2nd ed. (Englewood Cliffs, N.J.: Prentice-Hall, 1970), pp. 80–85.

[6] Rensis Likert, *New Patterns of Management* (New York: McGraw-Hill, 1961).

[7] Keith Davis, *Human Relations at Work,* 2nd ed. (New York: McGraw-Hill, 1962), pp. 235–257.

FIGURE 12-1
The Linking Pin

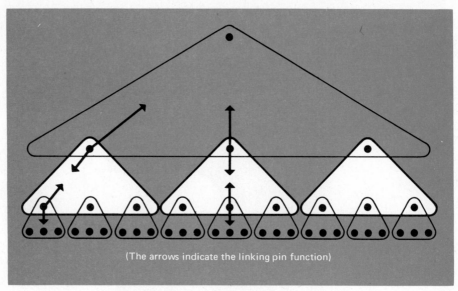

(The arrows indicate the linking pin function)

Source: Rensis Likert, *New Patterns of Management* (New York: McGraw-Hill, 1961), p. 113. Copyright © 1961 by McGraw-Hill Inc. Used with permission of McGraw-Hill Book Co.

2. *They provide status and social satisfactions that group members might not otherwise enjoy.* In a large corporation, many individual employees may feel they are just anonymous workers to their employers. To the fellow members of their groups, the same employees are welcome friends who share their jokes and gripes, eat with them, and possibly play tennis or cards with them after work.

3. *They help their members communicate.* To stay informed about matters that may affect their livelihood, informal group members develop their own channels of communication alongside the formal channels established by management. In fact, managers often turn to the informal system to convey information "unofficially" — for example, to squelch rumors about a possible takeover by another company.

4. *They affect the work environment.* By persuasion or threats, informal group members make fellow workers conform to group norms of behavior and work standards. This function may work to the detriment of the organization — overly enthusiastic employees, for example, may be quickly "set straight" by their fellow employees. But this function can also benefit the organization — lazy or careless employees may likewise be told to "shape up" by their fellow workers.

Disadvantages of Informal Groups. Informal groups can also present managers with a number of problems:

1. *Resistance to change.* Perpetuating values preserves the integrity of the group and adds stability to the work situation. But when carried too far, it

FIGURE 12-2
Informal Groups
within the
Organization

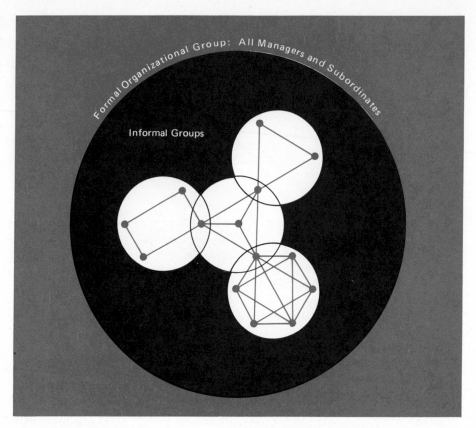

can become an immovable barrier to change. For example, minority employees who have just been hired by the organization may have a difficult time being accepted by existing informal groups. (We will discuss overcoming resistance to change in Chapter 15.)

2. *Conflict*. Providing social satisfaction may enhance the work environment, but it may also conflict with management's needs. For example, many people believe that a coffee break increases productivity. But if the informal group stretches it out for an extra 15 or 20 minutes every morning, the members' gain in social satisfaction may lead to the employer's loss in production.

3. *Rumor*. Every organization must come to grips with the grapevine—the informal group's communication system that dispenses truth and rumor with equal dispatch. When employees are not well informed on matters that directly affect them, they may tend to spread false rumors that undermine the morale of the organization.

4. *Conformity*. Informal groups usually act as reference groups. Thus, they encourage conformity among their members. Individuals may be reluctant to act differently, creatively, or aggressively, because they do not wish to lose

the approval of their group. As a result, the organization suffers, because its members show less initiative and creativity in their work.

CHARACTERISTICS OF GROUPS IN ORGANIZATIONS

The tasks of managers in dealing with groups are (1) to determine when and how groups can be utilized most effectively to achieve organizational goals, (2) to manage groups so that they perform at a high level, and (3) to overcome the disadvantages associated with groups. In order to accomplish these tasks, managers must be aware of and deal with a number of characteristics that are common to groups. We will describe these characteristics in this section.

Informal
Leadership

Task

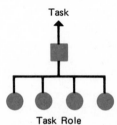

Task Role

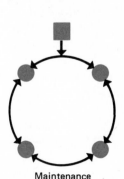

Maintenance
Role

The formal leader of a group is, of course, appointed or elected to head the group. Leaders of informal groups, on the other hand, tend to emerge gradually as group members interact. Usually, the man or woman who speaks up more than the others, who offers more suggestions than anyone else, or who gives direction to the group's activities becomes the informal leader. Even in formal groups, such self-confident, assertive individuals often develop into rivals of the formally chosen leaders, thereby weakening the leader's hold on the group membership.[8]

Both formal and informal leaders play two basic roles: a task role and a group building and maintenance role. In the *task role,* the leader directs the group toward completion of the activities it is seeking to accomplish. As sales managers, for example, our task role would include hiring and firing personnel, assigning territories, and supervising the training of new sales force members. In the *group building and maintenance role,* the leader is concerned with fulfilling the social needs of the group by encouraging feelings of group solidarity. For example, if as sales managers we settle some nonwork-related dispute between salespeople, we are acting in a maintenance role. Proper exercise of this role enables the leader to keep members attached to the group over extended periods of time.

Ideally, the group leader plays both roles successfully, enabling the group to perform with a high degree of effectiveness. In practice, however, a single leader will often be unable to assume both roles; in such cases, a second person closes the gap by taking over the neglected function (usually the maintenance role).[9] We will be discussing these roles further in Chapter 17, "Leadership."

[8] Bertram H. Raven and Jeffrey Z. Rubin, *Social Psychology: People in Groups* (New York: Wiley, 1976).

[9] See Walter H. Crockett, "Emergent Leadership in Small, Decision-Making Groups," *Journal of Abnormal and Social Psychology,* Vol. 51, No. 3 (November 1955), pp. 378–383; Kenneth D. Benne and Paul Sheats, "Functional Roles of Group Members," *Journal of Social Issues,* Vol. 4, No. 2 (Spring 1948), pp. 42–49; and Edgar F. Borgatta, Robert F. Bales, and Arthur S. Couch, "Some Findings Relevant to the 'Great Man' Theory of Leadership," *American Sociological Review,* Vol. 19, No. 6 (December 1954), pp. 755–759.

Group Norms
and Conformity

Over time, group members establish expectations about how they and the other members of the group will behave. They will exert pressure on each other to ensure that these expectations will be met. For example, an executive who comes to work in sneakers when all the other executives are wearing black shoes will at the very least be subjected to questions about the unusual attire and perhaps even ridicule from peers for this violation of group norms. The possibility of rejection by the group is usually enough to ensure that members will conform to their group's expectations—which is why the executive is unlikely to come to work in anything but black shoes.

When an individual does not conform to group norms, the other members of the group will initially try to persuade the deviant to conform. Frequently, the members will try to reason with the deviant or make pointed jokes at his or her expense. If this approach fails, the members are likely to escalate their pressure. If the norm being violated is seen as an important one, they will use criticism, sarcasm, ridicule, and finally ostracism—total rejection of the individual through the "silent treatment." Where the deviant behavior touches on a truly sensitive area for the group—as with the rate-buster who exceeds the group's output norms—the deviant may be physically assaulted.

Such enforced conformity has its negative side, because it may stifle initiative and innovation and reduce productivity. Yet conformity also has its positive side: it maintains predictable patterns of work, nurtures teamwork, and defends group and individual interests. For managers, the problem has never been how to prevent group pressures—which are inevitable—but how to channel them into constructive activities. Here, as in so many other areas of employer-employee relationships, one answer has been to encourage employee participation in decisions that affect their interests. In this way, the group members are less likely to define themselves as being antagonistic to management.

Group
Cohesiveness

Group *cohesiveness,* or solidarity, is an important indicator of how much influence the group as a whole has over individual members. The more cohesive the group—that is, the more positive individuals feel about their membership in the group—the greater the potential influence of the group. Individual group members are not likely to violate the norms of a group to which they are strongly attached.

Group cohesiveness tends to develop in a circular fashion: individuals will join groups whose members they admire or identify with. Once they become members of a group, individuals will tend to feel an even closer sense of identification with other group members. Thus, highly cohesive groups often have less tension and hostility than noncohesive groups. For this reason, they are potentially more productive than noncohesive groups.[10]

[10] See Kenneth N. Wexley and Gary A. Yukl, *Organizational Behavior and Personnel Psychology* (Homewood, Ill.: Irwin, 1977), and P. C. Andre de la Porte, "Group Norms: Key to Building a Winning Team," *Personnel,* Vol. 51, No. 5 (September-October 1974), pp. 60–67.

GROUP PERFORMANCE

Two major aspects of group performance that are frequently important to managers are: (1) the relationship between group cohesiveness and performance, and (2) the differences between group and individual problem solving and decision making.

The first aspect is especially important for managers when they are dealing with informal groups. As we have mentioned, group norms may encourage either high or low productivity by group members. In highly cohesive groups, such norms are likely to be especially influential. Thus, managers' success or failure in meeting their organizational objectives may depend on how well they manage the cohesive groups with which they must deal.

The second aspect—differences in effectiveness between groups and individuals—is especially important for managers who work with task groups and committees. These groups are formed to solve problems and make decisions. Managers who know when to use groups for specific tasks and who can lead these groups effectively will be able to generate better decisions and problem solutions.

Group Cohesiveness and Group Performance

Many studies have been made of informal work groups whose members' individual output can be accurately measured (such as bricklayers, assembly-line workers, and typists). These studies have found that highly cohesive groups tend to have more *uniform* output among their individual members than members of less cohesive groups. That is, in cohesive groups, person-by-person productivity will stay within a narrow range—for example, from eight to ten typed pages per hour. Groups with low cohesion will have a much wider range of output among their members, reflecting the groups' weaker social control.

A corollary of this finding is that if their norms favor high output, then cohesive groups will be uniformly high producers. On the other hand, if their norms favor low output, cohesive groups will be low producers. For noncohesive groups, where the pressure to conform is neither so strong nor so influential, the relationship between norms and output is usually a good deal more ambiguous.[11]

For managers, the importance of these findings lies in the fact that cohesive groups commonly set their own production standards. Where the group is antagonistic to management, it will restrict output to a level well below management standards. In factories, this sort of restriction often occurs in a work group that has been assigned to a job for which piece rates have been established. Members of such groups often believe that if management standards are reached or surpassed, a higher standard or lower piece rate will be forthcoming. They will therefore restrict their output. The group members may also

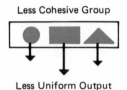

Cohesive Group

Uniform Output

Less Cohesive Group

Less Uniform Output

[11] See Wexley and Yukl, *Organizational Behavior,* pp. 126–127, and Raven and Rubin, *Social Psychology,* pp. 366–367, for a discussion of this topic and numerous supporting studies.

feel that if their actual output stays below the set level, management may offer a more favorable piece rate as an inducement to increase productivity.[12]

These facts lead to two obvious conclusions: (1) Managers must seek to minimize employee-management antagonism, perhaps by involving employees more in the decision-making process. Hopefully, informal group members will come to see themselves as part of the larger organization. (2) Once this is accomplished, managers must try to strengthen group cohesiveness. In this way, the social satisfaction of group members will be increased, and group performance will become more uniform and predictable.

One way of increasing group solidarity is to give the group members more say in selecting those they will work with. A study of Chicago-area construction workers found that once they were given a voice in co-worker selection, turnover dropped significantly, indicating greater job satisfaction. In this new cooperative atmosphere, the strengthened group cohesion led to higher output, with the construction firm recording a 5 percent savings in total production costs.[13]

Individual versus Group Problem Solving

Many studies have shown that group solutions to problems tend to be somewhat better than the average solutions of individuals. (The *best* individual solutions, however, are often superior to group solutions.) For example, the "Lost on the Moon" test with which we began this chapter has been given to individuals and to groups; the groups' solutions tend to be closer to those of the NASA experts than the individual solutions are. Part of the improved performance by groups results from the fact that in a group the chances of catching errors are sharply increased, since there are more people reacting to proposed solutions. Moreover, group members bring new information to the problem and also generate additional alternative solutions.

Despite the tendency for groups to perform well in problem-solving activities, managers will often have to make decisions on their own. Group decisions often take longer—meetings and discussions are time-consuming—and are usually more expensive because of the greater number of person-hours involved. Effective managers take the cost of making decisions into account in selecting a decision-making approach. Thus, they will often opt for an acceptable one-person decision quickly rather than seek a somewhat better group decision later. This is especially true for simple problems and even for technical ones where the manager has an adequate amount of information.[14]

For more difficult problems, such as new product development, group decision making may be necessary. Such problems can be solved only if a great deal of information is applied to them; and large amounts of information can be efficiently gathered and evaluated only by a group. In addition, as we dis-

[12] Lester Coch and John R. P. French, Jr., "Overcoming Resistance to Change," *Human Relations,* Vol. 1, No. 4 (1948), pp. 512–532.

[13] Raymond H. Van Zelst, "Sociometrically Selected Work Teams Increase Production," *Personnel Psychology,* Vol. 5, No. 3 (Autumn 1952), pp. 175–185.

[14] See Edward H. Bowman, "Management Decision-Making: Some Research," *Industrial Management Review,* Vol. 3, No. 1 (Fall 1961), pp. 56–63.

cussed in Chapter 7, there are problems whose solutions must be accepted by subordinates in order for the solutions to be effective. For example, a manager who tries to set up a work schedule without consulting subordinates is likely to encounter resistance to the schedule. Such problems require that managers and subordinates participate in seeking solutions as a group. In the following section, we will focus on how to make the group problem-solving and decision-making process work more effectively.

IMPROVING GROUP PROBLEM SOLVING

To improve group problem solving, we must first understand the strengths and weaknesses of groups. Every group brings to the problem-solving task some assets, some liabilities, and some factors that can be either positive or negative, depending on the skills of the group members and the discussion leader.[15]

Group Assets

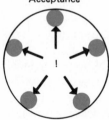

More Problem
Approaches

Greater Solution
Acceptance

Group problem solving has four major advantages:

1. *Greater knowledge and information.* Regardless of how much knowledge any one individual brings to the task, the total information possessed by all the members is bound to be greater. Thus, a design engineer might best be able to develop the blueprint for a new machine, but an assembly-line worker would have a better idea of how his or her fellow workers might react to it.

2. *More approaches to a problem.* There is no way of knowing beforehand which approach to a complex problem will best achieve the desired result. The more approaches being tried, the better the chance of finding the best solution. Obviously, five or ten people in a group will usually generate many more approaches than will any one person.

3. *Increased acceptance of solutions.* As we saw in Chapter 7, a decision will not be effective unless those who must implement it accept the decision and make it work. And many studies have shown that when people participate in solving a problem, they see the solution as "their own" and acquire a psychological stake in its success.

4. *Better comprehension of the decision.* When a manager makes a decision individually, he or she must relay it to those who have to carry it out. Failure of decisions to be implemented effectively has often been traced to garbled communications. But when those who must execute the decision have participated in making it, the chance of communication failure is reduced.

Group Liabilities

There are three major disadvantages to group problem solving:

1. *Premature decisions.* Most problem-solving groups come up with a number of suggested solutions, each of which gains some support and suffers some criticism. Frequently, the first solution to win appreciable support is

[15] Our discussion is based on Norman R. F. Maier, "Assets and Liabilities in Group Problem Solving," *Psychological Review,* Vol. 74, No. 4 (July 1967), pp. 239–249.

adopted — even though winning support may often have more to do with skillful presentation than with objective quality. Better solutions introduced *after* consensus has been tentatively reached are rarely given full consideration.

2. *Individual domination.* The group leader, whether informal or formal, frequently dominates the discussion and influences its outcome even if his or her problem-solving ability is poor. Such domination can put a damper on the work of the group's best problem solvers, thus stymieing the contributions they might otherwise make.

3. *Conflicting alternative solutions.* When the group tackles the problem initially, everyone agrees on the one major goal: finding the best possible solution. But as alternative solutions are proposed, the members begin to take sides. And as each side vies for support, winning the battle will often begin to take on greater importance than finding the best solution.

Factors That
Can Be Assets
or Liabilities

The five factors we will discuss here can prove to be assets or liabilities, depending on how the group leader handles the situation.

1. *Disagreement.* The clash of ideas that develops in a group can foster creativity and innovation, or it can breed resentment and hurt feelings. Skillful group leaders use disagreements to generate creative solutions ("I think both ideas are good; can we come up with a solution that incorporates both?"). When disagreements threaten to become harmful, skillful leaders put a stop to them.

2. *Conflicting interests.* Group members often disagree on solutions, because they approach the problem from different perspectives and with different goals in mind. For example, a group may consider the problem of how to reverse a poor profit situation for a particular product line. The sales manager, diagnosing the situation as a failure to break into specific markets, suggests more aggressive sales and promotion tactics. For the controller, on the other hand, the matter is one of costs getting out of hand; perhaps commissions should be cut. The group leader must organize the discussion in such a way that group members agree on the essence of the problem and the desired goals before solutions are proposed.

3. *Taking risks.* It is popular to assume that groups tend to be more "conservative" and cautious than individuals. There is considerable evidence, however, that in some situations groups make riskier decisions than individuals might make.[16] As management writers put it, in those situations group solutions tend to represent "risky shifts" from solutions that might be offered by individual group members. For example, in dealing with a hypothetical case in which an individual must decide whether to stay in a secure job or leave for one that

---

[16] Dorwin Cartwright, "Risk Taking by Individuals and Groups: An Assessment of Research Employing Choice Dilemmas," *Journal of Personality and Social Psychology,* Vol. 20, No. 3 (1971), pp. 361–378, and Dorwin Cartwright, "Determinants of Scientific Progress: The Case of Research on the Risky Shift," *American Psychologist,* Vol. 28, No. 3 (March 1973), pp. 222–231.

is less secure but that offers a higher salary, groups have been more likely than individuals to recommend the riskier option.[17]

4. *Time requirements.* As we mentioned earlier, group decisions take longer and are more expensive than individual decisions. But group decisions are also likely to be more effective than individual decisions. Thus, time can be an asset for group decision making because it permits full discussion of alternatives, and it can be a liability because it results in increased costs. The skillful group leader will minimize the costs and maximize the effectiveness of groups by preventing discussions from wandering into irrelevant issues and continuing once the major tasks have been accomplished.

5. *Changing minds.* Rarely, if ever, do all group members start with the same possible solution to a problem. To reach an agreement, some group members usually change the position they started with. This can be an asset or a liability, depending on whose mind is changed. If those with the most creative ideas are induced to change, the group winds up with a mediocre decision. If those with the least constructive views change their minds, the final decision is improved. The leader who has remained objective about the problem can influence the final decision when it is appropriate to do so by tactfully indicating his or her support for what appears to be the better solution.

Effective Group Leadership: One Perspective

Norman Maier has indicated how he believes leaders should behave in order to get the best performance from their groups.[18] His conclusions are based on his extensive research over a number of years into group problem solving.

Maier distinguishes between "problem-solving activity" and "persuasion." *Problem-solving activity* represents group interaction at its best: each member serves as a sounding board for the ideas of others. All group members participate in proposing and evaluating suggestions. The entire group gains from the open exchange of opinions. *Persuasion* follows a different pattern: each group member has a fixed point of view that he or she tries to "sell" to the others while closing his or her ears and mind to opposing views. Competition replaces cooperation; domination by a few articulate or aggressive individuals replaces participation by all.

From this perspective, a leader has one major task: to manage the discussion process so that the group engages in true problem solving. Maier feels

---

[17] See James A. F. Stoner, "A Comparison of Individual and Group Decisions Involving Risk" (Master's thesis, Massachusetts Institute of Technology, School of Industrial Management, 1961). There have been hundreds of studies published since the first "risky shifts" were demonstrated by Stoner in 1961. In spite of these extensive research efforts, the types of situations in which the phenomenon occurs and the cause and nature of the phenomenon are still unclear and remain a source of lively debate and continuing research. See also James A. F. Stoner, "Risky and Cautious Shifts in Group Decisions: The Influence of Widely Held Values," *Journal of Experimental Psychology,* Vol. 4, No. 4 (October 1968), pp. 442–459, and Russell D. Clark, "Group-Induced Shift toward Risk: A Critical Appraisal," *Psychological Bulletin,* Vol. 76 (1971), pp. 251–270.

[18] Maier, "Assets and Liabilities in Group Problem Solving," pp. 244–247.

TABLE 12-1
Effective and
Ineffective Group
Behaviors

Effective: Problem-Solving Activity	Ineffective: Persuasion
Trying out ideas on each other	Selling preformed opinions
Listening to understand	Listening to refute—or not listening at all
Willing to change one's position	Defending one's position to the end
All group members generally participating in discussion	A few group members dominating the discussion
Finding stimulation in disagreement	Reacting unfavorably to disagreement
Group members interacting and reaching consensus	Using one-to-one interaction for individual conversion

that leaders should focus entirely on this task and virtually give up the attempt to make substantive contributions themselves. True leaders, according to Maier, must forgo the temptation to sell their own solutions during the group working sessions—relying instead on the resources of the entire group (including their own nondominating suggestions). In this way initiative is encouraged, and group members will begin to regard themselves as members of the same team. (See Table 12–1.)

This author has seen and participated in groups led by managers who perform the leadership role as described by Maier. Those groups usually did outstanding work, and most of their members were highly satisfied to be in them. However, two things stand in the way of the universal application of Maier's ideas: managers do not easily accept the self-restraint such a role demands, and they do not always command the high level of interpersonal skill that must go with it.

TASK FORCES AND COMMITTEES

Comments and jokes about the time-wasting proclivities of committee work have always been popular among managers, who generally pride themselves on their individualism. Opponents of task forces and committees feel they have inflicted a crushing blow when they say something like "No committee painted the Mona Lisa or sculpted the Pietà." The reality of the matter is, however, that the kind of creative work an organization requires—problem solving and decision making—is often better done by a committee than by an individual. A committee or task force is usually the best means for pooling the expertise of different members of the organization and for channeling their efforts toward effective problem solving. And because of their collective information and authority, committees and task forces are frequently more likely than individuals to come up with workable solutions to problems.

The need for committees appears to have been widely recognized in organizations. As far back as 1960, Rollie Tillman found "that 94 percent of the firms with more than 10,000 employees reported having formal committees."[19]

[19] Rollie Tillman, Jr., "Committees on Trial," *Harvard Business Review,* May-June 1960, pp. 6–7 ff.

It is probable that the number and types of groups active in organizations have grown considerably since that time and that the average number of meetings per year has also increased. The greater complexity and rate of change in organizations today require the kind of information pooling and problem evaluation that committees and task forces can provide.

Functions of
Committees

Task forces and committees are used in organizations for a great variety of activities — such as managing the organization, handling its finances, developing its new products, or planning its advertising campaigns. (See Table 12-2.) The major functions of committees are:

1 To provide members with the opportunity to exchange views and information.
2 To make recommendations to a higher organizational level.
3 To generate ideas or problem solutions.
4 To make policy decisions for the organization.[20]

As a rule, committee membership (and the proportion of time spent working in committees) is greater for managers at the top levels rather than at the lower levels of the organization. (See Figure 12-3 on next page.) One reason for this is that only top-level managers have the authority to make policy decisions for the organization. In addition, the higher a manager's level, the larger the number of organizational subunits he or she affects. Higher-level managers, therefore, have a greater need than lower-level managers to inter-

TABLE 12-2
Survey of
Committee
Activities

Type of Committee	Percent of Total Committee Types Surveyed	Percent of Surveyed Members Serving on Each Type*	Average Number of Members	Average Number of Meetings per Year
General Management	30.3	77.4	8.6	27
Finance and Control	14.8	37.7	6.7	23
Marketing	9.3	23.9	7.4	24
Production	9.9	25.2	8.9	28
Labor and Personnel	15.4	39.4	7.1	14
Research and Development and New Products	9.8	24.9	8.2	18
Public Relations	2.2	5.5	7.4	9
Others	8.3	21.1	8.3	14

*Total adds up to more than 100 percent because many members serve on more than one committee.

Source: Rollie Tillman, Jr., "Committees on Trial," *Harvard Business Review*, May-June 1960, p. 12. Copyright © 1960 by the President and Fellows of Harvard College; all rights reserved.

[20] "Committees: Their Role in Management Today," *Management Review,* Vol. 46, No. 10 (October 1957), pp. 4–10 ff.

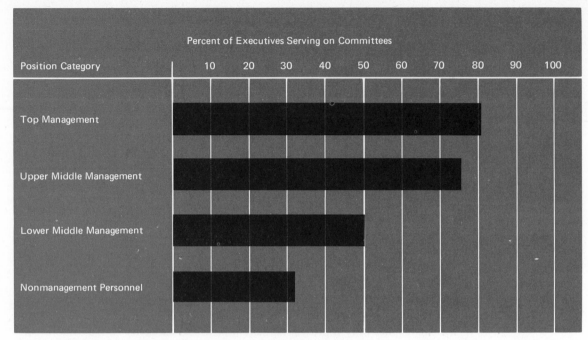

FIGURE 12-3   Survey of Executive Committee Membership

Source: Rollie Tillman, Jr., "Committees on Trial," *Harvard Business Review*, May-June 1960, p. 8.
Copyright © 1960 by the President and Fellows of Harvard College; all rights reserved.

relate their own work activities with those of other subunits. This need for close coordination between higher-level managers and their subunits is often met through committees and task forces made up of individuals from the different parts of the organization.

Types of Committees and Task Groups

There are four types of formal committees and task groups in organizations: task forces, standing committees, boards and commissions, and the plural executive. (See also our discussion of committees in Chapter 10.)

Task Forces. *Task forces*, or project teams, are formed to deal with a specific problem or task. They continue in existence only until the task is completed or the problem solved. Task forces are usually formed to deal with complex problems or tasks that involve a number of organizational subunits. For example, assume a computer firm develops a new memory device that cannot be manufactured by the firm's existing facilities. A special task force may then be organized to determine what new equipment will be needed, how it can be best obtained, and what changes it will require in the firm's work patterns. Such task groups are usually made up of representatives (or key decision makers) from the subunits involved plus whatever technical experts a problem or task requires.

Task forces may achieve their results in one of three ways:

1 By making recommendations to a senior executive to whom they are responsible.
2 By reaching decisions in a group when the senior executive is the formal leader of the group.
3 By the individual representatives of the various units committing their units to take specific actions in accord with the committee's conclusions.[21]

Standing Committees. *Standing,* or permanent, *committees* remain in existence to meet a continuing organizational need. Typical standing committees might be the finance committee or new products review committee in a company or an admissions committee in a college. Usually such committees either make formal recommendations to a higher-level manager or have the authority to make their own decisions for a limited organizational activity.

Boards and Commissions. *Boards* are made up of individuals who are appointed or elected to manage a public or private organization. School board members, for example, are elected by their community to set school policy, raise revenues, hire a principal, and perhaps even select schoolbooks. The board of directors of a corporation is selected by stockholders to oversee the management of the assets of the company, set company policies and goals, hire company officers to carry out those policies, and review the progress of the company toward those goals. *Commissions* are made up of individuals usually appointed by government officials to carry out administrative, legislative, or regulatory duties (the Federal Trade Commission and the Securities and Exchange Commission, for example).

While the other formal groups we have discussed are concerned with the internal needs of the organization, boards and commissions represent the interests of people outside the organization. School board members, for example, are responsible to the community; commission members are generally responsible to the public; board members are responsible to their stockholders and, increasingly, to the society of which they are a part. (See Chapter 3.) Thus, while boards and commissions manage the activities of others, they in turn are accountable to others for their actions.

The Plural Executive. The *plural executive,* or general management committee, is a formal committee that functions as a chief executive. That is, members of the plural executive are responsible as a group for the overall management of the organization, the way an organization president would be. The plural executive functions in a democratic fashion in the sense that its members have equal standing — no one member can formally overrule the majority decision of

---

[21] Note that in matrix organizations, which are discussed in Chapter 9, the project team may have its own budget and enjoy a great deal of autonomy in implementing solutions and decisions.

the group. Usually, the plural executive (like a chief executive) is responsible only to the board of directors.

Most authorities on management frown on the use of the plural executive. Management by committee can easily lead to power conflicts as executives compete with each other for influence and authority. It can also lead to excessive delays in reaching decisions, since committee meetings may be difficult to arrange and may take up a great deal of time once they have started. However, William Mylander reported that the plural executive arrangement at Du Pont appeared to work quite well. He attributed this to the fact that the Du Pont plural executive did not attempt day-to-day supervisory activity. Instead, it behaved more like a corporate board of directors by delegating overall supervisory responsibility to general managers.[22]

Advantages of Committees

Committees share some of the same advantages and disadvantages of all types of groups. However, because committees are so often composed of top-level managers, they also have unique strengths and weaknesses. We will discuss the assets and limitations of committees in this and the following section.[23]

The major advantages of committees are:

1. *Better quality decisions.* A committee brings together experts from a variety of fields who provide a breadth of knowledge and a range of perspectives far beyond the ability and scope of any individual decision maker. In addition, because all alternative proposals are evaluated by a number of top-level executives, hasty decisions are more likely to be avoided.

2. *Improved coordination.* In the course of committee discussion, members become increasingly aware of the extent to which the activities of their units affect the workings of the other units. From this awareness comes a new willingness to coordinate the work of all units in order to achieve the overall goals of the organization.

3. *Enhanced likelihood of acceptance.* Like other group members, the more committee members participate in the problem-solving activities of their committee, the more fully they are likely to commit themselves and their subunits to implementing committee decisions. The increased likelihood that committee decisions will be accepted means that these decisions will probably be more effective.

4. *Training managers.* All corporations are constantly on the hunt for executive talent. Committees serve as a training ground for young executives who, freed from the parochial concerns of their individual units, learn to think in terms of the wider issues that may one day confront them.

5. *Dispersion of power.* Many things can be done faster and with fewer

[22] William H. Mylander, "Management by the Executive Committee," *Harvard Business Review,* May-June 1955.
[23] Our discussion is based on Ernest Dale, *Planning and Developing the Company Structure* (New York: American Management Associations, 1952), and Ernest Dale, *Organization* (New York: American Management Associations, 1967).

complications under the direction of a single authority. However, too much authority concentrated in any one person's hands may lead to abuse of power, favoritism, and erroneous decisions. By spreading responsibility among its members, a committee reduces the chances of an unwise concentration of power in any one individual. In addition, a committee reduces the possibility that those adversely affected by committee decisions (such as a decision on salary increases) can complain of favoritism or bias.

Disadvantages of Committees

The major disadvantages of committees are:

1. *Waste of time and money.* Since one main purpose of committees is to permit members to exchange views and information, committee meetings cost the organization a great deal in terms of time and money. The time cost of eight people in a two-hour meeting, for example, comes to two person-days of work, *not* including preparation time. When salaries are included in the calculation, the monetary cost can be quite high (was that meeting really worth $300 or $500?).

With poorly managed meetings, the expense can seem exorbitant and the waste of time excessive. Yet there is another side to the story, as Alan Filley, Robert House, and Steven Kerr have noted.[24] A manager can obviously save time when he or she communicates with a number of subordinates in a meeting, rather than on a one-to-one basis. Nor do calculations of waste consider that the quality of communication and problem solving might well be higher in a group context.

2. *Individual domination.* Because formal committees are run by formal leaders who are usually the superiors of the other committee members, the danger is high that the group will be dominated by the leader. Such dominance may, of course, limit the committee's effectiveness. "Hidden agendas" may emerge as subordinates and other lower-level participants worry more about creating favorable impressions than about the problems the committee is supposed to solve.

3. *Premature agreements and mediocre compromises.* Like other group members, committee members may give little thought to any alternatives proposed after tentative agreement on a particular solution has been reached. In addition, executives angling for each other's support for their own pet projects may often go along with watered-down compromises.

In addition to these *political* pressures for compromise, there are also *psychological* pressures. As Irving Janis has noted, a cohesive group develops a tendency to experience "groupthink" (a term derived from George Orwell's *1984*) whereby the drive for consensus and compromise inhibits the potential dissenter or critic.[25] Because of the decline in objectivity and moral judgment that characterizes "groupthink," committee members may abdicate their

---

[24] Alan C. Filley, Robert J. House, and Steven Kerr, *Managerial Process and Organizational Behavior* (Glenview, Ill.: Scott, Foresman, 1976).

[25] Irving L. Janis, "Groupthink," *Psychology Today,* November 1971, pp. 43–46 ff. See also Irving L. Janis, *Victims of Groupthink* (Boston: Houghton Mifflin, 1973).

"What bothers me about these meetings is even though it's work, I have the nagging feeling I ought to leave and get back to work."

Sidney Harris/*The Saturday Evening Post*

responsibility for critically scrutinizing the pros and cons of alternative solutions. Janis suggests that the tendency toward "groupthink" contributed to the poor decisions made by presidential advisers on the Bay of Pigs invasion and Vietnam.

4. *Lack of responsibility.* Because no one committee member feels responsible for the committee's ultimate decision, members may behave less carefully than they would if they bore individual responsibility. In addition, if the committee's decision should go wrong in application, members might not work as hard to overcome the difficulty as they would in situations where they would be held individually accountable.

Making Committees and Task Groups Effective

Since committees play a necessary role in organizations, managers must learn to use committees effectively. Earlier we discussed some guidelines suggested by Maier on how to improve group performance. In this section, we will provide additional guidelines for managing committees. We will deal with (1) formal procedures for committee meetings, (2) guidelines for committee leaders, and (3) guidelines for committee members.

One word of caution: Committees differ greatly in their functions and activities. Thus, our general guidelines will not be appropriate in every case. For example, a highly directive committee responsible for communicating instructions from top management down to subordinates should be managed differently from a committee whose major task is to solve complex managerial problems on a continuing basis. The suggestions below are oriented toward problem-solving committees, which must be managed flexibly if the skills of the members are to be mobilized most effectively.

Formal Procedures. There are several formalities that are frequently useful in helping committees operate effectively:[26]

a. The committee's goals should be clearly defined, preferably in writing. This will focus the committee's activities and reduce the time devoted to discussing what the committee is supposed to do.

b. The committee's authority should be specified. Can the committee merely investigate, advise, and recommend, or is it authorized to implement decisions?

c. The optimum size of the committee should be determined. With less than five members, the advantages of group work may be diminished. With more than ten or fifteen, the committee may become unwieldy. While size will vary with the circumstances, the ideal number of committee members for many tasks seems to range from five to ten.

d. A chairperson should be selected on the basis of his or her ability to run an efficient meeting—that is, his or her ability to encourage the participation of all committee members, to keep the committee meetings from getting bogged down in irrelevancies, and to see that the necessary paperwork gets done.

e. Appointing a permanent secretary to handle communications is often useful.

f. The agenda and all supporting material for the meeting should be distributed before the meeting. When members study each item beforehand, they are more likely to stick to the point and to be ready with informed contributions.

g. Meetings should be started on time, and the time at which they will end should be announced at the outset.

Guidelines for Committee Leaders. Most studies of committee effectiveness have found that it ultimately depends on how well the committee is run. Committee leaders play key roles, because they are the ones who set up many of the formal procedures outlined above and who control the pace and focus of committee discussions.

The first task of committee leaders is to acquaint themselves and the members of their committee with the problem at hand. This done, leaders should set up an agenda and schedule for committee meetings so that members can prepare themselves for the meetings in advance.

Not all leaders and committees will benefit from Maier's recommended leadership style, described earlier in this chapter. Thus, an important task of committee leaders is to determine the decision-making style with which they are most comfortable and which is most suitable for the committee's task. Leaders should also try to see that both types of leadership roles—task and maintenance—are provided, either by them or by other committee members.

[26] Cyril O'Donnell, "Ground Rules for Using Committees," *Management Review,* Vol. 50, No. 10 (October 1961), pp. 63–67. See also Tillman, "Committees on Trial," pp. 168–172, and Dale, *Planning and Developing,* pp. 90–92.

These general guidelines aside, there are a number of specific guidelines to help leaders manage committee discussions effectively. For example, leaders should avoid statements like: "Here is the problem. This is what *I* think should be done about it." Such statements will focus the entire discussion on the leader's ideas, rather than on the ideas of committee members. A better statement is: "Here is the problem. What do *you* think we ought to do?" Committee leaders should also try to avoid statements like "I don't think that idea would work," or "You'll have to do better than that." Such discouraging responses can bring the flow of ideas to a halt.

To obtain the full benefits of a committee, it is obviously desirable to encourage the participation of all committee members. Leaders should tactfully discourage discussion monopolizers. They should also encourage less aggressive members to participate by asking them questions directly.

Finally, leaders should try to keep committee discussions from wandering. They can do this by periodically summing up the discussion or by asking questions that will refocus the discussion on the committee's task.[27]

Guidelines for Committee Members. For Jay Hall, the author of our chapter-opening moon test, the group decision process has one basic aim: to resolve conflicts creatively by reaching a consensus. He defines consensus not as unanimity but as a condition in which each member accepts the group's decisions, because they seem most logical and feasible. Hall offers five guidelines to help group members achieve consensus:[28]

1. State your position as clearly and logically as you can—but do not argue for your own position. Listen to and ponder the other members' reactions before you push your point.

2. If discussion between some members should get bogged down on any one point, do not treat it as a win-or-lose proposition for the people involved. Instead, seek out the next most acceptable alternative.

3. Do not yield on any point just for the sake of harmony. Accept a solution only when it is based on sound logic.

4. Shun techniques that bypass logic for the sake of reducing conflict (such as majority vote, flipping a coin, bargaining, and averaging). When a dissenting member finally goes along with the group, don't make up for this by letting the yielder have his or her own way on some other point.

5. Root out differences of opinion and pull everyone into the discussion. It is by airing the widest range of opinions and by drawing on all available information that the group can come up with high-grade solutions.

Working with college students and with management executives, Hall found that groups trained to apply this five-step decision-making process did con-

---

27 Alan C. Filley, "Committee Management: Guidance from Social Science Research," *California Management Review,* Vol. 13, No. 1 (Fall 1970), pp. 13–21. See also George M. Prince, "How to Be a Better Committee Chairman," *Harvard Business Review,* January-February 1971, pp. 98–108.
28 Hall, "Decisions, Decisions, Decisions," p. 86.

sistently better in solving problems than untrained groups. Usually the trained groups would even outperform their best individual member—an outcome he defined as "synergy." (Synergy is usually defined as "a condition in which the whole is greater than the sum of its parts.") Hall's guidelines encourage the maximum participation of group members and the search for the best possible problem solutions. Thus, they would be most useful for committees working on a task that requires an ingenious or creative solution.

Summary

Groups are an inevitable part of organizational life. A manager's task is to improve group performance so that the effectiveness of the group and the satisfaction of its members will be increased.

There are both formal and informal groups in organizations. *Formal* groups are made up and directed by management for some organizational objective. They include command groups, task forces, and committees. *Informal* groups emerge in the organization with or without the encouragement of management.

Group members provide each other with support and protection. In turn, they expect each other to conform to group norms. Members who violate group norms may be subjected to a variety of pressures, ranging from attempts at persuasion to physical assault.

The threat of rejection or punishment by the group is particularly effective in enforcing conformity in highly cohesive groups. Thus, members of cohesive work groups are likely to conform to their groups' productivity standards.

Groups are generally better at problem solving than the average individual: they bring a greater amount of information to a problem, generate a large number of alternative solutions, and make it more likely that the solution will be accepted. However, group problem solving is also more time-consuming and costly than individual problem solving. Thus, a manager will not use a group problem-solving approach in every instance. If a group approach is called for, effective managers encourage the active participation of group members and avoid trying to dominate the group.

Aside from command groups, the four types of formal organizational groups are task forces, standing committees, boards and commissions, and the plural executive. Advantages specific to these types of groups are that they help develop managers and avoid excessive concentration of power in a single individual. Specific disadvantages include the possibility of political maneuvering or mediocre compromise and the danger that accountability for decisions will be difficult to determine.

Guidelines for making committees effective include: (1) the need to establish certain formal procedures; (2) the need to select a committee leader who is knowledgeable about the task at hand and skilled in interpersonal relationships; and (3) the need for committee members to try to listen to all points of view and avoid settling for illogical or unworkable compromises.

Review Questions

1. What are the three basic types of groups in organizations? Which type of group do you think is most important? Why?
2. What are reference groups? Why is it important for managers to be aware of them? Can you identify your own reference groups?
3. Why do you think informal groups emerge in organizations? What organizational needs do they serve? What member needs do they serve?

4. How do informal leaders emerge in informal and formal work groups?
5. What are the two leadership roles?
6. How do group members try to enforce conformity?
7. What is the relationship between group cohesiveness and group performance? How can group cohesiveness be increased?
8. On what bases would a manager decide whether to use individual or group problem solving?
9. What are the possible assets and liabilities of group decision making and problem solving?
10. What is the "risky shift"?
11. According to Maier, how can the manager improve the effectiveness of a group's problem-solving activities?
12. What is a task force? What are the different types of committees and their functions?
13. What are the advantages and disadvantages of task forces and committees?
14. What formal procedures will help make committees effective? How can committee leaders and members help make committees effective?

CASE STUDY: THE OFFICE AT THE TOP

"Great idea. A fantastic new concept in organizational structure. Should have thought of it earlier." Such were the musings of Patrick A. Doyle, board chairman of the Aristo Insurance Company, as he read business releases of group management at such firms as General Electric, Borden, and Continental Can. "We'll be the first to adapt the innovation to the insurance industry."

Doyle, about to retire, felt that the group management concept would be a fitting and lasting contribution in his name. He had run across the concept and realized that earlier it would have helped him immeasurably in the many difficulties he had experienced. "This idea would ease the burden of those to follow," he thought. Consequently, Doyle's last official act before retirement was the creation of the "corporate office," along with the names of those to occupy it.

As Doyle had discovered, the "corporate office" or "office of the president" originated to relieve the burden on the president in the face of increasing organizational diversification, decentralization, technology, and product complexity. The concept, when used successfully, is not an alleviation of the president's job through increased delegation or distribution of his tasks, but rather it is to facilitate the execution of his tasks and decisions that are generally major issues or problems. As such, it allows group executive expertise to concentrate collectively in solving organizational problems in planning, control, and evaluation. It furthermore satisfies the need for coordination and input at the executive level.

Upon Doyle's retirement, James Griffin, Doyle's appointed successor as board chairman and chief executive officer, along with the president and vice presidents of finance, marketing, underwriting, claims, and research, constituted the corporate office. Chairman Griffin hailed the corporate office "as a process by which the seven of us can bring our own backgrounds, intelligence, and judgment to company problems. In

Case reprinted with permission from *Contemporary Management Incidents,* by Bernard Deitzer and Karl Shilliff (Columbus, Ohio: Grid, Inc., 1977), pp. 34–35.

effect," announced Griffin, "this is to be a group problem solving body, and when the group discusses major problems of finance or underwriting or marketing, brought to us by the various committee members, the consensus decision reached by the deliberations of the seven of us will then be issued by me, the board chairman. All of us will share equal responsibility for the decision."

Upon its installation, the corporate office began to meet every day for approximately two to three hours, discussing problems and issues brought to the committee by the seven members. Sometimes the more technical or involved problems consumed the entire day.

However, all is not well at Aristo. Recently the president resigned to take a similar post with another insurance firm. Net income has drastically plummeted since the inception of the office, and the subordinates who report to the various vice presidents are disgruntled because they rarely see their bosses "who always seem to be in committee meetings, trying to solve more and more problems of the company."

Case Questions
1. Can you identify the organizational problem at Aristo?
2. How would you restructure the top management?

Chapter 13

Organizational Design for Changing Environments

Upon completing this chapter you should be able to:

1. State the importance of finding the organizational design that is appropriate for your organization.

2. Describe classical and neoclassical approaches to organizational design and identify their limitations.

3. Identify the key variables in the contingency approach to organizational design and explain how each variable can affect organizational structure.

4. Differentiate between mechanistic and organic organizational systems.

5. Explain why the concept of organizational climate is important to managers.

6. Identify the factors that influence organizational climate.

7. Describe one model of how organizations change over time and how organizational structure must be redesigned to cope with these changes.

In Chapter 9 we noted that the organizational structure of many large corporations changed as their goals and the environment in which they operated changed. General Motors, for example, had a highly centralized structure when it produced a small variety of products and when demand for these products was still limited. As market demand increased — due in part to increases in population and personal income — GM's line of products became more diversified. It then became more efficient for GM to adopt a more decentralized organizational structure. In short, GM's structure changed as its situation changed.

The question of what is the "correct" type of organizational structure for a given situation has long been an important one for managers in all types of organizations. President Carter promised to "reorganize the federal bureaucracy" when he ran for election in 1976. He argued — and apparently many people agreed — that the way some federal agencies were structured made them ineffective in meeting human needs. Many college administrators have had to cut back or eliminate some departments in order to deal with declines in student enrollments. And, as the General Motors example suggests, business managers are under continuing pressure to restructure their organizations to make them more efficient and effective.

The search for the right organizational design is not an idle one. The consequences of an inappropriate structure can be inefficiency and high cost (as in the case of an organization with a span of management that is too narrow) or even outright failure of the organization. For example, when the Pennsylvania Railroad merged with the New York Central Railroad to form Penn Central, the opportunities for a larger, more efficient operation seemed very promising. However, the two companies never merged their organizations into one sound structure. The result was rivalry and costly duplication of effort, both of which contributed to the financial collapse of Penn Central in the early 1970s.

In this chapter we will deal with three major topics: (1) the broad question of how to design an organization so that it "fits" with the environment in which it operates; (2) how the structure and other elements of the organization help create its "climate" or "personality"; and (3) how organizations evolve and change as they increase in size.

We should emphasize that the design process we will be describing is rarely neat, rational, and precise. Designing the organization is, first of all, a *continuous* process, because environments and organizations inevitably change over time. Thus, large changes may be required occasionally (if, say, our organization is purchased by another company), while smaller changes may be needed more frequently (if, say, we want to find the right kind of integrating mechanism between two departments). Second, changes in structure will usually involve a great many trial-and-error attempts, accidents, and political realities, rather than a purely rational approach. For example, it may be logical to cut back a particular department, but if the head of that department has strong allies on the board of directors, the cutback may be impossible to

315

achieve. In other words, like most complex managerial problems, the problem of organizational design is not one we will be able to solve once and for all.

EARLY APPROACHES TO ORGANIZATIONAL DESIGN

Early management writers attempted to find the "one best way" or the "universal" approach to designing their organizations. They tried to discover a set of principles which, if followed by managers, would yield an organizational structure that would be efficient and effective in most situations. Such an approach implied that organizational structure was unaffected by the organization's environment—that a sound structure would enable the organization to succeed regardless of external conditions.

Today, management writers have moved from a "one best way" approach toward organizational design to a contingency approach. They argue that an organization is closely interdependent with its environment, and that in different situations, different structures will be more effective. A manager's task, according to this approach, is to isolate the variables that affect his or her organization and then to design the organization appropriately.

We will be discussing these key variables in this chapter. As background for our discussion, we will review briefly the early management approaches to the organizing process. (These were described, in part, in Chapter 2.) We will then deal with more recent perspectives on how an organization should be designed.[1]

The Classical
Approach to
Organizational
Design

The sociologist Max Weber[2] and management writers Frederick Taylor and Henri Fayol were major contributors to the so-called classical approach to organizational design. This approach suggested that the most efficient and effective organizations had a hierarchical structure based on a legalized, formal authority. (Weber called an organization with such a structure a *bureaucracy*.) Members of the organization were guided in their actions by a sense of duty to the organization and by a set of rational rules and regulations. When fully developed, according to Weber, such organizations were characterized by specialization of tasks, appointment by merit, provision of career opportunities for members, routinization of activities, and a rational, impersonal climate.

The word "bureaucracy" has today taken on many negative connotations. The early management writers, however, found much to commend bureaucracy as an organizational design. Weber in particular praised its rationality, its establishment of rules for decision making, its clear chain of command, and its promotion of people for their ability and not because of favoritism or whim.

---

[1] For the overall perspective in this section, the author is indebted to Kenneth N. Wexley and Gary A. Yukl, *Organizational Behavior and Personnel Psychology,* Chapter 3 (Homewood, Ill.: Irwin, 1977), and Y. K. Shetty and Howard M. Carlisle, "A Contingency Model of Organizational Design," *California Management Review,* Vol. 15, No. 1 (Fall 1972), pp. 38–45.

[2] Max Weber, *Economy and Society* (New York: Bedminster Press, 1968).

He also admired the clear specification of authority and responsibility, which he believed made it easier for the organization to evaluate performance and distribute rewards fairly.

Of course, Weber, Taylor, and Fayol developed their theories at a time when organizations that were approaching their bureaucratic model were considered modern and efficient. The other types of organizations that existed at the time seemed far less impressive to these writers. However, it soon became evident that some of the major advantages of the bureaucratic structure were also possible disadvantages. For example, the safeguards against favoritism and bias could be too rigidly imposed by such means as adhering excessively to rules and procedures. Such an inflexible approach could depersonalize managers and subordinates.

Criticisms of the Classical Approach. The classical bureaucratic model is most frequently criticized in the following areas:

1. It neglects the human aspects of organization members, who are assumed to be motivated only by basic economic incentives. As the educational levels, affluence, and work expectations of organization members have risen over time, this criticism has become more severe.

2. It does not take into account rapidly changing and uncertain environments. Formalized bureaucratic organizations have difficulty changing their rigidly installed procedures.

3. As the organization grows in size, top managers become progressively out of touch with realities at the lower levels of the organization. This problem is compounded when technology changes rapidly. As new workers enter the organization, they are likely to have technical skills that surpass those of their superiors higher up in the organization. Some of these differences in technical skills may be offset by the advantages that top managers have in terms of experience, wider perspective, and more access to information at higher levels. Even so, rapid technological changes cast doubt on the assumption that upper-level managers automatically have greater ability than their lower-level counterparts.

4. As organizational procedures become more formalized and individuals become more specialized, the danger increases that the means will become confused with the ends. Specialists, for example, in concentrating on their own finely tuned goals, may lose sight of the fact these goals are not ends in themselves but a means toward reaching the broader goals of the organization.

Victor Thompson[3] has also criticized the bureaucratic structure for its tendency to encourage what he calls "bureaupathology." The competitive nature of life in bureaucracies, the fact that managers in them must meet high standards of performance, and the fact that managers' subordinates may have more technical knowledge than they do can make many managers feel insecure. Some may try to protect their authority and position by behaving in an aloof, ritualistic way. Such behavior, according to Thompson, is "pathological"

---

[3] Victor A. Thompson, *Modern Organization* (New York: Knopf, 1961).

Drawing by Chas. Addams; © 1976 The New Yorker Magazine, Inc.

because it prevents the organization from meeting its goals. For example, managers who wish to avoid giving deserving subordinates a large raise in order to stay within higher-level budget guidelines may protect themselves from subordinates' demands by acting cold and aloof. The result may be a breakdown in communication between managers and subordinates. Thompson believes that bureaucratic structures permit these kinds of counterproductive, personal insecurities to flourish.

The Neoclassical Approach

Early human relations researchers and behavioral scientists attempted to deal with what they saw as the major inadequacy of the classical bureaucratic model: the neglect of the human element within the organization. They argued that an industrial organization has two objectives—economic effectiveness *and* employee satisfaction.

As we discussed in Chapter 2, the initial impetus for this point of view was provided by the Hawthorne studies, which suggested that merely showing an interest in employees could result in increased productivity. Thus, the human relations researchers and behavioral scientists argued that the bureaucratic structure could be improved by making it less formal and by permitting more subordinate participation in decision making. Because they did not reject the classical model, but only tried to improve on it, these researchers are called neoclassicists by some writers. Major contributors to the neoclassical approach

318

were Abraham Maslow, whose work we will describe in Chapter 16, and Douglas McGregor,[4] Chris Argyris,[5] and Rensis Likert,[6] whose work we will describe in the following sections.

Douglas McGregor. McGregor believed that the vertical division of labor that characterized organizations was based in part on a set of negative assumptions about workers that many managers held. He referred to these assumptions as Theory X. As we described in Chapter 6, Theory X assumptions include the notions that most people have little ambition, desire security above all, and will avoid work unless they are driven to it by orders and threats. The rigid, formal hierarchy in organizations, according to this view, is designed to maintain managers' power, influence, and authority over subordinates.

McGregor suggested that organizations based on what he called Theory Y assumptions would meet the human needs of organization members and utilize their potential much more effectively. Theory Y assumes that people can find a great source of satisfaction in work, that they can be committed to organizational goals for the sake of achievement rather than because of the threat of punishment, and that they can learn not only to accept but to seek responsibility. Organizations structured according to Theory Y assumptions would allow members a great deal more independence than bureaucratic organizations. They would also allow more lower-level participation in decision making and greater openness in communication between managers and subordinates.

Chris Argyris. Argyris was concerned with the fact that managers in a formal organization had near-total responsibility for planning, controlling, and evaluating the work of their subordinates. For example, bureaucratic managers would have complete authority to set work schedules and reward or fire workers. Argyris argued that such domination of the workplace by managers would cause subordinates to become passive and dependent. In addition, subordinates would tend to experience a decreasing sense of responsibility and self-control.

To Argyris, such conditions are incompatible with the human need for self-reliance, self-expression, and accomplishment. Members of the organization—particularly at lower levels, where very little initiative is allowed—will become dissatisfied and frustrated in their work as these needs are blocked. The result, suggested Argyris, is not only increased unhappiness among organization members but also increased problems in meeting organizational goals. For example, dissatisfied workers may leave the organization, resulting in high

---

[4] Douglas McGregor, *The Human Side of Enterprise* (New York: McGraw-Hill, 1960).

[5] Chris Argyris, *Personality and Organization* (New York: Harper & Brothers, 1957), and *Integrating the Individual and the Organization* (New York: Wiley, 1964).

[6] Rensis Likert, *New Patterns of Management* (New York: McGraw-Hill, 1961); *The Human Organization* (New York: McGraw-Hill, 1967); and Rensis Likert and Jane Gibson Likert, *New Ways of Managing Conflict* (New York: McGraw-Hill, 1976).

turnover rates, or they may commit acts of sabotage, increasing costs. More often, they will insist on higher wages, because their work is so psychologically unrewarding.

As an alternative, Argyris argued for an organizational design that better meets human needs and increases the satisfaction of organization members. Like McGregor, he favors allowing subordinates a much greater degree of independence and decision-making power and creating a more informal and flexible organizational climate. He also favored a wider use of matrix-type organizational structures, which allow for the creation of project teams. (See Chapter 9.)

Rensis Likert. Likert shared the perspectives of McGregor and Argyris. In his research on effective group performance, he found that traditional authoritarian managers were less able to motivate their subordinates to high standards of achievement than managers who actively supported their subordinates' feelings of worth and importance. Based on these findings, Likert created a model to describe different organizational designs and their effectiveness.

In Likert's model, an organization can be based on one of four systems. *System 1* represents the traditional organizational structure. Power and authority in the System 1 organization are distributed strictly according to the classical management-subordinate relationship. A manager at one level in the hierarchy tells members of a lower level in the hierarchy what to do, and so on down the chain of command.

FEELINGS OF WORTH AND IMPORTANCE

System 4 organizations, in contrast, involve much greater group participation in supervision and decision making. Group members who would be affected by a decision or problem engage in the decision-making or problem-solving process together. To create feelings of mutual support and ease communication throughout the organization, some individuals in each work group also belong to other work groups. Thus, the work groups in the organization are linked.

High Performance Goals

As in System 1 organizations, managers would still be held accountable for their group's performance. However, the primary task of System 4 managers would not be to make quality decisions and then delegate responsibility for carrying them out. Instead, the managers' primary task would be to build a *group* that can make quality decisions and carry them out effectively. In Table 13-1, System 1 and System 4 organizations are contrasted according to a variety of characteristics. Systems 2 and 3 are intermediate stages between these two extremes. (See Chapter 17.)

System 4 represents Likert's view of how an organization should ideally be designed and managed. To reach System 4, according to Likert, organizations need to (1) obey the "principle of supportive relationships," (2) use group decision making where appropriate, and (3) set high performance goals.

Group Decision Making

The *principle of supportive relationships* suggests that the managers and activities of the organization should cause individual members to view their experiences as adding to their personal sense of worth and importance. Through the use of group decision making and high performance goals, man-

320

	System 1	System 4
Leadership Processes	Low superior-subordinate trust and confidence. Subordinates do not feel free to discuss important job subjects with superiors who do not involve subordinates in problem solving.	High superior-subordinate trust and confidence. Subordinates discuss job subjects candidly with superiors, who virtually always involve subordinates in problem solving.
Communication Processes	Information flow is predominantly downward, with superiors holding it to a minimum and subordinates being suspicious of it. Upward communication is limited and inaccurate. Lateral communication is restricted because of peer hostility and suspicion. Superiors and subordinates are psychologically distant and perceive each other inaccurately.	Information flows freely and accurately in all directions. Subordinates accept or candidly question downward communication. Superiors and subordinates are psychologically close and perceive each other accurately.
Interaction-Influence Processes	Limited subordinate-superior interaction characterized by fear and distrust. Limited influence by subordinates except through "informal organization" and unionization.	Extensive friendly interaction between subordinates and superiors as well as high trust and confidence. High influence by subordinates directly and through unionization.
Decision-Making Processes	Decisions made by superiors or higher levels with little or no knowledge of lower-level problems or involvement by subordinates.	Decisions made by group participation and usually consensus with high awareness of lower-level problems.
Goal-Setting Processes	Goals established by orders from superiors.	Goals normally established by group participation.
Control Processes	Primary concern for performance of control functions is restricted to very top levels.	Concern for performance of control functions is felt throughout the organization.

TABLE 13-1   Characteristics of System 1 and System 4 Organizations

agers can help build this feeling of support. Group members come to feel that they are responsible for decisions which affect them and that they are an integral part of the organization. The setting and attainment of high goals enable organization members to develop a sense of pride and accomplishment.

Limitations of the Neoclassical Approach. The neoclassical approach to organizational design suggests that organizations should encourage much greater subordinate participation in decision making, more open communication, and less status difference between managers and subordinates. However, while these approaches compensate for some limitations in the traditional classical model, they are also open to criticism. Common criticisms of the neoclassical approach are:

1. The neoclassicists share the classical assumption that there is "one best way" to design an organization. They overlook environmental, technological, and other variables that might affect an organization's design.

2. Theory Y, like Theory X, oversimplifies human motivation. Not everyone is motivated by the nonmonetary aspects of work, nor can all work be made intrinsically challenging and rewarding.

3. Coordinating decentralized, fragmented groups to achieve organizational goals may be more difficult than the neoclassicists suggest, particularly when the objectives of lower-level employees are not consistent with the goals of upper-level managers.

CONTINGENCY APPROACHES TO ORGANIZATIONAL DESIGN

As we have already suggested, research and writing since the early 1960s have caused many of today's management theorists to doubt that there is a single, ideal way to design an organization. Advocates of the current contingency approaches suggest that the structure that will be most appropriate for an organization will depend on the particular circumstances in which that organization finds itself.

The key variables that can affect the organization and thus help determine what its structure should be are its strategy, the technology it uses to carry out its activities, the environment in which it operates, and the characteristics of its members. The manager's job, according to the contingency approach, is to establish an effective fit between the organization's structure and those variables. We will be discussing each of these variables, and how each can affect organizational design, in this section.

Strategy and Structure

In Chapter 9, we suggested that "structure follows strategy" — that the overall, long-term goals of an organization will help determine its design. Here we will present a diagram that summarizes how a strategy is formulated and that points out the relationship between strategy and structure. Our diagram is a simplified one and so does not attempt to cover all aspects of an organization's environment (see Chapter 3) or the entire strategy-making process (see Chapter 5). It does suggest a way of looking at strategy and structure that is applicable to any type of organization.[7]

As Figure 13-1 indicates, an organization's environment has at least four major aspects — social, political, technological, and economic. Each aspect

[7] The author is indebted to Professor Thomas P. Ference and his colleagues at Columbia University's Graduate School of Business for the basic form of this figure. See also Harold J. Leavitt, "Applied Organization Change in Industry," in W. W. Cooper, H. J. Leavitt, and M. W. Shelly II, eds., *New Perspectives in Organization Research* (New York: Wiley, 1964).

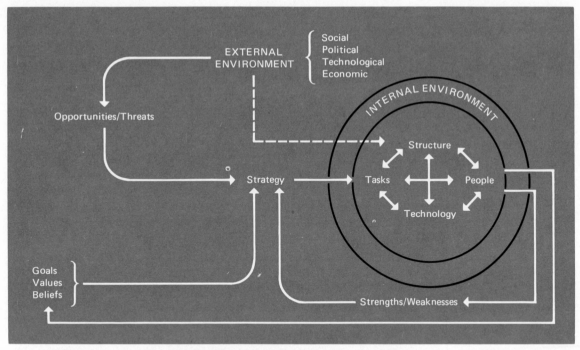

FIGURE 13-1   A Model of Strategy Formulation for Organizations

presents organization members with a set of opportunities and threats that will help determine the strategy of the organization. For example, a recent phenomenon in our society has been the growing number of students interested in taking business courses. College administrators who wish to increase student enrollments might, therefore, include expansion of the business department as part of their strategic plan. Conversely, there has been a growing decline in liberal arts enrollments. Colleges that have their major strength in this area might have to make expansion of their job placement program a part of their strategic plan to maintain enrollments.

The strengths and weaknesses of the organization and the goals, values, and beliefs of organization members (particularly the top managers) are the other major inputs to the organization's strategy. For example, a hospital with a strong team of heart specialists on its staff is more likely to expand its research program into heart disease than to expand its cancer research program.

The strategy finally selected by the organization will be a major determinant of the tasks that members of the organization will perform. These tasks, in turn, will help determine the organization's structure. Highly technical and creative tasks, for instance, may require a matrix-type organizational design.

To be effective, the organization's structure will also be determined by people and technology within the organization, as shown by the double-headed arrows in the diagram. For example, organization members who require a great deal of close supervision may not be able to work effectively within a highly decentralized organizational structure. The structure will also have to be compatible with the external environment, as the dashed arrow suggests. Multinational companies in northern European countries, for instance, have been facing increasing legal and political pressures to allow greater worker representation on their boards of directors.

Task-Technology and Structure

A number of research studies have confirmed that an organization's tasks and the technologies necessary to accomplish them are major determinants of organizational structure. Some of the most influential studies in this area were the South Essex studies carried out by Joan Woodward and her colleagues in the mid-1960s.[8] The purpose of the studies was to find out if the classical principles of management being taught in British schools were actually being practiced by managers and if application of these principles had any effect on an organization's success. The one hundred manufacturing firms studied ranged in size from 11 to about 40,000 employees, though most firms had fewer than 1,000 employees.

A preliminary analysis by Woodward and her co-researchers found that there seemed to be no relationship between the success of a firm and the degree to which it adhered to the classical principles of management. Managers in some successful firms, for example, appeared to violate the classical "span of management" principle by having a very large number of subordinates reporting to them; managers in some unsuccessful firms did not seem to violate this principle.

Puzzled by the lack of consistency between adherence to organizational principles and organizational performance, the researchers then turned to the technological processes used by the firms. They wanted to see if there was some relationship between a firm's technology and its structure and if this relationship in some way accounted for a firm's performance. They divided the firms into three basic groups, based on their production technology: (1) unit and small batch production, (2) large batch and mass production, and (3) process production.

Unit production refers to the production of individual items tailored to a customer's specifications. For example, custom-made clothes are produced in single units. The technology used in unit production is the least complex of all groups, since the items are produced largely by individual craftsmen. *Small batch production* refers to products that are produced in small quantities in separate stages, such as machine parts that are later assembled. *Large batch* and *mass production* refer to the production of large quantities of products, sometimes on an assembly line (as with automobiles). *Process production* refers to the production of materials that are sold by weight or volume — such

---

[8] Joan Woodward, *Industrial Organization* (London: Oxford University Press, 1965). See also Karl O. Magnusen, "A Comparative Analysis of Organizations," *Organizational Dynamics,* Vol. 2, No. 1 (Summer 1973), pp. 16–31; Charles Perrow, *Organizational Analysis* (Belmont, Calif.: Wadsworth, 1970); and James D. Thompson, *Organizations in Action* (New York: McGraw-Hill, 1967).

as chemicals or drugs. These materials are usually produced with highly complex equipment that operates in a continuous flow.

Using these three categories, Woodward reanalyzed the firms she was studying. She found that there were a number of relationships between the technological process a firm was using and its structure, such as:

1. *The more complex the technology*—going from unit up to process production—*the greater the number of managers and management levels.* In other words, complex technologies lead to tall organizational structures. More complex technologies require a greater degree of supervision and coordination; thus, more managers and a large number of management levels are necessary. (See Figure 13-2.)

FIGURE 13-2
Technological Complexity and Management Levels

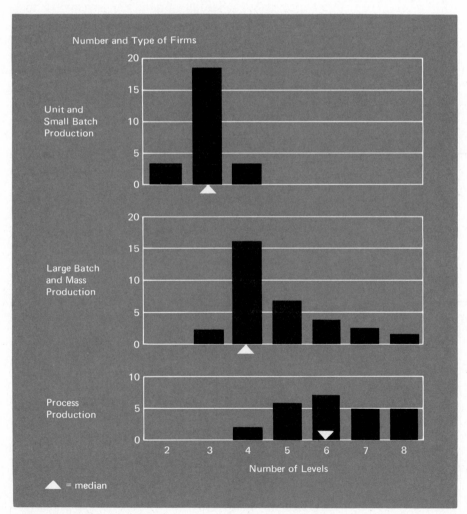

Source: Joan Woodward, *Industrial Organization* (London: Oxford University Press, 1965), p. 52. Used by permission.

NARROW SPAN

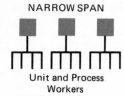

Unit and Process
Workers

WIDE SPAN

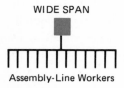

Assembly-Line Workers

2. *The span of management of first-line managers increases from unit to mass production and then decreases from mass to process production.* Lower-level employees in both unit and process production firms tend to do highly skilled work. As a result, they tend to form small work groups, making a narrow span inevitable. Assembly-line workers, on the other hand, usually perform similar types of unskilled tasks. Large numbers of such workers can be supervised by one manager.

3. *The greater the technological complexity of the firm, the larger the clerical and administrative staffs.* The larger number of managers in technologically complex firms require supportive services—to do the additional paperwork, for example, or to handle nonproduction-related work, such as personnel administration. In addition, complex equipment requires more attention in terms of maintenance and production scheduling to keep the equipment in operation a high proportion of the time.

Woodward then examined the firms in each technology category to see if their success or failure was related to their structure. She found that the successful firms in each category did in fact have similar structural characteristics, which tended to cluster around the median value for those characteristics at each technological level. For example, if the median span of management in process firms was 9, the successful process firms would have spans near that number. Unsuccessful firms, on the other hand, would have structural characteristics well above or below the median in each category.

The significance of this finding is that *for each type of technology there were specific aspects of organizational structure that were associated with success.* In other words, the successful firms were those with the appropriate structure for their level of technology. For mass production firms, the appropriate structure conformed to the classical management principles. In the other two types of firms, however, the appropriate structure did *not* conform to classical guidelines.

Woodward's studies provide impressive evidence of the influence of technology on organizational structure. Some recent research, however, suggests that the impact of technology on structure is strongest in small firms (which the firms that Woodward studied tended to be). For large firms, the impact of technology seems to be felt mainly at the lowest levels of the organization.[9]

External Environment and Structure

Every organization must deal with events in the external environment, such as changes in supply and demand, technological developments, and actions by competitors. In examining the effects of the environment on organizational design, we will find it useful to distinguish between three types of environments: stable, changing, and turbulent.[10] We will then discuss the structures appropriate for each type of environment.

---

[9] See, for example, D. J. Hickson, D. S. Pugh, and D. Pheysey, "Operations Technology and Organization Structure: A Critical Reappraisal," *Administrative Science Quarterly,* Vol. 14 (1969), pp. 378–397.

[10] Ross A. Webber, *Management* (Homewood, Ill.: Irwin, 1975), pp. 433–435.

Organization

Stable Environment

The Stable Environment. A stable environment, as its name implies, is one that shows little or no unexpected or sudden change. Product changes occur infrequently; those modifications that are made can be planned well in advance. Market demand is steady with only minor and predictable fluctuations. Laws that affect the particular organization or product have remained the same for an extended period and are unlikely to be changed abruptly. New technological developments are unlikely to occur, so research budgets are either minimal or nonexistent.

Because of the increasing rate of technological change, stable organizational environments are becoming fewer and examples harder to find. Still, they do exist. There are companies realizing a steady profit spinning cotton twine on 60-year-old machinery. And it has been a long time since a spectacular change occurred in the manufacture of such items as toothpicks, manhole covers, and violins.

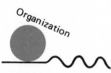

Changing Environment

The Changing Environment. In a changing environment, innovation may occur in any or all of the areas previously mentioned—product, market, law, or technology. Such changes are, however, unlikely to take the top managers of the organization completely by surprise. The trend of changes is likely to be apparent and predictable, and organizations will be able to adjust fairly easily to the trend. For example, law firms are in a changing environment, because lawyers must acquaint themselves with each new law that is passed. However, the basic body of law changes very gradually. Other examples of organizations in a changing environment include many service, construction, and appliance industries.

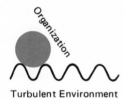

Turbulent Environment

The Turbulent Environment. When competitors launch new, unexpected products, when new laws are passed without appreciable warning, and when technological breakthroughs suddenly revolutionize product design or production methods, the organization can be said to be in a turbulent environment.

Few organizations face a permanently turbulent environment. If a rapid and radical change does occur, organizations usually pass through only a temporary period of turbulence before making an adjustment. For example, hospitals had to adjust to a sudden increase in demand for their services when Medicaid legislation was passed. Similarly, many companies have undergone a turbulent period due to the passage of pollution-control laws and the energy crisis. Some firms, however, do experience almost constant turbulence—many electronics and computer companies, for instance, have to deal with a rapid rate of technological change in their fields.

Matching the Structure to the Environment. Tom Burns and G. M. Stalker have distinguished between two organizational systems: mechanistic and organic.[11] In a *mechanistic* system, the activities of the organization are broken

---

[11] Tom Burns and G. M. Stalker, *The Management of Innovation* (London: Tavistok Publications, 1961).

down into separate, specialized tasks. Objectives and authority for each individual and subunit are precisely defined by higher-level managers. Power in such organizations follows the classical bureaucratic chain of command that was described earlier.

In an *organic* system, job skills are more likely to be used in a group setting rather than on one specific task. There is less emphasis on taking orders from a superior or giving orders to subordinates. Instead, members communicate across all levels of the organization in order to obtain information and advice.

After studying a variety of companies, Burns and Stalker concluded that the mechanistic system was best suited for organizations in a stable environment, while organic systems were best suited for organizations in a turbulent environment. Organizations in changing environments would probably use some combination of the two systems—say, a mechanistic structure with an organic-type subdivision in research or other areas most affected by change.

In a stable environment, there is little need for organization members to have a flexible array of skills, since each member is likely to continue to perform the same task. Thus, skill specialization is appropriate. In turbulent environments, however, jobs must constantly be redefined to cope with the ever-changing needs of the organization. Organization members must be skilled at solving a variety of problems, not at performing a set of specialized activities. In addition, the creative problem-solving and decision-making processes required in turbulent environments are best carried out in groups in which members can communicate openly with other members. Thus, for turbulent environments, an organic system is appropriate.

The findings of Burns and Stalker were supported and extended by Paul R. Lawrence and Jan W. Lorsch.[12] Lawrence and Lorsch examined ten companies, measuring the degree of differentiation and integration these companies exhibited in relation to the type of external environment in which they operated. They used the word *differentiation* to refer to the degree to which managers of different functional departments varied in their cognitive and emotional orientation. (See Chapter 10 for Lawrence and Lorsch's description of how managers of different departments or activities vary in their attitudes and working styles.) *Integration* referred to the degree to which members of various departments in the organization worked together in a unified way.

Lawrence and Lorsch hypothesized that departments in organizations such as plastics manufacturing companies, which were operating in unstable environments, would be more differentiated than departments in environmentally stable organizations, such as container manufacturing companies. They further reasoned that not all departments would be affected to the same extent by an unstable environment, and that this would cause departments within the same organization to become differentiated. For example, the research department

Differences in Managerial Orientation

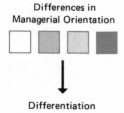

↓

Differentiation

Departmental Cooperation

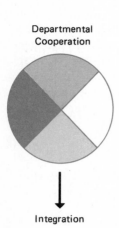

↓

Integration

---

[12] Paul R. Lawrence and Jay W. Lorsch, *Organization and Environment* (Homewood, Ill.: Irwin, 1967).

of a firm might deal directly with a great deal of change and turbulence, because of the constant development of new products. The managers of that department might use an organic-type structure. On the other hand, the sales department in that same firm, with an established list of customers, might not be as affected by change. That department might therefore be organized along more formal, mechanistic lines.

Lawrence and Lorsch also hypothesized that high-performance organizations in each type of environment would have a greater degree of integration than lower-performance companies. They believed that effective cooperation and coordination within an organization would make it more likely that an organization would be successful.

Their findings after analyzing the companies in the study confirmed their hypotheses. The firms operating in an unstable environment were the most highly differentiated and the firms operating in a stable environment were the least differentiated of the companies studied. In addition, the high-performance organizations in both types of firms had a higher degree of integration than low-performance organizations. Those successful organizations with a high degree of differentiation were able to integrate their operations effectively by using a variety of integrating mechanisms, such as committees and task forces.

The Lawrence and Lorsch study lent further support to the idea that an organization whose internal structure is appropriate for its environment will achieve higher performance than an organization whose structure is inappropriate. Another study that demonstrated the importance of designing an organization to fit its environment was carried out by Morse and Lorsch.[13] In this study, four departments of a large company were evaluated. Two of these departments, which manufactured containers, operated in a comparatively certain environment. The other two departments were in the uncertain environment associated with communications research. In each pair, one department had been evaluated as highly effective and the other as less effective.

Morse and Lorsch found that the most effective manufacturing department was structured in a mechanistic fashion, with clearly defined roles and duties, while the most effective research department was structured in an organic fashion, with roles and duties loosely defined. On the other hand, the less effective manufacturing department was structured in an organic way, while the less effective research department was mechanistically structured. In short, the structures of the most effective departments fit with their environments, while the structures of the less effective departments did not.

People and Structure   There is also a relationship between the attitudes, experiences, and roles of organization members and the structure of the organization. Our discussion of this topic will be divided into the two categories that cover all the people in an organization — managers and subordinates.

[13] John J. Morse and Jay W. Lorsch, "Beyond Theory Y," *Harvard Business Review,* May-June 1970, pp. 61–68.

Managers and Structure. In previous chapters, we have mentioned the importance of managerial values in determining the strategy of an organization. The organization's managers—especially the top managers—influence the choice of strategy directly through their preferences for certain goals and certain ways of getting things done. Their selection of strategy will, in turn, affect the kind of structure that emerges in the organization.

Personal preferences of managers will also influence the organizational structure directly. Most managers have personal preferences for specific types of organization, for ways of relating to subordinates, customers, and other managers, and for ways of attacking problems. These preferences translate directly into various types of organizational structures. For example, a manager with strong Theory X values will prefer a more traditional organizational structure, while a manager with Theory Y values may prefer a more organic system.

Other important influences on structure may result from managers' personal attitudes toward authority, their regard or disregard for formality, and their past experiences (positive or negative) with different types of organizational design. Some writers believe that in recent years there has been a growing dissatisfaction with the depersonalized, mechanistic concept of organizational authority. This dissatisfaction, if widely felt, could cause managers to opt for a more humanistic structure that places less emphasis on coercion and career mobility and a greater emphasis on collaboration and personal growth.[14]

Subordinates and Structure. Such factors as employees' level of education, background, degree of interest in work, and availability of work alternatives outside the organization will influence how an organization should be structured. For example, highly educated individuals who have excellent outside alternatives and who enjoy their work are likely to be more appropriately organized in an organic structure. Individuals with low levels of education, doing boring or repetitive work, might be better organized in a more mechanistic structure.

Today, rising affluence and levels of education among subordinates are exerting pressure on managers to develop ways of making organizational structure compatible with the individual needs of employees. In addition, job mobility has been increasing: each year 20 percent of our population moves to a new address. Many individuals are deciding that it is not necessary to stick with an unrewarding job just because it is close to home.

In times of high unemployment, as in the recession of the mid-1970s, individuals may be more likely to accept whatever structure they are in, because they feel fortunate to be working at all. But, in general, the combination of more money to spend, more education, and more mobility are adding up to new perspectives on work. Growing numbers of people will require greater involvement and participation in helping the organization achieve its goals.

Many companies are taking active steps and are experimenting with new

[14] See Warren G. Bennis, "The Coming Death of Bureaucracy," in Patrick E. Connor, ed., *Dimensions in Modern Management* (Boston: Houghton Mifflin, 1974), pp. 496–505.

ideas to provide a more rewarding environment for their employees. The programs for job enrichment and job enlargement, described in Chapter 9, are explicit examples of the attempts being made to alter the organizational structure and work processes to take account of individual needs. Although the best known of these programs are the experiments being carried out in Sweden in plants such as Volvo, they have also been a feature of some American companies (AT&T and IBM, for example) for quite some time. It would seem likely that the number of such programs will increase in the future.

Conclusion. We have seen how strategy, technology, external environment, and people must all be considered in designing any organizational structure. Because of these factors, certain types of structures are more appropriate and effective in certain situations. In addition, since these factors change over time, managers must continue to be aware of them as they manage (and redesign) their organizations.

ORGANIZATIONAL CLIMATE

Joan Caulfield was discussing her first job after graduation: "Maybe I shouldn't have joined Omni in the first place. During the campus interview, I kept feeling there was something wrong, but I couldn't put my finger on it. I felt the same when I visited their head office. But everything else pointed to Omni: exciting initial projects, a terrific boss with whom I really hit it off, and an offer that was $2,500 higher than any other I got. So they really wanted me and my skills. Everything fit but the 'fit.' Six months later I quit. I still don't know why but I felt miserable there.

"Now I'm a fast-tracker at STR with two big promotions in less than three years. And I love it here. I knew right away that STR was for me. I still don't know what makes the difference between here and Omni; sometimes I guess you have to trust the vibrations."

Caulfield was describing her reactions to what we can call "organizational climate." Every organization has a kind of "personality," which comes from the interaction of the strategic, environmental, technological, and human variables discussed in the preceding section. This climate is, in turn, an important determinant of how the organization performs and how the members of the organization interpret and respond to their experience within the organization.

Definition and Importance of Organizational Climate
Organizational climate has been defined in a number of ways by a number of different writers. Forehand and Gilmer provided one useful definition when they stated that organizational climate refers to

the set of characteristics that describe an organization and that (a) distinguish the organization from other organizations, (b) are relatively enduring over time, and (c) influence the behavior of people in the organization.[15]

[15] Garlie A. Forehand and B. Von Haller Gilmer, "Environmental Variation in Studies of Organizational Behavior," *Psychological Bulletin*, Vol. 22 (1964), pp. 361–382.

This definition is echoed by DuBrin, who points out that organizations have "personalities" and that organizational climate is a measure of that personality:

Every organization has properties or characteristics possessed by many other organizations; however, each organization has its own unique constellation of characteristics and properties. *Organizational climate* is the term used to describe this psychological structure of organizations. Climate is thus the "feel," "personality," or "character" of the organization's environment.[16]

One of the difficulties of defining organizational climate is that the subject itself is a complex one. (Some writers, for example, find the concept so complex that they prefer to discuss the *multiple climates* in an organization.)[17] The task of establishing an accepted method of *measuring* organizational climate has also turned out to be a difficult one. However, from our own experiences, we are aware of the fact that different organizations can be experienced in very different ways. For example, all of us have known classes in which the teacher was "strict" and in which our mood and behavior were far different than in classes in which the teacher was more flexible and friendly. Organizations have their own feel or tone about them that can at times be described as almost an "aura." How we react to a specific organization is a result of how we perceive that organization's personality and how it fits in with our own personality and needs.

The concept of organizational climate is important to managers and individuals for three reasons: (1) there is evidence that some climates are likely to yield better results for specific tasks than other climates; (2) there is evidence that managers can influence the climates of their organizations or, more specifically, their own unit within the organization; and (3) the "fit" between the individual and the organization appears to play a significant role in determining the individual's performance and satisfaction within the organization.[18]

The way our own personality is likely to fit with that of an organization is a particularly important consideration when evaluating career opportunities. Since the way we fit with the organization will have a direct effect, either positively or negatively, on our performance and satisfaction, it is important to be aware of the concept of climate and choose our organization and department carefully. In addition, because we are all influenced by our environment, we should recognize that the climate of the organization we join will, to some

[16] Andrew J. DuBrin, *Fundamentals of Organizational Behavior* (New York: Pergamon Press, 1974), pp. 331–361.

[17] See, for example, Benjamin Schneider, "Conceptualizing Organizational Climates," *Research Report #7*, Department of Psychology, University of Maryland (May 1974). See also Don Hellriegel and John W. Slocum, Jr., "Organizational Climate," *Academy of Management Journal*, Vol. 17, No. 2 (June 1974), pp. 255–280, which contains numerous references to organizational climate studies.

[18] See, for example, H. Kirk Downey, Don Hellriegel, and John W. Slocum, Jr., "Congruence Between Individual Needs, Organizational Climate, Job Satisfaction and Performance," *Academy of Management Journal*, Vol. 18, No. 1 (March 1975), pp. 149–155.

extent, shape and mold us. The longer we stay in a given environment, the more likely we are to have feelings, attitudes, beliefs, and values which are consistent with that environment. We should ask ourselves not only "Will we 'fit' there?" but also "Is this what we want to *become*?" This point was made with a vengeance by Kurt Vonnegut, Jr., in *Mother Night,*[19] in which the "hero" becomes a Nazi propagandist as a cover-up for his spy activities against the Germans. In the process, he acquires many of the attitudes of the enemy against whom he is working. As Vonnegut says in his introduction to the book, "We are what we pretend to be, so we must be careful about what we pretend to be."

Determinants of Organizational Climate

When some aspect of the organization is altered, the change may influence the climate of the organization in desired or undesired ways. For example, a new president taking over the organization may change its structure. This structural change may cause a change in climate, which in turn may influence such factors as employee effort, performance, or satisfaction. (See Figure 13-3.) In order to manage their organizations effectively, managers need to recognize how they can influence organizational climate.

FIGURE 13-3
Determinants and Influences of Organizational Climate

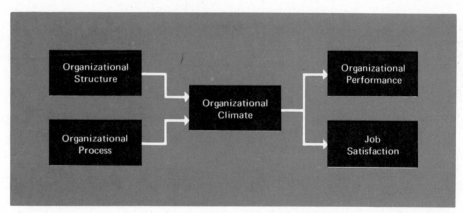

Source: Edward E. Lawler III, Douglas T. Hall, and Greg R. Oldham, "Organizational Climate: Relationship to Organizational Structure, Process and Performance," *Organizational Behavior and Human Performance*, Vol. 11, No. 1 (February 1974), p. 142. Used by permission.

What are the factors that can influence organizational climate? Obviously there are many. We will list a few of the major factors below.[20]

1. *Economic conditions.* When economic conditions are good, organizations "relax." More adventuresome projects may be undertaken, and a general feeling of confidence is experienced by organizational members. When economic conditions worsen, budgets become tighter and caution replaces confidence.

2. *Leadership style.* Managers' attitudes and approaches to their subor-

[19] Kurt Vonnegut, Jr., *Mother Night* (New York: Harper & Row, 1961).
[20] DuBrin, *Fundamentals of Organizational Behavior,* pp. 334–340.

dinates will have a major impact on organizational climate. The leadership style of top managers is particularly important, since it will be adopted by junior managers who perceive it as the "correct" way to act.

3. *Policy*. Organizational policy, whether written or implied, creates impressions and perceptions of the organization over a period of time. For example, an organization in which there is a policy of promotion from within may have a more competitive climate than an organization that usually fills top positions from outside.

4. *Values*. The values of the organization's managers will, over time, greatly affect organizational climate. A company that places a high value on the welfare of its employees, for example, will probably have higher-than-average pension, hospitalization, and recreational benefits. Such a company may develop a much warmer, friendlier climate than an organization in which company profits are valued more than employee satisfaction. However, some employees may also find the company too paternalistic.

5. *Organizational structure*. A company organized into strictly divided functional departments, with a clear ranking of managers by title, may develop a climate characterized by rigidity, traditionalism, and an emphasis on by-the-book procedure. Conversely, less mechanistic structures may result in flexible, innovative, and informal climates.

6. *Characteristics of members*. Organizational climate can be greatly influenced by the characteristics of the people in the organization. For example, such characteristics as the average age of members, the prevalent clothing style, the proportion of female managers, and even the length of hair worn by male managers can influence the overall personality of the organization and affect members' attitudes and behavior.

7. *Nature of the business*. We will naturally expect to find a different climate in a funeral home than in a modern dance studio. Although these examples are extreme, the nature of any business will influence the type of employees it attracts and the ways in which they behave.

8. *Life stage*. Younger organizations tend to have a less formal climate than their mature counterparts.

A MODEL OF ORGANIZATIONAL GROWTH AND CHANGE

George Abbott has been president of his publishing company since he founded it twenty-five years ago. When the company was small, George's informal style of management helped create a warm family atmosphere that encouraged hard work and long hours. It was also efficient at the time for George to handle most of the company's problems himself. Today, however, the company has grown in size. George's informal style causes confusion among company managers, who do not have a clear idea of their responsibilities. George's insistence on handling most problems himself results in delays and frustrations for employees throughout the company.

Burns Electronics Company has been a successful, diversified organization for many years. It is structured along product lines, with a separate management hierarchy responsible for each family of products. Overall direction for the company is still provided by top managers at central headquarters. In recent years, the efforts by top managers to improve coordination and control throughout the company have aroused resentment among division managers. They feel they are getting bogged down in a mountain of reports and in endless meetings.

Earlier in this chapter, we discussed the fact that an organization's structure must fit with its strategy, technology, environment, and employees. As the above examples suggest, however, these factors will change over time. The structure that suits an organization during one stage in its life cycle may not be suitable during another stage. Periodically managers may have to alter the organizational structure to fit the changing needs and circumstances of their organization.

Larry E. Greiner has developed a model to describe how organizations change over time and how these changes affect management practices and organizational structure.[21] He suggests that organizations move through five developmental phases (described later). Each phase is made up of two stages, which Greiner labels as evolution and revolution. The term *evolution* is used to describe prolonged periods of growth where no major upheaval occurs in organization practices. The term *revolution* is used to describe those predictable periods of substantial turmoil in organization life.

Greiner argues that each evolutionary stage causes its own revolution. For example, as a company evolves into a more centralized structure, managers begin making demands for decentralization. These demands may eventually grow to the point where a "revolutionary" change in structure will be required. Since each phase of development influences the following phase, knowing where an organization is located in its growth process can help managers anticipate and prepare for the next revolutionary crisis.

Greiner lists five key dimensions as essential for building a model of organizational growth and change:

1 *Age of the organization.* Organizational problems and the way management deals with them can vary significantly over periods of time. On the other hand, time may also tend to institutionalize management values. For example, over a period of years, such factors as management attitudes and employee behavior become more predictable and harder to change.

2 *Size of the organization.* As the organization grows in terms of number of employees and revenues, its problems and approaches to these problems change markedly. Problems of coordination and communication increase, new levels of management are likely to emerge, and tasks can become more interrelated.

3 *Stages of evolution.* After surviving a revolutionary crisis, Greiner suggests that most companies have from four to eight years of relative calm and steady growth.

[21] Larry E. Greiner, "Evolution and Revolution As Organizations Grow," *Harvard Business Review*, July-August 1972, pp. 37–46.

4 *Stages of revolution.* Companies do not always survive periods of turbulence in a healthy fashion. As Greiner points out, the annual *Fortune* 500 list of the most successful companies has shown many changes since the list was first compiled. Managers in a revolutionary period of their organizations must develop new patterns of management that will enable them to enter the next evolutionary period.

5 *Growth rate of the industry.* The speed at which the evolutionary and revolutionary stages arrive will depend to a large extent on the growth rate of the company's industry. Rapidly expanding markets, for instance, accelerate the need for change; new employees have to be hired, and plant facilities have to be expanded. The organization's structure must be adapted to meet these new conditions.

The Five Phases of Growth

As shown in Figure 13-4, Greiner describes five phases of evolution and revolution through which an organization passes. Table 13–2 on page 338 shows the organization practices that are characteristic of each phase.

Phase 1: Creativity. In its earliest stage, an organization's activities are usually centered around the development of products and markets. Top managers' energies are devoted to these ends, rather than to overall management of the company. Communication between managers and subordinates is frequent and informal. Organization members may work long hours for low pay in anticipation of future benefits.

As the company grows through its evolutionary stage, it becomes increasingly difficult to handle the rapidly swelling staff by the old informal methods. Leaders become more and more overworked and harried. A crisis in leadership leads to the first revolution. The founders, frequently incapable of or unwilling to change their managerial style, may have to step aside in favor of a strong manager who can refocus the organization's activities. Companies who do not solve these problems are likely to fail at this point.

Phase 2: Direction. Under a strong and capable business manager, a period of sustained growth may be anticipated. A functional organizational structure is introduced, separating production from marketing and leading to more specialization. Accounting systems, incentives, budgets, and work standards are adopted. Communication becomes more formal as management becomes more divided between upper-level policy makers and lower-level functional specialists.

These lower-level managers, however, become increasingly frustrated and demand more autonomy and room to exercise their own initiative. With upper-level managers reluctant to give up the responsibility, a new revolutionary period is at hand.

Phase 3: Delegation. The successful company will install an effective decentralization program in answer to the problems in Phase 2. Greater responsibility is given to lower-level managers. Top executives stay out of day-to-day operations, often concentrating on acquiring new units for the organization. Communication from the top is less frequent.

Decentralized managers are able to penetrate new markets, respond faster

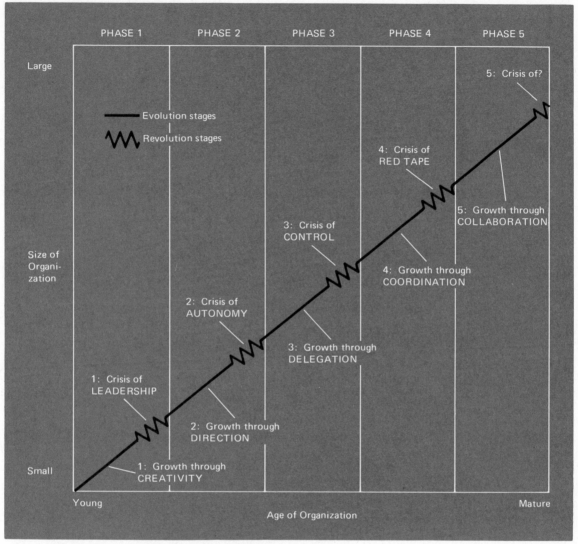

FIGURE 13-4 The Five Phases of Growth

Source: Larry E. Greiner, "Evolution and Revolution As Organizations Grow," *Harvard Business Review*, July-August 1972, p. 41. Copyright © 1972 by the President and Fellows of Harvard College; all rights reserved.

to customers, and develop new products. Eventually, however, top managers attempt to return to a centralized structure, because they sense a loss of control. This attempt usually fails and brings on the Phase 3 revolution. The company must find a new solution to its coordination problems.

Phase 4: Coordination. The evolutionary period in Phase 4 is characterized by the installation of formal systems for achieving coordination, under the

Category	Phase 1	Phase 2	Phase 3	Phase 4	Phase 5
Management Focus	Make and sell	Efficiency of operations	Expansion of market	Consolidation of organization	Problem solving and innovation
Organization Structure	Informal	Centralized and functional	Decentralized and geographical	Line-staff and product groups	Matrix of teams
Top Management Style	Individualistic and entrepreneurial	Directive	Delegative	Watchdog	Participative
Control System	Market results	Standards and cost centers	Reports and profit centers	Plans and investment centers	Mutual goal setting
Management Reward Emphasis	Ownership	Salary and merit increases	Individual bonus	Profit sharing and stock options	Team bonus

TABLE 13-2 Organization Practices during Evolution in the Five Phases of Growth

Source: Larry E. Greiner, "Evolution and Revolution As Organizations Grow," *Harvard Business Review*, July-August 1972, p. 45. Copyright © 1972 by the President and Fellows of Harvard College; all rights reserved.

initiation and administration of top management. Decentralized units are merged into product groups, each of which is expected to show a satisfactory return on its invested capital. Numerous staff personnel are added to initiate control and review programs for line managers.

These changes encourage more efficient use of company resources, and field managers learn to justify their actions more carefully to headquarters. Tension gradually builds, however, between line and staff and between headquarters and the field. In addition, a red-tape crisis occurs as rules and regulations begin to interfere with problem-solving activities.

Phase 5: Collaboration. In response to Phase 4 problems, a more flexible and behavioral approach to management becomes necessary. Groups and interdivisional teams are created to perform tasks and solve problems. Headquarters staff is reduced, and the remaining staff experts join field teams as consultants. Managers are trained in behavioral skills so that they can improve group performance.

Many companies today are in this stage of evolution. We can only speculate as to what the next revolutionary phase will bring. Greiner suggests that the revolution will center around the psychological saturation of employees who grow emotionally and physically exhausted by the intensity of teamwork and the heavy pressure for innovative solutions. There may also be pressure for labor representation on management boards, as already exists in many European countries.

In summary, Greiner's perspective suggests three major points that are of interest and importance to managers:

1. There is no single organizational structure that will be appropriate indefinitely. The organization *grows out* of a given structure, even though it was the correct one for the circumstances that prevailed when it was designed.

2. As an organization grows, periods of comfortable growth and smooth operation will alternate with periods of turbulence and frustration.

3. The redesign that solves the problems of one stage sets the groundwork for the problems of the next stage.

The implications of these points are that part of the task of managers is to recognize the life stage their organization is in so that they can better anticipate the types of problems with which they and their organization will be confronted.

Summary

Classical management writers tried to find the "one best way" of designing an organization. They tended to favor a bureaucratic, hierarchical structure that was based on legalized formal authority and that was characterized by task specialization. However, such a structure is relatively inflexible and neglects the human and environmental factors that can affect the organization.

Neoclassicists such as McGregor, Argyris, and Likert tried to improve the classical model. McGregor suggested that organizational structures based on Theory Y values would increase both the productivity and satisfaction of organization members. Argyris argued that there was a need for a more informal organizational design that would give members greater independence and power. Likert favored what he called a System 4 organizational structure, which would permit greater group participation in supervision and decision making. Although these approaches enriched the classical model, they also overlooked technological and environmental variables that can affect the organization, and they simplified the complexity of human motivation.

Contingency approaches to organizational design stress the need to fit an organization's structure to its strategy, technology, environment, and people. An organization's strategy affects its structure, because strategy will determine the types of tasks that employees will perform. Task-technology will affect structure, because some structures are more appropriate for a given technology and set of tasks than are other structures.

The external environment of an organization will also affect its structure, since there are specific structures that have been found to be most effective in particular environments. Mechanistic designs tend to be most appropriate in stable environments, while organic designs tend to be most appropriate in turbulent environments.

Organizational design will also be affected by the people in the organization, depending on such factors as their level of education and work involvement. Managers' attitudes and values will directly influence structure, since managers have the ultimate responsibility for designing the organization. The increasing demand of employees for greater job satisfaction and participation is also likely to have an effect on structure.

The interaction between an organization's structure, strategy, environment, technology, and people will determine the organization's climate or personality. This climate can affect the productivity and satisfaction of organization members. Factors that influence climate include economic conditions, leadership style and values, organizational policy and structure, and the characteristics of organization members.

Organizational design is a continuous process, because organizations (and environments) change over time. Greiner hypothesizes that organizations progress through five phases of growth: creativity, direction, delegation, coordination, and collaboration. Each phase begins with an evolutionary period of relatively calm growth and concludes with a turbulent revolutionary crisis that managers must solve if the organization is to continue its growth and evolution.

Review Questions

1. What are the advantages and disadvantages of the classical bureaucratic model of organizational design?
2. What is meant by "bureaupathology"? Can you think of any examples of bureaupathology? How do you think it can be resisted or overcome?
3. According to the neoclassical approach, what should be the objectives of an industrial organization? What are the limitations of this approach?
4. According to McGregor, how would an organization structure based on Theory Y assumptions differ from an organization based on Theory X assumptions?
5. According to Argyris, what are the consequences of the domination of the workplace by higher-level managers?
6. According to Likert, what are the differences between a System 1 and a System 4 organization? What is Likert's principle of supportive relationships?
7. How are strategy and structure interrelated?
8. What were the relationships Woodward found between the technological process a firm used and its structure?
9. What are stable, changing, and turbulent environments? Which organizational system is best suited for each environment?
10. What are differentiation and integration? Which types of organizations are likely to be highly differentiated?
11. How did Morse and Lorsch support and extend the work of Burns and Stalker?
12. How can the attitudes and values of managers and subordinates affect organizational structure?
13. What is organizational climate? Why is it important to understand the concept?
14. What are the major factors that affect organizational climate?
15. According to Greiner, what are the five developmental phases of organizations? What are the major problems of each phase? What problems do you think today's managers will face during the next developmental phase of their organizations?

CASE STUDY: PROBLEMS IN PLANT DEMOCRACY

General Foods Corporation had experienced productivity and morale problems among blue-collar workers in one of its traditionally organized pet food plants. To prevent these problems from arising in the new Topeka, Kansas plant it built in the early 1970s, the company organized the plant so that workers would perform many of the tasks formerly assigned to management—making job assignments, supervising, and even deciding pay raises. Work responsibility for each phase of the new plant's operations was assigned to worker teams who were under the direction of a "coach" rather than a foreman. Team members handled a variety of tasks, such as manufacturing, equipment maintenance, and quality control, thereby eliminating the need for many managerial personnel. Status differences between managers and workers were blurred—for example, managers no longer had reserved parking spaces.

The new system was regarded by GF management as a model for the future. Costs and turnover were lower than in traditionally organized plants, and some employees stated the plant was the best place they had ever worked. However, major problems soon developed at the plant. Many managers and technical personnel resented the system, because they felt their own authority and expertise were being challenged. Competition between teams and team leaders developed. Workers felt uncomfortable about deciding pay raises for their fellow workers. As a result of such pressures, some aspects of the plant system were changed: the number of management positions was increased, supervision was stiffened, and several plant functions were returned to managers.

When GF opened another plant in 1976 next to the Topeka plant, it did so without implementing some of the elements in the Topeka system. As a result, according to one observer, members of the Topeka plant came to feel that GF's management was not fully committed to the changes it had made at the Topeka plant. In addition, GF seemed reluctant to give Topeka employees bonuses as a reward for the system's financial success, because of possible resentment at other GF plants. Morale problems at the plant reportedly increased. Managers also seemed to have suffered, since they felt GF was unprepared to promote innovative managers who had been involved in and supported the system at Topeka. By 1977, the system still seemed productive and desirable but appeared to some observers to be deteriorating. One manager predicted, "The future of that plant is to conform to the company norm." (Reported in *Business Week,* March 28, 1977, pp. 78–82.)

Case Questions

1. What mistakes do you think GF management made in instituting the new system at Topeka? What would you have done?
2. Could the problems at the plant have been prevented or minimized? How?
3. Would the Topeka system have worked better in a smaller firm or in a nonfactory environment, such as an office? Why or why not?
4. What do you think GF management should do now?

Chapter 14

Managing Organizational Conflict and Creativity

Upon completing this chapter you should be able to:

1. Identify three views of organizational conflict.
2. Distinguish between functional and dysfunctional conflict.
3. Describe the sources of the various types of conflict.
4. Identify the consequences of organizational conflict.
5. Identify and describe methods for stimulating, reducing, and resolving conflict.
6. Describe the creative process in individuals and in organizations.
7. Explain how creativity can be stimulated and encouraged in organizations.

The vice president of a large midwestern oil refinery met one morning with senior managers in the engineering department. The purpose of the meeting was to draft a proposal for the creation of a committee to plan the company's plant operations and capital expenditures for the coming year. It was no secret that the proposal was the vice president's pet project.

To start the ball rolling, the vice president circulated a first draft of the proposal. Most of the ensuing discussion centered on the wording of the draft. One manager, however, was apparently unsure that there was a real need for such a committee. He kept raising a series of questions about why the committee was being created and how it would affect senior department head responsibilities. After a short while the vice president, visibly impatient with these questions, remarked, "I don't see why you're so worried about all this. I strongly believe the committee will benefit our company, and I expect reasonable people will have no problem adjusting to it." The manager hesitated, then quickly replied, "My objections could be resolved just by changing a few words in the draft." The vice president agreed to make these minor changes in the proposal, then looked up and said, "I take it there is common agreement now." No one dissented.

At first glance, it would seem that nothing unusual or harmful occurred at this meeting. Most members of the group obviously wanted to avoid clashing with a powerful superior. Where conflict threatened, the vice president moved quickly to make sure it would not arise. After the new committee had been in operation for several months, however, it became clear that the meeting's lone dissenting manager had raised valid questions. The committee took up a great deal of time, its decisions seemed mediocre and unpopular, and department heads resented the loss of power to plan their own operations and expenditures. By discouraging conflict at the meeting, the vice president lost the opportunity to determine the weaknesses in the proposal and to develop improvements.

THREE VIEWS OF CONFLICT

Stephen P. Robbins has identified three basic attitudes toward conflict in organizations: traditional, behavioral, and interactionist.[1]

The *traditional* view of conflict was that conflict was unnecessary and harmful. Early managers and management writers generally thought that the appearance of conflict was a clear signal that there was something wrong with the organization. They believed that conflict would develop only if managers failed to apply sound management principles in directing the organization or if managers failed to communicate to employees the common interests that bind management and employees together. If these failures were corrected, according to the traditional view, the organization should operate as a smoothly functioning integrated whole. For example, Frederick Taylor, whom we dis-

---

[1] Stephen P. Robbins, *Managing Organizational Conflict* (Englewood Cliffs, N.J.: Prentice-Hall, 1974).

cussed in Chapter 2, believed that if the principles of scientific management were applied, the age-old conflict between labor and management would disappear.

The *behavioral* view of conflict is that conflict is a frequent occurrence in organizational life. Organization members are human beings, after all, with needs and interests that can often clash. Managers of different departments, for example, may have conflicts over priorities and resource allocations. Subordinates may argue with superiors over whether or not work can be completed in the allotted time. Subordinates at the same level may disagree over the best way to complete an assigned task. The behavioral view does suggest that conflict can sometimes be functional because it can pinpoint problems and lead to better problem solutions. However, behavioralists also see conflict mainly as something harmful, to be resolved or eliminated once it arises.

Current thinking (the *interactionist* view) about conflict among most management writers and growing numbers of managers is that conflict in organizations is inevitable and even necessary, no matter how organizations are designed and operated. This view still suggests that much conflict is, in fact, dysfunctional: it can harm individuals and can impede the attainment of organizational goals. But some conflict can also be functional because it may make organizations more effective. For example, one functional aspect of conflict is that it leads to a search for solutions. Thus, it is often an instrument of organizational innovation and change. (See Table 14-1.)

From this perspective, the task of managers is not to suppress or resolve all conflict but to *manage* it, so as to minimize its harmful aspects and maximize its beneficial aspects. Such management may even include the *stimulation* of conflict in situations where its absence or suppression (as in our chapter opening example) may hamper the organization's effectiveness, creativity, or innovation. In this chapter, we will deal with such questions as: What types

TABLE 14-1 Old and Current Views of Conflict	Old View	Current View
	Conflict is avoidable.	Conflict is inevitable.
	Conflict is caused by management errors in designing and managing organizations or by trouble-makers.	Conflict arises from many causes, including organizational structure, unavoidable differences in goals, differences in perceptions and values of specialized personnel, and so on.
	Conflict disrupts the organization and prevents optimal performance.	Conflict contributes to *and* detracts from organizational performance in varying degrees.
	The task of management is to eliminate conflict.	The task of management is to manage the level of conflict and its resolution for optimal organizational performance.
	Optimal organizational performance requires the removal of conflict.	Optimal organizational performance requires a moderate level of conflict.

of conflict are functional or dysfunctional? How does conflict arise in organizations? How can conflict be stimulated, reduced, or resolved? And, finally, how can the creativity of individuals and organizations be stimulated by managers?

CONFLICT, COMPETITION, AND COOPERATION

The subject of conflict has been made difficult to understand because of the different definitions and conceptions of conflict that exist.[2] We will define the term in a way that will allow us to discuss the constructive, functional aspects of organizational conflict.

Organizational *conflict* is a disagreement between two or more organization members or groups arising from the fact that they must share scarce resources or work activities and/or from the fact that they have different status, goals, values, or perceptions. Organization members or subunits in disagreement attempt to have their own cause or point of view prevail over others.

Our definition is intentionally broad. It does not indicate how severe the disagreement is, in what manner the conflicting parties seek to prevail, how the conflict is managed, and what the outcomes of the conflict are. The answers to these questions will determine the extent to which conflict is functional or dysfunctional for the organization.

One of the many semantic difficulties that exists in the area of organizational conflict is distinguishing between conflict and competition. We can base the distinction between these concepts on the ability of one party to keep the other from attaining its goals. *Competition* exists when the goals of the parties involved are incompatible but the parties cannot interfere with each other. For example, two production teams may compete with each other to be the first to meet a quota. (Obviously, both teams cannot come in first.) If there is no opportunity to interfere with the other party's goal attainment, a competitive situation exists; however, if the opportunity for interference exists, and that opportunity is acted upon, then the situation is one of conflict.

Cooperation occurs when two or more parties work together to achieve mutual goals. It is possible for parties to experience conflict and cooperation at the same time. (In other words, the opposite of cooperation is not conflict but no cooperation.) For example, two parties may agree on goals but disagree strongly on how to attain those goals. In fact, when we speak of managing conflict, we mean that managers should try to find the most effective balance between conflict and cooperation.

Functional and
Dysfunctional
Conflict

Conflict, as we have defined it, is inherently neither functional nor dysfunctional. It simply has the potential for improving or impairing organizational performance, depending on how it is managed. For example, managers in a

[2] See, for example, Stuart M. Schmidt and Thomas A. Kochan, "Conflict: Toward Conceptual Clarity," *Administrative Science Quarterly*, Vol. 17, No. 3 (September 1972), pp. 359–370.

company may be in conflict over how the annual budget is to be divided among their departments. Properly handled, such conflict could lead to new sharing arrangements that might benefit the entire organization. For instance, more money might be allocated to the managers with the most productive departments. (In such a case, the managers who would receive less money than usual might feel that the conflict was dysfunctional; but, overall, the organization would benefit.) Other functional outcomes might be that (1) the managers find a way to use the money they receive more effectively; (2) they find a better way to cut down on expenses; or (3) they improve the whole unit's performance so that additional funds become available to all of them. It is also possible, however, that the outcome of the conflict will be dysfunctional. For example, cooperation between the managers may break down, making it difficult to coordinate the organization's activities.

The relationship between organizational conflict and performance is illustrated in Figure 14-1. As indicated, there is an optimal, highly functional level of conflict at which performance is at a maximum. When the level of conflict is too low, organizational performance stagnates. The organization changes too slowly to meet the new demands being made upon it, and its survival is threatened. When the level of conflict is too high, chaos and disruption also endanger the organization's chances for survival. We will be looking more closely at potentially functional and dysfunctional outcomes of conflict later in this chapter.

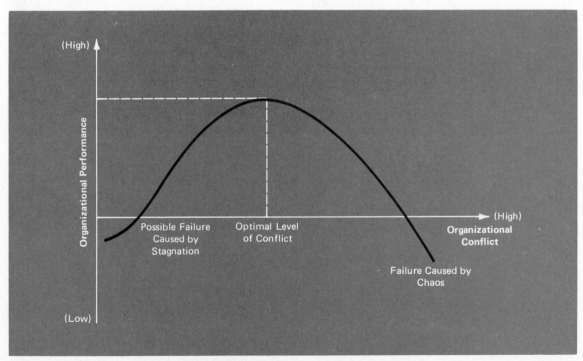

FIGURE 14-1   Organizational Conflict and Organizational Performance

Types of Conflict   There are five types of conflict possible in organizational life:

1   Conflict within the individual
2   Conflict between individuals
3   Conflict between individuals and groups
4   Conflict between groups in the same organization
5   Conflict between organizations

The fourth type, conflict between groups in the same organization, is the type of conflict with which we will be most concerned in this chapter. We will discuss the other types briefly below.

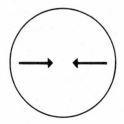

Conflict within the individual is a special case not covered by our original definition of conflict. It occurs when an individual is uncertain about what work he or she is expected to perform, when some work demands conflict with other demands, or when the individual is expected to do more than he or she feels capable of doing. We will discuss this type of conflict in Chapter 20. We mention it here because this type of conflict will often influence how an individual responds to other types of organizational conflict. For instance, an individual who is experiencing strong inner conflict may, because of stress, react to a routine organizational conflict in a disruptive, dysfunctional way.

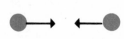

Conflict between individuals in the same organization is frequently seen as being caused by personality differences. More often, such conflicts erupt from role-related pressures (as between managers and subordinates) or from the manner in which people personalize conflict between groups. ("Your people are always dumping extra work on me," one supervisor will tell another. "I'm not ready for those parts, and I don't want you to have them piled up in my department.")

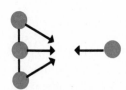

Conflict between individuals and groups frequently is related to the way individuals deal with the pressures for conformity imposed on them by their work group. (See Chapters 2 and 12.) For example, an individual may openly resent being punished by his or her work group for exceeding or falling behind the group's productivity norms.

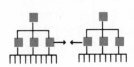

Conflict between organizations is considered an inherent and desirable form of conflict in our economic system, at least if the conflict is restricted to economic competition. Such conflict has been recognized to lead to the development of new products, technologies, and services, lower prices, and more efficient utilization of resources. Government laws and regulatory agencies exist to promote functional conflict (through antitrust legislation, for example) and to manage the dysfunctional aspects of such conflict, such as false advertising.

SOURCES OF ORGANIZATIONAL CONFLICT

The sources of organizational conflict discussed here are related most clearly to intergroup conflict. However, they also apply to some extent to conflict between individuals and between individuals and groups. The major sources of organizational conflict include: the need to share scarce resources; dif-

347

ferences in goals between organization units; the interdependence of work activities in the organization; and differences in values or perceptions among organization units.[3]

Shared Resources

If every unit in an organization had access to unlimited amounts of manpower, money, materials, equipment, and space, the problem of how to share these resources would hardly arise. The potential for conflict exists because these vital resources are limited. They must be allocated, so some groups inevitably will get less than they want or need. Lack of cooperation or even direct conflict can result as organization groups fight for the greatest possible share of available resources. Even if it were possible to allocate resources strictly according to the productivity of each group, managers would still argue about the relative importance of their group to the organization.

Differences in Goals

As we described in Chapters 10 and 13, organization subunits tend to become differentiated, or specialized, as they develop dissimilar goals, tasks, and problems. Such differentiation frequently leads to conflicts of interests or priorities, even when the overall goals of the organization are agreed upon. The sales department, for example, might want low prices to attract more customers, while the production department might want higher prices to allow it some leeway in meeting manufacturing costs. The purchasing department might want to order in large quantities to lower the unit cost, while the finance department might want to maintain low inventories to have capital available for investment. Because members of each department develop different goals and points of view, they often find it difficult to agree on programs of action.

Interdependence of Work Activities

Work interdependence exists when two or more organization units depend on each other in order to complete their respective tasks. In such a case, the potential for a high degree of conflict or friendliness exists, depending on how the situation is managed. Sometimes conflict arises when all the groups involved are given too much to do. Tension among the various group members will increase, and they may then accuse each other of shirking their responsibilities. Conflict may also flare up if the work is evenly distributed but the rewards are dissimilar. Potential for conflict is greatest, however, when one unit is unable to begin its work until the other unit completes its job. ("How can we meet our production quota if your people don't get those parts to us on time?")

Differences in Values or Perceptions

The differences in goals among the members of the various units in the organization are frequently accompanied by differences in attitudes, values, and perceptions that can also lead to conflict. For example, first-line supervisors who must get shipments out in a short period of time may be inclined to give in to

---

[3] See James G. March and Herbert A. Simon, *Organizations* (New York: Wiley, 1958); Richard E. Walton and John M. Dutton, "The Management of Interdepartmental Conflict," *Administrative Science Quarterly,* Vol. 14, No. 1 (March 1969), pp. 73–84; and Andrew J. DuBrin, *Fundamentals of Organizational Behavior* (New York: Pergamon Press, 1974).

© 1973 by Chicago Tribune-News Syndicate. Reprinted by permission.

union shop stewards on some issues rather than risk a slowdown. Higher-level managers, concerned with long-range management-union considerations, might want to avoid setting precedents on those issues and may try to restrict the flexibility of first-line supervisors. Younger managers may resent being given routine tasks, while older, higher-level managers may see such tasks as a necessary part of training. Members of the engineering department might value quality products, sophisticated design, and durability, while members of the manufacturing department might value simplicity of design and low manufacturing costs. Such incompatibility of values can lead to conflict. ("It would be too expensive to do it your way." "But we'd lose our reputation for quality if we did it your way.")

Other Sources of Conflict

Individual Styles. Some people enjoy conflict, debate, and argument; and when kept in proportion, mild forms of discord can stimulate organization members and improve their performance. A few individuals, however, manage their conflicts, debates, and arguments in such a way as to escalate them into battles that are quite disruptive. People who are highly authoritarian, for example, or low in self-esteem may anger their colleagues or overreact to provocation. In general, the potential for such intergroup conflict is highest when organization members differ markedly in such characteristics as work attitudes, age, and education.

Organizational Ambiguities and Communication Problems. Intergroup conflict can sometimes stem from ambiguously defined work responsibilities and unclear goals. One manager may try to expand the role of his or her subunit; this effort will usually trigger a defensive reaction from the other units involved. Also, if members of different groups know little about each other's jobs, they may unwittingly make unreasonable demands on each other. These demands may in turn trigger conflict.

Communication breakdowns are a common cause of intergroup conflict. For example, the same phrase may have different meanings to different groups; undefined use of that phrase may lead to harmful misunderstandings. In one case, the management of a large mining corporation decided to modernize its equipment. The union was told that "no employees would lose their jobs." On this basis, the union agreed to cooperate. A few months later, as some old functions were eliminated, a group of rock crushers were removed from their machines and transferred to warehouse jobs. The union struck. It had interpreted "job" to mean "task responsibility," while management had interpreted "job" to mean "employment." (See Chapter 18.)

CONSEQUENCES OF ORGANIZATIONAL CONFLICT

In a classic study of intergroup conflict, Muzafer Sherif and his colleagues divided a boys' camp into two groups, stimulated intense conflict between the groups, and observed the changes in group behavior that occurred.[4] The results of his study have since been confirmed by others, and it has become possible to show that groups that have been placed in a conflict situation will change in predictable ways. We will list and describe these changes here:

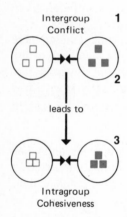

Intergroup Conflict

leads to

Intragroup Cohesiveness

1 *Rise in cohesion.* As a rule, group members in an intergroup conflict situation close ranks and put aside former disagreements. ("We've got to pull together!") The rise in cohesion stimulates greater efforts, but the pressures toward conformity that develop may discourage creativity and fresh approaches to problems.

2 *Rise of leaders.* When conflict becomes intense, individuals in the group who can most contribute to victory become more important. Those people who are more aggressive, able, or articulate than others are given increased power by the group. Rivalry for leadership decreases, and the group works harder to overcome "the enemy."

3 *Distortion of perception.* Group members' perceptions of their own group and the opposing groups become distorted. They regard their own skills and performance as superior to those of other groups. They also rationalize or dismiss their own shortcomings and emphasize those of competitors. ("You're all greedy," thinks the management representative at the outset of collective bargaining. "You're all cheap," thinks the union official.)

4 *Rise of negative stereotypes.* As each side belittles the other's ideas, the differences *between* the groups are seen as *greater* than they actually are, while the differences *within* each group are seen as *less* than they actually are.

5 *Selection of strong representatives.* To deal with the other side, each group selects representatives that it believes will not cave in to pressure from the other group. Each group will also perceive its own representatives in a highly positive way and opposing representatives in a negative way.

6 *Development of "blind spots."* Competitive struggle adversely affects the rivals' ability to grasp and think accurately about their respective positions. Strong group identification, heightened by fear of defeat or sellout, blinds both sides to the similarities in their proposals that, if recognized, could make a settlement possible.

[4] A short summary of the research is found in Muzafer Sherif, "Experiments in Group Conflict," *Scientific American,* November 1956, pp. 54–58. See also Muzafer Sherif and Carolyn W. Sherif, *Groups in Harmony and Tension* (New York: Octagon, 1966).

Once the conflict is over, there are different consequences for winners and losers. Leaders of the winning group normally strengthen their hold over the group. Growing smug and complacent, winners may rest on their laurels, resisting any change in their ways of doing things. Conversely, defeated groups tend to split into factions as old leaders are challenged by new aspirants to leadership. Losers also become more amenable to finding new ways of behaving and operating. For both winners and losers, the negative stereotypes engendered by win-lose conflict can become so severe as to make future intergroup cooperation extremely difficult to attain.[5]

Conflict of a less intense kind can have a more constructive impact. New, more effective leaders may make themselves known. Modified goals may help the organization adjust to change. And conflict may be institutionalized so that disagreements can be aired without damaging the organization. In some organizations, for example, department heads freely air their differences in committee meetings but abide by committee decisions once they are made.

Functional and Dysfunctional Consequences

Three factors determine whether or not the outcome of a given dispute will be, on balance, functional or dysfunctional: the level of conflict, the organizational structure and climate, and the way in which the conflict is managed. We will discuss the first two factors below; the last factor — which is the most important from our point of view — is the subject of the next section.

The Level of Conflict. Moderate levels of conflict have far greater potential for desirable outcomes than high levels. With moderate conflict, the rival groups will more likely learn to interact in constructive, problem-solving ways. As the level of conflict rises, however, so does the temptation to engage in destructive acts directed toward the rival group. David Mechanic describes a case in a mental hospital where ward attendants agreed to take on some of the administrative duties of the ward physicians in exchange for inclusion in the decision-making machinery.[6] When the physicians reneged on their part of the agreement, conflict escalated to the point where attendants disobeyed orders and deliberately withheld information essential to the physicians. Such high levels of conflict are almost always destructive to the organization.

Organizational Structure and Climate. In general, the more rigid the structure and climate of the organization, the less beneficial conflict is likely to be. Conflict can call attention to the problem areas of an organization and can lead to better ways of getting things done. (Figure 14-2 on next page is a model of how conflict can improve organizational performance.) However, if an organization

---

[5] See, for example, Robert R. Blake and Jane S. Mouton, "Reactions to Intergroup Conflict Under Win-Lose Conditions," *Management Science,* Vol. 7, No. 4 (July 1961), pp. 420–435, and Robert R. Blake, Herbert A. Shepherd, and Jane S. Mouton, *Managing Intergroup Conflict in Industry* (Houston: Gulf Publishing, 1964).

[6] David Mechanic, "Sources of Power of Lower Participants in Complex Organizations," *Administrative Science Quarterly,* Vol. 7, No. 3 (December 1962), pp. 349–364.

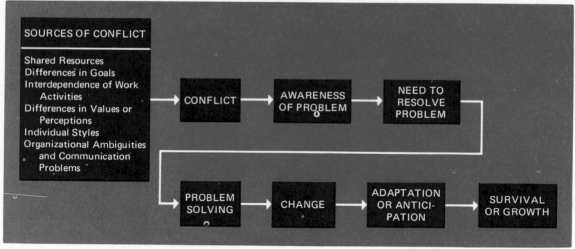

FIGURE 14-2 A Model of Functional Conflict

rigidly resists change, the conflict situations may never be relieved. Tensions will continue to mount, and each new conflict will split organization subunits further apart.

Unresolved conflict can also adversely affect informally structured organizations, where subunits depend a great deal on each other for information (rather than receiving most of their information from higher up). In a conflict situation, communication between subunits can break down, leaving each subunit unable to reach soundly based decisions.[7]

METHODS FOR MANAGING CONFLICT

In this section, we will discuss three forms of conflict management: (1) stimulating conflict in units or organizations whose performance is lagging because the level of conflict is too low; (2) reducing or suppressing conflict when its level is too high or counterproductive; and (3) resolving conflict.

Conflict Stimulation Methods   Most of us have been taught since childhood to avoid conflict or even disagreement. We have all heard statements like: "Stop fighting!" "It's better to turn the other cheek," or "Why don't you be nice and give in?" However, the tendency in our culture to paper over dissension is not always productive, as Elise Boulding has demonstrated.[8] In an experiment, Boulding formed a series

---

[7] See Joseph A. Litterer, "Conflict in Organization: A Re-examination," *Academy of Management Journal,* Vol. 9, No. 3 (September 1966), pp. 178–186, and William G. Scott and Terence R. Mitchell, *Organization Theory,* 3rd ed. (Homewood, Ill.: Irwin, 1976), Chapter 11.

[8] Elise Boulding, "Further Reflections on Conflict Management," in Robert L. Kahn and Elise Boulding, eds., *Power and Conflict in Organizations* (New York: Basic Books, 1964), pp. 146–150.

of groups to tackle a problem. Some groups contained a planted member prepared to challenge the majority view, some groups did not. Without fail, those groups that harbored a conflict-stimulator analyzed the problem more perceptively and came up with better solutions than the others. Yet, when the groups were instructed to drop one member, every group that had a planted dissident chose that dissident to be dropped, despite the clear evidence that the conflict was beneficial. Such resistance to conflict, in themselves and in others, is one of the obstacles that managers have to overcome in stimulating productive conflict.

Situations in which conflict is too low are those where people are afraid to "rock the boat." Rather than trying to find new and better ways of getting things done, group members passively accept things the way they are. Events, behavior, and information that could stir up people to do a better job are ignored; group members tolerate each other's weaknesses and lack of performance. Managers of such groups who become alarmed that their units seem to be drifting often find that stimulating competition and conflict can have a galvanizing effect.

Before offering some conflict stimulation suggestions, we should note that the attitude of top managers toward conflict is of critical importance in its safe encouragement and control. Openly stating that conflict is desirable—"I'd like to see you two take the time to fight these things out between yourselves until you reach a decision you like, rather than just smoothing things over"—will encourage organization members to surface disagreements they might otherwise suppress. Openly stating the rules of conflict—"If you're completely deadlocked, call in a third party for help before you come to me"—will help keep conflict to functional levels.

Conflict stimulation methods include:[9]

1. *Bringing in outsiders.* A frequently used method of "shaking up" a stagnant unit or organization is to bring in people whose backgrounds, values, and managerial styles vary significantly from the prevalent norms. Edmund G. Brown, Jr., governor of California, resorted to this method in 1977 when he put consumer representatives on state regulatory boards, which had long been dominated by individuals closely connected to the industries being regulated.

2. *Going against the book.* Excluding individuals or groups from communication to which they are officially entitled, or adding new groups to the information network, may redistribute power in the organization and thus stimulate conflict. For example, a nursing home administrator who was concerned about the passivity of patients provided them with information about their condition. They then felt more confident about disagreeing with their doctors about their treatment and took a more active role in improving their own health.

3. *Restructuring the organization.* Breaking up old work teams and departments and reforming them so that they have new members or responsibili-

[9] Robbins, *Managing Organizational Conflict,* Chapter 9.

ties will create a period of uncertainty and readjustment. Conflict that arises during this period may lead to improved methods of operation as members try to find ways to adjust to their new circumstances. Fostering a more open climate may also lead to conflict as organization members are encouraged to air their views.

4. *Encouraging competition.* Offering bonuses, incentive pay, and citations for outstanding performance will foster competition. If competition is maintained at a high level, it may lead to productive conflict as one group struggles hard to outdo the other.

5. *Selecting appropriate managers.* Some work groups may be overly passive because their managers are too authoritarian and do not allow opposing viewpoints to be raised. Other groups may need an active manager to shake them out of their lethargy. Finding the right manager for the particular group can encourage useful conflict where none exists.

Conflict
Reduction
Methods

Most managers are more frequently and intensely concerned with reducing rather than stimulating conflict. In this section, we will discuss methods that reduce the antagonistic feelings associated with conflict. Thus, these methods manage the level of conflict by "cooling things down." However, they do not normally deal with the basic issues that gave rise to the original conflict.[10]

Sherif and his colleagues, in the study we mentioned earlier, stimulated conflict at a boys' camp by assigning boys to separate groups and encouraging competition and rivalry between groups. When the conflict had become very intense and disruptive, they experimented with a variety of ways of restoring harmony. First, they tried three methods that proved ineffective:

1. They provided each group with favorable information about the other group. However, this information was so at odds with the negative impressions induced by the conflict that the boys rejected it.

2. They increased pleasant social contacts between the groups by having them eat together and watch movies together, for example. But friction worsened as the rival group members jostled and shoved each other and called each other names.

3. They asked the group leaders to negotiate and provide their respective groups with favorable information about the other. But the leaders felt they might be dethroned if they tried to reconcile their differences. Even in adult intergroup conflict, agreements worked out between representatives can be limited by group members' suspicions that the agreements are "sellouts."

Two methods that were tried did work. In the first effective method, the researchers substituted superordinate (superior) goals that both groups accepted for the competitive goals that had kept them apart. For example, the boys were told the camp could "not afford" to rent a movie all had asked for. Both groups then joined in a fund-raising drive to pay for the rental. This joint effort effectively lowered the level of conflict.

---

[10] See Bertram H. Raven and Jeffrey Z. Rubin, *Social Psychology: People in Groups* (New York: Wiley, 1976), Chapter 10.

The second effective method was to unite the group to meet a common "threat" or "enemy." For example, a camp truck was rigged to break down on the way to a campout. Neither group could tow the truck in for repairs on its own; working together, they were able to do so. Such common acts eventually created mutual cooperation and friendship between group members.

In the boys' camp study, these methods were successful in restoring harmonious relations between the two groups because the original sources of conflict had been artificially created by the researchers. Thus, the combination of diverting the boys' attention from their disagreements and providing them with shared experiences of successful cooperation were effective means of removing conflict. In normal situations, however, where conflict is not artificially created, diverting the groups' attention is likely to be more difficult to accomplish. Furthermore, the unresolved conflict will remain once the diversions have been exhausted. For these reasons, conflict reduction methods may be unsatisfying ways of dealing with conflict in organizations.

Conflict Resolution Methods

There are three types of conflict resolution methods: dominance or suppression, compromise, and integrative problem solving.[11] These methods differ very substantially in the extent to which they yield effective and creative solutions to conflict. They also differ in the extent to which they leave parties in the conflict able to deal with future conflict situations.

Our discussion of these methods focuses on the actions that managers can take to deal directly with the conflicting parties. Other possible methods for resolving conflict include changes in organizational structure—so that, for example, conflicting members or units are separated or a grievance agency is set up. In addition, some of the coordinating mechanisms we discussed in Chapter 10—such as liaison individuals and committees—can also be used to resolve conflict.

Dominance and Suppression. Dominance and suppression methods usually have two things in common: (1) They repress conflict, rather than settle it, by forcing it underground; and (2) they create a win-lose situation in which the loser, who is usually forced to give way to higher authority, winds up disappointed and hostile. Suppression and dominance can manifest themselves in the following ways:

Forcing. When the person in authority says in effect, "Cut it out—I'm the boss and you've got to do it my way," argument is effectively snuffed out. Such autocratic suppression will often lead to indirect but nonetheless destructive expression of conflict, such as malicious obedience. Once, for example, when a supervisor suggested that an assignment be delayed until a performance audit could pinpoint suspected deficiencies, the production manager snapped: "Keep your nose out of things until I tell you otherwise." A few mornings later

---

[11] See Robert R. Blake and Jane S. Mouton, *The Managerial Grid* (Houston: Gulf Publishing, 1964), and Paul R. Lawrence and Jay W. Lorsch, *Organization and Environment* (Homewood, Ill.: Irwin, 1967).

a cutting machine broke down in the supervisor's unit. Machine and operator stayed idle the entire day before the production manager found out about it. "Why didn't you call the maintenance crew?" the manager asked the supervisor. "You told me to keep my nose out of things until I heard from you," the subordinate shot back. Malicious obedience is merely one of many forms of conflict that can fester where conflict suppression is the rule.

Smoothing. Smoothing is a more diplomatic way of suppressing conflict. Instead of forcing acceptance of a solution, the manager tries to talk one side into giving in. Where the manager has more information than the other parties and is simply making a reasonable suggestion, this method can be effective. But if the manager is simply favoring one side, the losing side is likely to feel resentful.

Avoidance. If quarreling groups come to a manager for a decision, but the manager avoids taking a position, all the groups involved are likely to go away dissatisfied. Pretending one is unaware that conflict exists is a frequent form of avoidance. Another form is refusal to deal with conflict once it has surfaced.

Majority rule. Trying to resolve group conflict by a majority vote can be effective if members regard the procedure as fair. But if one voting bloc consistently outvotes the other, the losing side will feel dominated or suppressed.

Compromise. Through compromise, managers try to resolve conflict by finding a middle ground between two or more positions. Unlike suppression, this method has the advantage that conflicting parties are less likely to feel latent hostility over the compromise. From an organizational point of view, however, compromise is a weak conflict resolution method because it will not usually lead to a solution that will best help the organization achieve its goals. Instead, the solution reached will simply be the one that both parties in the conflict can live with.

Special forms of compromise include *separation,* in which opposing parties are kept apart until they agree to a solution; *arbitration,* in which conflicting parties submit to the judgment of a third party (usually the manager); *resort to rules,* in which the deadlocked rivals agree to "go by the book" and let the rules decide the conflict outcome; and *bribing,* in which one party accepts some compensation in exchange for ending the conflict. None of these methods is very likely to leave all parties to the conflict fully satisfied nor to yield creative solutions.

Integrative Problem Solving. With this method, intergroup conflict is converted into a joint problem-solving situation that can be dealt with through problem-solving techniques. Parties to the conflict together try to solve the problem that has arisen between them. Instead of suppressing conflict or trying to find a compromise, the parties openly try to find a solution they all will want to accept. Managers who impart to their subordinates the feeling that all members and groups in the organization are working together for a common goal, who encourage the free exchange of ideas, and who stress the benefits of finding the optimum solution in a conflict situation are more likely to achieve integrative solutions.

There are three types of integrative conflict resolution methods: consensus, confrontation, and the use of superordinate goals.

In *consensus,* the conflicting parties meet together to find the best solution to their problem, rather than trying to achieve a victory for either side. As we discussed in Chapter 12, group consensus will often yield a more effective solution than a solution offered by any one individual. (See, for example, the "Lost on the Moon" discussion in that chapter.)

In the technique of *confrontation,* the opposing parties air their respective views directly to each other. The reasons for the conflict are examined, and methods of resolving it are sought. With skilled leadership and a willingness to accept the associated stress by all sides, a rational solution to the conflict can frequently be found.

We noted earlier that appeal to a higher-level goal can be an effective conflict reduction method if it distracts the attention of the parties in conflict from their separate and competing goals. The establishment of *superordinate goals* can also be a conflict *resolution* method if the higher-level goal that is mutually agreed upon incorporates the conflicting parties' lower-level goals. For example, two academic departments in a university had been engaged in a lengthy and destructive conflict over their relative shares of grants from a university research fund. The animosity continued for a number of years until a group of young faculty members from each department submitted a joint proposal for a large grant from a government agency. When the proposal was accepted, the two departments started to turn more of their attention to ways of increasing grants from outside agencies and reduced their competition for the university research funds.

LINE AND STAFF CONFLICT

One of the most common forms of organizational conflict is the conflict between line and staff members. Because of its frequency, and because of the importance of achieving effective line-staff collaboration in modern organizations, we will discuss this type of conflict here.

The root of the conflict lies in the fact that line and staff members view each other and their role in the organization from different viewpoints.[12] Line and staff members, like members of the other differentiated units in the organization, have different time horizons, goals, interpersonal orientations, and approaches to problems. (See Chapter 10 for Lawrence and Lorsch's discussion of differentiation.) These differences enable line and staff members to accomplish their respective tasks effectively; but the differences also increase the likelihood of conflict between them.

[12] Louis A. Allen, "The Line-Staff Relationship," *Management Record,* Vol. 17, No. 9 (September 1955), pp. 346–349 ff.

The View from the Line

Line members frequently see staff members as having four major failings:

1. *Staff members overstep their authority.* Because line managers bear ultimate responsibility for results, they tend to resent staff intrusion on their prerogatives. (A typical complaint: "The efficiency experts are standing over the shoulders of my people and telling my people what to do. They're undermining my authority.")

2. *Staff members do not give sound advice.* Staff members may be cut off from the day-to-day operational realities that line members confront. Their suggestions may therefore lack applicability. ("Their ideas might sound good in their ivory-tower offices, but what do they know about the real problems in the plant or in the field?") Some staff members contribute to this stereotype by recommending ideas that worked well in other organizations but would not be suitable for their own organization.

3. *Staff members steal credit from line members.* "When things go wrong," say the line managers, "we get the blame. But when things go right, they take the bows." Staff members can take advantage of their position, because they frequently have greater access to the top managers than do line members.

4. *Staff members have narrow perspectives.* Staff members tend to be specialists—industrial engineers, labor relations experts, and so on. As such, say line managers, they have a limited perspective and fail to relate their suggestions to the organization's overall needs and goals.

The View from the Staff

Staff members have analogous complaints about line members. They see line members as having three major failings:

1. *Line managers do not use staff properly.* Line managers resist calling in a staff expert, because they like to retain authority over their subunit or because they fear admitting openly that they need help. As a result, staff may be called in only when the situation has completely deteriorated. ("I wouldn't have to work so hard," says the labor relations director, "if the plant manager had called me in *before* relations with the union had gotten so messed up.")

2. *Line managers resist new ideas.* Staff members are usually the first to be aware of useful innovations in their area of expertise. Line managers, however, resist making changes. They are therefore seen by staff members as overly cautious and rigid.

3. *Line managers give staff members too little authority.* Staff members often feel that they have the best solutions to problems in their specialty. They therefore resent it when their suggestions are not supported and implemented by line managers.

Other Line-Staff Differences

Differences in style and other characteristics often exacerbate conflicts between line and staff. For example, Melville Dalton found that staff members tend to be younger, better educated, more ambitious, more individualistic, and more concerned with their dress than line members.[13] Alvin W. Gouldner

---

[13] Melville Dalton, "Conflicts between Staff and Line Managerial Officers," *American Sociological Review,* Vol. 15, No. 3 (June 1950), pp. 342–351.

has classified organization personnel in terms of what he called "cosmo-politans" and "locals."[14] His two categories correspond roughly to the "staff" and "line" distinction. "Cosmopolitan" staff members are committed to their work for its intrinsic qualities; they are likely to feel closer to specialists in similar activities outside the organization than to other members of their own organization. "Local" line members identify themselves and their career aspirations more closely with their organizations and are less committed to specialized job skills and outside reference groups. Such differences may be seen as "lack of loyalty" by line members and "provincialism" by staff members.

Reducing Line-Staff Conflict

Edward C. Schleh and other management writers have suggested ways in which the dysfunctional aspects of line-staff conflict can be reduced:[15]

Line and staff responsibilities should be clearly spelled out. In general, line members should remain responsible for the operating decisions of the organiza-tion; in other words, they should be free to accept, modify, or reject staff recommendations. On the other hand, staff members should be free to give advice when they feel it is needed—not only when line members request it.

Integrate staff and line activities. Staff suggestions would be more real-istically based if staff members consulted line members early in the process of developing their suggestions. Such staff-line consultation would also make line members more willing to implement staff ideas.

Educate line to use staff properly. Line managers will make more effective use of staff expertise when they know what the specialist can do for them. Schleh suggests that staff members describe their functions to line conference groups or brief line members individually.

Hold staff accountable for results. Line members would be more amena-ble to staff suggestions if staff members were held liable for the failure of those suggestions. Accountability would also increase the likelihood that staff members would develop their suggestions more carefully.

MANAGING ORGANIZATIONAL CREATIVITY

Creativity has become an important part of organizational life. Like functional conflict, creativity enables the organization to find new and better ways of doing things. And in this age of tough competition, resource scarcity, and high labor and equipment costs, anything that leads to more efficient and effective operations increases an organization's chances to survive and succeed. Crea-tivity also enables the organization to anticipate change. Such an ability has

---

[14] Alvin W. Gouldner, "Cosmopolitans and Locals: Toward an Analysis of Latent Social Roles—I," *Administrative Science Quarterly,* Vol. 2, No. 3 (December 1957), pp. 281–306.

[15] Edward C. Schleh, "Using Central Staff to Boost Line Initiative," *Management Review,* Vol. 65, No. 5 (May 1976), pp. 17–23. See also Allen, "The Line-Staff Relationship," pp. 375–376.

become extremely significant as new technologies, products, and methods of operation make old ones obsolete.

Like functional conflict, creativity flourishes best in a dynamic, tolerant atmosphere. Creative people can be bothersome; they question how things are done, they upset routine, and their ideas require checking and shaping. To encourage and manage creativity, managers must have a working knowledge of the creative process, know how to select people with creative ability and how to stimulate creative behavior, and be able to generate an organizational climate in which creativity can be nurtured.

Creativity and Innovation

Some management writers distinguish between creativity and innovation. They define *creativity* as the generation of a new idea and *innovation* as the translation of such an idea into a new product, service, or method of production. In Lawrence B. Mohr's words, creativity implies "bringing something new into being; innovation implies bringing something new into use."[16]

Such a distinction can be a meaningful one in organizational life. The skills required to generate new ideas are not the same as those required to make these ideas a reality. To make full use of its ideas, the organization may need both creative and innovative personnel. In addition, creativity alone contributes little or nothing to organizational effectiveness unless the creative ideas can in some way be used or implemented. Thus, in organizations, the creative process must include both creative and innovative elements: A new idea must indeed be created, but it must also be capable of implementation and actually implemented before the organization will benefit from it.

Steps in the Creative Process

In this section we will describe the creative process as it takes place within the individual. (See also the box "Precepts for Creative Problem Solving" in Chapter 7.) In later sections, we will describe the process by which managers manage the creativity of individuals and groups.

It is convenient to divide the creative process into the following five steps:[17]

1 *Sensing.* The individual selects a problem to work on or, more likely, becomes aware that a problem or disturbance exists. ("I'm really getting bogged down in these monthly reports. Isn't there a better way to do this?")

2 *Immersion or preparation.* Having sensed or selected the problem, the individual "wallows" in it—recalling and collecting information that seems relevant and dreaming up hypotheses without evaluating them. ("I seem to recall that other companies do this differently. Perhaps they only require bimonthly reports.")

---

[16] Lawrence B. Mohr, "Determinants of Innovation in Organizations," *American Political Science Review,* Vol. 63, No. 1 (1969), p. 112. See also Donald W. MacKimmon, "The Nature and Nurture of Creative Talent," *American Psychologist,* Vol. 17, No. 7 (July 1962), pp. 484–495.

[17] See John F. Mee, "The Creative Thinking Process," *Indiana Business Review,* Vol. 31, No. 2 (February 1956), pp. 4–9, and Frederic D. Randall, "Stimulate Your Executives to Think Creatively," *Harvard Business Review,* July-August 1955, pp. 121–128.

3 *Incubation or gestation.* After assembling the available information, the individual relaxes and lets his or her subconscious mull over the material. This is a little-understood but big step in the creative process. The individual will often appear to be idle or daydreaming during this period, but his or her subconscious is in fact trying to arrange the facts into a new pattern.

4 *Insight or illumination.* Often when least expected—while eating, falling asleep, or walking—the new, integrative idea will flash into the individual's mind. ("A preprinted checklist! That way I can give my boss the right information without taking up all my time.") Such inspirations must be recorded quickly, because the conscious mind will usually forget them.

5 *Verification and application.* The individual sets out to prove by logic or experiment that the idea can solve the problem and can be implemented. Tenacity may be required at this point, since new ideas may be initially rejected as fallacious and impractical, only to be vindicated later on.

Individual Creativity

Individuals differ in their ability to be creative. Highly creative people, for example, tend to be more original than less creative people. If asked to suggest possible uses for automobile tires, noncreative people might say "buoys" and "tree swings"; creative people might say such things as "eyeglass frames for an elephant" or "halos for big robots." Creative people also tend to be more flexible than noncreative people—they are able and willing to shift from one approach to another when tackling a problem. They prefer complexity to simplicity and tend to be more independent than less creative people, sticking to their guns stubbornly when their ideas are challenged. Creative people also question authority quite readily and are apt to disobey orders that make no sense to them. Motivated more by an interesting problem than by material reward, they will work long and hard on something that intrigues them.[18]

There are a number of tests that do a fairly good job of measuring creative ability.[19] These tests offer organizations some guidance for selecting individuals who will be most effective in situations that require creativity—new product development, research, and advertising, for example. However, these tests are of limited value to an organization because they are much less successful in predicting creative *behavior*. If a test establishes a person's ability to write, but that person never puts a word on paper, he or she is of no value as a writer. People who have modest creative ability that they utilize to the fullest would contribute more to an organization than highly creative people who never use their talent.

Because there are practical difficulties associated with administering tests for creativity, and because it is hard to predict which people will actually behave in a creative way, it is generally more practical for managers to concentrate their main efforts on helping people utilize whatever creative potential

[18] Gary A. Steiner, ed., *The Creative Organization* (Chicago: University of Chicago Press, 1965).

[19] See, for example, J. P. Guilford, "Creativity: Its Measurement and Development," in Sidney J. Parnes and Harold F. Harding, eds., *A Source Book for Creative Thinking* (New York: Scribner's, 1962), pp. 151–168.

they possess, rather than attempting to select especially creative people. For specific fields that require a high degree of creativity—such as advertising or most types of R&D work—trying to select creative people might still be useful. But for improving the creativity and innovation of the organization as a whole, it is more practical to manage people so that their creative *behavior* is increased, regardless of their initial creative *ability*.

Stimulating
Individual and
Group Creativity

The methods of stimulating creativity that we will discuss in this section— brainstorming, synectics, and creative decision making—are designed to be used in groups. However, the principles that underlie these methods can also help individuals improve their creativity.[20]

Brainstorming. We discussed brainstorming in Chapter 8, in connection with forecasting. However, the technique is used more frequently for developing creative ideas for new products, for advertising campaigns, and for possible solutions to various types of complex problems.

Brainstorming attempts to prevent judgment or criticism from inhibiting the free flow of ideas. Group members are assembled, presented with the problem, and encouraged to produce as many ideas or solutions as they can. No evaluation is permitted. Even impractical suggestions are well received and recorded, since they may stimulate more useful recommendations or may in the end prove workable. Because brainstorming creates a freewheeling, uninhibited climate, participants usually can produce a wide range of ideas.

Donald W. Taylor, Paul C. Berry, and Clifford H. Block compared the effectiveness of groups and individuals who used the brainstorming technique.[21] (In individual brainstorming, the individual produces ideas without criticizing or evaluating them.) They found that individuals working alone usually developed more and better ideas than the same number of people working together in a group. The authors concluded that, despite the free atmosphere of brainstorming sessions, group members still inhibit one another's creativity and thus limit the range of ideas that are produced.

The fact that brainstorming group sessions, as opposed to individual sessions, are still used in organizations may be because managers are unaware of studies like those of Taylor and his colleagues. It may also be easier for managers to arrange group sessions, which generally are stimulating for the participants, than to induce individuals to brainstorm on their own.

Synectics (The Gordon Technique). This technique was developed by William J. Gordon when he was a member of Arthur D. Little, Inc., a well-known

---

[20] See Charles S. Whiting, "Operational Techniques of Creative Thinking," *Advanced Management,* Vol. 20, No. 10 (October 1955), pp. 24–30.

[21] Donald W. Taylor, Paul C. Berry, and Clifford H. Block, "Does Group Participation When Using Brainstorming Facilitate or Inhibit Creative Thinking?" *Administrative Science Quarterly,* Vol. 3, No. 1 (June 1958), pp. 23–47.

research and consulting firm.[22] It was designed to help the firm invent new products for its clients. (The company has developed many consumer and industrial products, such as new breakfast cereals, packaging materials, and construction methods, for its clients.) While the object of a brainstorming session is to generate as many ideas as possible, synectics aims for only one radically new idea focused on a specific problem area.

In synectics, only the group leader knows the exact nature of the problem. In this way quick, easy solutions are avoided, and participants do not have a chance to become overly enamored of their own ideas. Group discussion is organized around a subject that is related to the problem but that does not reveal what the problem actually is. For example, if the problem is to produce a new toy, the leader might suggest play or enjoyment as the discussion area. The session might open with give-and-take on the meaning of play and what types of play lead to the greatest enjoyment. Eventually, under the cautious direction of the leader, the discussion might focus on what kinds of new toys children would find most enjoyable.

The Group Process for Creative Decision Making. According to Andre L. Delbecq, groups can be organized for three different decision-making situations: for making routine decisions, for compromise or negotiated decisions, or for creative decisions.[23] Each type of group would be organized and managed in a different way.

Creative group decision making is appropriate when there is no apparent or agreed-upon method of solving a problem. According to Delbecq, creative decision groups should be composed of competent personnel from a variety of backgrounds and should be directed by a leader who can stimulate creative behavior. The group problem-solving process is somewhat akin to brainstorming in that discussion is spontaneous, all group members participate, and the evaluation of ideas is suspended at the beginning of the session so as not to discourage suggestions. The main difference is that brainstorming *avoids* decision making, whereas reaching a decision is the aim of the creative decision-making group. The creativity of group members is fostered by a permissive atmosphere in which originality, unusual ideas, and even eccentricity are encouraged. (See box on next page.)

Organizational Creativity and Innovation

Just as individuals differ in their ability to translate their talents into creative, innovative behavior, so do organizations differ in their ability to translate the talents of their members into new products, processes, or services. To enable their organization to use creative talent most effectively, managers need to

[22] See William J. Gordon, *Synectics* (New York: Collier Books, 1968), and George Prince, *The Practice of Creativity* (New York: Harper & Row, 1970).

[23] Andre L. Delbecq, "The Management of Decision-Making within the Firm: Three Strategies for Three Types of Decision-Making," *Academy of Management Journal,* Vol. 10, No. 4 (December 1967), pp. 334–335.

Creative Group Decision Making	
Group Structure:	The group is composed of heterogeneous, generally competent personnel who bring to bear on the problem diverse frames of reference, representing channels to each relevant body of knowledge (including contact with outside resource personnel who offer expertise not encompassed by the organization), with a leader who facilitates creative (heuristic) processes.
Group Roles:	Behavior is characterized by each individual exploring with the entire group all ideas (no matter how intuitively and roughly formed) that bear on the problem.
Group Processes:	The problem-solving process is characterized by: —Spontaneous communication between members (not focused in the leader). —Full participation from each member. —Separation of idea generation from idea evaluation. —Separation of problem definition from generation of solution strategies. —Shifting of roles, so that interaction which mediates problem solving (particularly search activities and clarification by means of constant questioning directed both to individual members and the whole group) is not the sole responsibility of the leader. —Suspension of judgment and avoidance of early concern with solutions, so that emphasis is on analysis and exploration, rather than on early solution commitment.
Group Style:	The social-emotional tone of the group is characterized by: —A relaxed, nonstressful environment. —Ego-supportive interaction, where open give-and-take between members is at the same time courteous. —Behavior that is motivated by interest in the problem, rather than concern with short-run payoff. —Absence of penalties attached to any espoused idea or position.
Group Norms:	—Are supportive of originality and unusual ideas, and allow for eccentricity. —Seek behavior that separates source from content in evaluating information and ideas. —Stress a nonauthoritarian view, with a relativistic view of life and independence of judgment. —Support humor and undisciplined exploration of viewpoints. —Seek openness in communication, where mature, self-confident individuals offer "crude" ideas to the group for mutual exploration without threat to the individual for "exposing" himself. —Deliberately avoid credence to short-run results, or short-run decisiveness. —Seek consensus, but accept majority rule when consensus is unobtainable.

Source: Andre L. Delbecq, "The Management of Decision-Making within the Firm: Three Strategies for Three Types of Decision-Making," *Academy of Management Journal*, Vol. 10, No. 4 (December 1967), pp. 334–335. Used by permission.

CREATIVITY

New Idea

INNOVATION

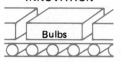

New Product

be aware of the process of innovation in organizations and to take steps to encourage this process. (See Table 14-2 on next page for an analysis of the characteristics of the creative individual and organization.)

The organizational creative process involves three steps: idea generation, problem solving or idea development, and implementation.[24]

Generation of Ideas. The generation of ideas in an organization depends first and foremost on the flow of people and information between the firm and its environment. For example, the vast majority of technological innovations have been made in response to conditions in the marketplace. If organization managers are unaware that there is potential demand for a new product, or that there is dissatisfaction with already existing products, they are less likely than other managers to seek innovations. It is therefore important for managers to remain in close touch with their organization's environment.

Outside consultants and experts are important sources of information for managers, because they are frequently aware of new products, processes, or service developments in their fields. New employees and other individuals within the organization are also an important source of ideas, particularly if they are constantly exposed to information outside their immediate work setting (as in a research department).

Problem Solving. Unlike idea generation, information that aids in problem solving usually is developed within the organization. The techniques described earlier, such as brainstorming, represent formal methods that managers can use to tap the ideas of organization members.

Individuals in the organization may also volunteer ideas on an informal basis. These individuals could include technical specialists employed by the firm who have access to outside information. They will also include other creative or knowledgeable individuals whose talent or familiarity with the details of a problem will enable them to suggest solutions. In both cases, the organizational climate and structure must encourage the free expression of ideas. For example, rigidly structured organizations that inhibit communication between departments will often keep potentially helpful people from knowing that a problem exists. By creating barriers to communication, such organizations may also prevent problem solutions from reaching the managers who need them. (See Chapter 13.)

Implementation. The implementation stage of the creative process in organizations consists of those steps that bring a solution or invention to the marketplace. For manufactured goods, these steps include engineering, tooling, manufacturing, test marketing, and promotion.

[24] James M. Utterback, "Innovation in Industry and the Diffusion of Technology," *Science*, February 15, 1974, pp. 620–626.

TABLE 14-2 Characteristics of the Creative Individual and Organization	The Creative Individual	The Creative Organization
	Conceptual fluency... is able to produce a large number of ideas quickly	Has idea people Open channels of communication *Ad hoc* devices: suggestion systems; brainstorming; idea units absolved of other responsibilities Encourages contact with outside sources
	Originality... generates unusual ideas	Heterogeneous personnel policy Includes marginal, unusual types Assigns nonspecialists to problems Allows eccentricity
	Separates source from content in evaluating information... is motivated by interest in problem... follows wherever it leads	Has an objective, fact-founded approach Ideas evaluated on their merits, not status of originator *Ad hoc* approaches: anonymous communications; blind votes Selects and promotes on merit only
	Suspends judgment... avoids early commitment... spends more time in analysis, exploration	Lack of financial, material commitment to products, policies Invests in basic research; flexible, long-range planning Experiments with new ideas rather than prejudging on "rational" grounds; everything gets a chance
	Less authoritarian... has relativistic view of life	More decentralized; diversified Administrative slack; time and resources to absorb errors Risk-taking ethos... tolerates and expects taking chances
	Accepts own impulses ...playful, undisciplined exploration	Not run as "tight ship" Employees have fun Allows freedom to choose and pursue problems Freedom to discuss ideas
	Independence of judgment, less conformity	Organizationally autonomous
	Deviant, sees self as different	Original and different objectives, not trying to be another "X"
	Rich, "bizarre" fantasy life *and* superior reality orientation	Security of routine... *allows* innovation...; "Philistines" provide stable, secure environment that allows "creators" to roam Has separate units or occasions for generating vs. evaluating ideas... separates creative from productive functions

Source: Reprinted from *The Creative Organization*, edited by Gary A. Steiner, by permission of The University of Chicago Press. © 1965 by The University of Chicago. All rights reserved.

For innovation to be successful, a high degree of integration is usually required among the various units of the organization. Technical specialists, who are responsible for the engineering side of the new product, must work with administrative and financial specialists, who are responsible for keeping the cost of innovation within practical limits. Production managers, who are helping to refine the specifications of the new product, must work with marketing managers, who are responsible for test marketing, advertising, and promoting it. Proper integration of all these groups is necessary for a quality innovation to be produced on time, on budget, and for a viable market. Organizations that are too rigidly structured may have a difficult time integrating their activities; thus, their ability to innovate effectively will be limited. For this reason, many management writers believe that the best structure for innovation is the matrix-type organizational structure, which encourages interdepartmental communication and integration. (See Chapter 9.)

Establishing a Climate for Organizational Creativity

As we suggested earlier, creativity is best nurtured in a permissive climate, one that encourages the exploration of new ideas and new ways of doing things. Such a climate is difficult for many managers to accept. They may be uncomfortable with the continuing process of change, which is a necessary accompaniment of creativity. They may also be concerned that in a permissive atmosphere, discipline or cost control may break down.

How can managers take these real feelings and concerns into account and yet create a climate that will encourage creativity? The steps listed below suggest a possible answer:[25]

1. *Overcome resistance to change.* Before organization members will encourage change, they must believe that change will benefit them and the organization. This belief is more likely to arise if members participate with their managers in making the decisions for change that will affect them. (See our discussion on overcoming resistance to change in Chapters 6 and 15.)

2. *Encourage new ideas.* The managers in the organization, from top managers to lower-level supervisors, must make it clear in word and deed that they welcome new approaches. Managers who closely supervise every action of subordinates encourage their subordinates to follow orders rather than to experiment. Managers whose first reaction to new ideas is negative ("It won't work") will quickly turn off the flow of ideas. To encourage creativity, managers must be willing to listen to their subordinates' suggestions. They must also be willing to convey the most promising suggestions to higher-level managers.

3. *Permit more interaction.* A permissive, creative climate is fostered if individuals are given an opportunity to interact with members of their own and other work groups. Such interaction will encourage the exchange of useful information, the free flow of ideas, and fresh perspectives on problems.

[25] See Richard E. Dutton, "Creative Use of Creative People," *Personnel Journal,* Vol. 51, No. 11 (November 1972), pp. 818–822 ff., and H. Joseph Reitz, *Behavior in Organizations* (Homewood, Ill.: Irwin, 1977), pp. 214–220, 242–249.

4. *Tolerate failure.* A great many new ideas prove impractical or useless. Effective managers accept and take into account the fact that time and resources will be invested in experimenting with many new ideas that will not work out.

5. *Provide clear guidelines and objectives.* Organization members who are given clear goals will be stimulated to meet them. Their creativity will have a purpose and direction. Supplying guidelines and objectives will also give managers some control over the time and money invested in creative behavior.

6. *Offer recognition.* Creative individuals are motivated to work hard on tasks that interest them. But, like all individuals, they enjoy being rewarded for a task well done. By offering recognition in such tangible forms as bonuses and salary increases, managers demonstrate that creative behavior in their organizations is valued.

Summary   There are three views of organizational conflict. In the traditional view, all conflict is seen as a harmful result of the failure to apply management principles. In the behavioral view, conflict is seen as a natural but usually undesirable part of organization life. The interactionist view suggests that conflict is not only inevitable but sometimes even necessary for the organization to survive.

There are various types of conflict. Conflict between groups in the same organization may be caused by their need to share scarce resources and work activities and by their differences in goals, values, or perceptions. Individual style differences as well as organizational ambiguities and communication problems may also contribute to group conflict. Line and staff conflict is an important example of organizational conflict.

Effects of conflict include a rise in group cohesion, selection of strong leaders and group representatives, and the development of distorted perceptions about one's own group and the opposing group. Whether or not these and other consequences will prove functional or dysfunctional will depend on the level of conflict, the organizational structure and climate, and the way in which the conflict is managed.

The management of conflict may include conflict stimulation, reduction, or resolution. Conflict stimulation methods include bringing outsiders into the organization, encouraging competition, restructuring the organization, and redistributing power among the organization work groups. Conflict reduction methods include establishing superordinate goals and uniting the conflicting groups to meet a common threat.

Undesirable or ineffective conflict resolution methods include compromise and the suppression of conflict. Integrative problem solving, on the other hand, allows managers to resolve conflict in a way that most benefits the organization and does the least harm to conflicting individuals or groups.

The management of organizational creativity requires an understanding of the creative process and how it can be stimulated. In individuals, the creative process can be divided into five steps: sensing, immersion, incubation, insight, and application. Individual or group creativity can be stimulated through brainstorming, synectics, and creative group decision making.

Effective organizational creativity and innovation follow a three-step procedure: idea generation, problem solving, and implementation. This procedure is facilitated by an organizational structure and climate that encourage (1) the free flow of communication between the organization and its environment; (2) the free flow of communication among organization members; and (3) the integration of organizational activities.

Review Questions

1. What are the traditional, behavioral, and interactionist views of conflict? With which view do you agree? Why?
2. What is the difference between conflict and competition?
3. What are the five types of conflict possible in organizations? Under what conditions will each type of conflict arise?
4. Why does differentiation often lead to conflict?
5. What are the effects of organizational conflict on group attitudes and behavior? What factors determine whether these effects will be functional or dysfunctional?
6. What are the consequences of a very low level of organizational conflict? What methods of conflict stimulation can managers use?
7. What ineffective conflict reduction methods did Sherif attempt?
8. What two conflict reduction methods that Sherif used proved effective? Why might these methods be ineffective in organizations?
9. What are the three types of conflict resolution methods? In what ways can these methods be manifested? Which method is usually best? Why?
10. From what viewpoints do line and staff members view each other and their role in the organization? How can line-staff conflict be reduced?
11. Why do you think creativity is important in organizational life?
12. What is the difference between creativity and innovation?
13. What are the steps in the creative process in individuals?
14. What techniques can be used to stimulate individual or group creativity?
15. What are the three steps in the organizational creativity process? How can each step be facilitated or inhibited?
16. How can managers establish an organizational climate that encourages creativity?

CASE STUDY: CHIEFLAND MEMORIAL HOSPITAL

Mr. James A. Grover, retired land developer and financier, is the current president of Chiefland Memorial Hospital's board of trustees. Chiefland Memorial is a 200-bed voluntary short-term general hospital serving an area of approximately 50,000 persons. Mr. Grover has just begun a meeting with the administrator of the hospital, Mr. Edward M. Hoffman. The purpose of the meeting is to seek an acceptable solution to an apparent conflict-of-authority problem within the hospital between Mr. Hoffman and the Chief of Surgery, Dr. Lacy Young.

The problem was brought to Mr. Grover's attention by Dr. Young during a golf match between the two men. Dr. Young had challenged Mr. Grover to the golf match at the Chiefland Golf and Country Club; but it turned out that this was only an excuse for Dr. Young to discuss a hospital problem with Mr. Grover.

The problem that concerned Dr. Young involved the operating room supervisor, Geraldine Werther, R.N. Ms. Werther schedules the hospital's operating suite in accordance with policies that she "believes" to have been established by the hospital's administration. One source of irritation to the surgeons is her attitude that maximum utilization must be made of the hospital's operating rooms if hospital costs are to be reduced. She therefore schedules in such a way that operating room idle time is minimized. Surgeons complain that the operating schedule often does not permit them

Case reprinted with permission from *Critical Incidents in Management,* 3rd ed., by John M. Champion and John H. James (Homewood, Ill.: Richard D. Irwin, Inc., 1975), pp. 40–42.

sufficient time to complete a surgical procedure in the manner they think desirable. More often than not, insufficient time is allowed between operations for effective preparation of the operating room for the next procedure. Such scheduling, the surgical staff maintains, contributes to low-quality patient care. Furthermore, some of the surgeons have complained that Ms. Werther shows favoritism in her scheduling, allowing some doctors more use of the operating suite than others.

The situation reached a crisis when Dr. Young, following an explosive confrontation with Ms. Werther, told her he was firing her. Ms. Werther then made an appeal to the hospital administrator, who in turn informed Dr. Young that discharging nurses was an administrative prerogative. In effect, Dr. Young was told he did not have authority to fire Ms. Werther. Dr. Young asserted that he did have authority over any issue affecting medical practice and good patient care in Chiefland Hospital. He considered this a medical problem and threatened to take the matter to the hospital's board of trustees.

As the meeting between Mr. Grover and Mr. Hoffman began, Mr. Hoffman explained his position on the problem. He stressed the point that a hospital administrator is legally responsible for patient care in the hospital. He also contended that quality patient care cannot be achieved unless the board of trustees authorized the administrator to make decisions, develop programs, formulate policies, and implement procedures. While listening to Mr. Hoffman, Mr. Grover recalled the position belligerently taken by Dr. Young, who had contended that surgical and medical doctors holding staff privileges at Chiefland would never allow a "layman" to make decisions impinging on medical practice. Dr. Young also had said that Mr. Hoffman should be told to restrict his activities to fund raising, financing, maintenance, housekeeping — administrative problems rather than medical problems. Dr. Young had then requested that Mr. Grover clarify in a definitive manner the lines of authority at Chiefland Memorial.

As Mr. Grover ended his meeting with Mr. Hoffman, the severity of the problem was unmistakably clear to him, but the solution remained quite unclear. Mr. Grover knew a decision was required — and soon.

Case Questions
1. Why do you think conflict has developed at Chiefland Memorial?
2. Would establishing clear lines of authority solve all the problems described in the case? Why or why not?
3. What should Mr. Grover do?

Chapter 15

Managing Organizational Change and Development

Upon completing this chapter you should be able to:

1. Identify two constructive responses to change pressures and suggest when each approach is appropriate.

2. Describe internal and external forces for organizational change.

3. Summarize the six phases of the organizational change process.

4. Identify the sources of resistance to change and the ways this resistance can be overcome.

5. Describe the three major approaches to change.

6. Describe a model of individual change.

7. Describe the organizational development approach to change and the assumptions and values upon which this approach is based.

The observation that we live in a world of change has been made so often and so consistently that it has become a cliché. Nevertheless, like many clichés, the observation is a true one. In the past few decades:

— Technological innovations have multiplied.
— Basic resources have progressively become more expensive.
— Competition has sharply increased.
— Communications have reduced the time needed to make decisions.
— Government regulation has widened and intensified.
— Environmental and consumer interest groups have become highly influential.
— The drive for social equality has gained momentum.
— The economic interdependence of the world's countries has become more apparent.

These and many other changes have confronted managers and their organizations with a host of new challenges.[1] How well managers meet these challenges — and those that are sure to come in the future — can determine whether or not their organizations will survive.

RESPONSES TO CHANGE PRESSURES

There are many nonconstructive ways that managers can respond to pressures for change — for example, by denying that they exist, resisting them, or avoiding them. The companies that were suddenly forced to close down in the winter of early 1977 because of natural gas shortages — even though those shortages had been predicted for years — clearly had avoided responding to changes in the environment in a constructive way. Similarly, those companies that lose millions of dollars in lawsuits because of discriminatory hiring and promotion practices or pollution law violations are paying the price for denying or resisting change in social values and government regulations.

To deal constructively with change, there are two major approaches that managers can take: (1) They can *react* to the signs that changes are needed. With this approach, managers make piecemeal, small changes to deal with particular problems as they arise. (2) They can develop a program of *planned* change. Through this approach, managers deal not only with present difficulties but also with anticipated difficulties that are not yet clearly observable.

The first response — which is simpler and less expensive than the second response — was appropriate for organizations as a whole when the pace of change was slower, when the environment was not as competitive, and when organizations were smaller and less complicated. Today, such a response is appropriate only for the small, day-to-day adjustments that are an integral part of the manager's job. Examples of such adjustments are easy to find: a

[1] For an early description of the new pressures confronting managers, see Peter F. Drucker, "Management's New Role," *Harvard Business Review*, November-December 1962.

sales form is modified because the old layout led to many errors in specifying quantity and price; young managers are having difficulty with tasks involving financial analysis, so a two-week seminar on financial analysis is arranged; two managers, working together on a high-priority project, temporarily move into adjoining offices until the project is completed. These small changes require minimal planning because they can (and should) be handled in a quick, uncomplicated manner. We will not deal specifically with this response to change here, because we are really dealing with it throughout the book in our descriptions of the daily problems and decisions that managers confront.

The second, planned response to change has been defined by John M. Thomas and Warren G. Bennis as "the deliberate design and implementation of a structural innovation, a new policy or goal, or a change in operating philosophy, climate, and style."[2] Such a response is appropriate when the entire organization or a major portion of it must prepare for or adapt to change. Because of the nature and extent of change in our world, this type of planned change is needed more frequently in today's organizations than it was in organizations of the past.

Planned change is usually greater in scope and magnitude than reactive change. It involves a greater commitment in time and resources; it requires more skills and knowledge for implementation to be successful; and it can lead to more problems if implementation is unsuccessful. Because of the scale and complexity of planned change, we will be dealing with it in some detail in this chapter. We will look at some of the forces that bring about change, the processes of organizational change, and the various approaches to organizational change, with a particular emphasis on what is called "organizational development."

FORCES FOR CHANGE

We will start this section with a brief review of the points discussed in Chapters 3 and 5 concerning the pressures for change that organizations experience, the increase in these pressures for change, and the multiplicity of forces for change. We will examine these forces in terms of their origin outside or within the organization.

External Forces Organizations depend on and must interact with their external environment in order to survive. The external environment is the source of their raw materials and personnel; it is also the recipient of their goods or services. Anything that interferes with the organization's ability to attract the human and material resources it needs or to market its products becomes a pressure for change.[3]

[2]John M. Thomas and Warren G. Bennis, eds., *The Management of Change and Conflict* (Baltimore: Penguin Books, 1972), p. 209. There are many other definitions of planned organizational change. See, for example, Gene W. Dalton, Paul R. Lawrence, and Larry E. Greiner, eds., *Organizational Change and Development* (Homewood, Ill.: Irwin, Dorsey Press, 1970).

[3]H. Joseph Reitz, *Behavior in Organizations* (Homewood, Ill.: Irwin, 1977).

373

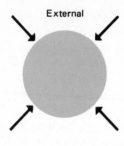

External

The list of changes at the beginning of this chapter are examples of external forces for change. The rising cost of petroleum products, combined with anti-pollution legislation, has caused automobile manufacturers to concentrate on improving the gas mileage and reducing the size of their cars. The banning of cyclamates and saccharin created pressure on diet food and beverage companies to search for a new artificial sweetener. The discovery of the effect of aerosol propellants on the atmosphere led to a change in the packaging and marketing of a wide variety of products. There are an enormous variety of external forces, from technological discoveries to competitive action, that can pressure the organization to modify its structure, goals, and methods of operation.

Internal Forces

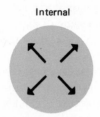

Internal

Pressures for change may arise from a number of sources within the organization, particularly from new managerial policies, technologies, and employee attitudes and behavior. For example, a top manager's decision to seek a higher rate of long-term growth will affect the goals of many departments and may even lead to some reorganization. The introduction of automated equipment to perform tasks that had required human labor may call for a complete change in work routine, incentive programs, and personnel procedures. Worker dissatisfaction, as manifested in high turnover rates or strikes, may lead to many changes in management policies and practices.

Needless to say, external and internal forces for change are often linked. This link is particularly strong with respect to changes in values and attitudes, which affect people throughout society. Some of these people enter the organization and cause it to change from within. For example, many of the changes we described in earlier chapters in this unit—such as job enrichment programs and the trend toward greater subordinate participation in decision making—represent a response in part to changes in people's attitudes toward authority and work satisfaction.

THE PROCESS OF ORGANIZATIONAL CHANGE

In this section, we will describe one model of planned organizational change. We will also discuss the sources of resistance to planned change in organizations and the ways of overcoming that resistance.

A Model of Organizational Change

Many models of organizational change have been proposed.[4] Each offers its own set of insights and guides to action. The model we have chosen to describe in detail was proposed by Larry E. Greiner.[5] We have selected his model because it emphasizes the role of the change agent and the need to implement

[4]See David A. Kolb and Alan L. Frohman, "An Organization Development Approach to Consulting," *Sloan Management Review,* Vol. 12, No. 1 (Fall 1970), pp. 51–65, and Ronald Lippitt, Jeanne Watson, and Bruce Westley, *Planned Change* (New York: Harcourt, Brace & World, 1958).

[5]Larry E. Greiner, "Patterns of Organization Change," *Harvard Business Review,* May-June 1967, pp. 119–130.

change carefully and gradually. We may define the *change agent* as the individual, usually brought in from outside the organization or department, who is responsible for taking a leadership role in initiating and managing the process of change. The individual, group, or organization that is the target of the change attempts is called the *client system.*

Greiner's model is based on two key ideas, which he derived from his review of studies of successful organizational change efforts: (1) successful change depends basically on a *redistribution of power* within the structure of an organization; and (2) power redistribution occurs through a *developmental process of change.* As illustrated in Figure 15-1 on the next page, Greiner breaks this developmental process down into six phases.

Phase 1: Pressure and Arousal. This phase occurs when top managers are subjected to severe internal and external pressures of the type we described earlier. For example, profits may be declining and employee morale may be low. Severe pressures such as these are usually necessary before top managers recognize the need for a large-scale change in the organization. If the pressure is comparatively slight — as when profits are high but employee turnover is also higher than desired — top managers will be tempted to see the situation as a temporary one, rather than admit that they are not doing their jobs effectively.

For a change program to be successful, it is important that top managers recognize the need for change. The involvement and support of top managers will be necessary to keep the organization's change effort adequately funded, motivated, and focused on the organization's overall interests.

Phase 2: Intervention and Reorientation. Even though aroused to take action, top management may not recognize the limits of its ability to analyze and solve the organization's problems. This task may be assigned to a change agent. Although the change agent is frequently a consultant from outside the organization, Greiner does not suggest that change projects can be carried out only by outsiders. Inside staff people, often from organizational development departments, are capable of managing the change process. However, outside specialists bring several advantages with them. They are likely to be specially trained in the process of planned change and can devote all their time to managing that process without being distracted by day-to-day managerial reponsibilities. They are unlikely to have their own special interests within the organization to protect. They are in a better position to observe the situation objectively. Finally, outside specialists stand a good chance of being regarded as experts and listened to (or confided in) by the organization's managers.

Phase 3: Diagnosis and Recognition. In this phase, managers and the change agent work together to gather information about the organization's problems. For this step to be successful, managers must share their power with subordinates. Top managers who decide on their own what changes are needed may do so without correct or adequate information. In addition, as we shall see,

375

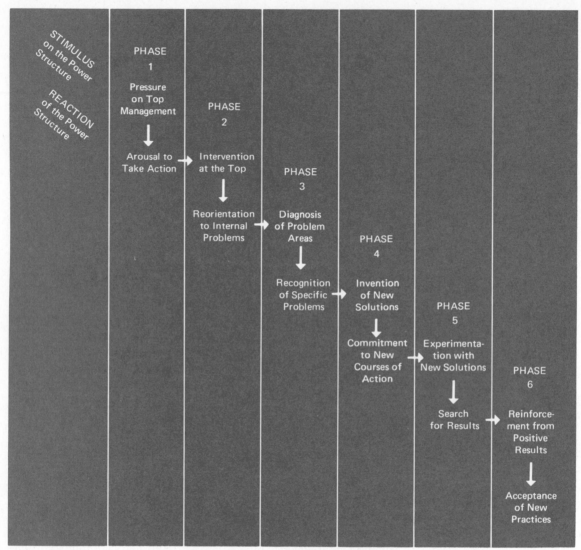

FIGURE 15-1 Dynamics of Successful Organizational Change
Source: Larry E. Greiner, "Patterns of Organization Change," *Harvard Business Review*, May-June 1967, p. 126. Copyright © 1967 by the President and Fellows of Harvard College; all rights reserved.

they may arouse resentment when trying to implement changes. On the other hand, delegating complete authority for change to subordinates may leave those subordinates without sufficient guidance. Ideally, according to Greiner, managers and subordinates should participate in making change decisions.

Phase 4: Invention and Commitment. The tendency of organization members to attack new problems with the same old methods (which may be a part of the problem) makes it necessary to invent new solutions and obtain full commitment to them. Usually, the change agent will play an active role in helping managers and subordinates collaborate in finding new problem solutions that all can endorse and support.

Phase 5: Experimentation and Search. Before large-scale changes are implemented fully, a period of experimentation and testing usually takes place. Alternative solutions are introduced and evidence that the solutions are or are not working efficiently is actively sought out by people at every level of the organization. For example, before dividing a single sales force into separate product sales forces, it might be a good idea to test the sales force split in one region before implementing it on a national basis.

Phase 6: Reinforcement and Acceptance. If appropriate changes have been properly tested and implemented, they should result in improved organizational performance. This improvement will reinforce organization members and cause them to work hard to keep the changes successful. Acceptance of the changes may also bring with it permanent changes in procedures. For example, the concept of manager-subordinate collaboration is likely to continue as an accepted part of day-to-day problem solving in the organization rather than fade away as a temporary method of creating change.

RESISTANCE TO CHANGE

A major obstacle to the implementation of new policies, goals, or methods of operation is the resistance of organization members to change. The fact that an outside change agent is often necessary for change programs to be successful is an indication of how strong such resistance can be. We will group the sources of resistance to change into three broad categories: uncertainty about the effects of change, unwillingness to give up existing benefits, and awareness of weaknesses in the changes proposed.[6] (See also Chapter 6.)

1. *Uncertainty about the causes and effects of change.* Quite aside from the practical problems that change brings (such as the need to acquire new skills), organization members may psychologically resist change because they wish to avoid uncertainty. The traditional ways of doing things offer precedents that can guide members' actions; the consequences of the traditional ways are at least well known and predictable. Unwillingness to give up tasks and relationships that are familiar may cause resistance to change.

The sense of being manipulated that people feel when their jobs are changed

---

[6] See Herbert Kaufman, *The Limits of Organizational Change* (University, Alabama: University of Alabama Press, 1971); Edgar F. Huse, *Organization Development and Change* (St. Paul: West Publishing, 1975); Alvin Zander, "Resistance to Change—Its Analysis and Prevention," *Advanced Management*, Vol. 15, No. 1 (January 1950), pp. 9–11; and Alton C. Bartlett and Thomas A. Kayser, eds., *Changing Organizational Behavior* (Englewood Cliffs, N.J.: Prentice-Hall, 1973).

without their consultation and involvement may also lead to resistance. Change imposed from the outside or on personal grounds ("This is the way I want things done") will be interpreted by subordinates as a sign that they have not done their jobs properly. They will feel pressured and uncertain about why the changes are being made. Thus, instead of seeing the changes as a more effective way of reaching common objectives, organization members may resent change.

2. *Unwillingness to give up existing benefits.* While appropriate change should benefit the organization as a whole, it is also likely to affect adversely some organization members or units. The typesetters who will be replaced by a computerized typesetting system, the sales manager who is reassigned to a less desirable territory, the hospital administrator who is afraid that using paraprofessionals will diminish the quality of medical care, and the college dean who will have to yield some responsibilities to a committee are all likely to resist change. For some individuals, the cost of change in terms of lost power, prestige, salary, quality, or other benefits will not be sufficiently offset by the rewards of change.

3. *Awareness of weaknesses in the changes proposed.* Sometimes organization members will resist change because they are aware of potential problems that have apparently been overlooked by change initiators. This form of resistance is obviously a very desirable one. It represents a type of functional conflict (see Chapter 14) that managers should recognize and use to make their change proposals more effective. For example, the head of the sales department may resist a decentralization plan because he or she knows that the sales managers do not wish to relocate. Changing the plan—perhaps by increasing incentives to relocate—may prevent the organization from losing experienced personnel.

In some organizations, managers may be too eager to impose change for change's sake. The objections to change by cooler heads will enable the organization to maintain its stability while the change proposals are evaluated more fully.[7]

| Overcoming Resistance to Change | The existence of resistance to a change proposal is a signal to managers that there is something wrong with the proposal or that mistakes have been made in the way the proposal has been presented. The problem for managers is to determine the actual cause of resistance and then remain flexible enough to overcome it in an appropriate manner. |

Many types of resistance can be overcome by involving subordinates in change discussions and decisions. Lester Coch and John French, whose study we described in Chapter 7, found that resistance to change can be reduced or eliminated by having the people affected participate in the design of the change.[8]

[7] See Robert Albanese, "Overcoming Resistance to Stability," *Business Horizons,* Vol. 13, No. 2 (April 1970), pp. 35–42.
[8] Lester Coch and John R. P. French, Jr., "Overcoming Resistance to Change," *Human Relations,* Vol. 1 (1948), pp. 512–532.

Paul Lawrence subsequently completed research that found effects similar to those in Coch and French's study.[9] Lawrence suggested that in order to avoid resistance, managers had to take into account what he called the social effects of change. For example, change imposed from above would be likely to cause people to feel that their knowledge and skill were being ignored. Such a method of implementing change would be likely to generate resistance.

Collaborating with subordinates in change decisions—or at least adequately explaining change proposals—will be useful in overcoming the first type of resistance, which is caused by uncertainty. It will also be extremely effective with the third type of resistance, which results from awareness of weaknesses in the change proposals. Manager-subordinate participation will allow objections to surface calmly and openly. The objections can then be evaluated and, where appropriate, improvements can be made in the change program.

Special tact may be needed in overcoming the second type of resistance, which is caused by employees who are unwilling to give up existing benefits. Encouraging more participation in change formulation and decision making may, in this case, merely have the effect of strengthening resistance and encouraging the employees to block the proposed changes with more vigor. Participation is not always a cure-all, a sure-fire method. In extreme circumstances, it may be necessary to spring unpleasant changes on subordinates and then work toward helping them understand and accept the new conditions.

APPROACHES TO ORGANIZATIONAL CHANGE

In the previous section, we described a model of how the impetus for change develops in an organization and how the change process is carried out. In this section, we will discuss the various elements of the organization to which the change process can be applied. Specifically, we will try to answer the question "What aspects of the organization can be changed?"

Harold J. Leavitt suggests that an organization can be changed by changing its structure, its technology, and/or its people.[10] Changing the organization's *structure* involves rearranging its internal systems, such as its lines of communication, work flow, or managerial hierarchy. Changing the organization's *technology* means altering its equipment, engineering processes, research techniques, or production methods. Changing the organization's *people* involves changing the selection, training, relationships, attitudes, or roles of organization members. Because we have already dealt with structure and technology to some extent in earlier chapters of this unit, we will deal with them only briefly here. Our main focus will be on change efforts aimed at the people

---

[9]Paul R. Lawrence, "How to Deal with Resistance to Change," *Harvard Business Review,* January-February 1969, pp. 4–12 ff.

[10]Harold J. Leavitt, "Applied Organization Change in Industry: Structural, Technical, and Human Approaches," in W. W. Cooper, H. J. Leavitt, and M. W. Shelly II, eds., *New Perspectives in Organization Research* (New York: Wiley, 1964), pp. 55–71.

in the organization; in particular, we will emphasize organizational development (OD) programs, which attempt to change an organization's climate.

Interdependence
of the Three
Approaches

Before we begin our discussion, we should note that all three elements in the organization — its structure, technology, and people — are highly interdependent. A change in one element is very likely to affect the other elements as well. (See Figure 15-2.) Thus, an effective change program is likely to be one that anticipates the interaction of these three elements and attempts to change all three to whatever extent is appropriate. Those change programs that focus on only one of the three elements have been found to have low records of success.[11]

FIGURE 15-2
Interdependence of
the Three Change
Approaches

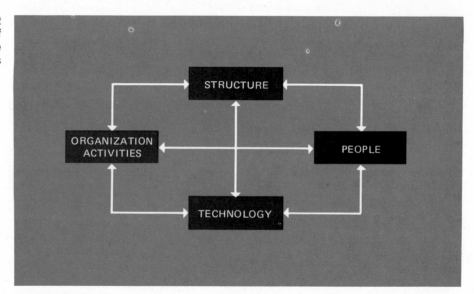

Source: Adapted from Harold J. Leavitt, "Applied Organization Change in Industry: Structural, Technical, and Human Approaches," in W. W. Cooper, H. J. Leavitt, and M. W. Shelly II, eds., *New Perspectives in Organization Research* (New York: John Wiley & Sons, Inc., 1964), p. 56. Used by permission.

Normally, the greater the amount of change that managers desire, the higher the likelihood that the change efforts will have to involve all three elements in order to be effective. For example, let us assume we are managers in a large manufacturing company and wish to increase sales in two product categories, proprietary drugs and personal care products. To achieve our goal, we might conclude that a major structural change will be required. The sales force will have to be divided into two separate units so that the efforts of salespeople will be more focused and so that accountability for each product line

[11]See, for example, Frank Friedlander and L. Dave Brown, "Organization Development," *Annual Review of Psychology,* Vol. 25 (1974), p. 314, and John P. Campbell and Marvin D. Dunnette, "Effectiveness of T-Group Experiences in Managerial Training and Development," *Psychological Bulletin,* Vol. 70, No. 2 (August 1968), pp. 73–104.

will be easier to determine. Such a structural change may well involve techno-logical changes. For instance, new computer programs may have to be used to transfer the old marketing and sales information into more appropriate formats; or new sales techniques and procedures may be developed to increase the professionalism of the sales force. In addition, people changes are also likely to be required. Some new sales personnel may have to be hired and trained, and previously hired personnel will have to be retrained or reassigned. Individuals who are unable to adjust to the new circumstances might have to be transferred or even replaced.

Structural Approaches

According to Leavitt, efforts to bring about organizational change through changes in structure can be divided into three groups. In the first group are structural changes created through the application of the classical organiza-tional design principles described in Chapter 2. The classical theorists sought to improve the performance of organizations by clearly and carefully defining the job responsibilities of organization members. They emphasized creating appropriate divisions of labor and lines of authority. Today, many managers can still improve the performance of their organizations by changing manage-ment spans, the chains of command, areas of responsibility, management levels, and the like.

Changing organizations through decentralization is another structural approach to change. This approach is based on the idea that creating smaller, self-contained organizational units will increase the motivation of the members of those units and help them to focus their attention on the highest-priority activities. The intended result is increased profitability for each unit. An added advantage of decentralization is that it permits each unit to adapt its own structure and technology to the tasks it performs or to its external environment.

The third structural approach to change aims at improving organizational performance by modifying the flow of work in the organization.[12] This approach is based on the reasoning that proper work flow and grouping of specialties will lead directly to an improvement in productivity and are likely to improve morale and work satisfaction as well.

Technological Approaches

Systematic application of the technological approach to change began with the work of Frederick Taylor and his *Scientific Management* (see Chapter 2). Taylor and his followers attempted to analyze and refine the interactions be-tween workers and machines so that the efficiency of the workplace would be increased. Through such methods as time and motion studies and the setting of piece rates, Taylor and later industrial engineers tried to improve organiza-tional performance by redesigning work operations and reward systems.

Although technological changes are sometimes introduced into an organi-zation by themselves, they are often difficult to implement successfully. A common problem with technological change is that it often proves incompat-

[12] See E. Chapple and Leonard R. Sayles, *The Measure of Management* (New York: Macmillan, 1961).

ible with the organization's structure. This incompatibility may create resentment and dislocations among organization members. For example, Trist and Bamforth found that decreased satisfaction and performance followed the introduction of technological innovations in a mining operation.[13] The miners, who had performed a variety of tasks in small, closely knit work groups, were forced to work on more specialized tasks in a much larger, less cohesive group when the technical advances were implemented. The result was low productivity, more accidents, and a high turnover rate.

To increase the chances that technological change will succeed, many managers attempt to implement both technical and structural changes simultaneously. By so doing, they hope to make the organization's structure more compatible with its technology.

Combining Technological and Structural Approaches. Combined technological and structural (or *technostructural*) approaches to change attempt to improve performance by changing some aspects of an organization's structure and technology. For instance, in the mining operation mentioned above, many of the original small work groups were eventually reintroduced in ways that would be compatible with the new mining machinery. This technostructural approach to change proved successful, as morale and productivity improved dramatically.

Job enlargement and job enrichment programs, which we discussed in Chapter 9, are other examples of technostructural approaches to change. In these programs, the tasks that make up a job, the ways the tasks are performed, and employee relationships are altered to improve employee satisfaction and perhaps to increase productivity. In job enrichment, the activities from a vertical slice of the organization are combined in one job to make it more challenging (thereby stimulating the jobholder's drive). Under job enlargement, various tasks at the same level of the organization are combined to provide employees with greater variety on the job and increase their sense of work involvement.[14]

People Approaches
Both the technical and structural approaches attempt to improve organizational performance by changing the work situation. They are based on the assumption that creating an appropriate work situation will cause employee behavior to become more productive. The people approaches, on the other hand, attempt to change directly the behavior of employees by focusing on their attitudes and skills. These approaches are based on the assumption that improving the attitudes and skills of employees will, in turn, cause employees

---

[13] E. L. Trist and K. W. Bamforth, "Some Social and Psychological Consequences of the Longwall Method of Coal Getting," *Human Relations,* Vol. 4, No. 1 (February 1951), pp. 3–38.

[14] See Friedlander and Brown, "Organization Development," pp. 320–324; W. Warner Burke and Harvey A. Hornstein, eds., *The Social Technology of Organization Development* (Fairfax, Va.: NTL Learning Resources, 1972); and Harvey A. Hornstein et al., *Social Intervention: A Behavioral Science Approach* (New York: Free Press, 1971).

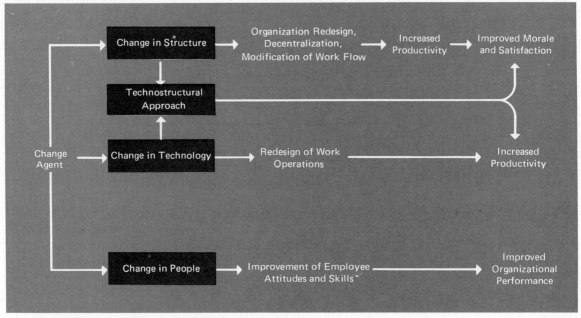

FIGURE 15-3   The Three Change Approaches

to perform more effectively. The new attitudes and skills may also encourage the employees to take the lead in changing the organization's structure and technology, leading to still more improvement in organizational performance.

People change efforts have been directed at individuals, groups, or organizations as a whole. At the *individual level,* examples of people change efforts include management development programs (which we will discuss in Chapter 19) and sensitivity training of key persons in the organization. For example, an opportunity to attend a sensitivity training group (or "T-group") might be made available to a manager whose personal style is seen as too aggressive by other organization members. Trainers of T-groups adopt a very permissive, nondirective style, giving group members a chance to learn how they react to others and how others react to them. In the group, the manager might learn new ways of relating to subordinates because of the unstructured interactions and frank feedback to which he or she would be exposed. Because a T-group is an intense experience for almost anyone who attends one, dramatic improvements in self-awareness and sensitivity to others sometimes do occur. However, it is also recognized that the experience has undesirable impacts on some participants. Therefore, most organizations are very careful to assure potential participants that attendance is voluntary.

At the *group level,* people change efforts may involve "team-building" activities in which new and improved methods of working as a group are learned. Team-building activities are normally conducted by an internal or external consultant trained in behavioral science methods. T-groups have also been used to bring about changes in the ways group members interact. However, their popularity with ongoing work groups has declined because of concern about their effectiveness for this purpose and because work group members are often uncomfortable about attending a T-group with their superiors or colleagues.

At the *organizational level,* people approaches may involve an organization-wide MBO program, which we discussed in Chapter 6. (Of course, MBO can also be used on a more selective basis by managers to change individual and group behaviors.) Organizational development is another major people approach that is used for the organization as a whole. We will be discussing OD in the last major section of this chapter.

A Model of Individual Change. Change approaches that focus on changing the attitudes, skills, and knowledge of individuals are frequently based on a model first described by Kurt Lewin[15] and later elaborated by Edgar Schein. Lewin noted that there are two major obstacles to successful change programs on the individual level. The first major obstacle is that individuals are unwilling to alter their long-established attitudes and behaviors. A manager who is told that he or she needs to learn newly developed production techniques will frequently accept this information with little or no difficulty. If the same manager is told that he or she is too passive in dealing with others, the manager is much more likely to resent and resist this information. Suggesting the need to make a change in managerial style or attitude is likely to be perceived as threatening to one's self-image and as an indication of past inadequacy.

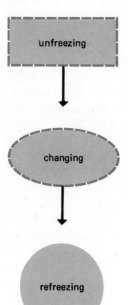

The second major obstacle that Lewin noted was that change frequently lasts only a short time. After a brief period of trying to do things differently, individuals generally return to their traditional pattern of behavior. Because of these obstacles, Lewin believed that successful change efforts required three elements: a period of *unfreezing* of old attitudes, a period of *moving* to a new attitude and a new level of performance, and, finally, a period of *freezing,* when the new attitude and performance level are made permanent.

Edgar Schein elaborated on this model, based largely on his readings and his research into the subject of brainwashing. He saw the successful change process as occurring in three phases:

(1) *Unfreezing:* an alteration of the forces acting on the individual, such that his stable equilibrium is disturbed sufficiently to motivate him and to make him ready to change; this can be accomplished either by increasing the pressure to change or by reducing some of the threats or resistance to change.

(2) *Changing:* the presentation of a direction of change and the actual process of learning new attitudes. This process occurs basically by one of two mechanisms: (a) *identification*—the person learns new attitudes by identifying with and emulating some other person who holds those attitudes; or (b) *internalization*—the person learns new attitudes by being placed in a situation where new attitudes are demanded of him as a way of solving problems which confront him and which he cannot avoid....

[15] Kurt Lewin, "Frontiers in Group Dynamics: Concept, Method, and Reality in Social Science," *Human Relations,* Vol. 1, No. 1 (1947), pp. 5–41.

(3) *Refreezing:* the integration of the changed attitudes into the rest of the personality and/or into ongoing significant emotional relationships.[16]

There are many examples of this change process in operation. New army recruits, for example, are quickly pressured to give up their relaxed civilian roles through a variety of enforced commands, rules, and dress regulations. In the T-groups we mentioned earlier, unfreezing takes place when individual managers are confronted by a warm, supportive atmosphere and new ways of relating to others. This type of atmosphere lowers resistance to change. The individual's identification with the tough sergeant or, in the T-group, with the effective group trainer will usually facilitate the change process. Finally, refreezing takes place when the changes are stabilized—that is, when the army code and life-style become accepted by "veterans" or when a new way of relating to others becomes a part of the manager's personal style.

THE ORGANIZATIONAL DEVELOPMENT APPROACH

The change approaches we have been discussing are particularly appropriate for immediate problems in the organization: an existing structure is leading to excessive paperwork and delayed higher-level decisions; a work-flow design is causing an excessive number of product defects; a new manager's style is irritating subordinates and causing high turnover. In sum, the approaches discussed in the preceding section help remove short-term problems that threaten the profitability or smooth functioning of the organization.

Organizational development (OD), the change approach we will describe in this section, is not designed to solve a single or temporary problem in the organization. It is a longer-term, more encompassing change approach designed to move the entire organization to a higher level of functioning—that is, to improve greatly the performance and satisfaction of organization members. While organizational development may frequently include structural, technological, and people changes, it actually seeks to make more fundamental changes in the way the organization operates.

Organizational development has been defined by Wendell French and Cecil Bell as

a long-range effort to improve an organization's problem-solving and renewal processes, particularly through a more effective and collaborative management of organization culture—with special emphasis on the culture of formal work teams—with the assistance of a change agent, or catalyst, and the use of the theory and technology of applied behavioral science, including action research.[17]

---

[16] Edgar H. Schein, "Management Development as a Process of Influence," *Industrial Management Review,* Vol. 2, No. 2 (May 1961), pp. 62–63. See also Ronald Lippitt, Jeanne Watson, and Bruce Westley, "The Phases of Planned Change," in Newton Margulies and Anthony P. Raia, eds., *Organizational Development* (New York: McGraw-Hill, 1972).

[17] For our discussion of OD we are heavily indebted to Wendell L. French and Cecil H. Bell, Jr., *Organization Development* (Englewood Cliffs, N.J.: Prentice-Hall, 1973).

The phrase *problem-solving processes* in the above definition refers to the organization's methods of dealing with the threats and opportunities in its environment. For example, managers might choose to solve the organization's problems on their own, or they might participate with subordinates in problem solving and decision making.

Through a *renewal process,* the organization's managers can adapt their problem-solving style and goals to suit the changing demands of the organization's environment. Thus, one aim of OD is to improve an organization's self-renewal process so that managers can more quickly find a management style that will be appropriate for the new problems they are facing.

Collaborative management means management through subordinate participation and power sharing, rather than through the hierarchical imposition of authority.

The term *culture* means the same thing as climate, which we discussed in Chapter 13. An organization's climate is its personality—the norms, attitudes, values, and types of interaction that prevail within the organization.

Action research refers to the way OD change agents go about finding out what aspects of the organization need to be improved and how the organization can be helped to make these improvements. Briefly, action research involves (1) a preliminary diagnosis of the problem by OD change agents; (2) data gathering to support (or disprove) the diagnosis; (3) feedback of the data to organization members; (4) exploration of the data by organization members; (5) planning of appropriate action; and (6) taking appropriate action.

Characteristics of the OD Process
As described by French and Bell, there are eight major characteristics that are typical of most OD programs. We will list and discuss these characteristics in this section.

1 *OD is an ongoing, dynamic process.* OD does not represent a quick, easy solution to an organization's problems. The OD process actually requires a considerable investment in time and money. (The organizations that use OD are therefore likely to be at least moderately successful.) OD practitioners may initially suggest a strategy for change to organization members. That strategy will be laboriously tested against the feelings and experiences of organization members and modified accordingly. Eventually, a final change strategy will emerge. Implementing that strategy may take several years.

2 *OD is a form of applied behavioral science.* OD change agents consciously attempt to apply research findings from the behavioral sciences, including psychology, sociology, and political science. For example, if the organization's reward system is seen as ineffective, they may apply the finding that in certain situations money incentives will promote productivity.

3 *OD is a normative, reeducative process.* As we shall see, OD practitioners share certain normative assumptions and values about how organization members should relate to each other. For example, they believe in open communication between organizational groups and in subordinate participation in problem solving. OD practitioners also believe that meaningful change is unlikely to take place unless the traditional assumptions and norms of organization members are replaced by more

appropriate norms and assumptions. Thus, OD change agents will work together with organization members to explore a variety of new attitudes, values, and ways of relating to others.

4 *OD takes a systems view of organizations.* As described in Chapter 2, a systems approach to organizations sees the various parts of the organization as being interrelated. OD practitioners are aware that organizational problems may have many causes, each requiring attention. They must also take into account the fact that a change in one part of the organization may affect the other parts. Thus, OD is usually implemented on an organization-wide basis.

5 *OD actions are data-based.* The actions or interventions of OD change agents are not based on what top managers see as the organization's problems or even on the initial assumptions made by the change agents themselves. Instead, the interventions are based on the change agents' research into the feelings and opinions of organization members about the organization's problems. Through attitude surveys, for example, the OD change agents may find that members resent the organization's authoritarian climate or its promotion system.

6 *OD is based on people's experiences.* OD practitioners do not base their actions on abstract management theories but on the real, day-to-day experiences of organization members. For example, they will frequently schedule a meeting after a work activity and invite members to discuss what they liked and disliked about that activity and how it was performed.

7 *OD emphasizes goal setting and planning.* As we frequently mentioned in our chapters on planning, the setting of specific, measurable goals motivates organization members and helps focus their activities. OD change agents help members learn how to set personal goals and work toward achieving them. For example, an individual's goals might be to "reduce conflict in my interactions with others and earn a promotion within three years." OD change agents may also work with managers and subordinates to help set up an MBO program to improve organizational performance.

8 *OD focuses on intact work teams.* OD practitioners believe that intact work teams provide the most effective means of achieving organizational goals. They also believe that such teams are most satisfying to their members. Most OD change agents therefore concentrate their activities on improving the performance and relationships within work teams.

OD Assumptions and Values

According to French and Bell, most practitioners of OD are in broad agreement on a number of assumptions concerning people's needs and aspirations as individuals, as group members, as group leaders, and as members of organizations. We will discuss some of these assumptions below.

People as Individuals. One of the most basic assumptions upon which OD is based is that people have a natural desire for personal development and growth. A major objective of OD is to provide the environment that supports and encourages that growth.

Another basic OD assumption is that most people not only have the potential to make a greater contribution to the organization but also have the desire to do so. OD aims to overcome those organizational factors that do not encourage or allow members to contribute more toward the achievement of organiza-

Cartoon by Leo Cullum

tional goals. For example, OD change agents may encourage greater communication about important organizational problems, in order to make it easier for employees to provide creative ideas to solve those problems.

People as Group Members and as Leaders. OD practitioners assume that it is important for people to be accepted by their work group. Without such acceptance, the performance and satisfaction of group members will suffer. In addition, OD practitioners note that the climate in most groups and organizations does not encourage the open expression of feelings by people. The necessity of suppressing feelings, OD practitioners believe, has a negative effect not only on group members' willingness and ability to solve problems constructively but also on their job satisfaction. For these reasons, OD concentrates on helping to foster trust and support among group members in order to improve group members' satisfaction and performance.

People as Members of Organizations. OD practitioners assume that the way in which work groups are linked is a strong influence on how satisfying and effective they are. For example, if communication between work groups is limited to their managers, coordination and cooperation are likely to be less effective than if all the members of the work groups could communicate.

A second OD assumption about organizations is that the policies followed and the methods practiced by the managers of large organizational groups (particularly upper-level managers) will have an effect on the manner in which the smaller groups operate, and vice versa. This influence can also work horizontally. For example, if one department presses for staggered work hours, other departments can be expected to follow.

A third OD assumption is that high-conflict strategies — those that are based on one group or department winning at the expense of another — have little chance over the long run of leading to organizational success. Instead, it is more desirable to try to find an approach, strategy, or problem solution that will be accepted by all the groups involved. (See Chapter 14.)

Values of OD Change Agents. The values of OD change agents influence the kinds of changes they will suggest. While these values are by no means universally held, there are four beliefs that most change agents share:

1 Satisfying human needs and aspirations is the primary purpose of organizational life. Change agents are therefore directly concerned with the self-fulfillment of people in organizations.

2 Encouraging the awareness and development of feelings as an integral part of organizational life will improve organizational growth and performance. Equally important, the job and personal satisfaction of the people within the organization will be enriched.

3 The role of the change agent is not to be a passive observer but to be actively involved in the organization. The agent also must be committed to research in order to be more accurate and effective in helping to select the organization's change program.

4 The equalization of power within the organization is seen by many change agents as not only desirable but necessary for long-run organizational growth and stability.

We should note that not all situations require power equalization. In some organizations, as in certain universities, hospitals, and city administrations, the top-level administrators may have a need for enhanced power in order to operate more effectively.

Types of OD Activities

Change agents have many techniques and intervention approaches at their command, not all of which will be used in every change program. In this section we will describe seven of the most widely used OD activities, as outlined by French and Bell.

1. *Diagnostic activities.* These activities are carried out in order to ascertain information about the organization and its people. Diagnostic tools may include interviews, questionnaires, psychological tests, and group meetings.

2. *Team-building activities.* These activities are designed to analyze the teams in an organization and to help them improve their effectiveness. For example, OD change agents may try to better communication between group members.

3. *Intergroup activities.* These activities are meant to improve the working relationship of interdependent groups. Emphasis is usually placed on effectively coordinating the groups' joint efforts and goals.

4. *Survey-feedback activities.* These activities are an important part of diagnostic activities. Information on attitudes, problems, perceived opportunities, and other important data are collected from organization members through surveys. This information is then reported back to organization members (with individual identities protected) so that members can determine what actions need to be taken to solve the problems and exploit the opportunities uncovered in the surveys.

5. *Education and training activities.* The aim of these activities is to increase the satisfaction and performance of organization members by adding to their skills and knowledge. For example, individuals may be taught technical skills to improve their job performance, or they may be helped to improve their interpersonal skills so that they can function more effectively in groups.

6. *Technostructural activities.* This type of intervention involves examining the technical and structural parts of the organization to see how they are affecting the performance of organization members. If necessary, new and more effective technical or structural patterns may be set up.

7. *Process consultation activities.* The primary purpose of these activities is to give organization members, particularly managers, new insights into human interrelationships in organizations and to help members develop new skills in recognizing and dealing with organizational problems. Group decision-making techniques, effective leadership roles, and functional conflict are examples of subjects that OD change agents and organization members might deal with together.

Grid OD. One of the more publicized OD techniques, the so-called "grid OD," makes systematic use of several of the OD activities described above. The grid OD approach is based on the Managerial Grid developed by Robert Blake and Jane Mouton.[18]

The Managerial Grid is based on the concept that there are two key variables found in organizations: concern for *production* and concern for *people.* The grid identifies possible combinations of these two variables.

As shown in the accompanying illustration, concern for people is the vertical axis of the grid, while concern for production is the horizontal axis. At

---

[18] See Robert R. Blake and Jane S. Mouton, *The Managerial Grid: Key Orientations for Achieving Production through People* (Houston: Gulf Publishing, 1964), and *Building a Dynamic Organization through Grid Organization Development* (Reading, Mass.: Addison-Wesley, 1969). Note that Grid is a registered service mark of Scientific Methods, Inc., and is used by permission.

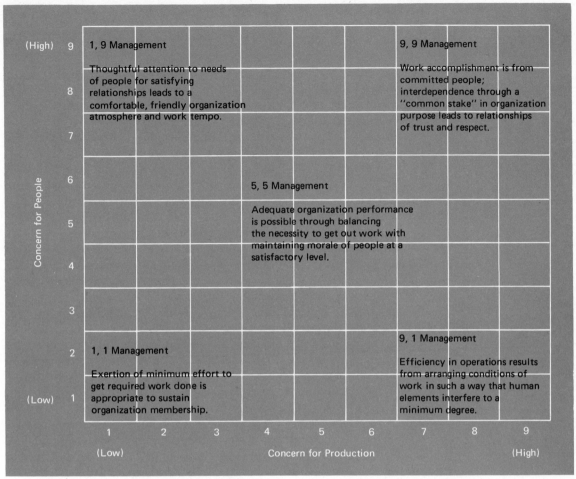

FIGURE 15-4 The Managerial Grid

Source: *The Managerial Grid* by Robert R. Blake and Jane Srygley Mouton (Houston: Gulf Publishing Company), p. 10. Copyright © 1964. Reproduced with permission.

the lower left-hand corner is what can be called a "1,1 management style" — low concern for both production and people. The 1,1 managers may place primary emphasis on staying out of trouble; they simply pass along orders from superiors. The 1,9 management style — high concern for people but low concern for production — is in the upper left-hand corner. The 1,9 managers may try to create a secure, happy environment for their subordinates and assume that they therefore will not be able to achieve the organization's production goals. High concern for production and low concern for people — the 9,1 management style — is in the lower right-hand corner. The 9,1 managers may see the personal needs of organization members as irrelevant or even harmful to organizational goals; they may therefore use their authority to pressure their subordinates to meet high production quotas. At the middle of the grid is the

5,5 management style—a compromise between concern for people and concern for production. The 5,5 managers may try to find a middle-of-the-road position to balance the needs of organization members and goals. In the upper right-hand corner is the 9,9 management style—high concern for people as well as for production. This style is widely considered to be the most effective of all. The 9,9 managers try to develop cohesive, committed work groups so that both high production and high satisfaction will result.

In grid organizational development, change agents use the concepts of the grid to encourage managers to reexamine their own style and work toward 9,9 effectiveness. A grid OD program commonly has six phases:

Phase 1: Training. This phase usually occurs after top managers in a fairly successful organization become convinced (1) that their organization has too little vitality; (2) that there is a gap between the organization's performance and potential; and (3) that grid OD should be examined as a possible solution for the organization's problems. During this phase, several key managers attend a week-long seminar to learn about grid concepts and how they are applied. In seminar sessions, they assess their own managerial styles and work on improving such skills as team development, group problem solving, and communication. After appropriate instruction, these key managers will work to implement the grid program throughout their organization.

Phase 2: Team Development. In this phase, the trained managers transfer their knowledge of and experience with Managerial Grid concepts to the work situation. Managers and their immediate subordinates are helped to work together to explore new managerial styles and operating procedures. Emphasis is placed on improving both manager-subordinate relationships and team effectiveness so that the team will operate on the 9,9 grid level.

Phase 3: Intergroup Development. The purpose of this phase is to change the relationship between the organization's work groups from one of conflict to one of cooperation in meeting organizational goals. The techniques used in this phase are similar to the group conflict reduction methods described in Chapter 14: intergroup tensions are dealt with openly, and joint problem-solving procedures are developed.

Phase 4: Organizational Goal Setting. In this phase, grid OD involves matters of concern to the entire organization, such as labor-management relations, promotion policies, productivity, and budgetary guidelines. Usually, top managers of the organization will work together to create a model of what the organization ideally should be like. They will then tentatively set a series of goals that are designed to help the organization move toward the top managers' ideal. These goals will be tested, evaluated, and refined by managers and subordinates working together throughout the organization.

Phase 5: Goal Attainment. In this phase, organization members seek to make the ideal model a reality. Members of the various components of the organization examine how their activities *should* be carried out in order to achieve excellence. They then proceed to take whatever corrective action is necessary so that they can begin to attain their subunit's—and ultimately the organization's—ideal goals.

GRID OD

Training

Team Development

Intergroup Development

Organizational Goal Setting

Goal Attainment

Stabilization

Phase 6: Stabilization. Eventually, the results of all the phases are evaluated to determine which areas of the organization still need improvement or alteration. Efforts are made to stabilize positive changes and to identify new areas of opportunity for the organization.

Evaluation of the grid OD approach is difficult because of the complexity, scope, and long-term nature of the program. However, one study found that such a program led to significant improvements in organizational effectiveness in terms of productivity and profits. In addition, managers involved in the program reported that it led to positive changes in their attitudes and behavior.[19]

Conditions for Successful OD Programs

French and Bell have identified eleven conditions that they believe are necessary in order for an OD program to be successful:

1. *Recognition by top or other managers that the organization has problems.* Without such recognition, it is highly unlikely that the necessary time, effort, and money will be invested in OD.

2. *Use of an outside behavioral scientist-consultant.* As we suggested earlier, internal change agents are unlikely to have the experience or freedom required to implement a change program.

3. *Support and involvement by top-level managers.* Only top managers have the authority to overcome initial resistance to change that can develop in the organization. In addition, top managers can readily keep all organization units informed about OD.

4. *Use of action research.* Without data, an OD program may be misguided. Furthermore, the fact that organization members respond to surveys or questionnaires creates a feeling of involvement in the program.

5. *Early successes.* If the first OD changes are implemented and prove successful, organization members will be motivated to make larger-scale changes.

6. *Education of organization members about OD.* People are likely to feel manipulated if they do not understand the reasons for changes. Making behavioral science knowledge widely available will minimize this barrier to change.

7. *Acknowledgement of managers' strengths.* Managers who have already tried to practice good management techniques are likely to resent an OD change agent who overplays the "expert" or "teacher" role.

8. *Involvement with managers of personnel departments.* Personnel managers have as their primary responsibility the management of the organization's human resources. Thus, their advice and cooperation are essential in implementing changes in such areas as employee evaluation and promotion and salary policies.

9. *Development of internal OD resources.* Change agents cannot possibly assume indefinite or total responsibility for the organization's change efforts.

---

[19] Robert R. Blake et al., "Breakthrough in Organization Development," *Harvard Business Review,* November-December 1964, pp. 133–155.

Eventually, the organization's managers must begin to take over the change agents' role.

10. *Effective management of the OD program.* Change agents and client must work together to coordinate and control the OD program. Otherwise, the organization's change effort may lose its impetus and become fragmented.

11. *Measurement of results.* The success of the organization in meeting its human and organizational goals must be monitored. Success in a particular subunit will suggest that the OD program is working; failure will suggest that the program needs to be modified. Data on results provide change agents and managers with important feedback on the organization's change efforts.

Summary   There are several ways in which managers can deal with the changes that may confront them and their organizations. Constructive approaches to change include reacting to change and planning for change. The former approach is appropriate for the day-to-day changes a manager must make. The latter approach is necessary when a major part or all of the organization needs to change. The need to change may be created by forces outside or within the organization.

Greiner's model of organizational change suggests that successful change depends on a redistribution of power within the organization. He divides the developmental process of change into six phases; pressure and arousal, intervention and reorientation, diagnosis and recognition, invention and commitment, experimentation and search, and reinforcement and acceptance.

Resistance to change may be based on uncertainty about the causes and effects of change, unwillingness to give up existing benefits, and awareness of weaknesses in the changes proposed. Most of the resistance can be overcome by collaborating with subordinates in change decisions.

Leavitt has suggested that an organization can be changed by modifying its structure, technology, and/or its people. *Structural* changes may involve the application of classical management principles, decentralization, or changes in work flow. *Technological* changes may involve redesigning work operations. *Technostructural* changes combine technical and structural elements. *People* changes attempt to improve the attitudes, skills, and knowledge of organization members.

People change approaches may involve the organization's individuals or groups. On an individual level, change may involve three elements: *unfreezing* of old attitudes, *changing,* and *refreezing* of new attitudes. On an organization-wide level, change may require the *organizational development* approach. In this approach, the principles of behavioral science are applied in an effort to educate members of the entire organization in new ways of relating to one another and of meeting personal and organizational goals. OD change agents assume that people can most effectively satisfy their own needs and those of the organization in cooperative, intact, and high-performing work teams.

Grid OD is a six-phase OD program based on the concepts of the Managerial Grid. It uses a variety of OD activities to bring about a high level of concern for people *and* production in the organization.

Review Questions
1. What are some nonconstructive responses to change pressures? Can you think of some examples of these nonconstructive responses in any of our society's political, business, or nonprofit organizations?
2. What are two constructive responses to change pressures? When is each approach likely to be used?

3. What are some internal and external sources of change in organizations?

4. What are the two key ideas upon which Greiner's model of change is based? What are the six phases of this model?

5. What are the three categories of resistance to change? Which type of resistance should be encouraged? How may each type be dealt with or overcome?

6. What are the three structural approaches to change?

7. What do technostructural approaches to change attempt to do? Why were these approaches to change developed? What are some examples of technostructural change approaches?

8. How does the assumption underlying the people approach to change differ from the assumption underlying the structural and technical approaches?

9. What obstacles to change caused Lewin to devise his model of individual change? According to Schein, what are the two mechanisms through which individuals learn new attitudes?

10. What are the eight major characteristics of the OD process?

11. What are the values upon which OD is based? Which of these values do you share?

12. Which are the most widely used OD activities?

13. What are the five types of managerial styles indicated on the Managerial Grid?

14. What are the six phases of grid OD?

15. According to French and Bell, what conditions are required for a successful OD program?

CASE STUDY: PROGRESS ON PURPOSE

Carl Bolling is a participant in the company's training program titled Systems and Procedures Studies. The participants meet once weekly for two hours over an eight-month period. The program is staffed by a local college professor.

As part of the requirements of the program, each participant is required to undertake a work-study project of his own choosing with the idea of critically analyzing the work activities observed and suggesting improvement for them through the application of techniques and ideas learned in the program. It was stressed by the professor at the beginning of the program that the "human element" was one of the prime factors to pay attention to when undertaking such a study.

Carl Bolling has the title of Planning Engineer. In this capacity, he engages in coordinating activities between the operating, production, and engineering departments. His selected work-study project for the training program deals with the purchase and order of heavy equipment for installation in new plants being constructed by the company. It concerns specifically the control of costs associated with purchased equipment that sometimes sits crated on a new plant location for weeks before it is ready for installation, Carl Bolling had analyzed the scheduling procedures of the construction department and the purchasing procedures of the operating department plus the required specifications and design of equipment by the engineering department. It was his opinion that thousands of dollars yearly could be saved by the company if the construction and operating departments would adopt the formal planning and purchasing procedures that he proposed. He felt convinced that his analysis of the problem was sound and his analysis of potential cost savings accurate.

Case from Francis J. Bridges, Kenneth W. Olm, and J. Allison Barnhill, *Management Decisions and Organizational Policy,* 2nd ed. (Boston: Allyn and Bacon, Inc., 1977), pp. 629–630. Reprinted by permission of the publisher.

Upon submitting his work-study project to fellow participants in the training program, he felt pleased that the group and the professor endorsed his project as "sound" and "well done." Upon submitting his proposal to his immediate boss, the vice president of engineering, he was gratified to know that the vice president planned to propose the introduction of his new procedures at the next meeting of the executive management committee.

Two weeks later the vice president of engineering called Bolling to his office and told him his suggested planning and purchasing procedures had been presented to the executive management committee. The reaction had been violent! They resented a mere planning engineer crossing functional lines and making recommendations in areas other than his own. They disliked the implication that their activities were costing the company thousands of dollars yearly, and they told the vice president of engineering that, in the future, he (Bolling) would be considered *persona non grata* in their departments.

The vice president of engineering suggested to Bolling that maybe it would be best if he were transferred to another division in the company. At least he would not run the risk of meeting these executives personally.

Case Questions
1. Could Bolling have avoided the problem brought about by his proposal? How?
2. How should the vice president of engineering have handled Bolling's proposal?
3. What do you think of the vice president's suggestion that Bolling should transfer to another division?
4. What do you think Bolling should do now?

Part **IV**

Leading

Case on Leading

WESTON UNIVERSITY

In early 1969, Thomas Ball had left the deanship of a prestigious West Coast college of business administration to assume the presidency of Weston University, succeeding Dr. Harold Powers. Weston had for several decades maintained a reputation as the leading private university in the Middle West. In recent years, however, its reputation had begun to weaken. This had not been in any way due to President Powers' abilities as an academician; in fact, it was his reputation as a scholar that had most impressed Weston's Board and resulted in his being offered the presidency. Rather, his problem had stemmed from a lack of leadership ability. He had found it difficult to handle the sometimes unpleasant tasks necessary to keep Weston's faculty productive and respected. Perhaps benefiting from the problem of Dr. Powers, the Board had conducted its search for his successor on the premise that academic standing alone was not a sufficient qualification for the office of president. They had felt their new president would have to combine an interest in upgrading Weston's academic standing with the business acumen necessary to implement the actions required to achieve this excellence. With these qualifications, the Board's search had identified Thomas Ball as a strong candidate, and he had been offered the position.

In the first several months of his tenure, the Board had every reason to be pleased with its choice. They were particularly impressed with Ball's professional approach to developing a long-range plan for the college. However, some of the deans of Weston's schools had quietly expressed disappointment that Ball had not consulted them more closely in the development of the plan. To be sure, he had asked each of them what his goals were for his particular school, and each had implied that he most wanted his school to be part of a first-rate institution, such as Weston had been in the past. The deans had also expressed the need for additional money for more competitive salaries, for a larger teaching staff, and for increased support of faculty research. Each had noted that Weston's salary scale was shamefully low, and almost all of them could cite the names of promising young faculty members who had been lost to other universities that had enticed them away with promises of higher salaries and other perquisites. Thomas Ball was convinced that in terms of prestige, work load, facilities, and environment, Weston could successfully compete with most of the institutions now pirating his faculty. But in terms of salary scale for both initial-level appointments and higher-level positions, as well as in terms of the criteria used for salary advances, Weston was definitely lagging behind other schools. Fortunately, Weston's plant facilities were in

Case copyright © 1970 by the Trustees of The Institute for Educational Management.

satisfactory shape, so President Ball felt that he could budget the funds necessary for salary increases during the coming academic year. He was concerned, however, with Weston's system of salary raises. Under President Powers, a fixed percentage of Weston's yearly income had been apportioned for raises in faculty salaries. This percentage was divided into equal amounts for each member of the teaching staff. In the early days of President Powers' tenure, department chairpersons had submitted recommendations that raises not be given to particular faculty members whose teaching or publication activities were undistinguished, but these recommendations had been rarely heeded by the president. Consequently, every faculty member could count on at least a token raise each year. This practice of "raises for all each July" had been followed without interruption by Dr. Powers throughout his fifteen-year tenure. Upon assuming the presidency, however, Dr. Ball concluded that something had to be done to institute a meaningful merit system.

After considerable thought and study on the matter, President Ball developed the following incentive program:

— one-third of the faculty would receive "significant" raises based on meritorious teaching *and* publication.
— one-third of the faculty would receive a "token" raise based on the rising cost of living.
— one-third of the faculty would receive no raise.

At the next meeting of the Council of Deans, President Ball presented his plan. After outlining his proposal, the president invited discussion on the plan.

"Mr. President," said Dean Mayer of the Medical School, "I can see what you're trying to accomplish, and I agree with what you are trying to do. The idea of promoting and giving raises on the basis of merit makes a lot of sense to me. Weston is on the brink of a new era and only the best faculty should have a place here. We've tried different methods in the past of recruiting and retaining the best teachers and researchers. However, for some time now, it's been no secret that once appointed, faculty members had found a home at Weston. Dismissals were, and still are, rare, while resignations are not so rare when other universities come around with more money in hand. Under President Powers, it was impossible to go outside the salary range to attract a new professor, or to go beyond a modest raise to retain a good professor."

"I disagree," said Dean Hunter of the College of Arts and Sciences. "I doubt whether you can ever in retrospect determine why a given professor did not choose to come to Weston, or why another one left here. It might indeed be the money, but it might also be for any one of a number of other reasons that we can only guess at. I think you've jumped at money as being the primary motivation, and I think you're wrong. Academic people tend to be rather liberal and unconcerned with finances. For example, they have always been in the forefront of support for such measures as Social Security, Medicare, and the guaranteed annual wage. I don't mean to sound rude, but some might argue that you're confusing an academic community with a business community."

"I don't think that your generalizations about academic people would really stand up when you got down to actual cases," answered President Ball. "In fact, it seems to me that the evidence right here at Weston belies your argument that faculties are not motivated by money. I understand that young teachers have left Weston 'because of the money' to go to other universities for as little as $200 to $300 a year more. Pardon me if I sound rude also, but it seems to me that Weston's faculty, like most, seem to be rather hypocritical on the subject of money. They seem to feel that it is vulgar to discuss it, or to admit that they're motivated by it, when, in fact, they are. Of course, I'm not naive enough to think that they're motivated solely by dollars. I recognize that a person will not demand as high a salary from a prestigious school as from a second-rate one. Unfortunately, I'm afraid that we cannot console ourselves with that fact, since I think we would all agree that Weston is no longer prestigious enough for that phenomenon to work here. We must therefore compete in all ways—in teaching loads, in course preferences, in research facilities and grants, in graduate assistantships, and in salary. Salary is only one part of this, but I feel it can play an important role. Money may not necessarily be all important by itself, but I believe it is psychologically important. It's a method of showing a person that you value him or her. A raise is like a good grade on a report card. It's important to people as a way in which the university can acknowledge that they are doing a good job. Most people need to know that their work is being acknowledged and recognized, and money is probably the best way of accomplishing this, even in an academic environment. And don't overlook the value of a high-quality faculty. If we can attract some 'stars' by paying them a competitive salary, this will help in recruiting promising young professors. Good people attract good people—and keep them."

"Mr. President," said Dean Kaufman of the School of Fine Arts, "even if we all were in agreement with you, we'd still be leery about implementing a merit system after so many years. How is this merit system going to work? Who would do the evaluating?"

"The department chairpersons would," answered President Ball. "They would then pass their recommendations on to you for approval."

"This will be very difficult to sell to the department chairpersons," said Dean Hunter. "In fact, it could really hurt your relations with the faculty, Mr. President. What you're proposing will throw this campus into turmoil. You're doing fine now, sir; why rock the boat?"

"We have to look ahead to a greater university, and we must be able to pay for those who will make it great. We must separate the wheat from the chaff and, quite frankly, harass those on tenure who don't measure up. I recognize the difficulties here, but the job must be done if Weston is to achieve the level of academic excellence that I envision."

"But, you can't expect such a radical change to take place overnight," said Dean Kaufman. "It takes time for change in an academic community.

Suppose you succeeded in driving out the tenured deadwood; we can't have a faculty made up entirely of 'stars.' We need some 'good soldiers,' some warm bodies to do the basic chores of teaching. If, for example, some of our English Composition professors on tenure were to leave as a result of this salary policy or because they were embarrassed by their younger colleagues, we would have to go out and recruit replacements and would have to pay them far more than we pay our present group."

"I agree," said Dean Hunter. "Can we morally fire people who have been here for years and are too old to begin fresh again? And, we *would* be firing them if we succeeded in embarrassing them into leaving."

"This may sound very callous," said President Ball, "but I firmly believe that it is better to fire someone who has become deadwood, for the sake of both the university and the professor himself. It is good for the university for the obvious reasons: first, you can hire for a small percentage more a person of higher ability; next, it takes the extra weight the old professor wasn't carrying off the shoulders of his colleagues by making their classes smaller since everyone won't be trying to avoid one professor; and, finally, the students are no longer cheated out of an education in the professor's area of concentration. I think that it can also be of benefit to the person fired. Most incompetent teachers are aware they're incompetent, and firing them just might give them the impetus to seek the kind of job in which they will be both happy and productive. If, on the other hand, some people are not aware of their incompetence, then it's about time someone told them."

"This is all fine, but it still doesn't solve the problems of evaluation," said Dean Kaufman. "How are we to evaluate, Mr. President? Research? Teaching? Personal character? Committee work? I wouldn't know how to discriminate. It's difficult enough to do an appraisal when a person comes up for promotion, but to do it every year for every person where money is concerned is frightening."

"Mr. President," said Dean Lang of the Engineering School, "it may be all well and good for some of the deans to favor this plan, but I would have a revolution in my place. I have enough trouble keeping the faculty happy as it is with the endless squabbles over equipment, teaching loads, and space. Trying to appraise scientists, and that's everyone on my faculty, is impossible. I think that *you* ought to do the evaluating. If one wanted to be legalistic about it, we could say that, as chief executive, it's your responsibility."

"I appreciate your problem," said President Ball. "However, your suggestion that I do the evaluating would be highly unfair to the faculty and would, as the students say, be essentially a cop-out. I don't know the faculty well enough to be able to judge them fairly. The department chairpersons are the best qualified to make the evaluations, and we have a double check in that all of you can review their decisions to make certain there are no gross miscarriages of justice. As for the actual evaluation, it won't be that difficult. I'm not asking you to grade them as narrowly as you do students. I suspect all of you could go through your faculty members right now and tell me which ones are incompetent, which are satisfactory, and which are exceptionally good. If this was a cocktail party, you'd probably be able to classify them easily, but you're afraid to make the decision because it involves money and the professors' feelings. An academic community may be somewhat isolated from the cold and cruel world, but part of your responsibility as a dean, and part of the responsibility of the department chairperson, is to handle difficult situations. If it were easy, you wouldn't have the prestige and additional money that goes with your positions. I feel strongly that this policy should be implemented, and I need your help in selling it to the various department heads. Please give it some thought. I'll be happy to hear any suggestions you might have that would achieve the same goal without causing the problems some of you think my plan might."

The generally antagonistic reaction of the deans to his proposal took President Ball by surprise. He felt that his plan was the obvious way to upgrade Weston's academic standing, and he was dismayed that there had been meaningful disagreement. In an effort to understand better what had transpired, President Ball called in Dr. George Henry, an old friend and a ranking member of the Psychology Department. He explained what had transpired and sought Dr. Henry's explanation of the reluctance of some of the deans.

"Part of the attraction of the academic life for these professors is the security and tranquility of campus life," answered Dr. Henry. "You're asking them to begin competing in a way that they fear will shatter that security and tranquility. In addition, the people who receive extra money will feel guilty for receiving it, because they'll know that, in effect, it'll be coming out of the pocket of a colleague who may be making a real contribution to Weston, but who may not be the greatest scholar in the world. This will also have the appearance of being a cleverly disguised purge on the part of the president and his deans, and the deans, not surprisingly, may not want to be associated with that. Faculty members are going to be asking who the president and his deans think they are to assume the role of God. You may be able to accept the lonely role of chief executive, but they might not."

"What do you think I ought to do?" asked the President.

"Quite frankly, I don't know," answered Dr. Henry. "The only thing I can recommend is for you to try to involve as many people as possible in this decision. However, if the response of the deans is any indication, this may be impossible. If you can't get more universal support than you have now, you may well have to scuttle the project. Frankly, Tom, the word has leaked out about your proposal, and it's causing unrest within the faculty ranks. You're going to have to do something very soon."

Following their discussion, President Ball spent some time reflecting on what Dr. Henry had said. He realized that he had to do something to broaden the backing for his plan, or he would have to give it up. Since he considered it to be the right course to follow, he knew he had to think of something soon to avoid further endangering faculty morale.

1. What effect do you think the old salary system had on professors' motivation, performance, and satisfaction? What effects is the new system likely to have, if it is instituted?
2. Do you agree or disagree with President Ball's arguments on why the new salary system should be instituted?
3. Who do you believe should evaluate Weston's professors?
4. How would you account for the deans' resistance to President Ball's plan?
5. What should President Ball do?

Chapter 16

Motivation, Performance, and Satisfaction

Upon completing this chapter you should be able to:

1. Identify and describe three theoretical approaches to motivation.
2. State how views of motivation in organizations have evolved.
3. Explain the systems view of motivation in organizations.
4. Describe the contributions of various theorists on motivation, and state how their work is related to motivation in organizations.
5. Explain the behavior modification approach to influencing behavior in organizations.
6. Describe two integrative approaches to motivation.

In this unit we will be discussing the third in our list of management functions, leading. The leadership function is the one in which the manager is most directly involved with subordinates; thus, leading is a central part of the manager's role, which involves working with and through others to achieve organizational goals. To a large extent, a manager's leadership ability—that is, a manager's ability to motivate, influence, direct, and communicate with subordinates—will determine the manager's effectiveness.

This chapter is concerned with how managers can motivate subordinates so that their performance and satisfaction will be increased. We are starting our unit on leadership with a chapter on motivation, because managers cannot lead unless subordinates are motivated to follow them. Chapter 17, "Leadership," describes the leadership styles that are available to managers and also discusses which is most effective in the various situations a manager is likely to confront. Chapter 18, "Interpersonal and Organizational Communication," is designed to help readers understand the importance of effective communication in organizations. Chapter 19, "Staffing and the Personnel Function," describes how managers recruit, select, train, and appraise the managerial and nonmanagerial employees that they need to help them and their organizations operate. Chapter 20, "Organizational Careers and Individual Development," is designed to help prospective managers plan their careers and inform them about some of the things they can expect as they enter and move up the organizational hierarchy.

THE IMPORTANCE OF MOTIVATION

Motivation—that which causes, channels, and sustains people's behavior—has always been an important and puzzling subject for managers. It is an important subject because managers, by definition, work with and through people. They need some understanding of why people behave as they do so that they can influence people to perform in ways that the managers find desirable. Motivation is a puzzling subject because motives cannot be directly observed or measured—they must be inferred from people's behavior. In addition, there are many theories, both old and new, about why people are motivated to behave as they do. These theories differ in what they implicitly suggest managers should do to obtain effective performance from the people around them. In our discussion, we will cover both old and new theoretical perspectives on motivation.[1] Thus, readers will gain an understanding of the current state of knowledge about motivation and its relationship to work behavior and satisfaction.

[1] For a major part of our discussion on motivation we are deeply indebted to the excellent coverage of the subject found in the following works: Richard M. Steers and Lyman W. Porter, eds., *Motivation and Work Behavior* (New York: McGraw-Hill, 1975), and Lyman W. Porter and Raymond E. Miles, "Motivation and Management" in Joseph W. McGuire, ed., *Contemporary Management: Issues and Viewpoints* (Englewood Cliffs, N.J.: Prentice-Hall, 1974), pp. 545–570.

Before beginning our discussion, we should note that motivation is not the only influence on a person's performance level. The other two factors that influence how well a person performs in a given situation are the individual's abilities and the individual's understanding of what behaviors are necessary in order to achieve high performance. This latter factor can be called "role perceptions." The relationship of all three factors to performance can be shown by the following equation:

Performance = f (motivation, ability, role perceptions)

If *any* one factor has a low value, performance level is likely to be low, even if the other factors are high.

For example, a young man may have an enormous desire to be an outstanding wide receiver (high motivation). He may also know exactly how to do the job well (high role perceptions) — for instance, he may understand the principles and strategies of football and may have figured out the best way to penetrate any defense formation. However, if he is slow, short, and without "good hands" (low ability), he is unlikely to perform well as a wide receiver even if his desire to do so increases.

This perspective is sometimes forgotten by many managers who tend to diagnose all performance problems as the result of "lack of motivation" or "not trying hard enough." Many performance problems are not of this nature, and driving or pushing someone to work harder is not very helpful if, for example, that individual does not have the training to do the job properly. Readers should keep in mind during our discussion that motivation is only *one* of the factors needed for high performance.

WAYS OF LOOKING AT MOTIVATION

It will be useful to our discussion to review some of the major ways of looking at and classifying motivation theories, since each of the various theoretical perspectives will shed light on how motivation influences work performance. One distinction that can be made is between *content* theories, which focus on the "what" of motivation, and *process* theories, which focus on the "how" of motivation.[2] *Reinforcement* theories represent a third approach, which emphasizes the ways in which behavior is learned.[3] Here we will introduce these approaches and indicate their basic similarities and differences. We will go into each one more deeply in later sections.

Content Theories   The content approach is associated with such names as Maslow, McGregor, Herzberg, Atkinson, and McClelland. Some of these names are familiar to managers (and to our readers) because these authors have strongly influenced

[2] See John P. Campbell et al., *Managerial Behavior, Performance and Effectiveness* (New York: McGraw-Hill, 1970).

[3] See Walter R. Nord, "Beyond the Teaching Machine," *Organizational Behavior and Human Performance,* Vol. 4, No. 4 (November 1969), pp. 375–401.

the field of management and have affected the thoughts and actions of practicing managers.

The content perspective stresses the importance of understanding the factors *within* individuals that cause them to act in a certain way. It attempts to answer such questions as: What needs do people try to satisfy? What impels them toward action? In this view, individuals have inner needs that they are driven, pressured, or motivated to reduce or fulfill. They may be motivated, for example, by the need for food, sex, security, achievement, or self-fulfillment. The particular need they have will determine the action which they take. That is, individuals will act or behave in ways that will lead to the satisfaction of their need. (See Figure 16-1.) For example, an employee who has a strong achievement need may be motivated to work extra hours in order to complete a difficult task on time; an employee with a strong need for self-esteem might be motivated to work very carefully in order to produce work of high quality.

At first glance, this approach to motivation seems simple: it suggests that managers can determine subordinates' needs by observing their actions, and that managers can predict subordinates' actions by becoming aware of their needs. In practice, however, motivation is a far more complicated concept. There are several reasons for this complexity.

First, needs differ considerably among individuals. Many ambitious managers, highly motivated to achieve power and status, have found it hard to understand that not all the people working under them are influenced by the same values and drives that they are. As a result, such managers find that trying to "motivate" these people is a frustrating and discouraging experience. Individual differences among subordinates enormously complicate a manager's motivational task.

Second, the ways in which needs are eventually translated into actions also vary considerably between one individual and another. One individual with a strong security need may "play it safe" and avoid accepting responsibility for fear of failing and being fired. Another individual with the same security need may seek out responsibility for fear of being fired for low performance.

FIGURE 16-1
A Content Theory
Model of
Motivation

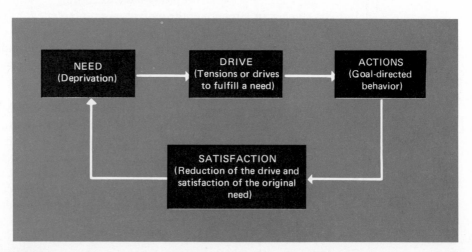

Third, individuals are not always consistent in the ways in which they act on their needs and in the needs that motivate them at any given time. One day we may give a challenging task to a subordinate, and that subordinate will outperform our highest expectations. Another time that same subordinate will seem lax and will perform in a mediocre manner.

Finally, the reactions of individuals to successful or unsuccessful fulfillment of their needs will differ. Some individuals with a high security need who fail to attain their goal (say, tenure at a university) may become frustrated and give up trying. Others may be motivated to redouble their efforts (say, by writing and publishing additional scholarly articles).

The more familiar we become with the people around us (and with ourselves), the more predictable will become the process by which needs are translated into actions. However, there are enough complexities and alternatives at each step in the process to cause us to make incorrect predictions a fair number of times.

Process Theories

Rather than emphasizing the content of needs and the driving nature of those needs, the process approach emphasizes *how* and *by what goals* individuals are motivated. In this view, needs are just one element in a process by which individuals decide how to behave. For example, individuals might see the strong possibility of receiving some reward (say, a salary increase) if they act in a certain way (say, by working hard). This reward will become an incentive or motive for their behavior.

Basic to process theories on motivation is the notion of *expectancy*—that is, what the individual believes is likely to occur as a result of his or her behavior. For instance, if the individual expects that meeting deadlines will earn praise from superiors and not meeting deadlines will earn disapproval, and if that individual prefers praise, then the individual will be motivated to meet deadlines. Conversely, if the individual expects that meeting deadlines will not earn praise, the individual may not be as motivated to meet those deadlines.

An additional factor in motivation, according to some process theorists, is the *valence* or strength of the individual's preference for the expected outcome. For example, if the individual expects that working hard to exceed production quotas will lead to promotion to supervisor and the individual strongly desires to be supervisor, then he or she will be motivated to exceed production quotas.

Reinforcement Theories

Reinforcement theories are associated with B. F. Skinner, operant conditioning, and behavior modification. These theories do not utilize the concept of a motive or a process of motivation. Instead, they deal with how the *consequences* of a past action influence future actions in a cyclical *learning* process. In this view, people behave the way they do because, in past circumstances, they learned that certain behaviors were associated with pleasant outcomes, and that certain other behaviors were associated with unpleasant outcomes. Because people generally prefer pleasant outcomes, they are likely to repeat behaviors that they have learned will have pleasant consequences. For example, individuals may be likely to obey the law—and a manager's legitimate instructions—because they have learned at home and at school that obedience to authority leads to praise and disobedience leads to punishment.

EARLY VIEWS OF MOTIVATION IN ORGANIZATIONS

In Chapter 2, we discussed how approaches to management have evolved since the industrial revolution. We noted that the circumstances of a manager's job changed over time—early managers, for example, dealt with subordinates' performance of relatively uncomplicated tasks, while many, if not most, of today's managers deal with individuals' performance of more complicated work. We also noted that knowledge about effective and ineffective managerial approaches and about the importance of social forces in the workplace grew over time. These changes affected the development of management thought.

In this section, we will elaborate somewhat on our discussion in Chapter 2, but with a focus on the underlying model or theory of motivation that managers tended to possess at different stages in the evolution of management thought. We will identify three major models: the traditional model, the human relations model, and the human resources model.[4] As we shall see, the beliefs that managers have about motivation are important determinants of how they attempt to manage people.

The Traditional Model

The traditional model of motivation is associated with Frederick Taylor and the scientific management school. According to this school, an important aspect of the manager's job was to make sure that workers performed their boring, repetitive tasks in the most efficient way. To motivate workers to perform their jobs successfully, managers had at their disposal a system of wage incentives—the more that workers produced, the more they would earn.

This motivational tool was based on the assumption or theory that workers were essentially lazy and could be motivated only with the promise of financial reward. In many situations, incentives were effective; over time, however, managers reduced the magnitude of the wage incentive that they offered workers. In addition, as efficiency rose, fewer workers were needed for a specific task. Layoffs became common, and workers began to seek job security rather than only temporary and minor wage increases.

The Human Relations Model

When it became apparent that the traditional approach to motivation was no longer adequate, management researchers and writers began to search for alternative explanations for employee behavior. Elton Mayo and the other human relations researchers found that the social contacts which employees had at work were important to them and that the boredom and repetitiveness of tasks were in themselves factors in reducing the motivation to work. They

---

[4] See Steers and Porter, *Motivation and Work Behavior,* pp. 15–20.

suggested that managers could motivate employees by acknowledging their social needs and by making them feel useful and important.

In response to these insights, organizations attempted to acknowledge the social needs of employees, and tried to motivate employees by increasing their job satisfaction. Employees were given some freedom to make their own decisions on the job. Greater attention was paid to the organization's informal work groups. More information was provided to employees about managers' intentions and about the operations of the organization.

The intent of managers, however, remained the same as in the traditional model: to have workers accept the work situation as established by the managers. In the traditional model, the workers were expected to accept management's authority in return for high wages made possible by the efficient system designed by management and implemented by the worker. In the human relations model, the workers were expected to accept management's authority because the supervisors treated them with consideration and were attentive to their needs.

The Human Resources Model

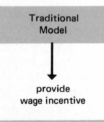

provide
wage incentive

cater to
employees'
social needs

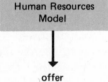

offer
increased
responsibility

Later theorists and researchers, such as Argyris, McGregor, Likert, and Maslow, criticized the human relations model as being simply a more sophisticated approach to the manipulation of employees. These theorists suggested that employees were motivated by a wide variety of factors—not only money, or the desire for satisfaction, but also the need for achievement and meaning in work. They argued that most individuals are already motivated to do a good job and that they do not automatically see work as undesirable. In fact, employees are likely to derive satisfaction from high performance (rather than perform well because they feel satisfaction, as in the human relations model). Thus, employees can be given far more responsibility for making decisions and carrying out their tasks, since they are already motivated to do well and are likely to meet organizational goals on their own.

The task of managers, according to the human resources model, is not to induce workers to comply with managerial objectives by bribing them with high wages, as in the traditional model, nor even to manipulate them with considerate treatment, as in the human relations model. Instead, it is to develop a shared responsibility for achieving organizational and individual objectives, with each individual contributing on the basis of his or her interests and abilities. (See Table 16-1 for a description of all three approaches.)

One fairly recent study of business managers found that managers today tend to believe in two models of motivation simultaneously. With their subordinates, managers tend to operate according to the human relations model: they try to reduce subordinates' resistance by improving morale and satisfaction. For themselves, however, managers prefer the human resources model: they feel their own talents are underutilized, and they seek greater responsibility from their superiors.[5]

[5] Raymond E. Miles, "Human Relations or Human Resources," *Harvard Business Review,* July-August 1965, pp. 148–163.

TABLE 16-1 General Patterns of Managerial Approaches to Motivation

Traditional Model	Human Relations Model	Human Resources Model
Assumptions		
1. Work is inherently distasteful to most people. 2. What they do is less important than what they earn for doing it. 3. Few want or can handle work that requires creativity, self-direction, or self-control.	1. People want to feel useful and important. 2. People desire to belong and to be recognized as individuals. 3. These needs are more important than money in motivating people to work.	1. Work is not inherently distasteful. People want to contribute to meaningful goals that they have helped establish. 2. Most people can exercise far more creative, responsible self-direction and self-control than their present jobs demand.
Policies		
1. The manager's basic task is to closely supervise and control his subordinates. 2. He must break down tasks into simple, repetitive, easily learned operations. 3. He must establish detailed work routines and procedures, and enforce these firmly but fairly.	1. The manager's basic task is to make each worker feel useful and important. 2. He should keep his subordinates informed and listen to their objections to his plans. 3. The manager should allow his subordinates to exercise some self-direction and self-control on routine matters.	1. The manager's basic task is to make use of his "untapped" human resources. 2. He must create an environment in which all members may contribute to the limits of their ability. 3. He must encourage full participation on important matters, continually broadening subordinate self-direction and self-control.
Expectations		
1. People can tolerate work if the pay is decent and the boss is fair. 2. If tasks are simple enough and people are closely controlled, they will produce up to standard.	1. Sharing information with subordinates and involving them in routine decisions will satisfy their basic needs to belong and to feel important. 2. Satisfying these needs will improve morale and reduce resistance to formal authority—subordinates will "willingly cooperate."	1. Expanding subordinate influence, self-direction, and self-control will lead to direct improvements in operating efficiency. 2. Work satisfaction may improve as a "by-product" of subordinates' making full use of their resources.

Source: Richard M. Steers and Lyman W. Porter, eds., *Motivation and Work Behavior* (New York: McGraw-Hill, 1975), p. 17. Copyright 1975 by McGraw-Hill Book Company. Used with permission of the publisher.

A SYSTEMS VIEW OF MOTIVATION IN ORGANIZATIONS

A SYSTEMS VIEW OF MOTIVATION

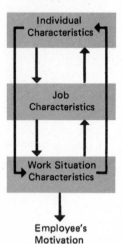

Employee's Motivation

Motivation is obviously a complex area that has been the subject of a number of conflicting theories and views. How, then, may managers utilize current knowledge about motivation to improve their understanding of the way in which motivation operates in organizations? Lyman Porter and Raymond Miles have suggested that a systems perspective on motivation will be most useful to managers.[6] By "systems perspective" they mean that there are three major variables in organizations that affect motivation, and that it is the relationship among these variables that ultimately determines the degree of motivation an employee will feel. Thus, they argue, it is necessary to take into account the "system," or whole, of the forces operating on the employee before the employee's motivation can be adequately understood.

As the accompanying table indicates, the three variables that Porter and Miles identify as affecting motivation in organizations are individual characteristics, job characteristics, and work situation characteristics. We will introduce these variables here and go on to discuss each in greater detail, using the appropriate theories referred to earlier.

Individual characteristics refer to the interests, attitudes, and needs that an individual brings to the work situation. It is obvious that individuals differ in these characteristics and that their motivations will therefore differ. For example, one individual might desire prestige, and so might be motivated by a job with an impressive title. Another individual might desire money, and so might be motivated to earn a high salary.

Job characteristics refer to the attributes of the employee's tasks. These characteristics include the amount of responsibility the individual is given, the variety of tasks the individual can perform, and the extent to which the job itself is satisfying. Presumably, a job that is intrinsically satisfying, for example, will be more motivating for many individuals than a job that is not.

Work situation characteristics refer to what happens to the individual in his or her work environment. Do colleagues encourage the individual to perform to a high standard, or do they encourage low productivity? Do superiors reward high performance, or do they ignore it? Does the organization itself manifest a concern for employees—through attractive fringe benefits and a genuinely informal and cooperative atmosphere, for example—or does the organization seem cold and indifferent to employees? These characteristics, too, can affect the motivation of employees.

Characteristics of the Individual

As we have already suggested, each individual brings his or her own interests, attitudes, and needs to the work situation. In this section, we will discuss some of the contributions made by writers such as Maslow, McGregor, and McClelland to our understanding of needs and motivation.

The Hierarchy of Human Needs. Maslow's hierarchy of needs (see Figure 16-2 on page 414) has probably received more attention and application to organi-

---

[6] Porter and Miles, "Motivation and Management," pp. 546–550.

TABLE 16-2   Variables Affecting the Motivational Process in Organizational Settings

Individual Characteristics	Job Characteristics	Work Situation Characteristics
1. Interests 2. Attitudes (Examples): 　—Toward self 　—Toward job 　—Toward aspects of 　　the work situation 3. Needs (Examples): 　—Security 　—Social 　—Achievement	Examples: 　—Types of intrinsic 　　rewards 　—Degree of 　　autonomy 　—Amount of direct 　　performance feed- 　　back 　—Degree of variety 　　in tasks	1. Immediate Work Environment 　a. Peers 　b. Supervisor(s) 2. Organizational Actions 　a. Reward practices 　　(1) System-wide rewards 　　(2) Individual rewards 　b. Organizational climate

Note: These lists are not intended to be exhaustive; they are meant to indicate some of the more important variables influencing employee motivation.

Source: Lyman W. Porter and Raymond E. Miles, "Motivation and Management," in Joseph W. McGuire, ed., *Contemporary Management: Issues and Viewpoints* (Englewood Cliffs, N.J.: Prentice-Hall, 1974), p. 547. Used by permission.

zational environments than any other theory of motivation. One of the reasons for this is that Maslow provides us with a theory that not only classifies human needs in a convenient way but also has direct implications for managing human behavior in organizations.[7]

Maslow views human motivation in terms of a hierarchy of five needs, which may be categorized as follows:

1   *Physiological needs,* which include the need for air, water, food, and sex.
2   *Security needs,* which include the need for safety, order, and freedom from fear or threat.
3   *Belongingness and love needs (or social needs),* which include the need for love, affection, feelings of belonging, and human contact.
4   *Esteem needs,* which include the need for self-respect, self-esteem, achievement, and respect from others.
5   *The need for self-actualization,* which includes the need to grow, to feel self-fulfilled, to realize one's potential.

According to Maslow, individuals will be motivated to fulfill the need that is *prepotent,* or most powerful, for them at a given time. The prepotency of a need will depend on the individual's current situation and recent experiences. Starting with the physiological needs, which are most basic, each need must be at least partially satisfied by the individual before he or she moves up the hierarchy to the next need stage.

[7] See Abraham H. Maslow, *Motivation and Personality,* 2nd ed. (New York: Harper & Row, 1970).

FIGURE 16-2
Maslow's
Hierarchy
of Needs

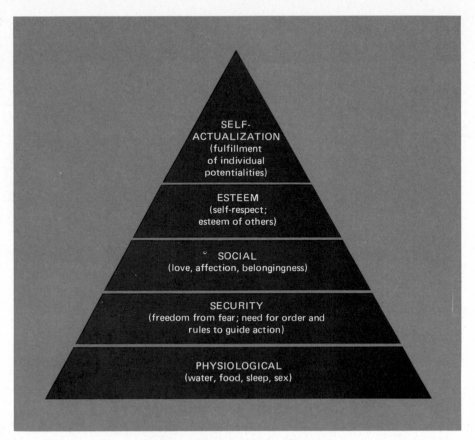

The practical implications of this theory for motivation in organizations are many. For example, unless employees are provided with the means to gratify their basic, physiological needs with a wage sufficient to feed, shelter, and protect their families satisfactorily and with a safe working environment, managers will get little result from incentives designed to provide employees with esteem, feelings of belonging, or opportunities to grow. And when their basic body needs are taken care of, employees still must have their safety needs gratified with job security and freedom from coercion or feelings of arbitrary treatment. Clearly defined regulations and limits of responsibility—knowing exactly what is expected of them—are other examples of security-gratifying measures.

In the modern organization, both physiological and security needs are usually (but not always) taken care of satisfactorily. For this reason, most of our attention as managers will be concentrated on the motivational aspects of the next three categories: belongingness and love needs, esteem needs, and the need for self-actualization.

Needs for belongingness and love are perhaps most strongly felt in relation to the individual's parents, husband or wife, or children. In addition, they are experienced in social contexts—the need for warm relationships with friends, the feeling of being "one of the gang." The work environment is also a social environment, and the same needs for a feeling of belonging and affection apply. Unless employees feel that they are an integral part of the organization and that their fellow workers want them on the "team," they will be dominated by the need for belongingness and will be unlikely to respond to higher-order opportunities or incentives.

Maslow described two major types of esteem needs. The first is the desire for achievement, mastery, and competence. In organizational terms, people want to be well trained and good at their jobs; they also want to feel that they are achieving something important when they perform their jobs. The other type of esteem need is the desire for prestige, status, importance, and recognition. As managers, we will have many ways of fulfilling both these types of needs in our subordinates through such means as providing challenging work assignments, performance feedback, performance recognition, and personal encouragement, and by involving subordinates in goal setting and decision making.

When all these needs have been adequately met, according to Maslow, employees will become motivated by the desire for self-actualization. Employees motivated by self-actualization needs try to find meaning and personal growth in their work and actively seek out new responsibilities. Maslow stresses that individual differences are greatest at this level; any number of ways may be found to achieve self-actualization on the job. For some individuals, producing work of high quality may be a means for self-actualization. For others, self-actualization may come through developing creative, useful ideas. By being aware of the different self-actualization needs of subordinates, managers can more effectively motivate subordinates. They can select varying approaches that allow subordinates to achieve personal as well as organizational goals.

Douglas McGregor related Maslow's hierarchy to the management of work groups.[8] He pointed out that managers often regard informal work groups as hostile and a threat to the organization. They therefore try to overdirect and overcontrol employees and try to discourage the formation of informal groups. As a result, suggests McGregor, the social needs of employees are thwarted, causing the employees to feel uncooperative and resentful. In addition, the employees are unlikely to move beyond the belongingness level in the need hierarchy, and so will not be motivated to contribute more to the achievement of their own and the organization's goals.

The Urge to Achieve and Entrepreneurial Behavior. John W. Atkinson and his colleagues have proposed a model of motivation based primarily on the principle that all healthy adults have a considerable *reservoir of potential energy*.[9] How this energy is released and used depends on the strength of the individual's motivational drives and the situations and opportunities with which the in-

---

[8] Douglas McGregor, *The Human Side of Enterprise* (New York: McGraw-Hill, 1960).

[9] John W. Atkinson, *An Introduction to Motivation* (New York: Van Nostrand, 1964).

"Honeywell knows what makes people tick."

Drawing by Booth; © 1972 The New Yorker Magazine, Inc.

dividual is presented. More specifically, an individual's motivation to strive for a particular goal results from (1) the strength of the basic motive or need involved, (2) his or her expectancy of succeeding, and (3) the incentive value attached to the goal.

Atkinson's model related behavior and performance to three basic drives, which vary significantly among individuals: the need for achievement (referred to as *n Ach)*, the need for power *(n Pow)*, and the need for affiliation or close association with others *(n Aff)*. For example, an individual might be motivated by a high need for affiliation. If he or she is in a work environment where considerable interaction with other employees takes place, the individual's potential energy for affiliation will be released, and work enjoyment might be high. On the other hand, if the work environment is unfriendly or the individual must work alone, then the individual's affiliation need will not be met in the workplace, and so motivation to come to work might be low.[10]

David C. McClelland followed this line of reasoning and related it directly to business drive and management. Focusing in particular on the need for achievement, he found that a strong achievement need was related to how well individuals were motivated to perform their work tasks. McClelland also found

[10] See George H. Litwin and Robert A. Stringer, Jr., *Motivation and Organizational Climate* (Boston: Graduate School of Business Administration, Harvard University, 1968).

that the need for achievement could be strengthened, to some extent, through training. Thus, managers might be able to improve their own motivation and performance, or that of their subordinates, through the use of appropriate training techniques.

The need for achievement can be defined as a desire to excel or to succeed in competitive situations.[11] In his research, McClelland found that people with a high need for achievement have several characteristics of interest to managers:

1 They like taking responsibility for solving problems.
2 They tend to set moderately difficult goals for themselves and to take calculated risks.
3 They place high importance on concrete feedback on how well they are doing.

Thus, individuals with high achievement needs tend to be highly motivated in challenging and competitive work situations. They are not motivated where the work situation is routine and noncompetitive. Conversely, people with low achievement needs tend not to perform well in competitive or challenging work situations.

There is considerable evidence of the relationship between high achievement needs and performance. McClelland himself, for example, found that people who succeeded in competitive occupations were well above average in achievement motivation. Successful managers, who presumably operated in one of the most competitive of all environments, had a higher achievement need than other professionals.[12] Similarly, Herbert A. Wainer and Irwin M. Rubin found that the performance of companies with managers who had high achievement needs was better than the performance of companies where managers had lower achievement needs.[13] McClelland later claimed considerable success in teaching adults to increase their achievement motivation and, in turn, to improve their work performance.[14]

For managers, the implications of these findings are twofold. First, it is important to find an appropriate match between the individual and the job. Employees who manifest a high achievement need (or who are found to have such a need through personality testing) would probably be considerably underutilized and unmotivated working on routine, nonchallenging tasks. Employees with a low achievement need, on the other hand, would probably not perform

[11] For a good discussion of the achievement motivation in work situations, see Edward E. Lawler III, *Motivation in Work Organizations* (Monterey, Calif.: Brooks/Cole, 1973).

[12] See David C. McClelland, *The Achieving Society* (Princeton, N.J.: Van Nostrand, 1961), and "Business Drive and National Achievement," *Harvard Business Review,* July-August 1962, pp. 99–112.

[13] Herbert A. Wainer and Irwin M. Rubin, "Motivation of Research and Development Entrepreneurs: Determinants of Company Success," *Journal of Applied Psychology,* Vol. 53, No. 3 (June 1969), pp. 178–184. See also interview with David C. McClelland in "As I See It," *Forbes,* June 1, 1969, pp. 53–57.

[14] David C. McClelland, "Toward a Theory of Motive Acquisition," *American Psychologist,* Vol. 20, No. 5 (May 1965), pp. 321–333.

up to par in competitive or very challenging work situations. Second, managers can to some extent raise the achievement-need level of subordinates by creating the proper work environment—permitting their subordinates a measure of independence, providing them with tasks that gradually become more challenging, and praising and rewarding high performance.

Motivation to Maintain Consistency. We stated earlier that the characteristics which individuals bring to the workplace include their interests, attitudes, and needs. Abraham Korman suggests that among the attributes affecting motivation are the attitudes which people have toward themselves. A person's self-image, he found, will affect the job and task role which that person selects.[15] Specifically, an individual will select a job and perform it in a way that will harmonize with his or her self-image. For example, people who see themselves as creative will tend to select jobs that require creativity (such as copywriting) and to be motivated to perform those jobs in a creative way.

Abraham Korman's hypothesis is relevant to managers because it can help to predict work behavior. For example, individuals who are high in self-esteem may be expected to seek challenging tasks, to seek to perform those tasks well, and to derive satisfaction from successful performance. Selecting employees with high self-esteem and bolstering the self-confidence of subordinates are ways that managers might be able to encourage high performance. Korman also suggests that individuals will tend to associate with others whom they perceive as being similar to themselves. This information could be relevant to managers who are forming separate work groups.

Characteristics of the Job Task
The characteristics of the job and its associated tasks represent the second variable influencing motivation in organizations. Researchers in this area have attempted to discover what effects a particular job will have on the desire of an individual to perform that job well. The fact that routine, assembly-line-type jobs were increasingly shown to reduce employee motivation and increase dissatisfaction was a major reason why interest in this area developed. In addition, an important contribution to our understanding of the relationship between job characteristics and motivation was made when Frederick Herzberg introduced his two-factor theory. Herzberg's work created a great deal of interest in the role of motivation in the daily operations of organizations.

A Two-Factor Approach to Work Motivation. In the late 1950s, Herzberg and his associates conducted a study of job attitudes of two hundred engineers and accountants.[16] Subjects were asked to recall times when they felt exceptionally

---

[15] Abraham K. Korman, "Hypotheses of Work Behavior Revisited and an Extension," *Academy of Management Review,* Vol. 1, No. 1 (January 1976), pp. 50–63.

[16] Frederick Herzberg, Bernard Mausner, and Barbara Snyderman, *The Motivation to Work* (New York: Wiley, 1959). See also Frederick Herzberg, *Work and the Nature of Man* (New York: World Publishing, 1966), and "One More Time: How Do You Motivate Employees?" *Harvard Business Review,* January-February 1968, pp. 53–62.

good about their jobs, and times when they felt bad about their jobs. Herzberg then attempted to find what factors led to each type of reaction.

Based on the responses he received, Herzberg concluded that job satisfaction and job dissatisfaction do not come from the presence or absence of one set of factors. Instead, they come from two separate sets of factors, which Herzberg called "satisfiers" (motivating factors) and "dissatisfiers" ("hygiene" factors). The satisfiers—that is, the factors that motivated employees to perform well and led to their feelings of satisfaction—included achievement, recognition, responsibility, and advancement. The absence of these factors had little to do with the employees' dissatisfaction. The dissatisfiers included such factors as salary, working conditions, and company policy. Positive ratings for these factors did not lead to job satisfaction but merely to the absence of dissatisfaction.

According to Herzberg's theory, then, the satisfiers are related to the nature of the work (the job *content*) and the rewards that result directly from performance of the work tasks. The dissatisfiers or hygiene factors, on the other hand, come from the individual's relationship to the organization's environment (the job *context*) in which the work is being done. The most important of these factors is company policy, which is judged by the individual as being a major cause of inefficiency and ineffectiveness. (See box.)

Herzberg's theory has received considerable notice and acceptance. But it has also been criticized on a number of grounds. For example, Herzberg's "storytelling" method of collecting data, in which the subjects recounted satisfying and dissatisfying job events, assumes that people will report these experiences accurately. It has been argued that people may be more likely to take credit personally for satisfactions and blame dissatisfactions on outside influences, a phenomenon that would account for the content-context split that Herzberg found.[17] In addition, a number of subsequent research studies indicated that the two-factor theory oversimplified the relationship between

Satisfiers and Dissatisfiers in the Workplace		
Motivating Factors (The Work Content):	—Achievement —Recognition —The Work Itself	—Responsibility —Advancement and Growth
Hygiene Factors (The Work Context):	—Company Policy and Administration —Supervision	—Working Conditions —Working Relationships —Salary, Status, and Security

Source: Frederick Herzberg, "One More Time: How Do You Motivate Employees?" *Harvard Business Review,* January-February 1968, p. 57. Copyright © 1967 by the President and Fellows of Harvard College; all rights reserved.

[17] Victor Vroom, *Work and Motivation* (New York: Wiley, 1964).

satisfaction and motivation.[18] For example, it was found that job context factors, such as salary, *could* lead to job satisfaction, and that the absence of job content factors, such as achievement and recognition, *could* lead to job dissatisfaction. Furthermore, the same factors may result in job satisfaction for one person and job dissatisfaction for another.

Nevertheless, Herzberg's theory is still regarded as an important contribution to our understanding of the effects of job characteristics on satisfaction, motivation, and performance. Job enrichment programs, for example, which we discussed in Chapter 9, were strongly influenced by the work of Herzberg and his colleagues.

Characteristics of the Work Situation

The characteristics of the work situation make up the third set of variables that can affect job motivation. These variables can be conveniently divided into characteristics of the immediate work environment and characteristics of organizational actions.[19] We will introduce these two broad categories here. In the next section, we will describe in detail one approach that can help managers influence the work situation so that the job motivation of their subordinates will be increased.

Characteristics of the Immediate Work Environment. This category includes mainly the attitudes and actions of peers and supervisors. As we discussed in Chapters 2 and 12, numerous studies have found that peer groups in the work situation can have an enormous influence on the motivation and performance of individuals. Most people desire the rewards that peers can provide, such as friendship and approval. In order to obtain those rewards, they will behave in accordance with the norms and values of the peer group. For example, if the group favors high productivity, the individual will be motivated to perform well. If the group has an "us versus them" approach to management, and regards high producers as "rate-busters," the individual will not be motivated to perform well and may even be motivated to perform poorly.

Immediate supervisors also strongly influence the motivation and performance of employees. As we shall see in the next chapter ("Leadership"), supervisors control many of the rewards and penalties that are available in the workplace, from praise, salary increases, and promotion, to criticism, demotions, and dismissals. They also strongly affect job design and the work environment. Thus, supervisors play a critical role in influencing the job attitude and performance of their subordinates.

Characteristics of Organizational Actions. This category includes the overall personnel policies of the organization, the organization's methods for rewarding individual employees, and the organization's climate.

The organization's *personnel policies* with respect to such matters as wage

---

[18] Robert J. House and Lawrence A. Wigdor, "Herzberg's Dual-Factor Theory of Job Satisfaction and Motivation," *Personnel Psychology,* Vol. 20, No. 4 (Winter 1967), pp. 369–389.

[19] Porter and Miles, "Motivation and Management," pp. 553–556.

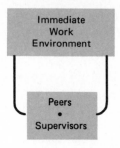

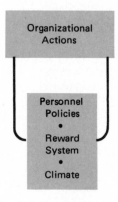

scales and employee benefits (vacations, pensions, and the like) generally have little impact on individual performance. Instead, these policies affect mainly the motivation of employees to remain with or leave the organization. Low wage scales, for example, might lead to a high turnover rate, while above-average wage scales might lead to a low turnover rate.

The organizational actions that generally have the greatest impact on the motivation and performance of individual employees are the *rewards* these employees are offered. Rewards such as bonuses, salary increases, and promotions can be strong motivators of individual performance, provided they are effectively administered: the reward or compensation the individual is being offered for improved performance must justify, in his or her mind, the extra effort improved performance requires; the reward must be directly associated with that improved performance so that it is clear to the individual (and to others in the work group) why the reward has been given; and the reward must be seen as fair by others in the work group so that they will not resent it and lower their own performance level.

Many organizations find it difficult to measure the performance of individuals accurately, especially in jobs that are not directly quantifiable as many production and sales jobs are. They therefore do not attempt to use extra compensation as a motivating factor. In addition, many organizations prefer to keep employees performing the same type of task at about the same salary level, in order to avoid creating resentment. Thus, in many organizations, bonuses, salary increases, and promotions are not used effectively as employee motivators.

Organizational *climate* — the "personality," "feel," or "character" of the organization's environment — is another factor that can influence employees. For example, a more traditional climate, in which lower-level employees are regarded as expendable, might be less motivating for such employees than a climate in which employees at all levels feel they are an integral part of the organization. We have discussed climate more fully in Chapters 13 and 14.

THE IMPACT OF PAST CONSEQUENCES ON BEHAVIOR

In this section, we will describe the operant conditioning/behavior modification approach to influencing behavior in organizations. This approach is associated with the name B. F. Skinner[20] and is the source of much controversy and emotional tension on the part of some commentators. Operant conditioning or behavior modification techniques, as we shall see, are based on the observation that the consequences of an individual's behavior in a given situation influence that individual's behavior in a future, similar situation. This implication that individual behaviors can be predicted from that individual's past experiences and present environment is disturbing to those who strongly believe in the notion that people freely choose how to behave. In addition,

[20] See, for example, B. F. Skinner, *Beyond Freedom and Dignity* (New York: Knopf, 1971).

operant conditioning or behavior modification techniques attempt to arrange the consequences of a person's behavior so that the person's future behavior will be influenced. This fact has given these techniques a certain manipulative, sinister, Machiavellian reputation.

In fact, one does not have to agree fully with the underlying assumptions of these techniques to see that they are a part of the daily interaction of people both within and outside organizations. Rewarding a child for going to bed on time, smiling at someone whose help we desire, frowning when someone says something with which we disagree, grading papers, and raising the salary of a highly productive employee are all familiar types of behavior modification. People act in these ways because they assume that the receivers of their actions will, in the future, behave in ways they find desirable.

Most managers would probably agree that work behavior is a learned activity. Individuals *learn* to be good managers, or they *learn* to be poor managers. They *learn* to perform a job well, or they *learn* to perform it poorly. The behavior modification approach in organizations focuses on establishing work situations — such as reward and recognition policies — that help subordinates learn work habits that are satisfying to them and that aid in the achievement of organizational goals.

Many studies on operant conditioning or behavior modification have been done. The results of these studies offer some very specific guides to what a manager should or should not do to help subordinates learn effective work habits. Before we discuss these guides, we will describe the essential elements of the operant conditioning approach.[21]

Operant Conditioning

The operant conditioning or learning approach to the management of organizational behavior is based on the "Law of Effect." In brief, the law states that behavior that is followed directly by a rewarding consequence tends to be repeated, while behavior that leads to a negative, or punishing, consequence tends not to be repeated. Thus, the frequency of the various kinds of behavior in the organization can be seen as contingent on the immediate consequences of those behaviors. If, for example, employees work hard to achieve organizational objectives and are directly rewarded with bonuses or extra privileges, they will tend to repeat their efforts when new objectives are set.

The operant conditioning process may be illustrated as follows:

$$S \longrightarrow R \text{ (Voluntary Behavior)} \rightarrow \text{Consequences} \rightarrow \begin{array}{l} \text{Future Voluntary} \\ \text{Response to Stimulus} \end{array}$$
$$\text{Stimulus} \quad \text{Response}$$

For our purposes, the stimulus would be a factor in the work environment, such as a task. The individual's response (or lack of it) to that task will lead to certain consequences (praise or disapproval). These consequences or rein-

---

[21] Our discussion is based on W. Clay Hamner, "Reinforcement Theory and Contingency Management in Organizational Settings," in Henry L. Tosi and W. Clay Hamner, eds., *Organizational Behavior and Management: A Contingency Approach* (Chicago: St. Clair Press, 1974), and Donald Sanzotta, *Motivational Theories and Applications for Managers* (New York: American Management Associations, 1977).

forcements will influence the individual's response the next time he or she is confronted with the same or a very similar stimulus.

The operant conditioning process suggests that if managers wish to change the behavior of a subordinate, they must change the consequences of that behavior. A person who is frequently late, for example, might be motivated to come in on time (a behavior change) if the manager expresses strong approval for each on-time or early appearance (change of consequences), rather than continuing to shrug the matter off. Lateness also may be stopped by expressing strong disapproval of the late arrival time. However, as we shall see, researchers believe that it is generally more effective to reward desired behavior than to punish undesired behavior.

For the consequences to influence a person's behavior, it is important that they be clearly related to that behavior. One reason why managers often fail to motivate subordinates is that the reinforcements which they offer subordinates are far removed from the subordinate's actions. For example, informing subordinates during the annual salary review that they have done a good job is probably a less effective motivator than praising them each time they perform a task particularly well.

Types of Reinforcement

There are various types of reinforcement or techniques that managers can use to modify the behavior of subordinates: positive reinforcement, avoidance learning, extinction, and punishment.

Positive Reinforcement. By definition, a consequence that is positively reinforcing is one that makes it more likely that a given behavior will recur. Reinforcers may be either primary or secondary. *Primary reinforcers* consist of biological satisfiers, such as water and food. They are innately rewarding, regardless of a person's past experience. *Secondary reinforcers* are those that are rewarding because of an individual's past experiences. Common secondary reinforcers are praise, promotion, and money; most individuals regard these as pleasant, and are therefore likely to repeat those behaviors that earn these rewards.

Because what is positively reinforcing varies among individuals, managers either need to develop a reward system that is appropriate for all the members of their work group, or they need to tailor their rewards to suit each individual. For example, offering increased responsibility as a reward for high performance will be effective only with those employees who have learned that exercising responsibility is a gratifying experience.

Avoidance Learning. Avoidance learning, or negative reinforcement, takes place when individuals learn to behave in ways that help them avoid or escape from unpleasant consequences. (Avoidance learning is thus distinguished from positive reinforcement, in which people learn to behave in ways that *gain* pleasant consequences.) Much lawful behavior in our society is based on avoidance learning: for example, people learn to park their cars legally in order to avoid a parking ticket. In the workplace, avoidance learning usually takes place when peers or supervisors criticize an individual's actions

("That report you did was really sloppy" or "When are you going to start carrying your share of the work load?"). The individual will try to improve his or her performance in order to avoid future criticism.

Extinction. Extinction and punishment are designed to reduce undesired behavior, rather than reinforce desired behavior. *Extinction* is the withholding of reward for undesired behavior so that the behavior will eventually disappear. The lack of reinforcement, if it occurs repeatedly, will cause the undesired response to become "extinct." For example, teachers often use extinction to control disruptive behavior in the classroom. By ignoring the disruptive students (rather than giving them extra attention in the form of frowns or comments), teachers avoid rewarding the disruptive behavior; eventually the students may try another type of behavior. In the workplace, extinction is commonly used to deal with overly inquisitive or moderately disruptive employees.

Punishment. Through punishment, managers try to change the behavior of subordinates by making sure that undesirable behavior leads to negative consequences. Giving harsh criticism, docking pay, denying privileges, demoting, and reducing an individual's freedom to do his or her job are common forms of punishment in the workplace.

Most ethical criticisms of behavior modification center around the technique of punishment. In fact, Skinner and other psychologists strongly recommend the use of positive reinforcement rather than punishment to change behavior. Punishment, by definition, only informs the individual what should *not* be done, rather than what should be done. Thus, one mistake may be followed by a new one as the individual seeks to find, by trial and error, the behavior that will not be punished. In addition, punishment causes the receiver of the punishment to feel resentment, a feeling that is usually counterproductive in the work environment. Most members of an organization are mature and are willing to be productive. For such individuals, positive reinforcement (combined with extinction) is a far more effective and humane method of changing behavior.

Learning Theory Techniques

Whether they realize it or not, managers are constantly influencing the behavior of their subordinates by the ways in which they withhold or offer rewards. In order to make their influence more effective, managers need to be aware of how the techniques of reinforcement can be best applied.

Perhaps the first general rule which managers need to be aware of is that what is rewarding to one individual is not necessarily rewarding to another. For example, many individuals may be influenced to work harder by the promise of more money, but for others the promise of time off would be far more rewarding. Managers must be alert to these differences and should try to determine what is reinforcing for each of their subordinates.

Another point which managers need to keep in mind is that some schedules of reinforcement are more effective than others. Under a *continuous reinforcement* schedule, the individual is immediately rewarded each time he or she manifests the desired behavior—for example, the individual is praised each time the work task is properly completed. Under a *partial reinforcement* schedule, rewards are provided intermittently—for example, through occasional praise for good performance and regular praise for exceptionally fine work. Continuous reinforcement has been found to lead to faster initial learning. Partial reinforcement, however, leads to a more permanent change in behavior.

Rules for Using Operant Conditioning. W. Clay Hamner has identified six rules for using operant conditioning or learning theory techniques. He points out that even though these rules make obvious sense, they are often violated by managers:[22]

1 Don't reward all individuals the same.
2 Be aware that failure to respond can also modify behavior.
3 Be sure to tell individuals what they can do to get reinforcement.
4 Be sure to tell individuals what they are doing wrong.
5 Don't punish in front of others.
6 Be fair.

We discuss these rules in the accompanying box.

Rules for Using Operant Conditioning Techniques
Rule 1: *Don't reward all individuals the same.* To be effective behavior reinforcers, rewards should be based on performance. Rewarding everyone the same in effect reinforces poor or average performance and ignores high performance.
Rule 2: *Be aware that failure to respond can also modify behavior.* Managers influence their subordinates by what they do not do as well as by what they do. For example, failing to praise a deserving subordinate may cause that subordinate to perform poorly the next time.
Rule 3: *Be sure to tell individuals what they can do to get reinforcement.* Setting a performance standard lets individuals know what they should do to be rewarded; they can then adjust their work pattern accordingly.
Rule 4: *Be sure to tell individuals what they are doing wrong.* If a manager withholds rewards from a subordinate without indicating why the subordinate is not being rewarded, the subordinate may be confused about what behavior the manager finds undesirable. The subordinate may also feel that he or she is being manipulated.
Rule 5: *Don't punish in front of others.* Reprimanding a subordinate might sometimes be a useful way of eliminating an undesirable behavior. Public reprimand, however, humiliates the subordinate and may cause all the members of the work group to resent the manager.
Rule 6: *Be fair.* The consequences of a behavior should be appropriate for the behavior. Subordinates should be given the rewards they deserve. Failure to reward subordinates properly or overrewarding undeserving subordinates reduces the reinforcing effect of rewards.

Source: Based on W. Clay Hamner, "Reinforcement Theory and Contingency Management in Organizational Settings," in Henry L. Tosi and W. Clay Hamner, eds., *Organizational Behavior and Management: A Contingency Approach* (Chicago: St. Clair Press, 1974).

[22] Hamner, "Reinforcement Theory and Contingency Management in Organizational Settings," pp. 96–98.

Fred Luthans and Robert Kreitner have described a *systematic* procedure for using the learning theory approach to manage organizational behavior.[23] As Figure 16-3 illustrates, the procedure involves five essential steps: identification, measurement, analysis, intervention, and evaluation.

Step 1, identification, involves specifying the behaviors that the manager considers undesirable. ("Tom is frequently late, despite repeated reprimands and attempts to explain to him why he should come in on time. His lack of punctuality may even have worsened.")

In step 2, measurement, the manager charts the frequency of the problem behavior over time. ("On the average, Tom is more than a half hour late three days a week.") Such measurement is a critical part of this approach, because it provides a base that will allow the manager to determine how successful he or she is in changing the subordinate's behavior. Frequently it will also provide insight into the circumstances associated with the behavior.

In step 3, analysis, the manager attempts to ascertain what factors are causing the existing behavior to continue. ("By coming in late, Tom is able to enjoy an extra half hour of sleep. In addition, he seems to feel that the work-pace starts slowly around here anyway.")

Step 4, intervention, involves (a) developing a strategy for changing the behavior, (b) implementing the strategy, and (c) measuring the frequency of the resulting behavior. ("Tom seems to enjoy our group's 15-minute work planning and review meeting each morning at 10 a.m. It's voluntary, but he rarely misses one. There's no reason why we can't hold the meeting at 9 a.m., so I'll reschedule it. And for the next month I won't comment if he comes in late. Nothing else seems to work, maybe this will.") A record is kept of the frequency with which the problem behavior is repeated. If a behavior change has occurred in the desired direction ("Tom has been late only twice in the last three weeks, and then only by a few minutes"), the manager selects a reinforcement schedule that will maintain the desired behavior—step 4d. ("Tom, I want you to know I think your comments at our morning meetings have really been helpful.")

In the last step, step 5, the manager evaluates how effective the entire procedure has been. Ineffective strategies are analyzed to see why they did not work or if there are other types of individuals or circumstances for which they might be appropriate. Effective strategies are filed away for possible future use.

Encouraging results have been reported in a number of studies of the effectiveness of behavior modification techniques. Luthans and Lyman, for example, found that supervisors trained in the five-step operant conditioning procedure were able to improve the performance of workers in their departments.[24] And one survey of ten major corporations, including Emery Air

---

[23] Fred Luthans and Robert Kreitner, "The Management of Behavioral Contingencies," *Personnel,* Vol. 51, No. 4 (July-August 1974), pp. 7–16.

[24] Fred Luthans and David Lyman, "Training Supervisors to Use Organizational Modification," *Personnel,* Vol. 50, No. 5 (September-October 1973), pp. 38–44.

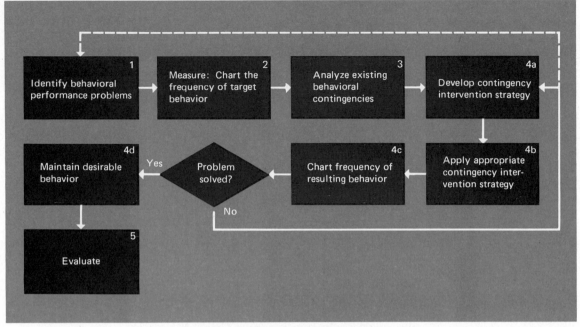

FIGURE 16-3 Steps in Organizational Behavior Modification

Source: Adapted from Fred Luthans and Robert Kreitner, "The Management of Behavioral Contingencies," *Personnel,* Vol. 51, No. 4 (July-August 1974), p. 13. © 1974 by AMACOM, a division of American Management Associations.

Freight, Michigan Bell, Standard Oil, and General Electric, found that positive reinforcement techniques resulted in major gains in efficiency, cost savings, attendance, or productivity.[25]

INTEGRATIVE APPROACHES

Each of the approaches to motivation that we have discussed so far tend to concentrate their reasoning and attention on one of the three sets of variables illustrated in our systems table at the beginning of the chapter (Table 16-2). In this section, we will look at two more integrative approaches that include two or more sets of variables in their analysis of motivation.

Most of our attention will be devoted to the expectancy/valence approach because of the considerable support it has received from research, the generality of its applications, and its relatively clear-cut implications for managers.

[25] W. Clay Hamner and Ellen P. Hamner, "Behavior Modification on the Bottom Line," *Organizational Dynamics,* Vol. 4, No. 4 (Spring 1976), pp. 2–21.

In addition, the expectancy/valence approach attempts to overcome criticisms sometimes directed at other motivational theories; namely, that their validity tends to rest on the assumptions that all employees are alike, that all situations are alike, and that there is one best way of motivating employees. The expectancy/valence approach makes a conscious attempt to account for differences between individuals and between situations.

Expectations, Outcomes, and Work Behavior

According to David Nadler and Edward Lawler, the expectancy/valence approach is based on four assumptions about the causes of behavior in organizations:[26]

1   *Behavior is determined by a combination of forces in the individual and in the environment.* Different people have different needs and expectations, formed by past experiences, that will influence their response to the work environment. Different types of work environments will usually make people behave in different ways.

2   *Individuals make conscious decisions about their own behavior in organizations.* These decisions may be about (a) *membership behavior* —coming to work, staying at work, being a member of the organization; or (b) *effort behavior*—how hard to work in performing their jobs.

3   *Different individuals have different types of needs, desires, and goals.* In other words, individuals are satisfied or rewarded by different outcomes. Understanding the individual's needs will lead to an understanding of how that individual can best be motivated and rewarded.

4   *Individuals make decisions among alternative plans of behavior based on their expectation of the extent to which a given behavior will lead to a desired outcome.* In other words, people tend to behave in ways that they believe will lead to rewards, and avoid behaving in ways that they see as leading to undesirable consequences.

The model that these assumptions lead to, which we shall refer to as the expectancy model, has three major components: performance-outcome expectancy, valence, and effort-performance expectancy.

Performance-Outcome Expectancy. When an individual engages in or contemplates a certain behavior, there is in that individual's mind the expectation of certain consequences from that behavior. For example, a worker who is thinking about doubling his or her output may expect that doubling the output will result in praise, more pay, or, perhaps, no reward at all. The worker may even expect that the outcome will be hostility from fellow workers. Each expected outcome will affect the individual's decision on whether or not to proceed with the contemplated behavior.

Valence. The outcome of a particular behavior has a specific valence (motivating power or value) for each specific individual. For example, the possibility

---

[26] David A. Nadler and Edward E. Lawler III, "Motivation—A Diagnostic Approach," in J. Richard Hackman, Edward E. Lawler III, and Lyman W. Porter, eds., *Perspectives on Behavior in Organizations* (New York: McGraw-Hill, 1977).

of transfer to a higher-paying position in another location may have a high valence for individuals who value money or who enjoy the stimulation of a new environment; it may have a low valence for individuals who have strong ties to their neighborhood, friends, or work group. The important point here is that valence is always determined by the individual and is not an objective quality of the outcome itself.

Effort-Performance Expectancy. The individual's expectations of how difficult it will be to achieve successful performance will also affect the individual's decision on whether or not to proceed with that performance. For example, an individual may be told that increasing sales by 50 percent will lead to a much-desired salary increase. Before deciding whether or not to pursue the sales increase, the individual must estimate the probability that he or she will be able to achieve it.

Given a choice, then, an individual will tend to select that level of performance which seems, to the individual, to have the best chance of achieving a valued outcome. The individual asks, in effect, "Can I do it?" and "If I do it, what will it bring me?" and "Is what it will bring me worth the effort of doing it?"

The answers the individual will give to these questions will depend to some extent on the types of outcomes expected. *Intrinsic* outcomes are those that accrue directly to the individual as a result of successful task performance. They include feelings of accomplishment, increased self-esteem, and satisfaction. *Extrinsic* outcomes, such as bonuses, praise, or promotion, are provided by an outside agent such as the supervisor or work group. In addition, a single level of performance may be associated with several outcomes, each having its own valence. (If I perform better, I will receive higher pay, be noticed by my supervisor, loved more by my spouse, and feel better about myself.) Some of these outcomes may even have valence because of the individual's expectation that they will lead to other outcomes. (If my supervisor notices the quality of my work, I may get a promotion.)

The theoretical working of the expectancy model in organizations is illustrated in Figure 16-4 on next page. The value of the expected reward to the individual (1) combines with the individual's perception of the effort involved in attaining the reward and the probability of achieving the reward (2) to produce a certain level of effort (3). This effort must be combined with the individual's abilities and traits (4) and his or her perception of the role or activities required for the task (5) in order to reach the performance level (6). The resulting level of performance leads to intrinsic rewards (or perhaps negative consequences if the performance level is lower than expected), which are inherent in the task accomplishment (7A), and perhaps to the extrinsic rewards (7B). The wavy line in the model leading to the extrinsic rewards indicates that those rewards are not guaranteed, since they are dependent on assessments of the individual's performance by supervisors and on the willingness of the organization to reward that performance. The individual has his or her own idea about the appropriateness of the total reward

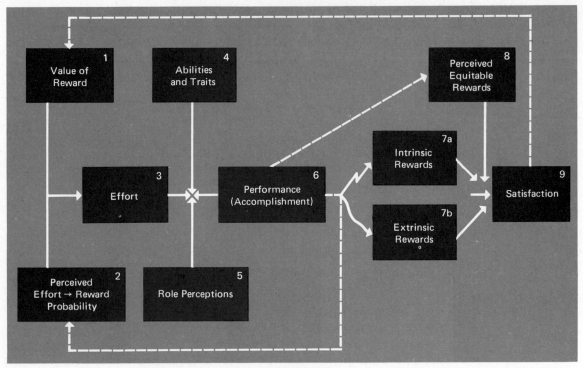

FIGURE 16-4 The Expectancy Model of Motivation

Source: Lyman W. Porter and Edward E. Lawler III, *Managerial Attitudes and Performance* (Homewood, Ill.: Richard D. Irwin, Inc. 1968), p. 165. Reproduced by permission of the publisher.

received (8), which, when measured against the rewards actually received, results in the level of satisfaction experienced by the individual (9). The individual's experience will then be applied to his or her future assessments of the value of rewards for further task accomplishment.[27]

Implications for Managers. Nadler and Lawler have suggested that the expectancy model presents managers with a number of clear implications on how to motivate subordinates. These include:

1 *Determine the rewards valued by each subordinate.* If rewards are to be motivators, they must be suitable for the individual. Managers can determine what rewards their subordinates seek by observing their reactions in different situations or by asking them what rewards they desire.

2 *Determine the performance you desire.* Managers must identify what performance level or behavior they want so that they can tell subordinates what they must do to be rewarded.

[27] Lyman W. Porter and Edward E. Lawler III, *Managerial Attitudes and Performance* (Homewood, Ill.: Irwin, Dorsey Press, 1968). See also Charles N. Greene, "The Satisfaction-Performance Controversy," *Business Horizons,* Vol. 15, No. 5 (October 1972), pp. 31–41.

3 *Make the performance level attainable.* If the subordinates feel the goal they are being asked to pursue is too difficult or impossible to reach, their motivation will be low.

4 *Link rewards to performance.* To maintain motivation, the appropriate reward must be clearly associated within a short period of time with successful performance.

5 *Analyze what factors might counteract the effectiveness of the reward.* Conflicts between the manager's reward system and other influences in the work situation might require that the manager make some adjustments in the reward. For example, if the subordinate's work group favors low productivity, an above-average award may be required to motivate a subordinate to high productivity.

6 *Make sure the reward is adequate.* Minor rewards will be minor motivators.

Implications for Organizations. The expectancy model also has a number of implications for organizations, according to Nadler and Lawler. These include:

1 *Organizations usually get what they reward, not what they want.* The organization's reward system must be designed to motivate the behaviors desired. Seniority benefits, for example, reward loyalty, not performance. Similarly, secret pay policies may fragment the work group and may make it impossible for employees to determine the link between pay and performance.

2 *The job itself can be made intrinsically rewarding.* If jobs are designed to fulfill some of the higher needs of employees (such as independence or creativity), they can be motivating in themselves. This implication is obviously the basis of many job enrichment programs. However, those individuals who do not desire enriched jobs should not be made to take them.[28]

3 *The immediate supervisor has an important role in the motivation process.* The supervisor is in the best position to define clear goals and provide clear, correct rewards for his or her different subordinates. The supervisor should therefore be given some training in the motivation process and should also be given enough authority to administer rewards.

Perceptions of Equitable Treatment and Work Behavior

Another model of job motivation, known as the "equity theory" or "inequity theory," is based on the thesis that a major factor in job motivation, performance, and satisfaction is the individual's evaluation of the equity or fairness of the reward he or she is receiving. In this model, equity is defined as a ratio between the individual's job inputs (such as effort or skill) and the job rewards (such as pay or promotion) *compared to the rewards others are receiving for similar job inputs.* The theory suggests that an individual's motivation, performance, and satisfaction will depend on his or her subjective evaluation of the relationship between his or her effort/reward ratio and the effort/reward ratio of others in similar situations.[29]

[28] See J. Richard Hackman et al., "A New Strategy for Job Enrichment," *California Management Review,* Vol. 17, No. 4 (Summer 1975), pp. 57–71.

[29] J. Stacey Adams, "Toward an Understanding of Inequity," *Journal of Abnormal and Social Psychology,* Vol. 67, No. 5 (November 1963), pp. 422–436. See also Paul S. Goodman and Abraham Friedman, "An Examination of Adams' Theory of Inequity," *Administrative Science Quarterly,* Vol. 16, No. 3 (September 1971), pp. 271–288.

Most discussion and research on equity theory center on money as the reward considered most significant in the workplace. People compare what they are being paid for their efforts with what others in similar situations receive for theirs. When they feel that inequity exists, a state of tension develops within them. People try to resolve this tension by appropriately adjusting their behavior. A worker who perceives that he or she is being underpaid, for example, may try to reduce the inequity by exerting less effort. Overpaid workers, on the other hand (also in a state of tension through perceived inequity), may work harder.

Because individuals differ, their methods of reducing inequity will also differ. Some individuals will resolve the inequity by rationalizing that their efforts were greater or lesser than they originally perceived them to be, or that the rewards are more or less valuable. For example, one person failing to receive a promotion may "decide" the previously desired job actually involved too much responsibility. Another may remove an inequity by quitting the job altogether. Still others may try to make those co-workers with whom they are comparing themselves change their behavior. Those work team members receiving the same pay but exerting less effort, for example, may be persuaded or coerced into working harder. Alternatively, high-performance workers may be discouraged in order to "stop making the rest of us look bad." For managers, equity theory has several implications, the most important of which is that, for many individuals, rewards must be *perceived* as fair in order to be motivating.

Summary   Motivation is an extremely significant subject for managers, since managers need to influence the motivation of people to achieve personal and organizational goals. However, people's abilities and role perceptions are also important factors in how well they will perform.

Theories of motivation can be characterized as content, process, or reinforcement. *Content* theories stress the importance of drives or needs within the individual as motives for the individual's actions. *Process* theories emphasize how and by what goals individuals are motivated. *Reinforcement* or learning theories focus on how the consequences of an individual's actions in the past affect his or her behavior in the future. These motivational theories have evolved as views of motivation have changed from the traditional model, which suggested that people are motivated by economic necessity, through the human relations model, which emphasized job satisfaction as a motivator, to the human resources model, which suggests that high performance leads to satisfaction. According to the latter model, individuals perform best when they are permitted to achieve personal as well as organizational goals.

The systems perspective on motivation identifies three variables that affect motivation in the workplace: individual characteristics, which include the interests, attitudes, and needs of the individual; job characteristics, which refer to the attributes inherent in the task; and work situation characteristics, which include the organization's personnel and reward policies, organizational climate, and the attitudes and actions of peers and supervisors.

Maslow, Atkinson, McClelland, and Korman are theorists who contributed to our understanding of the first variable, individual characteristics. Maslow theorized that individuals are motivated to fulfill a hierarchy of needs, with the need for self-actualization at the top. Atkinson suggested that individuals are motivated by the need for achievement, power, and/or affiliation. McClelland found that the need for achievement is most closely associated with successful performance in the workplace. Korman suggested that individuals are motivated to perform in ways that are consistent with their self-image.

Herzberg contributed to our understanding of the effects of the work task on motivation. He developed a "two-factor" approach to work motivation in which job satisfaction was attributed to factors related to the job *content* and dissatisfaction to factors related to the job *context*.

Characteristics of the work situation, particularly the actions of managers, have been shown to have a strong impact on motivation. Proper application of behavior modification techniques, which are based on learning theory or operant conditioning principles, has been found effective in leading to improved employee performance and satisfaction. Learning theory suggests that behavior that is followed directly by rewarding consequences is reinforced and therefore tends to be repeated, while behavior that is not rewarded or that is punished tends not to be repeated. Managers may use a variety of reinforcement techniques, such as positive reinforcement, avoidance learning, extinction, or punishment. The most effective technique, in terms of performance and satisfaction, has been found to be positive reinforcement combined with extinction. The positive reinforcement should, however, be tailored to fit the individual's preferences for particular types of rewards.

Integrative approaches to motivation include the expectancy/valence approach and equity theory. The expectancy model sees motivation, performance, and satisfaction as depending on the consequences the individual expects from the proposed performance, how much effort the individual expects the proposed performance will require, and the valence, or value, the offered reward has for the individual. Equity theory suggests that an individual's motivation, performance, and satisfaction depend on the individual's comparison of the rewards he or she is receiving with the rewards being received by others in the same situation.

Review Questions

1. According to content theories, what motivates people? What theorists are associated with the content approach? Why are content theories difficult to apply in practice?
2. What aspects of motivation do process theories emphasize? How do process theories relate the concepts of expectancy and valence to motivation?
3. How do reinforcement theories explain behavior? Why do you think the concept of motives should not be used in the reinforcement approach?
4. How have views of motivation in organizations evolved? How might each view affect the ways in which managers behave toward subordinates?
5. In the systems perspective, what three variables affect motivation in the workplace?
6. How is Maslow's hierarchy of needs related to motivation in organizations? How did McGregor apply Maslow's hierarchy to the management of work groups?
7. According to Atkinson, what three basic drives affect behavior and performance? How did McClelland relate Atkinson's work to management? What are the implications of his findings for managers?
8. According to Korman, how does a person's self-image affect his or her motivation?
9. What is Herzberg's two-factor approach to job satisfaction and dissatisfaction? Why has the approach been criticized?

10. How may an organization's climate and its personnel and reward policies affect motivation?
11. Why are operant conditioning techniques controversial? What is your own view of these techniques? Can you think of examples in your daily life in which you unknowingly use these techniques or allow them to be used on you?
12. How does the operant conditioning process work? What does this process suggest managers should do if they wish to change the behavior of a subordinate? What types of reinforcement techniques can managers use? Which technique is most effective? Least effective? Why?
13. What is the difference between a continuous reinforcement schedule and a partial reinforcement schedule?
14. What is the systematic procedure described by Luthans and Kreitner for using the learning theory approach to manage behavior?
15. Upon what assumptions is the expectancy/valence approach based?
16. What are performance-outcome expectancy, valence, and effort-performance expectancy? How do they determine what level of performance an individual will select? What implications does the expectancy model have for managers and organizations?
17. What does equity theory suggest about the motivation, performance, and satisfaction of individuals in the organization?

CASE STUDY: NO ROOM AT THE TOP

Lewis Latimer, supervisor of Special Test Operations, has a motivational problem created by organizational structure and work rules. The problem is a familiar one to many managers in business and industry, even if the titles here are different. Let Lew Latimer explain:

"My problem is easy to explain but beyond me in terms of solution. I'm a supervisor at an electronics company that manufactures desk-top electronic calculators. I head a group of about twenty special electrical test technicians. These employees don't test parts on the assembly line but conduct special electrical tests on completed units as directed by management. We do such things as: (1) conduct systems tests on field units; (2) conduct ongoing reliability testing; (3) conduct experimental testing for engineering; and (4) conduct special customer product testing (e.g., units for special applications).

"My people are electronics specialists typically, with military electronics backgrounds, or are graduates of electronic trade schools. Some have certificates of completion from junior colleges that specialize in the sciences. We train the people we hire on the use of our test equipment and procedures but require practical electronic test experience as an employment prerequisite.

"The company currently has three technician classifications. They are:

Technician C—*Trainee.* (Six months maximum.)
Technician B—*Equipment Test Technician.* Familiar with all usual systems tests. Can perform all tests without assistance other than use of test manuals. (Up to four years.)

Case from Robert D. Joyce, *Encounters in Organizational Behavior: Problem Situations* (New York: Pergamon Press, Ltd., 1972), pp. 148–150. Reprinted by permission of the publisher.

Technician A—*Senior Equipment Test Technician.* Must perform all functions of Technician B plus be able to calibrate test equipment and write test specifications. (No limit.)

"Most people are hired as Technician C, which is considered an entry-level position. If they learn their job well, they are promoted to Technician B at the end of six months. Technician B carries a higher pay scale and a limit of four years that the classification can be maintained. The purpose of this is to force an employee to qualify for a broader range of responsibility. The same is true for Technician A. Most people qualify for Technician A in about three years.

"So, in my department, the majority of employees are now in the top pay classification. It breaks out like this:

Technician C	1 person
Technician B	5 persons
Technician A	14 persons
Total	20 persons

"We're a young company in a fast-moving industry. We make a good, reliable line of calculators, and most of our employees are proud of their products and the company. This has certainly been true of my technicians. You couldn't find a more highly motivated bunch of people anywhere in the company.

"In recent months, attitudes have begun to change. Several of the employees have soured on the company and their jobs, after they reached the top of the pay scale for Technician A. For them, there's no place to go in the company and they know it.

"It's beginning to show up in their work too. A few of the employees are taking a much more casual attitude toward their work than they used to...the old team spirit is really gone. When five o'clock comes, the whole area is deserted. And these are people that I used to have to chase home each evening.

"I talked to Frank Duncan about the problem. Frank is my boss and the director of operations at our facility. I suggested that the most promising persons in the Technician A category should be allowed to move to the Junior Engineering classification. But Frank didn't care much for this solution. He said that all engineering classifications should be used only for professionals (he means college graduates), and that if we opened this classification to nonprofessionals (he means my technicians), morale problems will develop in other areas.

"Duncan said he would consider a Super-Grade classification for outstanding employees in the Technician A category, and asked me to write a new job description for this classification.

"For the moment I'm going along with that approach for lack of anything better, but I feel it is a short-range solution and the problem will be back with us in a year or so."

Case Questions
1. What is the fundamental issue(s) involved in this case?
2. What are the implications of the Super-Grade technician classification from the viewpoint of employee performance, job attitudes, and morale?
3. What are the implications of allowing technicians to move to a "professional" classification?
4. How else might this problem be resolved effectively?

Chapter 17

Leadership

Upon completing this chapter you should be able to:

1. Define and explain the leadership process.
2. Describe three major approaches to the study of leadership.
3. Distinguish between the two major leadership styles.
4. Summarize the situational factors that affect leadership effectiveness.
5. Describe three contingency approaches to leadership.

What makes an effective leader? Most people, when asked this question, would probably reply that effective leaders have certain desirable traits or qualities, such as charisma, foresight, persuasiveness, and intensity. And, indeed, when we look back on leaders like Napoleon, Washington, Lincoln, Roosevelt, and Churchill, it appears that such characteristics are a natural or necessary part of leadership. However, as we shall see, several thousand studies of leaders and leadership, some dating back to the nineteenth century, have failed to demonstrate that any trait or quality is consistently associated with effective leadership.[1] In spite of intensive research by social scientists, it appears that our knowledge of what it takes to be an effective leader and what effective leaders do is actually quite limited.

However, while understanding an apparently complex subject like leadership may be difficult, it is also challenging and potentially very rewarding. Leaders play a critical role in helping groups, organizations, or societies achieve their goals. For example, it is generally accepted that England might well have lost World War II had Neville Chamberlain remained as Prime Minister. Instead, the determined and inspiring leadership of Winston Churchill probably saved England and perhaps the rest of the world as well. Similarly, many business organizations that appear to be floundering achieve new vigor when their presidents are replaced. If we could identify the qualities that are associated with leadership, our ability to select effective leaders would be increased. And if we could identify effective leadership behaviors and techniques, we could presumably *learn* these behaviors and techniques, thereby improving our personal and organizational effectiveness.

Of course, leaders are not the only determinants of group or organizational performance—the skill, motivation, and ability of group members and the effect of environmental factors will also play a role. (For example, many well-managed baseball games have been lost because a ground ball took a bad hop, and many well-managed companies have suffered market setbacks because of a new discovery by a competitor.) Nor is group performance the only measure of a manager's effectiveness—employee satisfaction, for instance, can also be a result of a manager's leadership ability. Ultimately, however, managers and other leaders are judged by how well the goals of the group or organization they are leading have been achieved. Our emphasis in this chapter, therefore, will be on how managers (and other leaders) can lead their subordinates to more effective attainment of group or organizational goals.

DEFINING LEADERSHIP

Ralph M. Stogdill, in his survey of leadership theories and research, has pointed out that "there are almost as many different definitions of leadership

---

[1] See Ralph M. Stogdill, *Handbook of Leadership: A Survey of Theory and Research* (New York: Free Press, 1974).

as there are persons who have attempted to define the concept."[2] We will define *leadership* as the process of directing and influencing the task-related activities of group members. There are three important implications of our definition. First, leadership must involve *other people*—followers or subordinates. By their willingness to follow the leader, group members help define the leader's status and make the leadership process possible. Without followers or subordinates, a person's leadership qualities, if they existed at all, would be irrelevant.

Second, the leadership process involves an unequal distribution of *power* among leaders and group members.[3] Leaders can direct some of the activities of group members; that is, the group members are compelled or are willing to obey most of the leader's directions. The group members cannot similarly direct the leader's activities, though they will obviously affect those activities in a number of ways.

Third, our definition suggests that leaders can *influence* their followers or subordinates, in addition to being able to give their followers or subordinates legitimate directions. In other words, leaders not only can tell their subordinates *what* to do but also can influence *how* or in what manner the subordinates carry out the leader's instructions. For example, a manager may direct a subordinate to perform a certain task, but it may be his or her influence over the subordinate that will determine if the task is carried out properly.

The Nature of Leadership

Why do subordinates obey a manager? What are the sources of a leader's power and influence? We began to answer this question in Chapter 11 when we discussed the five bases of a manager's power. Briefly, these five bases are:

1 *Reward power*—the power to compensate or give awards for tasks satisfactorily completed.
2 *Coercive power*—the power to punish.
3 *Legitimate power*—the power of lawful or formal authority.
4 *Referent power*—the power to cause others to imitate one's personal style or behavior.
5 *Expert power*—the power of superior knowledge, ability, or skill.[4]

The greater the number of these influence sources available to the manager, the greater his or her potential for effective leadership. It is, for example, an obvious fact of organizational life that managers at the same level in the organizational hierarchy may differ widely in their ability to influence, motivate, and direct the work of subordinates. Although they may have the same legiti-

[2] Stogdill, *Handbook of Leadership*, p. 7. See also Fred E. Fiedler and Martin M. Chemers, "Leadership and Management," in Joseph W. McGuire, ed., *Contemporary Management: Issues and Viewpoints* (Englewood Cliffs, N.J.: Prentice-Hall, 1974), pp. 362–389.

[3] See Fred E. Fiedler and Martin M. Chemers, *Leadership and Effective Management* (Glenview, Ill.: Scott, Foresman, 1974).

[4] John R. P. French and Bertram Raven, "The Bases of Social Power," in Dorwin Cartwright, ed., *Studies in Social Power* (Ann Arbor, Mich.: University of Michigan, 1959), pp. 150–167.

mate power, managers are simply not equal in their reward, coercive, referent, or expert power.

In this chapter, we will attempt to extend further our understanding of leader effectiveness by discussing three major approaches to the study of leadership. The first approach sees leadership as a *trait*. This approach attempts to determine the traits (including the personality characteristics) possessed by successful leaders. The second approach attempts to identify the *behaviors* that are associated with effective leadership. Both these approaches assume that an individual with the appropriate traits or behaviors will emerge as the leader in whatever group situation he or she may be placed.

THE THREE APPROACHES TO LEADERSHIP

Trait

Behavior

Contingency

Current thinking and research leans toward a third approach, the *situational* perspective on leadership. This perspective assumes that the qualities that determine leader effectiveness will vary with the situation—the tasks to be accomplished, the skills and expectations of subordinates, the organizational environment, the past experience of the leader and the subordinates, and so on. An individual who is an effective leader in one situation might do very poorly in another. This perspective has given rise to so-called *contingency* approaches to leadership, which attempt to specify the situational factors that determine how effective a particular style will be. We will examine the contributions of all these approaches in the sections below.

THE SEARCH FOR LEADERSHIP TRAITS

The first systematic effort by psychologists and other researchers to understand leadership was the attempt to identify the characteristics of leaders. This approach is obviously a logical one: if only a few people are leaders, and so many are followers, then it seems likely that there is something within leaders that sets them apart from other people. This view of leadership—that leaders are born, not made—is in fact still popular (though not among researchers). After a lifetime of reading popular novels and viewing films and television shows, perhaps most of us believe to some extent that leaders are naturally braver, more aggressive, more decisive, and more articulate than other people. The image of the great commander, jaw jutting out, leading his men in a charge, or barking orders that are instantly obeyed is still a common and powerful one.

Aside from the evident logic and popularity of the idea that leaders are innately different from other people, the idea has certain practical implications as well. If the traits of leadership could be identified, then nations and organizations could become far more sophisticated in their leadership selection process. Only those people who possessed the designated leadership traits would be selected as politicians, officers, and managers. Presumably, organizations and societies would then be operated more effectively.

In their search for measurable leadership traits, researchers took two approaches: (1) they attempted to compare the traits of those who emerge as leaders with the traits of those who do not; and (2) they attempted to compare the traits of effective leaders with those of ineffective leaders.

"I've noticed, Jenkins, that you've been driving yourself of late—nice going!"

© 1976. Reprinted by permission of *Wall Street Journal* and Bo Brown.

Most studies on leadership traits are in the first category; and these studies have failed to uncover any traits that clearly and consistently distinguish leaders from followers.[5] Leaders as a group have been found to be *somewhat* taller, brighter, more extroverted, more intelligent, and more self-confident than nonleaders.[6] However, millions of people have these so-called leadership traits, but most of them obviously will never attain a leadership position; in addition, many established leaders did not and do not have these traits. (Napoleon, for example, was quite short, and Lincoln was moody and introverted.) It is also possible that individuals *become* more assertive and self-confident once they occupy a leadership position, and so even these traits

[5] See Victor H. Vroom, "Leadership," in Marvin D. Dunnette, ed., *Handbook of Industrial and Organizational Psychology* (Chicago: Rand McNally, 1976), pp. 1527–1551; Martin Blumenson and James L. Stokesbury, *Masters of the Art of Command* (Boston: Houghton Mifflin, 1975); Ralph M. Stogdill, "Personal Factors Associated with Leadership: A Survey of the Literature," *Journal of Psychology,* Vol. 25, No. 1 (January 1948), pp. 35–71; and R. D. Mann, "A Review of the Relationships between Personality and Performance in Small Groups," *Psychological Bulletin,* Vol. 56, No. 4 (July 1959), pp. 241–270.

[6] Interestingly enough, studies have also found that people who are *too* intelligent compared with other group members do not emerge as leaders—perhaps because they are too different or too far removed from the group. See Cecil A. Gibb, "Leadership," in Gardner Lindzey and Elliot Aronson, eds., *The Handbook of Social Psychology,* Vol. 4, 2nd ed. (Reading, Mass.: Addison-Wesley, 1969), pp. 205–282.

may not be reliable indicators of leadership ability. While personality measurements may one day become more exact, and certain traits may in fact become identified with leadership ability, the evidence thus far suggests that individuals who emerge as leaders possess no special traits.

Attempts to compare the traits of effective and ineffective leaders—the second category of leadership trait studies—are more recent and fewer in number. These studies, too, have generally failed to isolate traits that are strongly associated with successful leadership. One study did find that traits like intelligence, initiative, and self-assurance were associated to some extent with high managerial levels and performance.[7] However, even this study found that the most important trait related to managerial level and performance was the manager's supervisory ability—that is, his or her skill in using supervisory methods that were appropriate to the particular situation. In other words, the successful managers were those whose management approach was best suited for the needs and goals of their work group. Most other studies in this area also have found that effective leadership did not depend on a particular set of traits but on how well the leader's traits matched the requirements of the situation he or she was facing.[8]

THE BEHAVIOR OF LEADERS

When it became evident that effective leaders did not seem to have any distinguishing traits or characteristics, researchers tried to isolate the *behaviors* that made leaders effective. In other words, rather than try to figure out what effective leaders *were,* researchers tried to determine what effective leaders *did*—how they delegated tasks, how they communicated with and tried to motivate their subordinates, how they carried out their tasks, and so on. This approach to the study of leadership, like the trait approach, assumed that there was a "one best way" to lead. Unlike traits, however, behaviors can be *learned;* thus, researchers assumed that individuals trained in the appropriate leadership behaviors could lead more effectively.[9]

As we shall see, once research results were obtained, it became apparent that leadership behaviors that were appropriate in one situation were not necessarily appropriate in another. For example, an executive skilled at motivating creative individuals might be very successful in a consumer goods company in a highly competitive industry. Such a firm may depend on flamboyant marketing techniques, and so the executive's ability to manage creative people (like artists and copywriters) would be most useful. In an electronics company manufacturing specialized, high-quality components, such a manager would be less useful and perhaps even counterproductive; the company's success will

[7] See E. E. Ghiselli, *Explorations in Managerial Talent* (Pacific Palisades, Calif.: Goodyear, 1971).

[8] See Dorwin Cartwright and Alvin Zander, eds., *Group Dynamics,* 3rd ed. (New York: Harper & Row, 1968).

[9] See, for example, James Owen, "The Uses of Leadership Theory," *Michigan Business Review,* Vol. 25, No. 1 (January 1973), pp. 13–19.

likely depend on its ability to maintain product quality and service rather than on its marketing approach.

Nevertheless, despite evidence that effective leadership behaviors depended at least partially on the leader's situation, some researchers have reached the conclusion that certain management behaviors *are* more effective than others in a wide variety of circumstances. These researchers have focused on two aspects of leadership behavior: leadership functions and leadership styles.

Leadership Functions

This first aspect of the behavioral approach to leadership shifted the focus from the individual leader to the functions that leaders performed within their group. This perspective suggests that in order for the group to operate effectively, *someone* has to perform two major functions: "task-related" or problem-solving functions and "group maintenance" or social functions. Task-related functions might include suggesting solutions and offering information and opinions. Group maintenance functions include anything that helps the group operate more smoothly — agreeing with or complimenting another group member, for example, mediating group disagreements, or even taking notes on group discussions. (See also our discussion of leadership roles in Chapter 12.) Group members who are best able to perform these functions will presumably emerge as group leaders.

Studies in this area have found that most effective groups have some form of shared leadership in which one person (usually the manager or formal leader) performs the task function, while another group member performs the social function.[10] This leadership "specialization" occurs because an individual may have the temperament or skill to play only one role or because an individual will be preoccupied with one role at the expense of the other. For example, a manager focusing on the task function may present his or her ideas forcefully and encourage the group to make rapid decisions. The group maintenance function, on the other hand, requires that the individual remain responsive to the ideas and feelings of the other group members. An individual who is able to perform both roles successfully would obviously be an especially effective leader.

Leadership Styles

The second perspective on leadership behavior focuses on the style a leader uses in dealing with subordinates. Researchers have studied essentially two leadership styles: a task-oriented style and an employee-oriented style. In the *task-oriented* style, the manager directs and closely supervises subordinates to ensure that the task is performed to his or her satisfaction. The manager with this leadership style is more concerned with getting the job done rather than with the development and growth of subordinates. In the *employee-oriented* style, the manager tries to motivate rather than control subordinates. He or she encourages group members to perform their tasks by allowing group members to participate in decisions that affect them and by forming friendly,

---

[10] See Robert F. Bales, *Interaction Process Analysis* (Reading, Mass.: Addison-Wesley, 1951).

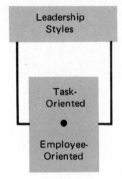

trusting, and respectful relationships with group members. Researchers at Ohio State University and the University of Michigan, and management writers such as Blake, Mouton, and Likert, have tried to determine which of these two leadership styles leads to the most effective group performance.

The Ohio State and Michigan Studies. At Ohio State, researchers studied the effectiveness of what they called "initiating structure" and "consideration" leadership behaviors. (These two terms correspond directly to task-oriented and employee-oriented styles, respectively.) They found that, as might be expected, employee turnover rates were lowest and employee satisfaction was highest under leaders who were rated high in consideration. Conversely, leaders who were rated low in consideration and high in initiating structure or task orientation had high grievance and turnover rates among their employees. (See Figure 17-1 below for the leadership styles studied at Ohio State.)

The researchers also found, however, that subordinates' ratings of their leaders' effectiveness did not depend on the particular style of the leader but on the situation in which the style was used. For example, Air Force commanders who were high on consideration were rated as *less* effective than task-oriented commanders. It is possible that the more authoritarian environment of the military, coupled with the air crews' belief that quick, hard decisions are essential in combat situations, would cause people-oriented leaders to be

FIGURE 17-1
Leadership Styles
Studied at Ohio
State

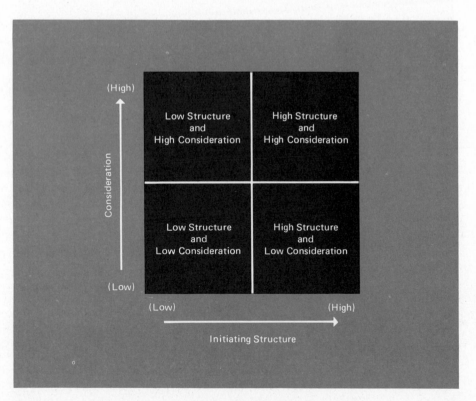

rated less effective. On the other hand, nonproduction supervisors and managers in large companies were rated more effective if they had high consideration.[11]

Researchers at the University of Michigan similarly distinguished between production-centered and employee-centered managers. Production-centered managers set rigid work standards, organized tasks down to the last detail, prescribed the work methods to be followed, and closely supervised their subordinates' work. Employee-centered managers encouraged subordinate participation in goal setting and in other work decisions and helped ensure high performance by inspiring trust and respect.

The Michigan studies found that the most productive work groups tended to have leaders who were employee-centered rather than production-centered. These studies also found that the most effective leaders were those who had supportive relationships with their subordinates, tended to use group rather than individual decision making, and encouraged their subordinates to set and achieve high performance goals.

The Managerial Grid and System 4 Management. The two management styles that researchers have identified—task-oriented and employee-oriented supervision—underlie two theories on effective management described in earlier chapters: Blake and Mouton's *Managerial Grid* in Chapter 15 and Likert's *System 4* approach to management in Chapter 13.

The Managerial Grid identifies five different types of management behaviors, based on the various ways that task-oriented and employee-oriented styles can interact with each other.[12] (See marginal figure and also Figure 15-4 in Chapter 15.)

Style 1,1 management, at the lower left-hand corner of the grid, is *impoverished management*—low concern for people and low concern for tasks or production. This style is sometimes called *laissez-faire* management, because the leader abdicates his or her leadership role.

Style 1,9 management, at the upper left-hand corner of the grid, is *country club management*—high concern for employees but low concern for production.

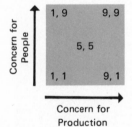

Concern for People

Concern for Production

Style 9,1 management, at the lower right-hand corner of the grid, is *task* or *authoritarian management*—high concern for production and efficiency but low concern for employees.

Style 5,5 management, at the middle of the grid, is *middle-of-the-road management*—an intermediate amount of concern for both production and employee satisfaction.

Style 9,9 management, at the upper right-hand corner of the grid, is *team*

---

[11] See Vroom, "Leadership," pp. 1530–1533.

[12] Robert R. Blake and Jane S. Mouton, *The Managerial Grid* (Houston: Gulf Publishing, 1964). For an early classification of leadership styles into authoritarian, *laissez-faire,* and democratic leadership, see Kurt Lewin, Ronald Lippitt, and Ralph K. White, "Patterns of Aggressive Behavior in Experimentally Created Social Climates," *Journal of Social Psychology,* Vol. 10, No. 2 (May 1939), pp. 271–299.

or *democratic management* — a high concern for both production and employee morale and satisfaction.

Blake and Mouton argue strongly that the 9,9 management style is the most effective type of leadership behavior. In fact, they suggest that a high task and employee orientation by the leader will, in almost all situations, result in improved performance, low absenteeism and turnover, and high employee satisfaction. However, as we shall see, other writers and researchers believe that situational factors do play a part in leader and group effectiveness.

Rensis Likert, again incorporating the basic style categories of task orientation and employee orientation, devised his own model of management effectiveness.[13] In this model, there are four possible leadership systems (see marginal figure). System 1 can be characterized as "exploitive" and "authoritative." The managers make all work-related decisions and order their subordinates to carry them out. Standards and methods of performance are also rigidly set by managers. Failure to meet the managers' goals results in threats or punishment. The managers feel little trust or confidence in subordinates, and subordinates, in turn, fear the managers and feel that they have little in common with them.

System 2 management is "benevolent authoritative." Managers still issue orders, but subordinates have some freedom to comment on those orders. Subordinates are also given some flexibility to carry out their tasks but within carefully prescribed limits and procedures. Subordinates who meet or exceed the managers' goals may be rewarded. In general, managers have a condescending attitude toward their subordinates, and subordinates are cautious when dealing with their managers.

System 3 management can be called "consultative." Managers set goals and issue general orders after discussing them with subordinates. Subordinates can make their own decisions about how to carry out their tasks, since only broad, major decisions are made by higher-level managers. Rewards, rather than the threat of punishment, are used to motivate subordinates. Subordinates feel free to discuss most work-related matters with their managers, who, in turn, feel that to a large extent subordinates can be trusted to carry out their tasks properly.

System 4 management, or "participative" management, is Likert's final and most favored management style. Under System 4, goals are set and work-related decisions are made by the group. If managers formally reach a decision, they do so after incorporating the suggestions and opinions of the other group members. Thus, the goal they set or the decision they reach may not always be the one they personally favor. To motivate subordinates, managers not only use economic rewards but also try to give their subordinates feelings of worth and importance. Performance standards exist to permit self-appraisal by subordinates, rather than to provide managers with a tool to control subordinates. Interaction between managers and subordinates is frank, friendly, and trusting.

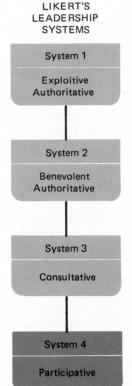

LIKERT'S
LEADERSHIP
SYSTEMS

System 1

Exploitive
Authoritative

System 2

Benevolent
Authoritative

System 3

Consultative

System 4

Participative

[13]See Rensis Likert, *New Patterns of Management* (New York: McGraw Hill, 1961), and *The Human Organization* (New York: McGraw-Hill, 1967).

Likert's studies found that organizational departments with low productivity tended to have leaders who used Systems 1 and 2 styles of management. On the other hand, high-producing departments in the organization tended to be those managed in the consultative or participative leadership style. He therefore concluded that System 4 management is the desirable form of management in a wide variety of work situations.

Is There a Universally Effective Leadership Style? The work of Blake, Mouton, and Likert would seem to suggest that a democratic, supportive, and high-goal-setting leadership style will be effective in most situations. The search for the "one best way" a leader should behave would therefore appear to be over. However, for most management writers and theorists, leadership behavior is still a complex, unresolved area of interest. There are two major reasons why the issue of which leadership style is most effective remains unresolved.

First, as we have already mentioned, the Ohio State studies found that the most effective leadership style varied with the situation. Other studies have similarly provided no clear evidence that a "System 4" or "9,9" style will consistently lead to improved group performance.[14] Likert himself recognized that the management style he favored had to be tailored to fit the types of subordinates and situations which managers faced.[15] It appears that there are simply too many kinds of leaders, subordinates, tasks, organizations, and environments for one style to apply in all cases.

The second reason why the issue of which leadership style is most effective remains unresolved is that the above styles are too general or ambiguous to guide managerial actions. How exactly should a manager go about increasing feelings of worth and importance among subordinates? Should a manager call a group meeting each time he or she needs to make a decision? How should a manager deal with subordinates who do not appear to be motivated by group standards and goals? A particular leadership style may be comfortable and useful for a specific manager, but it will not solve all the manager's individual, day-to-day leadership problems.

Robert Tannenbaum and Warren H. Schmidt were among the first theorists to describe various factors that they believe should influence a manager's choice of leadership style.[16] While Tannenbaum and Schmidt personally favor the democratic style, they acknowledge that managers need to take certain practical considerations into account before deciding how to manage. They suggest that a manager should consider three sets of "forces" before choosing a leadership style:

— forces in the manager
— forces in the subordinates
— forces in the situation

---

[14] See Stogdill, *Handbook of Leadership*, and Vroom, "Leadership."

[15] Likert, *New Patterns of Management*, p. 95.

[16] Robert Tannenbaum and Warren H. Schmidt, "How to Choose a Leadership Pattern," *Harvard Business Review*, May-June 1973, pp. 162–164 ff. (Reprint of March-April 1958 article.)

How a manager leads will primarily be influenced by his or her background, knowledge, values, and experience *(forces in the manager)*. For example, a manager who strongly values individual freedom may allow subordinates a great deal of independence in carrying out their job tasks. Conversely, a manager who believes that the needs of the individual must come second to the needs of the organization may take a much more directive role in his or her subordinates' activities. (See Figure 17-2.)

Characteristics of *subordinates* also must be considered before managers can choose an appropriate leadership style. According to Tannenbaum and Schmidt, a manager can allow greater participation and freedom under the following conditions:

—When subordinates crave independence and freedom of action
—When they want to have decision-making responsibility
—When they identify with the organization's goals
—When they are knowledgeable and experienced enough to deal with the problem efficiently
—When their experience with previous bosses leads them to expect participative management

Where these conditions are missing, managers may have to lean toward the authoritarian style. They can, however, vary their behavior once their subordinates gain self-confidence in working with them.

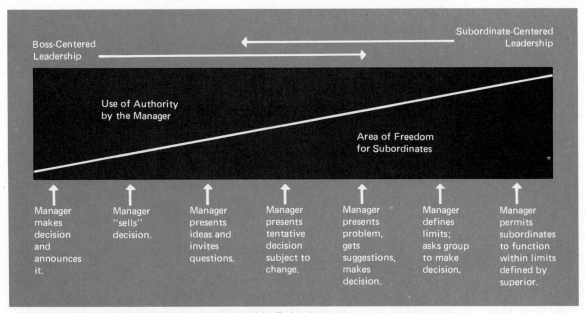

FIGURE 17-2   Continuum of Leadership Behavior

Source: Robert Tannenbaum and Warren H. Schmidt, "How to Choose a Leadership Pattern," *Harvard Business Review*, May-June 1973, p. 166. Copyright © 1973 by the President and Fellows of Harvard College; all rights reserved.

Finally, in choosing an appropriate leadership style, a manager must reckon with various *situational* forces: the organizational climate, the specific work group, the nature of the group's work tasks, the pressures of time, and even environmental factors, which may affect organization members' attitudes toward authority.

Most managers, for example, will move toward one or another leadership style in conformity with the type of behavior favored by the organization's hierarchy. If top management emphasizes human relations skills, the manager will incline toward an employee-centered style. If the decisive, take-charge style seems favored, the manager will tend to be task- rather than employee-oriented.

The specific work group will also affect the choice of style: a group that works well together may respond more to a free and open atmosphere than to close supervision. The same holds true for a group confident of its ability to solve problems as a unit. But if a work group is too large or too widely dispersed geographically, a participative management style may be difficult to use.

The nature of the problem and time pressures are other situational factors that may influence the choice of managerial styles. For example, a complex problem requiring highly specialized skills and knowledge that only the manager possesses may make direct instructions and close supervision necessary. Similarly, in situations where quick decisions are essential (as in emergencies), even democratic managers may revert to an authoritative leadership style.

To Tannenbaum and Schmidt, then, the particular leadership style a manager uses is not as important as the appropriateness of the style for the manager, his or her subordinates, and the work situation. The most effective leaders, in this view, are not authoritative or democratic but *flexible*—able to select a style that is comfortable for them and appropriate for the situation they are facing.

SITUATIONAL FACTORS IN LEADERSHIP EFFECTIVENESS

The trait and behavioral approaches were initiated in the hope that some factors could be found that were universally associated with leadership effectiveness. One of the major results of these research efforts was the discovery that effective leadership seemed to depend on a number of variables, such as organizational climate and managerial values and experience. No one leadership trait or style was most effective in all situations.

Researchers then took the next logical step: they tried to identify the factors in the situation that will influence the effectiveness of a particular leadership style. Since the early work of Tannenbaum and Schmidt, many researchers have added to and elaborated on the situational factors that will affect the leadership style a manager selects and how effective a particular style will be.

Before going on to discuss these factors, we should note that how the work situation will affect the manager will depend on his or her *perception* of the situation. The situation as it actually is may affect the manager only gradually. For example, a manager who believes that his or her subordinates are lazy and low in ability will manage them on that basis for a prolonged period, even if the subordinates are actually eager to work and have excellent skills. In order for the manager's leadership style to change to one that is more appropriate to the situation, the manager's perception of the situation will first have to change.

Factors that influence leader effectiveness include the leader's personality and past experience; the superior's expectations and behavior; the subordinates' characteristics, expectations, and behavior; the requirements of the task; the organizational climate and policies; and the expectations and behavior of peers.[17] (See Figure 17-3.) We should note that while these factors influence the leader, the influence process does *not* only work in one direction; the leader influences these factors in return. In short, the influence process is *reciprocal* — leaders and group members, for example, will influence each other and affect the effectiveness of the group as a whole.

FIGURE 17-3
Personality and Situational Factors That Influence Leadership Behavior

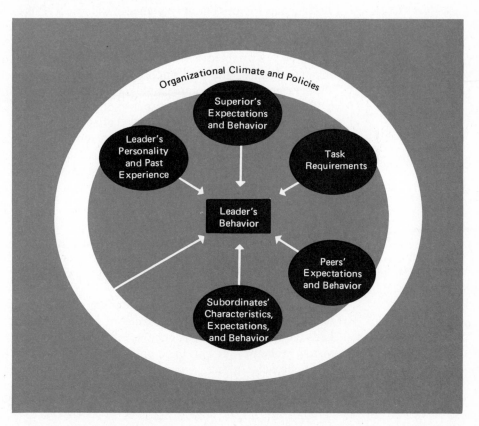

[17] See H. Joseph Reitz, *Behavior in Organizations* (Homewood, Ill.: Irwin, 1977), and Paul Hersey and Kenneth H. Blanchard, *Management of Organizational Behavior,* 2nd ed. (Englewood Cliffs, N.J.: Prentice-Hall, 1972).

The Leader's Personality and Past Experiences

As we have already suggested, the manager's values, background, and experiences will affect his or her choice of style. A manager who has had success in exercising little supervision, for example, or who values the self-fulfillment needs of subordinates may adopt a democratic style of leadership; a manager who distrusts subordinates or who simply likes to manage all work activities directly may adopt a more authoritarian role. In general, managers develop the leadership style with which they are most comfortable.

The fact that a manager's personality or past experience helps form his or her leadership style does not mean that the style is unchangeable. Managers *learn* that some styles work better for them than others; if a style proves inappropriate they can alter it. (They can also be helped to alter it through sensitivity training—see Chapters 15 and 19.) However, it is important to note that managers who attempt to adopt a style that is *very* inconsistent with their basic personality are unlikely to use that style effectively.

The Expectations and Behavior of Superiors

The leadership style that a manager's superiors reward is very important in determining the orientation a manager will select. For example, a superior who clearly favors a task-oriented style ("You really run a tight ship—keep it up") may cause the manager to adopt that type of leadership. A superior who favors an employee-oriented style ("You really seem to get to know your subordinates—I think that's an important thing for a manager to do") may cause the manager to adopt a more employee-centered orientation.

Because of their power to dispense organizational rewards, such as bonuses and promotions, superiors clearly will affect the behavior of lower-level managers. In addition, lower-level managers tend naturally to model themselves after their superiors. One study found that supervisors who learned new behaviors in a human relations training program tended to give up those behaviors quickly if they were not consistent with their immediate superior's leadership style.[18]

Subordinates' Characteristics, Expectations, and Behavior

Subordinates play a critical role in influencing the manager's leadership style—they are, after all, the people whom that style is supposed to affect. Ultimately, the response of subordinates to the manager's leadership determines how effective the manager will be.

The characteristics of subordinates affect the manager's leadership style in a number of ways. First, the *skills* of subordinates will influence the manager's choice of style: highly capable employees will usually require little supervision, while new or untrained employees will normally require a more directive approach. In fact, one study found that new leaders who were told that their subordinates were low performers managed in a much more authoritative manner than new leaders who were told that their subordinates were high

[18]E. A. Fleishman, "Leadership Climate, Human Relations Training, and Supervisory Behavior," *Personnel Psychology,* Vol. 6, No. 2 (Summer 1953), pp. 205–222.

performers.[19] Second, the *attitudes* of subordinates will also be an influential factor: some types of employees (such as military police) may prefer an authoritarian leader, while others (such as research scientists) may prefer to be given total responsibility for their own work.

The *expectations* of subordinates will also be a factor in determining how appropriate a particular style will be. Subordinates who have had employee-centered managers in the past may expect a new manager to have a similar style, and may react negatively to authoritarian leadership. Similarly, highly skilled and motivated workers may expect the manager not to "meddle." Employees faced with a brand-new task, on the other hand, will expect the manager's directives and will be upset if they are not forthcoming.

The reactions of subordinates to a manager's leadership style will usually let the manager learn how effective his or her style is. For example, the subordinates' confusion or resentment that often accompanies an inappropriate style will usually suggest to the manager that a change in style is required. Sometimes, however, a new manager may feel that changing the subordinates' expectations would be better than changing his or her own style — for example, the manager may be very reluctant to adopt an authoritarian approach. In such situations, it will normally require a great deal of time and patience on the manager's part before subordinates accept the new manager's style.

Task
Requirements

The nature of subordinates' job reponsibilities will also affect the type of leadership style a manager will use. For example, jobs that require precise instructions (such as computer keypunching) demand a more task-oriented style than jobs (such as university teaching) whose operating procedures can be left largely to the individual employees. Similarly, where a lot of cooperation and teamwork are involved, as in new product development, employees generally prefer people-centered supervision, whereas those working in isolation — truck drivers, for example — prefer more task-oriented direction.

Organizational
Climate and
Policies

As we noted in Chapter 13, every organization has its own "personality" or climate, which influences the expectations and behavior of organization members. Thus, the climate of the organization, as well as its stated policies, will also affect a manager's leadership style.

For example, in some organizations, climate and policy encourage strict accountability for expenses and results. Managers in such an organization will usually supervise and control their subordinates to make sure stated and implied organization guidelines are not being violated. In other organizations, the climate may be more employee-centered, with an emphasis placed on group cooperation and creativity. Similarly, during times of economic recession, the organization may encourage tighter controls and a more autocratic management

[19]G. F. Farris and F. G. Lim, Jr., "Effects of Performance on Leadership, Cohesiveness, Satisfaction, and Subsequent Performance," *Journal of Applied Psychology,* Vol. 53 (1969), pp. 102–110.

style, while in times of prosperity, a more relaxed, human relations approach may be favored.

Peers'
Expectations
and Behavior

One's fellow managers are an important reference group and source of rewards. Managers form friendships with their colleagues in the organization, and the opinion of these colleagues matters to them. In addition, the attitude of a manager's peers can often affect how effectively the manager will perform: hostile colleagues may compete aggressively for organization resources, harm the manager's reputation, and prove uncooperative in other ways. For these reasons, the reactions of his or her peers influence how the manager behaves toward subordinates. A manager who is comparatively lenient, for example, may well become more autocratic if other managers comment. ("You're letting your subordinates leave too early. My people are starting to complain." Or, "You're only giving two tests a term? Most instructors give four.") Regardless of his or her own inclinations, a manager will, to some extent, imitate the management style of his or her peers.

CONTINGENCY APPROACHES TO LEADERSHIP

The situational perspective on leadership identified various factors that can influence leadership behavior. The *contingency* approaches to leadership attempt (1) to identify which of these factors is most important under a given set of circumstances and (2) to predict the leadership style that will be most effective under those circumstances. In other words, the situational perspective suggests how managers *will* behave, and the contingency approaches suggest how managers *should* behave in order to lead most effectively. In the sections below, we will not review all the contingency models of leadership that have been developed (see Chapters 7, 13, and 15 for additional approaches). We will, however, review three of the more recent and well-known models.

Leadership Style
and the Work
Situation: The
Fiedler Model

The most thoroughly researched of the three contingency models we will discuss is the Fiedler model. Fiedler's basic assumption is that it is quite difficult for managers to alter the management styles that have helped them to develop successful organizational careers. For this reason, he believes it is inefficient or useless to try to change a manager's style to fit the situation. Since styles are relatively inflexible, and since no one style is appropriate for every situation, Fiedler suggests instead that the best way to achieve effective group performance is to match the manager to the situation or to change the situation to fit the manager. For instance, a comparatively authoritarian manager can be selected to fill a post that requires a more directive leader; or, the job can be changed so that the authoritarian manager is given more formal authority over subordinates.

The leadership styles that Fiedler contrasts are similar to the employee-centered and task-oriented styles discussed earlier. What differentiates his model from the others is the measuring instrument he used. Fiedler measured leadership style on a simple scale that indicated "the degree to which a man described favorably or unfavorably his least preferred co-worker (LPC)"— the employee with whom the person could work least well. It is this measure that locates an individual on the leadership style continuum. According to Fiedler's findings, "...a person who describes his least preferred co-workers in a relatively favorable manner tends to be permissive, human relations-oriented and considerate of the feelings of his men. But a person who describes his least preferred co-worker in an unfavorable manner—who has what we have come to call a low LPC rating—tends to be managing, task-controlling, and less concerned with the human relations aspects of the job."[20]

According to Fiedler, then, a high LPC manager wants primarily to have warm personal relations with his or her co-workers. He or she will regard such emotional ties with subordinates as an important part of being an effective manager. The low LPC manager, on the other hand, has a different set of goals. Above all, he or she wants to get the job done; the reactions of subordinates to his or her leadership style is simply not as important as the need to maintain production. Should the low LPC manager feel that a harsh style is necessary to maintain production, he or she will not hesitate to use it.

Leadership Situations. Fiedler has identified three elements in the work situation that will help determine which leadership style will be effective: leader-member relations, the task structure, and the leader's position power. Fiedler did not include in his studies other situational variables we have already discussed, such as employee motivation (Chapter 16) and the values and experiences of leaders and group members.

The quality of *leader-member relations* is the most important influence on the manager's power and effectiveness, according to Fiedler. If the manager gets along well with the rest of the group, if group members respect the manager for his or her personality, character, or ability, then the manager may not have to rely on formal rank or authority. On the other hand, if the manager is disliked or distrusted, then the manager may be less able to lead informally and may have to rely on directives to accomplish group tasks.

Task structure is the second most important variable in the work situation. A highly structured task is one in which step-by-step procedures or instructions for the task are available; group members therefore have a very clear idea of what they are expected to do. Tasks in an appliance repair shop, for example, tend to be highly structured because detailed repair manuals exist. Managers in such situations automatically have a great deal of authority: there are clear

---

[20] Fred E. Fiedler, "Engineer the Job to Fit the Manager," *Harvard Business Review*, September-October 1965, p. 116. See also Fred E. Fiedler, "The Contingency Model." in Harold Proshansky and Bernard Seidenberg, eds., *Basic Studies in Social Psychology* (New York: Holt, Rinehart and Winston, 1965), pp. 538–551, and "Validation and Extension of the Contingency Model of Leadership Effectiveness," *Psychological Bulletin*, Vol. 76, No. 2 (August 1971), pp. 128–148.

guidelines by which to measure worker performance (the refrigerator is either repaired or it isn't) and the manager can back up his or her instructions by referring to the rulebook or manual. When tasks are unstructured, on the other hand, as in committee meetings, group member roles are more ambiguous, because there are no clear guidelines on how to proceed. The manager's power is diminished, since group members can more easily disagree with or question the manager's instructions.

The leader's *position power* is the final situational variable identified by Fiedler. Some positions carry a great deal of power and authority. The presidency of a firm, for example, like most upper-level management positions, is heavily endowed with legitimate, reward, and coercive power. The chairperson of a fund-raising drive, on the other hand, has little power over volunteer workers. Thus, high position power simplifies a leader's task of influencing subordinates, while low position power makes the leader's task more difficult.

Matching the Situation to the Leader. As can be seen in the bottom part of Figure 17-4, there are eight possible combinations of these three variables in the work situation: Leader-member relations can be good or bad; tasks may be structured or unstructured; and position power may be strong or weak. A well-liked leader of a bomber crew, for example, would be in category 1 of the figure, while a disliked temporary committee chairperson would be in category 8.

Using these eight categories of leadership situations and his two types of leaders—high and low LPC—Fiedler reviewed studies of over eight hundred groups to see which type of leader was most effective in each situation. (Among the groups studied were basketball teams, executive training workshops, and Air Force and tank combat crews.) He found that low LPC leaders—those who were task-oriented or authoritarian—were most effective in extreme situations where the leader either had a great deal of power and influence or had very little power and influence. High LPC leaders—those who were employee-oriented—were most effective in situations where the leader had moderate power and influence. (See Figure 17-4.)

For example, a respected head of a research team would have only moderate influence over team members; this influence would be based largely on the fact that the team respects the leader. Research tasks are relatively unstructured, and so the leader would have little influence over the way the work would be organized and performed. In addition, the leader's position power is low, because team members would regard themselves as colleagues rather than subordinates (category 4). An authoritarian style would therefore be ineffective; team members would resent it, and it would stifle the flow of research ideas. A supportive style, on the other hand, would encourage high performance by the group. However, a well-liked commander of a tank crew (category 1) would lead most effectively with an authoritarian style. Tank crew members would not expect nor would they appreciate being consulted each time the commander had to make a routine decision. ("Should we fire?")

Subsequent research has failed either to verify or disprove Fiedler's model,

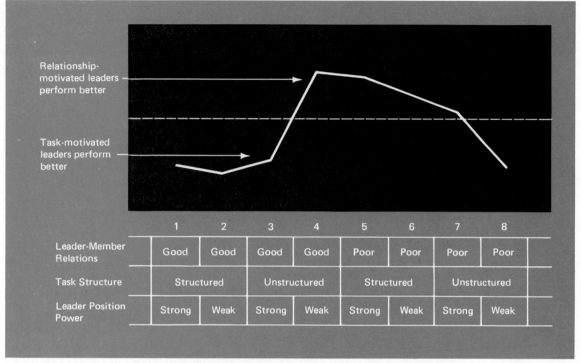

FIGURE 17-4 How the Style of Effective Leadership Varies with the Situation

Source: Fred E. Fiedler and Martin M. Chemers, *Leadership and Effective Management* (Glenview, Ill.: Scott, Foresman, 1974), p. 80. Copyright © 1974 by Scott, Foresman and Company. Reprinted by permission. Also copyright © 1965 by the President and Fellows of Harvard College; all rights reserved.

and researchers continue to disagree on the extent to which Fiedler's model is valid.[21] However, it is widely agreed that Fiedler has made a significant contribution to our understanding of how leaders and situations can be matched for effective performance.

A Path-Goal Approach to Leadership

Like the other variants of the contingency approach, the path-goal model tries to help us understand and predict leadership effectiveness in different situations. The model was formulated comparatively recently by Martin G. Evans[22] and Robert J. House.[23] Thus, it represents a new approach, and aspects of it are still evolving.

[21] See, for example, George Graen, James B. Orris, and Kenneth Alvares, "Contingency Model of Leadership Effectiveness: Some Experimental Results," *Journal of Applied Psychology,* Vol. 55, No. 3 (June 1971), pp. 196–201.

[22] Martin G. Evans, "Leadership and Motivation: A Core Concept," *Academy of Management Journal,* Vol. 13, No. 1 (March 1970), pp. 91–102.

[23] See Robert J. House, "A Path-Goal Theory of Leader Effectiveness," *Administrative Science Quarterly,* Vol. 16, No. 3 (September 1971), pp. 321–338, and Robert J. House and Terence R. Mitchell, "Path-Goal Theory of Leadership," *Journal of Contemporary Business,* Vol. 3, No. 4 (Autumn 1974), pp. 81–97.

The path-goal approach is based on the expectancy/valence model described in the previous chapter. (In brief, this motivation model states that an individual's motivation will depend on his or her expectancy of reward and the valence, or attractiveness, of that reward for the individual.) The path-goal approach focuses on the leader as a source of rewards. It attempts to predict how different types of rewards a leader can offer and the leader's different styles will affect the motivation, performance, and satisfaction of subordinates.

According to Evans, managers have at their disposal a number of ways to influence subordinates. The most important of these are the manager's ability to provide rewards and to clarify for subordinates what they must do to earn these rewards. In other words, managers can influence the availability of rewards ("goals") for their subordinates and can make clear the "paths" that subordinates must take in order to reach those "goals."

Evans suggests that the leadership style a manager possesses will help determine which rewards will be made available to subordinates. The manager's style will also influence subordinates' perceptions of what they have to do to earn those rewards. A manager with an employee-centered style, for example, will offer a wide range of rewards to subordinates — not only pay and promotion, but also support, encouragement, security, and respect. In addition, the manager with that style will be sensitive to individual differences among subordinates and will tailor the rewards he or she offers to the individual needs and desires of subordinates. A task-oriented manager, on the other hand, will offer a narrower, less individualized set of rewards. However, according to Evans, precisely such a manager will usually be much better than an employee-centered manager at linking subordinate performance to rewards. Subordinates of a task-oriented manager will know exactly the productivity or performance level they will have to attain in order to gain bonuses, salary increases, or promotions. Evans suggests that the style that will most motivate subordinates will depend on the types of rewards that subordinates desire. For example, subordinates who desire immediate satisfaction in the form of praise from their supervisor more than future satisfaction in the form of a bonus may be more effectively motivated by a supportive leadership style.

House and his colleagues have attempted to expand the path-goal theory by identifying the contingency variables that will help determine the most effective leadership style. The two variables they identify are the personal characteristics of subordinates and the environmental pressures and demands in the workplace with which subordinates must cope.

Personal Characteristics of Subordinates. The leadership style subordinates favor will, according to House, be partially determined by their personal characteristics. For example, studies cited by House suggested that individuals who believe the environment is affected by their behavior will favor a participatory leadership style. Individuals who believe events occur to them because of luck or fate will tend to find an authoritarian style more satisfying.

Another personal characteristic that House suggests will influence subordinate style preferences is the subordinates' evaluation of their ability. Subordinates who feel highly skilled and capable may resent an overly controlling manager. The directives of such a manager will be seen as counterproductive rather than rewarding. Subordinates who feel less skilled or able, on the other hand, may prefer the manager to be more directive. The manager's behavior will be seen by those subordinates as enabling them to carry out their tasks properly and therefore making it possible for them to earn organizational rewards.

Environmental Pressures and Demands. House identifies three environmental factors that help determine the leadership style which subordinates will prefer: the subordinates' tasks, the organization's formal authority system, and the subordinates' work group.

The nature of *subordinates' tasks* will affect leadership style in a number of ways. For example, an individual performing a structured task like equipment maintenance or a repetitive task like truck loading is likely to find an overly directive style redundant, since it is already clear exactly what needs to be done. An individual performing an unstructured task like personnel administration, on the other hand, is likely to appreciate at least some direction, because the direction will clarify what the subordinate must do to perform effectively. Similarly, where the task itself is already highly satisfying to a subordinate, consideration shown by the manager will have little effect on the subordinate's motivation. If the task is unpleasant, however, a display of support by the leader may add to the subordinate's satisfaction and motivation.

The *organization's formal authority system* usually clarifies for subordinates what actions are likely to be met with disapproval (exceeding the budget, for example) and what actions are likely to lead to rewards (coming in under budget, for example). In organizations where formal authority is overly rigid, an employee-oriented style is likely to be more motivating. In a very informal organization, some employees may prefer a directive manager who will let them know what they must do to earn tangible rewards.

The *subordinates' work group* will have a similar influence on which leadership style will be most effective. A cohesive, supportive work group, for example, will make an employee-centered leadership style less motivating, because subordinates will already be deriving satisfaction from the group. If groups are less cohesive, however, a supportive, understanding style may be more effective. In sum, as a general rule, the leaders' style will motivate subordinates to the extent that it compensates for what subordinates see as deficiencies in the task, authority system, or work group.

Because the path-goal theory of leadership is fairly new, research evidence for it is still inconclusive. However, the approach is considered highly promising, especially because it attempts to explain *why* a particular leadership style will be more effective in one situation than in another.

A Life Cycle
Theory of
Leadership

The final contingency approach to leadership we will discuss is Paul Hersey and Kenneth H. Blanchard's "life cycle theory."[24] From this perspective, the most effective leadership style varies with the "maturity" of subordinates. Hersey and Blanchard do not define maturity as age or emotional stability. Instead, they define maturity as desire for achievement, willingness to accept responsibility, and task-related ability and experience.

Hersey and Blanchard believe that the relationship between a manager and subordinates moves through four phases as subordinates develop and "mature," and that managers need to vary their leadership style with each phase. (See Figure 17-5.) In the initial phase—when subordinates first enter the organization, for example—a high task orientation by the manager is most appropriate. Subordinates have to be instructed in their tasks and familiarized with the organization's rules and procedures. A nondirective manager at this stage would simply cause anxiety and confusion among the new employees. However, a participatory employee relationship approach would also be inappropriate at this stage, according to Hersey and Blanchard, because subordinates cannot yet be regarded as colleagues.

As subordinates begin to learn their tasks, a task orientation by the manager remains essential, because subordinates are not yet willing or able to accept responsibility on their own. However, the manager's trust in and support of subordinates will probably increase, because the manager has become familiar with the subordinates and wishes to encourage further efforts on their part. Thus, the manager will also start to use an employee-oriented leadership style.

In the third phase, the subordinates' ability and achievement motivation are increased, and subordinates actively begin to seek greater responsibility. The manager will no longer need to be directive (indeed, close direction might be resented). However, the manager will continue to be supportive and considerate in order to strengthen the subordinates' resolve for greater responsibility.

As the subordinates gradually become confident, self-directing, and experienced, the manager can reduce the amount of support and encouragement he or she has been providing. The subordinates are "on their own" and no longer need or expect a close relationship with their manager.

The life cycle model has generated interest because it suggests that leadership style must be dynamic and flexible rather than static. The motivation, ability, and experience of subordinates must constantly be assessed in order to determine which style combination would be most appropriate. If the style is appropriate, according to Hersey and Blanchard, it will not only motivate subordinates but also help them move toward "maturity." Thus, as the manager develops his or her subordinates, increases their confidence, and helps

[24] Hersey and Blanchard, *Management of Organizational Behavior.* See also William J. Reddin, *Managerial Effectiveness* (New York: McGraw-Hill, 1970) on which Hersey and Blanchard base much of their work.

FIGURE 17-5
The Life Cycle
Theory of
Leadership

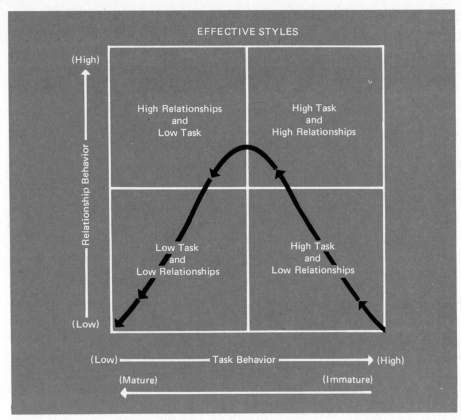

Source: Paul Hersey and Kenneth H. Blanchard, *Management of Organizational Behavior*, 2nd ed. (Englewood Cliffs, N.J.: Prentice-Hall, 1972), p. 135. Used by permission.

them master their work, the manager will constantly be shifting his or her style.

How Flexible Are Leadership Styles?

One of the major issues raised by the contingency perspective — which is currently favored by leadership theorists and researchers — is the extent to which managers are able to choose among leadership styles in different situations. The issue is important because how it is resolved will affect a wide range of management selection, placement, and promotion activities. If managers are flexible in their leadership style, or at least can be trained in a number of styles, then presumably they can operate effectively in a variety of leadership situations. If, on the other hand, managers are relatively inflexible in their leadership style, then they will operate effectively only in certain situations. They will therefore, according to the contingency perspective, be suited only for those management positions in which their style is appropriate or in which flexibility of style is comparatively unimportant (as in routinized, lower-level management positions). Such inflexibility would do more than hamper the careers of individual managers; it would also complicate enormously the organization's task of filling its management positions effectively.

Fred Fiedler, as we noted earlier, believes that leadership styles are quite inflexible. He is also very pessimistic about the possibility of training individuals to use different styles.[25] He suggests that the manager be *matched* to the situation—a task-oriented manager, for example, should be placed in a job where such an orientation would be most effective, as in a bookkeeping department, while an employee-oriented manager should be placed where group relationships are an important factor, as in a research department. Fiedler also suggests that the situation can be changed to suit the manager. (This procedure would obviously be more difficult and expensive.) An inappropriately authoritarian manager, for example, could be given subordinates who did not mind a directive style. If this is impractical, the work situation or the manager's position power might be altered to make it more appropirate for his or her authoritarian style. Where management training might be useful, according to Fiedler, is in helping managers recognize the style they use and in improving their skill in selecting a position that will be appropriate for them.

Victor H. Vroom and Philip W. Yetton are much more optimistic about the ability of managers to select an appropriate leadership style for each situation.[26] As we described in Chapter 7, Vroom and Yetton have developed a model that managers can use for selecting the proper amount of group decision making in a variety of problem situations. Briefly, the model suggests that the amount of subordinate participation in decision making which managers should select depends on: how much information or skill the manager possesses; whether or not a high-quality decision is required; the extent to which the problem is structured; and whether or not acceptance by the group is critical for the successful implementation of the decision. Thus, Vroom and Yetton suggest that managers can be flexible and adopt a number of styles, from making the decision solely on their own through various degrees of group participation in accordance with their analysis of the needs of the situation. Vroom and Yetton have even designed a training program to help managers understand how much group participation they normally like to use, to show them how to determine the most appropriate approach in a given situation, and to help them select the optimum amount of participation for future situations.

Several studies on leadership imply that managers actually do have a great deal of *potential* flexibility in responding to situational influences on their leadership style.[27] No reasonably alert manager, for example, whose subor-

[25] See Fred E. Fiedler, "The Trouble with Leadership Training Is That It Doesn't Train Leaders," *Psychology Today,* February 1973, pp. 23 ff.

[26] See Victor H. Vroom. "Can Leaders Learn to Lead?" in J. Richard Hackman, Edward E. Lawler III, and Lyman W. Porter, eds., *Perspectives on Behavior in Organizations* (New York: McGraw-Hill, 1977), pp. 398–408.

[27] See Farris and Lim, "Effects of Performance on Leadership, Cohesiveness, Satisfaction, and Subsequent Performance." See also Aaron Lowin and J. R. Craig, "The Influence of Level of Performance on Managerial Style," *Organizational Behavior and Human Performance,* Vol. 3 (November 1968), pp. 440–458.

dinates are clearly uncooperative and whose group's performance is declining will persist in using a leadership style without at least questioning its effectiveness. Thus, it is possible that individuals can learn how to diagnose a leadership situation and can alter their style, at least to some extent, to make their leadership more effective.

Summary   Leadership is an important subject for managers because of the critical role played by leaders in group and organizational effectiveness. *Leadership* may be defined as the process of influencing and directing the task-related activities of group members.

Three approaches to the study of leadership have been identified: the trait, behavior, and contingency approaches. The *trait* approach has not proved useful, since no major traits have been identified that consistently distinguish leaders from nonleaders or effective leaders from ineffective leaders.

The *behavior* approach has focused on leadership functions and styles. Studies have found that both types of leadership *functions*—task-related functions and group maintenance functions—have to be performed by one or more group members in order for the group to function effectively. Studies of leadership *styles* have distinguished between a task-oriented, authoritarian, or initiating structure and an employee-centered, democratic, or participative style. Studies at the University of Michigan and the work of Blake, Mouton, and Likert suggest that there may be a "one best way" for a leader to manage subordinates. Other studies, however, such as those performed at Ohio State University, suggest that the effectiveness of a particular style depends on the circumstances in which it is used. Tannenbaum and Schmidt, for example, maintain that a manager's choice of leadership style will be influenced by various forces in the manager, in his or her subordinates, and in the work situation.

The difficulty of isolating universally effective leadership traits or behaviors caused researchers to try to determine the situational variables that will cause one leadership style to be more effective than another. The major situational variables they identified include: the leader's personality and past experience; the expectations and behavior of superiors; the characteristics, expectations, and behavior of subordinates; task requirements; organizational policies and climate; and the expectations and behavior of peers.

The *contingency* approach to leadership attempts to identify which of these situational factors is most important and to predict which leadership style will be most effective in a given situation. The *Fiedler model* suggests that leader-member relations, task structure, and the leader's position power are the most important situational variables. The model predicts which types of leaders (high LPC or low LPC) will be most effective in the eight possible combinations of these variables.

The *path-goal* approach suggests that the most important leadership tool managers have is their ability to dispense rewards. The leadership style a manager uses will affect the types of rewards the manager offers and the subordinates' perceptions of what they must do to earn those rewards. The personal characteristics of subordinates, as well as the environmental pressures and demands to which they are subjected, will affect which leadership style subordinates actually or potentially find rewarding.

The life cycle theory of leadership suggests that leadership style should vary with the "maturity" of subordinates. The manager-subordinate relationship moves through four phases as subordinates develop achievement motivation and experience. A different leadership style is appropriate for each phase.

Fiedler suggests that leadership styles are relatively inflexible, and that therefore it is easier to match the leader to the appropriate situation or to change the situation to match the leader. Several other writers and researchers, however, believe that managers have a great deal of potential flexibility in their leadership styles and can therefore learn to be effective in a variety of situations.

Review Questions

1. In what ways, if any, have your views on leaders and leadership changed as a result of reading this chapter?
2. How is leadership defined in the text? What are the three implications of this definition?
3. Why was it logical for researchers to try to understand leadership by attempting to identify universal leadership traits? What two approaches did the trait researchers take? What did leadership trait studies reveal?
4. What leadership functions have to be performed in order for the group to operate effectively? Must the leader perform both functions?
5. What are the two basic leadership styles? What did the Ohio State and Michigan studies reveal about the effectiveness of each style?
6. What five types of management behavior are identified by the Management Grid? Which type do Blake and Mouton feel is most effective?
7. What are Likert's four management systems? What system does Likert believe is most effective?
8. How does the work of Blake, Mouton, and Likert differ from that of most contingency theorists?
9. According to Tannenbaum and Schmidt, what factors should influence a manager's choice of style? What are some of the practical considerations that they suggest managers need to take into account in selecting a style?
10. What situational factors in leadership effectiveness have been identified?
11. What basic assumptions underlie the Fiedler model? What measuring instrument did Fiedler use to differentiate leadership styles? What elements in the work situation determine which leadership style will be most effective? In what situations is a high LPC leader effective? In what situations is a low LPC leader effective?
12. On what model of motivation is the path-goal theory based? According to this theory, how do different style managers differ in their ability to influence or reward subordinates? What variables, according to this theory, help determine the most effective leadership style? Why?
13. What is the life cycle perspective on leadership? How should a manager's style vary in each of the four phases through which subordinates move?
14. Which leadership style do you believe would be most effective in influencing you? What style do you think you would be most likely to use? How flexible in style do you believe you are? Do you think your answers to these questions will affect your career choices and opportunities?

CASE STUDY: DECISION BY THE GROUP

John Stevens, plant manager of the Fairlee Plant of Lockstead Corporation, attended the advanced management seminar conducted at a large midwestern university. The seminar, of four weeks duration, was devoted largely to the topic of executive decision making.

Case reprinted with permission from *Critical Incidents in Management*, 3rd ed., by John M. Champion and John H. James (Homewood, Ill.: Richard D. Irwin, Inc., 1975), pp. 62–63.

Professor Mennon, of the university staff, particularly impressed John Stevens with her lectures on group discussion and group decision making. On the basis of research and experience, Professor Mennon was convinced that employees, if given the opportunity, could meet together, intelligently consider, and then formulate quality decisions that would be enthusiastically accepted.

Returning to his plant at the conclusion of the seminar, Mr. Stevens decided to practice some of the principles that he had learned. He called together the twenty-five employees of Department B and told them that production standards established several years previously were now too low in view of the recent installation of automated equipment. He gave the employees the opportunity to discuss the mitigating circumstances and to decide among themselves, as a group, what their standards should be. Mr. Stevens, on leaving the room, believed that the employees would doubtlessly establish much higher standards than he himself would have dared propose.

After an hour of discussion the group summoned Mr. Stevens and notified him that, contrary to his opinion, their group decision was that the standards were already too high, and since they had been given the authority to establish their own standards, they were making a reduction of 10 percent. These standards, Mr. Stevens knew, were far too low to provide a fair profit on the owner's investment. Yet, it was clear that his refusal to accept the group decision would be disastrous. Before taking a course of action, Mr. Stevens called Professor Mennon at the university for her opinion.

Case Questions
1. How could Mr. Stevens have avoided the situation he is now in?
2. What fundamental principle of organizational group decision making did Mr. Stevens violate?
3. If you were Professor Mennon, what advice would you give Mr. Stevens?

Chapter 18

Interpersonal and Organizational Communication

Upon completing this chapter you should be able to:

1. Define communication and state why it is important to managers.

2. Describe a model of the communication process.

3. Distinguish between one-way and two-way communication.

4. Summarize the barriers to interpersonal communication and explain how they can be overcome.

5. Distinguish between defensive and supportive communication.

6. Describe the factors that influence the effectiveness of organizational communication.

7. Explain the role of the "grapevine" in organizations.

8. State how the barriers to effective organizational communication can be overcome.

MEMO

TO: Eric Fenshel
FR: Jane Bryant
RE: Quarterly Report

As you know, your quarterly report is due in two weeks. I cannot emphasize how important it is that you get the report in on time. Division headquarters cannot proceed with its review unless reports from all district managers are in. However, you seem to be busy with the new marketing campaign. If you are unable to complete the report by the due date, you may take an extension. I will have to explain to headquarters why quarterly reports for my department are incomplete.

MEMO

TO: Jane Bryant
FR: Eric Fenshel
RE: Your recent memo

Your memo about my quarterly report came as something of a shock to me. Frankly, you don't "seem" to appreciate the amount of work this new marketing campaign requires. I have been working late every day *and* on weekends so that we can make our new product line a success. I had planned to ask for an extension for the quarterly report, but if the report is that important I'll make sure you get it on time. I just hope you don't expect the report and the marketing campaign to be as good as they should be.

The above exchange—by no means atypical—is an example of poor communication. Jane Bryant obviously had not clarified in her own mind what she wanted her memo to accomplish. On the one hand, she clearly wanted Eric's report to be in on time. On the other hand, she was aware that he was tied up with the marketing campaign and she felt the need to offer him an extension. Her unresolved conflict resulted in a stiff, confusing memo that must have frustrated Eric when he read it. Eric's memo, in turn, expressed his angry reaction and suggested that he would accomplish both his tasks inadequately. The result was that the individuals involved as well as the organization did not get what they needed.

THE IMPORTANCE OF COMMUNICATION

Effective communication is extremely important for managers for two reasons. First, communication is the necessary process by which the management functions of planning, organizing, leading, and controlling are accomplished. Second, communication is the activity to which managers devote an overwhelming proportion of their time.

The *process* of communication makes it possible for managers to carry out their task responsibilities. Information must be communicated to managers

THE FOUNDATION
OF THE
MANAGEMENT
FUNCTIONS

so that they will have a basis for planning; the plans must be communicated to others in order to be carried out. Organizing requires communicating with people about their job assignments. Leading requires managers to communicate with subordinates so that group goals can be achieved. Written or verbal communications are an essential part of controlling. In short, managers do not manage in isolation; they can carry out their management functions only by interacting with and communicating with others. The communication process is thus the foundation upon which the management functions depend.

A very large share of managerial time is devoted to the *activity* of communication. Managers are rarely alone at their desks thinking, planning, or contemplating alternatives. In fact, managerial time is spent largely in face-to-face or telephone communication with subordinates, peers, supervisors, suppliers, or customers. When not conferring with others in person or on the telephone, managers may be writing or dictating memos, letters, or reports—or perhaps reading memos, letters, or reports sent to them. Even in those few periods when managers are alone, they are frequently interrupted by communications from others. For example, one study of middle and top managers found that they could work uninterruptedly for a half hour or more only an average of once every two days.[1]

Henry Mintzberg, whose work we discussed in Chapter 1, has described the manager's job in terms of three types of roles.[2] Communication plays a vital part in each of these types:

1. In their *interpersonal roles,* managers act as the figurehead and leader of their organizational unit, interacting with subordinates, customers, and suppliers. They also make contact with peers in the organization. Mintzberg cites studies that indicate managers spend about 45 percent of their contact time with peers, about 45 percent with people outside their units, and only about 10 percent with superiors.

2. In their *informational roles,* managers seek information from peers, subordinates, and other personal contacts about anything that may affect their job and responsibilities. They also disseminate interesting or important information in return. In addition, they provide suppliers, peers, and relevant groups outside the organization with information about their unit as a whole.

3. In their *decisional roles,* managers implement new projects, handle disturbances, and allocate resources to their unit's members and departments. Some of the decisions that managers make will be reached in private, but they will be based on information that has been communicated to the managers. The managers, in turn, will have to communicate those decisions to others.

Mintzberg emphasizes that managers have a strong personal preference for oral communication. Oral communication is timely and current; it often informs the manager about immediate problems or opportunities. Written

---

[1] Rosemary Stewart, *Managers and Their Jobs,* (London: Macmillan, 1967).

[2] Henry Mintzberg, "The Manager's Job: Folklore and Fact," *Harvard Business Review,* July-August 1975, pp. 49–61. See also Henry Mintzberg, *The Nature of Managerial Work* (New York: Harper & Row, 1973).

communication, on the other hand, is often not sufficiently current. For example, only 13 percent of the mail received by chief executives in one of Mintzberg's studies was of immediate use to them. Because managers need to communicate quickly and receive information that is currently useful, they heavily favor oral communication. Studies cited by Mintzberg, for instance, suggest that managers spend from 66 to 80 percent of their total work time in oral communication.

In this chapter we will deal with the subject of communication in organizations. We will first present a model of interpersonal communication, describe the barriers to effective interpersonal communication, and suggest ways these barriers can be overcome. Second, we will show how the different types of communication channels that can exist in organizations will influence variables such as group performance, leader emergence, and group member motivation and satisfaction. Third, we will discuss problems of communication up and down the organization's chain of command. Fourth, we will discuss the informal channels of communication that develop in organizations. Finally, we will deal with means for overcoming organizational (rather than interpersonal) barriers to effective communication.

Before we begin our discussion, we should note that one of the major difficulties surrounding communication as a subject of study is in defining exactly what it is. One researcher uncovered as many as 95 definitions, with none of them widely accepted.[3] For our purposes, we will define *communication* as the process by which people attempt to share meaning via the transmission of symbolic messages. This definition calls attention to three essential points: (1) that communication, as we are using the term, involves *people,* and that understanding communication therefore involves trying to understand how people relate to each other; (2) that communication involves *shared meaning,* which suggests that in order for people to communicate, they must agree on the definitions of the terms they are using; and (3) that communication is *symbolic* — gestures, sounds, letters, numbers, and words can only represent or approximate the ideas they are meant to communicate.[4]

INTERPERSONAL COMMUNICATION

The
Communication
Process

The simplest model of the communication process is as follows:

$$\text{Sender} \longrightarrow \text{Message} \longrightarrow \text{Receiver}$$

This model captures three essential elements of communication; obviously, if one of the elements is missing, no communication can take place. For exam-

---

[3] F. E. X. Dance, "The 'Concept' of Communication," *Journal of Communication,* Vol. 20 (1970), pp. 201–210.

[4] See Lyman W. Porter and Karlene H. Roberts, "Communication in Organizations," in Marvin D. Dunnette, ed., *Handbook of Industrial and Organizational Psychology* (Chicago: Rand McNally College Publishing, 1976).

ple, we can send a message, but if it is not heard or received by someone, no communication has occurred.

Unfortunately, this simple model does not begin to suggest the complexity of the communication process. Most of us, for example, are familiar with the children's game of "Telephone." In this game, children arrange themselves in a row or circle. One child quickly whispers a message into the ear of another; that other child quickly whispers the message he or she has heard into the ear of another child, and so on down the line. The last child says the message out loud. Inevitably, the word or message the last child utters is not the same as the word or message that the first child had whispered. Thus, the game of "Telephone" illustrates one complexity in the communication process: the sender may send a message, but the receivers may "hear" or receive a message the sender did not intend.

Figure 18-1 illustrates a far more sophisticated model of the communication process. In our discussion below, we will describe each of the major elements of this model.[5]

Sender (Source). The *sender,* or source, is the initiator of the communication. In an organization, the sender will be a person with needs, desires, or information and a purpose for communicating them to one or more other people. A manager wishes to communicate information about an important production

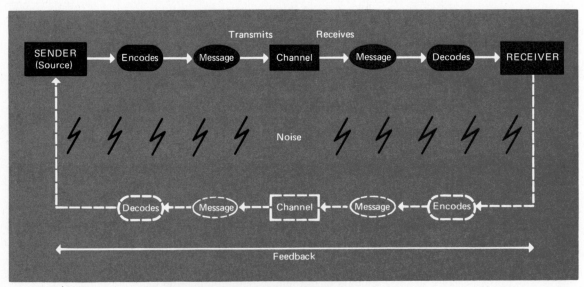

FIGURE 18-1   A Model of the Communication Process

[5]Our discussion will be based on William V. Haney, *Communication and Organizational Behavior,* 3rd ed. (Homewood, Ill.: Irwin, 1973); Joseph H. Reitz, *Behavior in Organizations* (Homewood, Ill.: Irwin, 1977); Andrew J. DuBrin, *Fundamentals of Organizational Behavior,* (New York: Pergamon Press, 1974); and James L. Gibson, John M. Ivancevich, and James H. Donnelly, Jr., *Organizations: Structure, Processes, Behavior* (Dallas: Business Publications, Inc., 1973).

deadline for the purpose of motivating other members of the department. A production-line worker speaks to the shop supervisor for the purpose of requesting additional help with a project. Without a reason, purpose, or desire, the sender has no need to send.

Encoding. The sender *encodes* the information to be transmitted by translating it into a series of symbols or gestures. Encoding is necessary because information cannot be transferred from one person to another except through representations or symbols. Since communication is the object of encoding, the sender attempts to establish "mutuality" of meaning with the receiver by choosing symbols, usually in the form of words and gestures, that the sender believes to have the same meaning for the receiver. Lack of mutuality is one of the most common causes of misunderstanding or lack of communication. In some Arab countries, for example, "yes" is indicated by a side-to-side shake of the head while "no" is indicated with a nod. American tourists who do not share these symbols can quickly experience or cause bewilderment when they converse with Arab citizens. Similarly, asking subordinates to work late on a project without specifying how late may lead to confusion as each subordinate privately decides what "late" means.

Message. The *message* is the physical form into which the sender encodes the information. The message may be in any form that can be experienced and understood by one or more of the senses of the receiver. Speech may be heard; written words may be read; gestures may be seen or felt. A touch of the hand may communicate messages ranging from comfort to menace. A wave of the hand can communicate widely diverse messages depending on the number of fingers extended. A letter, sprinkled with the perfume of its sender, will communicate a great deal to the receiver. Nonverbal messages are an extremely important form of communication, since they are often more honest or meaningful than verbal or written messages. For example, a manager who frowns while saying "Good morning" to a late-arriving subordinate is clearly communicating something more than a polite greeting.

Channel. The *channel* is the mode of transmission (such as air for spoken words and paper for letters); it is often inseparable from the message. For communication to be both effective and efficient, the channel must be appropriate for the message. Words carved in stone will convey an appropriately dignified and lasting message on a tomb; for office messages, however, such a channel is highly impractical. Similarly, saying good night by memo would clearly be inefficient. The receiver must be considered in selecting a channel: some people respond better to the formality of written words, others to the informality of spoken words.

Receiver. The *receiver* is the person whose senses perceive the sender's message. Just as a memo may be sent "to whom it may concern," or the chairman of the board may deliver a speech to the entire organization, there may be

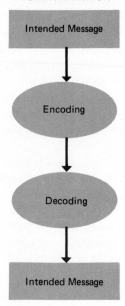

Intended Message

Encoding

Decoding

Intended Message

several individual receivers for any given message. Communication has not taken place if the message has not reached a receiver.

Decoding. *Decoding* is the process by which the receiver interprets the message and translates it into information that is meaningful to him or her. The decoding process is affected by the receiver's past experience, personal interpretations of the symbols and gestures used, expectations (people tend to hear what they want to hear), and mutuality of meaning with the sender. For example, the receiver cannot decode the message if it is not in a language he or she knows; conversely, if we tell close colleagues to "go jump in the lake" when they ask us for a favor, they are unlikely to decode this message literally because they are aware that what we really mean is "no." In general, *the more the receiver's decoding matches the sender's intended message, the more effective the communication has been.*

Noise. *Noise* is any factor that disturbs or confuses communication. Interference may arise at any stage of the communication process. The sender may be inarticulate or speak too softly to be heard clearly; the message may be distorted by other sounds in the environment; the receiver may be hard of hearing or not paying attention. While interference may occur during passage through the channel (a letter may be mistyped), most interference arises in the encoding and decoding stages.[6]

The urge to make sense of a communication is so strong that a puzzling or even nonsensical communication is often decoded by the receiver into a sensible statement that may have an entirely different meaning from the originally encoded message. For example, unclear instructions on how to perform a task may cause employees to "hear" different and incorrect instructions.

Feedback. *Feedback* is a reversal of the communication process in which a reaction to the sender's communication is expressed. Since the receiver now becomes the sender, feedback goes through the same steps as the original communication. Organizational feedback may be in a variety of forms, ranging from direct feedback, such as a simple spoken acknowledgment that the message has been received, to indirect feedback, which is a more complex countercommunication expressed through actions or documentation. For example, a straightforward request for a faster rate of production may be met directly with an assenting nod of the head or indirectly with record-breaking output or a union strike.

As the dotted lines in Figure 18-1 suggest, feedback is optional and may exist in any degree (from minimal to complete) in any given situation. In most organizational communications, the greater the feedback, the more effective the communication is likely to be. For example, early feedback will enable a manager to know if his or her instructions to a subordinate have been understood and accepted. Without such feedback, the manager might not know (until

---

[6] See Gibson et al., *Organizations: Structure, Processes, Behavior,* p. 167.

it is too late) whether or not the instructions were accurately received and carried out.

One-Way and Two-Way Communication

As our description of the communication process implies, communication may be one-way or two-way. In *one-way* communication, the sender communicates without expecting or asking for feedback from the receiver. Policy statements from top managers are usually examples of one-way communication. *Two-way* communication exists when the receiver can and does provide feedback to the sender. Making a suggestion to a subordinate and receiving a question or a countersuggestion in return is an example of two-way communication.

Harold J. Leavitt and Ronald A. H. Mueller conducted early experiments on the effects and effectiveness of one-way and two-way communication.[7] In these experiments, individuals were asked to describe an arrangement of geometrical shapes, such as those in Figure 18-2, to groups of listeners. The individuals were instructed to use words only. The listeners were asked to reproduce the diagrams from the individual's verbal descriptions. The experiments were conducted under conditions of one-way communication and two-way communication. In the one-way communication, the sender could not see or hear the group of listeners. In the two-way experiment, descriptions were still limited to words, but the sender was allowed to face the listeners and the listeners could question or comment freely.

FIGURE 18-2
Typical Patterns Used in Communication Experiments

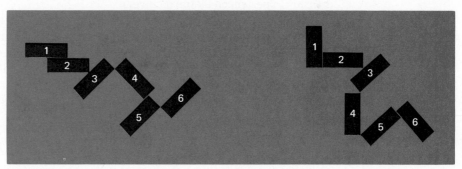

Source: Harold J. Leavitt, *Managerial Psychology*, 2nd ed. (Chicago: University of Chicago Press, 1964), pp. 141, 142.

The results of the experiments were as follows:

1. One-way communication takes considerably less time than two-way communication.

2. Two-way communication is more accurate than one-way communication (that is, the diagrams were more accurately reproduced when two-way communication was used). The feedback allows the sender to refine his or her communication for the receivers so that it becomes more precise and accurate.

[7]Harold J. Leavitt and Ronald A. H. Mueller, "Some Effects of Feedback on Communicating," *Human Relations,* Vol. 4, No. 4 (November 1951), pp. 401–410.

3. Receivers are more sure of themselves and of their judgments when two-way communication is used. The very fact that they are permitted to ask questions probably increases the receivers' self-confidence. In addition, they can use questions to clarify any doubts they may have.

4. Senders can easily feel attacked when two-way communication is used, because receivers will call attention to the senders' ambiguities and mistakes.

5. Although it is less accurate, one-way communication *appears* much more orderly than two-way communication, which often appears noisy and chaotic.

As Leavitt points out,[8] these results can provide guidelines for communication in organizations. If communication must be fast and accuracy is easy to achieve (as when informing employees about some minor change in the company's health plan), one-way communication is both more economical and more efficient. If an orderly, well-organized appearance is considered vital — as in a large, public meeting — one-way communication might also be more appropriate. In addition, one-way communication has political benefits, because it reduces the chance that the sender's mistakes will be recognized and challenged. Since the sender can place the blame for all mistakes on the receiver, the one-way approach is an attractive one for managers who need or want to protect their power.

Where accuracy of communication is important, however — as in instructions on carrying out complex tasks — the two-way method is almost essential. Without feedback from the receiver, the sender has little basis for judging the accuracy of the communication or the degree of understanding and comprehension experienced by the receiver.

In most situations, managers will have to create the most efficient mix of one-way and two-way communication, rather than decide which one form to use exclusively. Many managerial communications, such as straightforward statements of company rules, will require little or no feedback for managers to be assured of their accuracy. In other cases, such as formulation of organizational objectives, two-way communication is usually essential, at least to a certain degree.

Barriers to Effective Interpersonal Communication

— "I always give them a deadline, but they never pay any attention to it."

— "Management tells us the assignment is due before it really is."

— "How was I to know they'd *really* strike this time?"

— "We feel that management offers were not made in good faith."

The familiar ring to statements like these suggests the extent to which organizations can be hampered by poor communication. Some problems in communication are unique to organizations — they arise from the ways in which organizations are structured and operated. We will discuss these problems later in the chapter. In this section, we will focus on problems in interpersonal communication that can develop in any situation. We will emphasize barriers to effective

[8] Harold J. Leavitt, *Managerial Psychology,* 2nd ed. (Chicago: University of Chicago Press, 1964).

face-to-face oral communication, because of the importance of oral communication to managers. Many of these barriers, however, can apply to other forms of communication as well.

Leonard R. Sayles and George Strauss have identified a number of common barriers to interpersonal communication:[9]

1. *Hearing what we expect to hear.* Past experience leads us to expect to

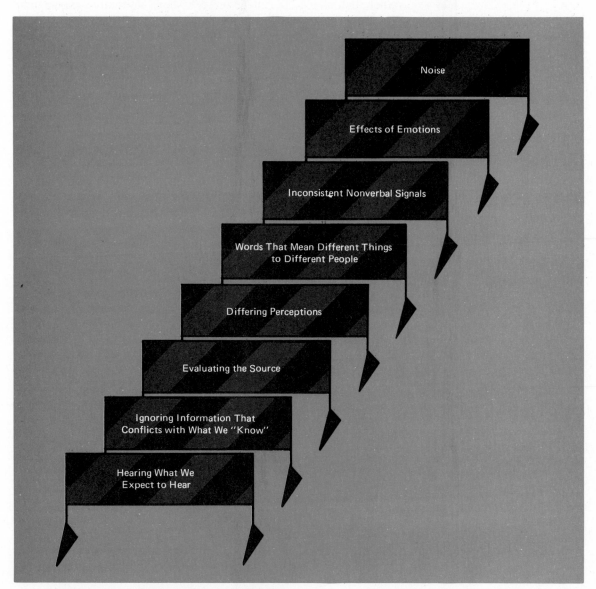

FIGURE 18-3   Barriers to Communication

[9]Leonard R. Sayles and George Strauss, *Human Behavior in Organizations* (Englewood Cliffs, N.J.: Prentice-Hall, 1966), pp. 238–246.

473

hear the same message in similar circumstances. Workers who are habitually criticized for their work are likely to hear a statement such as "You did a fine job on that" as a sarcastic put-down, even when it is genuinely meant as a compliment. They expect to be criticized, so they hear a criticism.

2. *Ignoring information that conflicts with what we "know."* When we hear a message that disagrees with our preconceptions, we are likely to ignore the message, rather than change our ideas or seek some alternative explanation. For example, a production manager may ignore a subordinate's warning that stocks of a necessary material are nearly depleted because he or she "knows" that an order for a new supply is certain to have arrived; or, a manager may ignore subordinates' expressed dissatisfaction because he or she "knows" that working conditions are excellent.

3. *Evaluating the source.* The meaning we apply to any message will be influenced by our evaluation of the message's source. Imagine the different ways you would decode the message "Relax — don't work so hard" if the source were (1) your mother, (2) your boss, (3) your doctor, or (4) someone strongly competing for your job.

In this example, evaluating the source may help the receiver to extract the meaning intended by the sender. In many cases, however, consideration of the source of the message will distort the message the receiver actually "hears." Labor-management relations are often fraught with such communication distortions. When neither side trusts the other, even the most positive communications are met with skepticism and are searched for hidden meanings or traps. (See also Chapter 19 for our discussion of the "halo effect.")

Managers usually cannot afford to accept every message they get at face value without evaluating the source. Some sources, after all, will prove themselves to be more reliable than others. The danger comes in being too quick to evaluate the message, with the result that the message is distorted before one has a chance to interpret it accurately. This tendency can also exert an undesirable influence on the sender, making him or her unduly cautious, defensive, or even aggressive, depending on how the manager's reaction is perceived. Psychologist Carl Rogers advises that people learn to listen to others with understanding:

> Real communication occurs, and this evaluative tendency is avoided, when we listen with understanding. What does that mean? It means to see the expressed idea and attitude from the other person's point of view, to sense how it feels to him, to achieve his frame of reference in regard to the thing he is talking about.[10]

4. *Differing perceptions.* Words, actions, and events are perceived in the light of the receiver's individual values and environmental pressures. If we congratulate a subordinate on arriving to work early, we may generate a feeling

---

[10]Carl R. Rogers and J. J. Roethlisberger, "Barriers and Gateways to Communication," *Harvard Business Review,* July-August 1952, p. 47.

"It looks OK to me."

Cartoon by George Dole

of pride and accomplishment. On the other hand, if that individual's work group considers early arrival as a sign of "buttering-up the boss," that individual may deliberately begin to arrive later in order to reestablish group identity.

5. *Words that mean different things to different people.* Words are symbols. As symbols, they may have different meanings for different people and in different situations. The word "telephone" to a person who installs telephones may signify job or task; to someone in the hospital, "telephone" may mean the possibility of companionship; to the junior executive moving into a private office for the first time, the word "telephone" may represent success. In order for effective communication to take place, the symbolic meaning of words has to be shared. Telling a superior "I'll be with you in a few minutes" can be confusing unless the superior already knows that by "a few minutes" we mean a half hour.

Further barriers to communication may result from the use of "jargon" or esoteric language known as "argot." People with special interests or knowledge, such as engineers or psychologists, are often unaware that not everyone is familiar with their specialized terms. Sometimes people will use jargon to exclude others or to create an impression of superiority — both of which make communication difficult.

Because words can often have strong symbolic significance, their misuse as labels can cause problems. If we label certain people as "slow" or "unreliable," for example, we begin to see them that way and encourage others to do so as well. Worse still, such labels become self-fulfilling prophecies: people labeled as slow and unreliable may begin to believe it themselves and act accordingly.

This self-fulfilling aspect of labels or beliefs is sometimes called "the Rosenthal effect" or "the Pygmalion effect."[11]

6. *Inconsistent nonverbal signals.* Tone of voice, facial expressions, and bodily postures can help or hinder attempts at communication. For example, residual anger from one situation may be unintentionally transferred to a totally unrelated encounter—the person who gets into a family argument at breakfast may arrive at work and "take it out" on unsuspecting subordinates by frowning and unintentionally talking in an angry voice.

7. *Effects of emotions.* Whatever emotion dominates our mood—anger, fear, happiness, anticipation—it will affect our interpretation of a relevant message. If, for example, we are in an atmosphere where we feel we are threatened with loss of power or prestige, we may lose the ability to gauge accurately the meanings of messages we receive and will respond defensively or even aggressively.

8. *Noise.* In order to function effectively, individuals must "screen out" many of the messages they receive during the day. No person could respond to every sound or gesture, even if he or she were aware of all of them. Sometimes, in the process of "screening out" the irrelevant, the relevant is also lost. The "boy who cried wolf" was eventually correct—unfortunately for him, his previous messages had been dismissed as noise. Similarly, a manager who labels every order as "urgent" may find subordinates slow to respond when a real emergency develops.

Overcoming the
Barriers to
Interpersonal
Communication

While complete and undistorted communication between two or more people is an ideal rather than a possibility, there are many techniques that can be used to improve communication and overcome some of the barriers we have described. Sayles and Strauss have identified a number of these techniques:[12]

Use Feedback. Two-way rather than one-way communication allows us to search for verbal and nonverbal cues from our receiver. The more complex the information we are trying to communicate, the more essential it is that we encourage our receivers to ask questions and to indicate areas of confusion. We can then adjust our speech pattern to the situation, speaking slower, allowing pauses, asking for questions from the receivers, and generally adjusting our approach to the receiver's preference and needs.

As receivers, we can improve communication by providing feedback through similar techniques of acknowledging, questioning, and restating the sender's message as we interpret it. At the same time, through careful and sensitive

---

[11] See Marshall B. Rosenberg, "Words Can Be Windows or Walls," in Walter R. Nord, ed., *Concepts and Controversy in Organizational Behavior,* 2nd ed. (Pacific Palisades, Calif.: Goodyear Publishing, 1976), pp. 485–490; Robert Rosenthal, "The Pygmalion Effect Lives," *Psychology Today,* September 1973, pp. 56–60 ff; Robert Rosenthal, "Teacher Expectations and Pupil Learning," in Robert D. Strom, ed., *Teachers and the Learning Process* (Englewood Cliffs, N.J.: Prentice-Hall, 1971).

[12] Sayles and Strauss, *Human Behavior in Organizations,* pp. 246–256.

observation, we may discover hidden meanings behind many communications. For example, is the worker who claims inability to handle a simple assignment really complaining about lack of training, lack of attention, or lack of pay?

Use Face-to-Face Communication. Accurate feedback is nearly always achieved more efficiently through face-to-face communication than through memos or letters. Furthermore, people are accustomed to expressing themselves more fully and with fewer reservations when talking rather than writing. The expression "speak freely" is familiar to us, while the injunction to "write freely" seems at odds with the actual practice of writing.

Be Sensitive to the Receiver's World. Individuals differ in their values, needs, attitudes, and expectations. Empathy with those differences will improve our understanding of others and make it easier to communicate with them. For example, we would not usually greet a superior with the phrase "what's happening?"—even if we do not mean to show disrespect—because we are aware that from the superior's view such a greeting could seem disrespectful.

Be Aware of Symbolic Meanings. As previously mentioned, different words acquire different meanings for different people. Remaining sensitive to these various meanings can minimize communication problems. If, for example, we are replacing an unpopular sales quota system with a new system in which reaching sales objectives is only one measure of productivity, we might do well to avoid the word "quota" entirely because of its negative association with the old system.

Use Direct, Simple Language. The more accurately our choice of words and phrases is tailored to the level of the receiver, the more effective our communication is likely to be.

Use a Correct Amount of Redundancy. If a message is important or complicated, it is probably necessary to repeat it in several different ways in order to ensure that the receiver will understand it. *Unnecessary* redundancy or the overuse of clichés should, however, be avoided, because they simply serve to dull the receiver's attention.

Moving from Defensive to Supportive Communication. One important approach to overcoming communication barriers was described by Jack R. Gibb.[13] Gibb suggests that the type of behavior or attitudes which people manifest will affect the way they communicate. Certain types of behavior will cause individuals to react defensively and inhibit communication, while other types will cause people to feel they are supported, thereby facilitating communication. The two categories of behavior identified by Gibb are listed in Table 18-1 on

---

[13] Jack R. Gibb, "Defensive Communication," *Journal of Communication,* Vol. 11, No. 13 (September 1961), pp. 141–148.

Defensive Behaviors	Supportive Behaviors
1. Evaluation	1. Description
2. Control	2. Problem orientation
3. Strategy	3. Spontaneity
4. Neutrality	4. Empathy
5. Superiority	5. Equality
6. Certainty	6. Provisionalism

Source: Jack R. Gibb, "Defensive Communication," *Journal of Communication*, Vol. 11, No. 13 (September 1961), p. 143.

this page. Behavior characterized by any of the qualities in the left column results in defensiveness by the receiver; those of the right column are seen as supportive and hence act to reduce defensiveness. We will deal here with each of the six pairs of behaviors.

Evaluation—Description. If the speaker's manner, expression, tone, or choice of phrase is interpreted as an attempt to make judgments about or evaluate the listener, then he or she will be on guard and prepared to defend himself or herself. This reaction is not without a basis in reality, since a high proportion of communication is, in fact, evaluative. As managers, we will often find it very difficult not to pass judgment on our subordinates automatically. Conscious effort is sometimes needed to avoid this defense-provoking behavior. Carl Rogers suggests an instructive way in which we can test the quality of our understanding:

> The next time you get into an argument…just stop the discussion for a moment and, for an experiment, institute this rule: "Each person can speak up for himself only *after* he has first restated the ideas and feelings of the previous speaker accurately and to that speaker's satisfaction."[14]

This technique inhibits the tendency that most of us have to formulate our reply mentally while the other person is speaking, instead of concentrating on trying to listen accurately to the message.

Control—Problem orientation. Statements, orders, or seemingly simple observations which are meant to control other persons by influencing their actions or beliefs carry the strong implication that the speaker has the better judgment, and therefore the listeners are, in some manner or other, inferior. This creates resistance. Methods of communicating an attempt to control may range from a threat-backed command to a simple disapproving frown. Since both imply that the receiver is not capable of making a wise decision without direction, both create defensiveness, even if the control is accepted. On the other hand, when the sender makes it clear that he or she is trying to join with the receiver in defining and solving a problem through cooperation and mutual

[14]Rogers and Roethlisberger, "Barriers and Gateways to Communication," p. 48.

agreement, a supportive climate is created, and an improvement in communication is almost inevitable.

Strategy—Spontaneity. If we think someone is "playing games" with us, rather than acting spontaneously, our usual reaction is defensive rather than supportive. Deceit and superficiality can "turn us off" to anyone from a potential date to a candidate for governor. Managers who have been superficially involved in sensitivity or management training frequently attempt to "act" spontaneously; the result is often a feeling of being manipulated on the part of the listener and results in defensive communication. Communication that appears to be genuine and honest, on the other hand, often creates a genuine and honest response.

Neutrality—Empathy. Communication that demonstrates empathy for the listener will produce highly favorable reactions. Conversely, a cold, clinical attitude will be seen as indifference by the listener and will lead to stiff, formal, less meaningful communication.

Superiority—Equality. As readers know from their own experience, individuals who act superior do not usually get open, honest, and friendly responses from the people around them. People rightfully want to protect their egos, and individuals who lecture them instead of talking to them will receive cold, formal replies. Those individuals who act as equals, on the other hand, and who indicate they trust and respect the listener, will usually receive honest, less defensive replies. Managers who want two-way communication with their subordinates must work hard to keep their rank from getting in the way.

Certainty—Provisionalism. When we try to impress others that we know all the answers and that nothing will shake us from our convictions, we are likely to get into arguments with people defending their own viewpoints. If, on the other hand, we indicate that we are willing to listen to other perspectives and consider other information, a supportive atmosphere is engendered and open communication is encouraged. People usually are willing to be flexible in the positions they take when they see that we are willing to be flexible in our point of view.

COMMUNICATION IN ORGANIZATIONS

> Because Christmas Eve falls on a Thursday, the day has been designated a Saturday for work purposes. Factories will close all day, with stores open a half day only. Friday, December 25, has been designated a Sunday, with both factories and stores open all day. Monday, December 28, will be a Wednesday for work purposes. Wednesday, December 30, will be a business Friday. Saturday, January 2, will be a Sunday, and Sunday, January 3, will be a Monday.—From an AP report on a Prague government edict.

All of the factors that we have discussed in relation to interpersonal communication also apply to communication within organizations. Effective communication in organizations, like effective communication anywhere, still involves getting a message from one person to another person (or perhaps to several persons) in an acceptably accurate form. However, as the above edict suggests, there are several factors unique to organizations that influence the effectiveness of communications. In this section we will deal specifically with how the realities of formal organizations can affect the communication process.

Raymond V. Lesikar has described four factors that influence the effectiveness of organizational communication: the formal channels of communication, the organization's authority structure, job specialization, and what Lesikar calls "information ownership."[15]

The *formal channels* of communication influence communication effectiveness in two major ways. First, the formal channels cover an ever-widening distance as organizations develop and grow. For example, effective communication is usually far more difficult to achieve in a large retail organization with widely dispersed branches than in a small department store. Second, the formal channels of communication inhibit the free flow of information between organizational levels. An assembly-line worker, for example, will almost always communicate problems to a supervisor rather than to the plant manager. While this accepted restriction in the channels of communication has its advantages (such as keeping higher-level managers from getting bogged down in information), it also has its disadvantages (such as keeping higher-level managers from information they should sometimes have).

The organization's *authority structure* has a similar influence on communication effectiveness. Status and power differences in the organization help determine who will communicate comfortably with whom. The content and accuracy of the communication will also be affected by authority differences among individuals. For example, conversation between a company president and a clerical worker may well be characterized by somewhat strained politeness and formality; nothing much of importance is likely to be said by either party.

Job specialization usually facilitates communication *within* differentiated groups. Members of the same work group are likely to share the same jargon, time horizons, goals, tasks, and personal styles. Communication *between* highly differentiated groups, however, is likely to be inhibited. (See Chapters 10 and 11.)

The term *information ownership* refers to the fact that individuals possess unique information and knowledge about their jobs. A darkroom employee, for example, may have developed a particularly efficient way to develop photoprints; a department head may have a particularly effective way of handling conflict among subordinates; a product manager may have a unique flair for devising marketing strategies. Such information is a form of *power* for the individuals who possess it; they are able to function more effectively than their peers. Many individuals with such skills are unwilling to share this infor-

---

[15] See Raymond V. Lesikar, "A General Semantics Approach to Communication Barriers in Organization," in Keith Davis, ed., *Organizational Behavior: A Book of Readings,* 5th ed. (New York: McGraw-Hill, 1977), pp. 336–337.

mation with others. As a result, completely open communication within the organization does not take place.

In the following sections we will discuss in some detail the effects of the organization's formal communication channels and authority structure on communication effectiveness. In addition, we will discuss the organization's *informal* communication system (the "grapevine"), which supplements the organization's formal communications network.

Communication Networks within the Organization

Some very interesting research has been carried out on communication channels in organizations and their effects on communication accuracy, task performance, and group member satisfaction. This research is interesting and important because managers have some influence over the way in which communication channels develop in their units. The formal authority structure, for example, which managers establish, will help determine who will interact with whom. Thus, managers can design their work units in such a way that effective communication will be facilitated.

There are a variety of ways in which organizations can design their communication networks or structures. Some communication networks may be rigidly designed—for example, employees can be discouraged from talking with anyone except their immediate supervisor. Such a network is usually designed to keep higher-level managers from being overburdened with unnecessary information and to maintain the higher-level managers' power and status. Other networks may be more loosely designed—individuals may be encouraged to communicate with anyone at any level. Such networks may be used wherever a free flow of information is highly desirable, as in a research department.

To test the effect of various communication structures, a series of experiments have been performed.[16] In a representative study in this series, five subjects were seated at a table and asked to solve different types of problems. The subjects were separated by partitions and could communicate with each other to solve the problems along communication lines controlled entirely by the researchers.

Figure 18-4 on page 482 illustrates four communication networks the researchers tested. In the "circle" network, for example, subject B could communicate (through the partitions) only with subjects A and C. To communicate with subject E, subject B would have to go through subject A or through subjects C and D. Subject C in the "star" pattern, on the other hand, could communicate directly with A, B, D, and E, although these subjects could not communicate directly with each other. Each of these networks can represent a real

---

[16] See Harold J. Leavitt, "Some Effects of Certain Communication Patterns on Group Performance," *Journal of Abnormal and Social Psychology*, Vol. 46, No. 1 (January 1951), pp. 38–50. Our discussion here is based on Reitz, *Behavior in Organizations;* Gibson et al., *Organizations: Structure, Processes, Behavior;* Leavitt, *Managerial Psychology;* and Marvin E. Shaw, "Communication Networks," in *Advances in Experimental Social Psychology*, Vol. 1, ed. Leonard Berkowitz (New York: Academic Press, 1964), pp. 111–147.

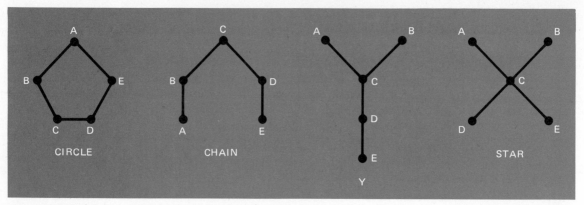

FIGURE 18-4   Types of Communication Networks

network in an organization. The "star" pattern, for example, might represent four salespersons (A, B, D, E) reporting to a district manager (C); the "chain" pattern might represent two subordinates (A and E) reporting to supervisors (B and D, respectively), who in turn report to the same supervisor (C).

The subjects in the experiments were given both simple and complex problems to solve. In one simple problem, subjects were each given a card with five symbols on it. Only one of the symbols was common to all of the cards. The group's task was to determine which was the common symbol. In a complex problem, subjects were each given five marbles with colors and patterns that were difficult to describe. Only one of the marbles was common to all of the subjects. Group members were asked to determine which was the commonly held marble.

The series of studies demonstrated that network *centrality* was the critical feature that determined whether a particular communication network was effective and/or satisfying to its members on a particular type of task. Some networks, such as the "Y" and "star," are highly centralized, with subject C at the central position. The "circle" and "chain" networks, on the other hand, are decentralized, with no one member able to communicate with all the other members.

In most tests, centralized networks performed faster and more accurately than decentralized networks, *provided the tasks were comparatively simple*. In the symbol task, for example, the person at the center (C) simply collected information from the other subjects about the card symbols they had and selected the common symbol. The centralized network was quicker for such tasks, because only minimal communication between the subjects was required. In addition, the central subject could solve the problem alone (after obtaining the necessary information). In the decentralized networks, however, the subjects had to communicate with each other far more extensively before they could determine the card symbol they all held.

For *complex* tasks, however, the decentralized networks were comparatively quicker and more accurate. In the marble task, for example, subject C in the centralized networks was soon overloaded with confusing information from the other subjects on the types of marbles they had. It was difficult for subject C to find which color and pattern of marble was held by all subjects. In addition, the other subjects often disagreed with the solution proposed by C, since the colors and patterns of the marbles were so ambiguous. In the decentralized networks, on the other hand, the subjects could more conveniently communicate information to each other and check on differing perceptions. They were therefore able to establish common labels for each type of marble more quickly and to arrive at the solution in less time.

The centrality of the networks also affected leader emergence and group member satisfaction. For both simple and complex tasks, centralized groups tended to agree that person C, occupying the central position, was the leader. Obviously, C emerged as the leader in centralized networks because the other group members were so completely dependent on C for their information. In decentralized networks, however, no one position in the network emerged as the leadership position.

Group member satisfaction, on the other hand, tended to be higher in decentralized networks for all types of tasks. In fact, satisfaction was highest in the "circle," next highest in the "chain," and then in the "Y." The least satisfied group members were in the "star" network. The reason for the greater satisfaction in the decentralized networks was the fact that members of those networks could participate in finding problem solutions. The only highly satisfied member of the centralized networks was the person at position "C," who played an active, leadership role.

These experiments have many implications for the relationships between organizational structure and communication. For example, an organization with mostly routine, simple tasks would seem to work most efficiently with a formally centralized communication network, while more complicated tasks seem to call for decentralization. Also, the emergence in the experiments of the most centralized position as the leader reinforces the idea that access to information is an important source of power in organizations.

Vertical Communication

Vertical communication consists of communication up and down the organization's chain of command. Downward communication starts with top management and flows down through management levels to line workers and nonsupervisory personnel. The major purposes of downward communication are to direct, instruct, and evaluate subordinates and to provide organization members with information about organizational goals and policies.

The main function of upward communication is to supply information to the upper levels about what is happening at the lower levels. This type of communication includes progress reports, suggestions, explanations, and requests for aid or decisions.[17]

---

[17] Kenneth N. Wexley and Gary A. Yukl, *Organizational Behavior and Personnel Psychology* (Homewood, Ill.: Irwin, 1977), pp. 58–71.

Problems of Vertical Communication. Downward communication passing through the formal hierarchy is likely to be filtered, modified, or halted at each level as managers decide what should be passed down to their subordinates. Upward communication is likely to be filtered, condensed or altered by middle managers who see it as part of their job to protect upper management from nonessential data originating at the lower levels. In addition, middle managers may keep information that would reflect unfavorably on them from reaching their superiors. Thus, vertical communication is often at least partially inaccurate or incomplete.

The importance to an organization of vertical communication was emphasized by a research survey conducted by Lyman W. Porter and Karlene H. Roberts in which they found that two-thirds of a manager's communication takes place with superiors and subordinates.[18] The studies mentioned by Porter and Roberts also found that the accuracy of vertical communication was aided by similarities in thinking between the superior and subordinate, but was limited by status and power differences between manager and subordinate, by a subordinate's desire for upward mobility, and by a lack of trust between manager and subordinate. For example, some studies suggest that communication is likely to be less open and accurate the higher the aspirations for upward mobility experienced by the subordinate. Such subordinates are likely to be ambitious, strongly opinionated, forceful, and aggressive. Consequently, they are often more concerned with defending their self-image than in reaching an agreement or an objectively accurate appraisal of a situation. They will also be less likely to communicate negative reports that may be interpreted as weaknesses in their performance or ability. Similarly, subordinates are more likely to screen out problems, disagreements, or complaints when they feel that their superior has the power to punish them in some way.

Even unambitious subordinates will be guarded in their communications if an atmosphere of trust does not exist between them and their superiors. The subordinates will conceal or distort information if they feel that their superiors cannot be trusted to react fairly or that they will use the information against them. The net result of all these communication problems is that higher-level managers will frequently make decisions that are based on faulty or inadequate information.

Problems in downward communication result when managers do not provide subordinates with all the information they need to carry out their tasks effectively. Managers are often overly optimistic about the accuracy and completeness of their downward communications; in fact, they frequently fail to pass on important information they receive (such as a higher-level change in policy) or to instruct subordinates adequately on how to perform their duties.

---

[18] Porter and Roberts, "Communication in Organizations," pp. 1573–1576. See also William H. Read, "Upward Communication in Industrial Hierarchies," *Human Relations,* Vol. 15, No. 1 (February 1962), pp. 3–15, and Karlene H. Roberts and Charles A. O'Reilly III, "Failures in Upward Communication in Organizations: Three Possible Culprits," *Academy of Management Journal,* Vol. 17, No. 2 (June 1974), pp. 205–215.

This lack of communication is sometimes deliberate—as we have already suggested, managers may withhold information to keep subordinates dependent on them. The net effect of incomplete downward communication is that subordinates may feel confused, uninformed, or powerless and may fail to carry out their tasks properly.

Lateral and Informal Communication

Lateral Communication

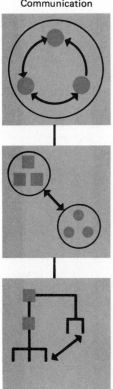

Lateral communication usually follows the pattern of work flow in an organization, occurring between members of work groups, between one work group and another, between members of different departments, and between line and staff. The main purpose of lateral communication is to provide a direct channel for organizational coordination and problem solving. In this way, it avoids the much slower procedure of directing communications through a common superior.[19] An added benefit of lateral communication is that it enables organization members to form relationships with their peers. These relationships are an important part of employee satisfaction.

A significant amount of lateral communication occurs outside the chain of command. Such lateral communication often occurs with the knowledge, approval, and encouragement of superiors. This encouragement is due to the fact that lateral communication often reduces the communication burden of superiors and also reduces communication inaccuracy by putting the relevant people in direct contact with each other.[20]

Another type of informal communication, which is not officially sanctioned, is the "grapevine." The grapevine in organizations is actually made up of several informal communication networks that overlap each other at a number of points—that is, some well-informed individuals in the organization are likely to belong to more than one grapevine network. Grapevines show admirable disregard for rank or authority and may link organization members in any combination of directions—horizontal, vertical, and diagonal. As Keith Davis suggests, the grapevine "flows around water coolers, down hallways, through lunch rooms, and wherever people get together in groups."[21] People at the lowest level of the organization, however, are least likely to receive grapevine information, perhaps because of their low status. For this reason, managers who wish to ensure that the lowest-level employees will receive certain information will often use written communications.

While the major function of the grapevine is to facilitate social relationships between organization members, it does have several work-related functions as well. For example, although the grapevine is hard to control with any precision, it is often much faster in operation than formal communication channels. Managers often use it to distribute information through planned "leaks" or

[19] Wexley and Yukl, *Organizational Behavior and Personnel Psychology*, pp. 60–61.

[20] See Richard L. Simpson, "Vertical and Horizontal Communication in Formal Organizations," *Administrative Science Quarterly*, Vol. 4, No. 2 (September 1959), pp. 188–196.

[21] Keith Davis, "Grapevine Communication among Lower and Middle Managers," *Personnel Journal*, Vol. 48, No. 4 (April 1969).

judiciously placed "just between you and me" remarks. (See also our discussion of informal groups and of rumor in Chapter 12.)

Keith Davis, who has extensively studied grapevines in organizations, has identified four possible types of grapevine chains.[22] (See Figure 18-5.) In the "single-strand" chain, person A tells something to person B, who tells it to person C, and so on down the line. This chain is least accurate at passing on information. (It is the equivalent of the chain in the "Telephone" game we described at the beginning of the chapter.) In the "gossip" chain, one person seeks out and tells everyone the information he or she has obtained. This chain is often used when information of an interesting but non-job-related nature is being conveyed. In the "probability" chain, individuals are indifferent about whom they offer information; they tell people at random, and those people in turn tell others at random. This chain is likely to be used when the information is mildly interesting but insignificant. In the "cluster" chain, person A conveys the information to a few selected individuals; some of those individuals then inform a few selected others.

Davis believes that the cluster chain is the dominant grapevine pattern in organizations: usually, only a few individuals, called "liaison individuals," will pass on the information they have obtained, and they are likely to do so only to individuals they trust or from whom they would like favors. They are

FIGURE 18-5
Types of
Grapevine
Chains

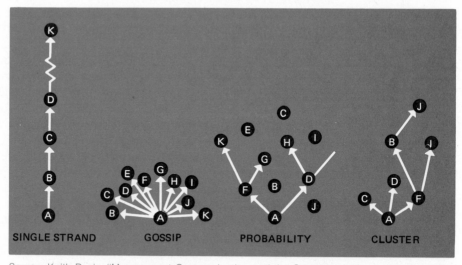

SINGLE STRAND   GOSSIP   PROBABILITY   CLUSTER

Source: Keith Davis, "Management Communication and the Grapevine," *Harvard Business Review,* September-October 1953, p. 45. Copyright © 1953 by the President and Fellows of Harvard College; all rights reserved.

[22]See Keith Davis, "Management Communication and the Grapevine," *Harvard Business Review,* September-October 1953, pp. 43–49; "Communication *within* Management," *Personnel,* Vol. 31, No. 3 (November 1954), pp. 212–218; and "Cut Those Rumors Down to Size," *Supervisory Management,* June 1975, pp. 2–6.

most likely to pass on information that is interesting to them, job-related, and, above all, timely. People do not pass on old information for fear of advertising the fact that they are uninformed.

In order to deal with the barriers to organizational communication, it is important first to recognize that communication is an inherently difficult process. For one thing, the verbal and visual symbols we use to describe reality are far from precise. A seemingly straightforward word like "job," for example, can be applied to anything from a child's newspaper route to the presidency of the United States. Words like "achievement," "effectiveness," or "responsibility" are even more vague in their meaning. This imprecision of language (and gestures) is one reason perfect communication is difficult, if not impossible, to achieve.

Another reason that communication is inherently difficult is that human beings perceive and interpret reality through the filter of their individual backgrounds, needs, emotions, values, and experiences. A production manager's memo to foremen asking for figures on absenteeism will be seen as a legitimate request by one foreman and as unnecessary meddling by another; a manager's instructions may seem coldly formal to some subordinates and appropriately polite to others; a quarterly report may be clear to one superior and confusing to another. Some writers, in fact, believe that most organizational barriers to communication are based on differences in the way people understand the communications they receive.[23]

Comprehending the innate barriers to communication and taking steps to minimize them are therefore the first steps toward improving a manager's ability to communicate effectively. For example, making explicit as many relevant aspects of a situation as possible will likely lead to a more effective and meaningful communication: a memo to members of the quality control department about the need to adjust inspection standards, for instance, will usually be better received if it states the practical reasons why the changes are necessary (such as an increased marketing emphasis on the organization's ability to deliver high-quality products). Such a memo will sound less like an autocratic directive and more like a frank request from one person to another. Similarly, the manager should not assume that the information left out of a communication will be known to the receiver. For example, a manager (or teacher) providing instruction should first check to see if the subordinates (or students) understand the specialized terms likely to be used. Finally, the manager should try to remain sensitive to the fact that some words are likely to have different meanings to the receiver than the manager intends. A memo asking employees to be more careful in their work, for example, is likely to be interpreted by employees as a statement that they have been sloppy. Communications that ask for improved employee performance have to be carefully and positively phrased in order to avoid causing hurt feelings and resentment.

---

[23] See, for example, Lesikar, "A General Semantics Approach to Communication Barriers in Organization," pp. 338–340.

The American Management Associations (AMA) has codified a number of communication principles into what it calls the Ten Commandments of Good Communication. These "commandments," which are designed to improve the effectiveness of organizational communication, are listed and summarized in the accompanying box.

The AMA principles provide us with useful guidelines on how the communication of individual managers can be improved. Management by objectives, which we discussed in Chapter 6, and organizational development, which we discussed in Chapter 15, can help improve communication in organizations as a whole. MBO emphasizes joint goal setting, performance feedback, and joint problem solving. Thus, MBO programs are particularly useful for improving downward communication in organizations and for creating an atmosphere of trust between managers and subordinates. OD approaches attempt to change an organization's climate or culture. In the process of bringing about this change, the organization's communication system will also be affected.

Ten Commandments of Good Communication

1. *Seek to clarify your ideas before communicating.* The more systematically we analyze the problem or idea to be communicated, the clearer it becomes.... Good [communication] planning must [also] consider the goals and attitudes of those who will receive the communication and those who will be affected by it.

2. *Examine the true purpose of each communication.* Before you communicate, ask yourself what you *really* want to accomplish with your message—obtain information, initiate action, change another person's attitude? Identify your most important goal and then adapt your language, tone, and total approach to serve that specific objective.

3. *Consider the total physical and human setting whenever you communicate.* Meaning and intent are conveyed by more than words alone.... Consider, for example, your *sense of timing*—i.e., the circumstances under which you make an announcement or render a decision; the *physical setting*—whether you communicate in private, for example, or otherwise; the *social climate* that pervades work relationships within the company or a department and sets the tone of its communications; *custom and past practice*—the degree to which your communication conforms to, or departs from, the expectations of your audience....

4. *Consult with others, where appropriate, in planning communications....* Such consultation often helps to lend additional insight and objectivity to your message. Moreover, those who have helped you plan your communication will give it their active support.

5. *Be mindful, while you communicate, of the overtones as well as the basic content of your message.* Your tone of voice, your expression, your apparent receptiveness to the responses of others—all have tremendous impact on those you wish to reach. Frequently overlooked, these subtleties of communication often affect a listener's reaction to a message even more than its basic content....

6. *Take the opportunity, when it arises, to convey something of help or value to the receiver.* Consideration of the other person's interests and

Successfully applied, OD will establish open, objective, and authentic communication between individuals and managers at all levels of the organization.

Summary   *Communication* may be defined as the process by which people attempt to share meanings via the transmission of symbolic messages. The process of communication is important to managers because it enables managers to carry on their management functions. The activity of communication, particularly oral communication, takes up a large portion of a manager's work time.

Elements of the proposed model of communication include the sender, encoding, message, channel, receiver, decoding, noise, and feedback. *Encoding* is the process by which the sender converts the information to be transmitted into the appropriate symbols or gestures. *Decoding* is the process by which the receiver interprets the message. If the decoding matches the sender's encoding, the communication has been effective. *Noise* is that which interferes with the communication. Types of noise include distraction and misinterpretation by the receiver. *Feedback* is the receiver's reaction to the sender's message; thus, it reverses the communication process.

---

needs — the habit of trying to look at things from his point of view — will frequently point up opportunities to convey something of immediate benefit or long-range value to him.

7. *Follow up your communication.* This you can do by asking questions, by encouraging the receiver to express his reactions, by follow-up contacts, by subsequent review of performance. Make certain that every important communication has a "feedback" so that complete understanding and appropriate action result.

8. *Communicate for tomorrow as well as today.* While communications may be aimed primarily at meeting the demands of an immediate situation, they must be planned with the past in mind if they are to maintain consistency in the receiver's view; but, most important of all, they must be consistent with long-range interests and goals. For example, it is not easy to communicate frankly on such matters as poor performance or the shortcomings of a loyal subordinate — but postponing disagreeable communications makes them more difficult in the long run and is actually unfair to your subordinates and your company.

9. *Be sure your actions support your communications.* In the final analysis, the most persuasive kind of communication is not what you say but what you do....For every manager this means that good supervisory practices — such as clear assignment of responsibility and authority, fair rewards for effort, and sound policy enforcement — serve to communicate more than all the gifts of oratory.

10. *Seek not only to be understood but to understand — be a good listener.* When we start talking we often cease to listen — in that larger sense of being attuned to the other person's unspoken reactions and attitudes.... [Listening] demands that we concentrate not only on the explicit meanings another person is expressing, but on the implicit meanings, unspoken words, and undertones that may be far more significant.

Source: Summarized from *Ten Commandments of Good Communication.* © 1955 by the American Management Associations.

489

Communication may be one-way or two-way. In two-way communication, unlike one-way communication, feedback is provided to the sender. One-way communication is faster than two-way and better protects the authority of the sender. Two-way communication, however, is more accurate and leads to greater receiver confidence. For complex organizational tasks, two-way communication is highly preferred.

Barriers to effective interpersonal communication include hearing what we expect to hear, ignoring information that conflicts with what we "know," evaluating the message in light of the sender's characteristics rather than focusing on the message's content, differences between people in their perceptions and use of language, and inconsistency between verbal and nonverbal cues. Many of these barriers can be overcome through the use of feedback, face-to-face communication, simple language, and redundancy, and by being sensitive to the receiver's feelings and expectations. Honest and meaningful communication also can be encouraged through the use of supportive behaviors that prevent people from reacting defensively.

The effectiveness of organizational communication will be influenced by the organization's formal channels of communication and authority structure, by job specialization, and by "information ownership." The formal channels may be rigid and highly centralized, with individuals able to communicate with only a few persons; or, they may be loose and decentralized, with individuals able to communicate with each other at any level. Experiments have found that centralized networks are faster and more accurate than decentralized networks for simple tasks, while for complex tasks decentralized channels are quicker and more accurate. Group member satisfaction is higher in decentralized networks.

Vertical communication is communication that moves up and down the organization's chain of command. Status and power differences between manager and subordinates, a subordinate's desire for upward mobility, and a lack of trust between manager and subordinates interfere with accurate and complete vertical communication.

Lateral communication improves coordination and problem solving and fosters employee satisfaction. Informal communication occurs outside the organizations' formal channels. A particularly quick and pervasive type of informal communication is the "grapevine."

Overcoming the barriers to effective organizational communication requires that individual managers acknowledge the difficulties inherent in the communication process. Making relevant information explicit and remaining sensitive to how a particular communication will affect its receiver can minimize some of these difficulties. Effectively implementing MBO programs and OD can improve communications throughout an organization.

Review Questions

1. What part does communication play in enabling managers to fulfill the three roles identified by Mintzberg? Why, according to Mintzberg, do managers favor oral communication?
2. What are the eight elements in the communication model? According to the model, what is effective communication?
3. Why is "mutuality of meaning" an important part of effective communication?
4. On what basis should managers select a channel or medium for their message?
5. What is "noise"? What factors in the organizational environment cause "noise"?
6. What differences have been found between one-way and two-way communication? Under what circumstances should each type of communication be used?
7. What are common barriers to effective interpersonal communication? How may these barriers be overcome?

8. According to Gibb, what behaviors lead to defensive communication? What behaviors lead to open communication?
9. What four factors influence the effectiveness of organizational communication? How do they exert this influence?
10. What have experimental studies revealed about the effects of different types of communication networks on task completion, leader emergence, and group member satisfaction?
11. What are the functions of vertical communication? How is accurate and complete vertical communication hindered?
12. What are the functions of lateral communication? Why is informal lateral communication usually desirable?
13. What is the function of the "grapevine"? Why do managers sometimes use the grapevine to convey information? What are some possible grapevine chains, according to Davis? Which chain is most likely to be used in organizations?
14. How may the barriers to organizational communication be overcome?

CASE STUDY: MY DOOR IS ALWAYS OPEN

Setting: The Production Manager's Office
Participants: Gilbert Steiner — Production Manager
Harold Terry — Production Scheduler
Time: Monday morning

Steiner: Good morning, Hal. Have a nice weekend?
Terry: Great, Mr. Steiner…took the family to the beach.
Steiner: Fine weekend for it…bet your kids enjoyed it.
Terry: They certainly did. My oldest boy loves the ocean.
Steiner: Billy?
Terry: *(surprised)* Yes, Billy. I didn't know you knew his name.
Steiner: You probably told me once.
Terry: You have a good memory.
Steiner: Thank you. Frankly, it's something I developed a long time ago. It's good management practice to get to know a little about your employees…their families…it brings you closer to them.
Terry: I can't argue with that…
Steiner: Sounds a little phony at first…I mean a person could sound like a fool overplaying the concerned boss and carrying on about an employee's arthritic dog, Jasper…but I mean real interest and concern in the man and his family.
Terry: I'm sure it pays dividends in employee loyalty and productivity.
Steiner: It certainly does. When you become a supervisor, I'm sure you'll realize it even more… *(pause)* Well, we'd better get started before the week is over.
Terry: Right. I've already checked the Final Assembly Department, and we should be able to ship the Fedderson order by Wednesday and the A-B-N Industries order by Thursday or Friday.
Steiner: Good. I'll hold you to that…
Terry: We do have a couple of problems though which I want to talk to you about.

Case from Robert D. Joyce, *Encounters in Organizational Behavior: Problem Situations* (New York: Pergamon Press, Ltd., 1972), pp. 2–5. Reprinted by permission of the publisher.

Steiner: Yes?

Terry: We can't ship to Ellis Industries as planned this week because...

Steiner: *(angrily)* What?

Terry: The parts we need still haven't arrived...

Steiner: Dammit, man! You told me that last week didn't you?

Terry: Yes, I did but...

Steiner: And do you recall what I told you?

Terry: You said it was my responsibility to make sure the parts came in.

Steiner: And you blew it!

Terry: Well, I did review the problem with Purchasing and they suggested...

Steiner: To hell with Purchasing! Those paperwork clerks only help foul up things worse. You should have contacted the vendor directly and... *(pausing and composing himself)* Look, Hai, you're a big boy. I don't have to do your job, do I?

Terry: Of course not, Mr. Steiner.

Steiner: Then you will get those parts this week won't you?

Terry: Yes, I'll get the parts.

Steiner: And you'll ship by Friday?

Terry: We'll ship by Friday.

Steiner: *(smiling)* Good. Management by results is the only thing that counts...don't you agree?

Terry: Yes, sir.

Steiner: *(serious)* Look, Hal, I guess I come down hard on you sometimes but it's because I expect a lot from you. How can you grow without challenge...without difficult objectives to reach?

Terry: I suppose you're right.

Steiner: I know I'm right. It's a philosophy I learned from my father years ago...results count, not words.

Terry: True.

Steiner: Anything else I should know? I don't care for lots of detail, but, at the same time, a person can easily get cut out of the communications loop if he gets too far from the action. And I don't like to get cut out of the loop.

Terry: Not really. Everything else is moving according to schedule. *(pauses)* The people in Shipping are a little upset though over the late Friday afternoon shipping schedules and were asking me if we in Manufacturing might not work out a more sequential shipping schedule. I thought that was information we could use, particularly with the planned production increase for next quarter...

Steiner: Ignore them. Those people are always complaining and they'll bend your ear all day if you let them. That's not information Hal, that's *noise* you're getting. When a shipping clerk stops complaining it means he's dead.

Terry: Yes sir.

Steiner: Anything else?

Terry: No. As far as I know we've covered everything.

Steiner: Hal, you know I like you. You've got tremendous potential in this department. I want to help you learn this business inside and out...I want to see you grow and develop...

Terry: Yes?

Steiner: Well, what I mean is...don't be reluctant to come to me if you have any problems which I can help you with...anything that you want to sit down and talk about...my door is always open.

Terry: Thank you, Mr. Steiner. *(turns to leave)*

Steiner: About that Ellis order...you did hear me didn't you?

Terry: Yes, sir, I heard you. We'll ship by Friday.

Case Questions
1. What barriers to open and effective communication did Gilbert Steiner create?
2. What was Steiner *really* communicating? Do you think he was aware of the effect his words would have on Terry?
3. What impact did Steiner's attitudes and values have on the effectiveness of his communication?
4. How might Terry have handled the conversation so that more meaningful information could have been exchanged?

Chapter 19

Staffing and the Personnel Function

Upon completing this chapter you should be able to:

1. Explain why staffing is an essential management function.

2. Summarize the staffing process.

3. State why human resource planning is important, what the aims of human resource planning are, and how the process of human resource planning is carried out.

4. Describe the process of recruitment both within and outside the organization.

5. Describe each step in the selection procedure.

6. Indicate why early job experiences have an effect on new employees' eventual success.

7. Describe the various types of training and management development programs.

8. Identify the four basic appraisal approaches and how appraisal can be managed so as to lead to improved employee performance.

The most important resources of an organization are its human resources—the people who supply the organization with their work, talent, creativity, and drive. Thus, among the most critical—and perhaps *the* most critical—leadership tasks of a manager are the selection, training, and development of people who will best help the organization meet its goals. Without competent people, particularly at the managerial level, organizations will either pursue inappropriate goals or find it difficult to achieve appropriate goals once they have been set.

Staffing is the management function that deals with the recruitment, placement, training, and development of organization members. In this chapter, we will deal with the staffing function in some detail. We will attempt to answer such questions as: How do organizations determine what human resources they need now and in the future? How can managers recruit and select people with the best potential for each position? How can managers train people so that they will perform effectively? Finally, What development programs will best assure a constant flow of managerial talent from lower to higher levels of the organization?

As we shall see, so many of the critical activities in staffing are closely related to such basic leadership tasks as motivating and communicating. For this reason, we have included staffing in our unit on leading, even though staffing is sometimes considered an entirely separate management function. We will be taking a "top-down" view of staffing and the personnel function in this chapter—that is, our emphasis will be on how managers recruit, select, train, and appraise lower-level managerial and nonmanagerial employees.[1] In the next chapter, "Organizational Careers and Individual Development," we will be taking a much more "bottom-up" view by describing how individuals can manage their own careers as they enter and move up the organizational ladder.

THE STAFFING PROCESS

As the diagram on the next page (Figure 19–1) suggests, the composition of an organization's work force changes over time. For example, managers in organizations do not stay in their positions permanently. Successful managers are usually promoted; many of those who are not promoted seek better jobs elsewhere. Unsuccessful managers are, in most cases, transferred or replaced. Thus, the organization and its managers must accommodate themselves to a constant, ongoing change of personnel.

[1] The following books, from which we have drawn some of the material in this chapter, treat the staffing of operatives as well as of professionals and managers: Wendell French, *The Personnel Management Process,* 2nd ed. (Boston: Houghton Mifflin, 1970); Robert L. Mathis and John H. Jackson, *Personnel* (St. Paul: West Publishing, 1976); and William F. Glueck, *Personnel* (Dallas: Business Publications, Inc., 1974).

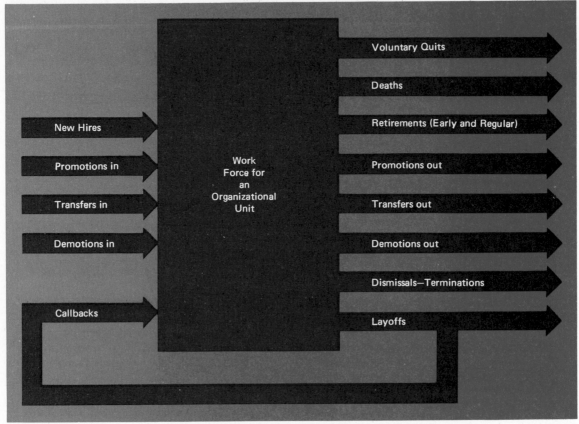

FIGURE 19-1   The Changing Composition of an Organizational Unit's Work Force

Source: Andrew F. Sikula, *Personnel Administration and Human Resource Management* (New York: John Wiley & Sons, Inc., 1976), p. 158. Used by permission.

The staffing *process* can be seen as a series of steps that are performed on a continuing basis to keep the organization supplied with the right people in the right positions at the right time. The steps or categories in this process include:[2]

1   Human resource planning
2   Recruitment
3   Selection
4   Induction and orientation
5   Training and development
6   Performance appraisal
7   Transfer, promotion, demotion
8   Separation

[2] See French, *The Personnel Management Process.*

Our chapter will be based on each of these categories. However, we will introduce and briefly describe all of the categories here.

Human Resource Planning. Human resource planning is designed to ensure that the personnel needs of the organization will be constantly and appropriately met. Such planning is accomplished through analysis of current and expected skill needs, vacancies, and department expansions and reductions. As a result of this analysis, plans are developed for executing the other steps in the staffing process. Human resource planning usually covers a period from six months to five years in the future.

Recruitment. Recruitment is concerned with developing a pool of job candidates, in line with the human resource plan. The candidates are usually located through newspaper and professional journal advertisements, employment agencies, and visits to college and university campuses.

Selection. The selection process involves evaluating and choosing among job candidates. Application forms, résumés, interviews, and reference checks are commonly used selection devices.

Induction and Orientation. This step is designed to help the selected individuals fit smoothly into the organization. Newcomers are introduced to their colleagues, acquainted with their responsibilities, and informed about the organization's policies and goals.

Training and Development. The process of training and development aims at increasing the ability of individuals and groups to contribute to organizational effectiveness. *Training* is designed to improve job skills; managers might be instructed in new decision-making techniques or the capabilities of data processing systems. *Development* programs are designed to educate employees beyond the requirements of their present position so that they will be prepared for promotion and able to take a broader view of their role in the organization.

Performance Appraisal. This step compares an individual's job performance against standards or objectives developed for the individual's position. If performance is high, the individual is likely to be rewarded (by a bonus, for example, or by more challenging work assignments). If performance is low, some corrective action (such as additional training) might be arranged to bring the performance back in line with desired standards.

Transfer, Promotion, Demotion. A *transfer* is a shift of a person from one job, organizational level, or location to another. Two common types of transfers are *promotion*—a shift to a higher position in the hierarchy, usually with added salary, status, authority, and opportunity—and *demotion*—a shift to a lower position in the hierarchy.

FIGURE 19-2
The Staffing
Process in
Organizations

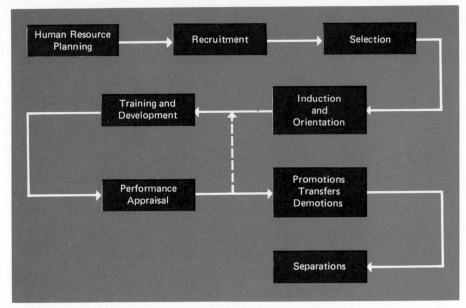

Separation. Separation, as the term implies, may involve resignation, layoff, discharge, or retirement. The type and quantity of separations can provide insights into the effectiveness with which the organization is managed. For example, too many resignations might signify a noncompetitive pay scale; recurrent layoffs might suggest poor integration of production with market demand; too many discharges might indicate poor selection or training procedures; and too many retirements might show poor management of the age mix among organization members. (Figure 19–2 illustrates the staffing process.)

HUMAN RESOURCE PLANNING

The need for human resource planning may not be readily apparent. After all, one might ask, if an organization needs new people, why doesn't it simply hire them? In fact, an organization's human resource needs can hardly ever be met as quickly or as easily as this question implies. An organization that does not plan for its human resources will often find that it is meeting neither its personnel requirements nor its overall goals effectively.

For example, a manufacturing company may purchase new automated equipment, but if the company has not started the process of hiring and training people to operate it before installation is begun, the equipment may remain idle for weeks or months. Similarly, an all-male, all-white organization that does not plan to increase the number of women and minority group managers working for it is likely to become the defendant in a civil rights lawsuit.

Planning Steps

There are four basic steps in human resource planning:[3]

1   *Planning for future needs.* How many people will the organization need to remain in operation for the foreseeable future?

2   *Planning for future balance.* How many people presently employed can be expected to stay with the organization? The difference between this number and the number the organization will need leads to the next step.

3   *Planning for recruiting and selecting or for laying off.* How can the organization attain the number of people it will need?

4   *Planning for development.* How should the training and movement of individuals within the organization be managed so that the organization will be assured of a continuing supply of experienced and capable personnel?

In order to accomplish these steps, the managers of a human resource planning program must consider a number of factors. The primary factor to be considered is the organization's strategic plan (see Chapter 5). The organization's basic strategy and the detailed goals, objectives, and tactics for making that strategy a reality will define the personnel needs of the organization. For example, a strategy of expansion will mean that additional personnel will have to be hired. A strategy of acquisition will suggest the need to hire managers who have had experience with the types of firms being acquired. Similarly, a strategy of automation will imply the need to reduce the number of production-line employees but increase the number of maintenance personnel.

Another factor to be considered by managers is possible change in the external environment of the organization (see Chapter 3). In a booming economy, for example, an organization might want to expand, and so its personnel needs will increase. At the same time, however, there may be fewer job candidates available because unemployment will be low. In a depressed economy, many organizations might want to cut back on the number of employees; however, if an organization wishes to expand, it is likely to have an increased number of candidates available (because of unemployment). There are a wide variety of other external changes that can affect the staffing function: technological changes, for instance, probably will increase the number of specialized personnel an organization will require; changes in union demands may affect layoff policies; and changes in government regulations can affect all personnel actions, from recruitment to separation.

In sum, the organization's internal environment—as exemplified by its strategic plan—as well as its external environment, will broadly define for managers the limits within which their human resource plan must operate. Once these broad limits have been established, managers can begin to com-

Internal Environment

Human Resource Plan

External Environment

---

[3] See Bruce P. Coleman, "An Integrated System for Manpower Planning," *Business Horizons,* Vol. 13, No. 5 (October 1970), pp. 89–95; Andrew F. Sikula, *Personnel Administration and Human Resource Management* (New York: Wiley, 1976); and Burckhardt Wenzel, "Planning for Manpower Utilization," *The Personnel Administrator,* Vol. 15, No. 3 (May-June 1970), pp. 36–40.

pare their future personnel needs against the existing personnel situation in order to determine what recruitment, training, and development procedures they will need to follow. The fact that the internal and external environments of an organization change means that managers must monitor these environments to keep their human resource plans up to date.

Forecasting and the Human Resource Audit

The central elements in human resource planning are forecasting and the human resource audit. *Forecasting* attempts to assess the future personnel needs of the organization. The *human resource audit* assesses the organization's current human resources. These two elements give managers the information they need to plan the other steps in the staffing process, such as recruiting and training.[4]

Forecasting. The primary emphasis of human resource forecasting is on the managerial and technical personnel the organization will need in order to maintain its growth and to exploit future opportunities. Thus, forecasters try to determine the number, type, and quality of people they will need to perform specific duties at a certain point in time; they try to specify the range of responsibilities that will have to be met; and they try to establish what skills and knowledge organization members will need. For instance, managers might forecast that subordinate participation in decision making is likely to become far more prevalent in the future. They may then plan to recruit greater numbers of managers who are especially skilled in human relations.

Forecasting obviously cannot be as precise as we would like it to be. However, it does serve as a reasonable guide for a manager's plans and actions. Human resource forecasts are usually short-range, covering a period of from six months to a year. (See Chapter 8 for a discussion of forecasting techniques.)

Human Resource Audit. Once the forecasts are completed, the next step is to obtain information about the organization's present personnel. This information will enable the planners to match the organization's personnel strengths and weaknesses against future requirements. Particular emphasis will be placed on locating existing skills and potential within the organization, since it will usually be more economical to promote from within than to recruit, hire, and train people from outside.

In a human resource audit, the performance of each individual in the organization is appraised. Members of each department may then be ranked according to the quality of their work. The information thus obtained will give upper-level managers an idea of how effective each department is. More

---

[4] See James W. Walker, "Forecasting Manpower Needs," in Elmer H. Burack and James W. Walker; eds., *Manpower Planning and Programming* (Boston: Allyn and Bacon, 1972); Noble S. Deckhard and Kenneth W. Lessey, "A Model for Understanding Management Manpower," *Personnel Journal*, Vol. 54, No. 3 (March 1975), pp. 169–175; and Eugene Schmuckler, "The Personnel Audit: Management's Forgotten Tool," *Personnel Journal*, Vol. 52, No. 11 (November 1973), pp. 977–980.

FIGURE 19-3   Management Replacement Chart

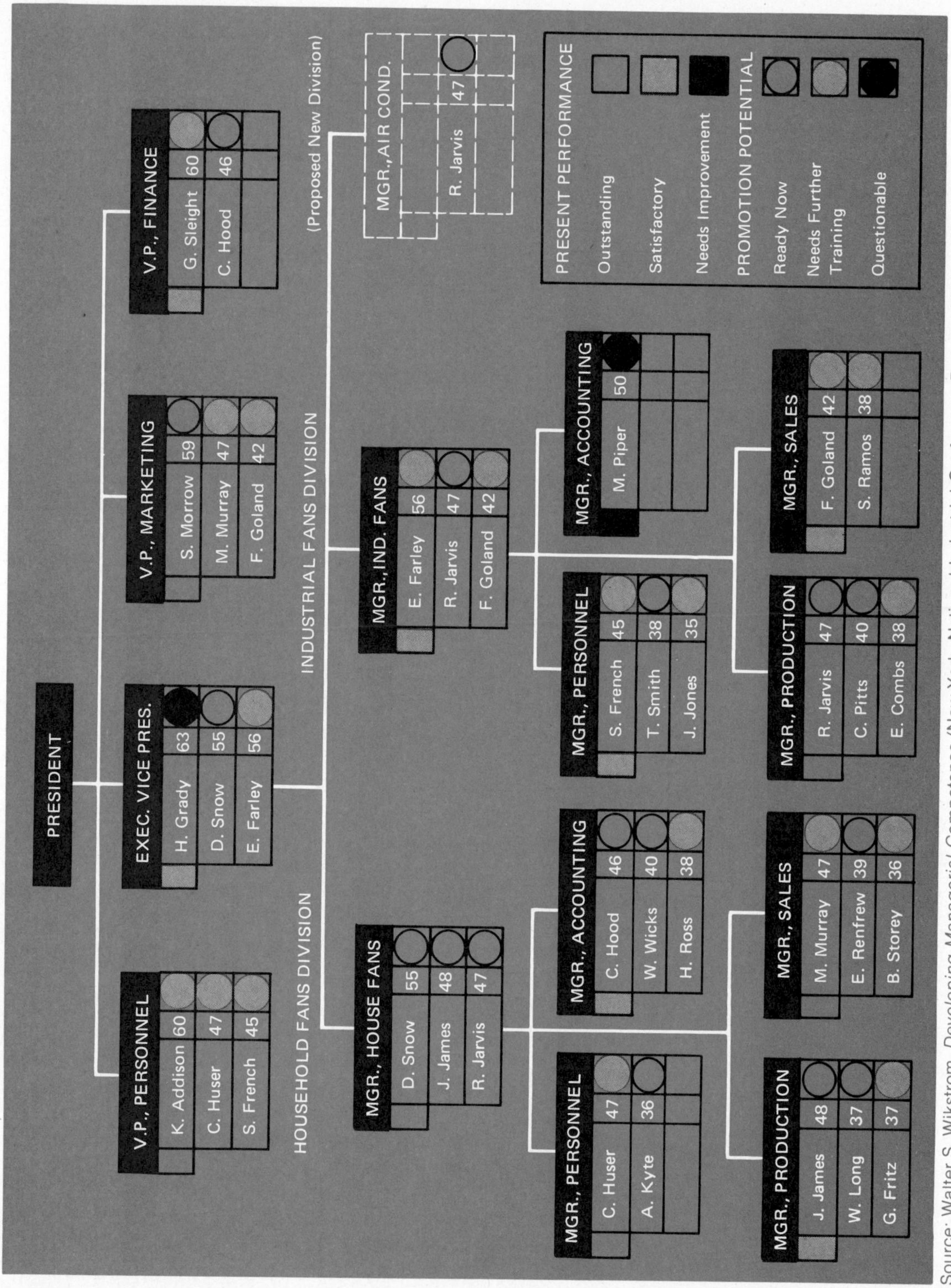

PRESIDENT

V.P., PERSONNEL
K. Addison	60
C. Huser	47
S. French	45

EXEC. VICE PRES.
H. Grady	63
D. Snow	55
E. Farley	56

V.P., MARKETING
S. Morrow	59
M. Murray	47
F. Goland	42

V.P., FINANCE
| G. Sleight | 60 |
| C. Hood | 46 |

(Proposed New Division)

MGR., AIR COND.
| R. Jarvis | 47 |

HOUSEHOLD FANS DIVISION

INDUSTRIAL FANS DIVISION

MGR., HOUSE FANS
D. Snow	55
J. James	48
R. Jarvis	47

MGR., IND. FANS
E. Farley	56
R. Jarvis	47
F. Goland	42

MGR., PERSONNEL
| C. Huser | 47 |
| A. Kyte | 36 |

MGR., ACCOUNTING
C. Hood	46
W. Wicks	40
H. Ross	38

MGR., PRODUCTION
J. James	48
W. Long	37
G. Fritz	37

MGR., SALES
M. Murray	47
E. Renfrew	39
B. Storey	36

MGR., ACCOUNTING
| M. Piper | 50 |

MGR., PERSONNEL
S. French	45
T. Smith	38
J. Jones	35

MGR., PRODUCTION
R. Jarvis	47
C. Pitts	40
E. Combs	38

MGR., SALES
| F. Goland | 42 |
| S. Ramos | 38 |

PRESENT PERFORMANCE
Outstanding
Satisfactory
Needs Improvement

PROMOTION POTENTIAL
Ready Now
Needs Further Training
Questionable

Source: Walter S. Wikstrom, *Developing Managerial Competence* (New York: National Industrial Conference Board, 1964). p. 99. Used by permission.

detailed audits may, in addition to performance appraisal, include such data as the age and education of each individual, his or her likely promotability, and what additional training is necessary.

For higher levels of management, the next step in the auditing process may be to develop a detailed succession plan. The *succession plan* will show the positions in the organization, present incumbents of those positions, likely future candidates for those positions, and the readiness of those candidates to take over those positions. (See Figure 19–3 on page 501.) Plans are usually developed in this level of detail only for upper-level managers. However, the need to compare existing human resources with future requirements applies to all levels of the organization.

RECRUITMENT

The purpose of recruitment is to provide a large enough group of candidates so that the organization will be able to select the qualified employees it needs. *General recruiting,* which is most appropriate for operative employees, takes place when the organization needs a group of workers of a certain type—for example, typists or salespeople. It follows comparatively simple, standardized procedures. *Specialized recruiting,* which is used mainly for executives or specialists, occurs when the organization desires a particular type of individual. In specialized recruiting, candidates receive individual attention over an extended period of time.[5]

The recruiting of college and MBA graduates falls somewhere between these two extremes. It resembles general recruiting in the sense that many candidates are stockpiled for a given group of openings and many may be hired with only a vague idea about their initial jobs—especially if the first "job" is membership in a management trainee program. However, to the extent that these campus recruits are more carefully screened and receive VIP treatment (plant or headquarters visits, interview lunches or dinners, personal follow-up on job offers, and so on), the process resembles the treatment given to managers and specialized personnel.

Job Analysis An important part of the recruiting process is developing a written statement of the content and location (on the organization chart) of each job. At the operative level, this statement is called the *job description;* at the managerial level, the statement is called a *position description.* Each box on the organization chart will be linked to a description that lists the title, duties, and responsibilities for that position. For example, a brief position description might read as follows: "Sales Manager: duties include hiring, training, and supervising small sales staff and administration of sales department; responsible for performance of department; reports to Division Manager."

[5] See Mathis and Jackson, *Personnel;* Sikula, *Personnel Administration and Human Resource Management;* and John B. Miner, *Personnel and Industrial Relations* (New York: Macmillan, 1969).

Once the position description has been determined, an accompanying job specification is developed. The *job specification* defines the background, experience, and personal characteristics an individual must have in order to perform effectively in the position. The job specification for Sales Manager might read: "Position requires BBA degree; five years' experience in sales and two years' supervisory experience; energetic, motivated individual with well-developed interpersonal skills." The job specification and position description together are called the *job analysis*.

Sources for Recruitment

Recruitment from Within. Many firms, such as IBM, General Foods, and Procter & Gamble, have a policy of recruiting or promoting from within the organization except in very exceptional circumstances. There are three major advantages of this policy. First, as we have already suggested, it is usually less expensive to recruit or promote from within than to hire from outside the organization. Second, a promotion-from-within policy may foster loyalty and inspire greater effort among organization members. Finally, individuals recruited from within will obviously be acclimated to the organization and may therefore perform more effectively. The major disadvantages of this policy are that it limits the pool of talent available to the organization; it reduces the chance for a fresh viewpoint to enter the organization; and it may encourage complacency because employees may assume that their seniority will assure their promotion.

There are a variety of ways in which organizations recruit from within. At lower levels of the organization, for example, seniority lists (sometimes required by union contract) may determine who will be selected for job openings. In some companies, the personnel department will *post* vacancy notices on bulletin boards and invite bids for these positions. This method has the disadvantage that some employees may avoid applying for fear of reprisal from their supervisors; in addition, unqualified candidates may require detailed explanations as to why they were not selected. This method does call attention, however, to qualified candidates who otherwise might be overlooked. Upper-level managers may also initiate a talent search within the organization. Employees who wish to be promoted will be asked to take appropriate tests or be interviewed. The information generated will be kept on file, and when a position opens up, the most qualified employees will be considered for it.

Outside Recruitment for Managers and Professionals. For most large companies, college and graduate school campuses are a major source of new managerial and professional talent. Almost all schools have a placement office; the company representative will usually work with the placement office to set up an interview schedule and to have company brochures distributed. A disadvantage of campus recruiting is that it tends to be quite expensive. Ten to fifteen interviews may be conducted for every candidate hired. In addition, a large proportion of those hired will not remain with the organization for more than two or three years.

Competition for middle management and professional talent is often no less vigorous than competition for market share. This competition is particularly intense in areas where top-quality ability is in short supply, as in advertising or investment analysis. Recruiters in such areas may buy large, expensive ads in newspapers and in national publications. Professional and middle management candidates may also be recruited via word of mouth and placement agencies.

A top-level vacancy often poses a complicated problem for an organization, because the right person for the position is usually not in the job market. He or she must be located in the upper reaches of some other firm, frequently a competitor, and induced to switch. Increasingly, corporate managements are turning to outside *executive search* firms. These professional recruiters are expected to locate three or four carefully sifted prospects who not only are highly qualified but who also can be enticed from their present positions by the right offer.

SELECTION

Ideally, the selection process is one of mutual decision making. The organization decides whether or not to make a job offer and how attractive the offer should be. The job candidate decides whether or not the organization and the job offer will fit his or her needs and goals. However, unless the job market is extremely tight, or the candidate is a highly qualified executive or professional, the selection process in practice will be more one-sided. Several candidates will be applying for each position, and the organization will, on the basis of a series of screening devices, hire the candidate it feels is most suitable.

The standard hiring sequence follows a seven-step procedure (see Figure 19–4):

1 Completed application form
2 Initial screening interview
3 Testing
4 Background investigation—reference checks
5 In-depth selection interviews
6 Physical examination
7 Job offer

Before we discuss each step briefly, the reader should note that the actual selection process will vary between organizations and between levels in the same organization. For example, the selection interview for lower-level employees may be quite perfunctory; heavy emphasis may be placed instead on the initial screening interview or on tests. In selecting middle- or upper-level managers, on the other hand, the interviewing may be extensive—sometimes lasting eight or more hours—and there may be little or no formal testing. Instead of initially filling out an application, the candidate may submit a résumé. Completion of the formal application may be delayed until after the job offer has been accepted.

FIGURE 19-4
Typical Events in the
Selection Process

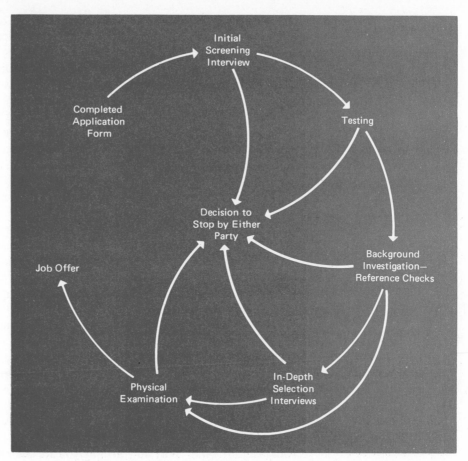

Source: Reprinted from *The Personnel Management Process*, 3rd edition, by Wendell French. Copyright © 1974 by Houghton Mifflin Company. Used by permission of the publisher.

The *application form* serves three purposes. First, it formally indicates that the applicant desires a position. Second, it provides the interviewer with the basic information he or she needs to conduct an interview. Third, it becomes a part of the organization's personnel information if the applicant is hired. Legally, the application form can request only information that has been shown to predict success in the job for which the candidate is applying. (It is illegal, for example, to request information on race or religion.)

The *initial screening interview* is used to make a quick evaluation of the applicant's suitability for the particular job. In effect, the initial interview determines for both the applicant and the interviewer whether or not the selection process should proceed. The applicant may be asked questions on his or her experience, salary expectations, relocation availability, and the like.

Through *testing,* the organization attempts to predict how well the candidate will perform on the job. For operative employees, tests will usually focus on mechanical aptitudes and skills (for example, a typing test). Some companies use a variety of personality and psychological tests for selecting managers.

To be effective, tests should be both reliable and valid. *Reliable* tests are those that yield roughly the same score each time they are taken by the same individual. Tests are *valid* when performance on the tests is closely associated with performance on the job. In recent years, tests used for selection purposes have come under criticism on the grounds that they represent invasions of privacy, are not reliable or valid, and lead to hiring and promotion discrimination. As a result of such criticism, fewer organizations are using tests as screening devices.

In a *background investigation,* the truthfulness of a candidate's résumé or application form will be checked, and further information will be sought from one or more of the candidate's references or previous employers. Such an investigation is useful, since studies have shown that as many as half of the applications submitted contain false or erroneous material.[6] Usually, the manager or interviewer will simply call the applicant's previous supervisor (with the applicant's permission), confirm the information the applicant has supplied, and ask the supervisor to rate the applicant's skills and abilities.

The *in-depth selection interview* is designed to fill in gaps on the candidate's application or résumé; find out more about the applicant as an individual; and, in general, obtain information of interest to the interviewer so that the suitability of the candidate for the job and the organization can be determined. Unlike the screening interview, which is usually conducted by a member of the personnel department, the in-depth interview is usually conducted by the manager to whom the candidate would report if hired. Typical questions in an in-depth interview might be: "Why did you choose your field?" "Why did you leave your last job?" and "Why do you think you are qualified for this position?" Because the in-depth interview is a crucial part of the selection process in many organizations, we will discuss it in greater detail below.

The *physical examination* will be one of the last steps in the selection process, unless the job involves heavy physical labor or stress. Physical examinations are designed to ensure that the candidate can perform effectively in the position for which he or she is applying, to protect other employees against a contagious disease, to establish a health record for the applicant, and to protect the organization against unjust workmen's compensation claims.

If an applicant successfully passes through these selection stages and still indicates a desire for employment, a *job offer* may be made. The salary offered should be competitive with salaries for similar jobs in other organizations and be compatible with the organization's existing salary structure. Too low an offer, if accepted, will cause the new employee to feel disgruntled when he or

---

[6] See, for example, Robert Hershey, "The Application Form," *Personnel,* January-February 1971, p. 38, and I. L. Goldstein, "The Application Blank: How Honest Are the Responses?" *Journal of Applied Psychology,* Vol. 55 (1971), p. 491.

she finds out what others are being paid. Too high an offer, on the other hand, may cause problems with existing employees.

Interviewing

For many positions, particularly in management, the in-depth interview is probably the most important factor in the organization's decision on whether or not to make a job offer and in the individual's decision on whether or not to accept the offer.[7] Nevertheless, a number of studies have documented the erratic and frequently invalid decisions made by interviewers.[8] The most effective interviews—that is, those that are best able to predict the eventual performance of applicants—are usually those that are planned carefully and in which the same questions are asked of all interviewees.[9] Most interviews, however, tend to be far less structured and deliberate.

Richard Nehrbass has identified three defects that typically keep interviews from being sources of accurate information about job applicants.[10] The first defect is the imbalance of power in the interview situation. The interviewer is likely to be experienced and at ease. The interviewee, on the other hand, who is probably inexperienced in the interview situation and to whom the job may represent a livelihood, a career, and an important part of his or her self-image, is likely to feel ill at ease. The interviewee may therefore behave in an uncharacteristically tense manner.

The second defect of interviews is that they frequently result in "phony" behavior. The applicant feels compelled to project an image that he or she thinks will be acceptable to the interviewer. Sometimes qualified applicants may be rejected because they put on an obvious act—they "always get along with people" or are "willing to work long hours." Less qualified applicants may be accepted because they happen to project a more realistic image.

The last defect Nehrbass identifies is the tendency of interviewers to ask questions that have no useful answers, such as "Why don't you tell me about yourself?" or "What do you think are your weaknesses?" Applicants are likely to regard such questions as a form of game playing and will therefore feel uneasy and give superficial replies. Nehrbass suggests that interviews which are much more focused on the requirements of the job and the actual skills and abilities of candidates will be better predictors of performance.

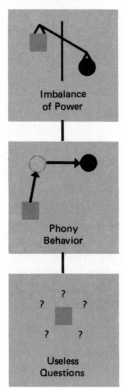

INTERVIEW
DEFECTS

Imbalance
of Power

Phony
Behavior

?
?   ?
?   ?

Useless
Questions

[7] See John D. Drake, *Interviewing for Managers* (New York: American Management Associations, 1972); Theodore Hariton, *Interview* (New York: Hastings House, 1970); George Shouksmith, *Assessment through Interviewing* (New York: Pergamon Press, 1968); and Norman R. E. Maier, *The Appraisal Interview* (New York: Wiley, 1958).

[8] See, for example, Eugene C. Mayfield, "The Selection Interview—A Reevaluation of Published Research," *Personnel Psychology,* Vol. 17, No. 3 (Autumn 1964), pp. 239–260; Edwin E. Ghiselli, "The Validity of a Personnel Interview," *Personnel Psychology,* Vol. 19, No. 4 (Winter 1966), pp. 389–394; and Orman R. Wright, Jr., "Summary of Research on the Selection Interview Since 1964," *Personnel Psychology,* Vol. 22, No. 4 (Winter 1969), pp. 391–413.

[9] See R. E. Carlson, D. P. Schwab, and H. G. Heneman III, "Agreement Among Selection Interview Styles," *Journal of Industrial Psychology,* Vol. 1 (1970), pp. 8–17.

[10] Richard G. Nehrbass, "Psychological Barriers to Effective Employment Interviewing," *Personnel Journal,* Vol. 56, No. 2 (February 1977), pp. 60–64.

Aside from these problems, the interview process may prove unreliable because of the differing objectives of the interviewer and interviewee. The prospective employer wants to sell the organization as a good place to work, and so may exaggerate the organization's strengths. The prospective employee wants to be hired, and so may exaggerate his or her qualities. With both parties distorting the truth, it becomes all but impossible for interviewer and applicant jointly to determine how well the individual is likely to "fit" with the organization.

Some organizations have attempted to reduce this problem by making certain that candidates are exposed to unattractive as well as attractive parts of the job. The so-called *realistic job interview,* in which applicants are given favorable and unfavorable information about the position, has been found to result in lower turnover rates and higher job satisfaction—without a decrease in the job acceptance rate.[11] (See Chapter 20.)

Manager Selection

The most important selection decisions made in organizations involve the selection of managers, because managers play a critical role in organizational success. The task of selecting managers is, however, a difficult one because of the complexity of the manager's job. Managers are required to utilize effectively a wide variety of skills and abilities; thus, accurate assessment of a management candidate's actual or potential skills and abilities is very hard to achieve.

In this section we will discuss briefly the selection of experienced managers and of nonmanagers with management potential from outside the organization. We will not discuss the selection of managers from within the organization at this point because we discuss promotion later in the chapter; however, we should note that promotion from within is a *comparatively* easy and reliable management selection task, because candidates will have a record of performance within the organization.

Experienced Managers. Organizations seek to hire experienced managers to fill their present management needs. A newly created post may require a manager with the kind of experience not available within the organization; an established post may exist and the talent to fill it is unavailable within the organization; a key position might suddenly open and there is no time to train a replacement; or, a top performer in a competing organization is sought to improve the organization's own competitive position.

The best predictor of future performance is past performance. Experienced managerial candidates will therefore be assessed to the greatest possible extent on their performance record. It is often difficult, however, to obtain verifiable data on a manager's past performance. Moreover, even when results are available, it is difficult for organization interviewers to judge how

---

[11] See John P. Wanous, "Effects of a Realistic Job Preview on Job Acceptance, Job Attitudes, and Job Survival," *Journal of Applied Psychology,* Vol. 58 (1973), pp. 327–332.

much of that performance is due to the manager. The manager may have had unusually able subordinates; the manager may simply have been lucky; or the manager may have sacrificed long-term results to achieve short-term, temporary profits. In short, the manager's past performance may or may not predict the manager's future performance with the organization. For these reasons, interviewers must frequently rely on other assessment tools.

The most important of these tools, as we have already stated, is the interview process—testing is not widely used to assess experienced managers. Experienced managers typically go through several interviews; their interviewers are almost always higher-level managers in the organization. Personnel managers are usually less aware of the detailed skills and abilities that the available position requires.

During the interview process, interviewers attempt to assess the candidate's suitability and past performance. Particular emphasis is placed on the candidate's personality: interviewers will try to determine how well the candidate seems to fit their idea of what a good manager should be. Personality traits frequently sought include: *intelligence*—the ability to grasp quickly complex material; *decisiveness*—the ability and willingness to make quick, accurate judgments; *emotional stability*—levelheadedness and ability to operate effectively under pressure: *self-confidence*—an air of assurance and self-esteem; and *interpersonal skill*—the ability to get along with and motivate others. The interviewers also attempt to assess how well the candidate's personality, past experience, and style of operating will "fit" in the organization.

Potential Managers. Potential managers usually enter the organization after being graduated from college. They will typically take entry-level positions—a research job or a staff job, or a membership in a training program. Their performance in these entry-level positions will have a strong influence on the type of managerial job they eventually will receive.

Assessing potential managers is even more difficult a task than assessing experienced managers, since potential managers must be judged on things they have not yet done. However, such an assessment is also extremely important, since the potential managers selected may well determine the future success of the organization.

Most assessments of prospective managers begin with a review of school grades. However, except for technical positions, school performance does not seem to be strongly associated with managerial performance. For this reason, many organizations are beginning to look for evidence of extracurricular managerial interest or experience—working on a campus journal, for example, or directing part of a community project. In addition, as we have already mentioned, candidates may be given a variety of tests to determine their suitability for the organization. Finally, like experienced managers, the prospective managers may be interviewed extensively to determine whether they have what the interviewers consider to be the appropriate personality traits for managers.

509

The Problem of Traits. We suggested in our chapter on leadership that measuring the presence or absence of certain traits was not a useful way of determining managerial effectiveness. Many different lists of so-called "desirable leadership traits" exist, and yet consistency among these lists is not very high. As John P. Campbell and his colleagues put it, "The various lists of desirable managerial traits . . . seem to include just about every human virtue."[12]

In reality, most managers have a mental model of the effective manager — they believe that a certain personal style, set of experiences, and problem-solving and decision-making approach will lead to high performance. They consciously or unconsciously use this model to assess candidates, particularly in job interviews. The net result is that managers often select candidates on the basis of a "gut feeling"; the candidates they select usually will be very much like themselves.

This use of "traits" or "gut feelings" in the selection process creates problems for individuals who differ from the accepted model — short people who do not fit the interviewer's idea that managers should be tall; fat people who are not as slim as managers "should" be; women or members of minorities whose behavior or attitudes seem idiosyncratic to the interviewer. The result for the organization is that potentially effective candidates — often with fresh ideas or approaches — may be lost.

In general, the likelihood of making good candidate choices is improved when several managers interview each candidate. The multiplicity of viewpoints made available through this approach lessens the possibility that effective managers will be lost to the organization because of one interviewer's bias or point of view. Another method that has proven effective in selecting qualified candidates is the assessment center, which we discuss next.

Assessment Centers

Assessment centers were originally used during World War II as a means of selecting OSS agents. Assessment centers have since been used with considerable success as devices for predicting the future management performance of both experienced and potential managers.[13] In the assessment center approach, candidates are asked to participate in a wide range of simulation exercises while trained observers note and assess the candidates' behavior. The most common exercise is the *in basket*. In this realistic simulation, the candidate is informed that he or she has just been promoted to a newly vacant position and will have to leave town soon to attend an important meeting. The candidate is given one hour to deal with the memos, letters, reports, telephone messages, and other materials in the previous incumbent's in basket. The candidate must handle each item in the most appropriate manner, and in many

---

[12] John P. Campbell et al., *Managerial Behavior, Performance, and Effectiveness* (New York: McGraw-Hill, 1970), p. 7.

[13] See Andrew J. DuBrin, *The Practice of Managerial Psychology* (New York: Pergamon Press, 1972), and Ann Howard, "An Assessment of Assessment Centers," *Academy of Management Journal*, Vol. 17, No. 1 (March 1974), pp. 115–134. An excellent description of the well-known AT&T assessment center can be found in Douglas W. Bray, Richard J. Campbell, and Donald Grant, *Formative Years in Business* (New York: Wiley, 1974).

cases will have an opportunity to explain or discuss his or her decisions in a follow-up interview.

In the *leaderless group discussion* exercise, the participants are given a problem to be solved by group decision. The way the candidates handle themselves in this situation helps to reveal their leadership qualities and interpersonal skills. Candidates may also participate in *management games* geared to the level of the job being filled, make oral presentations, and take any number of tests probing mental ability, general knowledge, and personality.

Assessment centers are not only excellent predictors of management potential but also can serve as part of a management development program. In fact, some graduate schools of business use some of the techniques to guide an individual's self-development program. However, the assessment center approach is so costly that its use tends to be restricted to a few relatively large, successful organizations. An assessment typically involves a number of assessors working with a small group of candidates over a period of several days.[14]

INDUCTION AND ORIENTATION

Induction and orientation are designed to answer the question, What information does a new employee need in order to function comfortably and effectively in the organization? Typically, induction and orientation will convey to the new employee three types of information: (1) general information about the daily work routine; (2) a review of the organization's history, purpose, and products, and how the employee's job contributes to the organization's needs; and (3) a detailed presentation, perhaps via brochure, of the organization's policies, work rules, and employee benefits.

Many studies have shown that employees feel anxiety when they first enter the organization. They worry about how well they will perform in the job; they feel inadequate compared to more experienced employees; and they are concerned about how well they will get along with their co-workers. For these reasons, effective induction and orientation programs are deliberately aimed at reducing the anxiety of new employees. Information on the job environment and on supervisors is provided, co-workers are introduced, and questions by new employees are encouraged.[15]

The Effects of Early Job Experiences
Early job experiences appear to play a very critical role in the individual's career with the organization. It is during these experiences that the individual's expectations and the organization's expectations confront each other. If these expectations are not compatible, dissatisfaction will result. As might be ex-

---

[14] For additional articles on assessment centers, see William C. Byham, "The Assessment Center as an Aid in Management Development," *Training and Development Journal,* Vol. 25, No. 12 (December 1971), pp. 10–12, and Allen I. Kraut, "A Hard Look at Management Assessment Centers and Their Future," *Personnel Journal,* Vol. 51, No. 5 (May 1972), pp. 317–326.

[15] See, for example, Earl R. Gomersall and M. Scott Myers, "Breakthrough in On-the-Job Training," *Harvard Business Review,* July-August 1966, pp. 62–72.

511

"Ah! The new blood!"

Drawing by Koren; © 1977 The New Yorker Magazine, Inc.

pected, employee turnover rates are almost always the highest among the organization's new employees.

David E. Berlew and Douglas T. Hall found that for management trainees the amount of challenge in the individual's first job was significantly correlated with the individual's subsequent career progress in the organization. Individuals who were initially given demanding tasks internalized high standards of performance and were better prepared for future assignments. Individuals who were given easy assignments appeared to be less motivated to perform at a high level. After five years, those individuals who were given demanding assignments when they entered the organization were, as a group, higher in the organizational hierarchy than new employees who were not given challenging assignments.[16] (See also our discussion of Berlew and Hall in Chapter 20.)

Stoner, Aram, and Rubin found a similar relationship between early job experiences and subsequent job performance. The individuals in this study were young MBA's and lawyers who had been given technical-assistance assignments in Africa. The initial reaction of the technical assistants to their jobs was assessed from informal letters that they sent back to the administrators of the assistance program within their first two weeks on the job. These initial

[16] David E. Berlew and Douglas T. Hall, "The Socialization of Managers," *Administrative Science Quarterly*, Vol. 11 (1966), pp. 207–223.

reactions correlated significantly with how well the job worked out for both employee and employer for the duration of the assignment.[17]

TRAINING AND DEVELOPMENT

The term *training,* as we have suggested, has been used most often to refer to the teaching of technical skills to nonmanagerial personnel. *Management development* usually refers to programs that attempt to improve the technical, human relations, and conceptual skills of managers. In our discussion of training and development, we will cover training briefly and then focus on management development.

Training Programs

The need to train new employees or individuals who are being promoted is self-evident; new jobs usually require training in new skills. In addition, the motivation of employees who have just been hired or promoted is likely to be high. Training becomes more problematic when it involves experienced employees who require additional training to make their performance more effective. The training needs of such employees are not always easy to determine, and when they are determined, the individuals involved may resent being asked to change their established ways of doing their jobs.

There are four procedures that managers can use to determine the training needs of individuals in their organization or subunit:

1 *Performance appraisal*—each employee's work is measured against the performance standards or objectives established for his or her job.

2 *Analysis of job requirements*—the skills or knowledge specified in the appropriate job description are examined. Those employees without necessary skills or knowledge become candidates for a training program.

3 *Organizational analysis*—the effectiveness of the organization and its success in meeting its goals are analyzed to determine where differences exist. For example, members of a department with a high turnover rate or a low performance record might require additional training.

4 *Survey of personnel*—managers as well as nonmanagers are asked to describe what problems they are experiencing in their work and what actions they believe need to be taken to solve them.

Once the organization's training needs have been identified, managers must initiate the appropriate training effort. There are a variety of training approaches that managers can use.[18] The most common of these approaches are *on-the-job training* methods. These include: *job rotation,* in which the employee, over a period of time, works on a series of jobs, thereby learning a

---

[17] James A. F. Stoner, John D. Aram, and Irwin M. Rubin, "Factors Associated with Effective Performance in Overseas Work Assignments," *Personnel Psychology,* Vol. 25, No. 2 (Summer 1972), pp. 303–318.

[18] See Glueck, *Personnel.*

broad variety of skills; *internship,* in which job training is combined with related classroom instruction; and *apprenticeship,* in which the employee is trained under the guidance of a highly skilled co-worker.

Off-the-job training takes place outside the actual workplace but attempts to simulate actual working conditions. This type of training includes *vestibule training,* in which employees work on the actual equipment and in a realistic job setting but in a different room from the one in which they will be working. The object is to avoid the on-the-job pressures that might interfere with the learning process. In *behaviorally experienced training,* some of the methods used in assessment centers—business games, in-basket simulation, problem-centered cases, and so on—are employed so that the trainee can learn the behavior appropriate for the job through *role playing.* Finally, off-the-job training may focus completely on the *classroom* with training seminars, lectures, and films.

Management Development Programs

Management development, as we have already suggested, is designed to improve the overall effectiveness of managers in their present positions and to prepare them for greater responsibility when they are promoted. Management development programs have become more prevalent in recent years because of the increasingly complex demands being made of managers and because letting experience alone train managers is too time-consuming and unreliable a process.

Early management development activities were program-centered. That is, a program would be designed and administered to managers regardless of individual differences among them. However, there is increasing recognition of the fact that managers differ in ability, experience, and personality. Thus, management development programs are becoming more *manager-centered*— that is, tailored to fit the unique developmental requirements of the managers attending. Before a program is selected, a *needs analysis* is made to identify the particular needs and problems of the manager or group of managers. The appropriate training activities are then recommended.[19]

As in other training programs, there are a number of on-the-job and off-the-job management development approaches.[20]

On-the-Job Methods. On-the-job methods are usually the preferred methods in management development programs. The training is far more likely than off-the-job training to be tailored to the individual, job-related, and conveniently located. There are four major on-the-job development methods: (1) coaching, (2) job rotation, (3) training positions, and (4) planned work activities.

Of these four methods, *coaching*—the training of a subordinate by his or her immediate superior—is by far the most effective management development technique. *Modeling* (or imitation) is a central part of all behavioral learning,

---

[19] See DuBrin, *The Practice of Managerial Psychology.*

[20] See Edward C. Ryterband and Bernard M. Bass, "Management Development," in Joseph W. McGuire, ed., *Contemporary Management: Issues and Viewpoints* (Englewood Cliffs, N.J.: Prentice-Hall, 1974), pp. 579–609.

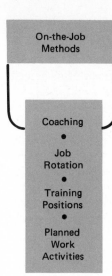

On-the-Job Methods

Coaching
•
Job Rotation
•
Training Positions
•
Planned Work Activities

and imitating the behavior of an outstanding manager is one of the easiest and best ways to learn good managerial habits. (Watching a poor manager, on the other hand, can teach one a few things to *avoid* doing but not what *should* be done.) When the manager does more than simply set a good example or act as a role model and takes an active part in his or her subordinate's development, then the training becomes even more effective.

Unfortunately, there are many managers who are either unable or unwilling to coach their subordinates. To be meaningful, on-the-job coaching must be tempered by considerable restraint—subordinates cannot develop unless they are allowed to work out their problems in their own way. Managers too often feel compelled to tell their subordinates exactly what to do, thereby negating the effectiveness of coaching. In addition, some managers feel threatened by the idea of coaching their subordinates, for fear of creating a rival. In reality, it is the *manager* who has much to gain from coaching subordinates, since a manager frequently will not be promoted unless there is a successor available to take his or her place.

Many firms, particularly those with MBO programs (see Chapter 6), make a point of training their managers in the fine art of coaching. Conscientious managers often keep a "development file" for each subordinate, indicating the training the subordinate is receiving, the skills the subordinate is acquiring, and how well the subordinate is performing. A record of *critical incidents*— situations in which a subordinate displayed desirable or undesirable behavior— may also be included. In discussing these incidents with the subordinate, managers can reinforce good habits ("You really handled that customer's complaint"), gently point out bad habits ("Do you think you should be firmer with the supplier?"), and identify the areas in which the subordinate needs further development.

The second on-the-job development technique is job rotation. *Job rotation* involves shifting managers from position to position so that they may broaden their experience and familiarize themselves with various aspects of the firm's operations.

Training positions are a third method used to develop managers. Trainees are given staff posts immediately under a manager, often with the title of "assistant to." Such assignments give trainees a chance to work with and model themselves after outstanding managers who might otherwise have little contact with them.

Finally, *planned work activities* involve giving trainees important work assignments as a means for developing their experience and ability. Trainees may be asked to head a task force or participate in an important committee meeting. In this manner they gain insight into how organizations operate and also improve their human relations skills.

Off-the-Job Methods. As we noted earlier, off-the-job techniques remove individuals from the stresses and ongoing demands of the workplace, enabling them to focus fully on the learning experience. In addition, they are given the opportunity to meet people from other departments or organizations. Thus, they will be exposed to useful new ideas and experiences and will have

Off-the-Job
Methods

Classes
•
University
Programs
•
Sensitivity
Training

an opportunity to make contacts that may be useful to them when they return to their jobs. The most common off-the-job development methods include in-house classroom instruction and management development programs sponsored by universities and other organizations, such as the American Management Associations.

Almost every management development program includes some form of *classroom instruction.* Specialists from inside or outside the organization are asked to teach trainees a particular subject. To counteract possible passivity and boredom, classroom instruction may be supplemented with case studies, role playing, and business games or simulations. For example, managers may be asked to play roles on both sides in a simulated labor-management dispute.

Some organizations send selected employees to *university-sponsored management development programs.* Many major universities have such programs, which range in length from about a week to three months or more. Some universities (such as MIT and Stanford) also have one-year, full-time study programs for middle-level managers. These managers usually have been slated for promotion; their organizations send them to these university programs to broaden their perspectives and prepare them for movement into general (as opposed to functional) management. University programs will often combine classroom instruction with case studies, role playing, and simulation.

Sensitivity training (or the T-group) is a controversial development technique used by some organizations. The purposes of sensitivity training are: (1) to increase an individual's understanding of his or her behavior and how others perceive that behavior; (2) to make the individual more sensitive to the feelings and opinions of others; and (3) to help the individual learn more effective, satisfying, and meaningful ways of relating to others. A typical T (for training) group is made up of ten to twenty people who meet for 3 to 6 hours daily over a period of one to two weeks. A qualified trainer will be present, but the trainer will intervene in group discussions only when it becomes appropriate to call the participants' attention to important behaviors or feelings that have been exhibited. Participants will be encouraged to select their own subjects for discussion, to express their reactions to the behavior of others in the group, and to analyze their own behavior and feelings. While members will initially experience anxiety—especially when their own actions are criticized—they usually learn to accept feedback about themselves and become more sensitive and open to the feelings of the other group members.

In the 1960s, T-groups were used extensively by many organizations in order to improve their managers' human relations skills. During that period, T-groups came under harsh criticism and no longer are used as widely. The criticisms of T-groups include the arguments that their effectiveness in improving managerial performance has not been demonstrated, that they can cause emotional damage in certain individuals, and that the behaviors they encourage are frequently not appropriate once individuals return to their organizations. However, most individuals who have participated in T-groups believe that T-groups can benefit emotionally healthy individuals by improving their attitudes and behavior.[21] Robert J. House, who has analyzed the available research on T-groups, suggests they can be used effectively by those organizations that both want and can tolerate managers who are more considerate of others and more outspokenly independent. House suggests that those organizations carefully screen individuals whom they wish to participate in such a program to make sure they can tolerate the anxiety of a T-group, and, most importantly, that the organizations make participation in the T-group purely voluntary.[22] (See also Chapter 15.)

Conditions for Effective Management Development Programs. One of the greatest difficulties in bringing about behavioral changes in a development program arises when the trainee returns to his or her job. If the on-the-job environment does not encourage or support the new behavior, the behavior will quickly disappear. In fact, the individual's performance can actually decline compared to his or her performance before the development program. This phenomenon has been observed in human relations training where individuals usually are taught to use more democratic, participative management styles. Those individuals whose supervisors do not favor such a style may become even more autocratic than they were before the training. (See Chapter 17.) For this reason, the support of top management and the trainees' supervisors is important in helping to make a training program effective.

Jack W. Taylor has identified a number of other mistakes that organizations need to avoid in order to make their development programs more useful.[23] These mistakes include:

1 *Placing the prime responsibility for training on staff.* Although staff departments can play a major role in developing and executing training programs, they should not be held accountable for developing an organization's human resources. It remains the *line* managers' responsibility to develop their human resources.

2 *Failing to equip managers for their training role.* Managers who are expected to develop or train their subordinates must be given training themselves in the appropriate developmental skills.

3 *Making a hasty needs analysis.* For the training program to be properly tailored to the individual, the needs analysis must be thorough.

4 *Substituting training for selection.* Training cannot create potential; it can only help to develop it. Managers need to select individuals who can benefit from a development program.

---

[21] See Edgar F. Huse, *Organization Development and Change* (St. Paul: West Publishing, 1975), and Dale Yoder, *Personnel Management and Industrial Relations,* 6th ed. (Englewood Cliffs, N.J.: Prentice-Hall, 1970). For an extensive review of the early research on sensitivity training, see John P. Campbell and Marvin D. Dunnette, "Effectiveness of T-Group Experiences in Managerial Training and Development," *Psychological Bulletin,* Vol. 70, No. 2 (August 1968), pp. 73–104.

[22] Robert J. House, "T-Group Training: Good or Bad?" *Business Horizons,* Vol. 12, No. 6 (December 1969), pp. 69–77.

[23] J. W. Taylor, "Ten Serious Mistakes in Management Training Development," *Personnel Journal,* Vol. 53, No. 5 (May 1974), pp. 357–362.

5 *Limiting training to the classroom.* Some experience in the work environment is necessary to make training successful.

6 *Trying to modify the trainee's personality.* Training can be used to change some dysfunctional behaviors. Using training to try to change a person's personality is both unproductive and unethical.

PERFORMANCE APPRAISAL

Performance appraisal is one of the most important tasks any manager has, yet it is one that most managers freely admit they have difficulty handling adequately. It is not always easy to judge a subordinate's performance accurately, and it is often harder still to convey that judgment to the subordinate in a painless or helpful manner.

Informal and Formal Appraisal

We will use the term *performance appraisal* to mean the continuous process of feeding back to subordinates information about how well they are doing their work for the organization. This process occurs both informally and systematically. *Informal appraisal* is conducted on a day-to-day basis. The manager spontaneously mentions that a particular piece of work was performed well or poorly; or, the subordinate stops by the manager's office to find out how a particular piece of work was received. Because of the close connection between the behavior and the feedback on it, informal appraisal quickly encourages desirable performance and discourages undesirable performance before it becomes ingrained.

Systematic appraisal occurs semiannually or annually on a formalized basis. Such appraisal has four major purposes: (1) it lets subordinates know formally how their current performance is being rated; (2) it identifies those subordinates who deserve *merit raises;* (3) it locates those subordinates who require additional training; and (4) it plays an important role in pinpointing those subordinates who are candidates for promotion.

It is important for managers to differentiate between the current performance and the promotability of their subordinates. Managers in many organizations fail to make this distinction; they assume that a person with the skills and ability to perform well in one job will automatically perform well in a different or more responsible position. This assumption is the basis of the well-known if somewhat overstated "Peter Principle," which suggests that individuals are successively promoted until they are placed eventually in a job that they cannot perform.[24]

Formal Appraisal Approaches

Who will be responsible for formal performance appraisals? In answer to this question, four basic appraisal approaches have evolved in organizations.

The first approach, *a superior's rating of subordinates,* is by far the most common one. However, other approaches are becoming more popular and can be a valuable supplement to appraisal by a superior.

[24] See Laurence F. Peter and Raymond Hull, *The Peter Principle* (New York: Morrow, 1969).

The Four Appraisal Approaches

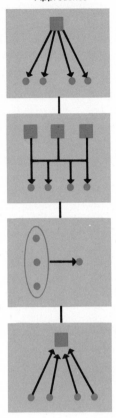

A group of superiors rating subordinates is the second most frequently used appraisal approach. Subordinates are rated by a managerial committee or by a series of managers who must complete separate rating forms. This approach, because it relies on the views of a number of people, is often more effective than appraisal by a single superior. However, it is time-consuming and often dilutes subordinates' feelings of accountability to their immediate superior.

The third appraisal approach is *a group of peers rating a colleague* — the individual is rated separately and on paper by his or her co-workers on the same organizational level. This approach is least common in business organizations because of the difficulty of asking employees to make appraisals on which raise or promotion decisions can be based. It is used mainly in the military, particularly in military academies, to identify leadership potential.

In the final approach, *subordinates' rating of bosses,* subordinates evaluate their superior's performance. This approach has a common analog in colleges, where students are often asked to evaluate their teacher on a number of performance measures. Although not widely used in business organizations, this approach is becoming a more common method of evaluating managers and helping them improve their performance.

Traditionally, appraisals have concentrated on an individual's personal characteristics, such as intelligence, decisiveness, creativity, and ability to get along with others. (See Table 19–1 on next page for an example of this approach.) Today, however, appraisals are increasingly based on the individual's performance — that is, on how well the subordinate is helping the organization achieve its goals. MBO (see Chapter 6) is an example of a performance-based appraisal approach that involves establishing specific objectives and comparing performance against those objectives.

Problems of Appraisal

In their studies of the performance appraisal process,[25] Herbert H. Meyer and his colleagues found that formal appraisals by managers are often ineffective in improving the performance of subordinates. Individuals who were formally given criticism about their job performance once or twice a year tended to become defensive and resentful. Their performance after the appraisal interview tended to decline.

Meyer and his colleagues suggest that the goal of appraisal should be to improve the future performance of subordinates, and that this goal is difficult to achieve if managers act in their traditional role of judge. Instead, Meyer and his colleagues argue, managers and each of their subordinates should set performance goals together, and then together evaluate progress toward those goals. Participatory appraisal, they found, leads to both greater satisfaction and performance on the job. Meyer and his co-workers also suggest that the

---

[25] Herbert H. Meyer, Emanuel Kay, and John R. P. French, "Split Roles in Performance Appraisal," *Harvard Business Review,* January-February 1965, pp. 123–129. See also Douglas M. McGregor, "An Uneasy Look at Performance Appraisal," *Harvard Business Review,* May-June 1957, pp. 89–94.

TABLE 19-1   Managerial Rating Scale

Performance Factor	Performance Level					
	FAR Exceeds Job Requirements	*Exceeds Job Requirements*	*Meets Job Requirements*	*Needs Some Improvement*	*Does Not Meet Minimum Requirements*	
Quality	Leaps tall buildings with single bound	Needs running start to leap tall buildings	Can leap only short buildings	Crashes into buildings	Cannot recognize buildings	
Timeliness	Is faster than a speeding bullet	Is as fast as a speeding bullet	Somewhat slower than a bullet	Can only shoot bullets	Wounds self with bullets	
Initiative	Is stronger than a locomotive	Is stronger than a bull elephant	Is stronger than a bull	Shoots the bull	Smells like a bull	
Adaptability	Walks on water consistently	Walks on water in emergencies	Washes with water	Drinks water	Passes water in emergencies	
Communication	Talks with God	Talks with the angels	Talks to himself	Argues with himself	Loses those arguments	
Career Potential	Belongs in general management	Belongs in executive ranks	Belongs in rank and file	Belongs behind a broom	Belongs with competitor	
Planning	Too bright to worry	Worries about future	Worries about present	Worries about past	Too dumb to worry	

Source: Anonymous

appraisal process should be a continuous one; that is, it should become part of the day-to-day interaction between managers and subordinates, rather than imposed on subordinates once or twice a year.

Aside from the tendency to judge subordinates, there are a number of other pitfalls managers need to avoid in order to make their formal and informal appraisal programs effective:

1 *Shifting standards.* Some managers rate each subordinate by different standards and expectations. A low-performing but motivated employee, for example, might be rated higher than a top-performing but seemingly indifferent employee. To be effective, the appraisal method must be perceived by subordinates as based on uniform, fair standards.

2 *Rater bias.* Some managers allow their personal biases to distort the ratings they give subordinates. These biases may be gross prejudices regarding not only sex, color, race, or religion but also other personal characteristics such as age, style of clothing, or political viewpoint. An increasing number of organizations try to deal with this problem by requiring documentation or explanations for rating reports.

3 *Different rater patterns.* Managers (like teachers) differ in their rating style. Some managers rate harshly, others rate easily. The lack of uniform rating standards is unfair to employees, who will become confused about where they stand; it is also unfair to the organization, since it will become difficult to decide which employees should be rewarded. Differences in rater patterns can be avoided through precise definitions of each item on the rating form.

4 *The halo effect.* There is a common tendency, known as the halo effect, to rate subordinates high or low on all performance measures based on one of their characteristics. For example, an employee who works late constantly might be rated high on productivity and quality of output as well as on motivation. Similarly, an attractive or popular employee might be given a high overall rating. Rating employees separately on each of a number of performance measures and encouraging raters to guard against the halo effect are two ways the halo effect can be reduced.

PROMOTIONS, TRANSFERS, DEMOTIONS, AND SEPARATIONS

Promotions Because the possibility of advancement serves as a major incentive for superior managerial performance, it is extremely important that promotions be regarded as fair—that is, based on merit and untainted by favoritism. Promotions are the most significant way to recognize superior performance; however, no manager should be promoted to a position in which his or her strengths cannot be applied. For example, a district manager who functions best in a post that requires independent judgment and quick decision making might be out of place in a higher-level staff post where final decisions would be the line manager's responsibility.

Even when promotions are fair and appropriate, they can still create a number of problems. One major problem is that organization members bypassed for promotion frequently feel resentful, which causes their morale and productivity to drop. Many organizations compound this resentment by turning the promotion process into a top-secret affair, thereby creating unrealistic expectations among all the lower-level members of the subunit. Making it clearer who the favored candidate is (if seniority is not a giveaway) and explaining the promotion once it is made will help subordinates accept the authority of the newly promoted manager.[26]

Another major problem in promotions is discrimination. Most people accept the need or at least the legal obligation to avoid racial, sex, or age discrimination in the hiring process. However, less attention has been paid to discrimination against women, the aged, and minority groups in promotion decisions. Despite laws such as the Civil Rights Act of 1964, which prohibits racial, sex, or religious discrimination, and the Age Discrimination Employment Act, which prohibits discrimination against the aged in employment opportunities, women and minority groups are still underrepresented in upper-level management positions, and older employees are sometimes passed over for promotion because of their age. *Affirmative action* programs, which seek to ensure that members of groups that have been discriminated against are groomed for advancement, have become more widespread. They are one means of overcoming the effects of past discrimination.

Transfers

Transfers serve a number of purposes. One purpose, which we have already mentioned, is to give people broader job experiences as part of their development. More often, transfers are used simply to move people to a high-priority position from one with a lower priority so as to meet organizational objectives more efficiently.

Transfers are also used when separation would not be fair or desirable. For example, if an individual is doing a good job in one position but is not considered promotable, he or she may be blocking the progress of lower-level managers. In a large firm, such an individual might be transferred to a job outside the major channels of promotion. Similarly, many middle managers "peak out" simply because there is no room for all of them at the top. Such managers may be shifted to other positions to keep their job motivation and interest high. Finally, inadequately performing employees may be transferred to other jobs simply because a higher-level manager is reluctant to demote or separate them.

Demotions and Separations

If a manager proves ineffective in a given position, that manager may be transferred, asked to go for retraining or further development, or fired.[27] The transfer may be a demotion, a shift to another same-level position, or even a promotion to a position with a more impressive title but with less responsibility.

---

[26] See George Strauss and Leonard R. Sayles, *Personnel,* 3rd ed. (Englewood Cliffs, N.J.: Prentice-Hall, 1972).

[27] See Frank Bird, "The Displaced Executive, or the Man on the Shelf," *MSU Business Topics* (Summer 1966).

Demotion is an infrequently used option, since in most cases the demoted manager and his or her former peers and subordinates find their continuing relationships difficult to handle.

Where demotion or other transfer is not feasible, it is usually better to separate than to let the poor performer stay on the job. It is helpful to keep in mind that poor performance does not necessarily mean incompetence. The corporate environment, the personality of the poor performer's superior, the lack of further advancement opportunities, the conviction that one has been treated unfairly can all contribute to lackluster performance. A surprising number of times, a man or woman dismissed from one firm becomes a solid success in another. Thus, no matter how agonizing separation decisions may be, the logic of human resource planning and management development frequently requires that they be made. When handled properly, separation can work out in the best interests of the individual who may reach his or her full potential in a different environment, as well as ensuring more effective management for the organization.

Summary   The *staffing process* includes (1) human resource planning, (2) recruitment, (3) selection, (4) induction and orientation, (5) training and development, (6) performance appraisal, (7) transfer, promotion, and demotion, and (8) separation.

Human resource planning includes planning for the future personnel needs of the organization, planning what the future balance of the organization's personnel will be, planning a recruitment-selection or layoff program, and planning a development program. Human resource plans will be based on *forecasting* and the *human resource audit*, in which the performance of each individual in the organization is appraised. To be meaningful, human resource plans have to take into consideration the strategic plan and the external environment of the organization.

General and specialized *recruitment* are designed to supply the organization with a sufficiently large pool of job candidates. Job recruits can be drawn from within or outside the organization. However, before recruitment can take place, a *job analysis*, consisting of the position description and job specification, must be made.

The *selection process* follows a seven-step procedure: completed job application, initial screening interview, testing, background investigation, in-depth selection interview, physical examination, and job offer. For managerial positions, the in-depth interview is probably the most important step. Ideally, it should be realistic and factually based. *Assessment centers* may also be used to select managers.

Induction and orientation help the new employee and the organization accommodate to each other. Giving new employees challenging responsibilities has been shown to correlate with future success.

Training teaches technical skills, while *development* is designed to improve a manager's technical, human, and conceptual skills. The need for training may be determined through performance appraisal, job requirements, organizational analysis, and employee surveys. Both training and development methods can be classified as on-the-job or off-the-job. *Coaching* is the most important on-the-job development method. Other development methods include job rotation, classroom teaching, and sensitivity training. Both training and development should be reinforced in the work situation.

Performance appraisal may be informal or systematic. To improve performance, appraisal should be based on goals mutually set by managers and subordinates. Problems of appraisal include shifting standards, rater bias, different rater patterns, and the halo effect.

To be useful as employee incentives, *promotions* must be fair. Discrimination in promotion, though illegal, has still not disappeared.

Transfers are used to broaden a manager's experience, to fill a high-priority position, and to relocate employees whom the organization cannot demote, promote, or fire. *Demotions* are an infrequently used option in dealing with ineffective managers. *Separations,* though painful, are more widely used and can sometimes prove beneficial to the individual as well as to the organization.

Review Questions

1. Do you agree with the statement that if the staffing of managers is performed, properly, then the staffing of operative employees will be performed properly also? Why or why not?

2. What are the steps in the staffing process? Are managers likely to be engaged in more than one step at the same time? Why or why not?

3. Why is human resource planning necessary? What are the objectives of such planning? What factors must managers of a human resource planning program consider? How do forecasting and the human resource audit aid the human resource planning process?

4. What is a job analysis?

5. What methods of recruitment can managers use? What are the advantages and disadvantages of recruitment from within?

6. What is the seven-step standard hiring sequence? Is this sequence the same under all conditions? Why or why not?

7. What are the defects of in-depth interviews? How can these defects be minimized?

8. What is an assessment center? What are some typical assessment center exercises?

9. What information are induction and orientation designed to provide?

10. How may new employees' work assignments affect their eventual success with the organization?

11. What is the difference between training and development?

12. How may managers determine the training needs of individuals in their organization? What training approaches and methods can managers use?

13. What is a needs analysis and when is it used?

14. What development approaches and methods can managers use? Which method is most effective?

15. Under what conditions can T-groups be used effectively?

16. How may the on-the-job environment affect the success or failure of a development program? What mistakes do organizations need to avoid in order to make their development programs useful?

17. What are the differences between systematic and informal appraisal? What are the four basic appraisal approaches? How may formal appraisal be made more effective in leading to improved performance? What appraisal pitfalls do managers need to avoid?

18. What are the problems associated with promotions? How may these problems be overcome?

19. When are transfers used in organizations?

CASE STUDY: QUINTESSENTIAL KELLY

Andrew Kelly has been employed by the Wearever Tire and Rubber Company for more than twenty-five years. Kelly is, despite his long service, only 43 years of age. He began employment in the mail room right after high school, received several promotions, and was, at the age of 21, transferred to the credit department. Kelly has been there ever since and is now the senior employee in a department of sixty people.

Kelly is the quintessential "valuable employee." His loyalty to the company has never wavered or been questioned. His attendance and punctuality records are virtually without blemish. He is a consistent worker, though "no genius," and has efficient work habits that only years of service bring to a man of his sort. Kelly is friendly but not gregarious. He makes no waves, and when he sees a problem, he takes care of it without comment. Kelly was often portrayed by his supervisors and colleagues as a "good soldier."

Robert Bennington, who had been credit manager for twenty-six years, has announced his retirement. Management is now faced with the problem of selecting his replacement. This is no easy task since Bennington and Kelly have been good friends for many years. The retiring manager has, as would be expected, recommended that his friend Kelly replace him. Top management, however, long ago pegged Kelly as "not good management material." While the people who originally rated Kelly have long since retired, the present management simply believes Kelly is not aggressive enough to be the effective leader of fifty-nine other workers.

Moreover, a younger man with five years of experience in credit has caught management's eye. Mike Fitzmaurice is 30 years old and "looks like management material." Too, he outclasses Kelly in education with an accounting degree from a prominent school of business, along with some additional work toward an MBA. From the start, Fitzmaurice has been a Wearever "junior executive" in the company's training program. He appears to make up for his limited experience with drive and originality. People at Wearever seem to think he can "go far."

Top management would like to promote Fitzmaurice to the position of credit manager but fears that the senior employee, Kelly, might be so offended that his effectiveness as a hard-working employee would be diminished. There is also the element of management's appearing ungrateful for Kelly's years of service. Other employees might come to believe that service counts for nothing. Wearever, like many other large firms, has rewarded worker longevity with a package of benefits, incentives, and often promotions.

The retirement of the credit manager has forced the issue. Wearever must now decide on either old reliable Kelly, or the bright newcomer Fitzmaurice.

Case Questions
1. Should the company promote Kelly on the basis of seniority and reliability? What are the risks if it does? What are the risks if it doesn't?
2. What alternatives exist beyond the simple Kelly-or-Fitzmaurice choice?

Case reproduced with permission from Bernard A. Deitzer and Karl A. Shilliff, *Contemporary Management Incidents* (Columbus, Ohio: Grid, Inc., 1977), pp. 72–73.

Chapter 20

Organizational Careers and Individual Development

Upon completing this chapter you should be able to:

1. Describe early career experiences and dilemmas that can influence your adjustment to an organization and your later career success.

2. State some causes of stress in organizations and how stress can be managed.

3. Explain the relationship between the life cycle and the way in which careers evolve over time.

4. Describe how an individual's position within the organization can change over time.

5. Explain what is meant by a "career plateau."

6. Summarize the career management activities and career tactics that are available to you.

In recent years there has been a growing interest in the study of managerial careers and in helping individuals understand how their careers will evolve over time. It has gradually become apparent that there are certain events and problems that recur at particular times over the course of a person's career—for example, when a person decides which organization to join, when a person starts work, when a person changes jobs, and so on. Because these recurring problems and events are somewhat predictable, it is possible for individuals to prepare for them beforehand. Thus, individuals who are knowledgeable about what they can expect may be in a better position than others to take an active role in managing their own careers.

In this chapter we will focus on how individuals can manage their own careers within organizations. Unlike the other chapters of this book (particularly Chapter 19), this chapter will not be concerned with how individuals manage other people's careers or the organization's resources. The emphasis will be on the *reader's* future development as a manager. We will describe the role of early organizational experiences on the individual's future performance and satisfaction; the early career dilemmas a young manager is likely to encounter; the career stages the individual is likely to pass through as his or her career evolves; and, finally, how individuals can take an active role in managing their careers so that they can achieve their career goals more completely.

EARLY ORGANIZATIONAL CAREER EXPERIENCES

The Formation of Expectations

Many young people are very disappointed in the first weeks or months on a new job. Some of the difficulties and surprises awaiting young people when they first enter an organization originate from the unrealistic expectations they acquired in the recruiting process. (See Chapter 19.) Recruiters and interviewers inflate the attractiveness of the job so as to secure a sufficient number of candidates to choose from. Applicants overstate their abilities and understate their needs to improve their chances of getting the job. Thus, each side offers a mixed bag of truths, half truths, and concealments—all likely to create problems when those hired begin to work. The new employees soon learn that the initial job is not as challenging as they had expected, that their treatment will not be so special after all, and that their ability to affect the organization is nowhere near what they had been led to believe.

The problem of inflated expectations can exist for anyone, but it may be especially severe for those young MBAs who have done particularly well in their studies and/or have graduated from prestigious business schools. They have become accustomed in graduate school to think of "the big picture," to fast, regular (and usually favorable) feedback on their performance, and to the challenging atmosphere of the university, and they expect to find the same conditions on their new job. More often than not, they perceive themselves as just additional cogs in a wheel—their skills and abilities unused and unsought.[1]

[1] See Lyman W. Porter, Edward E. Lawler III, and J. Richard Hackman, *Behavior in Organizations* (New York: McGraw-Hill, 1975), pp. 131–136, 172–178.

When the individual's expectations are inconsistent with the realities of the new job, the likelihood of the individual developing an effective and satisfying work role in the organization is considerably reduced. Edgar Schein found that almost 75 percent of one sample of MBA graduates had changed jobs at least once over a five-year period.[2] He also found that within five years most companies lose over half of the college graduates they hire. Schein attributes this high turnover to the clash between the graduates' expectations and the realities of the organization. Similarly, in their study of a small group of American business school graduates working in South America, John D. Aram and James A. F. Stoner found that job continuation and satisfaction were related to how closely the graduates' initial expectations matched the realities of their jobs.[3]

The Reality Shock Syndrome. Apparently, for many individuals, the disparity between initial job expectations and the hard realities of the job can be unpleasant and disconcerting. This clash between high expectations and frustrating on-the-job experiences has been characterized by Douglas T. Hall as "reality shock."[4] Hall suggests that reality shock produces a *syndrome of unused potential* in new job recruits. Six factors contribute to this reality shock syndrome, according to Hall:

1 Low initial challenge
2 Low self-actualization satisfaction
3 Lack of performance appraisal
4 Unrealistically high aspirations
5 Inability to create challenge
6 Threats to superiors

Low initial challenge. Recruiters often overstate the promise and challenge of the first job in order to attract the most promising candidates. Most organizations, however, start new employees on comparatively easy projects and only gradually increase the difficulty of the projects as the recruits gain training and experience. Thus, the new employees' expectations of early job challenge are not fulfilled.

Low self-actualization satisfaction. The recruiter promises growth and self-fulfillment on the job; more often than not, however, the organization rewards conformity to its customs and ways of doing things. Those recruits who desire more independence may therefore remain with the organization only a short time.

[2] Edgar H. Schein, "The First Job Dilemma," *Psychology Today,* March 1968, pp. 22–37.

[3] John D. Aram and James A. F. Stoner, "Development of an Organizational Change Role," *Journal of Applied Behavioral Science,* Vol. 8, No. 4 (1972), pp. 438–449. See also John Paul Kotter, "The Psychological Contract: Managing the Joining-Up Process," *California Management Review,* Vol. 15, No. 3 (Spring 1973), pp. 91–99, and James A. F. Stoner, John D. Aram, and Irwin M. Rubin, "Factors Associated with Effective Performance in Overseas Work Assignments," *Personnel Psychology,* Vol. 25 (1972), pp. 303–318.

[4] Douglas T. Hall, *Careers in Organizations* (Pacific Palisades, Calif.: Goodyear, 1976).

Lack of performance appraisal. Most organizations promise their new recruits that they will be given regular feedback on their performance. Most managers favor such feedback and believe that performance appraisal is necessary to motivate and train new employees. However, many managers, if not most, perform the appraisal task poorly with new employees or neglect it entirely. Young recruits are left in a state of confusion about how well they are doing and what they need to do to improve.

Unrealistically high aspirations. New college graduates and MBAs begin work eager to apply the modern skills and techniques they have been taught. Many such graduates believe that they already have the ability to perform at managerial levels well above their entry position. In fact, these recruits are generally unskilled in the practical application of the techniques they have learned in school, and their high aspirations and "classroom theories" are often resented by others in the organization. For example, no superior likes being made to feel that a skill he or she has been using is outdated. The fact that others do not rate them quite as highly as they rate themselves comes as a rude awakening to many young employees.

Inability to create challenge. Even though the first jobs young recruits are given are not challenging, they can often create challenge on their own — by doing the job in a new and better way, for example, or by having their superiors give them more to do. However, recent graduates are accustomed to having challenging assignments presented to them; they have little or no experience in creating challenge on their own. They may therefore accept a boring and dull assignment rather passively and neglect to take a more active role in defining their jobs.

Threats to superiors. As we have already suggested, a newcomer fresh out of college or graduate school may bring more technical expertise to a job than his or her superior possesses. In addition, the newcomer may be entering the organization at a salary that is much higher than the superior's initial salary was. For these reasons, the young recruits are often regarded as threats by their superiors, and the relationship between superiors and the new employees may be somewhat strained.

A particularly powerful cause of the "reality shock syndrome" is the realization by young employees that they must conform to the organization far more than they had anticipated. Each organization attempts to "socialize" its new employees so that they will accept its values, norms, and behavior patterns. A conservative organization, for example, may have fairly strict dress codes; an aggressively managed organization may have comparatively high sales quotas; a rigidly structured organization may limit the amount of communication that can take place between departments. To get ahead in the organization, or even to fit comfortably within it, new employees soon discover they must conform to these previously established patterns. Moreover, new entrants also discover that many of their ideas and innovations are strongly resisted. Organizations are usually much slower to change than young recruits anticipate, and even good suggestions are frequently ignored. Given these realities, it is hardly surprising that so many newcomers leave their first jobs a few months or a few years after they have been hired.

The Realistic Job Preview. To create more realistic expectations and to combat the high rate of turnover caused by reality shock, some organizations are giving their applicants and new employees a realistic job preview. As we mentioned in Chapter 19, the *realistic job preview* (or interview) attempts to inform recruits about the positive *and* negative aspects of the job for which they have applied. For example, recruits might be told that they will be supervised quite closely in their first job, rather than being given a large amount of independence. Or, the recruits might be told that some aspects of their jobs will be boring. Through such job previews, organizations hope to create more realistic initial expectations on the part of their applicants and new employees.

Studies of the realistic job preview have found that such previews are associated with more realistic job expectations and decreased job turnover. Moreover, job acceptance rates do not appear to be lower for applicants exposed to unfavorable information about the job than they are for recruits exposed only to positive job information.[5]

Early Job Experiences

As we noted in Chapter 19, the individual's early job experiences appear to be particularly important in influencing his or her adjustment to the organization and subsequent career success. Two aspects of the individual's early job experiences seem especially critical: the amount of challenge in the individual's first assignment and the actions of the individual's first supervisor.

Initial Job Assignment. The importance of the initial job assignment has been affirmed by a number of research studies. One study of 1,000 recent college graduates hired by a large manufacturing company found that about half had left the company within a three-year period. Those graduates who had left the company as well as those who had remained cited the lack of job challenge as the major cause of disenchantment with the firm.[6] David E. Berlew and Douglas T. Hall followed the careers of 62 junior executives over the first five years of their employment. The researchers found that the degree of challenge the junior executives were given in their first jobs correlated closely with how successfully they performed subsequent assignments and with how their careers advanced.[7]

Berlew and Hall suggest that the successful accomplishment of challenging tasks causes individuals to internalize high performance standards. These standards are then applied to the individual's future work tasks. In addition, successful task accomplishment causes the organization's expectations for

---

[5] See, for example, John P. Wanous, "Effects of a Realistic Job Review on Job Acceptance, Job Attitudes, and Job Survival," *Journal of Applied Psychology,* Vol. 58, No. 3 (December 1973), pp. 327–337. See also J. Weitz, "Job Expectancy and Survival," *Journal of Applied Psychology,* Vol. 40, No. 4 (August 1956), pp. 245–247, and John P. Wanous, "A Job Preview Makes Recruiting More Effective," *Harvard Business Review,* September-October 1975, p. 16 ff.

[6] M. D. Dunnette, R. D. Arvey, and P. A. Banas, "Why Do They Leave?" *Personnel,* May-June 1973, pp. 25–39.

[7] David E. Berlew and Douglas T. Hall, *Some Determinants of Early Managerial Success,* Working Paper #81-64 (Cambridge, Mass.: Sloan School of Management, M.I.T., 1964).

"You're punctual, hard-working, dedicated, and loyal—what's your little game, Brickhouse?"

Marvin Tannenberg/*The Saturday Review*

individuals to increase—they will be given even more difficult and challenging assignments. Individuals who are given unchallenging jobs, on the other hand, neither internalize high standards nor receive as much recognition for their work. Yet, despite the evident importance of challenging job assignments, most organizations continue to provide their new employees with relatively routine initial assignments.

Actions of the First Supervisor. The influence of the first supervisor on a new employee's subsequent performance has also been noted by a number of researchers.[8] For the newcomer, the first supervisor embodies the virtues and defects of the organization itself. If the supervisor is found wanting by the new employee, the organization obviously will be regarded as an undesirable place

[8] See, for example, Schein, "The First Job Dilemma," and Sterling J. Livingston, "Pygmalion in Management," *Harvard Business Review*, July-August 1969, pp. 81–89.

to work. Nevertheless, despite the undeniable impact of an employee's initial supervisor, most companies entrust the handling of incoming graduates to men and women who have not been trained for the task.

Special training, patience, or insight is required by supervisors of new employees for a number of reasons. First, new employees are likely to make a higher-than-average number of mistakes; impatient supervisors may overreact to these mistakes and dampen the new employees' self-image and enthusiasm. Second, insecure supervisors often control new employees too closely—either to keep them from making mistakes or to keep them from appearing too successful or knowledgeable. The result is that the employees may never be permitted to learn from their mistakes or may never achieve the recognition they deserve.

Finally, and most importantly, the expectations of supervisors will affect the new employees' attitudes and performance, since the employees will tend to fulfill those expectations regardless of their actual ability. If, for example, the supervisor looks upon the newcomers as potentially outstanding performers, he or she will treat them accordingly, thereby motivating them to do their best—and the supervisor's expectation will tend to be confirmed. Conversely, a supervisor who expects the newcomers to be poor performers will communicate these expectations directly or indirectly to the new employees, thereby triggering the indifferent performance that fulfills his or her negative expectations. For these reasons, the role of the supervisor in acclimating new employees to the organization is a critical one.

EARLY CAREER DILEMMAS

Based on a review of the literature and on an analysis of his own interviews with hundreds of young managers, Ross A. Webber has pinpointed three classes of career problems that typically plague managers early in their working lives: political insensitivity and passivity, loyalty dilemmas, and personal anxiety.[9] Webber suggests that the newcomer who is forewarned of these problems may either sidestep them entirely or keep their potentially damaging consequences to a minimum.

Political Insensitivity and Passivity — The struggle for and exercise of power are inevitable and probably essential parts of organizational life. Managers *seek* power because with power they can more easily achieve their personal and organizational goals. Managers *exercise* power in order to influence their subordinates to perform effectively and in order to protect the integrity of their units. For example, a manager is likely to resist strongly an inappropriate attempt by another manager to tell his or her subordinates what to do. The manager may, for instance, formally complain to the offending manager. Such an exercise of power does more than

[9] Ross A. Webber, "The Three Dilemmas of Career Growth," *MBA*, Vol. 9, No. 5 (May 1975) pp. 41–48. See also Abraham Zaleznik, "Power and Politics in Organizational Life," *Harvard Business Review,* May-June 1970, pp. 47–60.

simply protect the manager's ego; it helps maintain the healthy and useful differentiation between departments and keeps any one manager from achieving disproportionate influence within the organization. (See also Chapter 11.)

The formation of political alliances is also an integral part of organizational reality. Managers who can "play politics" well—that is, who are skilled in gaining the cooperation of superiors and peers—may obtain a proportionately larger share of organizational resources than other managers. As a consequence, they may be better able to maintain the performance of their units or even to expand their operations. The formation of political alliances also enables the alliance members to focus their energies more effectively and to make decisions more efficiently. For example, managers can often solve problems quickly by enlisting the informal cooperation of a colleague, instead of laboriously going through formal channels.

Young business school graduates are frequently insensitive to the role of "office politics" when they first enter an organization. The texts, lectures, and case studies on which their education is based often create the impression that organizational problems are always solved *rationally*—that objectively sound solutions, for example, will always be greeted with praise and that merit will quickly lead to salary increases and promotions. In reality, supervisors may ignore a newcomer's suggestion because they may see it as a threat to their position. Promotions and salary increases may depend on the new employee's having a higher-level "sponsor" or on how well the employee suits a supervisor's prejudices and values, rather than simply on merit alone. In addition, the promotion may occur only after several years have passed, rather than when the new employee feels he or she is ready.

Confronted with these realities, suggests Webber, new employees frequently become passive or withdrawn. Instead of seeking to understand their surroundings, forming their own political connections, and beginning to build a power base of their own, young managers often concentrate on their own narrow specialties and permit their careers to drift. The young manager who learns to accept organizational realities as they are, says Webber, can adapt more quickly to the organization and begin to manage his or her own career.

Loyalty Dilemmas

When young employees enter the organization, they are confronted with a number of demands on their loyalty from their superior. Webber suggests that there are five common ways in which loyalty can be defined by a superior:

1 Obey me.
2 Protect me and don't make me look bad.
3 Work hard.
4 Be successful, whatever it takes.
5 Tell me the truth.

Each of these definitions of loyalty is legitimate, because a certain amount of compliance with each is necessary to keep the organization functioning. However, these loyalty demands often conflict with reality as the young subordinate perceives it; moreover, if taken to an extreme, meeting these definitions of loyalty can cause the organization harm.

Obey Me. Usually, managers have a right to expect that their legitimate directives will be carried out. Disobedience, if carried too far, will prevent the organization from reaching its objectives. However, unquestioning obedience on the part of subordinates can lead to erroneous decisions. Subordinates who know, for example, that a superior's instructions are inappropriate but who proceed to obey them out of "loyalty" are doing their superior and organization more harm than good. Sometimes, loyalty even calls for disobedience of an unethical order or an order that is made in haste or anger. To a large extent, the Watergate break-in and cover-up occurred because subordinates were excessively obedient to illegitimate, higher-level directives.

Protect Me and Don't Make Me Look Bad. Managers are responsible for and are ultimately judged by the actions of their subordinates. As such, they have a right to expect that subordinates will consider their superiors' reputation as they carry out their work activities and interact with those outside their organizational units. Sometimes, however, this loyalty demand will cause subordinates to avoid taking necessary risks in order to ensure that harm will not come to their superiors. The subordinates may also cover up their mistakes rather than bringing them out into the open where they can be handled more effectively.

Work Hard. In the eyes of many managers, the best proof of loyalty to the organization is the willingness to work long and hard. However, if working overtime and on weekends causes morale to drop and subordinates to feel fatigued, the organization's performance may decline in the long run. Subordinates who are highly effective during regular work hours may be troubled by what they see as unrealistic work expectations on the part of their superiors.

Be Successful. "Get the job done no matter what" and "I don't care what you do as long as the bottom line shows a profit" are often implicit (if not explicit) parts of some managers' instructions to their subordinates. The result is that subordinates may feel a conflict between their organizational loyalty and their own ethical codes. If they disobey instructions, their careers might suffer; if they violate their ethics (or the law), guilt or scandal might result. The overseas bribes of Lockheed and of other corporations suggest that the demand to "be successful at all costs" is not uncommon.

Tell Me the Truth. It is obviously important for superiors to be told when a failure in their units is about to occur—not only so they can take steps to deal with the problem, but also so they can prepare to deal with their own superiors. All too often, however, telling a superior about an impending failure—especially when it is the subordinate's own fault—may lead the subordinate to be blamed or punished. In such a situation, newcomers often learn to apply their loyalty selectively, putting their self-protection before the needs of their superiors or the organization. As a consequence, failures may not be reported until it is too late to minimize their consequences.

Personal Anxiety

As their assignments grow more challenging, and salary increases and promotions signal recognition of their efforts, young managers derive greater satisfaction from their jobs. Webber suggests that, paradoxically, they also begin to feel anxiety about their growing commitment to the organization. The independence and integrity they valued as students and young managers sometimes conflict with the increasing demands made on them by their jobs. The manner in which they resolve this conflict will play an important role in influencing how their careers unfold.

Edgar Schein has described three ways in which an individual can respond to the organization's efforts to enforce compliance with its values and expectations:[10]

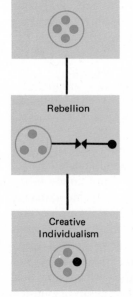

Conformity

Rebellion

Creative Individualism

1. *Conformity.* In this response, the individual completely accepts all the organization's norms and values. Total conformity represents a loss both for the individual and the organization. The individual loses his or her sense of identity and initiative, while the organization loses access to the diversity of opinion and ideas that its long-term health requires.

2. *Rebellion.* This response represents a complete rejection of the organization's values and expectations. The rebellious, extremely individualistic person either causes the organization to change or, more likely, voluntarily leaves the organization or is dismissed.

3. *Creative individualism.* In this type of response, the individual accepts the organization's important, constructive values and ignores those that are insignificant. Obviously, this response is difficult to maintain: the individual's decision about which norms are important may not be accurate, and the individual will probably suffer some criticism for violating even unimportant norms. Moreover, with each lateral transfer or promotion, new norms will come into play while others will lose their relevance. (The values of one's superior in a research department, for example, are likely to be somewhat different from those of one's superior in the sales department.) The individual will, therefore, have to make many choices about which values to accept over the course of his or her career. Nevertheless, the benefits of creative individualism are high: the individual maintains his or her integrity, independence, and personal sense of satisfaction, and the organization has access to the fresh ideas and objective viewpoints it needs.

Problems of Organizational Stress

The conflict that individuals feel between their independence and their commitment to the organization, the organizational pressures for conformity, and the day-to-day, ongoing demands of the workplace are factors that create considerable stress for many organization members—especially managers. In

[10] Edgar H. Schein, "Organizational Socialization and the Profession of Management," *Industrial Management Review*, Vol. 9, No. 2 (Winter 1968), pp. 1–16.

addition to these factors, there are various role conflicts that managers will often experience. These role conflicts, if they occur, can add considerably to managerial stress.

Daniel Katz and Robert L. Kahn suggest that an individual will experience *role conflict* when he or she is confronted with two or more incompatible demands. Katz and Kahn have identified six types of role conflict that they believe are fairly common in organizations:[11]

1. Intrasender conflict
2. Intersender conflict
3. Inter-role conflict
4. Person-role conflict
5. Role overload
6. Role ambiguity

Intrasender

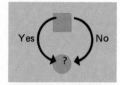

Intersender

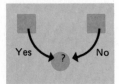

Inter-role

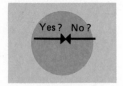

Person-Role

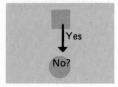

Intrasender conflict occurs when a single supervisor presents a subordinate with an incompatible set of orders or expectations. For example, a division manager orders a purchasing agent to buy materials immediately at a price that requires prior home office authorization, and then warns the agent not to violate the rulebook regulations.

Intersender conflict arises when orders or expectations from one person or group clash with the expectations or orders from other persons or groups. This can occur, for example, when a superior orders a foreman to engage in tighter supervision, while the work crew makes clear that any attempt to comply with this order will lead to serious trouble in the ranks.

Inter-role conflict occurs when the different roles played by the same person give rise to conflicting demands. In his roles as husband and father, for example, a man may be pressed to be home with his wife and family in the evening and on weekends. But in his role as loyal worker, the same man may have to put in a considerable amount of overtime to get his work done. This particular example of inter-role conflict is extremely common and often creates great tension both on the job and at home.

Person-role conflict occurs when on-the-job role requirements run counter to the individual's needs or values. An executive ordered to bribe a domestic or foreign official, for example, might find the assignment completely antithetical to his or her moral values. Yet his or her desire for career success might make refusal to carry out the order difficult.

In *role overload conflict,* the individual is confronted with orders and expectations from a number of sources that cannot be completed within the given time and quality limits. Should quality be sacrificed in the interests of time? Should some tasks be carried out and others ignored? If so, which tasks

[11] Daniel Katz and Robert L. Kahn, *The Social Psychology of Organizations* (New York: Wiley, 1966). See also Robert L. Kahn et al., *Organizational Stress: Studies in Role Conflict and Ambiguity* (New York: Wiley, 1964), and Andrew J. DuBrin, *Fundamentals of Organizational Behavior: An Applied Perspective* (New York: Pergamon Press, 1974), Chapter 4.

TABLE 20-1 Modern Methods for Coping with Stress

	Technique	Time	Benefits	Pitfalls
Transcendental Meditation	You meditate once or twice daily, using a word (mantra) or other focal point for achieving concentration. The mind is given a rest. and anxious or stressful thoughts rise to the surface and are dissipated.	Usually 20 minutes in the morning, 20 minutes in the evening. Becomes a permanent habit.	You feel relaxed, better able to face stressful situations. Work efficiency may improve.	In a few people, meditation produces fearful thoughts or anxiety attacks — or no result.
Encounter Group	Usually 10 or more people meet with a leader who encourages participation. Object is a clashing of emotions among members. In business T-groups and marriage encounter groups, you "let go," releasing feelings with little restraint.	Sessions last 1 to 2 hours, typically 4 to 6 sessions.	Helps those who can profit from a rough exchange. Teaches better coping with peers. Anxiety is freed, pretenses dropped.	If the leader is unskilled (many are), you may be shaken up, left with no solution for revealed emotional problems.
Transactional Analysis	Ten to 12 people meet with a therapist who guides them into emotional interaction. Leader explains parent-child-adult concept of TA and helps them achieve "I'm OK — you're OK" feelings about themselves and others.	Once-a-week meetings. 1 to 2 hours. Usually lasts 3 to 6 months.	Object is to practice TA concept in everyday life. Anxieties, physical stress symptoms relieved.	Too many groups are led by poorly trained people. Leader should be skilled, one who uses TA himself.
Erhard Seminars Training (est)	Groups of 250 meet in hotels. Leader follows rigid est training, often described as mind-blowing. This is a hard, seemingly cruel approach to self-awakening. It involves uncovering your hangups.	More than 70 hours crammed into two weekends.	You uncover your phoniness and false beliefs, learn to accept yourself. Some graduates have only praise for est.	Some can't cope with abrasive routine. Emotional problems uncovered may find no solution.
Biofeedback	Using electronically recorded information about your vital functions (blood pressure, heart rhythm, muscle tension), you learn to control functions and dampen stress.	One-hour sessions with therapist, weekly. Lasts 10 to 40 sessions.	You learn to eliminate stress, achieve deep relaxation. Control of ailments is uncertain.	If physical ailment calls for drug or other therapy, you may miss vital treatment.
Behavior Modification	Idea is that you can be taught to eliminate bad habits or fears by developing "normal" responses. Retraining is used to treat symptoms: fear of flying, stuttering, undue stress reactions, etc.	One-hour sessions with therapist, weekly. Lasts 20 to 30 sessions.	You get rid of the disabling fear, anxiety, or abnormality, without extensive psychotherapy.	There is no examination of causes, so some think treatment is superficial.

Source: Reprinted from the August 23, 1976 issue of *Business Week* by special permission. © 1976 by McGraw-Hill, Inc.

Role Overload

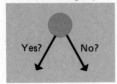

Role Ambiguity

should get priority? Dilemmas like these are a constant part of the manager's job.

Role ambiguity occurs when the individual is provided with insufficient or unclear information about his or her responsibilities. The individual is therefore uncertain about what he or she is "supposed" to do. Role ambiguity is often experienced by new managers who are given a set of duties and responsibilities without being told exactly how to carry them out. The stress experienced by the individual in such a situation can be considerable.

Because stressful situations are generally threatening ones, they give rise to what has been called the "fight or flight" response. That is, the organism experiencing stress prepares itself for running or fighting with an increase of adrenaline, faster breathing to increase the oxygen supply, a quickened heartbeat to pump more blood through the system, and so on. A moderate amount of stress may improve performance; for example, the nervous tension that students feel before an important exam may have a helpful, energizing effect. But the physiological overactivity that accompanies repeated bouts of sustained stress can leave the individual vulnerable to hypertension, headaches, ulcers, high blood pressure, heart disease, and other serious illnesses. Air traffic controllers, for instance, who work under the constant strain of life-and-death responsibility, suffer heavily from stress-induced diseases. Similarly, hard-driving, competitive, and impatient executives have been identified by some cardiologists as being especially prone to heart attacks.[12]

Because the physical and emotional damage caused by stress accumulates over time, the need to manage the strains of managerial work begins early in one's career. Specific, work-related stresses often can be dealt with by taking appropriate preventive measures. For example, new employees can obtain as much information as possible about their jobs so that they will not experience excessive role ambiguity as their careers progress. Similarly, the individual can become knowledgeable about the organization's power structure so that in a role overload situation he or she can make better decisions about whose orders can be temporarily ignored.

For the generalized stresses of a manager's job, there are a number of techniques that have recently become widely available. These are listed in Table 20-1 on the previous page.[13]

CAREERS OVER TIME

In this section we will try to help readers look ahead to future events in their careers. This task may be somewhat difficult, since ideas like the "mid-life crisis" or career "plateauing" will seem to have only limited meaning to young undergraduates. Nevertheless, for two major reasons it will be useful to the

[12] See Ogden Tanner, *Stress* (New York: Time-Life Books, 1976), and Meyer Friedman and Ray Rosenman, *Type A Behavior and Your Heart* (New York: Knopf, 1974).

[13] See also Herbert Benson, "Your Innate Asset for Combating Stress," *Harvard Business Review,* July-August 1974, pp. 49–60.

reader to understand how careers change over time. First, the career events we will describe are likely to be faced eventually by the reader, who will be better able to manage these events if he or she has some understanding of what is happening. Second, these events will be occurring to the reader's parents, boss, and older co-workers. If the reader is to deal with these individuals effectively, he or she must have insight into what these people are experiencing.[14]

Careers and the Life Cycle

There are a number of ways of looking at careers and the relationship between careers and the life cycle. Many theorists base their analysis of career events on psychologist Erik Erikson's famous theory of life stages.[15] Erikson has divided the individual's life into eight stages, four in childhood and four in adulthood. In each stage, the individual must successfully complete a "developmental task" before he or she can go on to the next stage.

Erikson's four adult stages are adolescence, young adulthood, adulthood, and maturity. (The childhood stages are not important for our discussion.) In the *adolescence* stage, the individual's developmental task is to achieve an ego identity. The individual tries to reconcile the differences between his or her self-perception and how he or she is perceived by others. Also, the individual attempts to select an occupation in which his or her skills and interests can be utilized. In the *young adulthood* stage, the individual attempts to develop satisfactory relationships or intimacy with others. This intimacy may involve a mate, a work group, or members of a common cause. In the *adulthood* stage, the individual is concerned with what Erikson calls generativity—the guiding of the next generation. For example, the person passes on his or her knowledge and values to children or students, or sponsors younger colleagues in the workplace. Finally, in the *maturity* stage, the person attempts to achieve ego integrity—the feeling that life has been satisfying and meaningful.[16]

The Levinson Model

A particularly interesting perspective on the evolution of careers is provided by Daniel Levinson and his colleagues.[17] In the Levinson model, adult life involves a series of crises that occur in a fairly predictable sequence every seven to ten years. We will describe these crisis stages and their career implications here. (See Figure 20-1 on next page.)

Age 16–22: Pulling Up Roots. In this period, the individual must successfully manage to break away from family ties and become his or her own person.

---

[14] Much of our discussion will be based on Hall, *Careers in Organizations,* pp. 47–64.

[15] See Erik H. Erikson, *Childhood and Society,* 2nd ed. (New York: Norton, 1963), pp. 247–274.

[16] Donald Super and his colleagues have divided vocational life into five stages; *growth* (birth–14), *exploration* (15–24), *establishment* (25–44), *maintenance* (45–64), and *decline* (65+). See Donald E. Super et al., *Vocational Development: A Framework for Research* (New York: Teachers College Press, 1957).

[17] Daniel J. Levinson et al., "The Psychological Development of Men in Early Adulthood and the Mid-Life Transition," in D. F. Hicks, A. Thomas, and M. Roff, eds., *Life History Research in Psychopathology,* Vol. 3 (Minneapolis: University of Minneapolis Press, 1974). See also Robert F. Pearse and B. Purdy Pelzer, *Self-Directed Change for the Mid-Career Manager* (New York: American Management Associations, 1975), and Gail Sheehy, *Passages* (New York: Dutton, 1976).

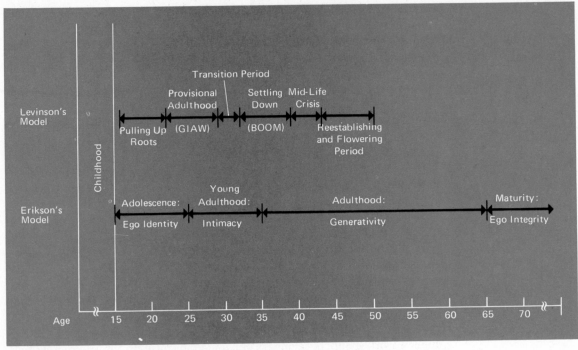

FIGURE 20-1   Careers and the Life Cycle

Individuals in this stage may still be at least partially dependent financially and emotionally on their parents. Those who gradually assert their independence can embark on their careers with some measure of self-sufficiency and confidence. Those who prolong parental ties, according to Levinson, often underperform in their careers.

Age 22–29: Provisional Adulthood. The individual in this stage has completed his or her education and begins to make commitments for the future. A lifestyle and career are selected. The individual becomes preoccupied, in Levinson's terms, with "Getting Into the Adult World" (GIAW). For those who are uncertain about the course they wish to follow, these years may be characterized by a dogged search for satisfactory career goals.

Age 29–32: The Transition Period. Sometime during this period the individual reviews his or her progress toward previously established personal and career goals. If progress has been satisfactory, the individual may continue on the same track. If not, radical changes and turmoil may result. Moves to a new geographic location, job or career changes, or divorces are comparatively common during this stage. Even seemingly successful individuals may feel that they have only one last chance to "break out" of their established pattern and to do what they really want to do with their lives.

Age 32–39: Settling Down. In these years, everything else is subordinated to job and career advancement. As Levinson puts it, the individual strives toward

"Becoming One's Own Man" (BOOM). Social contacts and friendships are cut or minimized to enable the individual to concentrate on gaining mastery of the job and on getting ahead. In place of friends, a young manager may seek a "sponsor" in the company who will help steer him or her toward the top. Those individuals who are uncomfortable with authority figures may have a particularly difficult time searching for and relating to a higher-level sponsor.

Age 39–43: The Potential "Mid-Life Crisis" Period. These years represent a second transitional period in which the manager again reviews his or her career progress. The manager who is satisfied with the way in which his or her career has developed will continue to work effectively. In fact, a certain pride in one's achievements and experience will begin to develop. But if his or her progress has not lived up to early dreams and expectations, the manager may experience a "mid-life crisis." Feelings of resentment, sadness, or frustration may cause the manager to lose his or her emotional equilibrium. The crisis may manifest itself in excessive drinking, in quitting the job and possibly wrecking one's managerial career, in flaunting a "middle-aged hippie" life-style, or in some other spectacular break with past behavior.

Age 43–50: The Reestablishing and Flowering Period. In this stage, the manager experiences a sense of contentment over past achievements. While career interest is still high, the manager becomes more open to other satisfactions that life can offer. Having reached a career pinnacle, the manager can relax his or her competitive drives, renew old social ties or develop new ones, and pay more attention to hitherto neglected family relationships. The major problem for the manager at this life stage involves relearning how to have relaxed, friendly relationships with others.

Careers within Organizations

Edgar Schein has offered a somewhat unique perspective on careers.[18] He emphasizes not only how the individual's behavior changes over the course of his or her career but also how the individual's positions and relationships within the organization can change over time. Schein focuses particularly on how the individual's movement through the various parts of the organization will affect his or her actions and the way in which he or she is perceived by the organization.

According to Schein, the organization can be viewed more usefully as a three-dimensional cone, rather than only as the traditional hierarchical triangle. (See Figure 20-2 on next page.) The three dimensions of the cone represent the different ways an individual can move through the various parts of the organization. *Vertical* movement up and down the organization represents hierarchical changes in one's formal rank or management level. *Radial* movement represents movement toward or away from the organization's "central core" or "inner circle" of power. *Circumferential* movement represents a transfer to a different division, function, or department.

[18] Edgar H. Schein, "The Individual, the Organization, and the Career: A Conceptual Scheme," *Journal of Applied Behavioral Science*, Vol. 7, No. 4 (1971), pp. 401–426.

FIGURE 20-2
A Three-
Dimensional
Model of an
Organization

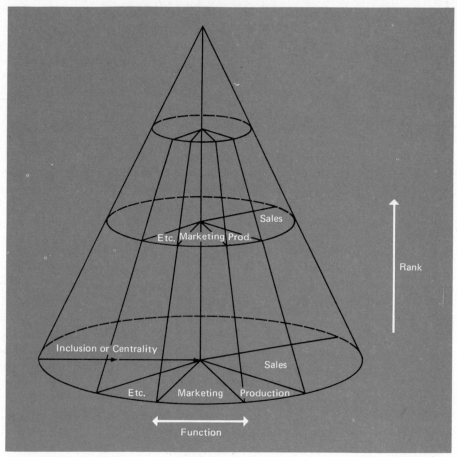

Source: Edgar H. Schein, "The Individual, the Organization, and the Career: A Conceptual Scheme," *Journal of Applied Behavioral Science,* Vol. 7, No. 4 (1971), p. 404. Copyright 1971 NTL Institute for Applied Behavioral Science. Reproduced by special permission.

Each of these types of movements, suggests Schein, involves passage through appropriate boundaries. *Hierarchical* boundaries separate one management level from another; *inclusion* boundaries separate groups closer to the center of power from those farther away; and *circumferential* boundaries separate one division or department from another. A central concept in this model is that for individuals to be permitted to cross these boundaries, they must first be accepted by the members of the group they are trying to join.

Schein suggests that different individuals within the organization might move through the organization in one or all of the three possible ways. An outstanding scientist, for example, might be promoted to ever higher levels (to keep him or her from leaving for a better job) without ever coming an inch closer to the core of administrative power. Conversely, a foreman of long standing who has moved radially toward the center of power by building good relationships with the production manager and other important managers may wield more influence within the organization than the higher-ranking scientist.

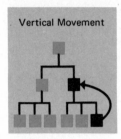

Vertical Movement

Radial Movement

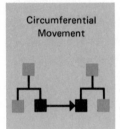

Circumferential Movement

Those destined for the upper levels of management may first move across a number of functional boundaries (such as production, sales, and finance) to acquire a generalist's background before they are promoted to a higher rank and allowed greater influence. Continued circumferential movement, without an upward passage through the boundaries of rank, may be the mark of an individual who is needed by the organization but who is not considered suitable for promotion.

To Schein, a person's career within the organization involves a series of passages or steps from one position in the "cone" to another. With each passage, the organization will attempt to influence the individual, and the individual will attempt to influence the organization in return. If, for example, the individual moves vertically or radially, the members of the individual's new department or power alliance will attempt to *socialize* the individual to their way of doing things. Acquiring the proper values and attitudes is considered an important part of a move to a higher level or a more powerful position. If the individual moves circumferentially, members of the new division or department will emphasize the *training* of the individual. Such a move requires that the individual be taught new skills more than new attitudes and values. Successful socialization or training will cause the individual to become accepted, and prepares the way for the individual to move on to the next position. (See Table 20-2 on next page.)

The individual's attempt to influence the organization is termed *innovation* by Schein. Innovation, Schein believes, will most likely occur when the individual is in the middle of a given stage of a career, rather than when the individual has just entered or is about to leave that stage. New arrivals, obviously, have still not become fully accepted; they therefore are comparatively powerless to induce change. People who are about to move to another position have "lame duck" status and therefore have less influence. At the middle of the stage, the individual is fully involved in his or her present job and therefore can recommend changes with some confidence and authority.

Schein also suggests that socialization (or training) and innovation continue throughout the person's career. He believes, however, that socialization is more prevalent during the early career stages, when the individual has not yet been fully acclimated to the organization. Innovation, the ability to influence the organization, is more prevalent at the later stages of the individual's career, when he or she has more experience and status.

The Career Plateau

The *career plateau* may be defined as "the point in a career where the likelihood of additional hierarchical promotion is very low."[19] The term has a negative connotation, because it seems to imply that the individual is no longer promot-

---

[19] Thomas P. Ference, James A. F. Stoner, and E. Kirby Warren, "Managing the Career Plateau," *Academy of Management Review,* Vol. 2, No. 4 (October 1977). Our discussion will be based on this source, on James A. F. Stoner, Thomas P. Ference, E. Kirby Warren, and H. K. Christensen, *Patterns and Plateaus in Managerial Careers—An Exploratory Study,* Research Paper No. 66 (New York: Columbia University, Graduate School of Business, 1974), and on E. Kirby Warren, Thomas P. Ference, and James A. F. Stoner, "Case of the Plateaued Performer," *Harvard Business Review,* January-February 1975, pp. 30–38 ff.

TABLE 20-2 Basic Stages, Positions, and Processes Involved in a Career

Basic Stages and Transitions	Statuses or Positions	Psychological and Organizational Processes: Transactions between Individual and Organization
1. Pre-entry	Aspirant, applicant, rushee	Preparation, education, anticipatory socialization
Entry (transition)	Entrant, postulant, recruit	Recruitment, rushing, testing, screening, selection, acceptance ("hiring"); passage through external inclusion boundary; rites of entry; induction and orientation
2. Basic training, novitiate	Trainee, novice, pledge	Training, indoctrination, socialization, testing of the person by the organization, tentative acceptance into group
Initiation, first vows (transition)	Initiate, graduate	Passage through first inner inclusion boundary, acceptance as member and conferring of organizational status, rite of passage and acceptance
3. First regular assignment	New member	First testing by the person of his or her own capacity to function; granting of real responsibility (playing for keeps); passage through functional boundary with assignment to specific job or department
Substages a. Learning the job b. Maximum performance c. Becoming obsolete d. Learning new skills, etc.		Indoctrination and testing of person by immediate work group leading to acceptance or rejection; if accepted, further education and socialization (learning the ropes); preparation for higher status through coaching, seeking visibility, finding sponsors
Promotion or leveling off (transition)		Preparation, testing, passage through hierarchical boundary, rite of passage; may involve passage through functional boundary as well (rotation)
4. Second assignment	Legitimate member (fully accepted)	Processes under no. 3 repeat
5. Granting of tenure	Permanent member	Passage through another inner inclusion boundary
Termination and exit (transition)	Old-timer, senior citizen	Preparation for exit... rites of exit (testimonial dinners, and so on)
6. Post-exit	Alumnus, emeritus, retired	Granting of peripheral status, consultant or senior advisor

Source: Edgar H. Schein, "The Individual, the Organization, and the Career: A Conceptual Scheme," *Journal of Applied Behavioral Science,* Vol. 7, No. 4 (1971), pp. 415–416. Copyright 1971 NTL Institute for Applied Behavioral Science. Reproduced by special permission.

able because of a lack of ability or some other flaw. In fact, reaching a career plateau is a normal organizational occurrence—just about everyone plateaus. Lack of ability, lack of skill in office politics, or inaccurate assessment by a superior *may* cause an individual's career to plateau. Usually, however, individuals plateau simply because there are far more candidates for higher-level positions than there are positions available. Since job openings become progressively more scarce as one ascends the organizational hierarchy, even highly successful managers eventually reach a career plateau.

In the early and mid-1970s, organizational growth slowed but the number of management candidates increased. These events have caused more attention to be given to the career problems faced by managers and their organizations when the managers plateau. Before we discuss these problems, we should note that for the individual manager the task of adjusting to a career plateau is frequently complicated by the mid-life crisis.[20] For the organization, the way in which the ongoing plateauing process is managed is likely to have a strong influence on how well the organization functions.

Management Career States. There are two main variables that can be said to define an individual's current career state. The first variable is the organization's evaluation of how promotable the individual is. The second variable is the organization's perception of how well the individual is performing in his or her present position. Based on these variables, four basic management career states can be identified:

1 *Learners or comers.* These are individuals who are considered to have advancement potential but who are presently not performing up to par. Members of training programs and recently promoted managers who have not yet mastered their new jobs are common members of this category.

2 *Stars.* These individuals are seen as doing outstanding work and are considered to have high advancement potential. They are sometimes placed on "fast-track" career paths and usually receive the greatest exposure to management development activities.

3 *Solid citizens.* These are managers who are seen as doing good or even outstanding work but who, for one reason or another, have little if any chance for further advancement. They may constitute the largest group of managers in most organizations and accomplish most of their organization's work.

4 *Deadwood.* These individuals are seen as having little or no chance for advancement, and their current performance is seen as marginal or inadequate. In some cases they may be shunted aside to a minor, dead-end post and then forgotten, or attempts may be made to rehabilitate them so that they will become solid citizens once again.

At any given moment, it is the solid citizens and deadwood who have plateaued—the comers and stars are still on an upward track. Since the solid citizens are effective plateauees—still performing satisfactorily—it might seem

---

[20] See Harry Levinson, "On Being a Middle-Aged Manager," *Harvard Business Review,* July-August 1969, pp. 51–60.

FIGURE 20-3
A Model of
Managerial
Career States

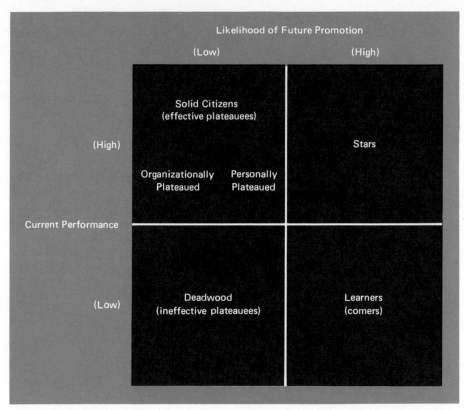

Source: Thomas P. Ference, James A. F. Stoner, and E. Kirby Warren, "Managing the Career Plateau," *Academy of Management Review,* Vol. 2, No. 4 (October 1977). Used by permission.

that the only problem for management is how to deal with the ineffective (deadwood) plateauees. And it is a fact that the latter do get more attention as candidates for rehabilitation or outright dismissal. Yet the solid citizens present management with a greater challenge than has generally been recognized. Once they realize they have reached a career plateau, the solid citizens may lose their motivation and gradually drift into the deadwood category—unless management takes steps to prevent this decline. (See Figure 20-3.)

As our discussion implies, these career states change over time. Newcomers usually enter the organization as learners. If they perform well, they move into the "star" category and become active candidates for promotion. With each promotion they temporarily move again into the "learner" category; as they master their jobs they again become "stars." As the years pass, however, increasing numbers of individuals reach their career plateau. The individuals may become plateaued for *organizational* reasons—fewer job openings exist at higher levels; younger or more qualified candidates may be sought by the organization for those higher-level jobs that are available; or the individuals may be regarded as too valuable in their present positions to be promoted. The individuals may also become plateaued for *personal* reasons—they may lack the technical or career skills needed to move to a higher position, or they may simply lack the desire for further promotion. Regardless of the reason for reaching their plateau, the individuals now become "solid citizens." They may remain effective until they retire, or until such factors as age, lack of motivation, or lack of new training causes their performance to decline.[21]

For our readers, the relevance of our discussion lies in the fact that if they become managers, they are very likely to pass through the various career states we have described until they reach their own plateau. It is important to keep in mind that solid citizens can be productive and successful for many years; for example, one can often maintain one's sense of growth and achievement by seeking new challenges or by obtaining transfers to other jobs at the same organizational level. In addition, there are options available if the plateau is unsatisfying—for instance, one can acquire additional training to become eligible again for promotion, or one can leave the organization for another that offers greater opportunity. It is also important to remember that one's bosses, co-workers, and subordinates will also be passing through the various career states. Understanding the process by which individuals become plateaued is useful in helping others deal with the experience.

INDIVIDUAL CAREER MANAGEMENT ACTIVITIES

While organizations can help individuals manage their careers,[22] career management is ultimately the individual's responsibility. Conscious career management by the individual can have many advantages: like organizations, individuals who plan for what they want to achieve are more likely to achieve their goals. They can focus their energies on the career goals they have selected, rather than drifting from job to job. In addition, they are less vulnerable to chance events and to having undesirable career decisions made for them by others. Finally, individuals who are competent in managing their own careers and who have well-thought-out goals and plans for reaching them tend to be somewhat more motivated and purposeful than others; thus, they are often more useful to their organizations and more likely to be successful within them.

Career Tactics   As we discussed earlier, many individuals are politically naive—they tend to underestimate the role that politics plays in organizational life. Thus, a very important part of developing an effective career strategy is coming to grips with the organization's political realities.

[21] See Laurence Peter and Raymond Hull, *The Peter Principle* (New York: Morrow, 1969). Peter and Hull suggest that the managerial career cycle ends when managers are promoted to their "level of incompetence": a job beyond their ability. It seems more reasonable to suggest that managers often plateau while they are still performing effectively and that even plateaued managers can still develop and grow.

[22] For example, under the guidance of Dr. Walter D. Storey, General Electric has developed career planning programs and a manual entitled *Career Action Planning,* and Arthur D. Little has developed a manual entitled *Effective Career Management.*

Alan N. Schoonmaker has suggested a number of tactics that individuals can use to advance their careers:[23]

— Do excellent work.
— Become visible.
— Present the right image.
— Avoid deadwood.
— Control resources, especially information.
— Develop good personal relationships.

To these tactics we will add three others suggested by Andrew J. DuBrin:[24]

— Be mobile.
— Help your boss succeed.
— Find a sponsor.

We will discuss all these tactics in this section.

Do Excellent Work. There can be little question that high performance and work excellence are the basic foundation of a career strategy. Great political ability by itself can sometimes cause a mediocre individual to rise above others who contribute more to their organizations; more often than not, however, such an individual will be quickly spotted as a low performer, and his or her career will not advance. As a general rule, the better your work, the greater your chances for organizational rewards. It is when you and your colleagues are performing at the same high level that your political ability can cause you to stand out.

Become Visible. In every classroom there are usually one or two students who get high grades without advertising that fact. Similarly, in organizations there are managers who contribute a great deal without anyone knowing about it. The difference is that school performance, as defined by tests and term papers, is easy to measure; organizational performance is usually much more difficult to evaluate. If you wish to be rewarded for your performance, you have to make sure your superiors are aware of it.

There are a number of ways that superiors can be informed about your actions without causing them to regard you as a braggart. These include sending memos to a superior when important projects have been completed; submitting short progress reports; and seeking evaluation and advice on one's work from the boss directly or from his or her colleagues. Making it known that you have received and rejected another job offer is, according to Schoonmaker, a particularly effective way of getting superiors to notice you.

[23] Alan N. Schoonmaker, *Executive Career Strategy* (New York: American Management Associations, 1971).
[24] DuBrin, *Fundamentals of Organizational Behavior*, pp. 147–158.

Present the Right Image. When you become visible, you want to be sure that you present the right impression. Hardworking individuals who appear slow or uncertain will often be perceived as lazy or indifferent, regardless of their actual performance. Individuals eager to "belong" to the organization but who dress in what, for the organization, appears to be an offbeat style may be regarded as nonconformists or "outsiders." Clothing, posture, tone of voice, and demeanor will play an important role in how individuals are perceived. It may seem phony and distasteful to you to try and present the "right" image. However, if you select an organization whose norms are compatible with yours, you should have to make only minor adjustments in your life-style in order to present the right impression.

Avoid Deadwood. Incompetent superiors, says Schoonmaker, can hinder your career. They may not appreciate your ability; their recommendations tend not to be taken seriously; their departments as a whole may be unfavorably regarded; and they are unlikely to be promoted, which means that at least one logical opening will not be available for you. Asking for a transfer is usually an ineffective method of leaving a department headed by an incompetent supervisor, since such a request is likely to be viewed as disloyal. A more effective method is to let another superior know that you can solve some problem plaguing his or her department; that superior may then arrange a transfer for you.

Control Resources, Especially Information. As we have already implied earlier in this chapter, knowledge is power. If you possess some information or expertise that people need, you are in a good position to bargain for favors and even advancement. If you are the organization's sole possessor of this information or expertise, you are in a particularly powerful position. Such knowledge or expertise is an effective instrument for helping others and for incurring their obligation to help you in the future.

Develop Good Personal Relationships. Ultimately, a successful political strategy depends on being able to get along with others. In organizations, these "others" do not mean only superiors but peers and subordinates as well. For example, individuals frequently create unnecessary difficulties for themselves by neglecting to form respectful, friendly relationships with their superiors' secretaries. Going over your supervisor's head to a superior, disagreements with your boss in public, personal criticisms, holding grudges, hostility, and revenge may be tempting, but they will not help your career.

Be Mobile. For those who aspire to top management, movement within the organization is highly desirable. Experience across the functional lines of an organization, for example, will help you develop the variety of skills you will need as a general manager. Experience at the different geographic locations of your organization will give you an understanding of the organization as a whole and may bring you to the attention of those at the very top. You should be aware, however, that high geographic mobility usually costs a great deal in terms of one's social and family relationships. You must strongly desire a top-level position in order to deal with the sacrifices that repeated moves require.[25]

If you are growing as much and as fast as you desire and are being appropriately recognized, then movement outside your organization is not an effective strategy. Joining another organization normally will require you to build a whole new set of alliances and relationships. On the other hand, if you are not gaining the experience and training necessary for advancement, if you have been placed in a dead-end job, or if you are not progressing as fast in responsibility and recognition as you desire, then leaving for a more challenging opportunity elsewhere is usually a better idea than waiting for things to improve where you are.

Help Your Boss Succeed. The more you help your boss — by doing good work, suggesting new approaches to problems, keeping him or her informed, and praising him or her to others — the more valuable to your boss you will be. You will then be more likely to get the approval and recommendations you need for a salary increase, promotion, or transfer to a more desirable job. In fact, becoming indispensable to an upwardly mobile boss can help you become part of an "advancement sandwich," in which your boss, you, and the subordinate that you train move up in the organization together.

Find a Sponsor. We have already mentioned the importance of having a higher-level sponsor as an organizational ally. Sometimes the sponsor will find you: the sponsor may be in a life stage in which he or she wishes to pass on knowledge to others, and if you seem to be sufficiently like the sponsor, he or she may encourage and help you. Usually, however, you will have to find a sponsor on your own. Attempting to meet as many superiors as you can (both on and off the job) will often enable you to find someone whose interests you share. Asking questions, trading information, and making yourself useful in other ways will help you to cement relations with a higher-level manager. Keep in mind that the responsibility for maintaining a relationship with a sponsor lies with you — you need the sponsor more than he or she needs you. The relationship with the sponsor must also be handled carefully, since losing a sponsor can put a crimp in your career. In addition, if the sponsor is not your boss, you have to make sure that your boss does not get the feeling you are going over his or her head or being otherwise disloyal.

Conscious Career Planning

While it can be extremely helpful to have a sponsor early in your career, it is also necessary to maintain responsibility for managing your own career. Sponsors may lose interest or retire, or you may leave for another organization; developing your own political and career skills is essential.

[25] See John F. Veiga, "The Mobile Manager at Mid-Career," *Harvard Business Review,* January-February 1973, pp. 115–119.

Schoonmaker has offered a nine-step career strategy.[26] Some of these sound rather harsh; they are, however, basically realistic. The nine steps are:

1. *Accept the fact that there are some inescapable and irreconcilable conflicts between you and your organization.* In short, what is good for the organization is not always good for you. So, being careful not to be disloyal, you must always recognize the need to look out for your own interests.

2. *Accept the fact that your superiors are essentially indifferent to your career ambitions.* Your superiors are ultimately responsible only for themselves and their units, and you should assume that they will help you only if doing so helps them achieve their own objectives. As Schoonmaker notes, the responsibility of your superiors to themselves and the organization would make any other attitude improper for them. Facing the truth that superiors will not take care of your career will free you to act in your own interests and help you avoid being manipulated by false promises and unrealistic expectations.

3. *Analyze your own goals.* Many people act to fulfill goals that they have been taught are important, rather than those that are really important to them. They therefore may spend their entire lives searching for an unattainable satisfaction. To get what you want, you first have to *know* what you want. Career management does not mean simply charting a series of promotions that end in an executive suite—it means planning to achieve *any* career goal that is meaningful to *you.*

4. *Analyze your assets and liabilities.* It is unrealistic to pursue goals that require abilities you do not have; it is foolish not to take advantage of those abilities you do have. Career goals that allow you to maximize your assets and minimize your liabilities will enable you to operate from a position of strength.

5. *Analyze your opportunities.* To reach your goals, you must first have the opportunity to reach them. Determining your opportunities requires you to make a cool-headed, systematic assessment of the types of positions that are available in your own and in other firms. Personal observations, tips from colleagues, and published information can help you analyze available opportunities.

6. *Learn the rules of company politics.* While good work is very important, it is the opinion others have about you and your work that may ultimately determine how successful you are. Developing political skill is therefore a key element of conscious career management. Noting and observing your organization's unwritten rules of politics (such as, "Get on the good side of the parts department manager—otherwise you'll never be able to keep your production schedule") is an important part of surviving in the organization and in getting ahead.

7. *Plan your career.* As we indicated earlier, a goal without a plan is little more than a daydream. Many managers select their goals without consciously determining how they are going to reach them; often, they fail to attain those goals because they drift indecisively from job to job or stay too long in one

[26] Schoonmaker, *Executive Career Strategy,* pp. 6–11.

position. Planning will enable you to make better decisions at each step of your career.

8. *Carry out your plan.* The best plan is useless if you avoid the responsibility for carrying it out. If your plan calls for you to ask for a raise, request a transfer, find another job, or turn down a job offer—do it.

9. *Chart your progress.* Very rarely does a career progress without a hitch— a sponsor may retire, the job market may change, a new colleague in the same department may prove to be a "star." Your goals are also likely to change somewhat over time—a promotion, for example, may suddenly seem less desirable if you are highly satisfied in your present job. Like organizational plans, career plans have to be revised periodically to keep up with current realities.

In fact, the entire career planning process (which includes *self-assessment*— learning what we want, what our needs and values are, what we like to do, and what we do well; *environmental assessment*—what opportunities and barriers exist inside and outside the organization; *conscious planning*—which includes the recognition that some opportunities will have to be surrendered and some goals revised; and *implementation, monitoring,* and *follow-up*) is very similar to many of the managerial activities we discuss throughout this book. Much of the purpose of managerial career planning activities is to help managers learn to apply to their own lives and careers the very skills they have developed and use in assisting and guiding their organizations.

Many books offer guidance on career planning.[27] In addition, a growing number of college and graduate schools of business offer full-credit courses in career planning and development for their management students. Graduate schools that have recently introduced such courses include the Harvard Business School, Columbia Graduate School of Business, Fordham Graduate School of Business Administration, and Northeastern University. The graduate school catalogues available by mail or in your placement office will indicate other schools where career planning courses are available.

Summary Certain events occur somewhat predictably over the course of a career. Understanding these events enables one to prepare for them and to take an active role in personal career management.

Early career experiences commonly include the formation of unrealistic expectations and "reality shock" when these expectations clash with frustrating on-the-job experiences. Low initial challenge, low self-actualization satisfaction, and lack of performance appraisal are some of the organizational factors contributing to reality shock. The realistic job preview is designed to create more realistic job expectations on the part of recruits.

Early job experiences appear to be strong influences on organizational adjustment and career success. The amount of challenge in the initial job assignment and the actions of one's first supervisor are particularly important career influences.

---

[27] Aside from Schoonmaker, see Arthur G. Kirn, *Lifework Planning,* 3rd ed. (Hartford, Conn.: Arthur G. Kirn & Assoc., 1974), and George A. Ford and Gordon L. Lippitt, *A Life Planning Workbook* (Fairfax, Va.: NTL Learning Resources Corp., 1972).

Career dilemmas that arise early in one's career include political insensitivity and passivity, loyalty dilemmas, and personal anxiety about one's growing commitment to the organization. The latter dilemma can sometimes be resolved through the use of "creative individualism," which permits the individual to accept only the most important values of the organization.

These career dilemmas as well as the daily demands of the job can cause considerable stress for managers. The feelings of stress will be accompanied by the role conflicts that managers commonly experience. Because of the physical and emotional damage that stress can cause, it is important to learn to manage stress early in one's career.

Researchers and management theorists have developed models of the career stages through which individuals must pass. Levinson and his colleagues, for example, have devised a model that describes adult life as a series of predictable crises that occur every seven to ten years. This model includes the concepts of pulling up roots; provisional adulthood; one transition period; settling down; the "mid-life crisis," which is a second transition period; and the reestablishing and flowering period.

Schein has devised a model that describes how the individual's positions within the organization can change over time. The model shows the organization as a cone in which vertical, radial, and circumferential movement can take place across different boundaries. With each movement, the individual is socialized or trained to fit into his or her new position. Schein believes individuals are most likely to be innovative at the midpoint of their tenure in a position.

Individuals reach a "career plateau" when they are no longer candidates for promotion. "Stars" and "learners" are still considered eligible for promotion; "solid citizens" and "deadwood," however, are considered to have reached their plateau. Almost everyone in an organization eventually reaches a plateau, usually because of the scarcity of positions available at the higher levels of the hierarchy.

Individual career management activities include the use of career tactics and conscious career planning. Career tactics include doing excellent work, becoming visible, and presenting the right image. Career planning, like many other types of planning, includes self-assessment, goal selection, and opportunity assessment.

Review Questions

1. Why do you think individuals develop unrealistic expectations about their first job? Why is this tendency particularly severe for business school graduates?
2. What is reality shock? What factors contribute to it?
3. What is a realistic job preview? Why are organizations using it?
4. What is the effect of the initial job assignment on organizational adjustment and career success? Why does the initial assignment have this effect?
5. How do the actions of superiors affect the satisfaction and performance of new employees?
6. What types of career dilemmas typically plague managers in their careers?
7. In what three ways can individuals respond to the organization's efforts to enforce compliance with its expectations? Which way do you think is best? Why?
8. What are the six types of role conflict identified by Katz and Kahn?
9. Why is it important to learn to manage stress early in one's career?
10. What is the Levinson model of an adult's working life?
11. According to Schein, what three types of movement are possible within organizations? What three types of organizational boundaries exist? How does the organization attempt to influence the individual who is making a position change? When can the individual most effectively influence the organization?

12. What is a "career plateau"? Why do people become plateaued? How are the four career states related to the career plateau?

13. Why is individual career planning important? What career strategies are available to individuals? Do these strategies seem harsh or unrealistic to you? Why or why not? What nine steps should be part of an individual's conscious career planning?

CASE STUDY: A TALK WITH KIRKEBY'S SON

"Did you want to see me?" Brad Kirkeby poked his head into the open doorway of his boss's office.

"Sure did, Brad. Come on in. I'll be finished with these overtime authorizations in a minute." Anthony Carboni continued initialing time cards while Kirkeby came in and sat down. Putting the cards in a neat stack to one side of his desk, Carboni looked up and smiled.

"Well, Brad, how's it going?"

"Boring as hell!"

Carboni retained his composure. He cared little for the disrespectfulness of so many young people and their total lack of tact. But Carboni had two reasons for restraint in this case. First, Brad Kirkeby was recently out of college and on an eighteen-month company rotational training program. He would be in Carboni's section for only another forty-five days. Secondly, Brad was the son of Lawrence Kirkeby, one of Lockport Aircraft's most capable designers.

"I'm sorry to hear that," replied Carboni. "What seems to be the problem?"

"I'm going out of my mind with blueprint check." Kirkeby's response was emphatic but not hostile.

"Well," said Carboni, "someone has to check blueprints."

"But why me?" replied Kirkeby. "Can't a draftsman or a clerk do it?"

"Oh, I suppose he could," said Carboni, "but this is the way we've always developed potential structure designers...by having them learn all phases of the business from the bottom up."

"No disrespect intended, Mr. Carboni, but that argument escapes me. It's like saying that if you want to be an actor, you have to have experience as a stagehand. I joined Lockport Aircraft to design airplanes, not to check blueprints."

"And so you will, Brad...eventually."

Kirkeby laughed. "Eventually...in time, Brad...wait your turn, Brad. In the long run it will all work out. Mr. Carboni, do you know what Lord Keynes, the famous British economist, said about the long run?"

"No," replied Carboni, growing less patient each moment.

"Lord Keynes said, 'In the long run we'll all be dead!' "

"Meaning?"

"Meaning that I don't want to die or retire before I'm given a meaningful job to do."

Carboni lit a small cigar and puffed several times while looking directly at Kirkeby.

"I'm trying to understand you, Brad," he replied at last. "But you are simply going

Case study from Robert D. Joyce, *Encounters in Organizational Behavior* (Elmsford, N.Y.: Pergamon Press, Ltd., 1972), pp. 151–154. Reprinted with permission of the publisher.

to have to adjust to the fact that you are out of college and in the real world now. It takes years of experience before you assume major structural design responsibility."

"That's because what they call experience in the Lockport Aircraft training program is merely a succession of routine tasks that could be done as well by a moron. Experience is learning and I'm not learning anything!"

"Look, Brad. I know you get all those aeronautical design theory courses in college and you expect to design planes your first week out of college. Face it, there's a certain amount of routine work in any job. Every day can't be a learning experience like it was in college."

"I don't see why not," replied Kirkeby. "If I was hired to eventually design planes, shouldn't I be working next to designers instead of piddling around with trivia?"

"The work in this section is hardly trivia!" Carboni was angry now but forced himself to keep from shouting. "But the work in this section is not the issue. You want to design airplanes like your father...right?"

"Right."

"Well," said Carboni, "your father has been with Lockport Aircraft for twenty-five years...eight years longer than I have. He started at the bottom and worked himself up step by step until, now, he's one of the most respected designers in the industry."

"My father is living proof of how ridiculous the system is. He had models at home when I was a boy...models he built in his spare time of wing and fuselage structures for as yet undreamed-of mach 1 and mach 1.5 power plants."

"Lawrence Kirkeby was always considered to be a very talented person," replied Carboni calmly.

Brad Kirkeby continued, "He was way ahead of his time. And what did this company have him doing for most of those years? Did they use his creative talents to design planes, or on research to advance the state of the art? No. That would have been too obvious. They made him waste nearly twenty potentially creative years on trivial assignments before he became a designer with the authority to control technical considerations."

"How naive can you be, Brad Kirkeby? Do you really believe that your father alone came upon this advanced design information and was frustrated for years by a repressive and unresponsive management?" Carboni was angry now and let it show as he continued.

"Sure your father was talented. That's how he got to be chief designer at Lockport Aircraft. But he was and is still a mortal like the rest of us. Lawrence Kirkeby made his share of mistakes along the line. It was only after years of detailing and understudy with our top designers that his own ideas began to evolve and his real talents began to show. That's when he was moved to a responsible design position."

Brad Kirkeby started to reply, but Carboni cut him off.

"That's the trouble with you kids nowadays. You want everything in life without having to pay the price for it. You tell me you're bored with your job and ought to be designing planes instead. For your information, there are at least thirty bright young men currently in the company who have already passed this apprenticeship that you consider so useless and are now on detailing and limited design activity. Do you suggest I pass them up and promote you to the head of the class, simply because you're bored with your present assignment?"

"Of course not, but..." Brad Kirkeby made an attempt to intervene.

"You're damned right I won't," shouted Carboni, answering his own question. "You've been in my section two months now and have turned in only mediocre work at best. You probably can justify that to yourself on the grounds that the work doesn't turn you on. Well, let me tell you something, Brad Kirkeby, talent is one hell of a lot more than just saying you have it. Talent is proving it in the work you do *now*...not the work you say you'll do next year or the year after! For all of your big talk about how great you are and how dull the work is, you have yet to prove to me you're anything but a phony!"

Case Questions

1. What issues are involved in this case?
2. To what extent do you agree with the basic position(s) taken by Brad Kirkeby?
3. To what extent do you agree with the basic position(s) taken by Anthony Carboni?
4. Can these two viewpoints be reconciled?
5. What is relevant job experience as you see it?

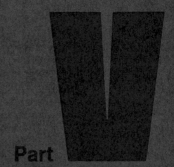

Part V

Controlling

Case on Controlling

BILL FRENCH, ACCOUNTANT

Bill French picked up the phone and called his boss, Wes Davidson, controller of Duo-Products Corporation. "Say, Wes, I'm all set for the meeting this afternoon. I've put together a set of break-even statements that should really make the boys sit up and take notice—and I think they'll be able to understand them, too." After a brief conversation about other matters, the call was concluded and French turned to his charts for one last checkout before the meeting.

French had been hired six months earlier as a staff accountant. He was directly responsible to Davidson and, up to the time of this case, had been doing routine types of analysis work. French was an alumnus of a liberal arts undergraduate school and graduate business school, and was considered by his associates to be quite capable and unusually conscientious. It was this latter characteristic that had apparently caused him to "rub some of the working guys the wrong way," as one of his co-workers put it. French was well aware of his capabilities and took advantage of every opportunity that arose to try to educate those around him. Wes Davidson's invitation for French to attend an informal manager's meeting had come as some surprise to others in the accounting group. However, when French requested permission to make a presentation of some break-even data, Davidson acquiesced. The Duo-Products Corporation had not been making use of this type of analysis in its review or planning programs.

Basically, what French had done was to determine the level of operation at which the company must operate in order to break even. As he phrased it, "The company must be able to sell at least a sufficient volume of goods so that it will cover all of the variable costs of producing and selling the goods; further, it will not make a profit unless it covers the fixed, or nonvariable, costs as well. The level of operation at which total costs (that is, variable plus nonvariable) are just covered is the break-even volume. This should be the lower limit in all of our planning."

The accounting records had provided the following information that French used in constructing his chart:

Plant Capacity—2,000,000 units
Past Year's Level of Operations—1,500,000 units
Average Unit Selling Price—$1.20
Total Fixed Costs—$520,000
Average Variable Unit Cost—$0.75

From this information, he observed that each unit contributed $0.45 to fixed overhead after covering the variable costs. Given total fixed costs of $520,000,

Case copyright © 1959 by the President and Fellows of Harvard College. Reproduced by permission.

he calculated that 1,155,556 units must be sold in order to break even. He verified this conclusion by calculating the dollar sales volume that was required to break even. Since the variable costs per unit were 62.5 percent of the selling price, French reasoned that 37.5 percent of every sales dollar was left available to cover fixed costs. Thus, fixed costs of $520,000 require sales of $1,386,667 in order to break even.

When he constructed a break-even chart to present the information graphically, his conclusions were further verified. The chart also made it clear that the firm was operating at a fair margin over the break-even requirements, and that the profits accruing (at the rate of 37.5 percent of every sales dollar over break even) increased rapidly as volume increased (see Exhibit 1).

Shortly after lunch, French and Davidson left for the meeting. Several representatives of the manufacturing departments were present, as well as the general sales manager, two assistant sales managers, the purchasing officer,

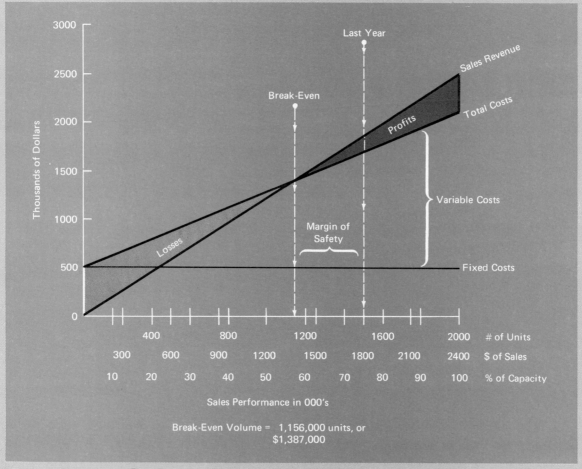

EXHIBIT 1   Duo-Products Corporation's Break-Even Chart — Total Business

559

and two men from the product engineering office. Davidson introduced French to the few men that he had not already met and then the meeting got under way. French's presentation was the last item on Davidson's agenda, and in due time the controller introduced French, explaining his interest in cost control and analysis.

French had prepared enough copies of his chart and supporting calculations so that they could be distributed to everyone at the meeting. He described carefully what he had done and explained how the chart pointed to a profitable year, dependent on meeting the volume of sales activity that had been maintained in the past. It soon became apparent that some of the participants had known in advance what French planned to discuss; they had come prepared to challenge him and soon had taken control of the meeting. The following exchange ensued (see Exhibit 3 at end of case for a checklist of participants with their titles):

Cooper: *(Production Control)* You know, Bill, I'm really concerned that you haven't allowed for our planned changes in volume next year. It seems to me that you should have allowed for the sales department's guess that we'll boost sales by 20 percent, unit-wise. We'll be pushing 90 percent of what we call capacity then. It sure seems that this would make quite a difference in your figuring.

French: That might be true, but as you can see, all you have to do is read the cost and profit relationship right off the chart for the new volume. Let's see — at a million-eight units we'd. . . .

Williams: *(Manufacturing)* Wait a minute, now!!! If you're going to talk in terms of 90 percent of capacity, and it looks like that's what it will be, you damn well better note that we'll be shelling out some more for the plant. We've already got okays on investment money that will boost your fixed costs by ten thousand dollars a month, easy. And that may not be all. We may call it 90 percent of plant capacity, but there are a lot of places where we're just full up and we can't pull things up any tighter.

Cooper: See, Bill? Fred Williams is right, but I'm not finished on this bit about volume changes. According to the information that I've got here — and it came from your office — I'm not sure that your break-even chart can really be used even if there were to be no changes next year. Looks to me like you've got average figures that don't allow for the fact that we're dealing with three basic products. Your report here [see Exhibit 2] on costs, according to product lines, for last year makes it pretty clear that the "average" is way out of line. How would the break-even point look if we took this on an individual product basis?

French: Well, I'm not sure. Seems to me that there is only one break-even point for the firm. Whether we take it product by product or in total, we've got to hit that point. I'll be glad to check for you if you want, but . . .

Bradshaw: *(Asst. Sales Mgr.)* Guess I may as well get in on this one, Bill. If you're going to do anything with individual products, you ought to know that we're looking for a big swing in our product mix. Might even start before we get into the new season. The "A" line is really losing out, and I imagine that we'll be lucky to

	Aggregate	"A"	"B"	"C"
Sales at Full Capacity (units)	2,000,000			
Actual Sales Volume (units)	1,500,000	600,000	400,000	500,000
Unit Sales Price	$1.20	$1.67	$1.50	$0.40
Total Sales Revenue	$1,800,000	$1,000,000	$600,000	$200,000
Variable Cost per Unit	$0.75	$1.25	$0.625	$0.25
Total Variable Cost	$1,125,000	$750,000	$250,000	$125,000
Fixed Costs	$ 520,000	$170,000	$275,000	$ 75,000
Net Profit	$ 155,000	$ 80,000	$ 75,000	-0-
Ratios:				
Variable Cost to Sales	.63	.75	.42	.63
Variable Income to Sales	.37	.25	.58	.37
Utilization of Capacity	75.0%	30.0%	20.0%	25.0%

EXHIBIT 2   Duo-Products Corporation's Product Class Cost Analysis (Normal Year)

hold two-thirds of the volume there next year. Wouldn't you buy that, Arnie? [*Agreement from the General Sales Manager*] That's not too bad, though, because we expect that we should pick up the 200,000 that we lose, and about a quarter million units more, over in "C" production. We don't see anything that shows much of a change in "B." That's been solid for years and shouldn't change much now.

Winetki: (*Gen. Sales Mgr.*) Bradshaw's called it about as we figure it, but there's something else here too. We've talked about our pricing on "C" enough, and now I'm really going to push our side of it. Ray's estimate of maybe half a million — four hundred fifty thousand I guess it was — up on "C" for next year is on the basis of doubling the price with no change in cost. We've been priced so low on this item that it's been a crime — we've got to raise, but good, for two reasons. First, for our reputation; the price is out of line class-wise and is completely inconsistent with our quality reputation. Second, if we don't raise the price, we'll be swamped and we can't handle it. You heard what Williams said about capacity. The way the whole "C" field is exploding, we'll have to answer to another half million units in unsatisfied orders if we don't jack that price up. We can't afford to expand that much for this product.

At this point, Hugh Fraser, administrative assistant to the president, walked up toward the front of the room from where he had been standing near the rear door. The discussion broke for a minute, and he took advantage of the lull to interject a few comments.

Fraser: This has certainly been enlightening. Looks like you fellows are pretty well up on this whole operation. As long as you're going to try to get all of the things together that you ought to pin down for next year, let's see what I can add to help you.

Number One: Let's remember that everything that shows in the profit area here on Bill's chart is divided just about evenly between the government and us. Now, for last year we can read a profit of about $150,000. Well, that's right.

561

But we were left with half of that, and then paid out dividends of $50,000 to the stockholders. Since we've got an anniversary year coming up, we'd like to put out a special dividend of about 50 percent extra. We ought to hold $25,000 in for the business, too. This means that we'd like to hit $100,000 *after* the costs of being governed.

Number Two: From where I sit, it looks like we're going to have to talk with the union again, and this time it's liable to cost us. All the indications are—and this isn't public—that we may have to meet demands that will boost our production costs—what do you call them here, Bill—variable costs—by 10 percent across the board. This may kill the bonus dividend plans, but we've got to hold the line on past profits. This means that we can give that much to the union only if we can make it in added revenues. I guess you'd say that that raises your break-even point, Bill—and for that one I'd consider the company's profit to be a fixed cost.

Number Three: Maybe this is the time to think about switching our product emphasis. Arnie Winetki may know better than I which of the products is more profitable. You check me out on this, Arnie—and it might be a good idea for you and Bill French to get together on this one, too. These figures that I have [Exhibit 2] make it look like the percentage contribution on line "A" is the lowest of the bunch. If we're losing volume there as rapidly as you sales folks say, and if we're as hard pressed for space as Fred Williams has indicated, maybe we'd be better off grabbing some of that big demand for "C" by shifting some of the facilities over there from "A."

That's all I've got to say. Looks to me like you've all got plenty to think about.

Davidson: Thanks, Hugh. I sort of figured that we'd get wound up here as soon as Bill brought out his charts. This is an approach that we've barely touched, but as you can see, you've all got ideas that have got to be made to fit here somewhere. I'll tell you what we should do. Bill, suppose you rework your chart and try to bring into it some of the points that were made here today. I'll see if I can summarize what everyone seems to be looking for.

First of all, I have the idea buzzing around in the back of my mind that your presentation is based on a rather important series of assumptions. Most of the questions that were raised were really about those assumptions; it might help us all if you try to set the assumptions down in black and white so that we can see just how they influence the analysis.

Then, I think that Cooper would like to see the unit sales increase taken up, and he'd also like to see whether there's any difference if you base the calculations on an analysis of individual product lines. Also, as Bradshaw suggested, since the product mix is bound to change, why not see how things look if the shift materialized as Sales has forecast.

Arnie Winetki would like to see the influence of a price increase in the "C" line, Fred Williams looks toward an increase in fixed manufacturing costs of ten thousand a month, and Hugh Fraser has suggested that we should consider taxes, dividends, expected union demands, and the question of product emphasis.

I think that ties it all together. Let's hold off on our next meeting, fellows, until Bill has time to work this all into shape.

With that, the participants broke off into small groups and the meeting disbanded. Bill French and Wes Davidson headed back to their offices, and French, in a tone of concern, asked Davidson, "Why didn't you warn me about the hornet's nest I was walking into?"

"Bill, you didn't ask!"

EXHIBIT 3
Duo-Products
Corporation's
List of Participants
in the Meeting

Bill French — Staff Accountant
Wes Davidson — Controller
John Cooper — Production Control
Fred Williams — Manufacturing
Ray Bradshaw — Assistant Sales Manager
Arnie Winetki — General Sales Manager
Hugh Fraser — Administrative Assistant
to President

Questions

1. What are the assumptions implicit in Bill French's determination of his company's break-even point?
2. On the basis of French's revised information, what does next year look like?
   a. What is the break-even point?
   b. What level of operations must be achieved to pay the extra dividend, ignoring union demands?
   c. What level of operations must be achieved to meet the union demands, ignoring bonus dividends?
   d. What level of operations must be achieved to meet both dividend and expected union requirements?
3. Can the break-even analysis help the company decide whether to alter the existing product emphasis? What can the company afford to invest for additional "C" capacity?
4. Is this type of analysis of any value? For what can it be used?
5. How might Bill French have improved his preparation for the meeting?
6. What can Bill do now to increase the chances that break-even analysis becomes a useful tool for his company?

Chapter 21

The Control Process

Upon completing this chapter you should be able to:

1. Explain why the control function is necessary.

2. Describe the link between planning and controlling.

3. State why managers need to find the right degree of control.

4. Describe the three different types of control methods.

5. Describe the steps in the control process.

6. Summarize the issues that managers have to deal with in designing a control system.

7. Explain the importance of "key performance areas" and "strategic control points."

8. Describe the characteristics of effective control systems.

As sales manager of the Top Drawer Office Supply Company, it is your responsibility to see that each division meets its sales quota. At the quarterly sales conference, Marsha Shore, regional sales manager of the western division, reports that her division "missed our total sales objective by 8 percent but expect to make that up when we surpass our objective for the next quarter."

Then you hear from Bruce Conacher of the eastern division: "Our figures for the quarter show that we exceeded our sales objective by almost 12 percent."

In evaluating the situation, you first consider the western division. Ms. Shore has an excellent record with the company and a proven record of reliability and accuracy in predicting future performance for her division. Mr. Conacher, although new to the job, more than met his objective this time, and it seems reasonable to assume he should be able to repeat his success. You therefore decide that no special action is needed.

Sometime later you receive the divisional profit and loss figures. You are more than a little surprised to find that the western division, in spite of missing its sales objective, shows a higher contribution to profits than the eastern division that more than met its objective.

Naturally, you investigate. And you find the answer: Mr. Conacher, in order to meet his sales objective, concentrated his division's efforts on large, established accounts, persuading them to place large orders and thus qualify for substantial quantity discounts. Result? High sales, minimum profits.

The situation is reflected in the next quarter's results when the eastern division, with most of its big accounts already overstocked, falls 18 percent below its quota. The western division, on the other hand, having spent a significant portion of its effort in the previous quarter on opening new accounts, is now reaping the benefit and, true to Ms. Shore's prediction, surpasses its objective by over 15 percent.

THE MEANING OF CONTROL

In this unit we will be describing the process of control, the various control methods that managers can use, and the ways in which the control process can be made effective. Why do we have a unit on control? Earl P. Strong and Robert D. Smith have described the need for control this way:

> There are a number of conflicting viewpoints regarding the best manner in which to manage an organization. However, theorists as well as practicing executives agree that *good management requires effective control*. A combination of well-planned objectives, strong organization, capable direction, and motivation have little probability for success unless there exists an adequate system of control.[1]

In other words, the information in the other parts of this book on planning, organizing, and leading, even if it were effectively applied, is not likely to help

[1] Earl P. Strong and Robert D. Smith, *Management Control Models* (New York: Holt, Rinehart and Winston, 1968), pp. 1–2.

managers achieve their goals unless the information on control is also applied effectively.

The Link between Planning and Controlling

Perhaps the simplest definition of management control is "the process through which managers assure that actual activities conform to planned activities." (See Chapter 1.) This definition has the advantage of pointing to the close link between *planning* and *controlling* the organization's operations, an association we first discussed in Chapter 4. In the planning process, the fundamental goals and objectives of the organization and the methods for attaining them are established. The control process measures progress toward those goals and enables managers to detect deviations from the plan so that they can take whatever remedial action is necessary (including a change in the plan). In fact, most good plans have controls (such as budgets) built into them. While the *functions* of planning and controlling should be kept distinct (so that neither function is slighted), the control process would be meaningless without previously established standards or goals.[2]

Our example at the start of this chapter illustrates the link between planning and controlling. The sales quotas represented the goals agreed to by upper management and the sales department; the quarterly sales conferences, during which sales managers reported on their progress toward those quotas, represented one of the company's control devices. In the example, short-term objectives were being met at the expense of long-term organizational goals. The control system did not detect that trade-off. It might have been useful in this case to build additional controls into the sales plan. For example, if the objectives had required that a certain percentage of the sales target be made up of new business, Conacher's concentration on established accounts would not have been acceptable; you, as sales manager, would therefore have been in a better position to anticipate the problems that Conacher's approach would create.

What Is Control?

Our simple definition of control suggests what control is intended to accomplish. It does not, however, indicate what control *is*. Robert J. Mockler has defined control in a way that indicates the essential elements of the control process:

> Management control is a systematic effort to set performance standards with planning objectives, to design information feedback systems, to compare actual performance with these predetermined standards, to determine whether there are any deviations and to measure their significance, and to take any action required to assure that all corporate resources are being used in the most effective and efficient way possible in achieving corporate objectives.[3]

[2] See Robert J. Mockler, *The Management Control Process* (Englewood Cliffs, N.J.: Prentice-Hall, 1972), and Douglas S. Sherwin, "The Meaning of Control," *Dun's Review and Modern Industry*, Vol. 67, No. 1 (January 1956), pp. 45–46 ff.

[3] Mockler, *The Management Control Process*, p. 2.

This definition divides control into four basic steps:

1 Establishing standards and methods for measuring performance
2 Measuring actual performance
3 Comparing performance against standards and interpreting any discrepancies
4 Taking corrective action (if appropriate)

We will briefly introduce these steps here and discuss them in greater detail later in this chapter.

Steps in the Control Process. The four basic steps in the control process and their relationship are illustrated in Figure 21-1. The first step is to *establish standards and methods for measuring performance.* Depending on the aspect of the organization to be controlled, this step could involve standards and measurements for everything from sales and production targets to worker attendance and safety records. For this step to be effective, the standards must be specified in meaningful terms and then must be accepted by the individuals involved. The methods of measurement should also be accepted and accurate. An organization may set an object to become the "leader in its field," but this standard will mean little more than verbal inspiration unless leadership is defined and an adequate way to measure it is established.

FIGURE 21-1
Basic Steps in the
Control Process

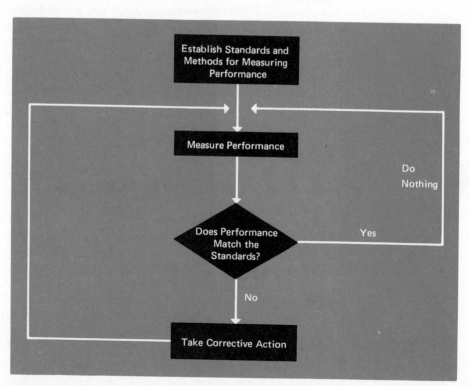

The second step is to *measure the performance*. Like all aspects of control, this is an ongoing, repetitive process, with the actual frequency dependent on the type of activity being measured. Safe levels of gas particles in the air, for example, may be continuously monitored in a manufacturing plant, while progress on long-term expansion objectives may need to be reviewed by top management only once or twice a year.

A fault to be avoided, however, is to allow too long a period of time to pass between performance measurements. Declining sales or production output is best discovered as soon as possible after it occurs, not at the end of a fiscal period when remedial action may be twice as costly or even impossible.

Does performance match the standard? In many ways, this is the easiest step in the control process to carry out. The complexities presumably have been solved in the first two steps; now it is simply a matter of comparing measured results with the target or standard previously set. If performance matches standards, managers may assume that "everything is under control," and, as Figure 21-1 shows, they do not have to intervene actively in the organization's operations. (They will, of course, have to continue the monitoring or measuring aspects of control, in case deviations subsequently develop.) Successfully achieved standards, however, do provide an opportunity for managers to translate this success into encouragement and motivation for the organization members involved in achieving them.

One part of this step that can increase its complexity is the need to interpret any deviations from the standard. Some deviations may be due to a temporary or unimportant circumstance, rather than to a real problem or flaw in the plan. Lower sales in July and August, for example, may be due to the fact that people are on vacation rather than to a loss of interest in the company's product.

The final step is to *take corrective action* if performance falls short of standards and the analysis indicates action is required. This corrective action may involve a change in one or more aspects of the organization's operations, or it may involve a change in the standards originally established. Unless managers see the control process through to its conclusion, they are merely monitoring performance rather than exercising control. The emphasis should always be on devising constructive ways to bring performance up to standard rather than merely to establish blame for past failures.

As our discussion of these steps implies, the control process must be carried out by managers throughout the organization. Because of the prominence of financial controls, some people assume that control responsibility can be left largely in the hands of accountants and controllers. Financial controls often do set the resource limits within which managers must operate, and many control methods involve budgets, profit and loss statements, and other financial tools. However, *all* managers need to exercise control to carry out their activities successfully. In addition, the control devices that managers use will often be nonfinancial in nature.

For example, such factors as absenteeism, employee turnover, sales force performance, new product development, plant safety, employee productivity, public relations, market share, and product quality—all important activities at every level of the organization—need to be controlled to make sure established standards or organization goals are being met. All of the factors we have just mentioned will be controlled, at least partially, through nonfinancial means. Product quality, for instance, will usually be controlled through periodic inspections and product testing. Public relations may be monitored through the number and type of customer complaints received.

THE IMPORTANCE OF CONTROL

It is impossible to imagine any organization completely devoid of control in the broadest sense of the term. If even the smallest organization is to function adequately, someone must be responsible for task initiation and completion. Employees must be "controlled" in the sense that they must carry out the assignments for which they are getting paid. The need for this level of control we may safely take for granted.

What we are concerned with in this section, of course, is the control necessary for an organization to achieve its objectives. What factors make control important for managers and their organizations? How much control do managers need to exercise?

Organizational Factors Creating the Need for Control

There are many factors that make control a necessity in today's organizations. Some of the most important of these factors include the changing environment of organizations, the increased complexity of organizations, the fact that organization members make mistakes, and the fact that managers need to delegate authority.[4] We will discuss these factors here.

Change. Suppose the Pinpoint Pencil Company, a supplier to our Top Drawer Office Supply Company, operated in a static market. Every year the company would make and sell the same number of pencils to the same customers. Manufacturing and labor costs would never vary, nor would availability and costs of materials. In other words, last year's results would govern this year's production. Planning and controlling for this company would quickly become automatic. In that sense, the active functions of planning and controlling would no longer be necessary.

Even in the most stable of industries, however, such a situation does not exist. Change is an integral part of almost any organization's environment. Markets shift; new products emerge; new materials are discovered; new regulations are passed. The control function enables managers to detect changes that are affecting their organization's products or services. They can then move to cope with the threats or opportunities that these changes represent.

[4] See Sherwin, "The Meaning of Control," p. 47; and Wm. Travers Jerome III, *Executive Control—The Catalyst* (New York: Wiley, 1961).

Complexity. The one-room schoolhouse and the small family business could be controlled on an informal, comparatively haphazard basis. Today's vast organizations, however, require a much more formal and careful control approach. Diversified product lines need to be watched closely to ensure that quality and profitability are being maintained; sales in different retail outlets need to be recorded accurately and analyzed; the organization's various markets, foreign and domestic, require close monitoring.

Adding to the complexity of today's organizations is the development of decentralization. For example, many organizations now have regional sales and marketing offices, widely distributed research facilities, or geographically separated plants. Such decentralization can simplify an organization's control efforts, since all the organization's operations no longer have to be controlled by central headquarters. Paradoxically, however, in order for decentralization to be effective, each decentralized unit's control activities have to be especially precise. Performance against established standards has to be watched closely so that general managers can appraise the effectiveness of the unit for which they are responsible, and so that corporate management can, in turn, appraise the effectiveness of the general managers.

Mistakes. If they or their subordinates never made mistakes, managers could simply establish performance standards and watch out for significant and unexpected changes in the environment. But organization members do make mistakes—wrong parts are ordered, wrong pricing decisions are made, problems are diagnosed incorrectly. A control system allows managers to catch these mistakes before they become critical.

Delegation. As we discussed in Chapter 11, when managers delegate authority to subordinates, their responsibility to their own superiors is not diminished. The only way managers can determine if their subordinates are accomplishing the tasks that have been delegated to them is by implementing a system of control. Without such a system, managers will be unable to check on subordinates' progress, and so will be unable to take corrective action until after a failure has occurred.

Finding the Right Degree of Control

The word "control" often has unpleasant connotations because it seems to threaten personal freedom and autonomy.[5] In an age when the legitimacy of authority is being sharply questioned, and when there is a widespread movement toward greater independence and self-actualization for individuals, the concept of organizational control makes many people uncomfortable. Yet, the need for control in organizations, as we have seen, is particularly acute today; in addition, organizational control methods are becoming more precise

---

[5] See G. H. Hofstede, *The Game of Budget Control* (Assen, The Netherlands: Van Gorcum, 1967), and Peter F. Drucker, *Management: Tasks, Responsibilities, Practices* (New York: Harper & Row, 1974), p. 494.

and sophisticated, particularly since computers have come into widespread use. How can managers deal with the potential conflict between the needs for organizational control and personal autonomy?

One way to deal with the seeming disparity between these two needs is to recognize that too many controls (that is, too many means or methods of control) will harm the organization as well as the individuals within it. Controls that bog down organization members in red tape or limit too many types of behavior will kill motivation, inhibit creativity, and, in the end, damage organizational performance. For example, in our chapter opening example, we noted that Mr. Conacher's problem could be avoided in the future by establishing a standard for at least a minimum percentage of sales to come from new accounts. This approach would probably be successful and might well be implemented by all regional sales managers as a result of Mr. Conacher's unfortunate experience. Alternatively, Top Drawer Office Supply Company might decide that this situation was basically the result of Mr. Conacher's inexperience in his new position and could be dealt with more appropriately by more careful coaching and training of new regional sales managers rather than by adding one more standard to the existing control system.

The degree of control that is considered extreme or harmful will vary from one organization to another. A machine shop, for example, may require much tighter controls than a research laboratory. Even within laboratories, some control variations will be found, since some experiments must be carried out under extremely precise conditions. Other experiments will not require such carefully controlled conditions. The economic climate may also affect the degree of control that is considered acceptable by organization members. In a recession, most people will accept tighter controls and restrictions; when things are booming, rules and restrictions will seem less appropriate. Regardless of the situation, excessive control will do more harm than good to the organization.

Inadequate controls will, of course, harm the organization by allowing resources to be wasted and by making it more difficult for organizations to attain their goals. However, individuals may also be harmed by inadequate controls; a decrease in control does not necessarily lead to an increase in personal autonomy. In fact, individuals may have even less personal freedom and autonomy, because they may not be able to predict or depend on what their co-workers will do. (Anarchy, the lack of any social or organizational controls, is not a situation of great personal freedom but one of massive uncertainty and unpredictability.) In addition, the lack of an effective system of organizational controls will mean that individual managers will have to supervise their subordinates much more closely, further reducing the freedom of those subordinates. If the lack of controls is extreme, the organization will likely fail, removing the freedom of members to pursue their personal goals within the organization.

Like most issues in management, then, the task for managers is to find the proper *balance*—in this case, between organizational control and individual freedom. With too much control, organizations become stifling, inhibiting, and

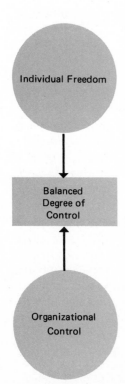

Individual Freedom

Balanced Degree of Control

Organizational Control

unsatisfying places in which to work; with too little control, organizations become chaotic, inefficient, and ineffective in achieving their goals.

Because organizations, people, environments, and technology keep changing, it is likely that any effective control system will require continuing modification and fine tuning for it to remain effectively balanced. For example, an organization's manufacturing or service divisions may employ relatively unskilled individuals who are not very interested in their work. The organization's control system might therefore require fairly frequent and detailed quality and productivity checks to compensate for the lack of worker interest. If the organization opened up a new operation to produce the same product or service in a different location, where the workers it hires are more skilled or more interested in the work, the control system might have to be redesigned to allow for the differences in the workers' skills and interests. For instance, fewer points of measurement might be used, the workers could be given more autonomy, and more responsibility might be placed on the workers to monitor and correct their own performance.

TYPES OF CONTROL METHODS

Most methods of control can be grouped into one of three basic types: steering controls, screening or yes-no controls, and post-action controls.[6] We will discuss these control types here. In later chapters, we will describe actual control techniques.

Steering Controls
Steering controls, or "feedforward controls," are designed to detect deviations from some standard or goal and to allow corrections to be made *before* a particular sequence of actions is completed.[7] The term "steering controls" is derived from the driving of a motor vehicle: the driver steers the car to prevent it from going off the road or in a wrong direction so the proper destination will be reached. In our chapter opening example, if the sales manager had been aware that Conacher was overloading his prime accounts in order to reach his sales quota, he or she could have instituted corrective action *during the quarter* in order to put him back on target. Obviously, to be usable, steering controls are dependent on the manager's being able to obtain timely and accurate information about changes in the environment or about progress toward the desired goal.

Yes-No or Screening Controls
This type of control provides a screening process in which specific aspects of a procedure must be approved or specific conditions met before operations may continue. If, in our chapter opening example, Conacher had been required to have all discounts over a specified amount approved by upper management,

---

[6] Our discussion is based on William H. Newman, *Constructive Control* (Englewood Cliffs, N.J.: Prentice-Hall, 1975), pp. 6–9.

[7] See Harold Koontz and Robert W. Bradspies, "Managing through Feedforward Control," *Business Horizons,* Vol. 4, No. 3 (June 1972), pp. 25–36.

that requirement would have been a yes-no control. More common examples of yes-no controls are quality control inspections, safety checks, and legal approval of contracts.

Because steering controls provide a means for taking corrective action while a program is still viable, they are usually more important and more widely used than other types of control. However, steering controls are rarely perfect—they do not catch all possible deviations from a plan or standard, nor are they always effectively applied. For these reasons, yes-no controls are particularly useful as "double-check" devices. Where safety is a key factor, as in aircraft design or the production of chemicals, or where large expenditures are involved, as in construction or aerospace programs, yes-no controls provide managers with an extra margin of security.

Post-Action Controls   As the term suggests, *post-action controls* measure results from a completed action. The causes of any deviation from the plan or standard are determined, and corrective action is applied to future activities that are similar to those that have already been completed. In our Top Drawer Company example, we would be exercising a form of post-action control by stipulating for our *next* quarter's objectives that 10 percent of the sales quota must come from new business. Post-action controls are also used as a basis for rewarding or encouraging employees (for example, meeting a standard may result in a bonus).

The flow of information and corrective action for all three types of control is shown in Figure 21-2. As can be imagined, the speed of information flow is a vital factor in efficient control, since the sooner deviations are discovered, the sooner corrective action can be taken. The accuracy of information is also extremely important, since corrective action for present or future activ-

FIGURE 21-2
Flow of Information and Corrective Action for Three Types of Control

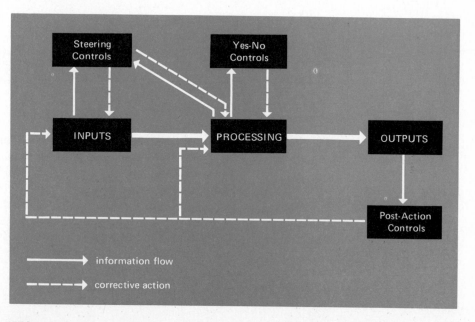

ities will be based on the information obtained from reports, computer print-outs, and other sources. We will be discussing management information systems in Chapter 24. (See also Chapter 18, "Interpersonal and Organizational Communication.")

There are other ways to classify controls besides the classification we have discussed. For example, Wm. Travers Jerome III has provided an interesting classification of control methods based on the uses to which the controls are put.[8] His classification appears in the accompanying box. Jerome suggests that groupings 1 through 3 are comparatively rigid in their application—little or no deviation from the established standard is desired. Groupings 4 through 8, on the other hand, allow organization members some latitude. They are designed to keep organizational activities broadly in line with organizational goals.

Controls Classified by Use

1. *Controls used to standardize performance* (for greater efficiency and lower cost). Examples: time and motion studies, inspections, production schedules.
2. *Controls used to safeguard assets* (from theft, waste, or misuse). Examples: authorization requirements, adequate recordkeeping.
3. *Controls used to standardize quality.* Examples: blueprints, inspections, statistical quality controls.
4. *Controls designed to limit authority exercised without top management's approval.* Examples: procedure manuals, policy directives, internal audits.
5. *Controls used to measure on-the-job performance.* Examples: output-per-employee reports, budgets, standard costs.
6. *Controls used for planning and programming operations.* Examples: sales forecasts, budgets, cost standards.
7. *Controls that allow top management to keep the firm's various plans and programs in balance.* Examples: master budget, policy manuals, committees, outside consultants.
8. *Controls designed to motivate organization members.* Examples: promotions, profit sharing, incentive bonuses.

Source: Adapted from Wm. Travers Jerome III, *Executive Control—The Catalyst* (New York: John Wiley & Sons, 1961), pp. 32–33. Used by permission.

The Importance of Steering Controls

The three types of control we have discussed—steering, yes-no, and post-action—are not alternatives to each other. Most organizations will use a combination of all three in attaining their goals. Steering controls are, however, particularly important. Just as outfielders cannot wait until a fly ball lands to see where they should have been standing, managers cannot afford to wait until all results are in before they begin to evaluate performance. If they do wait, they will usually find that it is too late to take corrective action. And where corrective action is still possible, it is likely to be far more costly than

---

[8] Jerome, *Executive Control*, pp. 32–34.

it would have been if it were taken earlier. For example, the sales decline in Conacher's division of the Top Drawer Company is not irreversible; a major effort to sign new customers will take time, however, and sales for the past quarter have already been lost. An earlier recognition of the problem would have permitted an earlier start on signing up new customers and probably would have resulted in higher sales for the quarter.

In addition to allowing managers to correct miscalculations, steering controls allow managers to take advantage of unexpected opportunities. Deviations from a standard or plan may, after all, take place in a *positive* direction; by becoming aware of these deviations before it is too late, managers can shift their organization's resources to where they will do the most good. For example, steering controls may detect greater than expected sales in a new product line; the number of those new products to be manufactured can then be increased.

DESIGN OF THE CONTROL PROCESS

In this section we will expand our description of the steps in the control process. Although much of our discussion will be appropriate to yes-no and postaction controls, our primary focus will be on the development of effective steering controls. Our emphasis is based on the fact that steering controls have the greatest potential for helping managers achieve constructive results.

The Control Process William H. Newman has provided a rich discussion of the procedures for establishing a control system.[9] We will describe his approach in terms of five basic steps:

1 Define desired results.
2 Establish predictors of results.
3 Establish standards for predictors and results.
4 Establish the information and feedback network.
5 Evaluate the information and take corrective action.

Before discussing these steps, we should note that they can be applied to all types of control activities—from monitoring the frequency with which articles are published by professors at a university to checking how often a shipping department meets its delivery dates.

Define Desired Results. The results that managers desire to obtain (or maintain) should be defined as specifically as possible. Goals expressed in vague or general terms such as "cut overhead costs" or "fill orders faster" are not nearly as constructive as "cut overhead by 12 percent" or "ship all orders within

---

[9] Newman, *Constructive Control*, pp. 12–25.

three working days." The latter phrasing not only provides managers with a basis for working out ways to estimate and implement necessary procedures but also includes a yardstick by which they can measure their success or failure in achieving their objectives.

Even objectives such as "improving customer relations," while hard to express in quantitative terms, can be defined more accurately by adding more specific details, such as "handle all complaints by letter within two days of receipt," "have sales manager pay a quarterly call on all accounts considered difficult by sales representatives," or "assure arrival of replacement parts within seven days of receipt of order." With effort, measurable objectives for most qualitative activities can usually be found.

Desired results, according to Newman, should also be linked to the individual responsible for achieving them. If the objective is "reduce shipping time by 10 percent," and the objective is not reached, who is responsible — the warehouse manager, the shipping clerk, or the truck drivers? The way to overcome this problem of accountability is to give the responsibility for obtaining the result to one person (such as the manager in charge of order processing) and to make sure that the person has the authority to achieve the desired result. If the objective is met, that person should be given the credit.

Establish Predictors of Results. The purpose of steering controls is to allow managers to correct deviations *before* a set of activities is completed, so that the goal of those activities can still be achieved. The deviations detected by steering controls must therefore be *predictors* of results; they must reliably indicate to managers whether or not corrective action needs to be taken. Otherwise, there would be no point to detecting or acting on those deviations. An important task of managers who are designing the control program is to find a number of reliable indicators or predictors for each of their goals.

Newman has identified several *early warning predictors* that can help managers estimate whether or not desired results will be achieved. Among these are:

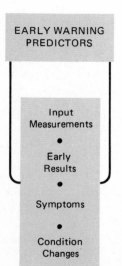

EARLY WARNING PREDICTORS

Input Measurements

•

Early Results

•

Symptoms

•

Condition Changes

1. *Input measurements.* There are certain key elements in any situation that will enable managers to forecast final results. For example, incoming orders will determine the number of items to be manufactured; raw material costs will directly affect future product prices; a worsening in economic conditions will very likely cause a decline in consumer demand. A change in these key inputs will suggest to managers that they need either to change their plans or to take some other corrective action.

2. *Results of early steps.* If early results are better or worse than expected, a reevaluation may be called for and appropriate action taken. The first month's sales of a new ice cream flavor, for example, may provide a useful indication of its future popularity.

3. *Symptoms.* These are conditions that seem to be associated with final results, but they do not directly affect those results. For example, whenever sales representatives get their sales reports in late, the sales manager may assume that quotas have not been met. An office manager may anticipate greater

employee productivity on rainy days, because he or she assumes that staff members will have sandwiches sent in rather than take a lengthy break for lunch. The problem with symptoms, as we have implied earlier, is that they are susceptible to very wrong or misleading interpretations.

4. *Changes in assumed conditions.* Original estimates are based on the assumption that "normal" conditions will prevail. Any unexpected changes, such as new government regulations, new developments by competition, or material shortages, will indicate the need for a reevaluation of tactics and goals.

Aside from early warning predictors, managers may use *past results* to help them make estimates of future performance. In this type of post-action control, performance on a previous cycle is used to make predictions and (if necessary) adjustments for the next cycle. For example, if a reduction in last year's market testing led to an above-average number of new product failures, market testing this year may be increased. As a general rule, the greater the number of reliable and timely predictors the manager can establish, the more confident the manager can be in making performance predictions.

Establish Standards for Predictors and Results. Establishing standards, or *pars,* for predictors and final results is an important part of designing the control process. Without established pars, managers may overreact to minor deviations or fail to react when deviations are significant. They may also fail to develop a clear idea of the results they desire.

To be meaningful, pars or standards must be appropriate for the particular circumstances. For example, receiving 200 customer complaints in a month when the service shop is in the process of reorganization is probably not as significant as receiving 50 complaints in a month when the shop should be functioning smoothly. Pars also need to be flexible in order to adapt to changing conditions. For instance, a new salesperson who proves to be an above-average performer should have his or her sales standard adjusted accordingly. Similarly, expected delivery times need to be adjusted if the local highway is being repaired.

Establish the Information and Feedback Network. The fourth step in the design of a control cycle is to establish the means for collecting information on the predictors and for comparing the predictors against their pars. As we shall see, the communication network works best when it flows not only upward but also downward to those who must take corrective action. In addition, it must be efficient enough to feed the relevant information back to key personnel in time for them to act on it.

To keep managers from getting bogged down in communications about how matters are progressing, control communications are often based on the *management by exception* principle. This principle suggests that the controlling superior should be informed about an operation's progress only if there is a significant deviation from the plan or standard. The superior can then concentrate fully on the problem situation. If matters are proceeding as planned (or with only minor deviations), there is no need for the superior to be informed.

Evaluate Information and Take Corrective Action. This final step involves comparing predictors to pars, deciding what action (if any) to take, and then taking that action. (See Figure 21-3 for the elements in a control cycle.)

Information about a deviation from par must first be evaluated; as we suggested earlier, some deviations are due to local or temporary circumstances and will not really affect the final result. Alternative corrective actions, if they are required, are then developed and evaluated. Sometimes the corrective action will be straightforward and obvious: if a supplier runs out of raw material, for example, another supplier will have to be located. At other times, a multifaceted, complex action will become necessary. For instance, if there is an industry-wide raw materials shortage, alternative materials may have to be found, products may have to be redesigned, and previously established goals may have to be revised. These changes may require that the entire planning and controlling cycle be started anew.

FIGURE 21-3
Elements in
a Control Cycle

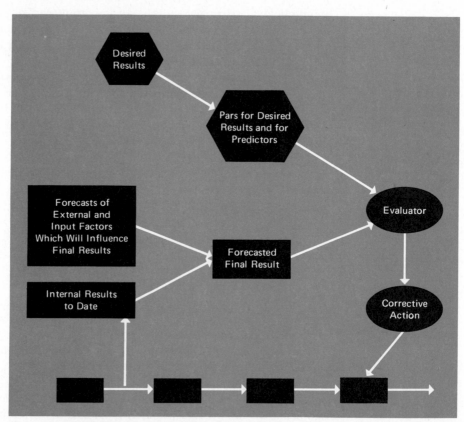

Source: Based on William H. Newman, *Constructive Control* (Englewood Cliffs, N.J.: Prentice-Hall 1975). p. 13. Used by permission.

Critical Issues in Establishing a Control System

Jerome E. Schnee and Thomas P. Ference have described a number of critical issues that must be dealt with when establishing a control system.[10] We will describe six of these issues:

1 *What types of measures are to be used*
2 *How many measures are to be used*
3 *Who establishes the measures and standards*
4 *How flexible the standards are to be*
5 *How frequently measurements will be taken*
6 *What direction feedback will take*

Types of Measurement. If managers could always measure performance directly, then their task of establishing a control system would be enormously simplified. Unfortunately, performance is difficult to measure directly for many types of activities. The quality of a research group's ideas, for example, may be difficult to determine with any degree of accuracy. Managers may therefore find it necessary to measure what appear to be components or correlates of performance. The productivity of the research group, for instance, might be measured by the number of progress reports it issues.

The danger inherent in this method is that managers may select something that is easy to measure rather than something that is really correlated with performance. An endless stream of progress reports from the research group, for example, might well indicate a *lack* of real progress, since significant research breakthroughs might not allow time to write a series of reports or would be communicated in a single technical paper. Another danger is that managers may encourage the correlated behavior rather than the work performance itself. For example, research group members might spend their time writing reports instead of doing research if they know their performance is being judged by the frequency of their reports.

Another measurement approach involves monitoring the activities that appear to lead to performance. For example, sales performance might be judged by the number of calls the salesperson makes or by the number of days he or she spends on the road. This type of measurement is often regarded as irrelevant or annoying by the persons being controlled. It also runs the danger that managers will concentrate on *means* (the number of calls) at the expense of *ends* (the number of actual sales).

Most types of measurement are based on some form of established standards.[11] Such standards may be *historical*—that is, based on records and information concerning the organization's past experiences. Sales standards,

---

[10] Our discussion of these issues is based largely on Schnee and Ference's lecture notes, supplemented with the author's experience; thus, it may not reflect their perspectives with complete accuracy.

[11] See Robert N. Anthony and John Dearden, *Management Control Systems,* 3rd ed. (Homewood, Ill.: Irwin, 1976), and Arthur E. Mills, *The Dynamics of Management Control Systems* (London: Business Publication Ltd., 1967).

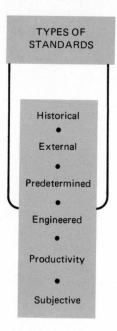

TYPES OF
STANDARDS

Historical
•
External
•
Predetermined
•
Engineered
•
Productivity
•
Subjective

for instance, are often historical in nature—the salespeople are expected to increase sales by a certain amount each year. A problem with historical standards is that past performance may have been poor; in addition, circumstances may have changed since past data were compiled.

External standards are those derived from other organizations or other units of the same organization (such as the company's various sales offices). The difficulty here is in finding organizations or units that are similar enough to make the external standards meaningful. Wherever possible, *predetermined* standards should be used. These standards (or budgets) are developed in the planning process; they are based on careful study and analysis of the organizational units' internal and external environments.

Engineered standards, concerned with machine capabilities, are often supplied by machine manufacturers. Time and motion studies are useful in setting *assembly-line productivity* standards, if the cost of the engineer who will perform these studies will be offset by the savings in efficiency, *and* if employees are willing to accept the new standards. Even professional tasks that are repetitive in nature, such as some surgical procedures or the drafting of simple wills, may have reasonable time standards set for them. For other types of tasks, *subjective* standards, which are based on a manager's discretion, may be established. Such subjective standards become more appropriate as the complexity of a task increases.

The Number of Measurements. As we have already suggested, managers need to develop a control system that is balanced. There need to be enough measures of performance to detect important deviations and to guide behavior in the desired direction; but too many performance measures will cause excessive effort to be devoted to control and will cause subordinates to feel overcontrolled. When a system is not functioning as well as desired, managers are frequently tempted to add more control measures. Sometimes this approach is useful, particularly when organizational units are exceeding their budgets, and deadlines and quotas are being missed. Frequently, however, adding more controls simply causes the few measures that are really important to be neglected. It is hard to focus on the major determinants of performance and the top priority items when a multitude of performance measures exist.

Authority for Setting Measures and Standards. Performance standards can be set with or without the participation of the people whose performance is being controlled. We have discussed the advantages of subordinate participation in the standard-setting process in a number of places throughout our text (see Chapters 6, 7, and 15, for example). When standards are set unilaterally by upper-level managers, there is a danger that employees will regard those standards as unreasonable or unrealistic; they may then refuse to meet them.

Even with participation, standard setting can degenerate into a form of game playing if managers and subordinates do not believe they have common goals. For example, subordinates may seek to negotiate low standards so that they will be able to achieve them easily; managers may seek to set unrealisti-

"We hate to pry, Mr. Wilkinson, but we must know more than "for a deal" before we lend you four million dollars."

Reprinted by permission of Bill Hoest

cally high standards initially in the hope of motivating subordinates to greater effort.

Flexibility of Standards. Managers need to determine whether or not standards should be uniform throughout the similar units of the organization. Sales territories, for example, may be considered roughly equivalent, and so the performance of salespeople may be measured against a uniform standard. (In other words, the person with the largest number of sales in the measurement period will be considered the best salesperson for that period.) Often, however, allowances must be made for the different circumstances each organizational unit or member must face. For instance, when sales territories are not comparable, a salesperson's performance may be judged by the past sales history of his or her specific territory.

Managers need to make a similar decision about the extent to which qualitative versus quantitative measures will be used in the control system. For some tasks (such as envelope stuffing), performance may be accurately and easily measured in quantitative terms. For other tasks (such as research and development activities), both qualitative and quantitative measures will have to be used. Obviously, precise qualitative measures are extremely difficult to establish, but even rough measures are usually better than none at all.

Frequency of Measurement. How frequently and when performance should be measured depends on the nature of the task being controlled. Quality control of items coming off an assembly line often requires hourly monitoring, because the quality of the raw materials or parts entering the assembly line may change during the day. Product development, on the other hand, may be measured on a monthly basis, since significant changes are unlikely to take place on a daily basis.

Managers are often tempted to measure performance at some convenient time, rather than when the performance to be controlled should be measured. For example, they may wish to check product quality at the end of the workday, to check plant safety arrangements over a weekend when the plant is empty, or to evaluate employees only during an annual review period. Such a temptation should be avoided, since inaccurate measurements may result. For example, assembly-line employees may be especially careful with the last run of items on the assembly line if they know a quality inspection will take place at the end of the day. Random inspection during the workday would probably provide more realistic measures of product quality.

Direction of Feedback. The purpose of control is to ensure that present plans are being implemented and that future plans will be developed more effectively. If the control system provides information merely for superiors to check up on their subordinates, the effectiveness of the system is lost—the people whose actions are being controlled may never find out what they are doing wrong and what they need to do to perform more effectively. In addition, the individuals being controlled will see the control system as punitive and not as an encouragement to improved performance.

The individuals whose actions are being monitored are usually in the best position to take whatever corrective action is necessary, because they are closest to the activities being controlled. Thus, a well-designed control system will usually include feedback of control information to the individual or group performing the controlled activity. The same information will not necessarily be provided to the individual's or group's superior.

KEY PERFORMANCE AREAS

In order for upper-level managers to establish effective control systems, they must first identify the key performance areas of their organization or unit. *Key performance* or *key result areas* are those aspects of the unit or organization that *have* to function effectively in order for the entire unit or organization to succeed. These areas usually involve major organizational activities or groups of related activities that occur throughout the organization or unit—for example, its financial transactions, its manager-subordinate relations, or its manufacturing operations. The broad controls that upper managers establish for these key

582

performance areas will help define the more detailed control systems and standards of lower-level managers.[12]

General Electric's
Key Result Areas

The General Electric Company developed its own list of key result areas and established standards for them.[13] (The eight areas are listed in the accompanying box.) We will discuss each of these areas here to illustrate how one organization used the concept of key performance areas to design its control system. Other organizations, of course, will have their own list of key result areas.

General Electric's Key Performance Areas

1. Profitability
2. Market position
3. Productivity
4. Product leadership
5. Personnel development
6. Employee attitudes
7. Public responsibility
8. Balance between short-range and long-range goals

1. *Profitability.* To develop a profitability standard that it could apply to all its decentralized operations, General Electric first examined traditional methods of profit measurement. For example, it studied the possibility of judging profit by the rate of return on investment (see Chapter 22) or by the percent of earnings to sales. (If earnings were $200 million on sales of $1 billion, the company would be considered to have earned a 20 percent profit by this measure.) These traditional measures were considered unsatisfactory for GE's operations. Profits expressed as a percent of sales ignored both the cost and the long-term importance of capital investment. In addition, this measure did not take into account the different circumstances under which GE's different product lines had to operate—some product lines were expected to have higher earnings as a percentage of sales than others. Thus, the same standard could not be applied to all of them. Measuring profits by the return on investment proved unsatisfactory, because, among other things, it would encourage managers to improve the *ratio* of profit to investment rather than the total *amount* of profits earned. For example, a manager of a unit with a very high rate of return of 30 percent might forgo an exceptionally attractive

[12] See Paul M. Stokes, *A Total Systems Approach to Management Control* (New York: American Management Associations, 1968).

[13] See *Planning, Managing, and Measuring the Business* (New York: Controllership Foundation, 1955). See also Jerome, *Executive Control,* pp. 217–240, upon which our discussion is based.

investment that would add considerably to the total profits of the whole company but would slightly lower that unit's rate of return. In addition, managers could give the appearance of increased profitability in the short run by subcontracting projects instead of making those capital investments that were necessary for longer-run competitive strength.

General Electric finally decided to use *total* dollar profits, minus a charge for capital investment, as its profitability measure. This measure takes into account the cost of investment; in addition, it makes managers focus directly on increasing dollar profits rather than on improving the appearance of profitability.

2. *Market position.* While profitability is a significant measure of performance, it is not the only effective or meaningful measure. Market position — where a firm stands relative to other companies — is also an important performance indicator. For example, an entire industry may be expanding, and so the profitability of a company within that industry may increase; if that company's market share is declining, however, it may mean that other companies' products are more acceptable to the public. That company's future profitability may therefore be threatened.

General Electric developed a comparatively simple measure of market position for its different products or services — the percent of available business each product or service had. A decline in market position would signal managers that either product satisfaction had decreased relative to competitors' products or that all available markets for the product were not being fully exploited.

3. *Productivity.* General Electric sought to find a measure that would reliably indicate if it made efficient use of its resources. The difficulty of devising such a measure lies in the fact that productivity will be affected by a number of factors — for example, the amount of work performed by employees, the efficiency of a plant's design, or the extent of automation.

Two of the productivity measures that GE finally developed included the payroll and depreciation dollar costs of goods produced. The payroll dollar cost measure provided an indicator of the efficiency with which labor was being used. The depreciation dollar cost indicated how efficiently the company's machinery and equipment were being used.

4. *Product leadership.* Product leadership was defined by GE as the ability to lead an industry in the engineering, manufacturing, and marketing of new products and in the improvement of existing products. Determining product leadership by this definition involves a number of subjective or qualitative measures. For example, engineers might consider their products to be leading the industry if those products are technologically complex and reliable; production personnel might see leadership in terms of low cost or the lack of manufacturing defects.

To achieve some meaningful measure of product leadership, GE required an annual review of existing and planned products. In each of GE's businesses, members of the engineering, manufacturing, marketing, and finance departments evaluate the cost, quality, and market position of a product. If these product factors are not up to par, then improvements are planned.

5. *Personnel development.* By "personnel development," General Electric meant what we have called human resource planning and development in Chapter 19. Such planning and development involves providing for the present and future personnel needs of the company, particularly its ongoing and expected need for managers and specialists.

For GE, the first step in measuring the effectiveness of personnel development is to assess the company's staffing process — for example, to determine if recruitment and on-the-job training programs are well-designed and proceeding according to plan. The effectiveness of development programs is also assessed. For instance, the number of existing managers and specialists who are graduates of company programs can be determined; too low a number might indicate those programs are ineffective either in locating qualified organization members or in helping members develop their abilities and skills.

6. *Employee attitudes.* The attitudes and motivation of employees, as we suggested in previous chapters, is a critical element in an organization's success or failure. Such attitudes are usually measured on an organization-wide basis by such indicators as absenteeism and turnover. From GE's point of view, such indicators are not completely satisfactory, since they become evident only *after* a serious problem has developed. In addition, they do not suggest what the cause of the difficulty may be.

The approach developed by GE was to take attitude surveys of its employees on a regular basis. Employees in each work group filled out questionnaires anonymously; the results of the survey were made available to the group's members. These results allowed managers to pinpoint (and thus act on) problems in their work group or department before they got out of hand.

7. *Public responsibility.* GE defined public responsibility in terms of its relationship to its employees, suppliers, local communities, and business community. Indicators of how well it was carrying out its responsibilities to its employees included the degree of job security the company was providing, the number of job opportunities it made available, and the sufficiency of its wages. Responsibility to suppliers was measured by surveys of those suppliers; specifically, suppliers were asked to appraise their local GE plant as a customer. Each plant or business office's local community was also surveyed to determine public attitudes toward the company. In addition, more qualitative measures were used, such as the degree to which GE officials participated in local community activities.

As might be expected, the extent to which GE met its responsibility to the business community at large is more difficult to measure. Several ways to measure that responsibility have been proposed, however. These include attitude surveys of other companies with which GE does business and the number of gifts the company makes to charitable and educational organizations.

8. *Balance between short-range and long-range goals.* As our chapter opening example suggests, a major problem in organizations is ensuring that immediate goals are not attained at the expense of future profits and stability. One way managers can maintain the balance between short-term and long-term goals is to consider the ways in which the key performance areas are related. For example, an aggressive plan to achieve product leadership can

potentially lead to dissatisfaction on the part of overworked employees. Eventually, too high a rate of turnover may develop in the organization. In addition, the long-term implications of plans can be considered in the planning process. New product development, for example, may require expenditures that will threaten the firm's future cash position.

Strategic Control Points

One important task in designing an effective control system at all levels of the organization is to isolate the points in the system where monitoring or information collecting should occur. The points selected should be the ones that are critical in determining the overall success of the activity being controlled. If such points can be located, then the amount of information that has to be gathered and evaluated can be reduced considerably.

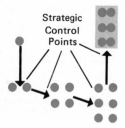

One useful way to find an operation's strategic control points is to locate those areas of the operation in which *change* occurs. For example, in an organization's system for filling customer orders, a change occurs when the purchase order becomes an invoice, when an inventory item becomes an item to be shipped, or when the item to be shipped becomes part of a truckload.[14] Since things are most likely to go wrong when such changes occur, monitoring change points is usually a highly effective way to control an operation.

A more important and useful method of selecting strategic control points is to focus on the most significant elements in a given operation. Usually only a small percentage of the activities, events, individuals, or objects in a given operation will account for a high proportion of the expense or problems that managers will have to face.[15] For example, 10 percent of a manufacturer's products may well yield 60 percent of its sales; 20 percent of its inventory items may account for 70 percent of the total dollar value of the inventory; 2 percent of an organization's employees may account for 80 percent of its employee grievances; 20 percent of the police precincts in a city may account for 70 percent of the city's violent crimes; and 60 percent of an auto assembly-line's quality control problems may involve a small number of parts. No organizational control system can or should cover all elements of a given operation. By focusing on the operation's most expensive or significant elements, managers can apply their limited control resources most efficiently and effectively.

CHARACTERISTICS OF EFFECTIVE CONTROL SYSTEMS

In this section we will discuss the characteristics that have been shown to be associated with reliable and effective control systems. While the importance of these characteristics varies with individual circumstances, most control systems are strengthened if they are:

[14] Ray A. Lindberg, "The Unfamiliar Art of Controlling," *Management Services,* May-June 1969, pp. 15–20.

[15] See Drucker, *Management,* pp. 500–501, and C. J. Slaybaugh, "Pareto's Law and Modern Management," *Price Waterhouse Review,* Vol. 11, No. 4 (Winter 1966), pp. 26–33.

1   Accurate

2   Timely

3   Objective and comprehensible

4   Focused on strategic control points

5   Economically realistic

6   Organizationally realistic

7   Coordinated with the organization's work flow

8   Flexible

9   Prescriptive and operational

10   Acceptable to organization members

If a control system is missing even a few of these characteristics, it will probably be ineffective in helping the organization meet its goals.[16]

Accurate. Obviously, information on performance must be reasonably accurate in order for the organization to take appropriate corrective action. Inaccurate data from a control system can cause the organization to take action that will either fail to correct a problem or create a problem where none exists. For example, a foreman may report to a supervisor that parts are being damaged on one assembly line because "the people on that line are inadequately trained." In fact, the machines on that particular line may be at fault. The supervisor may devote time and resources to additional training that will not solve the problem and that may even be resented by the employees if it is perceived as unnecessary. Evaluating the accuracy of the information they receive is one of the most important control tasks that managers face.

Timely. Although this characteristic has been mentioned before, we are repeating it here to underline its importance. Information must be collected, routed to the appropriate destination, and evaluated quickly if corrective action is to be taken in time to produce improvements. Otherwise, managers may act too late, act incorrectly, or simply not act at all. In our chapter opening example, the relevant information about sales in Conacher's division reached the sales manager too late to take action for the quarter.

Objective and Comprehensible. Most readers have probably had the experience of finding an instruction or repair manual difficult to understand. The annoyance, confusion, or frustration such manuals cause make it difficult to function coolly and effectively. To be useful, the information used in a control system should be understandable and seen as objective by the individuals involved. The less subjective or ambiguous the control system is, the greater

---

[16] Our discussion in this section is based on William H. Sihler, "Toward Better Management Control Systems," *California Management Review,* Vol. 14, No. 2 (Winter 1971), pp. 33–39; Drucker, *Management,* pp. 489–504; John R. Curley, "A Tool for Management Control," *Harvard Business Review,* March 1951, pp. 45–59; and Strong and Smith, *Management Control Models,* pp. 17–18.

the likelihood that individuals will take the appropriate corrective action at the proper time. A difficult-to-understand control system will cause unnecessary mistakes to be made and will normally cause employee resentment.

Focused on Strategic Control Points. As we mentioned earlier, the control system should be focused on those areas where deviations from the standards are most likely to take place or where deviations would lead to the greatest harm. The system should also be focused on those points where corrective action can be most effectively applied. For example, it would obviously be absurd to control parts quality after the parts have already been packaged or shipped. Parts quality is most logically checked immediately after the parts come off the assembly line.

Economically Realistic. The cost of implementing a control system should be less or, at most, equal to the benefits derived from the control system. For example, if managers are spending $60,000 on control to realize a savings of $50,000, they need to redesign their control system. The best way to minimize waste or unnecessary expenditure in a control system is to do the *minimum amount necessary to ensure that the monitored activity will reach the desired goal*. For instance, in most organizations a sales manager would be wasting time and money if he or she insisted on receiving daily sales reports. Weekly or monthly sales reports are usually sufficient for effective control of a sales staff.

Organizationally Realistic. The control system, to be workable, has to be compatible with organizational realities. For example, there has to be an equitable balance between the effort necessary to attain the desired performance level and the reward for achieving it. Managers who set excessively high standards and try to induce subordinates to adhere to those standards may well find that their subordinates will simply stop reporting deviations. Status differences between individuals also have to be recognized. Individuals who have to report deviations to someone they perceive as a lower-level staff member may stop taking the control system seriously.

Coordinated with the Organization's Work Flow. Control information needs to be coordinated with the flow of work through the organization for two reasons. First, each step in the work process may affect the success or failure of the entire operation. Second, the control information must get to all the people who need to receive it. For example, an appliance company that receives parts from several of its manufacturing plants and assembles them in one central location needs to be sure that all parts plants are performing up to par. Plant managers also need to know when a serious problem develops in one of the other plants, since the work pace in their own plants may have to be adjusted.

Flexible. As we suggested earlier, few organizations today are in such a stable environment that they do not have to worry about the possibility of change and so can apply a rigid set of controls. For almost all organizations, controls must have flexibility built into them so that the organizations can react quickly to overcome adverse changes or to take advantage of new opportunities.

Prescriptive and Operational. Effective control systems ought to indicate, upon the detection of a deviation from standards, what corrective action should be taken. In other words, they must be focused on what should be done, rather than simply convey facts. The information must also be in a usable form when it reaches the person responsible for taking the necessary action. For example, information on plant-wide quality control is not as usable as quality control information that is focused specifically on an individual or work group.

Acceptable to Organization Members. Ideally, a control system should lead to high performance by organization members by encouraging their feelings of autonomy, responsibility, and growth. Often, however, obtaining timely and accurate information and taking corrective action will conflict to some extent with the individual needs of employees. In such a case, the control system should at least avoid discouraging employees to the point where they will lower their performance. For example, too many controls, or controls that are too rigid, will often cause the satisfaction (and usually the motivation) of employees to decline. Such a negative effect must be taken into account when the efficiency of a control system is assessed.

Summary

Control is the vitally important process through which managers assure that actual activities conform to planned activities. It involves four basic steps: (1) the establishment of standards and measures; (2) the measurement of results; (3) the comparison of results against standards; and (4) the taking of corrective action.

The changing environment of organizations, the increasing complexity of organizations, the fact that organization members make mistakes, and the fact that managers must delegate authority are among the factors that make control necessary. In order to be effective, however, control systems must be properly balanced: too much destroys initiative and enthusiasm; too little leads to inefficiency and waste.

Most control methods can be grouped into three basic categories: *steering controls,* which detect performance deviations before a given operation is completed; *yes-no* or *screening controls,* which ensure that specific conditions are met before an operation proceeds further; and *post-action controls,* in which past experience is applied to future operations. While all three are important, steering controls are particularly critical since they allow corrective action to be applied early enough to prevent failure or to take advantage of unexpected opportunities.

Establishing a control system using steering controls involves (1) defining desired results; (2) establishing predictors of results; (3) establishing standards for predictors and results; (4) establishing the information and feedback network; and (5) evaluating the information and taking corrective action.

In designing a control system, managers must decide on the types and number of measurements that will be used, who will set the standards, how flexible the standards will be, the frequency of measurement, and the direction that feedback will take.

Some organizations formally establish *key performance areas* upon which their

589

control systems are based. At General Electric, the key performance areas were profitability, market position, productivity, product leadership, personnel development, employee attitudes, public responsibility, and balance between short-range and long-range goals.

For a control system to be effective, it must be accurate, timely, objective, focused on *strategic control points,* economically realistic, organizationally realistic, coordinated with the organization's work flow, flexible, prescriptive, and acceptable to organization members. These characteristics can be applied to controls at all levels of the organization.

Review Questions

1. Why do you think the control function is important?
2. How are planning and controlling linked?
3. What are the four basic steps in the control process? What are the key considerations in each step?
4. What organizational factors do you think create the need for control?
5. Why is a "balanced" control system necessary? How do you think managers can find the "right" degree of control?
6. What are the three main types of controls? How is each type used? Which is most important? Why?
7. According to Newman, what are the five steps in designing a control system? How do managers go about carrying out these steps?
8. According to Schnee and Ference, what six issues do managers have to deal with in designing a control system? How might managers resolve these issues?
9. What types of control standards may managers use?
10. What is the "management by exception" principle?
11. What are "key performance areas"? How did General Electric go about defining its key performance areas?
12. What are strategic control points? How may managers locate them?
13. What are the characteristics of effective control systems? Which characteristics do you think are most important?

CASE STUDY: DURMONT'S SHOE INVENTORY HEADACHE

David Durmont had worked his way up from a clerk to manager of a retail convenience food store when the opportunity came along to buy a retail women's shoe store franchise. He thought that since he had been successful in one retail trade, he would also be successful in another. Plus, this gave him the opportunity to be his own boss.

Mr. Durmont learned that it was necessary to buy a minimum of 48 pairs of any style of shoe if he wanted to have a good selection of all the sizes with extras in the more common sizes. The franchisor suggested he start his store with at least 50 different styles. This gave him a beginning inventory of 2,400 pairs of shoes. The average cost per pair was $10, so his initial investment in inventory amounted to $24,000. The store itself was a turnkey operation with everything being furnished to the franchisee, except the inventory, for a monthly rental fee. Mr. Durmont had to borrow $12,000 to get started, on which he agreed to make monthly payments of at least $400.

Case reprinted with permission from *Contemporary Management Incidents* by Bernard A. Deitzer and Karl A. Shilliff (Columbus, Ohio: Grid, Inc., 1977), pp. 106–107.

Sales were brisk during the grand opening of the store and continued on as forecasted by the franchisor. David was very pleased with the sales. However, he found that after he had sold about half, or 24 pairs, of any given style of shoe, he was running out of certain sizes. By the time he had sold 32 pairs, he had to quit displaying that particular style because the customer would get disturbed if he had styles on display but their size was not available. He tried to alleviate the problem by reordering the sizes he was out of, but found that most of the time he couldn't reorder, because the manufacturer had discontinued that particular style. It was either out of style or out of season. Therefore, he had to order the new styles that kept changing with the seasons.

As time went on, David Durmont found that his inventory of shoes kept growing, making it difficult not only to pay the $400 a month on his loan but also to pay for the new purchases of shoes. He had to keep ordering as the seasons changed and the new styles kept coming. By the end of the first year he had sold about 4,800 pairs of shoes, but his inventory consisted of 16 or so pairs of 150 different styles that were either out of season or were out of so many sizes they could no longer be displayed. Therefore, the customers did not know he had them.

An analysis of his sales and purchases showed that, after selling 32 pairs of any given style of shoe, he had to replace that style with a new style of 48 pairs. On the average, each two months he would sell 800 pairs of shoes. This would deplete about 25 styles to the point that they could no longer be displayed. So, to replace the 25 styles that were depleted, he had to order 1,200 pairs (25 styles times 48 pairs per style). If things keep going at the same rate the second year as they have the first year, he is going to end up the second year with 7,200 pairs of shoes at a cost of $72,000, two-thirds of which are going to be out of style, out of season, and out of sufficient sizes to display.

David Durmont never had this problem in the food business because there he could sell every item he bought on a first-in, first-out basis. He could reorder any item that was running low. None of the food items came in sizes that could no longer be displayed when certain sizes had run out. Every item he had in the food store could be displayed.

Case Question   1. What is the solution to David Durmont's shoe inventory headache?

Budgetary Methods of Control

Upon completing this chapter you should be able to:

1. Explain why budgets are one of the most important control devices that managers use.

2. Identify the various *responsibility centers* that exist in organizations.

3. Describe the budgeting process.

4. Identify the various types of budgets an organization can use.

5. Summarize two special approaches to budgeting.

6. Describe the potentially functional and dysfunctional aspects of budgets and how the dysfunctional aspects might be overcome.

Budgets are formal statements of the financial resources set aside for carrying out specific activities in a given period of time. They are the most widely used means for planning and controlling activities at every level of an organization. A budget indicates the expenditures, revenues, or profits planned for some future date. The planned figures become the standard by which future performance is measured. (See Chapter 4.) Most readers will already have had some contact with budgets; they will certainly have very early contact with budgets when they begin their careers.

Why are budgets such a fundamental part of many organizations' control programs? There are several reasons.[1] First, and most important, budgets are widely used because they are stated in monetary terms. Dollar figures can be used as a common denominator for a wide variety of organizational activities — hiring and training personnel, purchasing equipment, manufacturing, advertising, and selling. They can be used by the organization's existing accounting system to cover all departments. Thus, budgets can be a particularly comprehensive, convenient, and flexible control device. In addition, the monetary aspect of budgets means that they can directly convey information on a key organizational resource — capital — and on a key organizational goal — profit. They are, therefore, heavily favored by profit-oriented companies.

The second major reason budgets are the most widely used control tool is that they establish clear and unambiguous standards of performance. Budgets cover a set time period — usually a year. At stated intervals during that time period, actual performance will be compared directly with the budget. Frequently, deviations can be quickly detected and acted upon. In addition, by submitting budgets to a higher authority for approval, managers commit themselves to reaching the budgeted objectives. Thus, their responsibility for those objectives is clear. If specified results are not obtained, or if cost limits imposed by the budget are exceeded, the manager responsible for the budget will be held accountable.

For these reasons, budgets are not only a major *control* device but also one of the major means of *coordinating* the activities of the organization. In devising budgets (or any other type of plan), managers will take into account information provided by the subunits of their organization. The interaction between managers and subordinates that takes place during the budget development process will help define and integrate the activities that organization members will perform. Similarly, when final budgets are communicated to subunit members, the common objectives of the organization will often be clarified.

In this chapter we will describe more fully the role of budgets in a control system, the budgeting process itself, the different types of budgets managers have available, the benefits and drawbacks of budgets, and how those drawbacks can be overcome. Before we begin our discussion, we should note

---

[1]See Robert N. Anthony and John Dearden, *Management Control Systems,* 3rd ed. (Homewood, Ill.: Irwin, 1976), p. 453, and William H. Newman, *Constructive Control* (Englewood Cliffs, N.J.: Prentice-Hall, 1975), p. 91.

that line managers (and managers of staff departments) are normally responsible for developing their own budgets and approving those of their subordinates. However, accountants often play a significant role in formulating, evaluating, and approving budgets. They will also play an important part in comparing actual versus planned results as the budgeted activities take place. Readers should keep in mind, then, that managers will often have to answer for their budgets not only to superiors but also to accountants or other financial specialists.

RESPONSIBILITY CENTERS AND BUDGETARY CONTROL

Control systems can be devised to monitor organizational *functions* or organizational *projects*. Controlling a function involves making sure that a specified organizational activity (such as production or sales) is properly carried out. Controlling a project involves making sure that a specified end result is achieved (such as the development of a new product or the completion of a building). Budgets can be used for both types of systems. In this chapter, however, we will emphasize the use of budgets to control functions rather than projects; the former use of budgets is by far the more common one in organizations.[2] We will discuss methods for controlling projects in Chapter 23.

Responsibility Centers

Any organizational or functional unit headed by a manager who is responsible for the activities of that unit is called a *responsibility center*. All responsibility centers use resources (inputs or costs) to produce something else (outputs or revenues). Depending on how these inputs and outputs are measured by the control system, there are four major types of responsibility centers: revenue centers, expense centers, profit centers, and investment centers. We will describe these briefly here; the types of budgets used in these centers will be described more fully later.

Revenue Centers. *Revenue centers* are those organizational units in which outputs are measured in monetary terms but are not directly compared to input costs. Examples of such units are sales and marketing departments. Budgets, or sales quotas, are prepared for individual salespeople and the revenue center as a whole; sales orders or actual sales are then compared with these budgets so that the effectiveness of individual salespeople or the center can be determined. The effectiveness of the center is not judged by how much revenue exceeds the costs of the center (in terms of office space and salaries, for example); comparing inputs to outputs is how a profit center is measured. Sales departments, for example, are not normally considered profit centers because they have very limited influence over such factors as product cost, product design, or marketing strategy. It is usually unreasonable, therefore, to give such units a profit-making responsibility.

[2]Our discussion will be based on Anthony and Dearden, *Management Control Systems*, Chapters 5, 6, and 8.

Expense Centers. In *expense centers,* inputs are measured by the control system in monetary terms but outputs are not; thus, budgets will be devised only for the input portion of these centers' operations. Organizational units commonly considered expense centers include administrative, service, and research departments.

There are two categories of expense centers: engineered and discretionary. *Engineered* expenses are those for which costs can be calculated or estimated with high reliability—for example, the costs of direct labor or raw material. *Discretionary* expenses are those for which costs cannot be reliably estimated beforehand (research costs, for example) and must depend to a large extent on the manager's judgment (or discretion). In both cases, actual input expenses will be measured against budgeted input expenses at review time.

Profit Centers. Performance in a *profit center* is measured by the numerical difference between revenues (outputs) and expenditures (inputs). Such a measure is used not only to determine how well the center is doing economically but also how well the manager in charge of the center is performing. Thus, profitability measures are one of the means by which managers of profit centers are motivated to high performance.

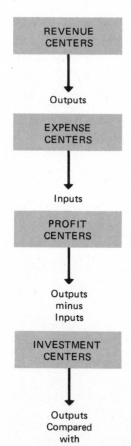

A profit center is created whenever an organizational unit is given responsibility for earning a profit. In a divisionalized organization, in which each of a number of divisions is completely responsible for its own product line, the separate divisions are considered profit centers. Stated simply, the expenditures of all a division's subunits are totaled and then subtracted from the revenues derived from that division's products or services. The net result is the measure of that division's profitability.

In nondivisionalized organizations, or *within* a division, individual departments may also be made into profit centers by crediting them for revenues and charging them for expenses. A manufacturing department, for example, would normally be considered an expense center. Allowing the manufacturing department to "sell" its products at an agreed-upon price (called a *transfer price*) to the sales department would be one way to turn that department into a profit center. The difference between the transfer price and the manufacturing cost per unit would represent the manufacturing department's "profit." Presumably, the more units the sales department sold, the more it would want to "purchase" from the manufacturing department (and the higher the manufacturing department's profits would be). The head of manufacturing might, therefore, be more motivated to improve product quality and customer service if his or her department were considered a profit center.

Investment Centers. The control system in an *investment center* does not measure only the monetary value of inputs and outputs; it also assesses how those outputs compare with the assets employed in producing them. Let us assume, for example, that a new hospital requires a capital investment of $20 million in property, buildings, equipment, and working capital. In its first year, the hospital has $2 million in labor and other input expenses and $4 million in revenue. The hospital would *not* be considered to have earned a $2 million profit for two reasons: a deduction from revenues would have to be made to allow for depreciation of buildings and equipment; and the cost of that investment, in terms of what *could* have been earned if the funds had been invested elsewhere, would have to be taken into account. In this way, a much more accurate picture of profitability would be obtained. Any profit center can, in fact, be considered an investment center as well, because its activities will require some form of capital investment. However, if a center's capital investment is minor (as in a consulting firm) or if its managers have no control over capital investment, it may be more appropriately treated as a profit center.

Two ways the effectiveness of an organization's use of its total assets (capital investment) can be measured are: through a return-on-investment ratio and through residual income. The *return-on-investment ratio* is simply a fraction in which net income (revenues minus expenses) is the numerator and total assets is the denominator. In our hospital example, the return on investment (ROI) before allowance for depreciation is 10 percent — $2 million ÷ $20 million — an inadequate return from an investment standpoint. *Residual income* is found by subtracting an interest charge (say, 10 percent) from the net income. This interest charge may be based on the interest being *paid* (to lenders) for the assets used in the investment; on the amount of income that could have been *earned* if the investment assets had been invested in some other activity; or on both, depending on the proportion of the investment assets borrowed.

ROI is the more widely used measure of investment effectiveness in organizations, mainly because it allows organizations to determine easily when a division or department is not profitable. However, different units frequently require widely dissimilar capital investments and often have different ROI targets. Thus, some companies do not find it meaningful to compare such units on their ROI. Instead, they use the residual income method, because it allows units with different profit objectives to be judged by one standard.

THE BUDGETING PROCESS

In this section, we will describe the budgeting process briefly. We will focus on four key areas: the ways in which budgets are drawn up and approved; the role played by the budget department and budget committees; the ways in which budgets are revised; and problems that commonly occur when budgets are being developed.[3]

How Budgets Are Drawn Up and Approved

The budgeting process usually begins when managers receive top management's economic forecasts and sales and profit objectives for the coming year. These will usually be accompanied by a timetable stating when budgets must

---

[3] See Gordon Shillinglaw, *Managerial Cost Accounting,* 4th ed. (Homewood, Ill.: Irwin, 1977); Jeremy Bacon, *Managing the Budget Function* (New York: National Industrial Conference Board, 1970); and Anthony and Dearden, *Management Control Systems,* pp. 457–462.

be completed. The forecasts and objectives provided by top management will represent guidelines within which other managers' budgets will be developed.

In a few organizations, budgets are imposed by top managers with little or no consultation with lower-level managers. Together with the controller, top managers in those organizations not only establish overall goals but also work out detailed objectives and budgets for all management levels and responsibility centers. Subordinates are sometimes given an opportunity to offer counter-proposals, but these may or may not be accepted.[4]

Most companies, however, now believe that budgets should be prepared, at least initially, by those who must implement them. These budgets are then sent up the hierarchy for approval by superiors. This type of "bottom-up" budgeting has five distinct virtues:

1   Supervisors and department heads at the lower levels of responsibility have a more intimate view of their needs than those at the top.
2   Lower-level managers can provide more realistic breakdowns to support their proposals.
3   Managers are less likely to overlook some vital ingredient or hidden flaw that might subsequently impede implementation efforts if they develop the budgets for their own units.
4   Managers will be more strongly motivated to accept and meet budgets that they have had a hand in shaping.
5   Morale and satisfaction are usually higher when individuals participate actively in making decisions that affect them.[5]

Because of these virtues, the budgets devised by lower-level managers will sometimes contain more ambitious objectives than would have been imposed by top managers.

The process by which lower-level managers participate in developing budgets very much resembles the multilevel planning process we described at the end of Chapter 5. Supervisors prepare their own budget proposals within the limits defined by upper management. These are reviewed by department heads, who meet and negotiate with lower-level supervisors if they feel changes are necessary. When lower-level budgets are finalized, department heads draw up their department budgets and submit these to their superiors for approval. The entire process continues until all the budgets are finalized and assembled into one integrated package by the controller or budget director. This organization-wide budget is submitted to the president (or budget committee) for further review, alteration, or approval. Finally, the master budget goes to the board of directors. The plan goes into effect when the board approves it.

[4]See Chris Argyris, "Human Problems with Budgets," *Harvard Business Review,* January 1953, pp. 97–110, for a good description of this process.
[5]See, for example, Selwin W. Becker and David Green, Jr., "Budgeting and Employee Behavior," *Journal of Business,* Vol. 35, No. 4 (October 1962), pp. 392–402.

The Role of
Budget
Personnel

Developing budgets is basically the function of line managers. Staff people from a planning group or budget department may provide information and technical assistance, but the main responsibility for budgets remains with line personnel. (Managers of staff departments will, of course, be responsible for their own department budgets – see Chapter 11.)

Many organizations have formal budget departments and committees. These groups are likely to exist in large, divisionalized organizations in which the division budget plays a key role in planning, coordinating, and controlling activities. The *budget department,* which generally reports to the corporate controller, provides budget information and assistance to organizational units, designs budget systems and forms, integrates the various departmental proposals into a master budget for the organization as a whole, and reports on actual performance relative to the budget.

The *budget committee,* made up of senior executives from all functional areas, reviews the individual budgets, reconciles divergent views, alters or approves the budget proposals, and then refers the integrated package to the board of directors. Later, when the plans have been put into practice, the committee reviews the control reports that monitor progress. In most cases, the budget committee must approve any revisions made during the budget period.

How Budgets
Are Revised

Obviously, no manager can be allowed to revise a budget whenever he or she pleases; otherwise the entire review and approval process would be a charade. Still, because budgets are based on forecasts, which can easily go wrong, some provision must be made for necessary revisions. In cases where the budget is used primarily as a planning tool, formal updating periods may be established at stated intervals. Where the budget is a main part of the control and evaluation mechanism, revisions are limited to cases where deviations have become so great as to make the approved budget unrealistic. The aim is to build reasonable stability and firmness into the budget without being excessively rigid.

Comparisons of actual performance with budgets are known as reviews or *audits.* To be effective, audits depend on a regular, accurate flow of data from organizational units. Unit managers will regularly submit monthly or weekly progress reports, unless a problem requires immediate attention. (Daily reports may be used in special situations, as when a new product is being market tested.) Usually these reports are audited on a monthly basis by those individuals with control responsibility. If deviations are detected, the appropriate managers will be asked to explain them and to specify the corrective action they plan to take. Serious deviations, as we have already suggested, require that the budget be revised.

Some Problems
in Budget
Development

There are a number of anxieties that commonly arise during the budget development process. During that process, the organization's limited resources are allocated, and managers may fear that they will not be given their fair share. Tension will heighten as competition with other managers increases. Managers are also aware that they will be judged by their ability to meet or beat budgeted standards, and so are anxious about what those standards will be. Conversely, their superiors are concerned with establishing aggressive budget objectives, and so will often be anxious to trim their subordinates' expenditure requests or to raise their revenue targets.

Henry L. Tosi has described four important reactions to these budget development anxieties: political behavior, dysfunctional reactions toward budget units, overstatement of needs, and the development of covert information systems.[6]

Political Behavior. Political activity may increase sharply when budgets are being developed as managers try to influence resource allocations. Managers may withhold information until the last minute in order to magnify its importance, ingratiate themselves with superiors, or attempt to gain influence in other ways. If such political behavior results in one unit getting more than it really needs or deserves, the performance of other units and the organization as a whole may be hindered.

Dysfunctional Reactions to Budget Units. Supervisors who are unhappy with resource allocations are not really in a position to vent their anger on their superiors, who determine their promotions, bonuses, and salary increases. Instead, they will usually take out their hostility on the staff personnel who compile the budget data and assemble the final budget figures. They may, for example, make it hard for budget personnel to get the timely and accurate information they need. As a result, the entire budgeting process may suffer.

Overstatement of Needs. To protect themselves in the struggle for resources and to compensate for the fact that cuts are often made in requested amounts, some managers pad their budget estimates. Managers who submit requests based only on their actual needs will then suffer if their requests are automatically cut along with those of other managers. In that case, they quickly learn to pad their requests as well. The result is that the entire budgeting process becomes tainted by "game playing."

Slack is often built into budgets as a hedge against unforeseen events. For example, in preparing their budgets, some school systems build in conservative income and excessive expenditure estimates as a safety margin.[7] Sometimes, however, the slack can be quite considerable. For example, one study found that the operating expenses budgeted for divisions overstated expected expenses by as much as 25 percent.[8] Such overstatements suggest that the budgeting process is not functioning as well as it should.

---

[6]Henry L. Tosi, Jr., "The Human Effects of Budgeting Systems on Management," *MSU Business Topics,* Vol. 22, No. 4 (Autumn 1974), pp. 53–63.

[7]See John F. Hulpke and Donald A. Watne, "Budgeting Behavior: If, When, and How Selected School Districts Hide Money," *Public Administration Review,* Vol. 36, No. 6 (November-December 1976), pp. 667–674.

[8]Michael Schiff and Arie Y. Lewin, "Where Traditional Budgeting Fails," *Financial Executive,* Vol. 36, No. 5 (May 1968), pp. 51–52 ff. See also M. Dalton, *Men Who Manage* (New York: Wiley, 1959), pp. 31–52, for an interesting discussion of how managers distort budget reports for their own ends.

Covert Information Systems. When budgets are kept secret, managers will often try to find out how their allocations compare with others by developing covert or informal information sources — secretaries, budget staff members, or colleagues. The danger for the organization does not lie in the fact that secrecy may be breached but in the very real possibility that inaccurate information will be spread through the grapevine. The rivalry and tension between organizational units may therefore be increased.

Tosi suggests that organization-wide participation in the budgeting process often minimizes these types of anxiety reactions. When all managers are involved in budget development, they are more likely to be satisfied with their resource allocations.

TYPES OF BUDGETS

In this section we will describe the various types of budgets an organization can use. Before we begin our discussion, we should note that the comprehensive budgets of an organization are usually divided into two parts: operating budgets and financial budgets. The *operating budgets* indicate the goods and services the organization expects to consume in the budget period; they usually list both physical quantities (such as barrels of oil) and cost figures. The *financial budgets* spell out in detail the money the organization intends to spend in the same period and where that money will come from. Figure 22-1 shows the operating and financial components of a manufacturing firm's comprehensive budget. Each rectangle in the diagram represents one or more of the types of budgets we describe below. These different types of budgets make up the firm's overall budgetary plan.[9]

Budgets Based on Responsibility Centers
The most common types of budgets parallel three of the responsibility centers discussed earlier — expense, revenue, and profit.[10]

Expense Budgets. There are two types of expense budgets, one for each of the two types of expense centers — engineered cost budgets and discretionary cost budgets.

Engineered cost budgets are typically used in manufacturing plants; however, they can be used by any organizational unit in which output can be accurately measured. These budgets usually describe the material and labor costs involved in each production item, as well as the estimated overhead costs.

Engineered cost budgets are designed to measure efficiency: exceeding the budget will mean that operating costs were higher than they should have been. Responsibility for the budget (and therefore for cost overruns) generally rests

[9] See Shillinglaw, *Managerial Cost Accounting*, pp. 136–137.
[10] Our discussion is based on Anthony and Dearden, *Management Control Systems*, pp. 186–188, 454–457.

FIGURE 22-1
Budget
Components

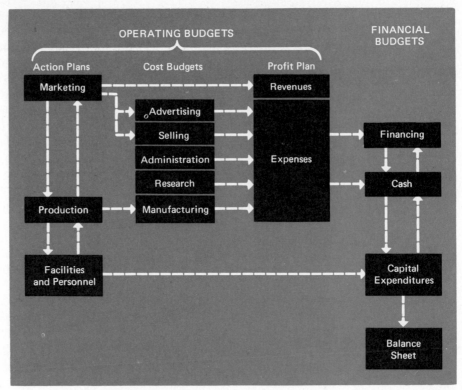

OPERATING BUDGETS

FINANCIAL BUDGETS

Action Plans   Cost Budgets   Profit Plan

Marketing

Advertising

Selling

Administration

Research

Production   Manufacturing

Facilities and Personnel

Revenues

Expenses

Financing

Cash

Capital Expenditures

Balance Sheet

Source: Gordon Shillinglaw, *Managerial Cost Accounting,* 4th ed. (Homewood, Ill.: Richard D. Irwin, Inc., 1977), p. 137. Reproduced with permission of the publisher.

with the operating manager, who is supposed to make reliable cost estimates when developing the budget and who controls many of the variables (such as productivity) that will affect manufacturing efficiency.

Discretionary cost budgets are typically used for administrative, legal, accounting, research, and other such departments in which output cannot be accurately measured. Managers of such departments try to control costs by setting limits on the tasks that will be performed and on the level of effort that will be used to carry out those tasks. Actual department expenses are periodically compared to budgeted expenses so that higher-level managers will be informed if a cost overrun occurs.

Unlike engineered cost budgets, discretionary cost budgets are not used to assess efficiency, because performance standards for discretionary expenses are difficult to devise. For example, if the market research department exceeds its budget, it will often be difficult for managers to determine how that department's work could have been performed more efficiently. In addition, managers of discretionary expense centers usually cannot exceed their budgets without higher-level approval. Managers of engineered expense centers, however, normally do not require higher-level approval to exceed their budgets.

Revenue Budgets. *Revenue budgets* consist of the expected quantity of sales multiplied by the expected unit selling price of each product. The revenue budget is the most critical part of a profit budget, yet it is also one of the most uncertain, because it is based on projected future sales. Companies with a large volume of back orders or where sales volume is limited only by the companies' productive capacity can make firmer revenue forecasts than companies that must reckon with the swings of an unstable or unpredictable market. However, marketing and sales managers of even these latter companies can control the quality and quantity of their advertising, service, personnel training, and other factors that affect sales. This control gives them some influence over sales volume and frequently enables them to make reasonably accurate sales estimates.

Revenue budgets are meant to measure marketing and sales effectiveness. But since marketing and sales managers ultimately have far less control over sales than operating managers have over costs, they are not normally expected to achieve the same degree of success in reaching their targets. Thus, revenue budgets are a less useful tool for managerial evaluation than are cost budgets.

Profit Budgets. A *profit budget* combines cost and revenue budgets in one statement. It is used by managers who have responsibility for both the expenses and revenues of their units. Such managers frequently head an entire division or company. The profit budgets, which are sometimes called *master budgets,* consist of a set of projected financial statements and schedules for the coming year. Thus, they serve as annual profit plans.

Profit budgets have three main uses:

1. They plan and coordinate overall company or division activities. For example, they make it possible to integrate the use of manufacturing facilities with sales forecasts.

2. They provide benchmarks that are useful in judging the adequacy of expense budgets. For example, if the budget indicates that profits will be low, the expense budget might be revised downward.

3. They help assign responsibility to each manager for his or her share of the overall organization's performance. For example, the head of the manufacturing department will be held accountable for the manufacturing expenses in the budget.

Financial Budgets

The *capital expenditure, cash, financing,* and *balance sheet budgets* integrate the financial planning of the organization with its operational planning. These budgets, prepared with information developed from the revenue, expense, and operating budgets, serve three major purposes. First, they verify the viability of the operating budgets ("Will we generate enough cash to do what we are planning to do?"). Second, their preparation reveals financial actions that the organization must take to make execution of its operating budgets possible ("If events conform to plans, we'll be short of cash in October and November; we'd better talk to our bankers this month about a line of credit to cover that period"). Third, they indicate how the organization's operating plans will affect its future financial actions. If these actions are difficult or undesirable to take, appropriate changes in the operating plans may be required. ("In order to make our planned capital expenditures, we will have to arrange major borrowings in the capital markets in the next twelve months. But our economists say that will be poor timing; we had better rethink the expansion of our unit in Texas.")

Capital Expenditure Budgets. *Capital expenditure budgets* indicate the future investments in new buildings, property, equipment and other physical assets the organization is planning in order to renew and expand its productive capacity. Formulation of the capital expenditure budget reveals important projects the organization will undertake and some of the more significant cash requirements the organization will face a number of years into the future. Because of the long useful life of buildings and equipment and their relative inflexibility, the choices made on new capital expenditures are not easily altered. Thus, the decisions in the capital expenditure budget are frequently among the more important ones for the organization.

Cash Budgets. *Cash budgets* bring together the organization's budgeted estimates for revenues, expenses, and new capital expenditures. The development of the cash budget will frequently reveal information about the *level* of funds flowing through the organization and about the *pattern* of cash disbursements and receipts. The level or pattern may require managerial action. For example, preparation of the cash budget may show that the firm will be generating a great deal more cash than it will be using during the next year. This information may encourage management to move more aggressively on its capital expenditure program or even to consider additional areas of investment. Alternatively, development of the cash budget may show a very satisfactory cash position throughout the year with the exception of one or two months when disbursements exceed receipts by a considerable amount. Short-term borrowing would then be arranged in advance to cover those months.

Financing Budgets. *Financing budgets* are developed to assure the organization of the availability of funds to meet the shortfalls of revenues relative to expenses in the short run and to schedule medium- and longer-term borrowing or financing. These budgets are developed in conjunction with the cash budget to provide the organization with the funds it needs at the times it needs them.

Balance Sheet Budgets. The *balance sheet budget* brings together all of the other budgets to project how the balance sheet will look at the end of the period if actual results conform to planned results. This budget, also called a *pro forma* balance sheet (see Chapter 23), can be thought of as a final check on the organization's planned programs and activities. Because it is based entirely on the other budgets, it does not require managers to make any new projections or decisions. However, analysis of the balance sheet budget may suggest problems or opportunities that will require managers to alter some of the other budgets. For example, the balance sheet budget may indicate that the company has planned to borrow more heavily than is prudent. This information might lead to a reduction in planned borrowing and reduced capital expenditures on the one hand, or—alternatively—to the decision to issue additional stock to obtain some of the desired financing.

Variable versus Fixed Budgets

One difficulty with budgets is that they are often inflexible. Thus, they may be seen as inappropriate for situations that change in ways beyond the control of those responsible for achieving the budgeted objectives. For example, an expense budget based on annual sales of $12 million may be completely off track if sales of $15 million are achieved. The expense of manufacturing will almost always increase if more items are produced to meet the larger demand. It would therefore be unreasonable to expect managers to keep to the original expense budget.

To deal with this difficulty, many managers resort to a *variable* budget. (This type of budget is referred to by a variety of names, such as flexible budgets, sliding-scale budgets, and step budgets.) Where *fixed* budgets express what individual costs should be at *one* specified volume, variable budgets are cost *schedules* that show how each cost should vary as the level of activity or output varies. For instance, a variable budget might indicate that expenses will rise an additional $10,000 for every ten items produced over a certain amount. Variable budgets are, therefore, useful in identifying in a fair and realistic manner how costs are affected by the amount of work being done. For this reason, they are widely used in businesses not only to plan and control activities but also to help evaluate managerial effectiveness.

Fixed, Variable, and Semivariable Costs. There are three types of costs that must be considered when variable budgets are being developed: fixed, variable, and semivariable costs.[11]

Fixed costs are those that are unaffected by the amount of work being done in the responsibility center. These costs accumulate only with the passage of time. For example, for many organizational units, monthly salaries, insurance payments, rent, and research expenditures will not vary significantly for moderate ranges of activity. (See Figure 22-2.)

Variable costs are expenses that vary directly with the quantity of work being performed. The obvious example of a variable cost factor is raw materials—the more goods produced, the greater the quantity (and cost) of raw materials required.

Semivariable costs are those that vary with the volume of work performed but *not* in a directly proportional way. In other words, semivariable costs

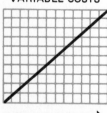

FIXED COSTS

VARIABLE COSTS

Quantity of Work

---

[11] We are indebted to Glenn A. Welsch, *Budgeting: Profit Planning and Control*, 4th ed. (Englewood Cliffs, N.J.: Prentice-Hall, 1976), for our treatment of this topic.

FIGURE 22-2
The Variable and
Fixed Components
of Total Cost

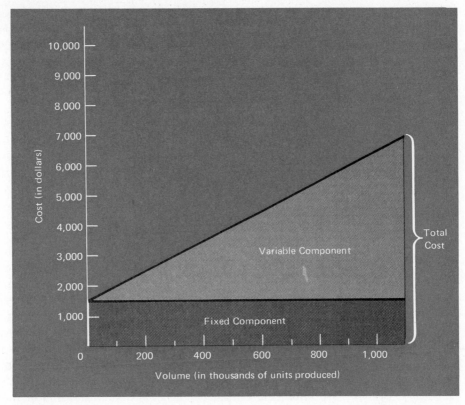

contain a mix of both fixed and variable elements. Semivariable costs often represent a major part of an organization's expenses. For example, over the long term, labor costs are usually semivariable—the number of personnel hired (or laid off) will rarely be based directly on day-to-day changes in production. Similarly, the cost of the total sales effort often does not vary directly with the number of products sold.

Devising Variable Budgets. In devising their budgets, managers must try to break down their total costs into the above categories. It would be a waste of time and effort to devise variable budgets when most costs are fixed; and it would result in poor budget estimates to devise fixed budgets when most costs are variable. Isolating the fixed and variable elements in their total costs, on the other hand, allows managers to devise more accurate and useful budgets.

The problem in devising variable budgets is that cost variability is often difficult to determine. Usually managers will use one or more of the following three methods to determine their variable costs:

1 *Direct estimates.* Managers estimate which components of their expenses are variable, either by exercising their judgment based on past experience or by relying on studies performed by industrial engineers.

605

2 *High and low point method.* Two budgets are developed — one for maximum assumed output and one for minimum assumed output. The difference in cost between these two budgets divided by the difference in volume will yield the variable rate.

3 *Correlation method.* Monthly data on the organization's past output and cost variability are assembled. Projections based on these data and on conditions in the present are made to estimate future cost variability.

Variable budgets are used most appropriately in responsibility centers where operations are repetitive, where there are a large number of different expenses, and where these expenses can be accurately estimated. The main disadvantage of variable budgets is that they are often quite expensive to prepare.

SPECIAL APPROACHES TO BUDGETING

In this section we will describe two special approaches to the budgeting process. The first approach is known as PPBS — Planning-Programming-Budgeting System. The federal government attempted to implement PPBS in the mid- and late 1960s in order to improve its entire budgeting system. Even though this attempt was abandoned in 1971, the Defense Department has continued to use PPBS. Some state and local governments also have implemented the PPBS approach. The second approach we will describe is zero-base budgeting (ZBB). While this approach was initially developed by a corporation, President Carter has since mandated its use for the 1979 federal budget. PPBS and ZBB are infrequently used by business organizations. For this reason, our focus will be on the application of these approaches to nonprofit organizations and federal, state, and local governments.

PPBS The Planning-Programming-Budgeting System was originally introduced to the Department of Defense in 1961. Because of its apparent success, it was extended to the rest of the federal government in 1965. The system was designed to identify costly duplication of programs by different departments and agencies, to analyze the potential impact of government programs, and to tie in those programs more closely with the annual budget. The system did not prove successful throughout the federal government for the reasons discussed below. However, it continues to be used in many types of governmental and educational institutions and offers many advantages over traditional budgeting systems.[12]

There are five basic steps in the Planning-Programming-Budgeting System:[13]

[12] Peter A. Pyhrr, *Zero-Base Budgeting* (New York: Wiley, 1973).

[13] Robert N. Anthony and Regina E. Herzlinger, *Management Control in Nonprofit Organizations* (Homewood, Ill.: Irwin, 1975). See also George A. Steiner, "Program Budgeting," *Business Horizons,* Vol. 8, No. 1 (Spring 1965), pp. 43–52; Samuel M. Greenhouse, "The Planning-Programming-Budgeting System," *Public Administration Review,* Vol. 26, No. 4 (December 1966), pp. 271–277; and Allen Schick, "A Death in the Bureaucracy: The Demise of Federal PPBS," *Public Administration Review,* Vol. 32, No. 2 (March-April 1973), pp. 146–156.

1. *Specify and analyze basic objectives in each major area of activity.* The aim of this step is to force government or nonprofit agencies to ask themselves: "What are we really trying to accomplish?" For example, the objective of the Defense Department is *not* to win wars but to deter attacks on the United States and its allies. From this perspective, it becomes possible to analyze the various elements in defense programs to see which accomplish these objectives most efficiently and effectively. If the higher goals of the department are not kept in mind, its various programs and weapons systems are difficult to compare directly.

2. *Analyze the output of a given program in the light of the specified objectives.* In this step, agencies try to answer the question, "How well is this program achieving its objectives?" To take our Defense Department example again, the measure of a program's effectiveness would *not* be the quantity of weapons being built but whether or not these weapons are providing increased security.

3. *Measure the total cost of the program for several years ahead.* Agencies often embark on a program based on the costs of that program for a year or two. In fact, costs of most programs—particularly in government—grow enormously over a period of years. A new weapons program, for example, may involve an initial $25 million in research and design costs. The manufacture and maintenance of the weapons developed in the program may eventually lead to costs of several hundred million dollars annually. Projecting costs into the future enables managers to make budget decisions in the present that are more realistically based.

4. *Analyze the alternatives.* In this step, managers try to analyze which of the alternatives available to them will most effectively and efficiently achieve the stated objectives. This step is the most crucial one in the entire PPBS approach. In the Defense Department example, the analysis might involve comparing the effectiveness and cost of improving and updating the existing B-52 bomber fleet with that of building a new fleet of B-1 bombers.

5. *Make the approach an integral part of the budgetary process.* The PPBS approach would only be a theoretical exercise if it did not become a basis for making budget decisions.

The Problems of Implementation. Changing and improving the governmental budgeting process proved to be a very difficult task. PPBS was never accepted by federal agencies outside the Department of Defense. In addition, Congress was generally critical of the approach and failed to give it the support it required.

What were some of the reasons for the failure to implement what appears to be an improved approach to budgeting? The most important reason was probably the opposition of the agencies and departments involved. Such resistance to change seems to develop whenever a new program is introduced without prior consultation with those affected by the change. (See, for example, Chapter 15.) In the case of PPBS, President Johnson's insistence that the approach be put to immediate use gave the various agencies and Congress too little time to prepare for it. Thus, agency heads and members of Congress were only vaguely aware of the advantages and techniques of the system they were supposed to supervise. Furthermore, the Federal Budget Bureau tried to implement the Defense Department's version of the system throughout the executive branch, even though that version's language and procedures were not completely appropriate for civilian agencies. If those agencies had been allowed to develop their own version of PPBS, it might have been more successful.

Zero-Base Budgeting

In the normal budgeting process, the previous year's level of expenditure is often assumed to have been appropriate. The task of individuals preparing the budget is to decide what activities and funds should be dropped and, more often, what activities and funds should be added. Such a process builds into an organization a bias toward continuing the same activities year after year—well after their relevance and usefulness may have been lost because of environmental changes or changes in the organization's objectives.

Zero-base budgeting, in contrast, enables the organization to look at its activities and priorities afresh. The previous year's resource allocations are not automatically considered the basis of this year's allocations. Instead, each manager has to justify anew his or her entire budget request. Whereas PPBS originated in a government agency, ZBB was developed by Texas Instruments, Inc. Later, President Carter introduced it successfully in Georgia when he was governor of that state; he is now attempting to implement it in the executive branch of the federal government.

In essence, ZBB involves allocating an organization's funds on the basis of a cost-benefit analysis of each of the organization's major activities.[14] The process involves three major steps:

1. *Break down each of an organization's activities into "decision packages."* A "decision package" includes all the information about an activity that managers need to evaluate that activity and compare its costs and benefits with other activities. Such information might include the activity's purpose, costs, and estimated benefits, *plus* the consequences expected if the activity is not approved and the alternative activities that are available to meet the same purpose.

2. *Evaluate the various activities and rank them in order of decreasing benefit to the organization.* Usually each manager will rank the activities for which he or she is responsible. These rankings are then passed on to a superior, who will (together with the lower managers) establish rankings for all the activities in his or her department. This process continues until rankings for all organizational activities are reviewed and selected by top managers.

3. *Allocate resources.* The organization's resources are budgeted according to the final ranking that has been established. Generally, funds for top-priority activities will be allocated fairly quickly; lower-priority items will be scrutinized much more carefully.

[14]See Peter A. Pyhrr, "Zero-Base Budgeting," *Harvard Business Review,* November-December 1970, pp. 111–121.

ZBB includes these benefits: managers must quantify each alternative and thereby provide the measures needed for comparisons; low-priority programs can be cut or eliminated with more confidence; and alternative programs and their advantages are presented with greater clarity for periodic review. However, the approach does have some drawbacks as well. One major problem is that bureaucrats are often very reluctant to submit their programs to such intense scrutiny. They may therefore inflate the importance of the activities they control. In addition, managers may fail to develop enough information to allow for a meaningful analysis of a decision package. These problems can often be overcome through training of managers in the ZBB approach and with effective administration of the entire program.

FUNCTIONAL AND DYSFUNCTIONAL ASPECTS OF BUDGET SYSTEMS

In Chapter 21, we noted that the word "control" has negative connotations for many people. The same holds true for the word "budget." However, like other types of control, budgets have many aspects with the *potential* to help organizations and their members reach their goals. How functional budgets turn out to be in practice will depend on how effectively managers conceive and carry out the budgeting process. It is particularly important that the budgeting process, like other types of control, be clear and acceptable to the people whose activities it is intended to control.

Potentially Functional Aspects of Budgets

V. Bruce Irvine has described some of the potentially functional aspects of budgets:[15]

1. *Budgets can have a positive impact on motivation and morale.* A basic human need is to belong to and be accepted by one's group. Budgets activate this motivational factor by creating the feeling that everyone is working toward a common goal.

2. *Budgets make it possible to coordinate the work of the entire organization.* Since a comprehensive budget is a blueprint of all the firm's plans for the coming year, top management can tie together the activities of every unit.

3. *Budgets can be used as a signaling device for taking corrective action.* One of the main purposes of any control system is to alert the appropriate organization members that a standard has been violated. If, for example, the expenses incurred exceed the budgeted ones by a significant margin, then managers know that some corrective action is probably needed.

4. *The budget system helps people learn from past experience.* Once the budget period is over, managers can analyze what occurred, isolate errors and their causes, and take steps to avoid those errors in the next budget period.

5. *Budgets improve resource allocation.* In the budgeting process, all requests for resources should be clarified and logically supported. The need

[15]V. Bruce Irvine, "Budgeting: Functional Analysis and Behavioral Implications," *Cost and Management*, Vol. 44, No. 2 (March-April 1970), pp. 6–16.

to quantify their plans forces managers to examine their available resources more carefully when considering how to allocate them.

6. *Budgets improve communication.* A plan cannot be put into effect unless it is communicated to those who must carry it out. In the process of developing the budget with those responsible for its implementation, managers can communicate their own objectives and plans more effectively.

7. *Budgets help lower-level managers see where they fit in the organization.* The budget gives these managers goals around which to organize their activities. In addition, it indicates what organizational resources will be made available to them.

8. *Budgets let new people see where the organization is going.* This aspect of budgets can enhance the morale of junior managers because it helps them become acclimated to the organization's goals and priorities. In addition, they can more easily determine the nature of their responsibilities.

9. *Budgets serve as a means of evaluation.* Performance can more easily (and often more fairly) be measured against previously approved benchmarks.

Potentially Dysfunctional Aspects of Budgets

Managers often find that unintended and unanticipated consequences arise from their budget systems. These dysfunctional aspects of their budget systems may interfere with the attainment of the organization's goals. In this section we will describe some of the dysfunctional aspects of the budgeting process that commonly develop.[16] (The more general problems associated with any control system will be discussed in Chapter 24.) The dysfunctional aspects of budgets we will discuss are: (1) differing perceptions of budgets by line members and by budget staff members; (2) mechanical difficulties with budgets; (3) problems in effectively communicating budgets; (4) problems in using budgets to motivate employees; and (5) problems that arise when too high or too low budget goals are set.

Differing Perceptions of Budgets by Line and Budget Staff Members. Based on his interviews with supervisors in four different companies, Irvine identified a number of reasons why budgets are often perceived as dysfunctional. It is important to note that these reasons depend less on organizational realities than on the supervisors' *perceptions* of those realities. The reasons are:

a. Budgets are used to evaluate results, but the causes of failure or success are frequently not investigated. Budgets would be regarded as more fair and useful if the reasons for budget deviations and mitigating circumstances were taken into account.

b. Budgets are useful for analyzing the past and charting the future, but they are seen as little help in handling the here-and-now problems that supervisors have.

c. Budgets are often too rigid. Sometimes the approved standards have been left unchanged for two or three years; meeting budget in such cases

[16]Our discussion is based on Irvine, "Budgeting: Functional Analysis and Behavioral Implications," and Argyris, "Human Problems with Budgets."

"I have before me, gentlemen, some figures that may shock you, as they did me."

Drawing by Modell; © 1977 The New Yorker Magazine, Inc.

would hardly represent efficient performance. Budgets need more "give" to make them responsive to internal or external environmental changes.

d. Sometimes, on the other hand, budgets are changed too frequently. As the supervisors in the study observed, if a standard is raised every time performance comes close to the original budget figures, how can they ever satisfy their superiors?

e. Budget staff members sometimes use incomprehensible jargon and specialized formats, making it difficult for managers to understand performance reports. Thus, they cannot adequately respond to criticisms of them included in budget staff reports.

Mechanical Considerations. Certain potentially negative effects of budgets can be traced to the mechanics of budgets and the budgeting process. For instance, there are expenses involved in installing and operating a budget system; if these costs outweigh the benefits obtained by the system, the organization's goals are not being effectively achieved.

The fact that budgets involve estimates of future costs and events may also lead to problems, since these estimates may prove to be grossly inaccurate. The unreliability of budget estimates is often increased, according to Irvine, when budgets are regarded as *ends* in themselves, rather than as *means* to a goal. For example, managers may attempt to keep expenses down throughout the organization by setting severe limits on how much any unit can increase this year's budget relative to last year's. Such a procedure might result in a situation in which activities that have recently increased in importance will be inadequately funded. When managers keep their ultimate goal in mind, they usually devise their budget estimates more carefully.

Problems frequently arise if budgets assign costs to one person when those costs are actually caused by another person. In such a case, the resentment that usually develops between the individuals involved may hinder the organization's effectiveness.

Communication and Budgets. Like other control devices, budgets are least effective when they are used punitively. Often, budget department members will report actual results directly to superiors; the employees whose performance is being controlled may not know how well they have conformed to the budget until their superiors call them in about a problem or perhaps not even until a performance appraisal takes place. As a result, employees will regard budgets purely as a rating tool or as a device for catching their mistakes. In addition, deviations may not be communicated to them until the budget period is over; as a result, employees never get the opportunity to learn from their mistakes and to take corrective action on their own.

However, when actual results are communicated swiftly and directly to the employees whose performance is being controlled, the employees can more easily determine what mistakes they have made. They can then act to correct those errors or at least avoid repeating them in the future. In addition, they will rely more confidently on the budget for guidance in their daily activities. Thus, quick communication of actual results is critical in making budgets effective training devices. (See Figure 22-3.)

FIGURE 22-3
The Importance of the Communication Factor When Using Budgets to Control and Motivate Employees

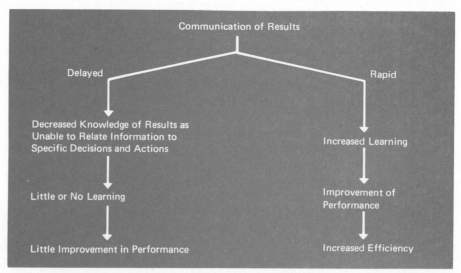

Source: V. Bruce Irvine, "Budgeting: Functional Analysis and Behavioral Implications," *Cost and Management* (Journal of the Society of Management Accountants of Canada), March-April 1970, p. 14. Used by permission.

The Motivational Impact of Budgets. One of the major reasons for the widespread use of budgets is that managers believe budgets are effective motivational devices. When budgeted standards are not met, it is assumed that people will be motivated to work harder to meet the standards next time and so earn organizational rewards. When high standards are set and made known to employees, managers believe the employees will be more motivated to attain those standards. In short, the budgeted standards are believed to create pressure on employees to perform up to par.

The motivational impact of budgets can be analyzed in terms of *force fields,* a concept developed by Kurt Lewin.[17] Lewin suggested that any behavior is the result of an equilibrium between opposing *driving* and *restraining* forces. For example, driving forces that would motivate an individual to work late at the office might include a pride in meeting deadlines, the need to impress colleagues, or the fear of organizational censure. Restraining forces might include fatigue, resentment at the amount of work involved, and the desire to be someplace else. The equilibrium between these forces will determine how late the individual stays.

Managers often try to motivate employees to high performance by increasing the driving forces – promising more rewards or applying verbal pressure, for example. However, while increasing the driving forces may sometimes raise performance, it often creates counteracting restraining forces that will prevent performance improvement or make any improvement only temporary. Also, the tension and resentment in the work situation is often increased. (The employees may work harder, for example, but they may not work more efficiently and may also enjoy work less.) Reducing the *restraining* forces does not have these disadvantages. Thus, it is usually preferable to decrease restraining forces in order to raise the level of performance.

The budgeting process often creates driving forces that increase the pressure on employees. With precise goals stated on paper, budgets leave little room for employees to escape censure if results fail to come up to par. In addition, as Irvine notes, there are a number of specific ways that managers use budgets to raise their subordinates' performance:

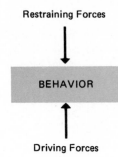

Restraining Forces

BEHAVIOR

Driving Forces

1 Budget "pep" talks
2 Red circles around poor showings
3 Production and sales drives built around the budget
4 Threats of reprimand
5 Induced feelings of failure if budgets are not met

---

[17]Kurt Lewin, "Group Decision and Social Change," in Eleanor E. Maccoby, Theodore M. Newcomb, and Eugene L. Hartley, *Readings in Social Psychology,* 3rd ed. (New York: Holt, Rinehart and Winston, 1958), pp. 197–211. See also Edgar F. Huse, *Organization Development and Change* (St. Paul: West Publishing, 1975). Force field analysis is a popular technique used by OD practitioners and is similar to the other techniques described in Chapter 15. It can be used by readers to analyze many types of change problems.

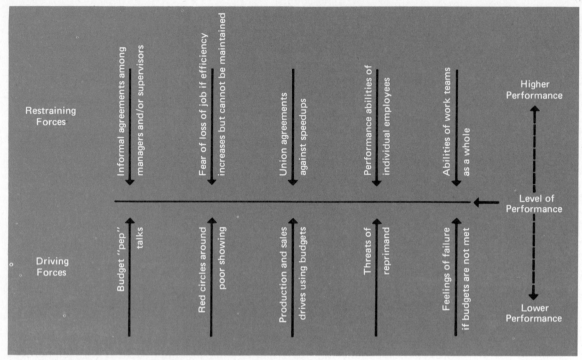

FIGURE 22-4   Force Field Analysis of Budgeting Situation

These pressures for increased efficiency are felt by employees, who will begin to resist and resent them. The employees will often try to find ways to minimize their growing work load and protect themselves from censure. Dysfunctional restraining forces may therefore be generated that counteract the pressures exerted by top management. For example:

—Employees may make informal agreements against speedups.
—Interdepartmental strife may increase, with every supervisor trying to blame budget deviations on someone else.
—Scapegoating may increase, as line people blame staff members for budget deviations, or production department members blame salespeople for a poor sales record.
—Managers may internalize the pressures, building up anxieties, tension, and resentment within themselves. Their work efficiency may therefore decline.
—Managers may try to manipulate results. For example, they may exaggerate their costs during one budget period so that their allocation during the next period will be increased.

Even if these opposing force fields stabilize at a higher level of production, the hostilities and suspicions generated by the conflicting pressures will now be directed toward keeping the new production level from rising again. Any new attempt to increase performance may be met by strikes, slowdowns, and other dysfunctional actions. (See Figure 22-4.)

To blunt the dysfunctional impact on motivation, Irvine suggests that management would do better if it reduced the forces that decrease performance rather than increased the pressures for greater performance. For example, the resentment that budget pressures generate can often be reduced when managers and subordinates meet, develop, and agree on budget standards together. Meetings can also be held to discuss any problems that employees anticipate with a particular budget and ways the budget can be improved. The budgets might also be used more openly as a positive rating device; budget staff members should be encouraged to credit publicly individuals who are coming in under budget, instead of just publicizing poor showings.

Goal Difficulty and Goal Achievement. Much of what management writers have noted about negative reactions to budgets is related to two common faults:

1 Budget goals may be perceived as too high—for example, a very high sales or production level may have been set.
2 The amount of resources allocated to attain the budgeted goals may be perceived as inadequate—for example, the expense budget may be too restrictive for the goals to be accomplished.

One generally accepted guideline for effective budgeting is to establish goals that are *difficult but attainable*. A goal too easily achieved will usually fail to motivate or encourage employees. In fact, the budgeting goals may provoke mediocre performance if they seem to indicate that management will be satisfied with mediocrity. Conversely, if the goals are set unrealistically high, they may actually discourage employees, who will see no point in trying to do the impossible. The employees may eventually give up or even quit their jobs altogether. If the goals are difficult but attainable, however, employees will often be challenged and inspired to improve their performance and meet the budgeted goals.[18]

Roger Dunbar has analyzed some of the research on goal setting.[19] He suggests that setting high goals will improve performance up to a certain point; eventually, however, the goals become unacceptable to employees, and their performance drops off sharply. Also, there is a point at which even increased performance becomes less profitable for the organization—as goals become more difficult to attain and are consistently missed, the cost of coordination increases. When the added cost of coordination nullifies the benefits achieved by higher performance, says Dunbar, then that higher performance is no longer profitable for the organization.

[18] See Andrew C. Stedry, *Budget Control and Cost Behavior* (Englewood Cliffs, N.J.: Prentice-Hall, 1960); Becker and Green, "Budgeting and Employee Behavior"; and Andrew C. Stedry, "Budgeting and Employee Behavior: A Reply," *Journal of Business,* Vol. 37, No. 2 (April 1964), pp. 195–202. Stedry suggests that the goals set should be unattainable but not so far out of reach that individuals give up. His approach has been criticized, mainly on the grounds that it would be difficult to apply in practice and that it may prove dysfunctional in the long run.
[19] Roger L. M. Dunbar, "Budgeting for Control," *Administrative Science Quarterly,* Vol. 16, No. 1 (March 1971), pp. 88–96.

Summary   Budgets are among the most widely used devices for controlling and coordinating the activities of an organization. The four major types of responsibility centers that budgets may control are revenue, expense, profit, and investment centers.

The budgeting process begins when top management sets the strategies and goals for the organization. Usually, lower-level managers will then devise budgets for their subunits within these guidelines set by top management. The budgets will then be reviewed by the superiors of those managers; the superiors will eventually integrate lower-level budgets into their own budget and send it up the chain of command for review. This process continues until the organization's overall budget has been approved by the board of directors. A budget department or budget committee may assist line managers in budget preparation and review.

The budget development process typically arouses anxiety among managers, who are usually concerned about the resource allocations they receive. The managers may engage in dysfunctional political behavior, react adversely to budget personnel, overstate their needs, and develop covert information systems in an attempt to obtain a higher budget allocation. Effective participation in the budgeting process usually reduces these reactions.

Overall organizational budgets may be *operating* or *financial*. Specific types of budgets include expense (engineered and discretionary), revenue, profit, cash, capital expenditure, and balance sheet budgets. Budgets may also be fixed, variable, or semi-variable. Two special budgeting approaches include PPBS, which attempts to evaluate organizational programs more closely, and ZBB, which attempts to base resource allocations on current rather than historical needs.

Budgets have potentially functional and dysfunctional aspects, depending on how the budgeting process is conceived and executed. Potentially functional aspects include improved coordination and communication, higher motivation and morale, and increased learning by lower-level managers. Potentially dysfunctional aspects include differing perceptions by line and staff members, mechanical problems, and unnecessary and harmful pressures on organization members. Some of these pressures may be reduced if high but attainable budget goals are set.

Review Questions
1. Why do you think budgets are so widely used in organizations?
2. What are the four major types of responsibility centers? What organizational units are commonly considered as belonging to each type of center? How is the performance of each center measured?
3. How are budgets drawn up, approved, and revised? What are the advantages of lower-level participation in the budgeting process?
4. What roles do budget departments and budget committees play in the budgeting process?
5. What four reactions may result from the anxiety that often accompanies budget development?
6. What types of budgets are used for three of the responsibility centers described in the text? What does each of these budgets consist of? What is each of these budgets designed to do?
7. What are cash, capital, expenditure, and balance sheet budgets? Why are they used?
8. What are variable budgets? What types of costs must managers consider when devising variable budgets? Why? How may variable costs be determined?
9. What are the five basic steps in PPBS? What does this type of budgeting seek to do? Why did the attempt to implement PPBS throughout all federal agencies fail?

10. What are the basic steps in ZBB? What is this type of budgeting approach designed to do?
11. What are the potentially functional aspects of budgeting?
12. What are the potentially dysfunctional aspects of budgeting? How do you think these may be overcome?

CASE STUDY: ORDERS FROM HEADQUARTERS

About a month ago Bruce Crawford, regional sales manager of the Aristo All-Lines Insurance Company, received a complaint from the firm's comptroller to the effect that the monthly expense reports of Crawford's agents were being turned in late to the home office, and, worse yet, the majority of them were incomplete and inaccurate. The comptroller, a vice president, furthermore advised that this practice had to be stopped immediately or he personally would take steps (such as returning expense reports unpaid) to correct the situation. The comptroller also emphatically pointed out that Aristo's organizational procedures manual gave explicit instructions on the monthly submission of expense accounts.

Crawford, who is responsible for ten subordinate district sales managers and some one hundred agents, thereupon felt that his weekly newsletter to the field would be the best medium for communicating the comptroller's message. So at the conclusion of his very next issue he wrote, "By the way, more attention must be given to the preparation and submission to the home office of agents' monthly expense accounts." He underlined each and every word.

Two months later Crawford received a long-distance phone call from the comptroller in which he sharply complained of at least twenty late and inaccurately completed expense accounts. All were being returned unpaid. And, "furthermore," warned the comptroller, "if you can't handle the problem, perhaps we should get someone out there who can."

Bruce Crawford, by this time embarrassed and irritated, personally phoned each of the twenty agents. All of the agents were quite upset with their returned expense sheets. And when Crawford reprimanded them for their inefficient practice of late submission, the consensus of their replies was: "We've been doing it this same way for months. Why is the comptroller complaining just now? Moreover, things are tough enough without him withholding our month's expenses." Crawford rubbed his chin and wondered what to do next.

Case Questions
1. What fundamental management issues are involved in this incident?
2. If you were Crawford, how would you handle the situation?

Case reprinted with permission from *Contemporary Management Incidents* by Bernard A. Deitzer and Karl A. Shilliff (Columbus, Ohio: Grid, Inc., 1977), pp. 159–160.

Chapter 23

Nonbudgetary Methods of Control

Upon completing this chapter you should be able to:

1. State why nonbudgetary methods of control are important to managers.

2. Describe various types of financial control methods, including financial statements, ratio analysis, and break-even analysis.

3. Describe the three types of auditing.

4. Explain how and why Gantt charts, milestone schedules, and PERT and CPM networks are developed.

As we discussed in the previous chapter, budgeting is a highly effective means for controlling the allocation and use of an organization's resources. There are, however, many organizational activities that are not ideally suited for budgetary methods of control. For example, while budgets are useful for controlling organizational functions, such as sales, they are not as useful for controlling the progress of organizational projects, such as a new product development program. Similarly, while budgets can establish measurable standards for specific parts of an organization, they are not as useful for monitoring the financial performance of the organization as a whole.

No single, unified method of control has, as yet, been devised for all of an organization's activities. There are simply too many types of activities in an organization, each requiring a different form of control, for any one control system to be effective. Instead, managers need to design a series of control methods and systems to deal with the differing problems and elements of their organization. These control systems will, however, be interrelated sufficiently to allow managers to coordinate the organization's activities and keep them focused on the organization's major goals.[1]

In this chapter, we will discuss the nonbudgetary methods of control that managers can use. We will focus specifically on (1) financial control methods, (2) audits, and (3) methods for project planning and control.

FINANCIAL CONTROL METHODS

Technically, budgeting can be classified as a financial control. Budgets, however, differ considerably in structure and use from the other financial methods that will be described in this section. The financial control methods we will discuss consist of a series of financial statements and methods that are used to evaluate or monitor how well a business organization is performing. Many of these methods may be effectively used by nonprofit institutions. However, we will concentrate on their application to business, where they tend to be not only more common but also more crucial to an organization's health and survival.

Financial
Statements

Essentially, financial statements document, in financial terms, the flow of goods and services to, within, and from the organization. They are prepared by accountants and form the organization's accounting record. Financial statements provide a means for controlling three major aspects of an organization's activities:

1   The *liquidity* of the organization—its ability to convert its assets into cash in order to meet its current financial needs and obligations.

2   The *general financial condition* of the organization—its long-term balance between debt and equity (the assets of the firm after its liabilities have been deducted).

[1] See William H. Newman, *Constructive Control: Design and Use of Control Systems* (Englewood Cliffs, N.J.: Prentice-Hall, 1975), pp. 6–9, 128–129.

3 The *profitability* of the organization—its ability to earn profits steadily and over an extended period of time.[2]

Financial statements are usually prepared *ex post* (in retrospect) to indicate what financial events occurred since the last statement. Depending on the company, the period covered by a financial statement could be the previous year, the previous quarter, or the previous month. As we suggested in Chapter 21, the usefulness of financial statements for applying control measures is limited by the fact that they cover only past events. For example, last year's income statement will be completed after all of last year's events have occurred; it cannot, therefore, be used to influence last year's income. The first quarterly or monthly statement for the new fiscal year, however, often can provide managers with useful information about trends or events; thus, corrective action may still be applied for the remaining periods of the year. Obviously, the more promptly these statements are prepared and communicated, the more potential they have for influencing effective managerial action before the year has elapsed.

The financial statements most often used on a regular basis by organizations are balance sheets and income statements. Cash flow statements and statements of the sources and uses of funds are also widely used in many organizations. We will describe these types of financial statements here.[3]

Balance Sheet. The message of a balance sheet is, "Here's how this organization stacks up financially *at this particular point in time.*" The point of time covered by our sample balance sheet, Figure 23-1, is indicated by the line "as of December 31, 1978."

In its simplest form, the balance sheet describes the company in terms of its *assets, liabilities,* and *net worth.* A company's assets range from money in the bank to the goodwill value of its name in the marketplace. The left side of the balance sheet lists these assets in descending order of liquidity. The normal breakdown of assets is between current assets and fixed assets. *Current assets* cover items such as cash, accounts receivable, marketable securities, and inventories—assets that could be turned into cash at a reasonably predictable value within a relatively short time period (typically one year). *Fixed assets* are the company's plant, equipment, property, patents, and other items used on a continuing basis to produce its goods or services. These represent assets that also have monetary value but are ones the company plans to continue to use for a number of years to produce its products or services.

Liabilities are also made up of two groups, current liabilities and long-term liabilities. *Current liabilities* are all debts, such as accounts payable, short-term loans, and unpaid taxes, that will have to be paid off during the current fiscal period. *Long-term liabilities* include mortgages, bonds, and other

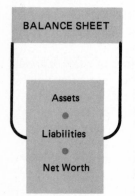

BALANCE SHEET

Assets
•
Liabilities
•
Net Worth

---

[2] See Earl P. Strong and Robert D. Smith, *Management Control Models* (New York: Holt, Rinehart and Winston, 1968), p. 55.

[3] See Strong and Smith, *Management Control Models,* and J. Fred Weston and Eugene F. Brigham, *Managerial Finance,* 5th ed. (Hinsdale, Ill.: Dryden Press, 1975).

CHAPNER METALS
Consolidated Balance Sheet
As of December 31, 1978

ASSETS			LIABILITIES AND NET WORTH		
Current Assets	$	950,000	Current Liabilities	$	600,000
Cash		50,000	Accounts Payable		475,000
Marketable Securities		350,000	Accrued Expenses		
Accounts Receivable		250,000	Payable		125,000
Inventories		300,000	Long-Term Liabilities		600,000
			Total Liabilities		1,200,000
Fixed Assets		1,250,000			
Land		50,000			
Plant and Equipment		1,500,000	Net Worth		1,070,000
Less Accumulated			Common Stock at Par		850,000
Depreciation		300,000	Accumulated Retained		
			Earnings		220,000
Other Assets					
Patents and Goodwill		70,000			
			Total Liabilities		
Total Assets		$2,270,000	and Net Worth		$2,270,000

FIGURE 23-1   The Balance Sheet

debts, which are being paid off gradually. The company's *net worth* is the residual value remaining after total liabilities have been subtracted from total assets.

Income Statement. While the balance sheet describes a company's financial condition at a given *point* in time, the income statement summarizes the company's financial performance over a given *interval* of time. The income statement, then, says "Here's how much money we're making" instead of "Here's how much money we're worth."

Income statements, such as Figure 23-2 on next page, start with a figure for gross receipts or sales and then whittle away at it by deducting all the costs involved in realizing those sales, such as cost of goods sold, administrative expenses, taxes, interest, and other operating expenses. What is left is the net income available for stockholders' dividends or reinvestment in the business.

Cash Flow and Sources and Uses of Funds Statements. In addition to the standard balance sheet and income statement, many companies are now reporting financial data in the form of a statement of cash flow or a statement of sources and uses of funds. Basically, these statements show where cash or funds came from during the year (from operations, reducing accounts receivable, and sale of investments, for example) and where they were applied (purchase of equip-

FIGURE 23-2
The Income
Statement

CHAPNER METALS
Statement of Income
For the Year Ended December 31, 1978

Net Sales		$3,500,000
Less Cost of Sales and Operating Expenses		
Cost of Goods Sold	$2,775,000	
Depreciation	100,000	
Selling and Administrative Expenses	75,000	2,950,000
Operating Profit		550,000
Other Income	15,000	
Gross Income		565,000
Less Interest Expense	75,000	
Income before Taxes		490,000
Less Income Taxes	196,000	
Income after Taxes		$ 294,000

ment, payment of dividends, and reducing accounts payable, for example). They should not be confused with income statements; cash flow statements show *how* cash or funds were used rather than how much profit or loss was achieved.

Financial statements are used by managers primarily to control the internal operations of their organizations. However, we should keep in mind that financial statements are also used by managers in their transactions outside the company. In addition, they are used by people outside the organization to evaluate the organization's strengths, weaknesses, and potential. For example, managers may go outside the company to borrow funds from bankers or to sell new stock to investors. Their organization's financial statements will influence and often determine whether or not they will succeed. The bankers will be particularly interested in the firm's liquidity, while investors (and long-term lenders, such as bond purchasers) will be interested in the firm's overall financial condition.[4]

Managers also use financial statements to compare their organization with other organizations. Thus, financial statements can help managers evaluate their own performance.

Human Resource Accounting. Traditional financial statements appear to neglect the human resources of the organization. The costs of hiring and training personnel, for instance, are treated simply as operating expenses. The

[4] See James C. Van Horne, *Financial Management and Policy,* 4th ed. (Englewood Cliffs, N.J.: Prentice-Hall, 1977), p. 672.

value of the organization's personnel—in terms of the skills and energy they provide the organization—are not included in traditional statements at all.

Human resource accounting is an approach tried by a few organizations that attempts to overcome this limitation in traditional financial statements. In this approach, the organization's human resources are regarded as an *investment*. Thus, the dollar costs of hiring and training personnel, for example, are regarded not merely as expenses but as positive contributions to the organization's future profitability. These costs may therefore appear in the assets column of a financial statement. Conversely, the loss of personnel through such means as separation or retirement may be treated as liabilities.

Ratio Analysis

For organizations as well as for individuals, financial performance is relative. An annual salary of $20,000 will be seen as high if the average salary in the individual's field or industry is $10,000, and low if the average salary is $30,000. Similarly, organizational profits of $1 million might be very high for a restaurant but very low for an oil company. For the "bottom line" on a financial statement to be meaningful, it must ultimately be compared with something else.

Ratio analysis seeks to extract information from a financial statement in a way that will allow an organization's financial performance or condition to be evaluated. It involves selecting two significant figures from a financial statement and expressing their relationship in terms of a percentage or ratio. That ratio can then be compared with a similarly formed ratio from another financial statement; in this way, the performance of the organization can be more meaningfully assessed.[5]

RATIO ANALYSIS COMPARISONS

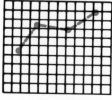

1. Over Time

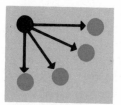

2. With Other Organizations

The ratio analysis comparisons can be made in one of two ways: (1) comparison over a time period—the present ratio compared with the same organization's ratio in the past (or with a future projection); and (2) comparison with other similar organizations or with the industry as a whole. The first type of comparison will indicate how the organization's performance or condition has changed; the second type will suggest how well the organization is doing relative to its competitors.

Because financial statements are expressed in numerical terms, people sometimes assume that the information obtained from them will automatically be precise in nature. However, many financial figures, such as those for depreciation, may be based on loose or unreliable estimates. In addition, accounting systems vary significantly from one organization to another. These factors need to be considered when ratios are being analyzed and compared. As a general rule, several of an organization's ratios need to be evaluated in order for a judgment of that organization's financial performance to be meaningful.

The ratios most commonly used by organizations may be divided into five major categories: liquidity, debt, coverage, profitability, and operating. We

[5] Our discussion is based on Strong and Smith, *Management Control Models*, pp. 67–71; Weston and Brigham, *Managerial Finance*, pp. 23–33; Van Horne, *Financial Management and Policy*, pp. 672–689; and R. M. S. Wilson, *Financial Control: A Systems Approach* (New York: McGraw-Hill, 1974), pp. 77–89.

will discuss the most prevalent types of ratios in each of these categories in the following sections. Readers should keep in mind that there are other ratio categories and other types of ratios.

Liquidity Ratios. Short-term lenders to a company want to be sure that the company has the ability to pay them back by converting assets quickly into cash. One measure of this ability is the company's *liquidity ratio*. Its purpose is to answer the question, "Does the company have enough cash or easily convertible resources available to meet present short-term obligations and still remain financially healthy?"

Perhaps the most common liquidity ratio is the *current ratio*. It is expressed by the fraction: current assets divided by current liabilities. For example, if an organization has current assets of $1.2 million and current liabilities of $500,000, its current ratio is 2.4. (In other words, its current assets are 2.4 times its current liabilities.) The higher the current ratio, the more funds there are available to meet obligations.

Debt Ratios. While liquidity ratios are used to measure a company's short-term financial condition, *debt ratios* are computed to assess its ability to meet long-term commitments. The simplest debt ratio is total debt to net worth (total debt ÷ net worth). An equally common form of debt ratio is total debt to total assets (total debt ÷ total assets). Debt ratios are easier to understand if we think of the result as a percentage. For example, if our company has a total debt, including current liabilities and bonds, of $500,000 and our total assets come to $1 million, our debt is 50 percent of assets. In other words, 50 percent of our company's assets is owed to creditors. If the industry average is 65 percent, we will probably have little problem borrowing more capital. If, on the other hand, it is 40 percent, potential creditors may feel that we have already overextended ourselves.

Coverage Ratios. Potential investors and lenders are interested in a company's ability to meet its present interest expenses—that is, the cost of its present financing. *Coverage ratios* are designed to indicate this ability. The *times interest earned ratio,* one of the standard coverage ratios (there are several), is computed by dividing earnings before interest and taxes by the total interest charges for the same period. The resulting figure will indicate how many times the company's earnings can meet interest expenses. Obviously, a company's failure to meet interest charges out of income can lead to financial difficulties and eventually even to bankruptcy. In most industries, an organization will have to be capable of covering its annual interest charges several times over in order for it to be able to obtain additional funding.

Profitability Ratios. One of the important tests of a public relations manager's skill is the ability to keep the public from crying "Rip-off!" when an increase in selling prices coincides with an announcement that the company has realized millions of dollars in profits. However, as all managers know, there are profits and there are profits. A profit of $4 million for example, is unimpressive if it

"Stop!"

Drawing by Stevenson; © 1976 The New Yorker Magazine, Inc.

is derived from total sales of $200 million or a capital investment of $500 million.

Profitability ratios are designed to put profit into perspective as a measure of the company's efficiency of operation. They may be expressed as the profit margin on sales—net profit after taxes ÷ total sales; as return on total assets—net profit after taxes ÷ total assets; or as return on net worth—net profit after taxes ÷ net worth. The return on net worth gives the rate of return on the stockholders' or owners' investment. Profitability ratios are usually expressed as percentages and, like other ratios, need to be compared with other time periods or industry averages in order to be meaningful.

Operating Ratios. Up to this point, we have categorized ratios by the *characteristics* they are designed to measure: liquidity, debt, coverage, and profitability. *Operating ratios* are ratios classified by organizational function or operation, such as manufacturing and sales. They measure how efficiently those operations are being carried out.

There are many ways that operating ratios may be used by managers to evaluate and control different aspects of their firm's activities. In analyzing the performance of their sales force, for example, managers may calculate this year's cost of operating the sales force as a percent of total sales. They can then compare that ratio to last year's ratio, to another sales division's ratio, or to a competitor's ratio. The use of this type of ratio can be refined even further. For example, a company that has been selling to wholesalers may decide to add salespeople to call on selected retail outlets. The company's managers can calculate how the ratio would be affected if sales remained the same; they can then determine how much sales will have to increase to bring the ratio back to the desired standard.

Some of the more common operating ratios are the inventory turnover ratio and the total assets turnover ratio. The inventory turnover ratio is defined as sales ÷ inventory. For example, if a company has sales of $1 million and an average daily inventory of $200,000, it may be said to be turning over its inventory five times. A high rate of inventory turnover is frequently a positive sign; it suggests that these assets are being used efficiently by the firm. A low rate may indicate that the organization's goods are becoming obsolete or are meeting increased competition.

The total assets turnover ratio is expressed as sales ÷ total assets. This ratio gives an indication of how effectively the firm's assets are being used. Too low a ratio may indicate the need for either an increased sales effort or possibly the liquidation of some of the company's less productive assets.

Operating ratios are, of course, only as good as the accuracy of the figures on which they are based. In addition, they require comparison figures in order to be meaningful. Industry averages and trends are often available from trade associations. Experienced managers will also frequently have a workable knowledge of the approximate ratios for competitive companies through their past experience or present contacts outside their own company. Major changes in company ratios over a period of time, or the development of company ratios that are significantly out of line with the rest of the industry, usually call for management attention.

Return on Investment. One particular approach to financial control that has received considerable attention and study in recent years is the Du Pont system of financial analysis.[6] The central ratio of the Du Pont system is the *return on investment* (ROI) ratio, which is expressed by the following formula:

$$\frac{\text{sales}}{\text{investment}} \times \frac{\text{profit}}{\text{sales}} = \text{ROI}$$

A more comprehensive breakdown of the system, somewhat modified from Du Pont's approach, is shown in Figure 23-3. The top line determines the profit margin on sales. The calculation starts with the cost of sales, including production, selling, and administrative costs. That total cost is subracted from total sales revenue to arrive at a net profit figure. Dividing net profit by total sales, as we saw in our discussion on profitability, yields the profit margin on sales.

[6] See Weston and Brigham, *Managerial Finance*, pp. 35–37.

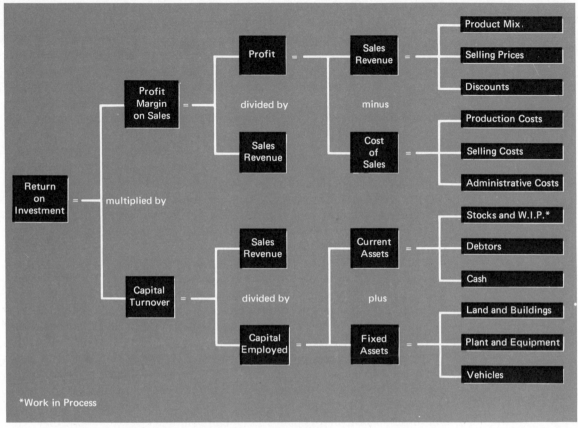

*Work in Process

FIGURE 23-3 Constituents of Return on Investment

Source: R. M. S. Wilson, *Financial Control: A Systems Approach* (New York: McGraw-Hill, 1974), p. 58. Used by permission.

The bottom line determines the total assets turnover ratio. It is arrived at by adding current assets to fixed assets, which equals total capital employed, and then dividing this total into the total sales revenue.

Such an ROI system can encourage management to adopt an integrated approach to assessing organizational efficiency. For example, if the ROI is low (relative to that of competitors or the organization in the past), managers can backtrack to find possible sources of the problem — say, a low turnover ratio. There are, however, two possible dangers in using the system. The first is that a satisfactory ROI may actually conceal weaknesses. An inefficient use of manufacturing assets, for example, might be offset by a particularly effective sales campaign and still result in a satisfactory ROI. If sales return to normal, the continued inefficient use of manufacturing assets will cause a marked decline in the ROI to appear. Once managers are aware of these possibilities, however, they can establish additional standards and controls at each point in the system.

The other danger is that concentration on ROI, with its emphasis on current sales and capital utilization, may tend to overshadow the company's long-term goals. Current return on capital, for example, may sometimes need to be sacrificed in order to build a firm foundation for future expansion. Once again, however, such pitfalls can be overcome by establishing additional standards and controls for the organization's other activities and goals.

Break-Even Analysis

Let us assume that you have been appointed financial manager of the Abacus Calculator Company. The company makes only one product, an electronic calculator, that it sells to distributors for $20 per unit. The variable cost of producing the calculators is $10 per unit. In addition, the company has annual fixed costs of $100,000. (See our discussion of fixed and variable costs in Chapter 22.) Obviously you do not need one of your company's calculators to figure out that a loss will result if only a few hundred units are sold and that you will make a great deal of money if two million units are sold. But at what precise point will your sales cover your costs?

Helping managers find that point and applying the information gained from it is the purpose of break-even analysis (also called cost-volume-profit analysis). Through break-even analysis, managers can study the relationship between costs, sales volume, and profits; they can specifically determine how changes in costs and volume will affect profits, and thus make more informed decisions about those variables.

The relationship between fixed costs, variable costs, units sold, and profit is most easily shown in a diagram sometimes referred to as a break-even chart or a profitgraph. Figure 23-4 illustrates such a graph for our calculator company, covering a sales period of one year. The graph shows that a net loss will result on sales of less than 10,000 units but that any sales above that figure will produce a profit. Our break-even point, then, is 10,000 units. (The reader may also wish to refer to our part opening case for another example of break-even analysis.)

Constructing a graph of this kind involves a fairly simple sequence of steps:

1 Calculate the total fixed costs for the chosen period.
2 Figure all variable costs per unit.
3 Determine the total cost curve by plotting the variable cost and adding the fixed cost to it. (You may also start with the fixed cost as a horizontal line and add the variable cost to it. Either way, the result is the same.)
4 Plot the total income from sales curve (selling price per unit times number of units).

The point at which the total sales curve crosses the total cost curve will be the break-even point.[7]

[7] The break-even sales volume can also be calculated with the following equation:

$$\text{Break-even volume} = \frac{\text{Fixed costs}}{\left(\begin{array}{c}\text{Sales revenue} \\ \text{per unit}\end{array}\right) - \left(\begin{array}{c}\text{Variable cost} \\ \text{per unit}\end{array}\right)}$$

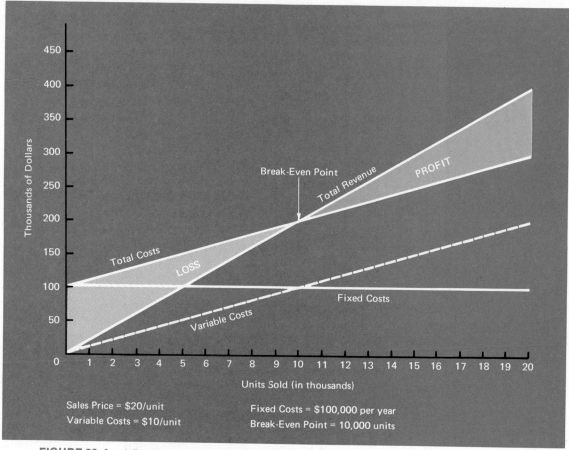

FIGURE 23-4 A Profitgraph for the Abacus Calculator Company

One of the quick and simple uses of break-even analysis is that it gives managers a rough profit and loss estimate for different sales volumes. Managers obtain this estimate simply by selecting the given volume along the horizontal axis and moving up vertically to discover the projected revenue and total costs for that volume. The graph can also be used to estimate the effect of changes in expenses and sales price. In our calculator company example, if fixed costs increase by $40,000, the break-even level would increase to 14,000 units. Alternatively, if the unit price of calculators drops to $15, the break-even point will move up to 20,000 units. In other words, a greater number of units will have to be sold in order for the company to realize a profit.

Break-even analysis can be used both as an aid in decision making and as a control device. The specific areas where break-even analysis can help in decision making include: (1) identifying the minimum sales volume necessary to prevent a loss; (2) identifying the minimum sales volume necessary to meet established profit objectives; (3) providing data helpful in decisions to drop or add product lines; and (4) providing information helpful in making decisions on the effect of raising or lowering prices.[8] As an aid to control, break-even analysis provides one more yardstick by which to evaluate company performance at the end of a sales period. ("Our sales reached $5 million this month; for that sales volume we had projected profits of $600,000, but our profits were only $500,000. We will need to find the causes of the difference.") Also, like other control measures, break-even analysis provides a basis for corrective action to improve performance in the future.

Limitations of Break-Even Analysis. One of the virtues of break-even analysis as an operational tool is its simplicity. Unfortunately, this same characteristic is the root of many of its weaknesses. Break-even analysis is based on several simple assumptions, all of which may affect the accuracy of the results. Among the more questionable of these assumptions are the following:

1 *That variable costs per unit are constant.* For moderate volume increases, existing facilities may have little trouble meeting the new demand. As production facilities approach capacity, however, bottlenecks and equipment problems may require large increases in variable labor costs to keep the equipment performing. Raw material costs may also rise because of increased production defects.

2 *That fixed costs are constant.* Costs that appear fixed may change in ways that are difficult to predict. For example, as volume rises, new equipment may have to be purchased to alleviate bottlenecks, additional clerical staff may be required to process orders, and additional staff people may be needed to improve coordination.

3 *That prices are constant.* Increased sales may be concentrated in a few customers who receive large quantity discounts; or, sales may be made at greater distances with the selling company deducting the additional transportation costs from revenues.

4 *That costs can be classified as fixed or variable.* In practice, many costs are quite difficult to classify. For example, if inventories increase to support the higher production levels and an additional warehouse must be leased, is that a fixed cost, since it will not increase or decrease with subsequent volume changes, or is it a variable cost brought about by the higher volume of production?

In spite of these weaknesses, break-even analysis has many positive uses as an aid in decision making and as a control device. While the information it provides may not be precisely accurate, it is usually close enough to reality to enable managers to use it effectively.

AUDITING

To much of the general public, the term "auditing" conjures up scenes of stern-faced individuals scrutinizing a company's books in order to find out who is cheating the company, how they are juggling the figures to cover it up, and how much they have already embezzled. While the discovery of fraud is, in fact, one

---

[8] Wilson, *Financial Control: A Systems Approach*, pp. 137–138.

important facet of auditing, it is far from being the only one. Auditing has many important uses, from validating the honesty and fairness of financial statements to providing a critical basis for management decisons.

In this section, we will discuss three types of auditing: external, internal, and management. The *external audit* is largely a verification process, performed by CPAs from outside the company, to check the accuracy, fairness, and honesty of the financial statements. The *internal audit,* carried out by people inside the company, has a somewhat broader scope and leads to an evaluation of the organization's financial control system and perhaps some aspects of managerial performance. The *management audit* is basically a different type of evaluation, aimed at a critical review of management policy and performance and not at the details of the control system. It may be conducted by outsiders or insiders.[9]

External Auditing

The traditional external audit involves the independent appraisal of the organization's financial accounts and statements. Assets and liabilities are verified, and financial reports are checked for completeness and accuracy. The audit is conducted by accounting personnel employed by an outside CPA firm or by chartered accountants. The auditors' purpose is *not* to prepare the company's financial reports; their job is to verify that the company, in preparing its own financial statements and valuing its assets and liabilities, has followed generally accepted accounting principles and applied them correctly.

EXTERNAL
AUDIT

↓

Organization's
Accounts and
Statements

The external audit plays a significant role in encouraging honesty not only in the preparation of statements but also in the actual operation of the organization. It is, in fact, a major systematic check against fraud within the organization. For people outside the organization, such as bankers and potential investors, the external audit provides the major assurance that the publicly available financial statements have been prepared honestly and in a manner consistent with accounting principles.

The external audit takes place after the organization's operating period is finished and its financial statements are completed. For this reason, and also because it focuses on a comparatively limited set of financial statements and transactions, the external audit does not make a major contribution to control of the ongoing operations of the organization. There is, however, one important exception: knowing that the audit will inevitably occur is a strong deterrent against actions that may lead to embarrassment (or an uncomfortable prison term) if they are discovered at the time the audit takes place.

Internal Auditing

The internal audit shares many of the objectives of the external audit. Both are intended, in broad terms, to verify the accuracy and reliability of the financial statements of the organization. The internal audit, however, goes deeper into the financial structure of the company, appraising it not only for accuracy but also for operational efficiency.

[9] See Wayne S. Boutell, *Contemporary Auditing* (Belmont, Calif.: Dickenson Publishing, 1970), and Arthur W. Holmes and Wayne S. Overmeyer, *Basic Auditing,* 5th ed. (Homewood, Ill.: Irwin, 1976).

INTERNAL AUDIT

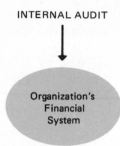

Organization's
Financial
System

The internal audit will evaluate how adequately the organization's control system is working toward realizing organizational objectives. It will evaluate several of the organization's reports for accuracy and usefulness, and will finally lead to recommendations for improvements in the control system. Because of the concentration on the operations of the organization, this process is also known as "operational auditing."

The internal audit is conducted by members of the organization. It may be carried out as a separate project by assigned members of the financial department or, in larger organizations, by a full-time internal auditing staff. The range and depth of the audit will also vary greatly, depending on company size and policy, from a relatively narrow survey to a broad, comprehensive analysis. This more complete internal audit will provide an appraisal not only of the organization's control system but also of its policies, procedures, and use of authority. It may also evaluate the quality and effectiveness of the managerial methods being used. In this broader sense, the internal audit may start to approach the management audit, which we discuss next.

Although the internal audit does provide management with useful information, it does have some limitations:

1. *Cost.* Internal audits can be expensive, particularly if they are carried out in depth.

2. *Skill.* Internal auditing involves more than simply gathering facts. Well-trained personnel are needed if the process is not to arouse resentment and if the results are to be useful to managers.

3. *Tact.* Even if the auditors are skilled, many employees may still regard auditing as a form of "snooping" or "checking up." If the auditors are not tactful and experienced in interpersonal communication, the audit may even have a negative effect on the employees' future motivation.

Management Auditing

MANAGEMENT AUDIT

Management's
and
Organization's
Overall
Performance

Management auditing provides a broader, more detailed evaluation of the organization than external or internal auditing. It involves a systematic appraisal of the overall performance of management and, consequently, of the entire organization. The form it takes will vary, but a thorough management audit inevitably requires a considerable commitment of time and resources. For this reason, companies that arrange management audits on a regular basis are unlikely to schedule them more frequently than once every three to five years. The audits are usually performed by experts from outside the organization in order to ensure that some of the more sensitive areas of management will be assessed objectively.[10]

Probably the best-known management audits are those conducted by the American Institute of Management. The A.I.M. audit is based on the evaluation of ten categories of the company's operation. These ten areas of appraisal are:

[10] See William T. Greenwood, *Business Policy: A Management Audit Approach* (New York: Macmillan, 1967).

1 *Economic function.* The audit assesses the value of the organization's goods and services to the public, as well as the contribution the organization makes to the national economy.

2 *Corporate structure.* Every company develops a structure of communication and authority through which it pursues its corporate objectives. The audit evaluates the efficiency and effectiveness of that structure.

3 *Health of earnings.* The company's profits are judged not simply for their quantity but also for qualities such as consistency and stability over the years. Such measures as the profits to assets and return on investment ratios are compared with those of other organizations in the same industry.

4 *Service to stockholders.* The audit evaluates the degree to which management carries out its obligations to provide stockholders with security for their investment, capital growth, reasonable dividends, and adequate information on the company's operations and progress.

5 *Research and development.* New ideas and product improvements are vital to a company's growth and stability. The A.I.M. audit evaluates the company's research and development facilities, management attitudes to R&D, and the organization's preparedness for future progress.

6 *Directorate analysis.* The company's directors are appraised, both for their individual contribution and for the way they work together as a team. Their integrity and acceptance of responsibility as company representatives are also considered.

7 *Fiscal policies.* The audit assesses the financial structure and soundness of the company and how effectively the company applies fiscal policies and controls to the achievement of short- and long-range company objectives.

8 *Production efficiency.* The organization's efficiency will help it maintain a strong competitive position over a long period of time. The audit assesses efficiency of production, as in a manufacturing firm, or operating efficiency, as in service companies such as banks.

9 *Sales vigor.* An effective sales effort is essential if a company is to realize its potential. Therefore, the enthusiasm, expertise, and efficiency of the sales force are assessed.

10 *Executive evaluation.* Although many of the other operational categories also involve executive evaluation, the A.I.M. audit directly judges the company's executives in this category for qualities such as ability, industry, and integrity.[11]

Obviously, these categories do not represent separate, isolated aspects of the company. Many activities are considered in more than one category, with varying emphases and viewpoints. Each category is given its own point score so that the A.I.M. audit arrives at a total figure by which the company can be compared to past performance or to industry standards.

The advantages of such audits include the facts that (1) they encourage a systematic reconsideration of where the organization should be headed in the next five or ten years; (2) they evaluate many measures of organizational per-

---

[11] Jackson Martindell, "The Management Audit," *Proceedings of the Annual Meeting, Academy of Management* (1962), pp. 164–171, and *The Appraisal of Management* (New York: Harper & Row, 1962). See also "How Good Is Your Company? Score Yourself," *Business Week,* February 24, 1951, for an example of an A.I.M. questionnaire and scoring system.

formance, as opposed to only one or two; and (3) they evaluate top management's performance, which other types of audits generally fail to do. The A.I.M. audit has been specifically criticized, however, for overemphasizing the economic and fiscal categories at the expense of the other categories.

There are differing views about the extent to which management audits should be future-oriented as opposed to present- and past-oriented. John C. Burton has suggested that the audit should avoid making forecasts and should concentrate instead on the organization's past and present performance (like the A.I.M. audit). The public, he argued, will be able to make its own prediction about the organization's future success or failure.[12] Robert B. Buchele, however, suggests that management audits need to be more future-oriented. Past performance is no longer a reliable indicator of future viability, he says, because the external environment of organizations is undergoing increasingly rapid changes.[13] And, in fact, several of the companies rated as excellent by A.I.M. audits experienced heavy financial losses due to poor preparation for technological changes or the actions of competitors.

Buchele's auditing approach focuses on aspects of the organization that he feels are the most relevant to predicting future success or failure. Among the more important of these, he includes the following:

- Rate of expansion or contraction of markets
- Determination of success potential for products the firm will be able to produce in the future
- Cost-benefit analysis of the R&D program
- Degree of coordination between R&D and long-range planning
- Flexibility and appropriateness to the future of the organization's manufacturing processes and skills
- Adequacy of the styles and characteristics of top management for meeting probable future challenges

Buchele does not, of course, suggest that the present and past record should be ignored. Management's past approaches to its future needs, for example, will help auditors estimate how prepared for the future the organization is today.

PROJECT AND PROGRAM CONTROL TECHNIQUES

The nonrepetitive project or program is becoming an increasingly frequent phenomenon in today's large organizations. As these projects also increase in scale, complexity, and cost, new methods for planning and controlling them have been and are being developed.

The best known of the older approaches is the Gantt chart, which was developed by Henry L. Gantt (see Chapter 2). This relatively simple chart has made

---

[12] John C. Burton, "Management Auditing," *Journal of Accountancy,* May 1968, pp. 41–46.

[13] Robert R. Buchele, "How to Evaluate a Firm," *California Management Review,* Vol. 5, No. 1 (Fall 1962), pp. 5–17.

a significant contribution to project management and is still a valuable and widely used control tool. It is also the foundation upon which the other, more sophisticated types of project and program control techniques – milestone scheduling, PERT, and CPM – are based.

The Gantt Chart   A Gantt chart is a graphic control method for a project with a specified completion date. An example is shown in Figure 23-5. The project is broken down into separate tasks or assignments, and estimates are made of the amount of time necessary to carry out each task. An estimated date is also included when each task must be completed in order for the final completion date to be met.

This information is translated into a pair of brackets for each task. Each bracket pair on the chart indicates the task's starting date and completion date. Within each set of brackets a contrasting bar is filled in representing the degree of accomplishment of that particular task. The result is a graphic representation of the state of each phase of the project on each day of the production period. In other words, the manager can see immediately what particular tasks are behind or ahead of schedule, and by how much. (In our example, shipping of Product B is a little behind schedule.) If the chart is kept up to date and reviewed daily, extra effort can be applied to those parts of the operation that are behind schedule before they get so far behind that the final completion date is threatened.[14]

FIGURE 23-5
Gantt Chart for
Manufacturing
Department

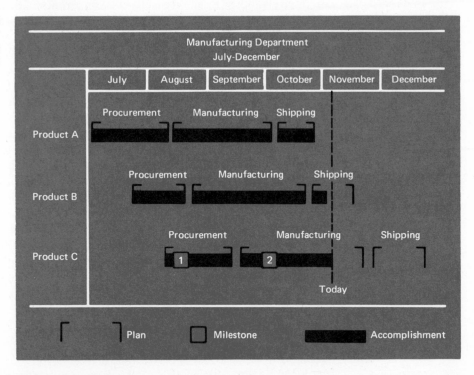

[14] See Strong and Smith, *Management Control Models*, pp. 83–95. See also Newman, *Constructive Control*, p. 60.

Milestone
Scheduling

If you select a date when a certain accomplishment, decision, or event is to take place and indicate that date on the horizontal bar of a chart, you have created a *milestone*.[15] The milestone date may be a date on which a decision is to be made concerning outside financing; it may be a date when announcement of the project to the trade press is planned; it may simply be a date when a thorough project progress review is scheduled. Usually, however, the milestone represents a selected date by which a certain phase of the entire project is to be completed. Milestones thus add detail to the information contained in the Gantt chart. They serve as formal review points where costs, progress, and the need for replanning or schedule modification can be reviewed. In Figure 23-5, we have added milestones to the bars for Product C to indicate (1) mailing out of final purchase orders and (2) completion of first quality inspection. The Gantt chart will show the relationship between milestones *within the same task* but does not show a direct relationship between milestones situated within different tasks. Modifying a Gantt chart to overcome this limitation leads to the formation of a network.[16]

Network
Analysis: PERT
and CPM

Gantt charts are appropriate for scheduling a series of unrelated activities, such as separate production runs in a job shop operation. The milestone method can be used to divide a major project into subactivities so that managers can achieve greater control. Neither approach, however, can adequately deal with the interrelationships among activities or events. These interrelationships form an important aspect of more complex projects and programs in which one activity or event will often depend on the successful completion of other activities or events. In such situations, some form of *network analysis* is necessary to ensure that the entire project or program is moving ahead as planned.

The two major forms of network technique are PERT, which stands for Program Evaluation and Review Technique, and CPM, the Critical Path Method. The systems were developed independently, although virtually at the same time, around 1957–58. PERT was first developed for the U.S. Navy in connection with the Polaris weapons system and is credited with reducing the completion time of the program by two years. CPM was developed by Du Pont in order to facilitate its control of large, complex industrial projects.

The two systems are similar in most essential respects. The main difference lies in the treatment of time estimates. PERT was created primarily to handle research and development projects in which time spans are hard to estimate with any degree of accuracy. Consequently, PERT time spans are based on probabilistic estimates. CPM, on the other hand, is usually concerned with projects that the organization has had some previous experience with. Time estimates, therefore, can be made relatively accurately.

---

[15] See James L. Riggs and Charles O. Heath, *Guide to Cost Reduction through Critical Path Scheduling* (Englewood Cliffs, N.J.: Prentice-Hall, 1966).

[16] See Robert J. Thierauf and Richard A. Grosse, *Decision Making through Operations Research* (New York: Wiley, 1970), and Robert W. Miller, *Schedule, Cost, and Profit Control with PERT* (New York: McGraw-Hill, 1963).

The use of both PERT and CPM has spread rapidly and made a significant impact on the planning and control of projects and programs. Both systems are most appropriate for controlling special, complex, nonrepetitive projects such as the development of a large weapons system, highway construction, shipbuilding, or the installation of a large-scale data processing system.[17] However, PERT and CPM have also proved useful in managing relatively simple projects.

Establishing and using a PERT or CPM system involve considerable expense, particularly if the system is computerized. In deciding whether or not to use a system, managers must determine to what extent the project to be controlled is time-critical. For example, projects such as reinforcing a weak dam, constructing a building at an Olympic site, or completing contracts that include penalty payment clauses are highly time-critical. The expense of a complete CPM or PERT system would probably be justified for such projects, since these systems make it much more likely that the projects will be completed on time.[18]

Developing the Network. There are a number of PERT and CPM techniques with different names and slight variations of methods. All, however, are essentially systems for planning, scheduling, and controlling projects. Their purpose is to divide the project into separate operations and then chart the order in which the operations should be carried out, when they should be started and completed, and when the entire project should be completed. Since PERT and CPM are basically similar in technique, we will discuss them together, pointing out the differences between them whenever appropriate.

Events
and
Activities

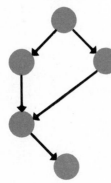

Translating a program into a PERT or CPM network involves essentially four requirements:[19]

1. The activity must be broken down into individual tasks. These tasks will then be put into the network in the form of events and activities. *Events* will usually be indicated in circles on the chart; they will represent those parts of the tasks to be accomplished at specific points in time. *Activities* will represent the time or the resources required to progress from one event to another. They will usually be indicated by arrows on the chart. For example, the official start of a design project would represent the chart's first event; the five weeks necessary to prepare preliminary blueprints would represent the chart's first activity.

2. Events and activities are placed in the chart in a highly logical, sequential, and integrated way. For example, each activity is preceded and followed by the appropriate events; no activity may start until its preceding event (or

[17] See Riggs and Heath, *Guide to Cost Reduction through Critical Path Scheduling,* pp. 16–20; Miller, *Schedule, Cost, and Profit Control with PERT,* pp. 1, 27–29; and Joseph Horowitz, *Critical Path Scheduling: Management Control through CPM and PERT* (New York: Ronald Press, 1967).

[18] Richard J. Schonberger, "Custom Tailored PERT/CPM Systems," *Business Horizons,* Vol. 15, No. 6 (December 1972), pp. 64–66.

[19] Robert W. Miller, "How to Plan and Control with PERT," *Harvard Business Review,* March-April 1962, pp. 93–104. See also Miller, *Schedule, Cost, and Profit Control with PERT,* pp. 32–38.

events) has been completed. Similarly, no event is considered completed until all the events leading up to it have been completed.

3. The length of time required for each activity is estimated and written in on the network. In CPM, as we indicated earlier, a single time estimate is established for each activity. In PERT, however, each activity may be assigned three time estimates, plus a fourth which is based on the other three. The first three estimates are known as the optimistic, most likely, and pessimistic time estimates. They are expressed in sequence above the arrow. The "optimistic" time estimate is the length of time in which the activity could be completed under ideal conditions; the "most likely" estimate is the normal time such an activity should take; the "pessimistic" estimate takes into account the possibility that just about everything will go wrong. The fourth time estimate, which appears beneath the arrow, indicates the length of time the activity is actually expected to take. It is based on a probability analysis of the other time estimates.

The times are shown on the network diagram as:

$$\frac{\text{optimistic, most likely, pessimistic}}{\text{expected}}$$

expressed, of course, in figures such as:

$$\frac{3,5,9}{5.3}$$

4. A critical path through the network must be determined. We will discuss this requirement in the next section.

To illustrate the construction of a network, we may use as an example the building of a custom-designed automobile.[20] The major tasks (events) in this job, their immediate predecessors, and their estimated time for completion are listed in Table 23-1. The building of the car frame, for example, which is listed as task "D," cannot begin before task "B," design, is completed.

The time indicated may be assumed to be relatively accurate since the estimates are based on ample amounts of past experience. A CPM approach will therefore be used. In the development of a new weapons system, for which accurate time estimates would be very difficult to make, a PERT system would be more applicable.

From the information in the table we can construct the network shown in Figure 23-6 on page 640. This network illustrates which jobs can be performed simultaneously and which must wait for predecessors to be completed. Once the automobile has been designed, for example, the different parts can be built at the same time. On the other hand, the body and accessories can be mounted only after the interior of the car has been built and the chassis has been road-tested.

[20] See also Ferdinand K. Levy, Gerald L. Thompson, and Jerome D. Wiest, "The ABCs of the Critical Path Method," *Harvard Business Review*, September-October 1963, pp. 98–108. I am indebted to Peter L. Pfister for this example.

TABLE 23-1
Sequence,
Predecessors, and
Time Requirements
of Car-Building
Tasks

Job Letter	Description	Immediate Predecessors	Normal Time (Days)
A	Start		0
B	Design	A	8
C	Order Special Accessories	B	0.1
D	Build Frame	B	1
E	Build Doors	B	1
F	Attach Axles, Wheels, Gas Tank	D	1
G	Build Body Shell	B	2
H	Build Transmission and Drivetrain	B	3
I	Fit Doors to Body Shell	G, E	1
J	Build Engine	B	4
K	Bench-Test Engine	J	2
L	Assemble Chassis	F, H, K	1
M	Road-Test Chassis	L	0.5
N	Paint Body	I	2
O	Install Wiring	N	1
P	Install Interior	N	1.5
Q	Accept Delivery of Special Accessories	C	5
R	Mount Body and Accessories on Chassis	M, O, P, Q	1
S	Road-Test Car	R	0.5
T	Attach Exterior Trim	S	1
U	Finish	T	0

Determining the Critical Path. The *critical path* is simply the longest path through the network in terms of the amount of time the entire project will take. It is determined by totaling the amount of time each *sequence* of tasks will take (as opposed to tasks that are performed simultaneously). The task chain with the longest time is the critical path. In Figure 23-6, the critical path is marked in the thicker arrows. You will see, for example, that once the path reaches B there are eight possible routes to R. Since we are looking for the longest path, the critical path will follow B, J, K, L, M, R, since that will add the most days (8.5) to the total.

The significance of the critical path lies in the fact that it will determine the total length of time, or completion date, for the entire project. If events on the critical path are delayed, then the entire project will be delayed, and the scheduled completion date will not be met.

Paths other than the critical path are called *subcritical*. These paths contain some slack since the total time for their completion is less than the critical path. One of the ways in which PERT and CPM provide for completion time to be reduced is to find ways to transfer resources from activities on the critical

639

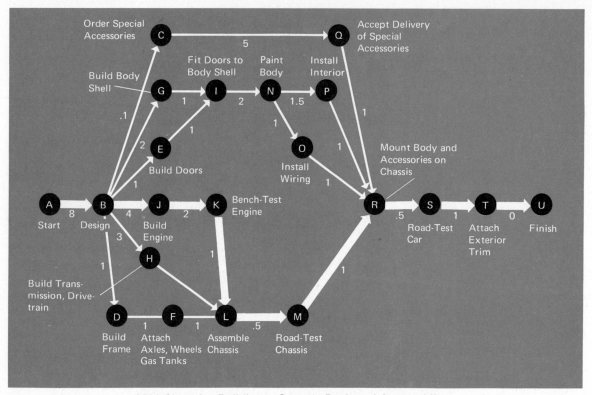

FIGURE 23-6 CPM Chart for Building a Custom-Designed Automobile

paths to activities on the subcritical paths. For example, if it were possible to reduce the number of car frame builders and increase the number of engine builders, the time taken for frame building (D) on the subcritical path might be increased by one day, while the time for engine building would be reduced by one day. Since engine building is on the critical path, this would reduce completion time by one day.

Delays on subcritical paths are less serious than delays on the critical path. They, too, must be carefully controlled, however, since serious delays can result in a subcritical path becoming the longest, and therefore the critical, path. It is also possible to have more than one critical path when different paths add up to the same number of days.

Extension of the PERT and CPM Techniques. So far we have discussed the main function of PERT and CPM: the determination and control of the time required to complete a project. The main benefit to be gained from these techniques is time — time saved through the initial scheduling of tasks and also time saved as the project progresses. Since time and cost are closely related, saving time usually also leads to savings in cost.

In addition to these "time is money" relationships, both PERT and CPM have been adapted and applied to the explicit treatment of costs. For example, an optimum cost efficiency schedule can be developed. It will help managers determine both the savings and the costs involved in achieving a shorter production schedule. Using extra labor to reduce the time span of an activity, for instance, may cost more in wages than would be received in a bonus for early completion.

Most of the extensions of PERT and CPM are more complex than the simple examples given here.[21] They do, however, make significant contributions to the usefulness of PERT and CPM to managers.

Advantages and Limitations of PERT and CPM

The increasing use of PERT and CPM is an indication of the fact that managers can gain significant advantages from them. These advantages include:

1. *Illustrating task relationships.* By providing a graphic representation of how the performance of each task is dependent on others, networks offer a distinct advantage over simpler graphs such as bar charts.

2. *Encouraging effective planning.* Drawing up a network requires that the project manager plan the project from start to finish in considerable detail.

3. *Pinpointing problem areas.* Bottlenecks and potential trouble spots are discovered early enough for preventive measures to be applied or for corrective action to be taken.

4. *Improving communication.* The network diagram provides a common frame of reference for all the different parties involved in a project, such as designers, managers, contractors, and other employees.

5. *Comparing alternative actions.* Managers are provided with an opportunity to compare different methods for reaching the project goal.

6. *Allowing concentration on key jobs.* By identifying critical tasks, CPM and PERT allow managers to apply their attention where it is most needed. At the same time, the network will indicate when other tasks are falling behind schedule. This will allow managers to take immediate action.[22]

7. *Creating flexibility.* In a complex project, the critical path may change a number of times as time estimates prove inaccurate. PERT and CPM provide managers with the ability to identify the current critical path on a continuing basis. Thus, they can keep their resources concentrated on those activities that are critical for completing the project on time.

There are also a number of limitations to PERT and CPM. The cost of setting up such systems, especially in terms of computer time, should obviously be considered before the systems are adopted. More importantly, these systems will certainly not help managers solve all their problems. Manager-subordinate relationships, relations with suppliers, difficulties with quality control — all the day-to-day pressures that make up the manager's job — will not be relieved by PERT or CPM. Nor will these systems substitute for managerial planning and control. In fact, the reverse is true. In order for the

---

[21] See Riggs and Heath, *Guide to Cost Reduction through Critical Path Scheduling,* and Hilliard W. Paige, "How PERT-Cost Helps the General Manager," *Harvard Business Review,* November-December 1963, pp. 87–95.

[22] These six points are from Horowitz, *Critical Path Scheduling,* pp. 10–12.

systems to be effective, they must be carefully planned and tightly controlled throughout a project.[23]

One common misconception is that PERT and CPM time estimates are firm and that they will automatically ensure completion of the project. However, these systems only indicate how events should occur. When unforeseen events occur—as they often do—managers will have to respond. The network schedules should always be regarded as tentative.

When properly constructed and used, PERT and CPM can provide valuable aids for planning and control. They are not, however, substitutes for effective management.

Summary

Nonbudgetary control methods are required for many types of organizational activities. These include financial controls, audits, and project and program control techniques.

Financial control methods include financial statements, ratio analyses, and break-even analysis. Commonly used *ex post financial statements* are balance sheets, income statements, and cash flow and sources and uses of funds statements. These statements are used by managers to control their organization's activities and by individuals outside the organization to evaluate its effectiveness. Common types of *ratio analysis* are liquidity, debt, coverage, profitability, operating, and return on investment ratios. These ratios may be used to compare the organization's performance against competitors or against its own performance in the past. *Break-even analysis* is designed to illustrate the relationship between costs, sales volume, and profits. It can be used both as a decision-making aid and as a control device.

There are three types of auditing methods. *External auditing* involves an independent appraisal of an organization's financial accounts and statements. *Internal auditing* is performed by organization members. This type of auditing appraises the organization's financial statements and operational efficiency. *Management auditing* involves a systematic appraisal of management and organizational performance in a number of categories.

Project and program control techniques include Gantt charts, milestone scheduling, PERT, and CPM. The *Gantt chart* graphically indicates the tasks involved in each project and the time it will take to complete them. *Milestones* on a Gantt chart indicate important dates in a project—usually when a certain phase of the project is to be completed. *PERT* and *CPM* networks illustrate not only the tasks involved in a project and the time it will take to complete them but also the interrelationships between those tasks. In this way, the project can be planned and integrated more effectively, and the project completion date can be determined and controlled more easily.

Review Questions

1. Why do you think managers need to understand and use nonbudgetary methods of control?
2. What are the three major uses of financial statements? How may financial statements be used as control devices?
3. What are the major types of financial statements? What information does each type provide?
4. What is ratio analysis? How may comparisons of ratios be made?

[23] See Bruce N. Baker and Rene L. Eris, *An Introduction to PERT-CPM* (New York: Irwin, 1964), and Peter P. Schoderbeck, "PERT Cost: Its Values and Limitations," *Management Services*, Vol. 3, No. 1 (January-February 1966), pp. 29–34.

5. What are the five major types of ratios used by organizations? What information is each type of ratio expected to provide?
6. What is the ROI ratio? What are its strengths and weaknesses as a measure of organizational efficiency?
7. What is the purpose of break-even analysis? What are the steps involved in creating a profitgraph? What is the break-even point? What are the benefits and limitations of break-even analysis?
8. What are the three basic types of audits? What is the purpose of each type? What ten areas does the A.I.M. audit appraise?
9. How is a Gantt chart constructed? How may milestones supplement a Gantt chart?
10. What limitation of the Gantt chart are PERT and CPM designed to overcome?
11. How are PERT and CPM networks developed?
12. What is the critical path? How is it determined?
13. What are the advantages and limitations of PERT and CPM?

CASE STUDY: GETTING THE BRADYS TO WORK

Mr. and Mrs. Brady are a young couple who are starting their careers. Each weekday morning they complete a set of activities that are necessary to get them both off to the office. An analysis of the project "Getting the Bradys to Work" reveals the following list of relevant activities, their duration, and their predecessor relationships:

Activity	Description	Duration (Minutes)	Immediate Predecessors
	Performed by Mr. Brady		
1	Alarm goes off	0	—
2	Get up, shut off alarm, turn up heat	2	1
3	Return to bed until wife finishes showering	14	2
4	Get up, shower, and shave	22	3, 13
5	Get dressed	10	4
6	Prepare breakfast	13	5
7	Eat breakfast	20	6
8	Brush teeth	3	7
9	Put on tie and coat	4	8
10	Pick up briefcase, hat, and lunch	3	9, 20
11	Warm up the car and get it out of garage	9	10
12	Leave for work with wife	0	11, 25
	Performed by Mrs. Brady		
13	Get up, shower	16	1
14	Blow-dry and comb hair	11	13
15	Apply makeup	4	14
16	Get dressed	9	15

Case adapted from Jerome D. Wiest and Ferdinand K. Levy, *A Management Guide to PERT/CPM,* © 1969, pp. 149–150. Reprinted by permission of Prentice-Hall, Inc.

Activity	Description	Duration (Minutes)	Immediate Predecessors
17	Straighten up bedroom	6	16
18	Feed the parrot	5	17
19	Eat breakfast	20	6, 18
20	Prepare and pack the lunches	25	19
21	Brush teeth	3	8, 20
22	Put on lipstick	2	21
23	Turn down heat, and pick up lunch	2	22
24	Lock front door	1	23
25	Get into car to go to work	2	11, 24

Case Questions

1. Draw an arrow diagram for the project "Getting the Bradys to Work."
2. Mark the critical path and state its length.
3. How early must the alarm go off if the Bradys are to leave for work in their car at 8:00 A.M.?
4. If the Bradys wanted to get more sleep by having the alarm go off later and still leave for work at 8:00 A.M., would it help them to:
   a. Take less time showering?
   b. Eat faster?
   c. Buy their lunch at work?
   d. Wait until they get to work to brush their teeth?
   e. Have Mrs. Brady rather than Mr. Brady prepare breakfast?
   f. Have Mr. Brady rather than Mrs. Brady prepare and pack the lunches?
5. Is there any time when Mr. Brady could read the newspaper for a few minutes without delaying his and Mrs. Brady's departure—without setting the alarm for an earlier time? Similarly, is there any time when Mrs. Brady could read the newspaper?

Chapter 24

Making Control Effective

Upon completing this chapter you should be able to:

1. State why an information system is an important part of a control system.

2. Describe how managers can evaluate the value and cost of information.

3. Explain why managers at different levels of the organization have different information needs.

4. Describe how a management information system (MIS) can be implemented effectively.

5. Identify the problems that can develop when a computer-based MIS is being implemented, and state the ways these problems can be overcome.

6. State how control systems may be effectively designed.

All the managerial functions—planning, organizing, leading, and controlling—are necessary for successful organizational performance. From this point of view, it is not useful to argue that one of the functions is more important than another: a complete breakdown in any one will prevent success. Nevertheless, we have suggested in this text that planning is particularly important, because it establishes the overall purpose and goals of the organization. If managers do not know where their organization is going, then their ability to organize, lead, and control will be severely hampered.

In a similar sense, establishing *effective* controls is also of special importance. It is the firmness and consistency with which managers monitor progress toward their goals that turn plans into reality. If managers do not stay "on track" and make the appropriate corrections and adjustments as they progress, all their work in the preceding management functions can become meaningless. Effective control plays a vital role in "making real" what managers have so carefully planned.

In this chapter, we have the following major aims: (1) To examine the way organizational information systems help provide the information required for effective control; (2) to analyze in some detail the workings of management information systems (MIS)—especially a computer-based MIS; and (3) to discuss the problems that generally arise when managers try to achieve effective control. We will emphasize management information systems for two reasons. First, the organization's information system is the critical part of its control system. How well the information system functions—that is, how quickly and accurately managers receive information about what is going right and what is going wrong—determines, to a large extent, how effective the control system will be.[1] Second, organizational information systems are undergoing major changes as a result of the progressively more extensive use of computers.[2] Computers offer managers considerable opportunities for improving their control systems. Thus, it has become increasingly important to understand how computer-based information systems should be designed, implemented, and managed.

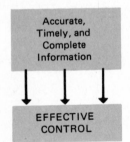

Accurate, Timely, and Complete Information

↓ ↓ ↓

EFFECTIVE CONTROL

INFORMATION AND CONTROL

To appreciate the central role played by information in making control effective, consider a modest-sized manufacturer of automobile replacement parts with annual sales of $10 million. Every year the firm's 350 employees service 20,000 customer orders. These orders must be processed, billed, assembled,

---

[1] Information systems are also important for effective planning. See Francois E. de Carbonnel and Roy G. Dorrance, "Information Sources for Planning Decisions," *California Management Review,* Vol. 15, No. 4 (Summer 1973), pp. 42–53.

[2] It has been estimated that American organizations spend $26 billion annually on computer information processing. See Paul A. Strassman, "Managing the Costs of Information," *Harvard Business Review,* September-October 1976, pp. 133–142.

packed, and shipped—adding up to some 400,000 different transactions that must be controlled.

And that is only the beginning. Management writes 25,000 checks annually. Half of these cover wages; most of the others pay for the 5,000 purchase orders issued every year. Costs are assembled from 17,000 time cards, 6,000 job orders, and 20,000 materials requisitions. Each year, that small $10 million firm is processing almost a million pieces of information related to its activities —and that figure does not include all the other pieces of control information being processed, such as those related to inventory and quality control.

The Computer Revolution

Before the widespread use of electronic computers, large amounts of valuable information about an organization's activities could not be used effectively by managers. The information either reached managers too late for them to take action on it, or it was simply too expensive to gather the information in a usable form.[3] Today, managers have at their command a wide range of data processing and information tools. In place of a few financial controls, managers can draw on a number of computer and other types of information systems to control activities in every area of their organization. On any number of performance measures, the information provided by these systems helps managers compare standards with actual results, detect deviations, and take corrective action before it is too late.

The introduction of computerized information systems has sharply changed management control in many organizations. Even a neighborhood retailer may now have computerized inventory, sales, billing, and other financial controls. In large organizations, complex electronic data processing (EDP) systems control entire programs and sets of operations. It is not unusual to find that computers have replaced bookkeepers, and that accountants and controllers routinely perform broader management functions than they ever have in the past.[4]

In order for managers to be sure that the computer-based information they are receiving is accurate, they need to understand the processes by which data are fed to, analyzed, and delivered by computers. Such an understanding is not difficult to achieve. One survey found that business firms were more successful in teaching basic information about computers to business graduates than they were in teaching basic business subjects to computer science graduates.[5] Contemporary managers do not need to learn how to program computers. However, they should understand how computerized information systems are developed; the capabilities, limitations, and costs of these systems; and the manner in which these information systems may be used.

[3] Earl P. Strong and Robert D. Smith, *Management Control Models* (New York: Holt, Rinehart and Winston, 1968), pp. 119–120.

[4] Robert J. Mockler, *The Management Control Process* (Englewood Cliffs, N.J.: Prentice-Hall, 1972), pp. vii, 73. See also "The Controller: Inflation Gives Him More Clout with Management," *Business Week*, August 15, 1977, pp. 84–95.

[5] Hirohide Hinomoto, "Education in Information Systems," *Academy of Management Journal*, Vol. 18, No. 2 (June 1975), pp. 402–407.

The Value and
Cost of Control
Information

In designing or improving a management information system, one of the issues that managers need to consider is whether the benefits of the proposed system justify its cost. The purpose of an MIS is to provide managers with the right information at the right time. Yet, if the savings that result from the information are outweighed by the cost of the information system — or if another system can provide the same or better information more cheaply or conveniently — then the system is not cost-effective. A problem that managers have in evaluating the cost-effectiveness of their information system is that the value of information is difficult to define in measurable terms.

Robert H. Gregory and Richard L. Van Horn have suggested that, for managers, the value of information depends on four factors: the information's quality, its timeliness, its quantity, and its relevance to management's ability to take action.[6] These factors should be weighed against the costs associated with instituting and operating an MIS so that the effectiveness of the MIS can be assessed.

Information Quality. To judge the quality of information, managers simply note how closely the reported facts correspond to reality. The more accurate the information, the higher its quality and the more securely managers can rely on it when deciding what action to take. However, the cost of obtaining information increases as the quality of the information desired goes up. Checking each item that comes off the assembly line, for example, is obviously more expensive than checking every hundredth item. How accurate the information needs to be will vary with the situation. But, in general, information of higher quality that does not add materially to a manager's decision-making capability is not worth the added cost. In our assembly-line example, it is only in unusual situations that managers will decide to have every item checked for defects, since periodic checking will normally reveal any problems before too many defective goods are produced.

Information Timeliness. For control to be effective, corrective action must be applied before too great a deviation from the plan or standard has taken place. Thus, the information provided by an information system must suggest action *in time* for that action to be taken. Just when information is considered timely, however, will depend on the situation. For example, information destined for top-level managers to monitor progress on long-range objectives may be considered timely if it arrives at quarterly intervals. The cost of making it available weekly would not be justified, since long-range plans are neither reviewed nor modified at such frequent intervals. However, middle and lower-level managers responsible for ongoing operations and activities may need weekly or even daily control information. The shop superintendent, for

[6] Robert H. Gregory and Richard L. Van Horn, "Value and Cost of Information," in J. Daniel Couger and Robert W. Knapp, *Systems Analysis Techniques* (New York: Wiley, 1974), pp. 473–489.

instance, needs a daily report on machine downtime if delays are to be minimized. The quality control managers must get a daily or weekly report on all customer rejections. On a monthly or quarterly basis, such information would merely be ancient history and of no value to the manager.

Timeliness may also be determined by company policy or by events, rather than by the calendar. Information on inventory, for example, is provided to the manager responsible for reordering only when a previously established minimum level for the inventory is being approached. Requiring inventory information on a calendar basis — such as every week — when inventory levels for most items are well above their reorder points would usually not be worth the added cost, since action would not be implied by the information.

Information Quantity and Relevance. Managers can hardly make accurate and timely decisions without sufficient information. Thus, a system that provides too little information can be ineffective, because it may lead managers to make wrong or late decisions that worsen problems instead of solving them. Conversely, managers may be inundated with large quantities of irrelevant and useless information. They may then overlook information on serious problems because they are bogged down or confused. Thus, information systems that provide managers with too much information can also prove ineffective, because they keep managers from reacting to problems on time. In addition, the cost of reports, staff analyses, computer processing, and the like can become prohibitive.

DATA

↓

Raw Facts

INFORMATION

↓

Analyzed Data

MANAGEMENT INFORMATION

↓

Information with Action Implications

In deciding just what level of information managers need, it is helpful to distinguish between data, information, and management information. *Data* are raw, unanalyzed facts, figures, and events from which information *can* be developed — the collection of orders received for product X in January, the inventory records for welding rods at the factory in Spokane, or the number of major surgical operations performed by a hospital on May 23. *Information* is analyzed or processed data that informs the recipient about a situation — for example, the information that the inventory of welding rods at the Spokane plant is equivalent to twelve days supply when the desired minimum inventory is ninety days supply (because of delays associated with ordering and delivery). *Management information* is information that has action implications; that is, it suggests in an accurate, timely, and relevant way that managers need to do something about a situation. The inventory information above is management information, because it implies the need for immediate action (such as increasing the inventory and determining how and why the inventory was allowed to fall to such a low level). The most cost-effective information, obviously, is management information, because it has a practical impact on a manager's ability to exercise effective control.

With the growing use of EDP systems, the problem of managers getting swamped by potentially interesting but basically unhelpful data and information has become very real. However, this difficulty is not an inevitable part of computer use in organizations. In fact, the capabilities of computers give them great power to *condense* information to only the most relevant, useful, and timely essentials. They can be programmed to report only those exceptional situations that require managerial attention. Unfortunately, this capability is not always utilized, and the idea that "more is better" dies slowly.

MANAGEMENT INFORMATION SYSTEMS

One of the difficulties associated with discussing MIS is the fact that there are so many definitions of it.[7] For our purposes, we will define an MIS as a formal method of making available to management the accurate and timely information necessary to facilitate the decision-making process and enable the organization's planning, control, and operational functions to be carried out effectively. The system provides information on the past, present, and projected future and on relevant events inside and outside the organization.[8]

In using the word "formal" in our definition, we do not mean to imply that the informal communications network has no place in the organization's control mechanism. In fact, a manager can often spot emerging problems *before* they show up in the formal control reports and printouts if he or she is keyed into the grapevine. (See Chapter 18.) The ability of managers to maintain effective informal communication channels, to sense the implications of the information those channels transmit, and to evaluate, decide, and act quickly on such information extends enormously the usefulness of the formal MIS. In our discussion, we will focus on the formal MIS, because it can be more directly designed and otherwise acted on by managers. We do not, however, minimize the importance of the informal information system.

Some definitions of MIS stress the role of computers and EDP—in some cases, defining an MIS as that part of the organization's information system directly associated with computer hardware and software. Narrowing the focus in this manner can sometimes be useful; but given such a limited definition, we can overlook too easily the major part of the organizational information system that may not be computerized. We will devote special attention to the computerized parts of an MIS, but we do not restrict our definition in that manner.

In the past, considerable discussion has been devoted to the desirability and feasibility of developing one all-encompassing, integrated system of management information. However, most authorities today regard an organization's MIS as a *series* of information systems of varying degrees of complexity, completeness, and scope. While these interrelated systems do interact and overlap to some extent, the possibility and even desirability of integrating the group into one "utopian" total system does not seem very great.

[7] John Dearden (in "MIS Is a Mirage," *Harvard Business Review*, January-February 1972, p. 90) has suggested that the concept of MIS "is embedded in a mish-mash of fuzzy thinking and incomprehensible jargon."

[8] See Walter J. Kennevan, "Management Information Systems," *Data Management*, Vol. 8, No. 9 (September 1970), pp. 62–64.

TABLE 24-1
Information
Requirements by
Decision Category

Characteristics of Information	Operational Control	Management Control	Strategic Planning
Source	Largely internal————————→		External
Scope	Well defined, narrow—————→		Very wide
Level of Aggregation	Detailed————————————→		Aggregate
Time Horizon	Historical———————————→		Future
Currency	Highly current————————→		Quite old
Required Accuracy	High—————————————→		Low
Frequency of Use	Very frequent————————→		Infrequent

Source: G. Anthony Gorry and Michael S. Scott Morton, "A Framework for Management Information Systems," *Sloan Management Review,* Fall 1971, p. 59. Reprinted by permission.

Designing
an MIS

Differing Information Needs at Different Management Levels. Robert N. Anthony has divided managerial activities into three basic categories:

1 *Strategic planning*—the development of an organization's overall goals and methods for achieving them.
2 *Management control*—the process of assuring that the organization's goals are being accomplished effectively and efficiently.
3 *Operational control*—the process of assuring that specific tasks are being accomplished effectively and efficiently.[9]

G. Anthony Gorry and M. S. Scott Morton have suggested that an organization's information system must provide the different types of information that these three managerial activities require.[10] For example, as shown in Table 24-1, the information sources for operational control will be based largely within the organization, while the information sources for strategic planning will be based largely outside the organization. (See Chapter 5.) Sources for management control will be more evenly balanced between internal and external ones.

We can think of the three categories of managerial activities as referring to the activities that take place at different levels of the managerial hierarchy (top, middle, and first-line). We can then analyze the different information needs of the various managerial levels. These differing needs will have to be taken into account when an MIS is being designed.

Strategic planning in most organizations is carried out by top managers. Thus, for top managers, the MIS must provide information upon which a strategic plan can be soundly based. For this task, external sources of informa-

[9] Robert N. Anthony, *Planning and Control Systems* (Boston: Harvard University, Graduate School of Business Administration, 1965).
[10] G. Anthony Gorry and Michael S. Scott Morton, "A Framework for Management Information Systems," *Sloan Management Review,* Vol. 13, No. 1 (Fall 1971), pp. 55–70.

Largely
External
Sources

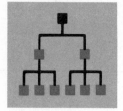

Internal
and
External
Sources

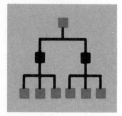

Largely
Internal
Sources

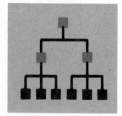

tion—on economic conditions, on technological developments, on the actions of competitors—assume paramount importance. This information does not have to possess great accuracy since strategic plans are broad rather than detailed in nature and because they require rough indications of future trends rather than exact statements about the past or present.

For the management *control* activities that top managers carry out, the sources of information must obviously be both internal and external. Top managers of corporations, for instance, will be concerned about the overall financial performance of their organizations. They will therefore need information on quarterly sales and profits, say, and on the sales and profits of competitors. Internal control reports for top managers will come in at monthly, quarterly, and sometimes even at annual intervals. Such a slow-paced information flow is possible because top managers will not be concerned with day-to-day operating control but with longer-range problems, plans, and performance.

Middle-level managers, such as division heads, will be concerned with the current and future performance of their units. They will therefore need information on important matters that will affect those units—large-scale problems with suppliers, abrupt sales declines, or increased consumer demand for a particular product line. Thus, the type of information middle-level managers will require falls somewhere between the extremes required by lower- and top-level managers. For instance, in devising and using break-even charts (see Chapter 23), middle-level managers will need to know about plant costs in some detail; they will also need broader-based information on economic conditions and expected market demand.

At the bottom of the pyramid, the MIS will have to provide frequent and highly detailed and accurate information so that the day-to-day operations of the organization can be controlled. A supervisor has to know if material wastage is exceeding the norm, if costly overruns are in the making, or if the machine time allocated for a job has expired; a chief engineer has to know if maintenance expenditures are going to exceed the budget; the head of the quality control department wants daily reports on the number of defects found; the local sales manager wants to know the number of customer calls the new sales rep has made that day. Obviously, accuracy of information is particularly important at this level, since the manager will frequently be required to take on-the-spot action.

How may the various needs of different managerial levels be translated into a management information system? One major company designed the manufacturing component of its MIS this way: *supervisors* receive daily reports on direct and indirect labor, material usage, scrap, production counts, and machine downtime; *superintendents* and *department heads* receive weekly departmental cost summaries and product cost reports; *plant managers* receive weekly and monthly financial statements and analyses, analyses of important costs, and summarized product cost reports; *divisional managers* receive monthly plant comparisons, financial planning reports, product cost summaries, and plant cost control reports; and, finally, *top managers* receive overall monthly and quarterly financial reviews, financial analyses, and summarized comparisons of divisional performance.

Guidelines for Effective Design. Many articles and books have described the systematic steps that should be followed in designing and implementing an MIS. Robert G. Murdick has reviewed a number of these sources and has adapted them to form his own model of how an MIS should be developed.[11] (See Figure 24-1 on next page.) His flow chart gives a good idea of the complexity and amount of work required for MIS development. In fact, the design and implementation of such an MIS would likely require a major team effort by managers and information systems designers over a period of two or three years. For the sake of simplicity, we may break down Murdick's model into four major stages:

1 A preliminary survey and problem definition stage (top of diagram)
2 A conceptual design stage (middle of diagram)
3 A detailed design stage (bottom left of diagram)
4 A final implementation stage (bottom right of diagram)

How can these steps in the MIS development process be carried out effectively? For our purposes, we can focus on five guidelines for effective MIS design: (1) make the user a part of the design team; (2) carefully consider the costs of the system; (3) favor relevance and selectivity of information over sheer quantity; (4) pretest the system before installation; and (5) train the operators and users of the system carefully.

1. *Make the user a part of the design team.* Most management writers agree that cooperation between the operating managers (those who use the information) and systems designers is not only desirable but necessary.[12] Managers at the various hierarchical levels have differing decisions to make, differing control responsibilities, and differing information needs; thus, the information system must be designed to direct appropriate information to each decision maker. However, the management scientists and staff specialists who design these systems often do not think like managers and may be unaware of the complexities that enter into a management decision. (See Chapters 8 and 11.) Unless the operating managers have a decisive voice as to how an MIS is designed, the information system can fail to provide needed information while simultaneously overloading them with other useless information.[13]

2. *Carefully consider the costs of the system.* To keep the MIS on track

[11] Robert G. Murdick, "MIS Development Procedures," *Journal of Systems Management,* Vol. 21, No. 12 (December 1970), pp. 22–26.

[12] See William R. King and David I. Cleland, "Manager-Analyst Teamwork in MIS," *Business Horizons,* Vol. 14, No. 2 (April 1971), pp. 59–68.

[13] See Arnold Barnett, "Preparing Management for MIS," *Journal of Systems Management,* Vol. 23, No. 1 (January 1972).

FIGURE 24-1 MIS Development

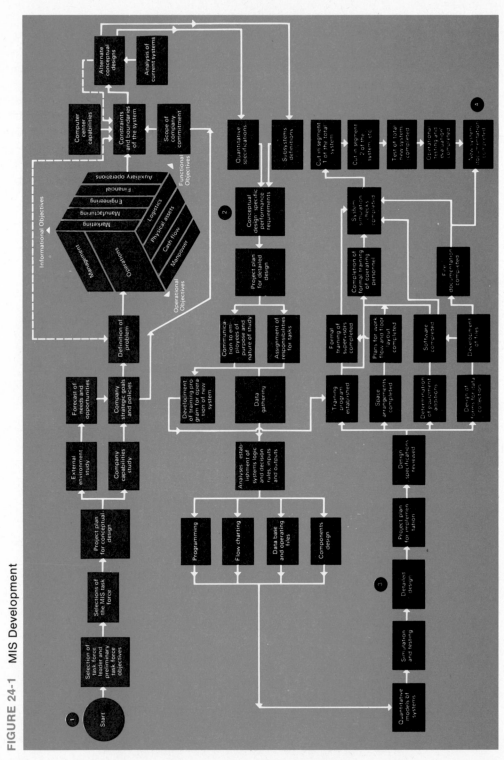

Source: Robert G. Murdick. "MIS Development Procedures," *Journal of Systems Management*, Vol. 21, No. 12 December 1970). pp. 24–25. Reprinted by permission.

and on budget, designers need to specify how the system will be developed—including benchmarks for time required, milestones to be reached, and costs. (See Chapter 23.) This component of the design stage is often neglected, because managers, particularly in nonprofit organizations, tend to justify the MIS on cost-saving grounds and may fear that documentation of the system's actual installation costs will discredit their original estimates. As a result, an unnecessarily expensive system may be implemented. This problem can be overcome by having managers justify the installation of a new system on a cost-benefit basis. In addition, the analysts should clearly specify in the design stage which units of the organization will be responsible for installing and operating the system. In this way, the appropriate managers can be held accountable for costs.[14]

3. *Favor relevance and selectivity over sheer quantity.* As we suggested earlier, a manager needs enough information for an informed decision; *more* information is not necessarily better information. In fact, information overload can often be a real headache to the manager who is too busy to isolate what he or she needs from a flood of irrelevant facts and figures. As a result, the manager may overlook what is truly important or be unable to digest the information in time to take the necessary action.[15]

A properly designed MIS will not supply managers with the routine details of an organization's daily activities. Such pieces of information as time sheets, customer orders, invoices, shipping tickets, requisitions, and work orders will normally not be reviewed by managers, except perhaps those at the lower levels of the organization. Instead, the MIS will *filter* or evaluate information so that only the most relevant information will be supplied to the appropriate manager. In addition, the effective MIS will *condense* information, so what is relevant can be absorbed in a short period of time.

4. *Pretest the system before installation.* This important step is another one that may be neglected by MIS designers. Even when managers and designers cooperate in the system's development, important factors may be overlooked; if these do not become apparent until the system is finally implemented, costly problems may arise and expensive changes may be necessary. For example, a computer may be installed to reorder parts automatically when inventory reaches a certain level. If the computer has been improperly programmed, it may reorder parts long before that level is reached, and the organization's inventory costs may skyrocket. Testing the computer may reveal the improper programming before funds are expended unnecessarily.

5. *Train the operators and users of the system carefully.* A training program for managers and MIS operators is important for two major reasons. First, even well-managed organizations experience turnover; if no provision for training in the operation and use of the MIS is made, then the organization

---

[14] Regina Herzlinger, "Why Data Systems in Nonprofit Organizations Fail," *Harvard Business Review,* January-February 1977, pp. 81–86.

[15] See Russell E. Ackoff, "Management Misinformation Systems," *Management Science,* December 1967, pp. 147–156.

will be at a loss when experienced personnel leave. Second, operators and users need to be trained so that the MIS can be used effectively. Operators need to understand just how much information managers at different levels need so unnecessary (and overly expensive) amounts of information will not be produced. Perhaps most importantly, *managers* need to understand how the MIS operates so they can control it rather than letting it control them. MIS technicians often gain power at the expense of managers when they are the only ones who understand how a system works.

Computers and MIS

The extent to which organizations handle both complex and simple activities is truly impressive. Our daily lives would be quite different without computers to handle such things as payrolls, telephone calls, stock market transactions, airline reservations, car rentals, billing, checking, and thousands of other activities. Large-scale projects such as the space exploration program and the development of nuclear power would have been simply impossible without the analytical speed and accuracy of the computer. Our discussion of management science in Chapter 8 and of PERT/CPM in Chapter 23 suggested other ways in which computers make themselves felt in industry and government.

The new generation of computers developed in the 1960s has increased the ability of managers to exercise control in two other ways. First, these computers permit *time-sharing,* which makes it possible for organizations that could not otherwise afford a large-scale computer system to plug into a central computer facility. The second breakthrough to result from improvements in computer technology was so-called *real-time* managerial control. This lightning-fast system of information retrieval makes it possible for the computer to "decide" about real events *while they are taking place.* With real-time systems, for example, airline tickets sales can be strictly controlled, with no ticket agent permitted to complete a transaction unless the computer verifies the space. Manufacturing firms can have up-to-the-minute production data at their disposal, and so can adjust their daily operations accordingly. Retailers can maintain current information on actual sales and inventory levels, and so can order additional shipments of fast-moving items immediately from suppliers. Firms may also use real-time systems for up-to-the-minute monitoring control of cash flow.

Problems in Implementing a Computer-Based MIS. Despite the growing use of computers in MIS and the many organizational problems they have solved, implementing a computerized MIS has generated a number of difficulties. This situation is hardly surprising. As readers of this text are already aware, implementing any type of significant change in an organization almost inevitably creates the opportunity for a host of problems.

In our discussion here, we will focus on the people problems rather than on the technical problems associated with implementing a computer-based MIS. The technical problems are obviously beyond the scope of an introductory management text. In addition, it is more important for most managers to know how to deal with the people problems. The major responsibility for solving complex technical problems will be assumed by the information system experts; the people problems are at least as difficult to solve and are no less likely to inhibit successful implementation of a computerized information system. The primary responsibility for their solution will fall upon managers.[16]

G. W. Dickson and John K. Simmons have suggested five major factors that will determine whether and to what extent the implementation of a new MIS will be resisted:

1. *Disruption of established departmental boundaries.* The establishment of a new MIS system often results in changes in a variety of organizational units. For example, inventory and purchasing departments may be merged to make use of the MIS more efficient. Such changes can create resistance on the part of department members, who may resent having to change the way they do things or with whom they work.

2. *Disruption of the informal system.* The informal communication network not only serves as a source of management information but also is a source of social satisfaction for network members. If the new MIS disturbs the informal structure, resistance may be generated. For example, organization members may prefer some of the earlier, informal mechanisms for gathering and distributing information and may resist the more formal arrangement of the new system.

3. *Specific individual characteristics.* People with many years of service with the organization have "learned the ropes" and know how to get things done in the existing system. They may tend to resist change more tenaciously than newer people who have been with the organization for a comparatively short period of time and who do not have as large an investment in organizational know-how and relationships. The very youth of the systems people may also contribute to implementation difficulties if their age and behavior encourage older, more experienced managers to band together against "those know-it-all whiz kids." Middle managers can also be expected to resist major system changes if they fear that computers will absorb the more enjoyable and rewarding of their middle management functions.

4. *The organizational climate.* If top management maintains open communications, deals with grievances, and, in general, establishes a climate of trust throughout the organization, resistance to the installation of a new MIS is likely to be less severe. (See Chapter 13.) However, if top managers are isolated or aloof from other organization members, then effective implementation of the MIS is likely to be hindered.

5. *How the change is implemented.* As we emphasized in earlier chapters, the manner in which changes are designed and implemented can affect how much resistance the changes will encounter. In general, when managers and subordinates make change decisions together, the likelihood of the changes being accepted is increased.

[16] Our discussion in this section is based on G. W. Dickson and John K. Simmons, "The Behavioral Side of MIS," *Business Horizons,* Vol. 13, No. 4 (August 1970), pp. 59–71.

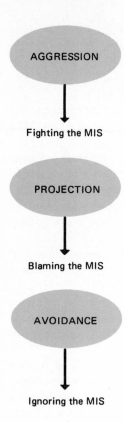

AGGRESSION

Fighting the MIS

PROJECTION

Blaming the MIS

AVOIDANCE

Ignoring the MIS

Dickson and Simmons have observed that the frustrations associated with the implementation of a new MIS can manifest themselves in three ways: by aggression, by projection, or by avoidance. *Aggressive* behavior may be manifested when individuals hit back at the object (or person) frustrating them. Aggression against a computer-based MIS has gone as far as sabotage—with systems components physically destroyed. A more common, if less dramatic, form of aggression against an MIS occurs when someone tries to "beat the system"—either by neglecting to record important information produced by the MIS or by supplying misinformation. Psychologically, *projection* occurs when individuals blame someone else for their own failings or difficulties. In our context, projection occurs when managers (or other individuals) blame the system for problems caused by human error or other factors unrelated to the system itself. *Avoidance* behavior is manifested when individuals defend themselves by withdrawing from or avoiding a frustrating situation. When managers ignore the output of an MIS in favor of their own information sources, they may be exhibiting avoidance behavior.

According to Dickson and Simmons, the frequency with which each type of behavior will be manifested will depend on the hierarchical level of the individuals and managers affected by the MIS change. (See Table 24-2 on next page.) The reason for this variation in behavior is that people at different levels of the organization will be affected by a computer-based MIS in different ways. Among lower-level nonclerical personnel, for instance, the installation of a new MIS may cause an increase in job complexity. For example, machinists may be required to fill out a series of punch cards on their daily output, instead of making a few verbal reports. They may resent this new task if it does not seem directly job-related. Thus, they may manifest aggressive behavior, such as "forgetting" to use the new system or making deliberate errors. On the other hand, clerical workers (like keypunchers), who will be working directly with the new system, are less likely to manifest aggression toward it; the MIS represents the major part of their job. They may, however, resist changes in the system through projection—for example, by making remarks about the new system's failings and inadequacies relative to the old system.

Operating management—which in our context may include both first-line and middle managers—generally experiences the greatest impact from a new MIS. The information supplied by the MIS to top managers will, after all, help determine how the operating managers are evaluated. The problem for operating managers is that they have less control over how and when this information is filtered, interpreted, and presented to their superiors; instead of supplying it directly to top managers, they supply it to the MIS, which is operated by staff specialists. This loss of control is a source of anxiety for managers. Other sources of anxiety for operating managers include the fact that a computerized MIS tends to allow more centralized decision making, which makes it easier for top managers to increase their control over the operating managers. In addition, there is always the possibility that a computer-based MIS will eliminate or substantially alter some first-line and even middle management jobs. Thus, the resistance of operating managers to the MIS may encompass all three types of psychological reactions: they may fight the

TABLE 24-2 Work Groups, MIS Interaction, and Probable Types of Dysfunctional Behavior

Organizational Subgroup	Relation to MIS	Probable Dysfunctional Behavior
Operating Personnel:		
Nonclerical	Provide system inputs	Aggression
Clerical	Particularly affected by clerical systems; job eliminated, job patterns changed	Projection
Operating Management	Controlled from above by information systems; job content modified by information-decision systems and programmed systems	Aggression, avoidance, and projection
Technical Staff	Systems designers and agents of systems change	None
Top Management	Generally unaffected and unconcerned with systems	Avoidance

Source: G. W. Dickson and John K. Simmons, "The Behavioral Side of MIS," *Business Horizons*, Vol. 13, No. 4 (August 1970), p. 63. Copyright 1970 by the Foundation for the School of Business at Indiana University. Reprinted by permission.

system (aggression); they may ignore it, sticking to their old communication channels and ways of using information (avoidance); or they may blame the system for failures caused by other factors (projection). Table 24-3 on page 660 illustrates the reasons why operating managers are especially likely to resist a computer-based MIS.

The top management in many organizations is, in the main, unaffected by and comparatively unconcerned with the implementation of an MIS. Top managers have much to gain from such a system, because it will enable them to make more informed decisions. However, they tend to avoid active involvement with it, perhaps out of unfamiliarity with or feelings of insecurity about computers. This lack of direction and support from top managers often exacerbates the difficulties other organization members have with the MIS.

Overcoming the Implementation Problems. No single approach will overcome all the implementation problems we have identified. Each situation must be separately diagnosed and its own individualized "cure" prescribed. Nevertheless, there are a number of factors Dickson and Simmons consider important in helping managers overcome implementation problems:

1. *User orientation.* Perhaps the most critical step in overcoming implementation problems is to ensure that in both design and implementation an MIS will be user-oriented. If the system's output fails to meet the users' needs with a minimum of adjustment and new learning, they will stick firmly, and logically, to their own systems, thereby reducing the chances that the MIS will eventually become useful to them. In addition, as we have stressed earlier, designers should be extremely careful not to burden organization members with a mass of data they cannot use effectively.

TABLE 24-3
Reasons for
Resistance to MIS
(by Working Group)

	Operating (Nonclerical)	Operating (Clerical)	Operating Management	Top Management
Threats to economic security		X	X	
Threats to status or power		X	X*	
Increased job complexity	X		X	X
Uncertainty or unfamiliarity	X	X	X	X
Changed interpersonal relations or work patterns		X*	X	
Changed superior-subordinate relationships		X*	X	
Increased rigidity or time pressure	X	X	X	
Role ambiguity		X	X*	X
Feelings of insecurity		X	X*	X*

X = The reason is possibly the cause of resistance to MIS development.
X* = The reason has a strong possibility of being the cause of resistance.

Source: G. W. Dickson and John K. Simmons, "The Behavioral Side of MIS," *Business Horizons*, Vol. 13, No. 4 (August 1970), p. 68. Copyright 1970 by the Foundation for the School of Business at Indiana University. Reprinted by permission.

2. *Participation.* Many implementation problems can be overcome (or avoided) if future users participate from the very beginning as welcome and important members of the MIS team. Operating managers should have a major say in the items to be included, the disposition of information, and possible job modifications. Above all, the technical "whiz kids" must be kept from taking over the entire implementation process. Otherwise, serious line-staff conflicts may develop.

3. *Communication.* The aims and characteristics of the system should be clearly defined and communicated. This task is more difficult than it sounds because the character of an MIS continually evolves and changes as it is being designed and implemented. Thus, the final nature of the MIS will not be known with precision at the outset. Nevertheless, a solid attempt must be made to achieve a broad understanding of the system's basic objectives and characteristics. Otherwise, team members and organization managers will differ constantly about what they expect the system to accomplish and how it will be operated.

4. *Redefinition of performance evaluation.* A new MIS may modify a manager's job to the point where old methods of performance evaluation no longer apply. For this reason, an MIS that calls for such job modification must be accompanied by a new and satisfactory reward system if management resistance to the MIS is to be avoided or overcome. Otherwise, managers will not know how their accomplishments will be measured and rewarded.

5. *New challenges.* The notion that a computer can do many of the things

a manager can do—and perhaps do them better—has a lot to do with the feelings of insecurity a computer-based MIS may arouse. One of the ways Dickson and Simmons suggest for overcoming the resistance occasioned by this insecurity is to publicize the new challenges made possible by the computerized system. A new MIS may well liberate many middle managers from some of their boring and routine work. Thus, they may have an opportunity to take a larger role in activities like long-range planning that have tended to be the exclusive prerogative of upper-level managers.

ESTABLISHING EFFECTIVE CONTROL SYSTEMS

In Chapter 22, we discussed the problem of dysfunctional reactions to budgets. Such reactions may apply to all types of control systems; most individuals will experience at least some discomfort at the prospect of having their performance monitored and reported to others. However, we also noted earlier (in Chapter 21) that when controls are of the "steering" kind and when progress toward goals is fed back to the individual whose actions are being controlled, this discomfort or resentment can often be reduced and even entirely eliminated. In a similar manner, when a joint goal-setting program such as MBO is implemented *effectively*—and many MBO programs fall far short of the ideal— much of the follow-up evaluation is perceived as helpful rather than punitive.

Nevertheless, even in well-managed control systems, there are a number of problems that seem to recur.[17] These problems hinder the effectiveness of the control system.

1. *Easily measured factors receive too much weight, while difficult-to-measure items are not given enough attention.* This problem arises because it is quicker and easier to measure the performance of those factors that can be quantified. For example, personnel turnover figures are often carefully checked, but little or no control may be exercised over whether or not the most qualified employees are being hired. As a result, the control system may concentrate on comparatively minor matters at the expense of more important organizational goals.

2. *Short-run factors may be overemphasized at the expense of long-run factors.* Long-run results are more unpredictable than short-run achievements; in addition, it is often difficult, if not impossible, to design measurements that can relate long-term results to specific current actions. Customer goodwill, for example, may be an important determinant of long-term growth, but managers have a hard time fitting it into a control system. The long-term growth and survival of the organization may therefore not be given the attention they need by the control system.

3. *Failure to adjust the control system to reflect shifts in importance of various activities and goals over time.* No organization can afford to neglect

---

[17] Our discussion in this and the following section is based on William H. Newman, *Constructive Control: Design and Use of Control Systems* (Englewood Cliffs, N.J.: Prentice-Hall, 1975).

such things as dependable quality, assured delivery, new product development, and the control of manufacturing and selling expenses. But at various stages of the company's growth, a shift in emphasis may be essential as one or another of these factors assumes a higher priority in the struggle for survival. In practice, managers tend to accept the usefulness of existing controls, rather than adjust them as situations change and new objectives emerge.

Guidelines for Effective Control

We have already discussed management information systems, which play an important role in establishing effective controls. William H. Newman has identified four other factors that need to be incorporated by the control system if it is to be effective and efficient:

1   Controls must be related to meaningful and accepted goals.
2   Tough but attainable pars (standards) must be set.
3   The number of controls must be limited.
4   The control system must be self-adjusting.

Relating Controls to Meaningful and Accepted Goals.   To be meaningful, a goal must reflect the language and activities of the individuals to whom it pertains. Top managers, for example, think naturally in terms of financial performance. At their level, it will be meaningful to relate at least some controls to quarterly financial results and budgets. First-line supervisors, however, may regard a budget as a nuisance concocted by front office "pencil pushers." For these supervisors, control relates to such tangible things as hours of work, number of products produced, percentages of rejects, downtime, and material wastage. In their eyes, controls will be meaningful if they relate to and provide timely and accurate data on operational, day-to-day activities.

For a control standard to work as intended, suggests Newman, it must also be accepted by organization members as an integral and fair part of their jobs. For example, the necessity to keep costs under budget should be accepted as normal and even desirable. As you will recall from our discussion of joint goal setting in Chapters 6 and 7, when the people who must meet standards have a major say in setting them, they are more likely to be committed to those standards. Participation in goal setting by organization members often causes the goals to become internalized—a part of their personal aims.

Set Tough But Attainable Pars.   A control target or standard has two basic aims: (1) to motivate, and (2) to serve as a standard against which actual performance can be compared. Obviously, a control system is most effective when it motivates people to high performance. Since most people respond to a challenge, successfully meeting a tough standard may well provide a greater sense of accomplishment than meeting an easy standard. However, if a target is so tough that it seems impossible to meet, it will be more likely to discourage than to motivate effort. Standards that are too difficult may, therefore, cause the performance of organization members to decline.

Newman argues that very tough but *potentially* attainable pars should be

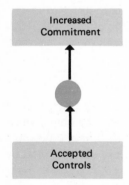

Increased Commitment

Accepted Controls

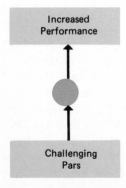

Increased Performance

Challenging Pars

"Management has asked us all to tighten our belts a bit."

Drawing by Booth; © 1971 The New Yorker Magazine, Inc.

established so that high performance will be encouraged even if the actual goals are missed. Some companies prefer to accomplish a similar objective by setting goals that are clearly achievable but establishing the expectation that most individuals will exceed the goal by 10 percent with reasonable effort, and that really solid performers will exceed the goal by 20 to 25 percent. Both these approaches to par setting are fine—*so long as they are well understood by everyone involved.*

Limit the Number of Controls. As the number of controls applied to an individual's work increases, the individual's actual autonomy and freedom in *how* and *when* the work is to be performed declines. At some point, the number of controls will be seen as so constraining and threatening by the individual that he or she will start thinking more in terms of self-defense than of performance. Rather than developing new and more effective ways to get the work done, and rather than seeking new responsibilities, the individual's attention will shift to ways to look good in those dimensions of the work that are being monitored. The resulting defensive maneuvers will frequently be at the expense of other important dimensions that are not as amenable to detailed measurement and control. If managers do not realize what is occurring, their

Limit Controls

response to this situation may well be to attempt to develop and *add* additional controls for the specific areas that are being neglected. Thus the cycle of "overcontrol" continues and expands.

The problem of excessive controls can be tackled in three major ways. First, controls should be focused on the major objectives to be achieved, such as sales, rather than on minor or unimportant matters, such as the amount of money being withdrawn from petty cash. This step alone will eliminate much of the waste and unnecessary pressures of "control for the sake of control." Second, minor targets can be stated in general terms rather than quantified absolutes. For example, instead of targeting personnel turnover at some definite percentage, the criterion could be to "maintain personnel turnover at a satisfactory level"—*satisfactory* being elastic enough to ease a manager's feeling of pressure. Finally, managers and other organization members should be allowed considerable leeway in terms of *how* they achieve their control objectives. For example, managers should have the authority to train their subordinates in their own way, so long as the desired results are achieved.

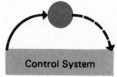

Emphasize Self-Adjustment

Emphasize Self-Adjustment. A control system, of course, has as its major goal to show when and where corrective action must be taken. Most managers accept this aspect of control but resent being told exactly how the corrective action should be applied. They prefer to take action on their own, rather than have it done for them by superiors or staff personnel. As was suggested in Chapter 21, steering controls are particularly useful in this regard, since they permit information to be fed back to the responsible individuals early enough to allow them to choose their own corrective actions. Through such feedback, effective control is maintained with no loss of managerial autonomy and pride.

Summary

Effective control is based on an effective management information system (MIS). An MIS may be defined as a formal method for providing managers with the information they need to carry out their tasks effectively. Computer-based management information systems are being introduced into growing numbers of organizations.

The value of information supplied by an MIS depends on the information's quality, quantity, timeliness, and relevance to management action. The cost of obtaining the information must be balanced against the information's benefits.

The information needs of managers differ with their hierarchical level. Top managers require information on *strategic planning*. Thus, their information sources will be largely external. Middle-level managers require information that will enable them to exercise *management control*. Thus, their information sources will be both external and internal. In addition, they will require a more rapid information flow. Lower-level managers, who are concerned with *operational control,* will require frequent, highly detailed, and accurate information—predominantly from internal sources.

Guidelines for an effective MIS include: (1) make the user part of the design team; (2) carefully consider the costs of the system; (3) favor relevance and selectivity over sheer quantity; (4) pretest the system before installation; and (5) train the operators and users of the system carefully.

There are a number of people problems that can arise when a computer-based MIS is being implemented. These problems are likely to develop if the MIS disrupts established departmental boundaries, if it disrupts the informal communication system, if individuals resist the system, if the organizational climate is not supportive, and if the change is implemented without manager-subordinate participation. The reactions of organization members to a computer-based MIS may include aggression, projection, and avoidance, depending on their organization level and how the MIS will affect them.

Problems with control systems that managers have to be particularly careful to avoid include overemphasizing measurable and short-term factors and failing to adjust the system to reflect changing priorities and circumstances. Guidelines to effective control include: (1) relate controls to meaningful and accepted goals; (2) set tough but attainable pars; (3) limit the number of controls; and (4) emphasize self-adjustment.

Review Questions

1. Why do you think an effective information system is a key part of an effective control system?
2. On what four factors does the value of information depend? How do managers weigh these factors against the costs of the MIS?
3. What are the differences between data, information, and management information? Which is most desirable for managers? Why?
4. What are the differing information needs at different management levels? How may an MIS be designed to meet these different needs?
5. What are the four major stages in developing an MIS? How may these stages be carried out effectively?
6. What were two major breakthroughs that resulted from the development of new computer technology in the 1960s?
7. What factors determine whether and to what extent the implementation of a computer-based MIS will be resisted?
8. In what three ways may individuals manifest the frustrations associated with the implementation of a computer-based MIS? How will the type and frequency of the behaviors manifested be affected by the hierarchical level of the individuals involved? How may these implementation problems be overcome?
9. What problems typically plague control systems?
10. What guidelines have been suggested for making control systems effective?

CASE STUDY: RUTGERS ELECTRONICS

The following conversation takes place in the office of the Vice President of Marketing of a medium-sized electronics company. MM (Modern Manager) in the dialogue below represents the VP of Marketing, while TT (Technical Type) represents the Manager of Data Processing.

MM: Let's review the situation briefly to put the problem in perspective. It was a year ago today that I told you I wanted a cathode-ray tube display in my office. We're in the electronics business, and I think we should be in the forefront of the people using our products. I indicated I wanted to be able to make inquiries of our customer file to find out the current status of customers, shipments, on order, and the like. I asked you when you thought you could have this set up for me and you said six months. Is that correct?

TT: I would have to say that your recollection is basically correct, but I think there are some real mitigating circumstances underlying the problem.

Case from Jerome Kanter, *Management-Oriented Management Information Systems*, 2nd ed., © 1977, pp. 299, 300. Reprinted by permission of Prentice-Hall, Inc.

MM: Before you get into that, let me continue for a minute. The terminal was not installed in six months as you indicated but three months later than that. The terminal was hooked up and could communicate with a local time-sharing company computer and also with an educational institution in the area, but it didn't communicate with our own data base. You indicated we could be ready on a week-to-week basis, but the fact of the matter is that another three months has passed and I still don't have any results. It's quite embarrassing to have people come into the office, ask about the CRT and what I can do with it. Frankly, I usually tell them what I wanted to do with it, and try to mix the tenses so they don't realize it's what I would like to do and not what I can do. I usually have to make some kind of excuse if they ask me to demonstrate it.

TT: What you say is true and I apologize for the lack of results, but I would like to review the circumstances. You remember when we started out with this project, I told you the terminal itself was the simplest part of our problem — like the iceberg analogy, 10 percent is visible above the surface (that's the terminal), while 90 percent is below the surface (that's the customer data base and communications software that provides the data to the terminal). Frankly, we've had one heck of a time developing the customer data base. That's where the problem lies. We had a tape file, and we've had to go to disk to facilitate on-line inquiry. We've also had problems keeping the file current and incorporating the information you wanted as well as the information desired by other parts of the organization.

MM: Are you saying that my demands have been given low priority?

TT: Not exactly, but I think you would agree that the first thing we must do is bill our customers accurately for the products and services they get from us, and then set up the accounts receivable so that we get the cash.

MM: That may be so, but it seems we should be able to do that type of thing with no trouble at all. When can I use my terminal the way you and I talked about it?

TT: I want to be frank with you because I'm well aware of your impatience and disappointment — I assure you I share your feelings. It's still difficult, despite our experience, to predict when we can have the system operable. You know our business has been growing and changing very rapidly, and the minute we think we've got the situation under control, something else breaks that impacts the system — a new sales division is added, or we add a new product line, and so on. I've discussed the matter with my systems people, and I think we can reasonably promise you that your CRT can be hooked on-line three months from today.

MM: If that's the situation, take the device out of my office. It's stupid to pay rent on a machine I'm not using. It's an expensive office toy when you get nothing from it. This time you tell me when you're ready to go; I've lost confidence that we'll ever make it.

Case Questions

1. Does MM really need the terminal to improve control of the company's marketing activities, or is it just an office toy?
2. Do you think the events which occurred in this situation are typical?
3. Do you feel TT's explanation of the delay is reasonable?
4. Do you think MM bears some of the blame for the problem?
5. How do you think TT should have handled the situation from the outset?
6. What should be TT's plan of action now?

Name Index

Subject Index